KU-518-718

Tuscany
& Umbria

Miles Roddis
Alex Leviton

Destination Tuscany & Umbria

Tuscany and Umbria, big sister and little brother, between them offer the quintessential Italian experience. One is popular and sophisticated, long a traveller's darling, the other more retiring, more of a country boy.

From Tuscany, the Renaissance swept across Europe, changing the continent's architecture, its perspective on painting and indeed on life itself. Ancient homeland of the Etruscans, Tuscany is the land of Dante, da Vinci, Michelangelo and Botticelli. Small wonder it was an essential port of call for 19th-century Grand Tourists.

Its majestic Renaissance cities are disproportionately rich in great art treasures. Florence, with its spectacular cathedral, unique Uffizi gallery and unparalleled array of other museums, merits a whole holiday to itself. Siena, its bitter rival over the centuries, offers the spectacular Piazza del Campo, the venue for Il Palio, surely the world's most vigorous horse race and just one of many colourful regional folk festivals and contests. And the famous Leaning Tower in Pisa isn't even the finest of the architectural wonders within its Piazza dei Miracoli...

But Tuscany is also the rounded green hills of Le Crete, the fertile vineyards, olive groves and gentle countryside of Il Chianti, and the picturesque hill towns such as San Gimignano and Volterra.

Umbria, styled the 'Green Heart of Italy', is a walker's and cyclist's paradise, most of its countryside remaining largely uncommercialised. The wild Valnerina region beckons visitors looking to get off the beaten track while those with a cultural agenda can savour Orvieto's spectacularly striped Duomo and pay respects to St Francis and Giotto at Assisi's renowned Basilica.

Highlights

Visit Pisa's (p149) three leading ladies: the baptistry, Duomo and Leaning Tower

Be entertained by the *sbandieratori* (flag-throwers) in Piazza del Campo (p198), the main square of Siena

OTHER HIGHLIGHTS

- Stand among the flowers that blanket the area surrounding Lago di Trasimeno (p288).
- Get an earful of some of the world's best-known jazz musicians who appear at the Umbria Jazz Festival (p273) in Perugia.
- Be seen in Porto Santo Stefano (p247), the ultimate fashionable resort town.
- A beautiful, steep, historic hill town, Montelpulciano (p234) does wonders for your calves.

Marvel at the sculptures in the cathedral (p199) of Siena, one of Italy's great Gothic structures

Experience Carnevale (p166) with the colourful floats in Viareggio

Sip on the locally produced, world-famous Chianti wine (p141)

Sculpture fans flock to Perugia (p267) to see the many scattered throughout the city

DAMIEN SIMONIS

Begin your day at the fountain in the Piazza del Comune, one of the many sights in Assisi (p281)

ROBIN CHAPMAN

Take a bird's-eye view of Lucca (p155), a village full of churches and good restaurants

Swim in the beautiful blue waters surrounding Isola d'Elba (p184)

JON DAVIDSON

JULIET COOMBE

Catch your breath at Piazzale Michelangelo (p109) and be bowled over by the view of Florence

Gaze up in awe at the campanile of Florence's famous Duomo (p87)

JOHN HAY

ALAN BENSON

Sample the amazingly rich and rare black truffles (p140)

Take in the rainbow façade of Orvieto's Gothic
cathedral (p335)

Time it right and catch the late afternoon
sun striking the many towers of San
Gimignano (p219)

Enjoy the sight of the Garfagnana Valley (p162) from the Apuane Alps.

8

DAMIEN SIMONIS

Imagine the performances put on at this 1st-century-BC Roman amphitheatre in Fiesole (p138)

Relax among the greenery of Il Chianti (p141)

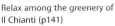

DAMIEN SIMONIS

Discover hidden wonders as you explore the pasturelands of Le Crete (p216)

Climb the marble Renaissance staircases that litter Spoleto (p311), the city of festivals and concerts

JEFFRE'

Contents

Regional Map Contents

Northwestern
Tuscany
p148

Florence
pp78-9

Eastern
Tuscany
p254

Central
Coast &
Elba
p175

Central
Tuscany
p195

Northern
Umbria
p267

Southern
Tuscany
p241

Southern
Umbria
p311

The Authors

MILES RODDIS

Miles updated the Tuscany and introductory chapters, apart from Food & Drink. This is his third Italian job for Lonely Planet and second trawl through Tuscany. Having researched places as disparate as Burkina Faso, these days he writes mostly about Mediterranean lands, living just across the pond in Spain. Miles has written or contributed to more than 25 Lonely Planet books, including *Europe on a Shoestring, Mediterranean Europe, Western Europe, France* and *Walking in France, Spain* and *Walking in Spain,* and *Italy.* He dreams of writing the Tuscany chapter of *Walking in Italy* next time.

My Tuscany & Umbria

If I had to choose, I'd fly into Pisa (p148), explore the town, and aim for Lucca (p155), my favourite Tuscan city – for its food, oval 'square' and wonderfully preserved city walls. Then I'd drop down to Siena (p195), before popping over the border to savour Orvieto (p333) and Perugia (p267). After that I'd head for Florence (p74). Three days there – absolute minimum – and I'd probably be wiped out for monuments and canvases. So I'd enjoy a little exercise and sybaritic excess walking Il Chianti (p141), sampling its wines and dining sumptuously every night. I'd then need a purge in the Apuane Alps (p173), where distractions are fewer and the walking more vigorous.

ALEX LEVITON

Alex updated her original Northern and Southern Umbria chapters, as well as Food & Drink, Transport and Directory. Alex accidentally found Italy on her way to and from Africa during her gap year in 1998. She fell for it and has since returned seven times, six of those visits spent falling passionately in love with Umbria, its people, nature, food, architecture and history. She is a freelance writer, journalist, editor and writing coach who lives in a tobacco warehouse loft in Durham, North Carolina, where she is searching for an Italian-language Scrabble partner.

Getting Started

Tuscany and Umbria offer some of the most diverse and rewarding landscapes in Italy. Tuscany has been on the international tourist trail since the days of the Grand Tour in the 19th century, while its neighbour, largely rural Umbria, has only been 'discovered' by foreign visitors in recent years, and still sees only a fraction of the numbers that swarm through Tuscany.

Pisa's Galileo Galilei airport is the major entry point if you fly in, and the city, with its breathtaking Piazza dei Miracoli, makes a good starting point. Florence, an unparalleled treasure house of art, is, of course, unmissable – though be prepared to jostle with several thousand others who feel the same way – while the towns of Siena and Orvieto are also both hugely popular. The Chianti region, world-famous for its wines, is also high on most visitors' lists.

If you prefer your countryside less trodden, head for the little-explored Casentino region in eastern Tuscany, the spectacular Garfagnana in the northwest, or southern Umbria.

See Climate Charts (p346) for more information.

Florence, understandably, is by far the most expensive place to stay, though there are a few economical options. Other places on the well trodden tourist trail tend to be relatively pricey, too; Chianti, for example, is particularly short on budget accommodation, but can easily be explored by day trip from Florence or Siena. Smaller towns and less-visited rural areas are significantly cheaper.

Main towns are interlinked by train or bus, but to explore the countryside in any depth it makes sense to hire a vehicle.

WHEN TO GO

Tuscany and Umbria pull in visitors year-round, though the busiest time is between May and September, when you will normally need to book accommodation in advance. August is best avoided: the weather's hot and clammy, especially inland, and huge numbers of Italians take their

---

DON'T LEAVE HOME WITHOUT...

- A small daypack
- Mosquito repellent and sun block
- Sturdy walking shoes or trainers
- A wi-fi adaptor to upload your pics daily and tell friends of the fun you're having from the privacy of your hotel room
- Lonely Planet's *Italian Phrasebook*
- A pocket knife (including corkscrew) for picnic time
- A photocopy of your passport and travel insurance policy (see p350)
- Your credit card PIN – you'll be needing it!
- An adaptor plug for electrical appliances (see p342)
- At least one set of smart casual clothes: Italians like to dress up when they go out, and some churches refuse admittance to the skimpily dressed. Perhaps a portable clothesline and travel iron too.
- A valid visa, should you need one (see p356)

holidays then. Coastal resorts in particular are often filled to capacity. The best time to visit is in the low season, from March to early May, and from late September to October, when the weather is pleasantly warm, prices are lower (often significantly so for hotels), and there are fewer tourists. Hotels' definitions of 'low' and 'high' season vary, so do phone around or search the Internet as you plan your break.

The Parco Nazionale delle Foreste Cantinesi and especially the Apuane Alps can be a real relief from the heat – although they are not immune from torrid weather. The Alps also happen to be Tuscany's wettest zone.

You may want to organise your trip to coincide with one or more of the many festivals that enliven the Tuscan and Umbrian calendars (see p348 and the relevant sections in the destination chapters).

COSTS & MONEY

Tuscany's popularity makes it expensive, especially in the cities, while Umbria's growing international profile has also pushed up prices. Wherever you go, accommodation will be far and away your most significant shell-out, and Florence is the place that will empty your pockets the quickest. A double room in a three-star hotel costs from around €90 upwards, while you'll pay around €18 for a dorm bed. In smaller towns there's decent accommodation from about €70. Some hotels throughout the region charge for parking, especially in Florence, where typical prices range from €5, if you're lucky, to upwards of €25. A three-course meal with wine will set you back roughly €30 per person. But it's quite acceptable to just go for a starter or one of the rich range of pasta dishes. Then, of course, there are pizzas aplenty, which cost as little as €5, plus *panini* and many other kinds of well-filled rolls and sandwiches.

Public transport in the region is relatively economical; the express bus service between Florence and Siena, for example, costs only €6.50. Do factor into your calculations admission prices to museums and galleries, which vary considerably and can easily skew your budget.

Ways to Save

If possible, avoid paying for breakfast at your hotel; you'll get much better value at a local café. Stand at the bar to drink your coffee or munch your croissant; prices can double, or even triple, if you sit down and are served at a table – resist the overtures of the occasional trying-it-on café owner, who may try to direct you to a table.

Read the fine print on menus (usually posted outside eating establishments) to check the *coperto* (cover charge) and *servizio* (service fee). Both are the norm, so you usually need to factor in at least €3 before you even open your mouth.

Check museums for free or discounted entrance fees. EU citizens aged under 18 or over 65 quite often get in free, while showing a student card can also frequently get you a discount.

If you're staying in a city for a while, consider investing in a weekly or monthly bus pass.

TRAVEL LITERATURE

Tuscany has been a favourite subject for travel writers for centuries. Umbria, on the other hand, is only beginning to attract international attention. We recommend the following:

A Small Place in Italy (Eric Newby) A delightfully witty, engaging account by this classic travel writer of life in I Castagni, the farmhouse he shares with his feisty Italian wife, Wanda.

LONELY PLANET INDEX

Litre of petrol €1.25

Litre of water €0.60

Bottle of Peroni beer €1.60

Souvenir T-shirt €15

Pizza €5-7

HOW MUCH?

Cappuccino €1.10

Gelato €1.50

Slice of pizza €1.20

Six-pack of Campari €6

Local phone call €0.20

TOP TENS

Festivals & Events

Few regions of Europe can rival Tuscany and Umbria for the variety and vigour of their local *festas*, many of them 20th-century revivals of ancient traditions. For a comprehensive listing, see p348.

- Carnevale (Viareggio), February–March (p166)
- Scoppio del Carro (Florence), Easter Sunday (p114)
- Corsa dei Ceri (Gubbio), 15 May (p297)
- Giostra dell'Archidado (Cortona), May or June (p263)
- Festival dei due Mondi (Spoleto), June–July (p314)
- Estate Fiesolana (Fiesole), June–August (p139)
- Il Palio (Siena), 2 July and 16 August (p212)
- Giostra del Saracino (Arezzo), June and September (p257)
- Sagra Musicale Umbra (Perugia), September (p273)
- Festa di San Francesco (Assisi), 3–4 October (p286)

Films

With its photogenic countryside, unparalleled architectural richness and downright sensuousness, Tuscany remains a favourite location for English-language film directors. See p39 for reviews.

- *A Room with a View* (1986) Director: James Ivory
- *The English Patient* (1996) Director: Anthony Minghella
- *Romeo & Juliet* (1968) Director: Franco Zeffirelli
- *The Talented Mr Ripley* (1999) Director: Anthony Minghella
- *Life Is Beautiful* (1998) Director: Roberto Benigni
- *Hannibal* (2001) Director: Ridley Scott
- *Tea with Mussolini* (1999) Director: Franco Zeffirelli
- *Much Ado About Nothing* (1993) Director: Kenneth Branagh
- *Under the Tuscan Sun* (2003) Director: Audrey Wells
- *Gladiator* (2000) Director: Ridley Scott

Wines

Chianti and the hill-top villages produce some of Italy's best and best-known reds, while Umbria's white Orvieto is as gorgeous as the town that bears its name. For more information on wines of the two regions, see p63.

- Brunello di Montalcino
- Vino Nobile di Montepulciano
- Orvieto Classico
- Vernaccia di San Gimignano
- Carmignano
- Chianti Classico
- Chianti Rufina
- Sagrantino di Montefalco
- Bianco di Pitigliano
- Vin Santo

ella Tuscany: The Sweet Life in Italy (Frances Mayes) Life's not always that sweet in Mayes' equel to *Under the Tuscan Sun,* written with the same sensual imagery.

ketches of Etruscan Places (DH Lawrence) An evocative collection of Lawrence's typically olourful observations on the Etruscan civilisation of central Italy.

he Tuscan Year: Tuscan Life & Food in an Italian Valley (Elizabeth Romer) Tuscan farm life, een through the eyes of a committed foodie, with plenty of recipes to add extra flavour to the text.

nder the Tuscan Sun (Frances Mayes) A best-selling example of the popular expat-literature enre, recounting Mayes' experience of restoring an old rural Tuscan villa, and her musings on local fe, love, cuisine and history.

anilla Beans & Brodo (Isabella Dusi) An enjoyable account of the author's efforts to join in ne close-knit community of Montalcino in southern Tuscany, with all its daily dramas and vibrant haracters.

NTERNET RESOURCES

Bella Umbria (www.bellaumbria.net) A comprehensive guide to the region, with an online otel-booking facility and email newsletter.

onely Planet (www.lonelyplanet.com) Cconcise information, postcards from other travellers nd the Thorn Tree bulletin board, where you can ask questions before you go, or dispense advice vhen you return.

mbria Tourism (www.umbriatourism.com) General information with links to other sites, ncluding various towns.

urismo in Toscana (www.turismo.toscana.it) The official Tuscany tourism website with xtensive information on accommodation, restaurants and the like.

uscany Life (www.tuscanylife.it) Slightly offbeat information on a range of topics, from wine outes and festivals to where to find 'aged trees'.

Itineraries

CLASSIC ROUTES

TUSCAN HILL TOWNS
Two days/Monteriggioni to Siena or Florenc

Start early in **Monteriggioni** (p217), just off the SS2 – you can see the whol town in half an hour and still have time for an espresso fix. From here it's 9km north to **Colle di Val d'Elsa** (p217). Go to the *alta* (high) part c town for a stroll and end up at the leafy piazza. It's a pretty run due wes of here to **Volterra** (p224), where you can check out the region's oldes town hall and have a late lunch, then head northeast to **San Gimignan** (p219), your overnight stop, along the more picturesque back road (se the boxed text, p223). Walk quickly around town before climbing up th Torre Grossa for an eye-popping panoramic view. Next morning, hea north to **Certaldo** (p144), where you can leave your vehicle and hop on th cable car up to the old part of town. Dip into the Palazzo Pretorio for quick peek at the frescoes and stay for lunch before putting your foot o the pedal and hitting the road south to **Siena** (p195) or north to **Florenc** (p74); either city is easily reachable within an hour.

This 85km itinerary is a good introduction to Tuscany's hill-top strongholds. With a vehicle you can leave the coach parties in your wake and cover all these towns in a couple of days. The drive, with plenty of breathtaking scenery, is almost as good as the arrival.

FIVE CITIES IN SIX DAYS

Six days/Siena to Assisi

This blockbuster trip kicks off with 24 hours in **Siena** (p195). Spend the morning 'doing' the Duomo group clustered around the cathedral. After lunch, lose yourself in the backstreets for a couple of hours, finishing up with a spot of retail therapy on Via di Città, before winding up at the magnificent Il Campo piazza. Hit a couple of museums before bedding down. Next day it's north to another heavy, **Florence** (p74), for a minimum of two days. Don't miss *David* and yet another Duomo, the Palazzo Pitti or the Uffizi. The following day hit the E35 to **Arezzo** (p254), arriving in plenty of time for lunch, or to buy picnic goodies at the market on Piazza Sant'Agostino. Wander around the old quarter, stopping for a cold beer on Piazza Grande overlooking the Romanesque Pieve di Santa Maria. Either stay overnight here or head south for **Perugia** (p267) in Umbria, dipping into the quintessential Tuscan hill town of **Cortona** (p262) with its steep medieval alleys, Renaissance art and stunning views. The road to Perugia passes the northern end of Lago di Trasimeno, where you should stop for refreshment (ice cream, anyone?) on the banks at Passignano. Once you hit Perugia, keep the blinkers on and aim straight for the medieval centre where, after a little shopping on Corso Vannucci, you can enjoy yet more cultural overload at the 13th-century ensemble around Piazza IV Novembre. From Perugia it's a mere 14km east to lovely, pink-stoned **Assisi** (p281).

It's possible, promise! The only problem is that you won't quite be able to do any place justice – especially the giants of Florence and Siena. But this 250km itinerary will give you a taste of the big-city scene – and it will help you to plan your next visit...You'll be surprised at how different each is.

UMBRIAN HISTORY & HILL TOWNS

Two to three weeks
Perugia to Assis

For a trek back through time start, in **Perugia** (p267) before heading
northeast to **Gubbio** (p294), the 'City of Silence', for a relaxing step into
the medieval epoch. Cut west to **Lago di Trasimeno** (p288) and **Tuoro** (p291)
where Hannibal taught the Romans a lesson in the Battle of Trasimeno
Then jump on the A1 south to **Orvieto** (p333), where the miracle-inspired
Romanesque and Gothic cathedral shimmers in the sun.

For the most ancient of ancient stone town walls and arches, head
to **Todi** (p322), **Amelia** (p331), **Narni** (p327) or all three, any of which will
inspire even the least artistically inclined to want to take a brush to can
vas. Wind your way quickly through Terni to the SS209 and meander
through the scenery mecca of the **Valnerina** (p317), making sure to stop
at San Pietro in Valle, where you can dine in an 8th-century abbey or
wander the ruins or local trails. Cross the mountain to **Spoleto** (p311)
filled with ancient stone staircases and a Roman theatre that houses the
world-famous Spoleto Festival. Take the SS75 to **Trevi** (p309), a Slow City
mired in a mix of afternoon naps, greying olive trees and vistas of the
Spoleto Valley.

Take the long way through the **Strada del Sagrantino** (trail of Sagrantino
wine; p330) through the impossibly charming wine towns of **Montefalco**
(p307) and **Bevagna** (p307) to get to hill-top **Spello** (p303). The last stop
heading back to Perugia is **Assisi** (p281), including a visit to Giotto's
fresco cycle in the St Francis Basilica. Take a moment to sit in the crypt
of St Francis, as you'll now understand how the beauty of Umbria could
so move him.

**Even if you just
cover one or two
legs of this
journey, you'll
most likely fall
madly in love with
the green heart
of Italy and its
relatively
untamed land.**

BEST OF THE REGION

**Two weeks to two months/
Circular route from Florence**

Starting in **Florence** (p74), move westwards to take in the towns of **Prato** (p134), **Pistoia** (p130), **Lucca** (p155) and **Pisa** (p148), making one of the last two an overnight stop. From here you might want to pop along to one of the beaches around nearby **Viareggio** (p165). The centre of Tuscany's white-marble industry, **Carrara** (p170), is a worthwhile stop, and you could easily lose yourself for several days in the northwestern corner of the region. The main attraction is the walking in the **Garfagnana** (p162), the **Apuane Alps** (p173) and the little-visited **Lunigiana** (p172).

Return to Pisa via **Barga** (p164) and **Bagni de Lucca** (p163), and travel along the coast, stopping at **Castiglioncello** (p180). Head inland from the coast, then south towards **Piombino** (p183), visiting towns such as **Suvereto** (p182) and **Massa Marittima** (p243). Unless it's August, when the island seethes, hop on the ferry for **Elba** (p184) from Piombino and spend a couple of days touring. Back on the mainland, head northeast to **Siena** (p195), where you should base yourself to take in the surrounding hill-top villages. Cross into Umbria and continue east to **Assisi** (p281), stopping next at **Spello** (p303) for a quick fix of the region's small-town charm. Next stop is **Spoleto** (p311), an unbeatable base for hiking. Carry on to the hill-top town of **Narni** (p327), where you can catch the highway back to **Perugia** (p267) and return to Florence, having a quick look at **Arezzo** (p254) en route.

This trip can be speedy or luxuriously slow, depending on how much time you have. The total number of kilometres you clock up depends entirely on how adventurous you are when exploring the Apuane Alps, Lunigiana and Elba (but you will probably manage at least 800km).

Few will have time to complete this 800km monster trip, but you might want to use it as a checklist, or pick off parts. If you do have the time and a sense of adventure, this route will provide you with a few more poetic superlatives to describe the region, as well as improve your map-reading skills.

TAILORED TRIPS

TUSCANY & UMBRIA FOR KIDS

Start your kiddie trip with Collodi's **Parco di Pinocchio** (p161), a theme park entirely devoted to Italy's best-known, and cheekiest, fictional character. Follow this by a paddle at the bucket-and-spade resort of **Viareggio** (p165). Hightail it to Pisa for a photo of the **Leaning Tower** (p150) for the family album (don't forget to include the classic holding-up-the-tower shots). From here, head for the fairytale city of **San Gimignano** (p219), good for

a frolic around its narrow streets and up to the old fortress. Next stop: Siena. Jump on the **Treno Natura** (p211) for a family-fun railway journey through the gentle Crete Senese countryside. Carry on to the **Museo della Mezzadria Senese** (p216) in Buonconvento with its multimedia presentation about what life was like living on the land. If antique farm tools sounds a bit heavy going for your two-year-old, swing east for the natural reserve at **Lago di Montepulciano**, where feathered friends like the purple heron make a change from feeding the ducks back home. Finally, dip into Umbria for a boat trip or swim at **Lago di Trasimeno** (p288).

TIPPLER'S TOUR

Kick-start this trip in **Il Chianti** (p141) country at a wine museum in **Rufina**, followed by a tour of the nearby Castello di Brolio vineyard (☎ 057 77 301). Take the E76 to **Montecarlo**, the main wine-producing town in the foothills of the Appenines. Try the local drop, *Montecarlo*, at Piccola Enoteca (Via Roma 26). The region south of Pisa is famous for its dry whites. Head for **Crespina** and try the light, crisp *Novello* at Enoteca Alisi Cristiana (Località Cenaia) in town. Next, sample the wines of the Etruschi Costa. Take Hwy 1 to **Bolgheri**, at the centre of this wine region. Enjoy a glug of the complex *Sassicaia di Bolgheri* cabernet at Enoteca Tognoni (Piazza Teresa 2). Weave your way southeast to lovely **Massa**

Marittima (p243), surrounded by vineyards, and treat your wine cellar to a couple of bottles of *Vino Monteregio*. It's a short hop from here to the Enoteca at **Montalcino's** (p228) Fortezza and a taste of the velvety *Brunello*. Next stop is **Montepulciano** (p234), home of the deliciously snooty *Vino Nobile*, which you can try at several wine cellars in town. Southeast of here is Umbria's main wine-producing area of **Torgiano** (p279), south of Perugia. Look for the aromatic *Rubesco Riserva*, one of Italy's finest wines.

This trip is recommended by car and, as it involves countless hectolitres of vino, with a designated driver.

WORLD HERITAGE SITES

This is the kind of itinerary you take pics of to *really* impress the folks back home! Each of the places we highlight features on Unesco's World Heritage list – a guarantee that a place is exceptionally worth seeing. Others we mention may not bear that international seal of quality, but won't fail to enchant. Begin with a serious slug of Renaissance and primarily religious culture in the historic centre of **Florence** (p74). Reserve your visit to the Uffizi Gallery in advance, start with the magnificent cathedral and its tower, then head towards Pisa, if you can tear yourself away. The easiest route is via **Lucca** (p155), relaxed and pedestrianised within the sturdy bastions of its intact city walls. In **Pisa** (p148), retreat a century or two to explore the Romanesque splendours of its Piazza dei Miracoli; that famous Leaning Tower is only one of a trio of medieval master-

pieces. Backtrack towards Florence, taking a detour to **Certaldo** (p144). A short jig south of here is the historic centre of **San Gimignano** (p219), a hill-top town like Certaldo where you can easily hang out for a few hours before hightailing it to the historic centre of **Siena** (p195), calling by **Monteriggioni** (p217), another walled medieval stronghold, on the way. You can't savour the Gothic treats of Siena and its Piazza del Campo in less than two days. From here, it's an easy run southwards to the historic centre of **Pienza** (p232), a tiny jewel of a village, which you can walk from one end to the other in 15 minutes or so. The cultural overload has been pretty severe so far, so it could be time to take a deep

breath of fresh air while exploring the gentle countryside of the **Val d'Orcia** (p231), Italy's latest attraction to receive World Heritage status. Hotel accommodation is fairly sparse hereabouts, so you might want to detour westwards to **Montalcino** (p228) or eastwards to **Montepulciano** (p234). Both these charming towns merit a lengthy evening stroll, have excellent restaurants, and offer superb, top-of-the-range local wines – once the driving day's over! From Montepulciano it's pretty much a straight line due east from here to your final destination, Assisi, over the border in Umbria. On the way, make the short detour northwards to **Castiglione del Lago** (p290), brooding over Lago di Trasimeno. Back on route, stop off in cosmopolitan **Perugia** (p267), another wonderfully preserved hill town. Your last port of call is **Assisi** (p281), equally stunning with a more spiritual air. Be sure to stay the night here: it's especially magical at dusk after the coach tours have left.

Snapshot

Tourism, especially from the US, is down, hoteliers in the big towns will tell you with a self-pitying shake of the head. The German and Brit settlers and second-homers of Il Chianti are upping sticks and heading for Mediterranean lands further east, where a plot can be bought for a snip, the estate agents and realtors will aver with a wring of their hands.

You won't even notice it. The cultural and scenic honey pots of Tuscany and Umbria still pull in visitors by the million, and a little extra personal space during high season is no bad thing. So don't fret for them. Numbers may have dropped just a bit, but both regions are still among Italy's most prosperous and both can fall back on significant agricultural and manufacturing bases, should tourism times ever get really hard.

One of Tuscany's greatest ecological issues remains marble extraction in the Apuane Alps. As in any debate there are two sides. The Carrara quarries have been worked since Roman times, but the rate of extraction today chews away huge chunks of the mountainside. Then again, Carrara marble is one of Tuscany's prestige exports, revered as the world's best. And the quarries employ more than 2000 workers who have little opportunity for alternative employment, beyond becoming waiters in resorts on the nearby coast.

On the positive side, Tuscany and Umbria, even though their people are traditionally opposed, like all Italians, to bureaucratic limitations upon perceived freedoms, have imposed strict controls on traffic in the historical heart of major cities. You park in Florence, Lucca and Pisa at your peril and the vehicle-free (to the extent that anywhere in anarchic Italy is *truly* car-free) streets, alleys and lanes are a sheer pleasure to walk.

Politically, both regions have traditionally favoured the left, and the April 2005 local elections continued this trend. Both Tuscany and Umbria elected presidents from l'Unione, a broad left-wing coalition. In common with six of Italy's eight regions, voters trounced the rival Casa della Libertà (Liberties House), whose principal partner is Prime Minister Silvio Berlusconi's Forza Italia party. Although the elections were on a regional scale, the vote was a resounding rejection for Berlusconi and his party and a rejection of the national government's unswerving support for Western intervention in Iraq and its failure to stem illegal immigration across both the Adriatic and Mediterranean Seas.

Forza Italia shared a bed with a ragbag of parties, ranging from benign middle-of-the-road social democrats to the neofascists of the Alleanza Nazionale (National Alliance) and the strident, parish-pump Lega Nord (Northern Alliance), a party which has little or no power base in the more nationally and internationally minded regions of Tuscany and Umbria.

FAST FACTS

Combined population: 4.35 million

Annual population growth: 0.07%

GDP per head: US$26,200

Inflation: 2.3%

Unemployment: 5.2%

Land area: 31,430 sq km

Vineyard area: 108,000 hectares

Annual wine production: 4.7 million hectolitres

History

ETRUSCANS & ROMANS

By the 8th century BC, the Etruscan civilisation was well established across central Italy and within 200 years the Etruscans had become the dominant power in what are today known as Tuscany and Umbria, overcoming the native Umbrians, as well as parts of Lazio. The Etruscan settlements, though, were largely independent of one another, held together in a loose confederation of 12 main cities, including Fiesole, Cortona, Volterra, Arezzo and Perugia. You can still see remnants of this fascinating culture, from extensive museum collections of bronzes and pottery to once richly adorned tombs scattered around the countryside. Florence's Museo Archeologico (see p102) has a fascinating collection. For an exciting recent tomb discovery, see the boxed text on p239.

Nobody really knows where these ancient people are originally from. The Greek historian Herodotus suggested that they migrated in waves from Asia Minor in the wake of the Trojan Wars, while others have claimed they were an indigenous tribe, originating on the Italian peninsula. Work still continues today on translating their archaic language, which may throw some more light on the matter, but in the meantime nearly all we know of them comes from archaeological records.

The rise of Rome spelled the end for the Etruscans; in 309 BC the Romans took Perusia (modern Perugia), a major Etruscan stronghold. This marked the start of a campaign of conquest that would eventually bring the whole of Etruria under Roman influence, firmly bound to the Eternal City through a system of compulsory alliances. The independent culture of the Etruscans was slowly eroded, and gradually their language died out. However, things didn't always go the Romans' way. In the late 3rd century, they faced their most dangerous foe, the Carthaginian leader Hannibal, who famously invaded the Italian peninsula with his army of elephants. In 217 BC the two forces met on the shores of Lago di Trasimeno, in what is now northern Umbria, and the Romans suffered a monumental defeat, losing as many as 16,000 men.

The 1st century BC saw a rapid expansion of the Roman Empire in Tuscany, with the founding of cities such as Florentia (Florence), Saena Julia (Siena) and Pistoria (Pistoia). Umbria too thrived under Roman administration, with the foundation of towns such as Hispellum (Spello), which grew wealthy on the passing trade of the Via Flaminia, one of Rome's most important roadways. From the 1st century AD onwards, Christianity spread rapidly through the two regions, and Umbria especially played an important role in the growth of monasticism; St Benedict, born in Norcia in 480, was one of the early pioneers.

THE EARLY MIDDLE AGES

By the 5th century AD, the Western Roman Empire was beginning to disintegrate, and Tuscany and Umbria succumbed to the might of the Gothic armies led by Totila. But the Eastern Roman Empire was still very much alive and well. Its emperor, Justinian, sitting in his capital Byzantium

www.mysterious etruscans.com has interesting and comprehensive information on the ancient and still poorly understood Etruscan civilisation.

In *Daily Life of the Etruscans*, Jacques Heurgon's up-to-date research attempts to unravel the mysteries of this archaic culture, investigating the origins of their language and religion.

TIMELINE	**8th century–6th century BC**	**309 BC**
	Etruscan civilisation is established across central Italy and reaches its peak of power and wealth	Rome takes Perugia, signalling the decline of the Etruscans and the rise of the Roman Empire

(Constantinople, today's Istanbul) was keen to recapture Italy. He sent his eunuch general, Narses, to face the barbarian horde, and in 552 these fresh invaders defeated and killed Totila near the modern town of Gualdo Tadino. Within only 20 years, though, the Lombards from the west wrested control of Tuscany and most of Umbria from Byzantine forces and established powerful dukedoms based around Lucca and Spoleto. They in turn were driven out in the late 8th century by the Franks, who also favoured Lucca as their power base. In 800 Charlemagne, leader of the Franks, formed an uneasy alliance with the papacy to create the Holy Roman Empire that was to be such a force in Europe over succeeding centuries. He installed the quaintly named margraves (roughly the equivalent of an English marquis) to rule the various districts on his behalf. In 978 Willa, the widow of Margrave Uberto, established the Badia, Florence's first abbey, and in 1000 her son, Ugo, took advantage of this family foothold and transferred his capital to Florence.

This was an unstable period fraught with provincial squabbles and regional rivalries. In Umbria, under the fairly nominal control of the Papal States, local lords feuding among themselves threw up defensive castles, several of which remain to this day. Over the border, 11th-century Tuscany saw the beginnings of the disastrous Imperial–Papal divisions that so dominated the Middle Ages in central Italy. Under the rule of Countess Matilda Canossa, the County of Tuscia (Tuscany) had achieved considerable independence from the empire. When hostilities broke out between Emperor Henry IV and Pope Gregory VII, Matilda sided with the pope, setting a precedent that would long resonate through Florentine history. Henry tried to have the pope deposed in 1077, but instead found himself at Matilda's castle of Canossa, in Emilia, dressed in sackcloth and imploring His Holiness to lift an order of excommunication.

Matilda's death in 1115 spelled the end of Tuscia as a political unit as the cities of Florence, Siena and Lucca flexed their muscles and declared their independence, the rest of erstwhile Tuscia coming under papal rule.

GUELPHS & GHIBELLINES

In the 13th century, the city-states of Pisa, Siena, Perugia and especially Florence, grew fat on the proceeds of trade, most notably textiles and banking. By 1300, Florence was one of the largest and richest cities in Europe with over 100,000 inhabitants. But peace, as so often throughout the history of the region, was at a premium. Political plotting and counterplotting brought increasing instability in the 14th century, and many cities divided into the opposing factions of the pro-empire Ghibellines and the pro-pope Guelphs. In reality, though, the divisions were as often based on family feuds, personal promotion and class antagonism as any lofty political ideology. This rumbling conflict broke out into open and bloody warfare, with Guelph Florence gaining the upper hand over Ghibelline Pisa, Siena and Arezzo.

Umbrian cities, developing into independent republics, also used the factional rivalries as an excuse for mercenary wars, land-grabbing and violent vendettas. But none had the resources of the great Tuscan cities and they all but destroyed themselves. The papacy, keen to exploit the weakness of these Umbrian cities, began to pick them off, starting with Spoleto

---

59 BC

Julius Caesar founds the colony of Florentia

AD 568

Lombards invade, turning Tuscany and Umbria into dukedoms controlled from Lucca and Spoleto

in 1354. Only Perugia managed to hold out against the papal forces, and Umbria slowly slid into the background of Italian power-politics.

The Black Death (bubonic plague) of 1348 ravaged the towns and countryside, decimating the population. Florence's woes were compounded by the collapse of two of its largest banks, but it soon bounced back, capturing Prato just three years later and – in a very Florentine way – simply buying Arezzo in 1384. Continuing its expansionist policy, it gobbled up Pisa some 20 years later.

It wasn't all plots, war and plague, though. This was also the age of St Francis of Assisi (see the boxed text, p281), when Dante and Boccaccio wrote and Cimabue and Giotto painted, their revolutionary artistic style laying the groundwork for the masters of the Renaissance.

The Fall of the Roman Empire: A New History by Peter Heather, recently released, ascribes the decline of the Roman Empire primarily to the impact of invading Huns from the Black Sea littoral.

THE RENAISSANCE

In 1434, Cosimo il Vecchio (The Elder – so called to avoid confusion with Cosimo I de Medici, who came later) started his career as the head of a wealthy banking family. This talented administrator then took effective control of the Florentine lands, thus introducing the lengthy and hugely influential rule of the Medici dynasty. Though extinct for some 250 years, the Medici remain a powerful presence in Tuscany to this day. There are few towns that don't boast at least one Medici-commissioned structure, while their heraldic shield with its six balls is a common sight.

Under Cosimo, a passionate patron of the arts, the humanist revolution in thinking and the accompanying Rinascimento (Renaissance) in the visual arts took off. These interrelated movements had been under way since the previous century, in, for example the work of artists such as Giotto. But the generous patronage of the Medici family was a catalyst that would turn Florence into the most innovative centre of the arts in all of Europe. New universities, open to disciplines other than theology, encouraged the serious study of a whole range of subjects. Much of the impetus came from the rediscovery of important, long lost ancient Greek and Latin texts. It was fomented too by contact with the decaying Byzantine Empire, that last vestige of the old Roman world and the repository of ancient learning and culture on the fringe of Europe. The Church Council of Florence in 1439 brought many Byzantine scholars to the city. Many others, seeing the rapidly approaching end of Constantinople as the Turks

The Merchant of Prato by Iris Origo brings medieval Tuscany vividly to life in a tale of domestic and business affairs based on the extensive correspondence of a 14th-century entrepreneur.

LEONARDO DA VINCI

Leonardo da Vinci (1421–1519) is the archetypal, open-minded, turn-yourself-to-anything Renaissance man. Primarily an artist (the way he preferred to define himself), he also turned his mind, whirring like one of the complex machines he designed, to everything from astronomy to zoology.

He had a particular interest in human anatomy and dissected over 30 corpses. There was no end to the man's inventiveness, revealed in his notebooks, with drawings and often detailed specifications for, among much more, a horse-drawn tank, a cog-driven mechanical calculator, a parachute, a submarine and a scheme for harnessing solar power. Most of his creations never got beyond the drawing board but today you can see accurate models of more than 50 of them in his home town of Vinci (p145).

1200–1300	1348
Florence, Siena and Perugia become wealthy through trade and banking; Florence is one of Europe's largest and richest cities	The Black Death (bubonic plague) wreaks havoc, decimating the population

advanced, were making their own independent way to western Europe. The rediscovery of classical learning soon became a rediscovery of classical art forms, while the study of science blossomed, led by that most famous of polymaths, Leonardo da Vinci (see the boxed text, p25).

Lorenzo il Magnifico (the Magnificent) continued his grandfather's work, expanding the city's power and continuing to patronise all things artistic (see below).

Lorenzo's death and his succession by his charmless son Piero in 1492 spelled the end, for the moment, of Medici rule and signalled the start of heated times for Florence.

Umbria, meanwhile, had declined into something of an agricultural backwater, disputed by petty princes and the papacy. Orvieto in particular became a favoured papal residence.

THE LATER MEDICIS

In 1494 Piero de' Medici was obliged to hand Florence over to the invading French king Charles VIII, before fleeing from an increasingly hostile population. The people had turned against the opulence and excesses of the Medici court and found a new champion in the dour Dominican monk, Girolamo Savonarola (see opposite), who became an increasingly strident voice in the short-lived republic, established after the expulsion of the Medici.

An altogether more subtle operator in the Republic was Niccolò Machiavelli (see the boxed text, p28), whose name has entered the English language – unfairly, as a result of character assassination by his many contemporary enemies – as a word for shifty, self-interested dealing.

The republic was soon over and the Medicis, headed by Giuliano, were back, returned to power backed by a Spanish-led army in 1512. Giuliano and his vicious successors never gained popularity and the family was once again sent packing in 1527, only to return once more in 1530, courtesy of a papal-imperial siege.

Cosimo I assumed power in 1537, determined to keep a key role for Florence in the affairs of a still-fractured Italy. A crucial moment came in 1555

Browse some of the fascinating documents of the Medici archives at www.medici.org.

The Rise and Fall of the House of Medici by Christopher Hibbert is a highly readable account of Florentine society during the centuries of Medici rule.

THE MAGNIFICENT MEDICI

At a time when freedom of expression was not always encouraged by the ruling elite, Lorenzo il Magnifico (the Magnificent) created a climate of tolerance in which the great Renaissance artists and scholars could flourish. Among others who enjoyed his patronage and protection were Michelangelo, Luca della Robbia, Botticelli and Leon Battista Alberti.

But his wisdom didn't stop at art and literature. Lorenzo's diplomatic skills brought a much-needed period of peace to the region. Soon after taking power, he managed to negotiate a settlement with the king of Naples, averting war and earning himself the respect of the Florentines into the bargain. A papal-inspired assassination attempt in 1478 – the Pazzi Conspiracy – only made him more popular. For the rest of his rule, he slowly reinforced, through peaceful means, the position of Florence as a great city-state.

Just as his popularity was coming under fire from the doom-laden Savonarola, Lorenzo died. The outpouring of grief in Florence marked the beginning of a new era as relative peace and prosperity gave way to political uncertainty, economic gloom and an artistic downturn.

1434

Cosimo de' Medici establishes Medici rule in Florence and encourages the birth of the Renaissance

1469–1737

Tuscany's fortunes rise and fall as the later Medicis continue to rule

---

SAVONAROLA

In the streets of Florence, and increasingly within the court of Lorenzo il Magnifico itself, people had begun to listen intently to the fanatical preachings of a Dominican monk called Girolamo Savonarola.

Born in Ferrara, Savonarola moved to Florence, where he preached against luxury, greed, corruption of the clergy and the very Renaissance itself. To him the Church and the world were corrupt and its rulers, oppressors.

In 1494, when Piero de' Medici fled, a republic was proclaimed and Savonarola was appointed its legislator. Under his severe, moralistic lead, the city underwent a kind of religious reform.

But his enemies were many and powerful. The corrupt Pope Alexander VI, of the infamous Borgia family, excommunicated Savonarola for preaching against him. Then, as the Florentine public turned cold on the evangelistic preacher, he began to lose the support of his dwindling political allies.

After refusing to undergo ordeal by fire, Savonarola was arrested. On 22 May 1498 in Florence's Piazza della Signoria (where today a plaque marks the spot), he was hanged and burned at the stake for heresy and his ashes scattered into the Arno.

---

when at long last Florence captured its old rival, Siena, after a year-long siege. Apart from Lucca and its modest possessions, Florence was now in control of the whole of Tuscany, and, in recognition of this, Pope Pius V conferred upon Cosimo the title of grand duke of Tuscany in 1569.

Though a ruthless despot, Cosimo did sort out the city's finances, build a fleet (which participated in the crushing defeat of the Turkish navy in the Battle of Lepanto in 1571) and promote economic growth across Tuscany with mining and irrigation programs for agriculture. Like his illustrious namesake, he was a patron of the arts and sciences, and also reformed the civil service. Tuscany and Florence also owe to him two of their most significant sights: the Uffizi (p94), built by him and designed to house all government departments in a single, more easily controlled building, and the Palazzo Pitti (p105), which he and his family acquired, moved into and embellished.

The Civilization of the Renaissance in Italy by Jacob Burckhardt is a classic 19th-century work on this vital period.

THE MEDICIS OF THE GRAND DUCHY

From the death of Cosimo I (1574) until that of the dissolute lout Gian Gastone de' Medici in 1737, the once glorious family continued to cling on to Tuscany though a long period of decline was setting in. Umbria at this time was a forgotten, rural corner of Italy with poor communications to the outside world, whose agricultural-based economy was suffering badly under the poor management of the papacy.

Cosimo I's two immediate successors, Francesco and Ferdinando I, between them managed to keep Tuscany out of trouble. They managed to restimulate the local economy, promote agriculture, build hospitals and bring some relief to the poor. And Cosimo II had the foresight to invite Galileo Galilei to Florence, where the scientist could continue his research under Tuscan protection (see the boxed text, p29).

Galileo's desiccated middle finger is preserved like a saintly relic in Florence's Museum of the History of Science (p97).

The lengthy reign of the humourless, anti-Semitic, anti-intellectual Cosimo III, from 1642 to 1723, was a real low-point in Tuscan history. The population was in decline, the economy a mess and taxes skyrocketing. The

---

1799	1860
Napoleon marches on Florence	Tuscany and Umbria join the Kingdom of Piedmont on the way to Italian unification

---

MACHIAVELLI'S MANOEUVRES

Born in 1469 into a poor offshoot of one of Florence's leading families, Niccolò Machiavelli got off to a bad start. His father, an impoverished, small-time lawyer was continually in debt, but was at least rich in books, which his son devoured.

Somehow the young Machiavelli managed to swing a post in the city's second chancery at the age of 29 and so embarked on a colourful career as a Florentine public servant. Our man must have shown early promise, as by 1500 he was in France on his first diplomatic mission in the service of the Republic.

Impressed by the martial success of Cesare Borgia and the centralised state of France, Machiavelli came to the conclusion that Florence needed a standing army.

The city, like many others on the Italian peninsula, used to employ mercenaries to fight its wars. The problem was that mercenaries had few reasons to fight and die for anyone. They took their pay and often did their best to avoid mortal combat. Machiavelli convinced the Republic of the advantages of a conscripted militia, which he formed in 1506. Three years later it was blooded in battle against the rebellious city of Pisa, whose fall was mainly attributed to the troops led by the wily statesman.

The return to power of the Medici family in 1512 was a blow for Machiavelli, who was promptly removed from office. Suspected of plotting against the Medicis, he was even thrown into the dungeon in 1513 and tortured. He maintained his innocence and, once freed, retired to his little property outside Florence a poor man.

It was in these years, far from political power, that he did his greatest writing. *Il Principe* (The Prince) is his classic treatise on the nature of power and its administration, a work reflecting the confusing and corrupt times in which he lived and a desire for strong and just rule in Florence and beyond.

Machiavelli never got back into the mainstream of public life. He was commissioned to write an official history of Florence, *Istorie Fiorentine,* and towards the end of his life he was appointed to a defence commission to improve the city walls and join a papal army in its ultimately futile fight against imperial forces. By the time the latter had sacked Rome in 1527, Florence had again rid itself of Medici rule. Machiavelli hoped that he would be restored to a position of dignity, but by now he was suspected almost as much by the Medicis' opponents as he had been years before by the Medicis. He died in 1527 frustrated and, as in his youth, on the brink of poverty.

---

pathetic figure of Gian Gastone signalled a sad end indeed to the Medici dynasty, and when he died in 1737, a foreigner, Francis, Duke of Lorraine and husband of the Austrian empress Maria Theresa, was appointed grand duke of Tuscany.

The world, and Florence in particular, have one more lasting reason to be grateful to the Medicis: Gian Gastone's sister, Anna Maria, bequeathed all the Medici property and their incomparable art collections to the grand duchy of Tuscany, on the condition that they never leave the city.

AUSTRIA & FRANCE IN CHARGE

The imperial Austrian couple, Empress Maria Teresa and Francis, paid a brief visit to Florence, leaving the grand duchy in the hands of the *reggenza* (regents), who brought a period of peace and order, enacting much-needed reforms and streamlining the civil administration. Pietro Leopoldo, who took over in 1765, proved to be an enlightened ruler, abolishing torture and the death penalty, suppressing the Inquisition,

---

and embarking on a number of plans for civic improvement. This was the golden age of the Grand Tour, when wealthy young men from all over Europe would travel through Italy to finish their education and find inspiration in the landscape, art and architecture.

Austrian rule ended abruptly in 1799 when Napoleon marched into Florence, making it the capital of the new 'Kingdom of Etruria' under Louis de Bourbon. The French reorganised Umbria in an attempt to stimulate the economy, and succeeded in bringing a new vigour to this moribund corner of the peninsula. But the grandly named Kingdom of Etruria was short-lived: in 1807, Napoleon changed his mind, ingested Tuscany into his French empire and installed his sister, Elisa, who reigned as grand duchess for a mere five years, before the Lorraine dynasty was reinstated.

TOWARDS ITALIAN UNITY

Grand Duke Ferdinando III proved to be one of the more popular Tuscan overlords. He pushed through a raft of reforms at every level of city and grand-ducal administration, and Tuscany became an ever-bigger draw for foreign artists and writers such as Byron and Shelley.

Under the rule of his son, Leopoldo II, the first long-distance rail line (Florence–Pisa–Livorno) and the first telegraphic link (Florence–Pisa) were both opened in the 1840s. In 1847, Lucca was transferred to the control of the grand duchy, ending centuries of Luccan independence.

The progressive political movements that were sweeping through Europe also found supporters in Italy. In 1848, when the whole continent seemed to be up in arms, there were insurrections in Pisa and Livorno, calling for a Tuscan constitution. Very soon came calls for a united Italian state, and

---

THE WORLD TURNS

'Eppur si muove' ('And yet it does move'), Galileo Galilei is said to have muttered after being compelled to recant his teachings on astronomy before the Inquisition in Rome in 1633. He was referring to the earth, whose prime position at the centre of the universe he had questioned. The earth rotated around the sun with the other planets, he insisted, just as the Polish astronomer Copernicus (who died the year before Galileo was born) had claimed.

Born in Pisa in 1564, Galileo studied at the monastery of Vallombrosa before taking up medicine at the University of Pisa. His fascination with mathematics and the study of motion led him to astronomy, and in 1610 he moved to Florence, where the Grand Duke offered him permanent residence to continue his research.

Galileo had been warned by conservative church authorities not to proceed with his wild claims, which, they felt, threatened the geocentric Christian view of the world and creation itself, not to mention the position of the Catholic Church within God's works. Galileo's own works were placed on the index of banned books and declared blasphemous.

All the same, he was given permission to write an 'objective study' and produced what is a triumph of reasoned argumentation in favour of his own theory. However, he was summoned before the Inquisition in Rome in 1632 in order to explain himself. Confined to internal exile in Florence until his death 10 years later, he continued to study, experiment, write books and correspond with other scientists across Europe.

He lies buried in Florence's Basilica di Santa Croce (p103).

1940	**1943**
Fascist Italy enters WWII on Nazi Germany's side	Italy surrenders

after mass demonstrations Leopold was forced out in 1859. The following year Tuscany and Umbria joined the Kingdom of Piedmont. Then, in 1865, Florence became the temporary capital of the newly independent Italy, until Rome was freed from papal rule and given the honour in 1870.

WWI & FASCISM

Florence: The Biography of a City by Christopher Hibbert is a fascinating, scholarly account of the great city's history and art.

Tuscany and Umbria at the beginning of the 20th century were, like much of Italy, poor and economically weak. Social discontent led to the growth of socialist and anarchist movements, while conditions in Umbria were worse still, compounded by mass emigration from the land. Florence, meanwhile, had never been more popular with foreign visitors, especially the British, and a thriving tourist industry quickly grew. EM Forster, DH Lawrence and Oscar Wilde were just some of the writers and artists who fell in love with the city of the Medicis.

Italy's decision to enter WWI in 1915 initially had little direct impact on Tuscany and Umbria, tucked far away from the front lines in the north. Like the rest of the country, however, they paid a high price in the lives of their young men sacrificed as cannon fodder.

By 1917 the situation on Italy's home front had become grim too. All basic products were strictly rationed and that winter, a harsh one, brought intense hardship as heating fuel was virtually unavailable.

Political turmoil following the end of hostilities was inevitable. By 1920 Benito Mussolini's Blackshirts had established branches in Florence, which in less than two years would become one of the Fascists' key strongholds. Tuscany became one of the single biggest sources of card-carrying Fascist members, and fascist violence in Florence became so alarming that Mussolini sent people in to shake out the local organisation and put a brake on the bloodshed.

WWII

Mussolini's decision to enter the war on the side of Germany meant disaster for Italy. Resistance groups began to operate in Tuscany almost immediately and the mountainous and hilly countryside was frequently the stage for partisan assaults and German reprisals. Allied bombers meanwhile caused heavy damage to coastal cities such as Piombino and Livorno. Pisa too was badly bombed – the Camposanto is a tragic monument to the conflict – while raids on Florence were comparatively light.

The British Abroad: The Grand Tour in the Eighteenth Century by Jeremy Black is a witty and well-researched book covering the pleasures and pitfalls of the nascent tourism industry in continental Europe, with quotes from early tourists.

By July 1944, free French troops had occupied the island of Elba. At the same time, Allied forces approached the German lines near Florence. At this point, the German high command decided to blow up the city's bridges, sparing only the Ponte Vecchio (some say it was Hitler who ordered it be spared). Allied troops moved into the city later that day, and Pisa and Lucca both fell to the Allies in the first days of September.

The Allies did not finally break through to the Po valley and force the Germans north until April 1945.

TO THE PRESENT

In the 1946 referendum on whether to institute a republic or a monarchy, Tuscans and Umbrians voted overwhelmingly, along with most of Italy, for a republic. Since then they have watched the comings and goings of

1946	2001
Italians vote in national referendum to abolish the monarchy and create a republic	Silvio Berlusconi's right-wing Casa delle Libertà (Liberties House) coalition wins absolute majority in national polls

national governments from a distance, concerned primarily with what's happening in their regions. The incumbent at the time of writing, Silvio Berlusconi, is a controversial and sometimes tactless media magnate, who is either loved or loathed by Italians, though he has managed to keep his right-of-centre coalition in power for longer than many of his predecessors.

Until the 1950s, Tuscany's economy remained largely based on agriculture, and was suffering from problems of rural depopulation. The advent of light industry saved the region from becoming an economic backwater and by the 1970s, tourism, fashion and banking had become important factors. Umbria, meanwhile, experienced little of the success of its bigger neighbour, and remained a quiet rural corner of Italy best known for its wines and truffles, though in recent years tourism has made inroads into the local economy and the region is beginning to enjoy increasing prosperity.

Both Tuscany and Umbria have limited autonomy and, with their strong regional loyalties and distrust of the central state, believe that more power should be devolved to the regions. Since the 1990s the regions, along with others, have been campaigning to this effect and with some success. It is now envisaged that more powers, including the crucial ability to raise revenue, will be slowly and quietly handed over to the regions.

It was only in 1992 that a Catholic Church commission acknowledged that the ecclesiastical judges who condemned Galileo's scientific theories as blasphemy made an error.

St Clare, a friend of St Francis and founder of the Poor Clares, became the patron saint of TV in 1958.

2003	**2004**
Italy takes up the six-month presidency of the European Union	The Val d'Orcia countryside is added to Unesco's World Heritage list

The Culture

REGIONAL IDENTITY

Tuscany and Umbria are at the geographic heart of Italy, and to many foreigners they represent the essence of the country. In many ways their people are the archetypal Italians: passionate, family-oriented, fond of food and wine, and fanatical – self-preening even – about their clothes and appearance. Tuscans especially are hard-working and proud of their long history of innovation and entrepreneurial spirit. Small-scale, family-run industries thrive in both regions, with tradition and quality still favoured over quantity. The two regions are among the richest in Italy and remain largely rural. The few cities apart, they're lands of small towns and villages with close-knit, ancient communities, where local matters and local gossip are of great concern and national politics are of secondary interest at best.

Italy as a modern nation state is a comparatively new creation, dating from only 1870. Before then, Tuscany and Umbria, though often fragmented into city states or under the boot of an alien occupier, whether from elsewhere in present-day Italy or abroad, had existed for centuries as separate entities. To this day, Tuscans and Umbrians, like most Italians, identify themselves first and foremost with their town and their region. Unless there's an international football match in the offing, you won't see many Italian tricolours flying except from government buildings, but you may well see streets festooned with the pennants of rival *quatiere* (quarters), the age-old division of cities such as Arezzo, Siena and Cortona. Here neighbourhood loyalty is strong, and events such as Il Palio and the Giostra del Saracino boost community spirit and give everyone an opportunity to indulge in the typical Italian passion for dressing up, as they strut about in doublets, fancy tights and felt hats.

Sport, of course, is a major passion, dominated by football, which is forever flickering on the TV. Rugby union is also gaining ground as the Italian team receives more international exposure and success. Food, too, is a popular topic of conversation, while the wines of Tuscany and Umbria are a source of much local pride and a subject upon which many express expertise.

Politically, both regions are left-leaning and the centre-left Ulivo Alliance, formed in 1995, has especially strong support in Umbria. As elsewhere in Italy, support for both the Communists and the parties of the far right has fallen off in recent years, and, like other Italians, the citizens of these two regions have an instinctive distrust of central government.

LIFESTYLE

Tuscans and Umbrians are particularly attached to their home ground and family. Such ties continue to influence how people do things in this part of the world. Many businesses are relatively small, family enterprises. From the great names in wine, such as Antinori, through to the flower-producing industry of Pescia and the small-scale farms of Umbria, most are run by families who pass on the business from generation to generation. Another consequence of this attachment to home and hearth is that people here tend to be much less mobile than in many other European countries, with many spending a lifetime living in the town of their birth.

The family remains the cornerstone of Tuscan and Umbrian society. Although the big extended families of the past are in most cases little more than a distant memory, family ties remain closely knit. Children

See www.regione
.toscana.it – the official
website of the regional
government, with all the
latest news and statistics.
The *'turismo'* section is in
English.

See www.regione
.umbria.it in Italian –
the official website
of Umbria's regional
government.

MUMMY'S BOYS

Although it's a well-worn stereotype, Tuscan and Umbrian men, like other Italians, have always loved mamma – and for much more than her fine cooking. In an age of rising house prices and job insecurity, increasing numbers are choosing to stay at home. Statistics suggest that up to 70% of single, unmarried men under 35 either still live with their parents or have moved back at some stage. Those who do leave the nest rarely go far, most remaining in their home town, and if marriage fails, a quarter of men return to their parents' abode.

For Luigi Barzini, whose 1964 book *The Italians* remains a classic, the family represented a 'stronghold in a hostile land'. That hostile land is a state that has little provision for unemployment benefits and other support that make it easier for youths in other countries to fly the nest – and stay out.

---

still typically remain at home until they reach their 30s, often leaving only when they get married.

Women – at least young women – are shaking off old stereotypes and are active in all departments of work and society. However, chauvinistic attitudes do remain, particularly in rural areas. Tuscans and Umbrians of both sexes are increasingly choosing to concentrate on studies or careers before getting married. They tend to have smaller families than in previous generations, through economic necessity and because, with the declining influence of the Catholic church and readily available birth control, they can, for the first time, take control of their bodies.

'To cook like your mother is good, to cook like your grandmother is better,' says the Tuscan proverb.

The age of consent for homosexuals in Italy is 16, and Tuscany and Umbria are usually tolerant of gay and lesbian communities, although outside Florence and Viareggio there is little 'scene' as such, and overt public displays of affection could meet with a negative response.

The stereotypical perceptions foreigners tend to have of Italians, while they inevitably contain a grain of truth, do not tell much of the story. The image of an animated, gesticulating people seemingly with plenty of time to kill is some distance from the truth.

Thrifty and hard-working, the Tuscans can also be a fairly reserved lot. To be swept up into Tuscan social life (as opposed to circles of resident Italians from other parts of the country) is no mean feat and a sign of considerable success. Umbrian society is also very close-knit and provincial in outlook, and outside the cities, not an easy one for foreigners to penetrate.

Italy and Its Discontents: Family, Civil Society, State: 1980-2001 by Paul Ginsborg is a thorough study of Italy's immediate past, analysing in particular the role of the family and the decline of Catholicism and communism.

POPULATION

Tuscany's population of just over 3.5 million includes some 80,000 foreigners who have made the region their home. Most people live in the northwest in an area bounded by Florence, Livorno, Massa and Pistoia. Prato province is the most crowded, with a little over 600 people per square kilometre.

Umbria, with a population of 834,000, is one of Italy's smaller regions, with over 70% of the people living in the northern province of Perugia. Though a largely rural region, these days only 7% of Umbrians are engaged in agriculture. Industries such as electronics in Terni or textiles in Perugia now draw a larger number of workers.

The make-up of the family unit is perhaps surprising in view of the traditional child-friendliness associated with Italians in general. In line with a national trend, approximately a third of Tuscan families are childless (Italy's birth rate is one of the lowest in Europe).

In recent years Italy has become a prime destination for immigrants, legal and otherwise, from North Africa, Albania and Kosovo, and Tuscany,

---

CLEAN AIR: THERE'S NO SMOKE WITHOUT FINE

In January 2005, Italy introduced a law, just as severe as anything that European pioneers Norway and Ireland have tabled, that effectively outlaws smoking in all enclosed public places.

The fine for maverick puffers ranges from a minimum of €27.50 to a savage €275. Higher penalties hit repeating offenders and those who light up in the presence of pregnant women, lactating mothers and bambini under 12. So if you really must puff, choose your company with care. If you do need a drag, you'll usually find a huddle of like-minded smokers, chatting away just outside the door.

Seriously, for nonsmokers it's a joy to savour rich regional cooking or sip a Campari, free of smoke. If Italians, anarchic by nature and resentful of all that's imposed by authority, can, for the most part ungrudgingly, accept such a radical overnight change, any nation can.

---

particularly Florence, is no exception. Prato, meanwhile, has a longstanding Chinese community, Italy's largest, while Chianti is a favourite with British, German and Swiss expats. Although migrants from the south of Italy traditionally favour northern cities such as Milan and Turin, Florence is also a popular spot.

SPORT
Football (Soccer)

Il calcio excites Italian souls more than politics, religion and good food all put together, and this fanatical devotion can be bewildering to some outsiders. The end of the 2004–05 season was a nail-biter for the region's two top-flight professional clubs. ACF Fiorentina, Tuscany's only Serie A (premier league) representative, hung on to its place in Italy's premier division by the straps of its boots, just avoiding relegation by winning its last game. Luckless Perugia, by contrast, was denied promotion to the big time from Serie B merely on goal average.

Fiorentina (see p126) may no longer be able to afford the likes of Roberto Baggio and Gabriel Batistuta in the line-up, but if you want to catch a game, you can see them in action at Florence's Stadio Comunale Artemio Franchi.

Rugby Union

While nothing quite competes with football, the popularity of rugby is at an all-time high, mainly thanks to Italy's participation in the Six Nations Championship. Italy's rugby team still has a long way to go before it can compete on equal terms with the world leaders in the sport, but it's constantly improving. You'll have to travel to Rome's Stadio Flaminio to catch a big game, but you may get a chance to see the Florence team play at the Centro Sportivo Universitario Val di Rose, in Sesto Fiorentino (www.firenzerugby.it in Italian), while other cities such as Perugia also have active teams. Perugia games can be seen at the Campo di Pian di Massiano. For further information go to www.rugbyperugia.it, in Italian.

Cycling

The Giro d'Italia has been held every summer since 1909. It is second only to the Tour de France in popularity and media coverage on the international cycling circuit. The precise route includes foreign stages and is constantly changing, but it always cuts through Umbria and the length of Tuscany. Italy's sports newspapers, *Gazetta dello Sport* and *Corriere dello Sport*, will have up-to-date details of the race if you want to follow the thrills and spills. Also try www.giroditalia.it.

MEDIA

In contrast to just about everything else in Tuscany and Umbria, there's very little to entertain you at the regional level, when it comes to the press and TV. That said, if you read Italian, you can feel the local pulse and pick up useful information about what's currently happening from the regional press.

Tuscany's leading newspaper is *La Nazione,* owned by media boss Andrea Monti Riffeser. It's based in Florence but also comes out in several regional versions, each giving extensive local coverage. In Umbria, *Corriere dell' Umbria* is the main read for the region.

There are no truly 'national' newspapers but major cities in Italy produce important dailies that have regional editions. The big three are *Corriere della Sera,* based in Milan, *La Stampa,* from nearby Turin, and Rome's *La Repubblica.* In their political stance, they cover the spectrum from centre-left *(La Repubblica)* to establishment-right *(La Stampa).*

You may well find the media considerably less objective than what you're accustomed to watching and reading, as too much of it is concentrated in too few hands. The TV scene is especially disquieting. The country's prime minister at the time of writing, Silvio Berlusconi, is also the richest man in Italy (and, incidentally, owner of AC Milan football club). He owns a fistful of newspapers and his Mediaset consortium runs a number of widely watched TV channels. Fact one: Italy has nearly 650 terrestrial TV stations, a fair proportion, admittedly, undisguised shopping channels or simply offering talking-head horoscopes and tarot readings. Fact two: official statistics indicate that the average Italian watches

The Dark Heart of Italy by Tobias Jones is a searing investigation into the culture of corruption and political malpractice in Berlusconi's Italy.

around four hours of TV a day. So viewers of Mediaset stations are fed the line of the party in power every hour...

The only other big TV player is the state-run entity, Radio e Televisione Italiane, which runs the three national channels, RAI 1, 2 and 3, none of them immune to government interference. Of these, RAI 3 offers the more serious programming.

In general, whatever channel you flick to, the quality is staggeringly poor, serving up a diet of tacky game shows with scantily clad, simpering hostesses, dire soaps and cheap imports.

Charles Richards' *The New Italians* gives an in-depth look at the paradoxical world of modern Italy and how Italians battle bureaucracy to make their country work.

There's the same conflict of powerful interest in the press world. The *Corriere della Sera* and *La Stampa* are both controlled by the Agnelli family, which owns Fiat automobiles. The country's leading daily financial paper, *Il Sole 24 Ore,* while meant to be independent, is actually owned by Confindustria, the national manufacturers' association, and another daily with national coverage *Il Giornale,* is edited by Silvio Berlusconi's brother.

Amazingly, most Italians seem unconcerned; only the political classes, especially on the left, are vocal about the situation, which former prime minister Massimo d'Alema has declared 'indecent'.

RELIGION

As elsewhere in Italy, Catholicism is the dominant religion, although the Vatican is no longer the same social force as it once was. Catholicism became the state religion at the time of Italian unification in 1870, and it wasn't until the 1929 Lateran Treaty between the Vatican and the Italian state was modified in 1985 that the Catholic Church lost that status.

As many as 85% of Italians still profess to be Catholic and roughly the same figure can probably be applied to Tuscany and Umbria. However, that percentage doesn't translate into church attendance, which has declined steeply in recent decades. Even so, religious rituals and rites of passage still play an important part in the lives of Tuscans and Umbrians, and first communions, church weddings and religious feast days are an integral part of society.

The Cambridge Companion to Modern Italian Culture by Zygmunt Baranski and Rebecca West (eds), is a comprehensive and invaluable collection of essays on all aspects of modern Italian culture, such as regionalism, mass media, feminism and religion, with suggestions for further reading.

There is also a small Protestant population, made up of various denominations, including Anglicans and Baptists and consisting mostly of the expat community, especially in Florence. Interestingly, Florence is one of the country's biggest centres of Buddhism, which has about 5000 followers throughout Tuscany. The city also has a small Jewish population.

It's estimated that there are around 500,000 Muslims in Italy, most of them recent arrivals. Not all, however, are from the immigrant community; a couple of Italian ambassadors to Saudi Arabia have embraced the faith.

ARTS

The regions' fantastic wealth of painting, sculpture and architecture is explored in the separate Art & Architecture chapter; here we explore the other arts, such as literature, film and music.

Literature

Long after the fall of Rome, Latin remained the language of learned discourse and writing throughout Italy, and the elevation of the Italian language to literary status was a long and gradual process.

The stirrings of Italian literature written in the vernacular began in Tuscany and Umbria in the beginning of the 13th century. One of the genres first created was spiritual poetry, which was concentrated in Assisi after the death of St Francis.

The first writer of real stature was Dante Alighieri (1265–1321), who wrote equally comfortably in both Italian and Latin. Born in Florence to a wealthy family, he was lucky to receive a rounded education, then became active in Florentine politics allying himself with the Guelph faction. Flexing his literary muscles, he began to write in a number of different styles and genres, covering everything from philosophy and politics to love. He was exiled from Florence in 1301 when the Ghibellines, the opposing group, took the reigns of power. He spent most of the rest of his life wandering Europe and composing, among much else, his *Divina Commedia* (Divine Comedy), the first great work written in Italian to stand the test of time.

Dante does not stand completely alone. Together with two fellow Tuscans, he formed the triumvirate that laid down the course for the development of a rich literature in Italian.

Petrarch (Francesco Petrarca; 1304–74), born in Arezzo to Florentine parents who had been exiled from their city at about the same time as Dante, actually wrote more in Latin than in Italian. *Il Canzoniere* is the distilled result of his finest poetry. Although the core subject is his unrequited love for a girl called Laura, the whole breadth of human grief and joy is treated with a lyrical quality hitherto unmatched. So striking was his clear, passionate verse, filtered through his knowledge of the classics, that a phenomenon known as *petrarchismo* emerged across Europe – the desire of writers within and beyond Italy to emulate him. His influence spread far and across time: the Petrarchan sonnet form, rhyme scheme and even subject matter was adopted by the English Metaphysical poets of 17th-century England, such as John Donne.

The Florentine Giovanni Boccaccio (1303–75), who ended his days in the hill-top town of Certaldo, was a contemporary and friend of Petrarch. His masterpiece, *Decameron,* was written in the years immediately following the plague of 1348, which he survived in Florence. Each of his 10 characters recounts a story in which a vast panorama of personalities, events and symbolism is explored.

During the second half of the 15th century, Lorenzo il Magnifico, the Medici ruler of Florence and patron of the arts *par excellence*, was also handy with a pen in his own right. Just as importantly, his enlightened approach to learning and the arts created a healthy atmosphere for writers to flourish.

Another outstanding writer of the Florentine Renaissance is Niccolò Machiavelli (1469–1527; see p28). Although known above all for his work on power and politics, *Il Principe,* he was a prolific writer in many fields. His *Mandragola,* for example, is a lively piece of comic theatre and a virtuoso example of Italian literature.

Tuscany and Umbria took a fairly long literary break during the 17th to 19th centuries, although Tuscany did give birth to Carlo Lorenzini (1826–90), better known to Italians of all ages under the pseudonym of Carlo Collodi (see the boxed text, p162), who was the creator of *Le Avventure di Pinocchio* – known to most non-Italians through the Disneyfied version, *Pinocchio.*

19TH CENTURY ONWARDS

Giosue Carducci (1835–1907) was one of the key figures of 19th-century Tuscan literature. Born in the Maremma, he actually spent the second half of his life in Bologna. Probably the best of his poetry was written in

www.greatdante.net explains all you wanted to know about the great poet, his life and works.

Too Much Tuscan Sun: Confessions of a Tour Guide by Dario Castagno is a light-hearted account by a native Tuscan, brought up in Britain, of his clients and some of their less endearing foibles.

the 1870s; it ranged in tone from pensive evocation of death (such as in *Pianto Antico*) or memories of youthful passion *(Idillio Maremmano)* to a kind of historic nostalgia. In many of these latter poems he harked back to the glories of ancient Rome.

Florence's Aldo Palazzeschi (1885–1974) was in the vanguard of the Futurist movement during the pre-WWI years. In 1911 he published arguably his best (although at the time little-appreciated) work, *Il Codice di Perelà* (Perelà's Code), an at times bitter allegory that in part becomes a farcical imitation of the life of Christ.

By the 1920s and '30s Florence was bubbling with activity as a series of literary magazines flourished, at least for a while, in spite of the Fascist regime. Magazines such as *Solaria,* which lasted from 1926 to 1934, its successor *Letteratura* (which began circulating in 1937) and *Il Frontespizio* (1929–40) gave writers from across Italy a platform from which to launch and discuss their work.

> The expat author Matthew Spender muses on the history of the region he has called home for 20 years, and shares his observations on contemporary Tuscan culture in *Within Tuscany: Reflections on a Time and Place.*

One of the founding authors of *Letteratura* was Alessandro Bonsanti (1904–84), much of whose writing is in the form of essays and literary criticism. Guglielmo Petroni (1911–93), from Lucca, was another contributor to *Letteratura*. Although a poet of some note in his day, he's chiefly recognised for his novel *Il Mondo è una Prigione* (The World Is a Prison, 1948), a vivid account of a political prison and one of the best accounts of the Italian Resistance. Mario Tobino (1910–91), from Viareggio, used his experience as director of a lunatic asylum to great effect in *Le Donne Libere di Magliano* (Free Women of Magliano), based upon life inside one such institution.

One of Italy's leading postwar poets was the Florentine Mario Luzi (1914–2005). His poetry concentrates on the anguish arising from the contrast between the individual and the broader universe.

Few women writers have reached the limelight in Tuscany but an important exception was Anna Banti (1895–1985). Her approach to her characters was psychological, delving deep into their minds, while simultaneously analysing the position of women in society.

Dacia Maraini (b 1936), for many years the partner of author Alberto Moravia, is Tuscany's most prominent contemporary female author, with some 10 novels and a fistful of plays to her credit. An interesting one is *Voci* (Voices), a mystery laced with disturbing social comment, where

---

NOVELS WITH A TUSCAN SETTING

Fictional titles in English aren't as prolific as the glut of autobiographical books, major and minor, about a writer's personal experiences in Tuscany, but the novel genre also threatens overload. There are two contrasting contemporary tales:

Tuscany for Beginners: A Novel (Imogen Edward-Jones) Yes, indeed a novel, not handy hints for newcomers. Recently released, this boisterous, racy, easy-on-the-brain story of life in a Tuscan B&B has more than a touch of Fawlty Towers.

Italian Fever (Valerie Martin) Here's yet another Tuscany-based novel that serves up mystery and romance aplenty as a young American discovers that the world is wider than New York.

The English novelist EM Forster wrote a pair of 20th-century classics that are set in Tuscany; both were made into successful films.

A Room with a View A comedy of manners exploring the emotional awakening of a prim young English lady as she encounters the vitality, beauty and passion of Florence.

Where Angels Fear to Tread Another 'clash-of-cultures' tale, telling the tragic story of Lilia, who defies family and class convention to marry a young Italian gigolo in 'Monteriano', a fictionalised version of San Gimignano.

BENIGNI'S WORLD

When people think about Italian cinema today, the image that undoubtedly comes to mind is Roberto Benigni's spirited and largely unintelligible Oscar acceptance speech in 1999. En route to the stage he conveyed his glee by jumping not just over, but on, the seats.

Until the momentous success of *La Vita é Bella* (Life Is Beautiful), Italian cinema had suffered an artistic and commercial slump. The Tuscan actor's approach to the delicate subject of the Holocaust quickly became the most successful foreign film ever in the US with a box-office take of some US$35.8 million. Benigni was also the first Italian and, indeed, non-English speaker to win the best actor Oscar.

With the exception of films such as *Cinema Paradiso, Ciao Professore!* and *Il Postino,* very few Italian films had succeeded in the international market over the preceding decade; it had been a long time since films by such cinematic greats as Fellini, Rossellini, Visconti, Antonioni and De Sica had held foreign audiences in thrall.

Benigni's success was just the kick-start the Italian film world needed; in 2001 Nanni Moretti took top prize at Cannes Film Festival for *La Stanza del Figlo* (The Son's Room) and Christian Comencini's *Il Piu bel Giorno della Mia Vita* (The Best Day of My Life) won the prize for best foreign film at the Montreal Film Festival the following year. In 2002 Benigni's *Pinocchio* was deemed by some critics – others panned it – one of the most beautiful of all Italian films with delightful costumes and storybook sets; the main criticism was that Benigni, at 50, was just too old for the part.

Benigni was born in 1952 in Misericordia, a small village in the province of Arezzo, and moved shortly after to Vergaio, a village of 3000 people 24km northwest of Florence. Here he joined the local virtuosos at the *casa del popolo* (town's social centre) perfecting that distinctly Tuscan dramatic technique of improvised rhyming stories. From this early training, he still maintains an admirable ability to improvise.

At age 20 Benigni moved to Rome where he worked in bars and theatres presenting his avant-garde monologue show to a bemused audience. Here he was discovered by Giuseppe Bertolucci, which eventually led to bringing Italian cinema, once again, to the screens of an international audience who had grown increasingly weary of the sanitised sentimentality of the Hollywood big screen.

---

the main character, a female journalist, embarks on the investigation of a murder.

Pisa-born Antonio Tabucchi (b 1943) has written more than a dozen novels, several translated into English, plus volumes of short stories. One such story is *Sostiene Pereira* (translated into English and titled, bizarrely, *Pereira Declares* for the US market and *Declares Pereira* in the UK). Set in prewar Lisbon, it was made into a charming film starring Marcello Mastroianni.

Cinema

Italian cinema has been enormously productive and has contributed an immense number of great works to the world of film. Tuscany's first claim to fame is as the place where the film projector was invented, one year before the Lumière brothers patented theirs in Paris. In 1895, poor Filoteo Alberini created his *kinetografo* (cinema projector) in Florence, but no-one paid much attention.

The biggest name to come out of Tuscany is Franco Zeffirelli (b 1923). His career took him from radio and theatre to opera production and film. He created the TV blockbuster *Jesus of Nazareth* (1977) and many film adaptations of operas, along with film hits such as *Romeo and Juliet* (1968), *Hamlet* (1990) and the semiautobiographical *Tea with Mussolini* (1999), set in and around Florence.

Room with a View, the film of EM Forster's novel, set in Florence, has magnificent shots of the city.

More recently, the director and actor Roberto Benigni (b 1952), from Arezzo, has made quite a name for himself, picking up three Oscars and successfully managing to create a genre all of his own: Holocaust comedy. He directed and starred in *La Vita é Bella* (Life Is Beautiful, 1998), about a father who protects his son in a concentration camp by pretending it's all a game. Charlie Chaplin's daughter, Geraldine, declared months after the Oscars that Benigni had inherited her father's cinematic poetry. Quite an accolade. Benigni shot parts of *La Vita é Bella* and his much less successful, almost painful-to-watch, rendition of *Pinocchio* (2002) at Papigno, an old factory near Terni converted into movie studios.

Umbria hasn't seen much in the way of the film industry. Their most recent claim to fame is actress Monica Bellucci, from Città di Castello, who recently starred as Mary Magdalene in Mel Gibson's *The Passion o, the Christ* and opposite Matt Damon in *The Brothers Grimm,* directed by ex-Monty Python comic Terry Gilliam. Zeffirelli's 1972 *Brother Sun, Sister Moon* (about the lives of St Francis and St Clare) was shot in Assisi. Historical drama queen Dame Maggie Smith starred in yet another film with gratuitous Italian countryside shots, *My House in Umbria,* a made-for-TV movie in 2003.

William Trevor's *My House in Umbria* is a tender novel about the relationships between the survivors of a terrorist bomb attack as they recuperate in the Umbrian countryside. In 2003 it was made into a film starring Dame Maggie Smith.

Music

Far and away Tuscany's most famous musical figure is Giacomo Puccini (1858–1924), composer of such well-loved opera classics as *Madame Butterfly, Tosca* and *La Bohème.* He was born in Lucca, where you can visit his house (see p158) or attend the annual music festival (for details consult www.puccinifestival.it) that honours him in nearby Torre del Lago.

On a quite different note, one of Italy's former leading pop bands Litfiba, was a Florentine product – its ex-singer Pero Pelù, now continues solo – and both Jovanotti, the country's most popular rap singer, and the singer Irene Grandi are also Tuscan. Siena-born Gianna Nannini is an extremely popular, internationally acclaimed and politically active Italian artist whose work ranges from rock albums to film soundtracks.

Indeed, Tuscany has produced plenty of bands and musicians, ranging from Marasco – a gritty, folksy singer from Florence who was big in the 1950s, through to Dirotto Su Cuba, a trip-hop band that has attracted a lot of attention around the country. In Umbria, jazz has gained an enormous following due to Umbria Jazz and the Spoleto Festival, both major events on the European jazz calendar.

Environment

THE LAND

If you think of Tuscany's coast as the base, the region forms a rough triangle covering 22,992 sq km. Crammed within that triangle is a remarkable variety of land forms, from mountains in the north and east to flat plains in the south, from islands off the coast to the hill country of the interior, all sliced through by river valleys.

Much of the coast facing the Tyrrhenian and Ligurian seas is flat, except for a stretch immediately south of Livorno and parts of the Monte Argentario peninsula.

In all, two-thirds of Tuscany is mountainous or hilly. The Apennines, shared with Emilia (part of the Emilia-Romagna region), close off the northern flank of Tuscany and run roughly from east to west (with a gradual southwards drop). The Apuane Alps (p173), an offshoot that rises from the coastal plain up in the region's northwestern corner, are renowned for their white marble deposits (see p170).

Inland and further south sprawl lower hill ranges, such as Monte Albano south of Pistoia, and Monte Pratomagno in the Arezzo province to the east. Separating them is a series of low river valleys, the most important of which is the Arno.

The most extensive lowlands are the inland Maremma Pisana, one-time swamps south of Pisa, and the Maremma, which extends down the coast and over the regional boundary with Lazio.

The River Arno, all 240 winding kilometres of it, is Tuscany's main river. It rises in Monte Falterona in the Apennines, flows south to Arezzo and then meanders northwest for a while. By the time it passes through Florence it is on a westwards course towards Pisa and finally the Ligurian Sea. It was once an important trade artery, but river traffic today is virtually nonexistent.

Of the seven islands scattered off Tuscany's coast, the central and eastern parts of Elba (p184), along with Giannutri (p248) and parts of Giglio (p248), are reminders of a great Apennine wall that collapsed into the sea millions of years ago. Capraia (p179), Montecristo (p193), western Elba and parts of Giglio were forced up by volcanic activity. The islands vary considerably, from the unexciting flatness of Pianosa (p193) to the rugged and rocky coastline of much of Elba.

Neighbouring Umbria is an undulating, landlocked region with an area of over 8400 sq km. Around 53% of its terrain is mountainous and most of the rest is decidedly hilly. The massive Umbrian-Marche Appenines are dominated by the Monti Sibillini (p321), whose highest peak, Monte Vettore, rears up to nearly 2500m. Other notable ranges include the Gubbio Appenines, the Monti Martani and the lower yet still impressive peaks of the Amerini and Spoleto clusters.

Less than 10% of Umbria is low lying. Through it, curling from north to southwest and bisecting the region, runs the Tiber River, which has been navigable for centuries. The second-longest river is the Nera. As it meets its Velino tributary, it forms the Cascata delle Marmore (Marmore Waterfalls; p317), a spectacular sight when the nearby hydro station lets water flow their way.

Umbria is also rich in both natural and artificial lakes. Lago di Trasimeno (p288), in the west, is the largest lake in central-southern Italy. Lake Corbara and Lago di Alviano (p333), these days more of a marshland, are artificial.

The impressive Cascata delle Marmore, plunging from a height of 165m, isn't a natural phenomenon – this waterfall was created by the Romans in the 3rd century BC.

The Dunarobba Fossil Forest, near Avigliano, is one of the oldest woods in the world, thought to date back almost two million years.

WILDLIFE
Animals

Cinghiale (wild boar) has been on Tuscan menus since the days of the Etruscans, and the rural areas of the region still teem with them. The only difference is that today most of them are the offspring of Eastern European boar, imported to make up for the depletion of local species. They also roam many of the regional nature parks in Umbria. Although they're common enough, you'll be lucky to spot them on walks in the countryside; they are busy avoiding their most dangerous predator – the armed hunter.

Where to Watch Birds in Italy, published by the Italian Bird Protection League (LIPU), highlights over 100 recommendations for species spotting.

Among other animals fairly common in the Tuscan and Umbrian countryside are squirrels, rabbits, foxes, martens, weasels and hares. The badger and the black-and-white-quilled *istrice,* a porcupine supposedly imported from North Africa by the ancient Romans for the dinner table, are rarer. In parks such as the Parco Regionale della Maremma (p245) there's a good chance of spotting roe deer, grazing at dawn or dusk.

Wolves, say some locals, still roam the hills between Volterra and Massa Marittima. Others reckon they're feral dogs. Either way, sightings are extremely rare. You've a better chance of seeing a real wolf in Parco Regionale del Monte Cucco (p299), where more survive, thanks to the rugged mountainous environment. The wildcat is another predator that roams the scarcely populated areas of Tuscany and Umbria, but it too is rare and hardly ever seen.

On a more slithery note, you can encounter several kinds of snakes. Most are harmless and will glide out of your way if you give them warning (by treading heavily as you approach). The only poisonous one is the viper, identified by its diamond markings. Rocky areas and the island of Elba are among its principal habitats.

Bird life is varied in Tuscany. The best time of year for twitchers is from November to March, when many migratory species linger in coastal nature reserves such as Lago di Burano (p249), Laguna di Orbetello (p247) and Monti dell'Uccellina (p245). As many as 140 species call Tuscany home or use it as a stopover. They include the black-winged stilt, buzzard, falcon, hawk, hoopoe, jay, kestrel, kingfisher, osprey, thrush, woodpecker and wren.

Birds of Britain & Europe with North Africa & the Middle East by Herman Heinzel et al, *Birds of Britain & Europe* by John Gooders and the exquisitely illustrated *Birds of Europe* by Lars Jonsson make excellent spotter's guides.

Umbria is also a great place to see a wide variety of bird life. Its extensive marshlands are an important stopping-off place for migratory species such as the grey heron, purple heron, bittern and spoonbill. In other parts of the region birds of prey, such as the golden eagle, goshawk, peregrine falcon, eagle owl and osprey, circle the skies.

Plants

Tuscan and Umbrian farmland is a visually pleasing mix of orderly human intervention and nature left more or less to itself. Everywhere, long lines of vines stripe the countryside, alternating with olive groves (olives were introduced in Etruscan times from the Middle East).

Tall, slender cypress and the odd flattened *pino marittimo* (cluster pine, found mainly on the coast) are among the most striking of the regions' call-sign trees. The cypress was introduced from Asia Minor in Roman times precisely for its decorative qualities.

Beech trees thrive in the cooler mountainous territory of the Apuane Alps, often competing for light and space with chestnuts. Thereabouts, hunting for chestnuts then roasting them is a favourite pastime on November weekends. In the Casentino (p260) and Vallombrosa areas of eastern Tuscany, deep, thick forests of pine, oak (one species of which is the cork oak, its bark important to the wine industry) and beech still cover large tracts of otherwise little-touched land. Other species include maple, hazelnut, alder and imported eucalyptus.

In Umbria, other trees of note down in the plains include willows, poplars and the black alder. Water lilies flourish in the rich marshlands while rare flowers such as the yellow poppy discreetly survive in Parco dei Monti Sibillini (p321).

Springtime, of course, is the brightest time of year in Tuscany and Umbria; whole valley floors and upland plains are awash in a technicolour sea of wild flowers, including jonquils, crocuses, anemones, gentians and orchids.

Down by the sea, Tuscan coastal and island areas boast typical Mediterranean *macchia* (dry, prickly scrubland).

NATIONAL PARKS

Three of Italy's 24 national parks are within Tuscany.

The Parco Nazionale dell'Arcipelago Toscano (p177), Europe's largest marine park, embraces the islands of Montecristo, Gorgona, Giannutri, Pianosa and part of Capraia, Elba and Giglio and seeks to protect both their fragile coastlines and the wild, mountainous hinterland of most.

Within the Parco Nazionale delle Foreste Casentinesi, Monte Falterona e Campigna (p260), on the border with Emilia-Romagna, is one of the most extensive and best-preserved forests in central Italy.

Well to the west and also shared with Emilia-Romagna, the recently created Parco Nazionale dell'Appennino Tosco-Emiliano protects the fragile mountain environment of the Appenines.

Tuscany also has three regional parks, one in the Apuane Alps, one in the Maremma and one on the heavily urbanised coast near Livorno.

Umbria has just one national park, the Parco Nazionale dei Monti Sibillini (p321), which takes its name from the principal mountain range in the area. But it makes up for this with a fistful of regional parks: Parco Regionale di Colfiorito, Parco Regionale del Trasimeno, Parco Regionale del Monte Cucco (p299), Parco Regionale del Monte Subasio, Parco Regionale del Fiume Nera and Parco Regionale del Tevere.

Other protected areas and places of naturalistic interest include La Valle Nature Oasis, La Cascata delle Marmore (p317), Fonti del Clitunno (Clitunno Springs) and Foresta Fossile di Dunarobba (Dunarobba Fossil Forest).

ENVIRONMENTAL ISSUES

One of the greatest ecological issues in the regions is marble extraction in the mountains of the Apuane Alps. The great white scars, which from the seaside look almost like snowfalls, are the result of many centuries' work.

Before WWII, the level of incursion was much slighter and marble miners eased blocks down to nearby villages with complex pulley systems. But today, the pace of removal has accelerated. About 1.5 million tonnes per year are scraped out and trundled away on heavy trucks. The extraction is disfiguring part of a nature reserve, the waste produced creates disposal problems and the heavy truck traffic compounds the problem. However, few voices seriously object to this prestigious industry. Carrara marble (p170) is sought after worldwide by everyone from architects to sculptors and the industry is a significant local employer.

Heavy industry never really came to Tuscany or Umbria, so the associated problems of air and water pollution elsewhere in Italy are not as

Flower-spotters will enjoy *Mediterranean Wild Flowers* by M Blamey & C Grey Wilson. *Trees of Britain & Europe* also makes a handy companion, while Paul Sterry's *Complete Mediterranean Wildlife* is a good general guide to the flora and fauna of the region.

For further information on national parks and other protected areas in Tuscany and Umbria visit www.parks.it. The World Wide Fund for Nature (WWF) has an Italian chapter at www.wwf.it.

RESPONSIBLE TRAVEL

Thanks to the temperate climate and stunning landscape, both Tuscany and Umbria are becoming increasingly popular with walkers and hikers. Unfortunately, the increase in the number of visitors has placed a great pressure on the natural environment. Please consider the following tips when walking and help preserve the ecology and beauty of the region.

- Don't light fires unless you're absolutely sure it's permitted and safe.
- Take all rubbish away with you, including cigarette butts, unless there are litter bins in the area. Don't bury your rubbish.
- Leave the wildlife alone.
- Be careful about where you go to the toilet and be sure to bury waste.
- Leave gates as you found them after you have passed through.
- Be attentive when passing through fields, particularly during periods of cultivation. Stick to the edges or obvious tracks and don't trample on crops.
- Keep to existing tracks to avoid causing erosion by disturbing the natural lay of the land.
- Don't pick grapes or olives on your way through vineyards or olive groves.

---

www.blueflag.org lists Tuscany's cleanest beaches.

Check out www.lipu.it (in Italian) for the Italian Bird Protection League (LIPU); visit its UK branch at www.lipu-uk.org. The European Federation Against Hunting (EFAH) can be found at www .efah.net. Its Italian equivalent is at www .abolizionecaccia.it (in Italian).

great here. That said, the medium- and light-industrial areas of Livorno, Piombino, suburban Florence, Perugia and along the Arno and Tiber rivers are far from hazard free. Heavy road traffic makes clean air a distant dream in much of the densely populated Prato-Pistoia area. Noise pollution can also be a problem in cities.

Umbria, where farming remains a significant occupation, is much less affected. The introduction of several hydroelectric plants and the manufacturing of chemicals, iron, steel and processed food have all taken their toll on the countryside, but on a much smaller scale and with a less detrimental impact on the environment.

The landscape of Tuscany and Umbria appears something of a work of art, with farmers alternating a patchwork quilt of farmland with stretches of forest. The post-WWII crisis in agriculture saw many farmers leave the land and in more remote spots, where wringing results from the earth was always a challenge at best, forest or scrub is reclaiming its territory. Sometimes this uncontrolled regrowth has a downside, helping propagate bushfires.

Regional government bodies in both Tuscany and Umbria are now taking a tougher line concerning the environment, partly in response to EU directives. Initiatives include reforestation and the promotion of environmentally friendly agricultural methods.

Tuscany & Umbria Outdoors

The beautiful landscapes of Tuscany and Umbria beg to be explored and enjoyed. Those who tear through the countryside on the highways miss out on a rich variety of outdoor activities that underscore the area's splendour.

Because Tuscany and Umbria are year-round destinations, there's something to do in every season, from adrenaline-inducing winter skiing to leisurely countryside walks. Families will be delighted to discover how accessible these activities are, while those in search of more demanding pursuits won't be disappointed either. There'll still be plenty of time left to lounge around the villa and sip chianti – which tastes all the better after a day outdoors.

WALKING

Tuscany and Umbria are eminently suited to walking and a common sight throughout the region is large organised walking groups, usually from the UK – frequently distinguishable at 200m by the floppy white sunhats they so often seem to go for.

The patchwork countryside of the centre, the wilder valleys and mountains south and northwest, and the dramatic Apuane Alps and Apennine ranges offer colourful variety. A truly ambitious trekker could undertake the 24-stage Grande Escursione Appenninica, an arc that takes you from the Due Santi pass above La Spezia southeast to Sansepolcro. Alternatively Umbria's Monti Sibillini are superb for walkers using Castelluccio as a base, with a choice of demanding backpack hikes to the summit or casual day hikes.

People have been traipsing across Tuscany since Adam was a boy, creating paths and trails as they went. One of the most important pilgrim routes in Europe during the Dark Ages was known as the Via Francigena (or Via Romea), which turned into something of a highway across Tuscany. Starting in the Magra River valley and winding through the wild Lunigiana territory of the northwest, the trail hugged the coast for a while before cutting inland to Siena via San Gimignano and then turning south to the Christian capital, Rome. Parts of the route can still be walked today.

Edizione Multigraphic produces good maps of Tuscany and the Apennines at 1:25,000.

Best Time of Year

Spring is undoubtedly the prettiest time to walk, while the colours of autumn have their own mellow appeal. Given that summertime continues into late October, you have lots of light for longer walks. After Tuscany's mad summer tourist rush, things begin to ease off by late September – all the more so out in the countryside.

If you're planning to go walking in the Apuane Alps or other mountain areas (such as Monte Vettore or the small Orecchiella reserve), the most pleasant (and safest) time is in summer. August, though, the time when most Italians take their holidays and trails get busy, is best avoided if you can be flexible. Lower terrain, by contrast, is best left untrodden in high summer as the heat can be oppressive, making even a crawl to the nearest air-conditioned bar a strain.

What to Take

For your average walks in the Tuscany-Umbria area you will need only a minimum of items. For easy, undemanding walks, a pair of comfortable trainers (runners) is often quite adequate. Otherwise, pull on either comfortable walking shoes or sturdy boots, depending on what kind of terrain you are planning to cover. A small daypack should contain an extra layer of clothing, in case temperatures drop, and some kind of wet weather gear. Depending on the season, sunblock, sunglasses and a hat are recommended. Obviously you need a map of the area, and a compass too if you're planning some serious stuff off the beaten track. Whatever the season, pack at least one bottle of water, allowing at least 1.5L per walker for a summertime day walk. A fistful or two of light, high-nutrition, easily assimilated food such as dried fruit or nuts can stave off hunger pangs.

For slip-in-the-pocket reference books about flowers, trees, birds and bigger mammals, check the sidebars in the Environment chapter.

Free camping is not permitted in the high mountains. That may seem like bad news to some, as you will need to plan your overnight stops around the availability of beds in *rifugi* (mountain huts). The upside is that you can leave tents, cooking gear and the like at your base accommodation. Bring your sleeping bag along as extra insurance against the cold.

But it's not just the cold – you need to be prepared for all kinds of weather in the mountains. You may start the day in splendid sunshine and heat, but that can easily change to cold and wet. Bear in mind that the Apuane Alps get the greatest concentration of rainfall in Tuscany.

Prime Spots

The Chianti (p141) region is popular for walkers of all levels. One of the classic walks takes you rambling over several days (perhaps as many as five or six) from Florence to Siena. Lonely Planet's *Walking in Italy* describes a stimulating three-day hike that passes through Greve and Radda. *Chianti Classico: Val di Pesa-Val d'Elsa,* a map at 1:25,000 published by Edizione Multigraphic, covers most of the area and has hiking trails superimposed.

Another area within easy reach of Florence for a day's walking is Il Mugello (p140), northeast of the city and extending to the border with Emilia-Romagna. *Sorgenti Firenze Trekking* (SOFT; Florence Spring Trekking) are a network of signed day or half-day trails crisscrossing the area. *Mugello, Alto Mugello, Val di Sieve,* produced by SELCA, is a decent map for hikers at 1:70,000.

For a day of history and hiking, you could walk from San Gimignano to Volterra or vice versa. The start and end points are fascinating medieval towns with reasonable transport links and plenty of accommodation. History buffs may want to walk in the tracks of the Etruscans, making a base in Suvereto or Campiglia Marittima. In a more structured way, at the Parco Archeologico di Baratti e Populonia (p183) you can follow the Via delle Cave, a signed two-hour walk that passes by a series of tombs and the quarries from which their building blocks were hewn.

Back on the spine of the Apennines, the Garfagnana (p162), up in the northwest, and Lunigiana (p172), spilling into Liguria, both offer exciting medium-mountain walking. Castelnuovo makes a good base and its **Centro Visite Parco Alpi Apuane** (www.parks.it/parco.alpi.apuane) is well stocked with information and maps.

You can enjoy these two areas in their own right or do a couple of limbering-up treks, then attack the Apuane Alps (p173). For serious hikes, they're stunning and challenging, but there are also possibilities for less arduous itineraries. To get a feel for the area, hop on the *Treno nei Parchi,* which is specifically geared towards hikers. Lonely Planet's *Walking in Italy* describes a couple of enjoyable multiday routes and *The Alps of Tuscany* by Francesco Greco presents many more. Edizione Multigraphic's *Parco delle Alpi Apuane* map at 1:50,000 covers the whole of the range. If your Italian is up to it, you might go for one of several

Italian guides on the mountains, such as *Alpi Apuane: Guida al Territorio del Parco* by Frederick Bradley and Enrico Medda.

The island of Elba is especially well geared for short walks and you will generally be able to plan your own routes quite easily. For more information contact **Il Genio del Bosco – Centro Trekking Isola d'Elba** (☎ 0565 93 08 37; www.geniodelbosco.it in Italian).

In Umbria, hiking in the scenic Monti Sibillini (p321) is wonderful, although there are relatively few marked trails. For information, contact the **Ente Parco Nazionale Monti Sibillini** (☎ 0737 97 27 11; www.sibillini.net). A good base for shorter day hikes is Castelluccio with a choice of trails leaving the village in several different directions; one of the most popular leads to the Lago di Pilato under Monte Vettore, the place, supposedly, where Pontius Pilate is buried. The Club Alpino Italiano (CAI) map *Parco Nazionale dei Monti Sibillini* covers the park at 1:25,000, as does the Edizione Multigraphic alternative of the same name.

Information

MAPS & BOOKS

In addition to Edizione Multigraphic and the CAI, the German cartographers Kompass produce 1:25,000 scale maps of various parts of Italy, including Tuscany and Umbria.

Walking in Tuscany, by Gillian Price is an excellent guide that describes over 50 walks and hikes of a none-too-strenuous nature (the text spills over into neighbouring Umbria and Lazio). Its ample selection takes you from Chianti country to the island of Elba, and to plenty of less explored parts of the Tuscan region as well.

However, it doesn't cover the more arduous trekking possibilities in the Apuane Alps in Tuscany's northwest. The series of *Guide dei Monti d'Italia,* grey hardbacks published by the Touring Club Italiano (TCI) and CAI, are exhaustive walking guides containing maps. *Walking and Eating in Tuscany and Umbria* by James Lasdun and Pia Davis provides 40 varied itineraries across these two central regions of Italy.

Organised Walking Holidays

Most major British adventure travel companies offer guided walking holidays in Tuscany, and usually Umbria too. They include:

ATG Oxford (www.atg-oxford.co.uk)
Headwater (www.headwater.com)
Inntravel (www.inntravel.co.uk)
Ramblers Association (www.ramblersholidays.co.uk)
Sherpa Expeditions (www.sherpa-walking-holidays.co.uk)

www.hiddenitaly.com
.au/walks takes you to an
Australian outfit that sets
up self-guided walking
tours in Tuscany and
Umbria.

CYCLING

Italy is generally a cycle-friendly country and Tuscany and Umbria are no exception. Most historic town and city centres are closed to traffic and there are plenty of places where you can rent a bike, buy your colour-coordinated Lycra and obtain advice on routes and itineraries. Whether you're out for a day's gentle pedalling around town with kids in tow, a weekend winery tour in Il Chianti with a bunch of friends or a serious workout on that muscle tone with a week or more of pedal power, Tuscany and Umbria provide plenty of cycling scope.

Cycling to Suit You

Matching the varied landscape, there is also a wide choice of roads and routes. Paved roads are particularly suited to high-tech racing bikes or travelling long distances on touring bikes. Country roads, known as *strade bianche,* have dirt surfaces covered with gravel for stability.

Back roads and trails are a further option, but only if you are fairly fit and have a quality multigear mountain bike, as this is mainly hilly terrain. There are also plenty of other challenges for the more ambitious cyclist: Monte Amiata is the perfect goal for aspiring hill climbers, while hilly itineraries with short but challenging climbs beckon from Umbria through to Il Chianti and Le Crete. Don't despair; there are also plenty of itineraries with gentler slopes for amateur cyclists and even for families with children.

Best Time of Year

The best time of year for serious pedalling is spring, not only because of the obvious advantage of a cooler temperature, but also because the scenery is at its most breathtaking at this time of year, with valleys drenched in poppies and wildflowers. However, Easter and the days either side of 25 April and 1 May, both national holidays, are best avoided.

Autumn is also a good season, although there's a greater chance of rain, which can lead to slippery roads and poor visibility.

What Type of Bike?

The most versatile bicycle for most of the roads here is a comfortable all-terrain bike capable of travelling over both paved and country roads and, even more importantly, able to climb hills without forcing you to exert yourself excessively. Ideally, it should afford a relaxed riding posture and be equipped with a wide range of gears, similar to a mountain bike's. If you don't have an all-terrain bike, you can simply modify a mountain bike by substituting its wide, grooved tyres with faster, narrower (1¼ inch) ones.

You may well find you are travelling along isolated roads that pass through fields or woodlands, so it's wise to be equipped with a kit for essential repairs. Always wear a helmet and have a detailed map of the area.

If you are bringing your own bike, check with your airline for costs and the degree of dismantling and packing required. Bikes can be transported by train in Italy, either with you or to arrive within a couple of days.

Prime Spots
IL CHIANTI

This is hard to describe without serious superlative overdose – just check out a Tuscany calendar and you'll get the picture. The picturesque SS222, known as the Strada Chiantigiana, runs between Florence and Siena, cleaving right through Chianti country. Although far from traffic-free, it's a scenic and popular cycling route.

More importantly, there are over 400km of traffic-free roads and plans are underway to develop the sport further with more trails and special cycle signposts to indicate directions, as well as offering information about accommodation, mechanical assistance and bicycle rental.

Parco Ciclistico del Chianti (☎ 0577 74 94 11; www.parcociclisticodelchianti.it), based in Gaiole in Chianti, is an ecologically committed local cycling organisation that offers both tailor-made and 'ready-to-ride' tours of around 40km.

AROUND SIENA

The hills around San Gimignano and Colle Val d'Elsa are another favourite venue for cyclists. A challenging route starts at Casole d'Elsa, following the road as it climbs to Monteguidi, then descending to cross the Cecina River before reaching the village of Montecastelli in the province of Pisa. An easier ride starts with a panoramic circuit around the town

www.parks.it is an excellent site, full of information about Tuscany and Umbria's national and regional parks, nature reserves and other protected areas.

WINDING DOWN, SOAKING IT UP

After a day on the hoof or in the saddle, nothing rivals a good long soak to ease the stiffness. From the hills of Tuscany and Umbria bubble restorative waters that people hereabouts have been using ever since Roman times. Nowadays the emphasis is upon curing and beauty treatments, but many spas also offer wellness programmes or simply the chance to dunk yourself in water fresh from their springs.

Following an active day in the Garfagnana you can relax in the thermal waters at Bagni di Lucca (p163). If you're heading back to the plains, the grander resort of Montecatini Terme (p133) has a huge choice of hotels and several health establishments. After walking or biking in Le Crete and the Val d'Orcia, a dip in the large pool at lovely little Bagno Vignoni (p232) rounds the day off nicely or, if you prefer more bustle, Chianciano Terme (p237) has spas and hotels aplenty. Umbria's main spa is at Terme di Fontecchio (p302), near Città di Castello, while Nocera Umbra (p299), not far from Gubbio, is a smaller but no less attractive option.

walls of Monteriggioni, carrying on to Colle Val d'Elsa and continuing towards San Gimignano and Volterra.

LE CRETE & VAL D'ORCIA

The rolling landscape here is similar to Il Chianti's, except that the woodlands are replaced by vast swathes of wheat fields. Cycling in Le Crete has been compared to sailing over a sea of land. Among the most stunning routes are the Monte Sante Marie road from Asciano to Torre a Castello and the Pieve a Salti road from Buonconvento to San Giovanni d'Asso. Both are unpaved and require all-terrain or mountain bikes. An alternative for cyclists with touring bikes is the legendary Lauretana road from Siena to Asciano and onwards towards Chiusure, Mont Oliveto Maggiore and Buonconvento.

MONTE AMIATA

Only die-hard peddlers should attempt to climb the steep flanks of this 1738m long-extinct volcano. The good news is that, at a mere 1370m, there is accommodation and a restaurant (Prato Le Macinaie) to revive you, roughly a 4km ride from the peak. You can attack the mountain by several routes: the easiest are those leading up from Arcidossa and Abbadia San Salvatore; the latter is a 14km uphill ride with a steady but reasonably slight gradient. The most difficult approach is Castel del Piano, 15km of unremitting uphill work with a steady, steep 7% gradient for the first 10km. But oh, the joy of whooshing down without a single turn of the pedals…

UMBRIA

The broad valleys of the Umbria region around Orvieto, Spello and Lago di Trasimeno are not too physically demanding and are well suited for cyclists who want to experience the beauty of the unique and varied landscape at a leisurely pace.

Information
MAPS & BOOKS

Edizione Multigraphic publishes a couple of series of maps designed for walkers and mountain-bike riders (*mulattiere,* or mule trails, are especially good for mountain bikes). The map at 1:50,000 is suited to two-wheelers. Ask for the *Carta dei Sentieri e Rifugi* or *Carta Turistica e dei Sentieri.*

The *Guida Cicloturistica del Chianti* by Fabio Masotti and Giancarlo Brocci has 20 cycling itineraries and 32 detailed maps of the Chianti

region. You can pick up a copy at the Siena tourist office. Another ex
cellent planning resource is the two volumes of Sergio Grillo and Cinzi
Pezzani's *Toscana in Mountain Bike,* between them they cover 69km o
off-road itineraries throughout the region.

Garfagnana by Bicycle by Lucia and Bruno Giovannetti has detaile
descriptions of key route features, a contour map, 27 itineraries fo
mountain bikes and five touring maps.

CYCLING ASSOCIATIONS

The Siena-based **Gli Amici Della Bicicletta** (☎ 0577 4 51 59; www.adbsiena.it in Italian
is an active, ecologically minded group that promotes cycling as a dail
form of urban transport and organises day-long and sometimes mor
extensive bicycle trips. It also dedicates considerable effort to developin
cycling paths and itineraries for visiting cyclists.

Cycling Tours

Florence by Bike (☎ 055 48 89 92; www.florencebybike.it), **Bicycle Tuscany** (☎ 055 2
25 80; www.bicycletuscany.com), **I Bike Italy** (☎ 055 234 23 71; www.ibikeitaly.com) an
The Accidental Tourist (☎ 055 69 93 76; www.accidentaltourist.com) all offer one-da
cycling excursions from Florence into Il Chianti, complete with cycl
hire. For more details, see p113. From Arezzo, **Alessandro Madiai** (☎ 33
649 14 81; torrequebrada@virgilio.it), himself a passionate cyclist, runs day an
overnight tours around the enchanting southern Tuscany countryside.

Several UK-based outdoor travel companies organise cycling trips t
Tuscany and Umbria. Among them are all of those we suggest for walkin
tours. Each does bike tours in either Umbria or Tuscany and, in mos
cases, both. Also well worth considering is the wondrously named **Th
Chain Gang** (www.thechaingang.co.uk), specialists in two-wheel travel.

In the US, **Ciclismo Classico** (www.ciclismoclassico.com) and **ExperiencePlus** (www
.xplus.com) each offers cycle tours in both Umbria and Tuscany.

SKIING

The region's skiing scene centres upon **Abetone** (www.abetone.com in Italian), on
the border with the region of Emilia-Romagna. While the Apennines are
smaller and less majestic than the Alps, they have a charm of their own
Abetone has some 51km of trails, 25 ski lifts and an average of 118cm
annual snowfall, supplemented by artificial snowmakers.

Best Time of Year

The ski season generally runs from December to late March. Abetone gets
pretty busy during weekends with people heading out here from Florence
and other nearby cities, such as Lucca and Pisa.

If you are here in March you may catch Pinocchio Sugle Sci, a keenly
contested ski competition for kids.

Prime Spots

A couple of shops on the main square in Abetone hire boots and skis –
you'll have to supply your own woolly hat. From here it is a couple of
minutes' walk to the chair lift that takes you to the top of Monte Selletta
(1711m). Here, there's a good choice of blue runs and a couple of red,
although the latter should pose little problem to even relatively novice skiers. On the contrary, they are exhilarating with dips that allow you to pick
up speed, followed by slower, flat sections where you can regain control.

Once you've warmed up with a couple of easy runs, ski across the face
of the ridge to lift 17, then take lift 15 and whoosh down the trail to lift

> **Abetone has some 51km of trails, 25 ski lifts and an average of 118cm annual snowfall, supplemented by artificial snowmakers**

18. This is the heart of the ski area with trails leading into all the valleys on the Tuscan side. It's also the access point for the Val di Luce (Valley of Light), a beautiful, appropriately named valley that has most of the area's more rewarding intermediate trails. If you head to the Alpe Tre Potenze (1940m), you will be rewarded with gorgeous panoramic views stretching all the way to the Tuscan coast.

Information

For ski-lift passes and more information contact the **Ufficio Centrale Biglietti** (☎ 0573 6 05 56; Piazza Piramidi, Abetone; 1-day weekday/weekend €25/29.50, 3-day weekdays €64, 1 week €120). You can also sign up for lessons with a trio of ski schools. **Scuola Sci Abetone** (☎ 0573 6 00 32), **Scuola Sci Montegomito** (☎ 0573 6 03 92) and **Scuola Sci Colò** (0573 60 70 77) each offers an hour's tuition for a minimum of €35.

WATER SPORTS

Enjoying the water doesn't necessarily involve any special effort or equipment but, if you want more than an idle paddle or swim, there are plenty of activities on offer. Diving facilities are generally of a high standard, and scuba-diving courses are not that expensive, with good rental gear widely available. Snorkelling is the low-tech alternative, and still allows you to get dramatically close to fascinating aquatic life. Although there are several areas that are excellent for diving, including Monte Argentario (Porto Ercole), the island of Elba is where most divers of all levels head. The main tourist office in Portoferraio carries a list of diving schools and courses on offer.

If you're into wrecks, you can dive at Pomonte where the *Elvisco* cargo boat is submerged at a depth of 12m. Alternatively, a Junker 52, a German plane from WWII, lies on the seabed near Portoferraio at a more challenging depth of 38m.

Typical prices are: one dive with guide €28; six dives €150; introductory snorkelling €50; and dive master course €500.

The coves of the Tuscan archipelagos and around Monte Argentario are superb for sailing, as well as windsurfing and kite surfing. You can rent equipment and receive instruction at the major resorts. Typically, a six-day sailing or windsurfing/kite surfing course costs from €125 (1½ hours per day).

Windsurfing is also very popular on the Costa Fiorita near Livorno. For information on sailing and windsurfing courses here, contact **Costa Fiorita Booking Centre** (☎ 0586 75 90 59; info@costafiorita.it). Further up the coast, Viareggio holds several annual sailing regattas, including the Coppa di Primavera in March and the Vela Mare Cup in May. For more information, check out the website: www.circolovelamare.it (in Italian).

Fishing in the sea is unlikely to lead to a very plentiful catch because of commercial overfishing that, in turn, has led to occasional fishing bans. For a more certain catch, you are better off heading for the trout farms and manmade lakes and streams, for which you will need a permit, available from the Federazione Italiano della Pesca Sportiva ed Attività Subacquee (with offices in every province), before you cast your line.

Best Time of Year

In Monte Argentario and Elba it's possible to enjoy most water sports, including diving, throughout autumn and winter as the water temperature remains relatively temperate year-round. For diving, however, it is still advisable to wear a semidry suit from November to October, switching to a regular wet suit in the summer.

Lago di Trasimeno abounds with water sports and outdoor activities. Ask for *Tourist Itineraries in the Trasimeno District*, a booklet of walking and horse-riding tracks, at the tourist office (p289).

Art & Architecture

The beauty of the Tuscan and Umbrian countryside is matched only by the extraordinary artistic output of its people. While Tuscany gained worldwide fame as one of the foremost creators of all things artistic, from the Middle Ages through the Renaissance, Umbria too has made its own more modest but significant contribution.

ARCHITECTURE
A Long, Long Time Ago...

The Etruscans (Peoples of Europe) by Graham Barker and Tom Rasmussen is the foremost book on Etruscan culture, drawing upon centuries of archaeological and architectural research to contemplate this advanced civilisation.

While the most prestigious ancient architecture lies outside the region, Umbria, and to a lesser degree Tuscany, still have a decent smattering of pre-Etruscan, Etruscan and Roman urban remains and necropolises (burial grounds). In Umbria, Amelia boasts 6th-century-BC town walls. Outside Perugia lies the Ipogeo dei Volumni burial site (p272) and near Orvieto is the Crocifisso del Tufo necropolis (p336). Etruscans often buried the dead with their worldly possessions. Much of the recovered loot from these two sites is on display in museums, such as the Museo Claudio Faina e Civico (p335) in Orvieto or the Museo Archeologico Nazionale dell'Umbria (p272) in Perugia. Perhaps the most imposing extant Etruscan monument is the Arco d'Etrusco (Etruscan Arch; p271), built as a gateway into Perugia.

The Etruscans dug intricate drainage systems for the marshy valleys of Umbria and Tuscany, allowing a more complex agricultural system. Each community needed a strategic viewpoint to watch over its crops, which led to the building of towns on top of tufaceous plateaus, thus, the birth of the Italian hill town.

A few Roman ruins remain in Umbria, fewer in Tuscany. The most complete example is in Carsulae (p327), a Roman village outside modern-day Terni, which was on the Via Flamini. Although you'll see much more extensive and intact Roman architecture elsewhere in Italy, many towns in the region have more than a trace of Roman architecture. In Tuscany, there are Roman baths and a theatre in Volterra (p226), an amphitheatre in Arezzo (p256) and Roman bath ruins in Fiesole (p139). In Umbria you'll find the grand amphitheatre in Spoleto (p313), sections of a Roman bridge and aqueduct in Narni (p328), and the city gates and well-preserved walls of Spello (p304). Bevagna (p307) in Umbria still has remnants of an amphitheatre and baths, and the town of Gubbio (p296) has a much-weathered Roman theatre.

In *Etruscan Places,* DH Lawrence traverses the Italian countryside, looking for ancient ruins and the meaning of life.

Romanesque

Emerging from the collapse of the Roman Empire and a battering by barbarian hordes invading from the north, Tuscany and Umbria, again at relative peace, furthered an architectural style that was classically influenced by Roman designs, having originated further northwest, in Lombardy. Characterised by simplicity, it was a model that would be adopted and adapted throughout western Europe.

The standard church ground plan typically follows that of Roman-era basilicas; a nave flanked by two aisles, no transept and between one and five apsidal chapels, topped by a simple dome. Initially, at any rate, churches tended to be bereft of decoration except on the semicircular apses and arches above doorways and windows. Beside the church there was often a free-standing, square-based bell tower, perforated by layers of semicircular arched windows.

OFF THE BEATEN TRACK

Avoid the long lines to see *David* at the Galleria dell'Accademia (p100) and the Uffizi Gallery (p94) by heading to these stunning examples of artistic genius.

- *Allegories of Good and Bad Government* by Ambrogio Lorenzetti in the Palazzo Communale (p198), Siena
- *The Legend of the True Cross* by Piero della Francesca in the Chiesa di San Francesco (p254), Arezzo
- The *Saint Francis Cycle* by Giotto and colleagues in the Basilica di San Francesco (p283), Assisi
- The frescoes by Masaccio, Masolino and Filippino Lippi in the Basilica di Santa Maria del Carmine's Cappella Brancacci (p108), Florence
- The original panels of the Fonte Gaia by Jacopo della Quercia in the Complesso Museale di Santa Maria della Scala (p209), Siena
- The Sagrestia Nuova (New Sacristy) by Michelangelo on display at the Basilica di San Lorenzo (p99), Florence
- The architecture of the Basilica di Santo Spirito (p107) by Brunelleschi in Florence
- The Bardi and Peruzzi Chapels by Giotto in the Basilica di Santa Croce (p103), Florence
- The *Last Judgement* fresco cycle by Luca Signorelli in the Chapel of Santa Maria di San Brizio, Orvieto cathedral (p335)
- Cimabue's *Crucifixion* in the Basilica di San Francesco (p283), Assisi

---

One of the earliest Romanesque examples in Umbria is the Tempietto del Clitunno (p316), near Spoleto. It was built between the 5th and 8th centuries AD, incorporating recycled materials from older structures. This convenient technique, known as *spolia* (literally re-using the 'spoils' from destroyed or looted monuments) is a common one across the centuries; you'll quite often see an anomalous hunk of pillar or recycled slab of inscribed tombstone poking out from a later structure. In Spoleto, most of the cathedral has been reconstructed but features, including its impressive façade, remain.

In Tuscany, the early rediscovery of the favourite Roman building material, marble, led to a more exuberant decorative style, the best examples of which are in Pisa (p148) and Lucca (p155). Key characteristics of the Tuscan variant are the two-tone marble banding and complex rows of columns and loggias in the façade. The cathedral in Carrara (p170), begun in the 11th century, was one of the first medieval buildings to be constructed entirely of marble, transported all the way from the Apuane Alps.

The baptistry (p89) in Florence, embellished in its marble casing, is a fine example of the pure lines of the Romanesque, thrown into relief by the Gothic frills and frets of the Cathedral (p87) next door. Overlooking Florence and the River Arno, the Chiesa di San Miniato al Monte (p109) is another splendid Romanesque structure. The Pieve di Santa Maria (p255) in Arezzo, with its richly columned façade, is a sterling example too.

Don't go to central Italy without your copy of *Art and Architecture in Italy: 1250–1400* by John White, a pre-eminent art history professor.

Gothic

The transition was gradual but by the beginning of the 13th century, the planners and masons of Tuscany and Umbria were introducing more and more Gothic features into their constructions (incidentally, it was 16th-century scholars who, with perplexing logic, named the style after the Goths, the destroyers of the Roman Empire).

What would several centuries later be styled 'Gothic' originated in the Île de France area around Paris and quickly spread south to Italy. Compared with their Romanesque predecessors, Gothic churches and palaces are truly colossal. The one element common to most is their great height. Soaring structures, it was felt, would lift mortal eyes to the heavens and at the same time remind people of their smallness compared to the grandeur of God. Rather than relying on the solidity of mass, they sought to capture an almost diaphanous light pouring through tall pointed windows. Churches in particular were richly adorned – pinnacles, statues, gargoyles and baubles, the busier, the better.

Check out www.great buildings.com/places /italy.html for a comprehensive list of prominent Italian buildings.

The central Italian interpretation of Gothic differs a little from the delicate lace stonework of the great Gothic cathedrals in northern Europe, such as Notre Dame in Paris. Although still of the same epic proportions, Gothic churches in Tuscany were relatively unadorned, except, that is, in their exuberant, creative use of that favourite local material, marble. Truly outstanding examples whose façades will indeed leave you feeling small – perhaps before the wonder of creation, certainly at the skill and daring imagination of their builders – are the cathedrals of Florence (p87), Siena (p199) and Orvieto (p335), plus the churches of Santa Croce (p103) and Santa Maria Novella (p97) in Florence.

Arnolfo di Cambio (1245–1302), the first great master builder in Florentine architectural history, designed the city's cathedral, and also Orvieto's with its equally stunning façade. He was also responsible for Florence's greatest civic structure in Gothic style, the Palazzo Vecchio (p92). Built of *pietra forte* (hard stone), its bobbly, rusticated surface of rough-hewn, protruding blocks is typical of many grand buildings in Florence. One of the most imposing medieval Italian government buildings, its only possible rival is the Palazzo Communale (p198) in Siena, built at the turn of the 14th century, with its slender Torre del Mangia.

At the Basilica di San Francesco (p283) in Assisi, constructed at a time of transition from Romanesque to Gothic, you can, if the crowds permit, see the two styles in close proximity. The lovely, more squat lower church was designed in Romanesque style, with safe, stolid walls and piers, and characteristic rounded arches. The upper church, by contrast, like a greyhound to a wombat, is a sublime example of soaring, sweeping Italian-Gothic architecture.

Florence & the Renaissance

The Italian Renaissance thrived first and foremost in Florence, peaking in the mid-16th century. Michelozzo di Bartolomeo Michelozzi (1396–1472) was commissioned by Cosimo de' Medici to build the Palazzo Medici-Riccardi (p99), a prestigious residence that would be in keeping with the family's stature. Three hefty storeys with the air of a fortress are topped by a solid roof whose eaves jut far from the walls. The lowest storey features rustication, as on the Palazzo Vecchio, which contrasts with the smooth stone of the upper levels. It's a structure that was to set the tone for civic building in Florence.

The Penguin Book of the Renaissance by JH Plumb analyses the successes of this astounding movement.

Other Renaissance palaces represent variations on the style and lend Florence its uniquely stern yet elegant feel. One example is the Palazzo Strozzi (p98), designed by Benedetto da Maiano (1442–97) with façade work by Giuliano da Sangallo (1445–1516). The style was echoed in buildings in other parts of Tuscany, especially the nearby northern towns of Prato (p134), Pistoia (p130) and Pisa (p148), and continued to be a model many years after the Renaissance proper was over.

Francesco di Giorgio (1439–1502) was about the only architect of note to come out of Siena during the Renaissance. An accomplished painter and sculptor too, his only lasting building is the Chiesa di Santa Maria del Calcinaio, a few kilometres outside Cortona. His was an original vision; he dropped the use of pillars and columns to separate aisles from a central nave. Instead, the building is a solid, two-storey construction with tabernacle windows on the second level.

Two of the most important Renaissance buildings in Umbria are the Palazzo Ducale (c 1470; p296) in Gubbio by Francesco Giorgio Martini and the Tempio di Santa Maria della Consolazione (1508; p323) in Todi, thought to have been designed by Donato Bramante (1444–1514).

FILIPPO BRUNELLESCHI

Enter Filippo Brunelleschi (1377–1446), one of the planet's most influential designers. It was Brunelleschi who brought the Renaissance to Florence, in architectural terms. But an even greater contribution of his was the very concept of the architect. Instead of acting as foreman, building on the fly, Brunelleschi designed formulae of perspective, mathematics and balance, and created buildings first on the drawing board, rather than on site.

Florence still has several of his creations, each a wonder of perspective and harmony: the portico of the Spedale degli Innocenti (Hospital of the Innocents, 1419; p102), considered the earliest work of the Florentine Renaissance; the Sagrestia Vecchia (Old Sacristy) in the Basilica di San Lorenzo (1428; p99); and his redesigned Basilica di San Lorenzo (1420) and Basilica di Santo Spirito (p107). The use of Corinthian columns, simple arches, usually a coffered ceiling over the wide nave and two-tone colouring (greenish-grey *pietra serena,* literally 'tranquil stone', and white plaster on the trim) are common elements. But Brunelleschi's most important work is the revolutionary cupola of Florence's cathedral (p87). Here, he uses his knowledge of architecture, science and art, along with a study of Roman construction – especially the dome of the Pantheon – to build this astonishing architectural feat.

MICHELANGELO

Born into a poor family, Michelangelo Buonarroti (1475–1564) entered the Medici household as a privileged student of painting and sculpture. In later years he also turned his attention to building design, although his architectural activities in Florence weren't that extensive. Indeed, much of his greatest work was done in Rome, where the majesty of the High Renaissance left even Florence trailing.

Before he took off for Rome, Michelangelo flexed his architectural muscles in Florence, designing the Sagrestia Nuova (New Sacristy) and the grand staircase and entrance hall for the Biblioteca Medicea Laurenziana, both in the Basilica di San Lorenzo (p99).

Mannerism

By 1527, with the sack of Rome by Charles V's imperial forces, the High Renaissance as an architectural force was over, war having depleted the funds and snuffed out the desire to continue creating in such quantity and on such a grand scale.

Mannerism (from the Italian *maniera,* meaning style or technique) bridges the gap between Renaissance and baroque. A term usually applied to painting, it is characterised in architecture by greater, sometimes gratuitous ornamentation. Antonio da Sangallo il Giovane (1485–1546), son of another Florentine architect and sculptor, worked mostly in Rome, although he returned briefly to Florence to build the Fortezza da Basso (p109) in 1534 for Alessandro de' Medici. Bartolomeo Ammannati (1511–92) expanded Florence's Palazzo Pitti (p105) into a suburban

Ross King's *Brunelleschi's Dome: How a Renaissance Genius Reinvented Architecture* chronicles how this hot-tempered Renaissance man constructed the largest bricks-and-mortar dome ever created.

Art and architecture were inextricably intertwined with mathematics and science in Renaissance Italy. Brunelleschi reinvented linear perspective by developing a system of drawing that allowed the accurate projection of three dimensions onto paper – science could now guide architecture.

palace for the Medici dukes and designed the Ponte Santa Trinità (p98). He also had a hand in the design of the Giardino di Boboli (p106).

Arezzo-born Giorgio Vasari (1511–74) left his mark in Florence with the creation of the Uffizi Gallery (p94) and the Corridoio Vasariano (p96), which links Palazzo Vecchio to Palazzo Pitti across the Arno. Bernardo Buontalenti (1536–1608) succeeded Vasari as architect to the Grand Duke of Tuscany. He designed the Forte di Belvedere (p109) and the Palazzo Nonfinito (p90) on Via del Proconsolo, which differs from Renaissance predecessors principally in the decorative flounces on its façade.

Baroque

The 17th century saw a construction slowdown throughout the region. This was the era of the baroque, which had more impact on décor than on architectural design. At its most extreme, particularly in Rome, such decoration was sumptuous to the point of giddiness – all curvaceous statuary, twisting pillars and assorted baubles.

These excesses are the exception rather than the norm in Tuscany, but some examples can be found in the villas near Lucca (p161), the cathedral in Pescia (p161), the frenzied interior of Florence's Basilica di Santa Maria del Carmine (p108) and the façade of its Chiesa d'Ognissanti (p97). The former, finished by Gherardo Silvani (1579–1675), is considered the finest piece of baroque architecture in Florence and a demonstration of the restraint typical of the city.

> Rudolf Wittkower's *Art & Architecture in Italy 1600-1750* is an excellent reference covering baroque art and architecture.

Urban Renewal to the Present

Urban renewal began in Tuscany and Umbria from the early 19th century. Napoleon's representative, Elisa Baciocchi, helped turn Lucca's walls (p158) into the velvet green garden area you see surrounding the old city today. Public works programmes got under way and many neoclassical buildings, bridges and *viali* (boulevards) were built. What had been the core of old Florence, where the Roman forum once stood, was flattened in the 1890s to make way for the grandiloquent Piazza della Repubblica (p92). Art Nouveau took off from the 1880s to the interwar period in the style known throughout Italy as Liberty (named after the eponymous London store). The town of Viareggio (p165) is rich in Liberty buildings, both grand and simple.

Sadly for a region so rich in the architecture of the past, it has seen little flourishing of architectural talent or visionary town planning since WWII. In Tuscany, cities such as Livorno and the suburbs of Florence, and in Umbria, Terni and, to a lesser extent, Foligno have seen block buildings replace the magnificent structures that were destroyed during Allied bombing in WWII. Nothing could be further from the ideals of Brunelleschi's finest structures than the soulless, fast-buck housing and light-industrial zones that now sprawl between Florence and Prato.

> An extensive virtual museum, the Web Gallery of Art at www.kfki .hu/~arthp/, showcases over 6500 pieces of European Renaissance, Gothic and baroque paintings and includes biographies of the artists.

PAINTING & SCULPTURE

Tuscany and Umbria were blessed – and cursed – with powerful cities that were effectively owned by prominent families or the Church. These rulers commissioned hired hands – Raphael, Signorelli, Pinturicchio and many more – to fresco their new palaces and churches. Tuscany and Umbria's art scene blossomed, spurred on not primarily by an aesthetic impulsion but more as a way of keeping alive in the minds of the faithful, who were more often than not illiterate, the stories and teachings of the Bible. Artists were regarded as tradesmen and art was devotional and instructive, especially in the Byzantine, Romanesque and Gothic days, when works were commissioned (though not always paid for) by the Church for religious institutions and purposes.

Antiquity
Etruscan art survives mostly in the form of ceramics, painted in an Eastern geometrical style. The Greek influence was also strong, particularly along the southern coast of Tuscany and into Lazio, where the inhabitants interacted with Greek traders. Great examples of ancient ceramics, funerary decorations and sculpture can be seen in the archaeological museums of Perugia (p272), Spoleto (p313) and Orvieto (p336), all in Umbria.

Check out www.artcyclopedia.com for a database describing the artistic movements and their major exponents.

Middle Ages
After the fall of Rome up until the 13th century, little original art was created in Tuscany or Umbria. As the cities freed themselves from imperial or feudal control in the course of the 12th century, so art began to free itself from the inherited rigidity of Romanesque and Byzantine norms. Gone were the solemn, otherworldly religious figures and the gold backgrounds representing heaven, and in were paintings that displayed emotions and real people.

In Tuscany, Pisa was in the ascendant. Master of Sardinia and a busy sea trade port, the city was more open to external influence and artistic interchange than inland cities such as Florence. The first artist of note to make an impact in Florence was Cimabue (c 1240–1302), who began painting in Pisa but travelled all over Tuscany. Cimabue painted the most realistic interpretation of St Francis (drawn from descriptions told to him by Francis' two nephews) in the lower basilica in the church of St Francis in Assisi (p283). Giorgio Vasari identifies him as the catalyst for change in painting, breaking free from the rigidity of Gothic and Byzantine models. In Florence, Cimabue's *Maestà* (Majesty; p94) amply demonstrates the transition from Byzantine-style iconography to a fresh exploration of expression and lifelike dimension.

Giotto di Bondone (c 1266–1337; usually known simply as Giotto), born in the Mugello northeast of Florence, was the key figure in the artistic revolution that was gathering pace in the run-up to the Renaissance and most of his Florentine contemporaries were influenced by him to some degree.

The story goes that the master Cimabue 'discovered' the young shepherd boy Giotto while walking his sheep one day. He saw a sketch the young boy was drawing and the rest, as they say, is history.

In sculpture, Nicola Pisano (c 1215–c 1278) was also something of a master to all who followed in Tuscany and Umbria. You'll see some of his best work in the baptistry (p151) in Pisa and the pulpit in Siena's cathedral (p199). He also sculpted the exquisite bas-reliefs on the Fontana Maggiore (Great Fountain; p269) in the centre of Perugia. He was succeeded by his son Giovanni Pisano (c 1248–c 1314), who often worked with him and who contributed to the cathedral in Siena.

Arnolfo di Cambio (c 1245–1302), a student of Nicola Pisano, architect of the cathedral and Palazzo Vecchio (p92) in Florence, also decorated the cathedral's façade. Some of this sculpture survives in the Museo dell'Opera del Duomo (p88), but the bulk was destroyed in the 16th century, when the cathedral was remodelled.

Another outstanding sculptor was Andrea Pisano (c 1290–c 1348), who left behind him the bronze doors of the south façade of Florence's baptistry (p89), where the realism of the characters combines with the fine linear detail of a Gothic imprint.

The Basilica di San Francesco, Assisi
All of the great masters of the day – Cimabue, Giotto, Pietro Lorenzetti, Simone Martini – were called in soon after St Francis' death in 1226 to create frescoes for the glorious new church being built in the new Italian

Gothic style. These paintings revolutionised art. The former Byzantine style typically presented solemn, two-dimensional religious figures against a gold background representing heaven. In the fresco cycle of the upper church, in addition to sky and nature, Giotto added something fresh in art – emotion and expressions.

The Sienese School

Although the focus of artistic life in Tuscany was concentrated upon Florence, its southern rival, Siena, also enjoyed a brief period of glory.

The only artist in Siena to hold a candle to Giotto was Duccio di Buoninsegna (c 1255–1318). Although still much attached to the Byzantine school, he introduced a measure of fluidity and expressiveness, qualities that have led some to compare him with Cimabue. Various examples of his work can be seen in Siena's cathedral (p199) and Florence's Uffizi (p94). Duccio's star pupil was Simone Martini (c 1284–1344), whose most celebrated work is the *Annunciazione,* created for the cathedral in Siena but now hanging in the Uffizi.

Other artists in Siena include the brothers Pietro (c 1290–c 1348) and Ambrogio Lorenzetti (died c 1348). Both worked in Siena and elsewhere; Pietro was particularly active in Assisi. Ambrogio's best-known work is the startling *Effetti del Buon e del Cattivo Governo* (Allegories of Good and Bad Government) in Siena's Palazzo Communale (p198).

Later, while the Renaissance and subsequent movements gripped Florence, Siena remained supremely indifferent and plugged on with largely Byzantine and Gothic models. You can see this in the work of such painters as Taddeo di Bartolo (1362–1422) and Giovanni di Paolo (1395–1482), who remained anchored in the late Gothic style, while in Florence artists such as Uccello, Verrocchio and Filippo Lippi were turning the painting world on its head.

www.pierodellafrancesca
.it will teach you about
Piero della Francesca
and his masterpieces,
including his fresco cycle
in Arezzo.

The Renaissance

With the Renaissance, artists allowed themselves more individual expression while both patrons and the public developed a greater aesthetic appreciation of art for its own sake, in addition to its didactic or devotional purposes. Artists rose in social standing and affluent lay people began to commission art, either for public places or their own homes. Themes broadened beyond the religious, embracing, for example, battle scenes, portraits (generally busts) and scenes from classical mythology.

The Renaissance, especially in Tuscany, saw an extraordinary and unique flourishing of painters and sculptors. Fra Angelico (c 1400–55), a Dominican monk, lived for a time in Florence's Convento di San Marco, whose museum today displays many of his finest paintings. Piero della Francesca (c 1420–92) is chiefly represented today in eastern Tuscany, in Arezzo's Chiesa di San Francesco (p254), with its magnificent fresco cycle, the *Legend of the True Cross,* and with a couple of sublime canvases in the Museo Civico (p259) of Sansepolcro, town of his birth. Luca Signorelli (1450–1523) from Cortona and a pupil of Piero della Francesca, painted the breathtaking *Last Judgement* fresco cycle in Orvieto's cathedral (p335).

In a painting ascribed
to Filippo Lippi within
Florence's Palazzo
Vecchio, is what appears
to be a flying saucer,
oval-shaped and topped
by pointy projections.

A trio of artists each inspired the other. Fra Filippo Lippi (c 1406–99) was a master of light and shadow with a keen eye for detail, skills that he passed to his son, Filippino Lippi (1457–1504). Both are well represented in Florence's churches and contributed to the fresco cycle, *Life of the Virgin Mary,* in Spoleto's cathedral (p313). Sandro Botticelli (1445–1510) was another product of this prolific father-and-son workshop, his flowing, ethereal figures seeming to float across the canvas.

In other artistic fields, Lorenzo Ghiberti (1378–1455), working primarily in bronze, is remembered especially for his north and east doors to Florence's baptistry (p89), the latter dubbed Porta del Paradiso (Door of Paradise) by an admiring Michelangelo. Donatello (c 1386–1466) trained at Ghiberti's prestigious workshop and produced a stream of sculpture hitherto unparalleled in its dynamism and force. Meanwhile, Siena's Jacopo della Quercia (1374–1438) was carving his way through Tuscany, working above all in Lucca and Siena, where he designed the Fonte Gaia (p198) in Il Campo. Although also active as a painter, Andrea del Verrocchio is best remembered for his sculpture (as well as being Leonardo da Vinci's mentor). His virtuosity can be admired in the sarcophagus he sculpted for the Medici family in the old sacristy of the Basilica di San Lorenzo (p99) in Florence. And throughout Tuscany, you'll come across glazed terracotta medallions and set pieces created by the prolific della Robbia family: father, Luca (1400–82), his nephew, Andrea, and Andrea's son, Giovanni.

Umbria's two most famous painters were Pietro Vannucci (c 1450–1523), better known as Perugino, and Bernardo di Betto (c 1454–1513), styled Pinturicchio. Perugino, born in Città della Pieve (which still houses much of his work), is known for painting soft classical figures. He did many of the frescoes in the Collegio del Cambio (p269) in Perugia and contributed to the Sistine Chapel in Rome. Pinturicchio, a student of Perugino, also painted frescoes in the Sistine Chapel, as well as the Borgia apartments at the Vatican. In turn, one of Perugino's students in Perugia was Raphael (1483–1520), who went on to study and paint in Florence, Siena and Rome.

LEONARDO DA VINCI

Born in a small town west of Florence, Leonardo da Vinci (1452–1519; see also p25) was the true rounded, multitalented epitome of Renaissance man. Painter, sculptor, architect, scientist, engineer and inventor, Leonardo brought to all fields of knowledge and art an original touch, often opening up whole new branches of thought. Paying little heed to received wisdoms, either Christian or classical, he read, wrote and created with unquenchable curiosity.

Such multifaceted study took up much of Leonardo's time, but he still found plenty to devote to what he saw as the noblest art, painting. One of his outstanding early works, the *Annunciazione,* now in the Uffizi (p94), already revealed his concern with light and shadow, and with its representation through chiaroscuro. Leonardo did much of his work outside Florence, spending some 20 years in Milan.

Visit www.italian-art .org, site of the Italian Renaissance Art Project (IRAP) for details on the movement and its artists.

MICHELANGELO

While Leonardo was in Milan, Michelangelo Buonarroti (1475–1564) was asserting himself as a rival painter, albeit of a very different kind. In contrast to Leonardo's smoky, veiled images, Michelangelo opted for greater clarity of line. As a young lad, he was taken in by Lorenzo de' Medici, who could spot talent when it presented itself. His greatest painting project was the ceiling of the Sistine Chapel in Rome. In Florence, there's relatively little of his work but the *Tondo Doni* (*tondo* means circular and Doni was the patron) in the Uffizi (p94) provides stunning insight into his craft.

See www.michelangelo .com/buonarroti.html – a site dedicated to the life and works of the artist.

Michelangelo was most prolific as a sculptor. And while he painted and built in Florence, his greatest gifts to the city were those he crafted from stone. After a stint in Rome, where he carved the remarkable *Pietà,* in St Peter's Basilica, Michelangelo returned to Florence in 1501 to accomplish one of his most striking commissions, the colossal statue of *David,* these days in the Galleria dell'Accademia (p100). Other masterpieces include his *Genio della Vittoria* (Genius of Victory) in the Palazzo Vecchio (p92) and the haunting sculptures that adorn the Medici tombs in the Basilica di San Lorenzo (p99).

High Renaissance to Mannerism

Fra Bartolommeo (1472–1517) stands out for such paintings as the *Apparizione della Vergine a San Bernardo* (St Bernard's Vision of the Virgin), now in the Galleria dell'Accademia (p100) in Florence. His art is quintessentially devotional, with virtually all incidental detail eliminated in favour of the central subject. By contrast, Piero di Cosimo (c 1461–1521) embraces both nature and mythology. Several of his works can be seen in Florence's Palazzo Pitti (p105).

The experimentation associated with the likes of Jacopo Pontormo (1494–1556) makes his work emblematic of Mannerism, that troubled search for a freer expression. In one of his earlier works, the *Visitazione* (Visitation) in the Chiesa della Santissima Annunziata (p102) in Florence, the figures seem almost furtive or preoccupied. His most famous painting remains his *Deposizione* (Deposition), a more mature work from the 1520s that's in the Chiesa di Santa Felicità (p105), also in Florence.

Il Rosso Fiorentino (The Redhead from Florence; 1494–1540) also worked on the SS Annunziata frescoes and several other projects elsewhere in Tuscany. His works too betray a similar note of disquiet and the flashes of contrasting light and dark create an unreal effect in his characters.

In rival Siena, Domenico Beccafumi (c 1484–1551) was one of the leading exponents of Tuscan Mannerism. Among his better-known works, the *Caduta degli Angeli* (Fall of the Angels) is full of disquiet and movement, to the point of blurring his images. It can be seen in the Pinacoteca Nazionale (p210) in Siena. Around the same time, Il Sodoma (1477–1549) was producing works of an altogether smokier style. (And yes, his nickname is exactly as it sounds, but it's debatable whether it was a corruption of his reputed family name 'Sodona', a horse-racing nickname or because, as Vasari, clearly no admirer or friend, writes, he was always surrounded by 'beardless young men'.) His paintings have a matte quality suffused with Mediterranean light. You can compare several of his works with those of Beccafumi in Siena's Pinacoteca Nazionale. He

Read The Renaissance *by Walter Pater for an idiosyncratic account of Italian art, much favoured by louche Victorian aesthetes.*

MOSTLY MADONNAS

As so much of the art of medieval and Renaissance Europe falls into distinct thematic groups, the titles of many paintings are nearly always the same. You will rarely see such stock titles translated into English in Tuscany, so a handful of clues follows.

A *Crocifissione* (Crucifixion) represents the crucifixion of Christ, one of the most common subjects of religious art. Another is the *Deposizione* (Deposition), which depicts the taking down of the body of Christ from the cross, while the *Pietà*, a particularly popular subject for sculptors, shows the lifeless body of Christ in the arms of his followers – the characters can vary, but the theme remains the same. Before all the nastiness began, Christ managed to have an *Ultima Cena*, or Last Supper, with the Apostles.

Perhaps the most favoured subject is the *Madonna col Bambino/Bimbo* (Virgin Mary with Christ Child). The variations on this theme are legion. Sometimes they are depicted alone, sometimes with various *santi* (saints), *angeli* (angels) and other figures. The *Annunciazione* (Annunciation), when the angel Gabriel announces to Mary the honour that has been bestowed on her, is yet another standard episode. When the big event occurred, lots of people, including the *Magi* (Wise Men), came to participate in the *Adorazione* (Adoration) of the newly born Christ.

pops up all over Tuscany, his most extensive work the haunting frescoes of the Abbazia di Monte Oliveto Maggiore (p216).

The variable works of Giorgio Vasari (1511–74) and his students are all over Florence. It was almost assembly-line production as he and his army of helpers ploughed speedily through commissions for frescoes and paintings. Vasari Incorporated was largely responsible for the decoration of the Palazzo Vecchio (p92). But Vasari's real claim to fame, and what he is most appreciated for today, is his monumental *Lives of the Artists*, a lively two-volume compendium of facts, unattested gossip and just plain fiction about the lives of his fellow Italian artists; it's still available in several English translations.

Baroque, Neoclassicism & the Macchiaioli

A full palette of artists continued to paint in Florence as the new century wore on, but few are of great note. Giovanni da San Giovanni (1592–1636) was the leading light of the first half of the 17th century and some of his frescoes remain in the Palazzo Pitti (p105). One much underestimated painter of the period was Cecco Bravo (1601–60), whose canvasses combine Florentine tastes of the period with a rediscovery of the soft, nebulous colours of Venice's Titian.

The arrival of artists from out of town, such as Pietro da Cortona and the Neapolitan Luca Giordano (1634–1705; see his complex *Allegory of Divine Wisdom* in Florence's Palazzo Medici-Riccardi, p99), imported the Baroque's predilection for hedonistic colour and movement to Florence. This, in contrast to the Mannerists, who had searched, often rather stiffly, for ways of breaking with, yet still remaining within Renaissance conventions.

Thereafter, the Florentine art scene remained sterile until the first intimations of Impressionism wafted down from Paris around the middle of the 19th century. In Florence, anti-academic artists declared that painting real-life scenes was the only way forward. The Macchiaioli movement lasted until the late 1860s and received its name (which could be translated as the 'stainers' or 'blotchers') from a disparaging newspaper article. Works by typical artists of the era such as Livorno-born Giovanni Fattori (1825–1908), Neapolitan Giuseppe Abbati (1836–68) and Silvestro Alga (1826–95), feature in Florence's Galleria d'Arte Moderna (p106).

Modern

Local star of the 20th century was Livorno-born painter and sculptor Amedeo Modigliani (1884–1920), with his elongated human forms and strong use of colour, but he scarcely qualifies, having decamped to Paris when only 22 and already more than half way through his tragically short life.

Several 20th-century Umbrian artists have taken centre stage. Futurist Gerardo Dottori (1884–1977), from Perugia, became known for *aeropittura,* or painting the sensation of flight. Alberto Burri (1915–95) began his abstract, impressionist painting directly onto burlap, or course hessian, while a prisoner of war in far-off Texas, and continued to use textured media throughout his career. He hails from Città di Castello (p300), where you can visit two art galleries housing much of his work (including an old tobacco warehouse for his larger pieces). Sculptor Leoncillo Leonardi (1915–68) worked mostly with ceramics and terracotta and dabbled in neocubism. Some of his work is displayed in Spoleto's Galleria d'Arte Moderna (p313).

Reading *The Lives of the Artists* by Giorgio Vasari before you head out to churches and museums brings the paintings – and the artists – to life. This contemporary view of the Renaissance artists includes all sorts of biographical (and often fictionalised) juicy titbits about the regions' most famous artists.

Food & Drink

Some of the most famous cuisine in the entire world is actually a result of poverty. While Medici banquets must have been grand affairs, most of the peasantry made do with much simpler fare. The dishes we crave today – pasta, risotto, vegetables – came to be because they were made from ingredients both abundant and cheap. To this day, visitors to Tuscany and Umbria still benefit from *la cucina contadina,* literally 'the farmer's kitchen'.

Lonely Planet's *World Food Italy* takes an in-depth look at the whole country's food history and culture.

STAPLES & SPECIALITIES
Tuscany

Tuscans love meat. Visit Florence's markets and you'll see more parts from more beasts than you knew existed. The pinnacle of all this carnivorous activity has to be the *bistecca alla fiorentina,* which is specially sourced from local white cattle, la Chianina. It's cut into T-bone steaks about 5cm thick and grilled over coals. *Bistecca* will come rare at a restaurant (forget well-done as it will be burnt on the outside) and you pay by *l'etto* (100g). In even the humblest of restaurants, your *bistecca* will probably cost more than €25, and will be enough to feed two people. While Chianina beef is becoming scarcer, you can still find it at many restaurants and markets.

Tuscans are jokingly called *mangiafagioli* or 'bean eaters', such is their passion for the humble legume. White *cannellini* beans and the dappled borlotti beans are favourites, and are often seen in soup, or served with sausages or braised meat.

Mary Ann Esposito explores Umbrian cooking in *Ciao Italia in Umbria: Recipe and Reflection from the Heart of Italy.*

Much of the food is based on the *pane toscano,* the fine-textured, salt-free bread. One of its uses is to thicken soups, which the Tuscans are famous for, such as *ribollita,* a 'reboiled' bean-and-vegetable soup that's flavoured with black cabbage and left to sit for a day before being served. The same *pane* is also used in *pappa,* a tomato-and-bread mush that has an extraordinary depth of flavour, and *panzanella,* a bread-and-tomato salad, which can appear as runny as a thick soup.

One local pasta is *pinci,* similar to the Umbrian *umbricelli,* served with *ragù* or *sugo* (sauce). *Pappardelle* – fresh, flat egg noodles cut wider than *tagliatelle* and thinner than lasagna sheets – are also common. The noodles are mostly flat, but sometimes come with a crinkled edge, and may be served *alla lepre,* moistened with a little hare or rabbit *ragù.*

While meat can dominate, the seafood of Tuscany is also great, and you'll see it displayed in restaurant windows throughout the area. Livorno leads the region with seafood, and it has created a seafood stew, *cacciucco,* which has to have five types of fish, one for each 'c' in the name. The name comes from the Turkish *kukut,* meaning 'small fry'.

A SNAIL'S PACE

Fast food as a concept doesn't sit easily with Italians, and it was here in 1986 that the first organised, politically active group decided to tackle the issue head-on. Symbolised by a snail, the Slow Food Movement now has more than 80,000 members in more than 100 countries. It has even spawned a sister movement, Slow City (see p340). It promotes good food and wine to be consumed (slowly, of course) in good company, and champions traditional cuisine and sustainable agricultural practices, including organic farming and using seasonal ingredients. The volunteer-run groups organise social programmes and educational outings with much feasting and frivolity. For more information, check out www.slowfood.com.

Cheese, or *caciotta*, the local name for cheese, is central to the cuisine, particularly *pecorino* (sheep's cheese). In fact, cheese was considered so important that in days gone by women used cheese-making as a dowry skill. The cheese of Pienza, a town near the Umbrian border, is one of the greatest *pecorini* in Italy.

Local sweets are few but memorable. *Panforte,* the Sienese flat, hard cake with nuts and candied fruit, is sensational. Instead of fancy sweets you'll see a range of dry-textured, often double-baked *biscotti* (biscuits) such as *cantucci,* which are usually studded with almonds. They're good, especially when dipped into *vin santo,* the local sweet wine. Another popular *biscotti* is *ricciarelli,* made with marzipan.

Umbria

The heart of Umbrian food is the hearth. Open wood fires are used for everything from *porchetta* (spit-roasted pig) to fish to bruschetta (grilled bread appetisers).

In Umbria it is the pig that reigns supreme, followed closely by *cinghiale* (wild boar). Hunting season is in the autumn and Umbrians embrace the activity with gusto. You will also find many meat dishes on the menu, including *agnello* (lamb) and *pesce* (fish) around Lago di Trasimeno.

Virtually every single Umbrian restaurant will serve at least one dish with the area favourite, *tartufo* (truffle). While the black truffle is considered a delicacy, the white truffle is even rarer, and the cost can reach thousands of euros. The local *pecorino* cheese is excellent, as is the mozzarella. *Pecorino di tartufo* is a semihard cheese studded with pieces of truffle.

Norcia, snuggled between Monti Sibillini and the Valnerina in Umbria's east, is a food-lover's dream. Look for a boar's head mounted outside a shop and you've found a *norcineria*. Its prosciutto (cured ham) is saltier and coarser, but more fragrant and complex than those of Parma and San Daniele. *Cinghiale* makes a decent prosciutto, but the *salsicce* (cured sausages) from it is even better. About 30 minutes from Norcia is Castelluccio, an ancient village set on a high plain amid a sea of wildflowers, and home to the implausibly delicate Castelluccio *lenticchie* (lentils), often paired with *salsicce di cinghiale* in a harmonised soup.

Umbria has its own pasta, most notably *umbricelli* (also spelled *ombricelli*), and *strangozzi* (*stringozzi* in some towns). Both are made by hand with the same water-based dough. *Umbricelli* is round and stringlike, but not as fine as spaghetti, while *strangozzi* is more squarish and very filling – the ultimate comfort food. Both *strangozzi* and *umbricelli* are often served with a meat, truffle or tomato sauce.

Umbria's chocolate is legendary. The Perugina chocolate company (now owned by Nestlé), based out of Perugia, sells the world-famous Baci, hazelnut 'kisses' covered with chocolate.

DRINKS
Wine

Tuscany produces six of Italy's DOCG wines (for more information on wine classification see p64): Brunello di Montalcino, Carmignano, Chianti, Chianti Classico, Vino Nobile di Montepulciano and Vernaccia di San Gimignano (the only white). It also boasts more than 30 DOC wines. Umbria's DOCG wines are Torgiano Rosso Riserva and Sagrantino di Montefalco plus more than a dozen DOC wines in eight different regions.

The best of the Tuscan wines, Chianti Classico, comes from seven zones in many different guises. The backbone of the Chianti reds is the Sangiovese, although other grape types are mixed in varyingly modest

Truffles produce a chemical that is similar to a sex hormone in pigs, which is why pigs are traditionally used to hunt them.

Butchers from Norcia were so well known for their craft during the medieval days that, to this day, a pork butcher anywhere in Italy is called a *norcino* and works in a *norcineria*.

WINE CLASSIFICATION

Since the 1960s wine in Italy has been graded according to four main classifications. *Vino da tavola* (table wine) indicates no specific classification; Indicazione Geografica Tipica (IGT) means that the wine is typical of a certain area; Denominazione di Origine Controllata (DOC) wines are produced subject to certain specifications (regarding grape types, method and so on); and Denominazione d'Origine Controllata e Garantita (DOCG) shows that wine is subject to the same requirements as normal DOC, but that it is also tested by government inspectors. These indications appear on labels.

A DOC label can refer to wine from a single vineyard or an area. DOC wines can be elevated to DOCG after five years' consistent excellence. Equally, wines can be demoted; the grades are by no means set in stone.

Further hints come with indications such as *superiore,* which can denote DOC wines above the general standard (perhaps with greater alcohol or longer ageing). *Riserva* is applied only to DOC or DOCG wines that have aged for a specified amount of time.

In general, however, the presence or absence of such labels is by no means a cast-iron guarantee of anything. Many notable wines fly no such flag. Many a *vino da tavola* or IGT wine is so denominated simply because its producers have chosen not to adhere to the regulations governing production. These sometimes include prestige wines.

Your average trattoria will generally stock only a limited range of bottled wines, but better restaurants present a carefully chosen selection from around the country. *Enoteche* (wine bars) usually present you with an enormous range of wines and a limited food menu.

Generally, if you simply order the *vino della casa* (house wine) by the glass, half-litre or litre, you will get a perfectly acceptable table wine to accompany your food.

quantities to produce different styles of wine. Chianti Classico wines share the Gallo Nero (Black Cockerel) emblem that once symbolised the medieval Chianti League. Generally, Chianti is full and dry, although ageing requirements differ from area to area, and even across vineyards.

The choice doesn't stop in the Chianti region. Among Italy's most esteemed and priciest drops is the Brunello di Montalcino (in Siena province). Until not so long ago, only a handful of established estates produced this grand old red, but now more than 140 vineyards are at it. The finished product varies a great deal and depends on soil, microclimate and so on. Like the Chianti reds, the Sangiovese grape is at the heart of the Brunello. It is aged in casks for four years and then for another two years in bottles.

Tuscany is largely, but not exclusively, about reds. Easily the best-known white is the Vernaccia di San Gimignano, which was a favourite of popes and artists as far back as the Renaissance.

An important development since the end of the 1980s has been the rise of Super Tuscans, a long-lived wine of high quality that follows the New World tradition of blending different mixes. Alongside, the Sangiovese vintners are growing Sauvignon, Merlot, Syrah and other grape varieties, and enclosing the mixes in French oak *barriques* (oak barrels). Keep an eye out for the names Sassacaia, Tiganello and Solaia. Since Super Tuscans veer from the strict norms of DOCG and DOC varietals, they were first given the classification of 'table wine', but several decades of fanfare and a few hundred awards have since changed that.

A regional speciality in both provinces that'll appeal to the sweet tooth is *vin santo* (holy wine), a dessert wine also used at Mass. It is traditionally served after dinner with almond-based *cantucci*.

Umbria has itself become a powerhouse of wines over the last two or three decades. There are four Le Strade del Vino (wine roads; see the boxed text, p68) in Umbria, encompassing the four major wine-growing regions:

If you're thinking of shipping wine back home, be prepared for a shock. It costs upwards of €150 to mail home a case, and that's before import taxes. Instead, ask for a *scatola* (wooden box) for around €10 and carry back home a half-dozen bottles.

Lago di Trasimeno; the triangle between Todi, Perugia and Spello; Bevagna and Montefalco; and the entire southwest from Narni to Orvieto.

Umbria was first recognised for its whites, most notably the dry Orvieto Classico, but the *grechetto,* a fruity and velvety straw-coloured white, is also gaining in fame.

However, Umbrian reds are making a strong showing. The Umbrian royals of wine are the Lungarotti family in Torgiano. Their Rosso Riserva became the first DOCG wine in Umbria. The Lungarotti family also run the fascinating Museo del Vino (p279) and its neighbouring *cantina,* where you can try a dozen Lungarotti wines.

Beer

The most common Italian beers are crisp, light Pilsener-style lagers, and younger Italians are happy to guzzle them down with a pizza. The main labels are Morena, Moretti, Peroni and Nastro Azzurro, all very drinkable, quite light and cheaper than the imported varieties. If you want a local beer, ask for a *birra nazionale* either in a bottle or *alla spina* (on tap).

Coffee

Coffee in Italy isn't like anywhere else in the world: it's much better.

An espresso is a small amount of strong, black coffee. It is also referred to as *un caffè.* You can ask for a *caffè doppio* (a double shot), *caffè lungo* ('long coffee') or *caffè Americano,* though the last two will usually just be an espresso with extra water run through the grinds so they can be bitter.

A *caffè corretto* is an espresso with a dash of grappa or some other spirit, and a *macchiato* ('stained' coffee) is an espresso with a dash of milk. You can ask for a *macchiato caldo* (with a dash of hot, foamed milk) or *freddo* (with a spot of cold milk). On the other hand, *latte macchiato* is warmed milk 'stained' with a spot of coffee. *Caffè freddo* is a long glass of cold, black, sweetened coffee. If you want it without sugar, ask for *caffè freddo amaro.*

Then, of course, there is the cappuccino (coffee with hot, frothy milk). If you want it without the froth, ask for *a cappuccino senza schiuma.* Italians tend to drink cappuccino only with breakfast and during the morning, never after meals.

It is difficult to convince barristas to make your cappuccino hot rather than *tiepido* (lukewarm). If you must, ask for it *ben caldo* (hot) or *bollente* (boiling) and wait for the same 'tut-tut' response that you'll attract if you order one after dinner.

Variations on the milky coffee menu include a *caffè latte,* a milkier version of the cappuccino with less froth. In summer the *cappuccino freddo,* a bit like an iced coffee, is popular. You will also find *caffè granita,* sweet and strong, which is traditionally served with a dollop of whipped cream.

Tea

Italians don't drink a lot of *tè* (tea), and generally do so only in the late afternoon, when they might have a cup with a few *pasticcini* (small cakes). It is generally served warm; if this doesn't suit your taste, ask for the water *molto caldo* (very hot) or *bollente.* The only herbal tea in Italy is chamomile, so if you don't want caffeine, ask for a *camomile.*

Water

Despite the fact that tap water is reliable throughout the country, most Italians prefer to drink bottled *acqua minerale* (mineral water). This is available either *frizzante* (sparkling) or *naturale* (still), and you will be asked in restaurants and bars which you would prefer. If you just want a

Pick up *A Traveller's Wine Guide to Italy* by Stephen Hobley for a guide to Italy's best wine-growing regions, including wine-tasting directions and advice.

Former sommelier Jonathan Nossiter's documentary film *Mondovino* follows the globalisation of wine-making in six countries, including interviews with industry giants and Tuscan family growers.

glass of tap water, you should ask for *acqua dal rubinetto,* although some Italians still equate this with asking to run a glass through the toilet.

CELEBRATIONS
Italy celebrates an unprecedented number of festivals, many of them originating from the region's pagan past.

Italians have always celebrated a harvest, the god of the sun, a wedding, a birth, anything. When Christianity arrived, they simply put the new God as the figurehead. Most of the festivals were wild affairs, such as the Saturnalia in Roman times, where a week of drunken revelry was marked by a pig sacrifice at the start and a human sacrifice at the end. Celebrations these days are more sedate affairs by comparison. But only slightly. The biggest

---

FIESTAS FOR FOODIES

Tuscans and Umbrians love to celebrate anything, especially food. The typical food festival is called a *sagra,* and one is celebrated in virtually every corner of Tuscany and Umbria. Some *sagra* feature their namesake, like the Sagra della Lumaca in Cantalupo, named after the snail, which has snails appearing in more dishes than you'd ever thought possible. Others might name themselves after the cherry, but will actually just be an excuse to get the town together for eating, dancing and general merriment (which isn't so bad, either). Here is a list of festivals where the food is all the rage.

January
Cioccolisit (☎ 0572 95 92 26) An artisan chocolate fair, held on the last weekend of January in Monsummano Terme, with top choco-makers and plenty of opportunities to taste.

February
Mostra Mercata del Tartufo Nero (☎ 0743 81 70 90) The Umbrian eating capital, Norcia, plies its delicious black truffle (and other locally produced edibles) on lucky visitors on the last weekend of February and first weekend of March.
La Festa dell'Olivo e la Sagra della Bruschetta Celebrate the pairing of toasted Umbrian bread topped with the ubiquitous olive and olive oil on the last Sunday of Carnevale in Spello.

March
Sagra della Polenta Dolce (☎ 0574 95 74 58) Sweet polenta is eaten as part of a Renaissance festival, now more than 430 years old, held in Prato on Easter Sunday.

April
Rassegna dei Proddotori della Pastorizia della Montagna Pistoiese (☎ 05773 6 88 81) Organised in collaboration with local cheese producers and the Slow Food Movement (see p62) this festival is held in the last weekend of April in Pistoia. There is plenty of tasting going on, as well as a large market.
Sagra della Fettunta (☎ 0572 6 71 94) Celebration of the typical bruschetta with olives, accompanied by Tuscan wine, held at the end of April and start of May in Montecatini Alto.

May
Sagra delle Ciliegie (☎ 0587 68 55 15) Cherry festival with tastings of typical local dishes, sweet and savoury, made with cherries. Lots of food stands, music and entertainment, held from 24 May to 2 June in Pisa.
Cantina Aperte (Umbria ☎ 0742 344 214, www.umbriadoc.com in Italian; Tuscany ☎ 055 290 684, www.movimentoturismovino.it in Italian;) Oenophiles might want to plan their trip around the last weekend in May, when every winery across the region is open to wine tasters. Other farm-produced tastings, folkloric festivals and music also dot the landscape.

festivals these days are at Natale (Christmas), Pasqua (Easter) and Carnevale (the period leading up to Ash Wednesday, the first day of Lent).

The classic way to celebrate any feast is to precede it with a day of eating *magro* (lean) because the feast day is usually a day of overindulgence. While just about every festival has some kind of food involved, many of them are solely food. The general rule is that a *sagra* (feasting festival) will offer food (although you'll normally be expected to pay), and at a *festa* (festival or celebration) you may have to bring your own.

WHERE TO EAT & DRINK

There seems to be one restaurant for every five residents in both Tuscany and Umbria. They are often small, with no more than eight or 10 tables.

June

Cena Medievale (☎ 0571 65 27 30) Festive medieval dinner with 500 of your newest friends, held in the beginning of June in Certaldo, Florence. An inordinately long table is set up along the town square, and €35 will buy you an evening of traditional dishes, music and dancing.

Palio dei Rioni (☎ 0575 65 82 78) Gastronomic fair celebrating local produce, held on the third Sunday in June in Castignion Fiorentino, Arezzo.

July

Festa del Calderone (☎ 0583 44 29 44) A stopping-off point for pilgrims in medieval days, this festival, on 25 July, commemorates the food hand-outs by cooking up enormous pots of pasta to feed the local folk. It is held in Altopascio, Lucca.

Sagra del Pesce (☎ 0565 6 32 69) Typical local seafood dishes are prepared in Piombino on the last weekend in July, culminating on the Sunday with a giant feed-the-masses frying pan of fried fish for all the townsfolk to enjoy.

August

Sagra del Bombolone (☎ 0583 64 10 07) Celebration of the famous *bombolone* (sweet doughnut), held from 1 August to 3 August in Sillicano-Camporgiano, Lucca.

Sagra delle Olive con Coniglio e Polenta (☎ 0583 80 58 13) Local Bagni di Lucca festival celebrating the traditional local dish: olives with rabbit and polenta. It is held on 14 and 15 August.

September

Festa dell'uva e del vino (☎ 0575 44 03 23) Open-air dinners with live entertainment and local wine, held in Arezzo on the third weekend in September.

October

Sagra della Lumaca (☎ 0742 36 02 79) On the last two weeks of October, in a beautiful medieval town just outside Bevagna, you'll find an entire festival devoted to dishes such as snail bruschetta, roasted snails and snail polenta.

November

Mostra del Tartufo Bianco (☎ 0571 4 27 45) White-truffle fair celebrated for more than 30 years on the last three weekends of November in San Miniato, Pisa. The record is held here for the largest truffle ever!

December

Sagra del Vine Brulè (☎ 0573 6 02 31) At 9pm on 30 December in Abetone, Pistoia, a giant cauldron of mulled wine is made, and most people arrive on skis.

Be sure not to judge an eatery by its tablecloth. You may well have your best meal at the dingiest little establishment imaginable.

What you think of as a bar back home is actually more of a neighbourhood fast-food and hang-out spot in Italy. They do serve alcohol, but most people only stop in for a quick *panini* (sandwich) or to chat with friends.

Restaurants come with many different names, so you might end up at a *ristorante* that's more of an *osteria*, or vice versa. Usually, they decide what connotation they'd like to have and go with that. Here's the breakdown:

Enoteca This is similar to an *osteria*, but the main focus is wine. The menu might consist of a few homemade dishes or cold entrées.

Osteria or hosteria The closest translation is 'tavern'. These are usually atmospheric restaurants that focus on wine or drinks.

Pizzeria Self-evident.

Ristorante Can be on the upmarket side and are often found accompanying hotels.

Trattoria Casual, often family-owned, serving local fare.

Quick Eats

Quick snacks abound throughout both provinces. A *fiaschetteria* may serve up small snacks, sandwiches and the like, usually at the bar while you down a glass of wine or two. It is a particularly Tuscan phenomenon. A *tavola calda* (literally 'hot table') usually offers cheap, preprepared meat, pasta and vegetable dishes in a buffet.

You'll also find numerous outlets where you can buy pizza *al taglio* (by the slice). Another option is to go to an *alimentari* (delicatessen) and ask them to make a *panini* with the filling of your choice. At a *pasticceria* (cake shop) you can buy pastries, cakes and biscuits.

Occasionally you will find places with no written menu. This usually means they change the menu daily. Inside, there may be a blackboard, or the waiter will tell you what's available. You might find you'll have your best meal in Italy in a place like this – or, possibly in a tourist area, the worst. Check inside first. The higher the number of locals, the higher the guarantee is for a good meal.

For tasting notes and global events, see www .italianwinereview.com.

An excellent food and travel portal is www .deliciousitaly.com.

For recipes, extensive descriptions of regional specialities and downloadable booklets try www.italianmade .com.

LE STRADE DEL VINO (THE WINE ROADS)

The kind wine folk of Tuscany and Umbria have made life that much easier for those with a healthy interest in wine by creating Le Strade del Vino, wine trails leading through the areas that grow wine. These trails generally follow back roads, passing by a plethora of vineyards. In Tuscany it's common to pass many *cantine aperte*, where you can taste, buy and immerse yourself in wine (sadly, not literally). Umbrian vintners are just starting to jump on the open-tasting bandwagon, but the well-marked routes also follow historic, cultural and natural treasures. It's a fantastic incentive to combine the sampling of a few wines and a glimpse into the traditional farming lifestyle of these rural provinces.

Each *strada* has its own distinct emblem, which you'll see on signposts in towns and throughout the countryside. Just look for a sign that has something resembling a bunch of grapes, and you're probably on the right track. Every *strada* has its own map, with listings of wineries and sometimes *agriturismi* (farm-stay accommodation), restaurants, wine-tasting *enoteche,* and even open olive mills or other gastronomic delights.

To date 14 Tuscan and four Umbrian *strade* have been marked out, which crisscross famous wine-production areas, such as Rufina and Montepulciano in Tuscany, and the Colli del Trasimeno and Strada dei Vini Etrusco Romana between Narni and Orvieto in Umbria. You can pick up maps and information at tourist offices or visit www.terreditoscana.regione.toscana.it/stradedelvino for Tuscany and www.umbriadoc.com (in Italian) for Umbria.

Global fast-food chains are slowly creeping into Italy. A McDonald's near the Spanish Steps in Rome sparked the Slow Food Movement – see p62. You'll find them in touristed areas, but with pizza *al taglio* and *panini* bars everywhere, you'll never have to eat at them if you don't want to.

VEGETARIANS & VEGANS

Menus around the region carry a bounty of vegetable-based dishes, and most eating establishments serve a good selection of antipasti (starters) and *contorni* (vegetables prepared in a variety of ways). Be aware that many sauces contain meat or animal stock.

Vegans are in for a much tougher time. Cheese is often added on top of dishes or in many sauces, so you have to say *'senza formaggio'* when you order. Many types of pasta are made with eggs.

EATING WITH KIDS

Maybe because Italy has one of the lowest birth rates in the world, children seem to be especially adored. While you'll be hard-pressed to find a children's menu anywhere, most restaurants are open to well-behaved children, and will sympathetically grant a request for *spaghetti con burro* (spaghetti with butter). Be aware of hyperactive sugar spikes: many Italian restaurants and *gelaterias* will give your child a treat before asking your permission.

Not every restaurant supplies highchairs, so ask when making a reservation. You won't see many babies in sit-down restaurants. For more information on travelling with your little ones, see p345.

It's believed that the Sangiovese grape – the principal variety in Chianti – was used as far back as the Etruscan period.

HABITS & CUSTOMS

Italians rarely eat a sit-down *colazione* (breakfast). It's generally a quick affair taken at a bar or café counter on the way to work. They tend to drink a cappuccino and eat a *cornetto* (croissant) or other type of pastry generically known as a brioche.

For *pranzo* (lunch), restaurants usually operate from 12.30pm to 3pm, but many don't like taking orders after 2.30pm. It's the main meal of the day, and most shops and businesses close for two or three hours every afternoon to accommodate it. People generally start sitting down to *cena* (dinner) around 7.30pm. It can be hard to find a place still serving after 11pm. Dinner is traditionally a simpler affair, but it is slowly becoming a fuller meal because of the inconvenience of travelling home for lunch every day.

Many restaurants shut one day a week. In some parts of Italy at least one day off is mandatory, but ultimately the decision on whether or not to enforce that rule rests with the *comune* (local council). The Florence *comune*, for instance, does not care what restaurateurs do (unless they close for three days or more in a week), so some skip the weekly break altogether.

A full meal consists of an antipasto, *primo piatto* (first course) and *secondo piatto* (second course), which is usually accompanied by a *contorno* (vegetable side dish). *Insalate* (salads) usually come after the main meal. A cheese course might come in place of a *primi* or as a dessert. Coffee is never served with a meal, always afterwards.

As a very general rule, the more languages the menu is in, the less traditional the food. Take along Lonely Planet's *Italian Phrasebook* and explore restaurants off the beaten path.

Numerous restaurants offer a *menù turistico* or *menù a prezzo fisso*, a set-price lunch that can cost as little as €10 (usually not including drinks) or up to €75 at the best restaurants. It can be a good deal at the better restaurants, especially when it is a speciality such as a *menù vegetariano* or *menù di tartufi*. The *menù turistico* is often a watered-down rip-off for tourists.

Most Italian restaurants add a *coperto* (cover charge) to the bill, usually 10%. Very few restaurants do not include a *coperto*, so check

---

DOS & DON'TS

Just as an Italian at our table would make few faux pas, most visitors at an Italian table get it right. We simply aren't that different. That's the good news. The bad news is that what constitutes 'good manners' alters – as it does everywhere – depending not only on who you're with, but where you are eating and the part of the country you're in.

- *'Buongiorno'* or *'Buonasera'* is the basic greeting in any bar or restaurant.

- Many restaurants expect patrons to dress in style. Change out of your trainers and sweatpants if you want good service.

- To eat long, thin pasta, twirl it up with a fork. *Never* use a spoon to assist. If you end up with a long piece, bite it off rather than slurp it up. Or order gnocchi.

- Keep your hands out of your lap. While you probably don't have to prove to anyone that you're unarmed, it still signifies good manners. Elbows on the table aren't acceptable, so go with the forearm or wrists.

- Don't expect a bread plate. Italians place their bread directly on the table or at the edge of their plates (just don't sop up your sauce with it unless you know your hosts very, very well).

---

your bill and tip 10% to 15%, depending on the level of service. Man Italians might round up the bill or tip for very good service, or in fine restaurants.

Smoking is now outlawed in all restaurants in Italy. This law has bee followed with surprising conformity. A few restaurants are run by die hard smokers, and you'll smell the telltale signs, but it's best to assum that you will not encounter any restaurants that allow smoking.

COOKING COURSES

Many people come to Italy just for the food, so it is hardly surprisin that its cookery courses are among the most popular in the world. Th website www.italycookingschools.com has hundreds of possibilities tha you can consider. Here are a few of our choices:

Casa Ombuto (☎ 348 736 38 64; www.italiancookerycourse.com) High on the hills of the Casentino valley stands Casa Ombuto. Seven-day courses are run by an inspiring husband-and-wife team in their cavelike *cantina*.

Cordon Bleu Perugia (See p273)

Lorenza de' Medici (☎ 0577 74 94 98; cuisineint@aol.com) Lorenza de' Medici teaches the art of Tuscan cuisine in an 11th-century former monastery in Il Chianti. Students learn about agriculture and the seasonal influence on food, and make excursions to local cheesemakers, wineries and food producers. This is a Rolls Royce course with prices to match.

Menfi (☎ 020 746 00 077; www.tastingplaces.com) Choose either a week in Tuscany, near Arezzo or a week in Umbria, in Orvieto; wine tasting and tours of the area are all part of the package.

Tutti a Tavola (☎ 0577 742 919; mimmaferrando@aliceposta.it) Five long-time friends known as 'The Flying Grandmothers' run this delightful cooking class out of their beautiful Tuscan farmhouse kitchens near Radda in Chianti. Three-day courses last most of the afternoon (some day include a market trip in the morning) and you eat your creation with the families and new friends that evening. Also arranges equally delightful accommodation.

Vallicorte (☎ 020 768 01 377; www.vallicorte.com) This is exactly what you need from a course a good group of people (matched by the coordinators), a charismatic instructor and a pair of amusing hosts in an ancient villa in Tuscany.

EAT YOUR WORDS

Get behind the cuisine scene by getting to know the language. For pro nunciation guidelines, see p372.

Sidebar notes:

When dining out at a restaurant, don't ask for grated cheese if you've ordered pasta with fish. It's considered uncouth.

If you can't afford her Badia a Coltibuono cooking school (about €5000 a week), you can at least afford *Tuscany: The Beautiful Cookbook* by Lorenza de' Medici (of *those* de' Medicis).

Useful Phrases

I'd like to reserve a table.
Vorrei riservare un tavolo.   vo·*ray* ree·ser·*va*·re oon *ta*·vo·lo

I'd like the menu, please.
Vorrei il menù, per favore.   vo·*ray* eel me·*noo* per fa·*vo*·re

Do you have a menu in English?
Avete un menù (scritto) in inglese?   a·*ve*·te oon me·*noo* (*skree*·to) een een·*gle*·ze

What would you recommend?
Cosa mi consiglia?   *ko*·za mee kon·*see*·lya

Please bring the bill.
Mi porta il conto, per favore?   mee *por*·ta eel *kon*·to per fa·*vo*·re

I'm a vegetarian.
Sono vegetariano/a.   *so*·no ve·je·ta·*rya*·no/a

I'm a vegan.
Sono vegetaliano/a.   *so*·no ve·je·ta·*lya*·no/a

Food Glossary

AT THE TABLE

aceto	a·*che*·to	vinegar
coltello	kol·*tel*·lo	knife
cucchiaio	koo·*kya*·yo	spoon
forchetta	for·*ke*·ta	fork
olio	*o*·lyo	oil
pepe	*pe*·pe	pepper
sale	*sa*·le	salt

STAPLES

aglio	*a*·lyo	garlic
burro	*boo*·ro	butter
formaggio	for·*ma*·jo	cheese
miele	*mye*·le	honey
pane	*pa*·ne	bread
panna	*pa*·na	cream
riso	*ree*·zo	rice
soya	*soy*·ya	soy
tartufo	tar·*too*·fo	truffle
uovo/uova	*wo*·vo/*wo*·va	egg/eggs
zucchero	*tsoo*·ke·ro	sugar

DRINKS

acqua	*a*·kwa	water
birra	*bee*·ra	beer
caffè	ka·*fe*	coffee
tè	te	tea
vino (rosso/bianco)	*vee*·no (*ross*·o/*byan*·ko)	wine (red/white)

MEAT & SEAFOOD

agnello	a·*nye*·lo	lamb
aragosta	a·ra·*go*·sta	lobster

carpaccio	kar·*pa*·cho	very fine slices of raw meat
coniglio	ko·*nee*·lyo	rabbit
cozze	*ko*·tse	mussels
frutti di mare	*froo*·tee dee *ma*·re	seafood
gamberoni	gam·be·*ro*·nee	prawns
granchio	*gran*·kyo	crab
pollo	*pol*·lo	chicken
polpi	*pol*·po	octopus
prosciutto	pro·*shoo*·to	cured ham
salsiccia	sal·*see*·cha	sausage
tonno	*tonn*·o	tuna
trippa	*tree*·pa	tripe
vitello	vee·*te*·lo	veal

VEGETABLES

asparagi	as·*pa*·ra·jee	asparagus
carciofi	kar·*cho*·fee	artichokes
carota	ka·*ro*·ta	carrot
cavolo	*ka*·vo·lo	cabbage
fagiolini	fa·jo·*lee*·nee	green beans
finocchio	fee·*no*·kyo	fennel
funghi	*foon*·gee	mushrooms
insalata	in·sa·*la*·ta	salad
melanzane	me·lan·*dza*·ne	aubergine
olive	o·*lee*·va	olive
patate	pa·*ta*·te	potatoes
peperoni	pe·pe·*ro*·nee	capsicums/peppers
piselli	pee·*ze*·lee	peas
pomodori	po·mo·*do*·ree	tomatoes
rucola	*roo*·ko·la	rocket
spinaci	spee·*na*·chee	spinach

GELATO FLAVOURS & FRUIT

amarena	a·ma·*re*·na	wild cherry
arancia	a·*ran*·cha	orange
bacio	ba·cho	chocolate and hazelnuts
ciliegia	chee·*lye*·ja	cherry
cioccolata	cho·ko·la·ta	chocolate
cono	*ko*·no	cone
coppa	*ko*·pa	cup
crema	*kre*·ma	cream
fragola	*fra*·go·la	strawberry
frutta di bosco	*froo*·ta dee *bos*·ko	fruit of the forest (wild berries)
limone	lee·*mo*·ne	lemon
mela	*me*·la	apple
melone	me·*lo*·ne	melon
nocciola	no·cho·la	hazelnut
pere	*pe*·ra	pear
pesca	*pe*·ska	peach
uva	*oo*·va	grapes
vaniglia	va·*nee*·lya	vanilla
zuppa inglese	*tsoo*·pa een·gle·ze	'English soup', trifle

Tuscany

Florence

Florence (Firenze), cradle of the Renaissance, is a city like no other. With its staggering wealth of world-class art and architecture and its rich history and culture, it's no wonder that this relatively small city on the banks of the Arno River is regularly besieged by tourists from around the globe. Dante, Michelangelo, Botticelli and da Vinci are just some of the big names who once lived and worked here, and their influence remains to this day.

The heart of Florence is immediately captivating, despite the industrial sprawl of its outskirts. The writer Stendhal was so dazzled by the Basilica di Santa Croce that he was barely able to walk for faintness. He is apparently not the only one to have felt so overwhelmed by the beauty of Florence – they say Florentine doctors treat a dozen cases of 'stendhalismo' each year.

Not everything, though, whiffs of history. That same sense of the aesthetic lives on today in the smartly dressed Florentines window-gazing at the designer shops along Via della Vigna Nuova and Via de' Tornabuoni (Florence is the home town for both Gucci and Ferragamo). And just watch them lounging with style on a café terrace or elegantly propping up a bar.

Should you feel the need to escape from all the Renaissance richness, Il Chianti, with its gentle countryside and fine wines, beckons from the south. Fiesole, in the low hills overlooking the city, is a breath of fresh air and an escape from the stifling summer heat of the plains.

You will need at least four or five days to do Florence any justice at all, but remember you can't see everything in just one visit.

HIGHLIGHTS

- Marvel at the art treasures of the **Uffizi** (p94) and **Museo del Bargello** (p90)
- Climb up to **Piazzale Michelangelo** (p109) for wonderful views of the city
- Visit the **Duomo** (p87), Brunelleschi's greatest legacy
- Eye up Michelangelo's *David*, posing in the **Galleria dell'Accademia** (p100)
- Indulge in some of Italy's finest wines on a tasting tour through **Il Chianti** (p141)
- Head for the hills and explore the Etruscan and Roman remains in **Fiesole** (p138)
- Drop by the spa town of **Montecatini Terme** (p133) for a spot of rest and relaxation

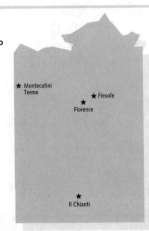

★ Montecatini Terme

★ Fiesole
★ Florence

★ Il Chianti

- POPULATION: 353,000

FLORENCE

HISTORY

Florence's history stretches back to the time of the Etruscans, who based themselves in Fiesole, and who may have had a settlement of some kind on the spot where the city now stands. What's certain is that it was Julius Caesar who founded the Roman colony of Florentia around 59 BC, making it a strategic garrison on the narrowest crossing of the Arno so he could control the Via Flaminia, which linked Rome to northern Italy and Gaul. Over succeeding centuries it grew to be an important centre of trade.

After the collapse of the Roman Empire, Florence fell under the sway of the invading Goths, followed by the Lombards and the Franks. The year AD 1000 marked a crucial turning point in the fortunes of Florence when Margrave Ugo of Tuscany moved his capital from Lucca to the city, introducing a period of great expansion. In 1110 Florence became a free *comune* (city-state) and by 1138 was ruled by 12 consuls, assisted by the Consiglio di Cento (Council of One Hundred), whose members were drawn mainly from the prosperous merchant class. Agitation among differing factions in the city led to the appointment in 1207 of a foreign head of state, known as the *podestà,* in principle aloof from the plotting and wheeler-dealing of the local cliques and alliances.

Medieval Florence was a wealthy and dynamic city-state, one of Europe's leading financial, banking and cultural centres and a major player in the international wool, silk and leather trades. The sizable population of moneyed merchants and artisans began forming guilds and patronising the growing number of artists who found lucrative commissions in this burgeoning city. But a political crisis was on the horizon.

The prolonged struggles between the propapal Guelphs (Guelfi) and the pro–Holy Roman Empire Ghibellines (Ghibellini) started towards the middle of the 13th century, with power passing from one faction to the other for almost a century. Into this fractious atmosphere were born the revolutionary artist Giotto and the poet Dante Alighieri, whose family belonged to the Guelph camp. In fact, young Dante even took part in the Battle of Campaldino (1289), which saw the defeat of Ghibelline Arezzo. Shortly afterwards the Guelphs themselves split into two factions, the Neri (Blacks) and Bianchi (Whites). The outspoken Dante, opting for the Bianchi, ended up on the wrong side and was expelled from his native city in 1302, never to return. In exile, he wrote his best-known work, *The Divine Comedy.*

In 1348 the Black Death spirited away almost half the population. This dark period in the city's history was used as a backdrop by Boccaccio for his *Decameron.*

The history of Medici Florence begins in 1434, when Cosimo de' Medici, a great patron of the arts, took the reins of power. His eye for talent and his tact in dealing with artists saw the likes of Alberti, Brunelleschi, Luca della Robbia, Fra Angelico, Donatello and Filippo Lippi flourish under his patronage. Many of the city's finest buildings are testimony to his tastes.

In 1439 the Church Council of Florence, aimed at reconciling the Catholic and Eastern churches, brought to the city Byzantine scholars and craftsmen, who they hoped would impart the knowledge and culture of classical antiquity. The Council, attended by the pope, achieved nothing in the end, but it did influence what was later known as the Renaissance. Under the rule of Cosimo's popular and cultured grandson, Lorenzo il Magnifico (1469–92), Florence became the epicentre of this 'Rebirth', with artists such as Michelangelo, Botticelli and Domenico Ghirlandaio at work.

But Florence's golden age was not to last, effectively dying along with Lorenzo in 1492. Just before his death, the Medici bank had failed, and, two years later, the Medicis were driven out of Florence. In a reaction against the splendour and excess of the Medici court, the city fell under the control of Girolamo Savonarola, a humourless Dominican monk who led a stern, puritanical republic, surprisingly supported by many leading artists and intellectuals, as well as common folk. In 1497 the likes of Botticelli gladly consigned their 'immoral' works and finery to the flames of the infamous 'Bonfire of the Vanities' in Piazza della Signoria. The following year Savonarola fell from public favour and was himself burned in the piazza as a heretic.

The republican government that followed was led by Piero Soderini. Its pro-French leanings brought it into conflict with the

---

THE RED & THE BLACK

Florence has two different parallel street-numbering systems: red or brown numbers (which usually have 'r' for *rosso,* or red, after the number) indicate commercial premises; black or blue ones are for private residences.

To compound the confusion, the black/blue numbers may denote whole buildings, while each red/brown number refers to one commercial entity – and a building may have several. It can turn you purple if you're hunting in a hurry for a specific address.

---

pope and his Spanish allies. In 1512 a Spanish force defeated Florence and the Medicis were reinstated. Their tyrannical rule endeared them to very few, and when Rome, ruled by the Medici pope Clement VII, fell to the emperor Charles V in 1527, the Florentines took advantage of this low point in the Medici fortunes to kick the family out again. Two years later, though, imperial and papal forces combined to lay siege to Florence, forcing the city to accept Lorenzo's great-grandson, Alessandro de' Medici, a ruthless transvestite whom Charles made Duke of Florence. Medici rule continued for another 200 years, during which time they gained control of all of Tuscany, though after the reign of Cosimo I (1537–74), Florence drifted into steep decline, headed by a succession of increasingly ineffective, decadent or just plain unpleasant characters.

The last male Medici, Gian Gastone, died in 1737, after which his sister, Anna-Maria, signed the grand duchy of Tuscany over to the House of Lorraine (at the time effectively under Austrian control). This situation remained unchanged, apart from a brief interruption under Napoleon from 1799 to 1814, until the duchy was incorporated into the Kingdom of Italy in 1860. Florence briefly became the national capital a year later, but Rome assumed the mantle permanently in 1871.

Florence was badly damaged during WWII by the retreating Germans, who blew up all its bridges except Ponte Vecchio. Devastating floods ravaged the city in 1966, causing inestimable damage to its buildings and artworks. However, the sal-

vage operation led to the widespread use of modern restoration techniques that have saved artworks throughout the country. In 1993 the Mafia exploded a massive car bomb, killing five, injuring 37 and destroying a part of the Uffizi Gallery. Just over a decade later, the gallery is undergoing its biggest-ever expansion, which will double its exhibiting area.

ORIENTATION

However you arrive, the central train station, Stazione di Santa Maria Novella, is a good reference point. Budget hotels and *pensioni* are concentrated around Via Nazionale, to the east of the station, and Piazza di Santa Maria Novella, to the south. The main route to the city centre from the train station is Via de' Panzani, and then Via de' Cerretani, about a 10-minute walk. You'll know you've arrived when you first glimpse the Duomo.

Most of the major sights are within walking distance – you can stroll across the city centre in about 30 minutes. From Piazza di San Giovanni around the battistero (baptistry), Via Roma leads to Piazza della Repubblica and continues as Via Calimala then Via Por Santa Maria to Ponte Vecchio. Take Via de' Calzaiuoli from Piazza del Duomo for Piazza della Signoria, the historic seat of government. The Uffizi is on the piazza's southern edge, near the Arno. Cross Ponte Vecchio, or Ponte alle Grazie further east, and head southeast to Piazzale Michelangelo for a fantastic view over the city.

Maps

One of the best of several commercial maps of the city is the red-covered *Florence* (€7), produced by the Touring Club Italiano at 1:12,500. A cutaway of the centre is scaled at 1:6500. Its green-covered *Tuscany* at 1:200,000 also costs €7.

INFORMATION
Bookshops

Edison (Map pp82-3; ☎ 055 21 31 10; Piazza della Repubblica 27r) Sells a variety of maps and travel guides. Also sells novels and nonfiction in English and other languages.

Feltrinelli International (Map pp80-1; ☎ 055 21 95 24; Via Cavour 12-20r) Good selection in English and major European languages.

Paperback Exchange (Map pp82-3; ☎ 055 247 81 54; www.papex.it; Via Fiesolana 31r) Vast range of new and

FLORENCE IN...

Two Days

Start your day with a cappuccino in **Caffè Gilli** (p124) in Piazza della Repubblica. Take a look around the splendid **Duomo** (p87) and adjoining **Baptistry** (p89). If you have a head for heights, you can also climb the **Campanile** (p88). Take in Piazza della Signoria, particularly the statuary in the **Loggia della Signoria** (p94). Linger as long as time allows in the **Uffizi Gallery** (p94), savouring some of the world's greatest Renaissance art. Then allow yourself a leisurely stroll along the Arno, crossing **Ponte Vecchio** (p105) for a glimpse of the Oltrarno district, where you could dine in one of the traditional Tuscan restaurants along Via Santo Spirito.

Start your second day with a visit to the **Museo di San Marco** (p101), with its frescoes by Fra Angelico. Next, give yourself a good stint in the **Galleria dell'Accademia** (p100), home to Michelangelo's *David*, before heading back to Via Cavour and visiting **Palazzo Medici-Riccardi** (p99). Round the day's sightseeing off with a *gelato*.

Four Days

Follow the above itinerary for the first two days. Use the morning of day three to delve into the **Museo del Bargello** (p90), then leave the city behind and head to **Fiesole** (p138) for great views over Florence. Spend the rest of the day exploring its Roman and Etruscan remains, walking in the hills and relaxing in one of the café/restaurants in the main square.

On day four, visit **Basilica di Santa Croce** (p103) and stop by **Enoteca Boccadama** (p123) for a light lunch and a glass of wine. In the afternoon cross again to Oltrarno and visit the fabulous collections in **Palazzo Pitti** (p105), followed by a stroll through the **Boboli Gardens** (p106).

One Week

Follow the previous itinerary, and on the fifth day visit **Palazzo del Bargello** (p90). In the afternoon take a tour of **Palazzo Vecchio** (p92). Head down to the Arno and cross Ponte alle Grazie to the San Niccolò area. Climb up to **Piazzale Michelangelo** (p109) for superb views over the city before descending for dinner in one of the cafés on Via dei Renai.

On day six take in the **Basilica di Santa Maria Novella** (p97) and the **Basilica di San Lorenzo** (p99), followed by a peek into the **Cappelle Medicee** (p99). The **Museo dell'Opera del Duomo** (p88) is well worth a visit too.

On day seven explore more of the Oltrarno area, with a visit to the **Basilica di Santa Spirito** (p107) and the **Basilica di Santa Maria del Carmine** (p108), with its frescoes by Masaccio.

econdhand books in English. Its bulletin board is a useful source of information about apartments for rent etc.

Emergency

Police Station (Map pp80-1; ☎ 055 4 97 71; Via ara 2) Report thefts at the foreigners' office here.

Tourist Police (Polizia Assistenza Turistica; Map pp82-3; ☎ 055 20 39 11; Via Pietrapiana 50r, Piazza dei Ciompi; ⏰ 8.30am-6.30pm Mon-Fri, 8.30am-1pm Sat) Don't get robbed on a Sunday!

Internet Access

Internet Point (Map pp82-3; ☎ 055 24 07 80; orgo degli Albizi 66r; per hr €3)

Internet Train (per hr €4) Borgo San Jacopo 30r (Map pp82-3; ☎ 055 265 79 35); Via dei Benci 36r (Map pp82-3; ☎ 055 263 85 55); Via dell'Oriuolo 40r (Map pp82-3; ☎ 055 263 89 68) There are more than 10 branches scattered throughout the city.

Internet Resources

City of Florence (www.comune.firenze.it) A useful portal for information on the city.

Firenze-Oltarno (www.firenze-oltrarno.net) For a taste of things south of the river. Lots of useful links.

Florence for Fun (www.florenceforfun.org) Good for accommodation and museum bookings, and well tuned in to Florence's nightlife.

Studentsville (www.studentsville.it) City life from a student perspective.

Laundry

Wash & Dry Laundrette (☎ 800 23 11 72; wash or dry €3.10; ⏰ 8am-10pm) Via de' Serragli 87r (Map p85); Via dei Servi 105r (Map pp80-1); Via del Sole 29r (Map pp82-3); Via della Scala 52-54r (Map pp80-1); Via Nazionale 129 (Map pp80-1) Has 10 branches, some with an Internet point.

(Continued on page 86)

A   **B**   **C**   **D**

1

To Amerigo Vespucci
Airport (3km);
Pistoia (30km)

To Villa Medicea di
Castello (3km); Teatro
della Limonaia (4km)

Viale Alessandro Guidoni

To Villa Medicea
di Careggi (1km)

7

Via M Mercati

Via Celso

Rifredi

Via di Novoli

**Ponte
di Mezzo**

Via A Tavanti

Via Giovan Filippo Mariti

Montug

Via Vittorio Ei

Via Francesco Baracca

To Tenax
(1.5km)

2

Torente Mugnone

Via Pietro Toselli

See Stazione & Around Map (pp80-1)

Viale Francesco Redi

Via C Colonna

Via dello Statuto

San Jacopino

Piazzale
delle Cascine

Canale Macinante

Ippodromo
delle
Cascine

Via Benedetto Marcello

Via delle Porte Nuove

Via del Ponte alle Mosse

Viale Belfiore

**Fortezza
da Basso**

Viale

3

5

Le Cascine

Viale degli Olmi

Viale Abramo Lincoln

A R N O

Stazione
Porta al Prato

Viale Fratelli Rosselli

Porta
al Prato

Stazione
di Santa
Maria
Novella

Viale Filippo Strozzi

Piazza
Indipen

To Depositeria
Comunale (2km);
Pisa (40km); Aeroporto
Galileo Galilei (42km)

Lungarno del Pignone

Via de'Vanni

Via Bronzino

Pignone

2

Via Solferino

Corso Italia

Lungarno Amerigo Vespucci

Ponte
della
Vittoria

See Central Florence
Map (pp82-3)

4

See Oltrarno & Nearby Quarters Map (p85)

Via Pisana

Ponte Amerigo
Vespucci

Piazza
Repub

Borgo San Frediano

Ponte alla
Carraia

Ponte
Santa
Trinità

Viale A Aleardi

**San
Frediano**

**Santo
Spirito**

Por
Vec

5

Piazza
Torquato
Tasso

**Giardino
Torrigiani**

Piazza
de' Pitti

Viale Francesco Petrarca

Bellosguardo

**Giardino
di Boboli
(Boboli
Gardens)**

Chiesa di
Leona

6

Viale Senese

Viale di Poggio Imperiale

Via di San Leon

To Certosa di
Galluzzo (3km);
Galluzzo (3km);
Siena (58km)

0 — 1 km
0 — 0.5 miles

SIGHTS & ACTIVITIES (pp86–110)
Chiesa di San Miniato al Monte.........1 E6
Mercato delle Cascine........................2 B3
Museo Stibbert..................................3 D1
Piscina Bellariva...............................4 H5
Piscina Le Pavoniere..........................5 A3

SLEEPING (pp114–19)
Camping Villa Camerata.....................6 H2
Ostello Villa Camerata...................(see 6)

ENTERTAINMENT (pp124–6)
Auditorium Flog.............................(see 7)
Cinema Poggetto...............................7 D1
Palazzo dello Sport Open-air Summer
   Cinema..8 G3
Stadio Comunale Artemio Franchi......9 G3

INFORMATION

Comune di Firenze Tourist Office	1	E6
Consorzio ITA	2	D5
CTS Travel Agency	3	F5
Farmacia Comunale (24-hour pharmacy)	4	D5
Feltrinelli International	5	F6
German Consulate	6	C6
Left Luggage Office	7	D5
Main Tourist Office	8	F5
Police Station	9	G3
Tourist Medical Service	10	F3
US Consulate	11	C6
Wash & Dry Laundrette	12	F5
Wash & Dry Laundrette	13	D5
Wash & Dry Laundrette	14	E5

SIGHTS & ACTIVITIES (pp86–110)

Amici del Turismo	15	F5
Basilica di San Lorenzo	16	F6
Basilica di Santa Maria Novella	17	E6
CAF Tours	18	E6
Cappelle Medicee	19	F6
Cenacolo di Sant'Apollonia	20	G4
Centro Lingua Italiana Calvino (CLIC)	21	C4
Centro Lorenzo de'Medici	22	E5
Chiesa della Santissima Annunziata	23	H5
Chiesa Russa Ortodossa	24	F2
Entrance to Galleria dell'Accademia	25	G5
Fortezza da Basso	26	D3
Galleria dell'Accademia	27	G5
Le Cascine	28	A5
Linguaviva	29	E5
Mercato Centrale	30	F5
Mondobimbo	31	H2
Museo Archeologico	32	H5
Museo di San Marco	33	G4
Palazzo Medici-Riccardi	34	F6
Spedale degli Innocenti	35	H5

SLEEPING (pp114–19)

Antica Dimora	36	G4
Cristina House	37	F3
Florence & Abroad	38	F4
Grand Hotel Baglioni	39	E6
Hotel Accademia	40	E5
Hotel Aprile	41	D6
Hotel Azzi	42	E5
Hotel Casci	43	F5
Hotel Globus	44	E5
Hotel Il Guelfo Bianco	45	G5
Hotel Loggiato dei Serviti	46	H5
Johanna I	47	G3

Johanna II	48	E2
Le Due Fontane	49	G5
Ostello Archi Rossi	50	E4
Ostello Spirito Santo	51	E5
Palazzo Benci	52	F6
Residenze Johlea I & II	53	G4

EATING (pp119–23)

Carabè	54	G5
Ì Tozzo di Pane	55	F4
Il Vegetariano	56	G4
Lobs	57	E5
Mario	58	F5
Nerbone	59	E5
Osteria dei Centopoveri	60	D6
Pasta Fresca Morioni	61	D6
Trattoria ZàZà	62	F5

ENTERTAINMENT (pp124–6)

Box Office	63	C4
Central Park	64	A5
Cinema Fulgor	65	D6
Ex-Stazione Leopolda	66	B5
Meccanò	67	A5
Palazzo dei Congressi Open-air Summer Cinema	68	E4
Teatro Comunale	69	B6

SHOPPING (pp126–8)

Officina Profumo-Farmaceutica di Santa Maria Novella	70	D6
Stockhouse Il Giglio	71	C6
Stockhouse One Price	72	D6

TRANSPORT (pp128–9)

Alinari (Cycle & Scooter Hire)	73	E4
ATAF Bus Stop (Nos 7, 13 & 70)	74	E5
ATAF local bus stop	75	E6
ATAF local bus stop	76	D5
ATAF Ticket & Information Office	(see 74)	
Avis Car Rental	77	C6
CAP & COPIT Bus Stations	78	E5
CentralSita Viaggi	(see 84)	
Florence By Bike	79	G4
Happy Rent	80	C6
Hertz Car Rental	81	D6
Lazzi Bus Station & Ticket Office	82	E5
Pre-booked Train Tickets Pickup	83	D5
SITA Bus Station	84	D5
Thrifty Rental	85	C6
Ticket Office	86	D5
Train Information Office	87	D5

See Oltrarno & Nearby Quarters Map (p85)

0 ————————— 200 m
0 ————————— 0.1 miles

E **F** **G** **H**

1

Largo
C Cantù

Via del Romitino

iazza
Muratori

Via Giovanni Lami

Viale dei Cadorna

Via Ponte
Rosso

●31

Ponte
Rosso

Via M di
Savoia

48🏠

Via delle Cinque Giornate

Via F Nievo

Via G C Abba

Piazza della
Vittoria

Via G C Vanini

Via X Febbraio

Via P Toscanelli

Parterre

2

Via della Cernaia

Via Francesco Crispi

Via F lli Ruffini

Via P Toscanelli

P

Via M di
Savoia

Via della Statuto

Via Francesco Puccinotti

Via XX Settembre

Viale Giovanni Milton

Via C Landino

Piazza
della Libertà

Piazza della
Costituzione

24

Via Lorenzo il Magnifico
10 🏠

Via Leone

37

Via P Politian

Via San Gallo

Viale Giacomo Matteotti

Palazzo
delle
Esposizioni

Viale Spartaco Lavagnini

47🏠

Via Duca d'Aosta

Via delle Mantellate

Ospedale
Militare

3

Via Bonifacio Lupi

Via Enrico Poggi

Via delle Ruote

Via d'Aosta

9

Via S Anna

Via Alfonso Lamarmora

Via G Dotti

Via Santa Caterina d'Alessandria

Via F
Bartolommei

79

56

Via di Campofregi

53

Via Salvestrina

Via Venezia

Via Luigi Salvatore Cherubini

e Filippo Strozzi

Via C Ridolfi

Piazza
della
Indipendenza

36

Via Cavour

Via Pier Antonio Micheli

o dei
ressi

Via del Prato

Via della Fortezza

Via Battaldi

Piazza del
Crocifisso

Via XXVII Aprile

38

Via Santa Reparata

Via San Gallo

Via G B Pira

**Giardino
dei
Semplici**

4

azzo degli
Alfari

50

73●

55

Via San Zanobi

20

Via degli Arazzieri

39

San Marco

Piazza
San Marco

Via Cesare Battisti

Università
degli
Studi di
Firenze

Via Giuseppe
Giusti

42🏠

12

Via Guelfa

Via B Cellini

Via Faenza

Via Nazionale

Via Panicale

Via Taddea

Via de' Ginori

Via Cavour

27

25

Via Ricasoli

23

5

Via Fiume

●29

57

59

Piazza del
Mercato
Centrale

45

46🏠

Piazza della
SS Annunziata

Via Laura

30

58

49🏠

14🏠

35●

Via della Colonna

51

22

3●

62

Via de' Pucci

43🏠

Via Cavour

54

Via dei Fibbiai

32

78

Via Sant'Antonino

44🏠

Borgo la Noce

8

15

Piazza
dell'Unità
Italiana

40🏠

52

Piazza
San Lorenzo

19

16

34

Via de' Gori

5

Piazza
Brunelleschi

Via degli Alfani

Via della Pergola

6

75

●18

Piazza
Madonna degli
Aldobrandini

17

39

Via dei Servi

Via de' Pucci

Via Ricasoli

Via de' Martelli

Via Bufalini

Piazza di Santa
Maria Nuova

Ospedale di
Santa Maria
Nuova

Via Nuova
de' Caccini

e Central Florence Map (pp82–3)

zza di
aria
yella

Via degli
Avelli

Via de' Panzani

Via del Giglio

Via F
Zanetti

Via de' Conti

Borgo San Lorenzo

Via de' Cerretani

Via de' Banchi

Duomo

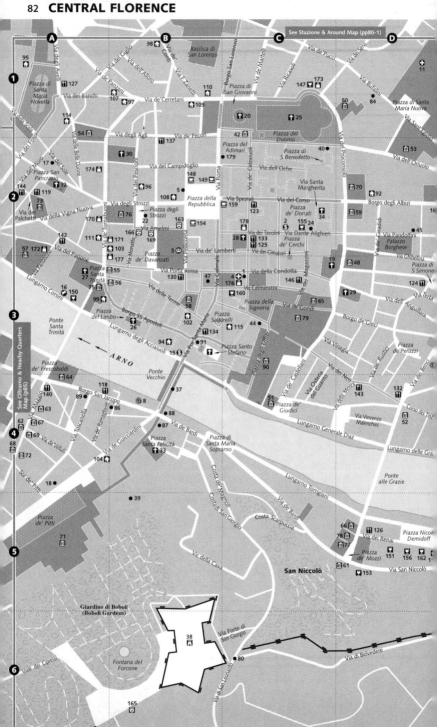

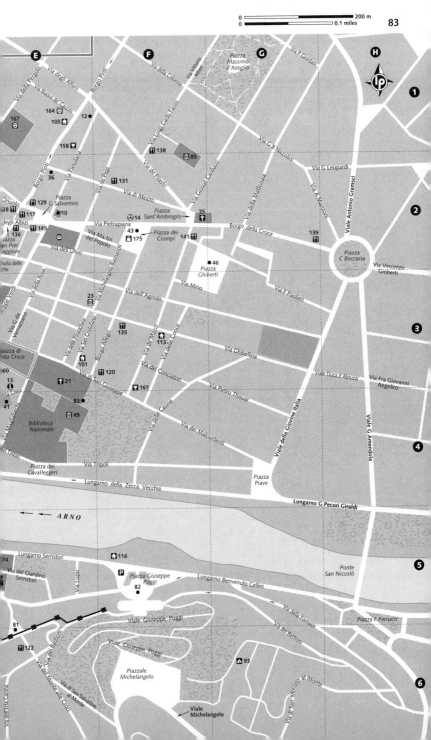

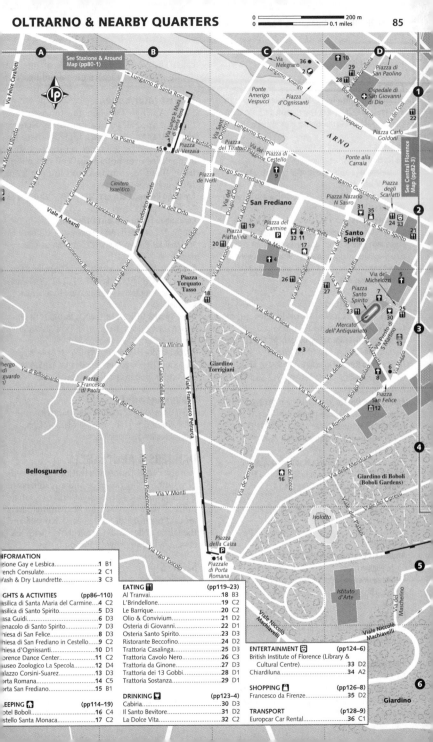

INFORMATION

...zione Gay e Lesbica	**1** B1
...ench Consulate	**2** C1
...ash & Dry Laundrette	**3** C3

...GHTS & ACTIVITIES (pp86–110)

...asilica di Santa Maria del Carmine	**4** C2
...asilica di Santo Spirito	**5** D3
...asa Guidi	**6** D3
...enacolo di Santo Spirito	**7** D3
...hiesa di San Felice	**8** D3
...hiesa di San Frediano in Cestello	**9** C2
...hiesa d'Ognissanti	**10** D1
...orence Dance Center	**11** C2
...useo Zoologico La Specola	**12** D4
...alazzo Corsini-Suarez	**13** D3
...orta Romana	**14** C5
...orta San Frediano	**15** B1

...EEPING (pp114–19)

...otel Boboli	**16** C4
...stello Santa Monaca	**17** C2

EATING (pp119–23)

Al Tranvai	**18** B3
L'Brindellone	**19** C2
Le Barrique	**20** C2
Olio & Convivium	**21** D2
Osteria di Giovanni	**22** D1
Osteria Santo Spirito	**23** D3
Ristorante Beccofino	**24** D1
Trattoria Casalinga	**25** D3
Trattoria Cavolo Nero	**26** C3
Trattoria da Ginone	**27** C3
Trattoria dei 13 Gobbi	**28** D1
Trattoria Sostanza	**29** D1

DRINKING (pp123–4)

Cabiria	**30** D3
Il Santo Bevitore	**31** D2
La Dolce Vita	**32** C2

ENTERTAINMENT (pp124–6)

British Institute of Florence (Library & Cultural Centre)	**33** D2
Chiardiluna	**34** A2

SHOPPING (pp126–8)

Francesco da Firenze	**35** D2

TRANSPORT (p128–9)

Europcar Car Rental	**36** C1

Scale: 0 — 200 m / 0 — 0.1 miles

(Continued from page 77)

Left Luggage
Stazione di Santa Maria Novella (Map pp80-1; per item for 12hr €3, for every 12hr thereafter €2; ☉ 6am-midnight) The left-luggage office is on platform 16.

Media
La Nazione (www.lanazione.it in Italian) Italian-language paper published in Florence; a useful source of local news.
La Repubblica (www.firenze.repubblica.it in Italian) Publishes a local version, which includes useful listings.
Toscana News (www.toscananews.com) A monthly tourist paper published in English and German, listing upcoming regional events and places of interest. It usually comes with its sister publication, *Chianti News* (www.chiantinews.it). The price is €0.50, though tourist offices give them away free.

Medical Services
Tourist offices have lists of doctors and dentists who speak various languages.
All'Insegna del Moro (Map pp82-3; ☎ 055 21 13 43; Piazza di San Giovanni 28) 24-hour pharmacy.
Dr Stephen Kerr (Map pp82-3; ☎ 055 28 80 55; www.dr-kerr.com; Via Porta Rossa 1; ☉ 3-5pm Mon-Fri) Resident British doctor.
Emergency Doctor (Guardia Medica; ☎ 055 47 78 91) For a doctor at night or on a public holiday.
Farmacia Comunale (Map pp80-1; ☎ 055 21 67 61; inside Stazione di Santa Maria Novella) 24-hour pharmacy.
Ospedale di Santa Maria Nuova (Map pp82-3; ☎ 055 2 75 81; Piazza di Santa Maria Nuova 1)
Tourist Medical Service (Map pp80-1; ☎ 055 47 54 11; Via Lorenzo il Magnifico 59; ☉ 24hr) Has English-speaking doctors, who will also make calls to hotels.

Money
American Express (Map pp82-3; ☎ 055 5 09 81; Via Dante Alighieri 22r)
Travelex (Map pp82-3; ☎ 055 28 97 81; Lungarno degli Acciaiuoli 6r)

Post
Central Post Office (Map pp82-3; Via Pellicceria) Off Piazza della Repubblica.

Telephone
Most public telephones accept both coins and phonecards (from €5; available from tobacconists and newsstands). Private call centres are much less expensive for international calls. The Via dei Benci branch of Internet Train offers cheap international calling.

Tourist Information
From April to October, the tourist office offers a special service known as **Florence SOS Turista** (☎ 055 276 03 82). It gives advice for tourists needing guidance on matters such as disputes over hotel bills. You can phone from 10am to 1pm and 3pm to 6pm from Monday to Saturday.
Amerigo Vespucci airport (Map pp78-9; ☎ 055 31 58 74; ☉ 7.30am-11.30pm)
Comune di Firenze Tourist Office (Map pp80-1; ☎ 055 21 22 45; Piazza della Stazione 4; ☉ 8.30am-7pm Mon-Sat, 8.30am-2pm Sun) Run by Florence's city council.
Consorzio ITA (Informazione Turistiche Alberghiere; Map pp80-1; ☎ 055 28 28 93; fax 055 247 82 32; ☉ 8.45am-9pm) Offers basic tourist information and books accommodation.
Main Tourist Office (Map pp80-1; ☎ 055 29 08 32; www.firenzeturismo.it; Via Cavour 1r; ☉ 8.30am-6.30pm Mon-Sat, 8.30am-1.30pm Sun)
Tourist Office (Map pp82-3; ☎ 055 234 04 44; Borgo Santa Croce 29r; ☉ 8.30am-7pm Mon-Sat Apr-Sep, to 5pm Oct-Mar, 8.30am-2pm Sun year-round)

Travel Agencies
CTS (Map pp80-1; ☎ 055 28 95 70; www.cts.it in Italian; Via de' Ginori 25r) The Florence branch of this national youth-travel organisation.

DANGERS & ANNOYANCES
Florence's most annoying feature is its crowds of visitors. Bring patience and a readiness to queue. While it's generally a safe city, single tourists should avoid the area immediately around Stazione di Santa Maria Novella and the Parco delle Cascine after dark. Pickpockets are active in crowds and on buses.

SIGHTS
Florence can seriously overwhelm. In fact, on one trip you'll only be scratching the surface of what this amazing city has to offer. Its wealth of museums and galleries house many of the most important and exquisite examples of Renaissance art, its architecture is unrivalled, and its warrens of narrow streets lead you off into the less explored but often fascinating side of modern Florentine life. Your only problem will be deciding what you can squeeze into one day. Thankfully, Florence is a compact city

> **QUEUE JUMPING**
>
> If time is precious and money not a prime concern, you can skip (or at least shorten) some of the museum and gallery queues by booking ahead. In summer especially, long queues can mean a sticky wait of up to four hours!
>
> For an extra €3 per museum, you can book a ticket in advance to any of the *musei statali* (state museums), which include the Uffizi Gallery, Palazzo Pitti, Museo del Bargello, Galleria dell'Accademia, Museo Archeologico and Cappelle Medicee. Simply, though not necessarily swiftly – you may find yourself in a long phone queue – phone **Firenze Musei** (☎ 055 29 48 83; www.firenzemusei.it; ☿ phone lines 8.30am-6.30pm Mon-Fri, 8.30am-12.30pm Sat). You are given a booking number and agree on the time you want to visit. When you arrive at the site at the allotted time, follow signs to a separate entrance for those with prebooked tickets, quote your booking number, pay and smile smugly at the perspiring hordes.
>
> For the Uffizi you can also buy tickets in advance at the gallery itself (also €3 per ticket supplement). In high season it's also well worth setting your alarm clock and being there, outside and waiting, by around 7.45am. When the doors swing open at 8.15am, they let the first stream in and you stand a very good chance of going with that first flow.
>
> If you prefer the electronic age, **Weekend a Firenze** (www.weekendafirenze.com) is an online service for booking museums, galleries, shows and tours. You pay €4.77 on top of the normal ticket price; reserve at least three days in advance. Print out the email confirmation they send and present it at the cashier's desk on the day of your visit.
>
> Many major hotels will also book entry tickets for you.

and nearly all the sights are within easy walking distance of each other.

Opening Times

As everywhere in Italy, museums and monuments tend to close on Monday, although since Florence is a year-round, week-through tourist destination, major monuments open daily. The main tourist office has a comprehensive list of opening hours.

WARNING

At most sights, the ticket office shuts 30 minutes before the advertised closing time. Also, in some places staff will usher you out at least 15 minutes before closing time, interpreting this as the moment when the door has to be bolted shut. Some churches enforce a strict dress code for visitors (no shorts, sleeveless shirts or plunging necklines).

FREE ENTRY & DISCOUNTS

If you carry an EU passport (and you'll need to have it with you) and are under 18 or over 65, admission to Florence's state museums is free. EU citizens aged between 18 and 25 pay half-price.

For one week of the year (usually in spring but the dates change), entry to *musei statali* (state museums) throughout Italy is made free. Since dates change it is impossible to

plan a trip around this, but keep your eyes open.

Duomo & Around

The **Duomo** (Cathedral; Map pp82-3; ☎ 055 230 28 85; ☿ 10am-5pm Mon-Wed & Fri, 10am-3.30pm Thu, 10am-4.45pm Sat, 1.30-4.45pm Sun) is an icon of Italy, ranking alongside Pisa's Leaning Tower and Rome's Colosseum. Brunelleschi's sloping, red-tiled dome dominates Florence's skyline, but it is only when you leave the crowded streets behind and approach the building from the piazza that you experience its breathtaking grandeur and the ordered vivacity of its pink, white and green marble façade.

The full name of this, the world's fourth-largest cathedral, is Cattedrale di Santa Maria del Fiore. Begun in 1296 by the Sienese architect Arnolfo di Cambio, it took almost 150 years to complete.

The present façade was raised only in the late 19th century to replace Arnolfo di Cambio's uncompleted original, which was pulled down in the 16th century. Its architect, Emilio de Fabris, was inspired by the design of the cathedral's flanks, which largely date from the 14th century.

The south flank is the oldest and most clearly Gothic part of the Duomo. The second doorway here is the **Porta dei Canonici**

(Canons' Door), a mid-14th-century High Gothic creation (you enter here to climb up inside the dome). Wander around the trio of apses, designed to appear as the flowers on the stem that is the nave of the church (and so reflecting its name – Santa Maria del Fiore, St Mary of the Flower).

The first door on the north flank beyond the apses is the early-15th-century **Porta della Mandorla** (Almond Door), so named because of the relief of the Virgin Mary contained within an almond-shaped frame. Much of the decorative sculpture that graced the flanks of the cathedral has been removed for its own protection to the Museo dell'Opera del Duomo, in some cases to be replaced by copies.

INTERIOR

The cathedral's vast interior, 155m long and 90m wide, and its sparse decoration come as a surprise after the visually tumultuous façade. Down the left aisle are two immense frescoes of equestrian statues dedicated to two *condottieri* (mercenaries), who fought in the service of Florence in the 14th century. The one on the left is of Niccolò da Tolentino (by Andrea del Castagno) and the other is of Sir John Hawkwood (by Uccello).

The 'divine' poet Dante has always been revered in his native Florence, and Domenico di Michelino's *Dante e I Suoi Mondi* (Dante and His Worlds), the next painting along the left aisle, is one of the most reproduced images of the poet and his verse masterpiece.

The festival of colour and images that greets you as you arrive beneath Brunelleschi's dome is the work of Giorgio Vasari and Frederico Zuccari. The fresco series depicts the *Giudizio Universale* (Last Judgment). Below the frescoes is the octagonal **coro** (choir). Its low marble enclosure surrounds the altar, above which hangs a crucifix by Benedetto da Maiano.

From the choir, the two wings of the transept and the rear apse spread out, each containing five chapels. The pillars delimiting the entrance into each wing and the apse are fronted by statues of Apostles, as are the two hefty pillars just west of the choir stalls.

Between the left (north) arm of the transept and the apse is the **Sagrestia delle Messe** (Mass Sacristy), its panelling a marvel of inlaid wood carved by Benedetto and Giuliano da Maiano. The fine bronze doors were executed by Luca della Robbia – his only known work in the material. Above the doorway is his glazed terracotta *Resurrection*.

Throughout, the stained-glass windows by Donatello, Andrea del Castagno, Paolo Uccello and Lorenzo Ghiberti positively glow.

A stairway near the main entrance of the cathedral leads down to the **crypt** (admission €3; 10am-5pm Mon-Fri, 10am-4.45pm Sat), where excavations have unearthed parts of the 5th-century Chiesa di Santa Reparata, which originally stood on the site. There's a small display of Roman pottery, architectural fragments and sections of the original mosaic floor, typical of early Italian churches. Brunelleschi's tomb is also here, beside the gift shop.

DOME

When Michelangelo went to work on St Peter's in Rome, he reportedly said: 'I go to build a greater dome, but not a fairer one'. You can climb up into the **dome** (enter by Porta dei Canonici; admission €6; 8.30am-7pm Mon-Fri, 8.30am-5.40pm Sat) to get a closer look at Brunelleschi's engineering feat – at the time, the biggest cupola ever built. The view from the top over Florence is breathtaking.

CAMPANILE

In 1334 Giotto designed and began building the graceful, 84m-high **campanile** (bell tower; Map pp82-3; admission €6; 8.30am-7.30pm) with its 414 steps, but died before it was completed.

Andrea Pisano and Francesco Talenti continued the work on the campanile. The first tier of bas-reliefs around the base are copies of those carved by Pisano, but possibly designed by Giotto, depicting the Creation of Man and the *attività umane* (arts and industries). Those on the second tier depict the planets, the cardinal virtues, the arts and the seven sacraments. The sculptures of the Prophets and Sibyls in the niches of the upper storeys are copies of works by Donatello and others. You can see all the originals in the Museo dell'Opera del Duomo.

MUSEO DELL'OPERA DEL DUOMO

This **museum** (Map pp82-3; Piazza del Duomo 9; admission €6; 9am-7.30pm Mon-Sat, 9am-1.40pm Sun), behind the cathedral, features many of the sculptural treasures that at one time adorned the Duomo, baptistry and campanile.

The first main hall is devoted to statuary that graced Arnolfo di Cambio's original Gothic façade, which was never completed. Pieces include several by Arnolfo himself, among them *Pope Boniface VIII, The Virgin and Child* and *Santat Reparata*. The long flowing beard of Donatello's *St John* stands out among the four mighty statues of the evangelists.

Out in the courtyard are displayed nearly all of the original 10 panels of Ghiberti's masterpiece, the *Porta del Paradiso* of the baptistry. Painstakingly restored after being damaged in the 1966 floods, they once again stand in all their glory.

On the mezzanine floor is the museum's best-known piece, Michelangelo's *Pietà*, a late work that he intended for his own tomb. Vasari recorded in his *Lives of the Artists* that, dissatisfied with both the quality of the marble and of his own work, Michelangelo broke up the unfinished sculpture, destroying the arm and left leg of the figure of Christ. A student of Michelangelo's later restored the arm and completed the figure.

Continue upstairs to the next main hall, where a pair of exquisitely carved *cantorie* (singing galleries), one by Donatello, the other by Luca della Robbia, face each other. Originally in the cathedral's sacristy, their scenes of musicians and children at play add a refreshingly frivolous touch amid so much sombre piety. Most striking of several carvings by Donatello are the haunted gaze of his *Prophet Habakkuk,* originally in the bell tower, and, in an adjoining room, his wooden representation of a gaunt, desolate *Mary Magdalene.*

Also on display is the equipment used by Brunelleschi to build the dome, as well as his death mask.

BAPTISTRY

The mainly 11th-century Romanesque **baptistry** (admission €3; noon-7pm Mon-Sat, 8.30am-2pm Sun) may have been built as early as the 5th century on the site of a Roman temple. One of the oldest buildings in Florence, it's dedicated, like many such constructions in Italy, to St John the Baptist (San Giovanni Battista) and counts Dante among the many famous personages who have been dunked and baptised in its font.

The octagonal structure with its stripes of white and green marble is chiefly famous for its three sets of gilded bronze doors, conceived as a series of panels in which the story of humanity and the Redemption would be told.

The earliest set of doors, which is now on the south side, was completed by Andrea Pisano in 1336. The bas-reliefs on its 28 compartments deal predominantly with the life of St John the Baptist.

A century later, Lorenzo Ghiberti toiled away for 20 years to get his set, on the north flank, just right. The top 20 panels recount episodes from the New Testament, while the eight lower ones show the four Evangelists and the four fathers of the Church.

Ghiberti returned almost immediately to his workshops and began turning out the eastern portals that face the cathedral. They took a full 28 years to complete, largely because of Ghiberti's intransigent perfectionism. On 10 panels, the bas-reliefs depict scenes from the Old Testament. So extraordinary were his exertions that, many years later, Michelangelo stood before the doors in awe and declared them fit to be the Porta del Paradiso (Gate of Paradise), which is how they remain known to this day.

Some of the doors are copies – the original panels are gradually being restored and displayed in the Museo dell'Opera del Duomo.

The interior of the baptistry recalls a Byzantine church. The two-coloured marble facing on the outside continues within, here enhanced by the geometrical flourishes above the Romanesque windows.

The single most arresting aspect of the decoration is its mosaics. Those in the apse were started in 1225, while the glittering spectacle in the dome was designed by Tuscan artists, including Cimabue, and carried out by Venetian craftsmen over 32 years towards the end of the 12th century. The stars of this vibrant ceiling are its *Christ in Majesty* and *Last Judgment.*

Donatello carved the tomb of Baldassare Cossa, better known as the antipope John XXIII, which takes up the wall to the right of the apse.

LOGGIA DEL BIGALLO

This elegant marble loggia was built in the second half of the 14th century for the Compagnia (or Confraternita) di Santa Maria della Misericordia, founded in 1244 to aid the elderly, the sick and orphans. Lost and abandoned children were customarily placed here so that they could be reclaimed by their families or put into the care of foster mothers. Members of the fraternity transported the sick to hospital and buried the dead in times of plague. Later, the Misericordia moved to its present position on Piazza del Duomo, from where to this day it continues its charitable vocation.

The loggia now houses a small **museum** (Map pp82–3; admission €1; 🕒 9am-5pm) containing a collection of artworks commissioned by the fraternity.

MUSEO STORICO-TOPOGRAFICO 'FIRENZE COM'ERA'

This **museum** (Map pp82–3; ☎ 055 261 65 45; Via dell'Oriuolo 24; admission €2.60; 🕒 9am-2pm Fri-Wed) may interest those who want to get an idea of how the city developed, particularly from the Renaissance to the modern day. Paintings, models, topographical drawings and prints help explain the history of the city.

From the Duomo to Piazza della Signoria

VIA DEL PROCONSOLO

Bernardo Buontalenti started work on the **Palazzo Nonfinito** (literally 'Unfinished Palace', Map pp82–3), a residence for members of the Strozzi family, in 1593. Buontalenti and others completed the 1st floor and courtyard, which is Palladian in style, but the upper floors were never completely finished, hence the building's name.

On the other side of Borgo degli Albizi stands the equally proud **Palazzo dei Pazzi**, constructed a century earlier and clearly influenced by Palazzo Medici-Riccardi. These days it's used as offices, but you're free to peek into the courtyard.

BADIA FIORENTINA

The 10th-century **Badia Fiorentina** (Florence Abbey; Map pp82–3; Via del Proconsolo; 🕒 church 6.30am-6pm, cloister 3-6pm Mon) was founded by Willa, the mother of Margrave Ugo of Tuscany. Ugo continued her work after experiencing a hellish vision of the punishment awaiting him in the afterlife should he not repent his sins. It is particularly worth a visit to see Filippino Lippi's *Appearance of the Virgin to St Bernard* (1485), to the left as you enter the church through the small Renaissance cloister. At the left end of the transept is

Mino da Fiesole's monument to Margrave Ugo. Stairs to the right of the altar lead up to an open gallery overlooking the cloister, decorated with 15th-century frescoes illustrating the life of St Benedict.

The church was closed for renovations at the time of writing.

MUSEO DEL BARGELLO

Just across Via del Proconsolo from the Badia is the gaunt exterior of the Palazzo del Bargello (Map pp82–3), also known as Palazzo del Podestà. Started in 1254, this palace was originally the residence of the chief magistrate, and then became a police station.

The **Museo del Bargello** (Map pp82–3; ☎ 055 238 86 06; Via del Proconsolo 4; admission €4; 🕒 8.15am-1.50pm Tue-Sat, 2nd & 4th Sun of the month) is inside and is one of Florence's true highlights with Italy's most comprehensive collection of Tuscan Renaissance sculpture. Canvases by Michelangelo grace the ground-floor Sala del Cinquecento (Room of the 1500s), notably his drunken *Bacchus* (executed when the artist was 22), a marble bust of *Brutus* and the *Tondo Pitti,* a large roundel of the Madonna and Child with the infant St John.

Other highlights are Benvenuto Cellini's playful marble *Ganimede* (Ganymede), Ammannati's sensuous *Leda* and Giambologna's much-imitated *Mercurio Volante* (Winged Mercury).

Upstairs is the majestic Salone del Consiglio Generale (Hall of the General Council). Among many works by Donatello are *San Giorgio* (St George), originally on the façade of the Chiesa di Orsanmichele and now within a tabernacle at the hall's far end, and *Marzocco,* Florence's heraldic lion that once stood in the Piazza della Signoria.

David (as in David and Goliath) was a favourite subject for sculptors. In this hall are two versions by Donatello: a slender, youthful image in marble, and the fabled bronze he fashioned in later years. The latter is extraordinary – the more so when you consider it was the first freestanding naked statue to be sculpted since classical times. Compare these slight, boyish Davids with Michelangelo's muscular warrior in the Galleria dell'Accademia. Also in this room are a couple of masterpieces by Luca della Robbia, including his delightful *Madonna della Mela* (Madonna of the Apple, c 1460), which once adorned Lorenzo il Magnifico's bedroom.

On the next floor there's a superb collection of terracotta pieces by the della Robbia family, including some of their best-known works, such as Andrea's *Ritratto Idealizia di Fanciullo* (Bust of a Boy, c 1475) and Giovanni's *Pietà* (1514). There is also a bronze collection, including another *Ganimede*, also by Cellini, and an arms gallery.

CHIESA DI SAN FIRENZE

The small medieval parish **church** (Map pp82–3) of San Firenze, which is currently closed to the public, is no longer recognisable in this baroque complex that is today home to law courts. The original church of San Firenze, on the right, was reduced to an oratory when the church on the left, dedicated to San Filippo Neri, was built. The late-baroque façade that unites the buildings was completed in 1775.

Across the piazza (on the western side) is the main façade of **Palazzo Gondi** (Map pp82–3). It was once the site of the merchants' tribunal, a court set up to deal with their quarrels. It is also now closed to the public.

CASA DI DANTE & AROUND

The **Casa di Dante** (Dante's House; Map pp82–3; ☎ 055 21 94 16; Via Santa Margherita 1; admission €3; ☒ 10am-5pm Wed-Mon, 10am-2pm Sun) was built in 1910 above the foundations of Dante's dwelling, so don't believe any claims that he actually lived in it! Those with a special interest in the poet may find the limited display inside mildly diverting. It was closed for renovations when we last passed by.

Just up the road is the 11th-century **Chiesa di Santa Margherita** (Via Santa Margherita), which houses some of the tombs of the Portinari family, relatives of Dante's muse, Beatrice, whom, it's claimed, he first espied here.

CHIESA DI ORSANMICHELE

Originally a grain market, this **church** (Map pp82-3; Via Arte della Lana) was formed when the arcades of a granary were walled in during the 14th century.

The *signoria* ordered the guilds to finance the decoration of the church, and they proceeded to commission sculptors to erect statues of their patron saints in niches and tabernacles around the building's exterior.

THE DELLA ROBBIA FAMILY

Some of the most beautiful and distinctive artworks of the Florentine Renaissance were produced by the prolific della Robbia family, headed by Luca (1399–1482), who first developed the process of glazing terracotta in the 1440s. He started out as a sculptor in marble, and one of his first major commissions was the wonderfully detailed marble *cantoria* (singing gallery; 1438) for the Duomo, now in the Museo dell'Opera del Duomo (p88). However, he soon turned his attention to the production of works based upon terracotta, and his methods long remained a closely guarded family secret. Essentially, they involved coating a terracotta statue in a thin layer of enamel, oxides and a lead glaze. Luca's workshop churned out a vast quantity of terracotta pieces, from simple blue and white Madonna reliefs for private homes to gigantic church altarpieces, as well as numerous *stemmi* (glazed heraldic emblems) for adorning the façades of guild houses across Florence. The durability of the new material made it ideal for decorating the outsides of public buildings.

Luca was aided by his nephew Andrea (1435–1525), whose most famous creations are the medallions of babies in swaddling clothes on the colonnade of the Spedale degli Innocenti (p102). Many of his works are also on show in the Museo del Bargello (opposite). Like his uncle, Andrea produced many Madonna and Child reliefs in a fairly standard, conventional portraiture. One way of telling Andrea's work apart, though, is the fact that he usually placed the Child to the left of the Madonna, whereas Luca placed him on her right.

Andrea's son Giovanni (1469–1521) continued the family tradition; you can see many of his finest pieces in the Museo del Bargello. Instantly recognisable, Giovanni's works are more elaborate than either Luca's or Andrea's, using a larger palette of colours. His bright greens, yellows, blues and browns are still fresh and vibrant, while the intricate garlands of fruit and flowers that border some of his works exemplify his flamboyant touch.

You'll come across works by the della Robbias all around Florence and elsewhere in Tuscany, inside and outside buildings, both ecclesiastical and secular.

The statues, commissioned over the 15th and 16th centuries, represent the work of some of the Renaissance's greatest artists. Some are now in the Museo del Bargello, though many splendid pieces remain, including Ghiberti's bronze *San Matteo* (St Matthew; in the middle on Via Arte della Lana). Donatello's *San Giorgio* (St George; last on the right on Via Orsanmichele) is a modern copy. The main feature of the interior is the splendid Gothic tabernacle, decorated with coloured marble, by Andrea Orcagna.

Unfortunately, the church is currently closed for renovation.

PIAZZA DELLA REPUBBLICA

Originally the site of a Roman forum and heart of the medieval city, this busy square was created in the 1880s as part of an ambitious plan of 'civic improvements' involving the demolition of the Mercato Vecchio, the Jewish ghetto and surrounding slums. A single column, once crowned with a statue by Donatello, is the sole surviving reminder of the old market area. Vasari's **Loggia del Pesce** (Fish Market; Map pp82–3) was saved, though, and has been re-erected on Via Pietrapiana (see p105). Today the square is flanked by a number of trendy and expensive restaurants and cafés.

MERCATO NUOVO

A stroll southwards down Via Calimala brings you to this loggia, built in the mid-16th century to protect merchandise such as wool, silk and gold that was traded here at the **Mercato Nuovo** (New Market; Map pp82-3; Via Porta Rossa). Nowadays, it's decidedly downmarket and shelters tacky souvenir and leather stalls.

At its southern end is the Fontana del Porcellino (Piglet Fountain) and the bronze statue of a boar, an early-17th-century copy of the Greek marble original in the Uffizi. Rub the porker's snout, throw a modest coin into the fountain and – so goes the legend – you're bound to return to Florence.

PALAZZO DEI CAPITANI DI PARTE GUELFA

Just off to the southwest of the Mercato Nuovo, this **palazzo** (Map pp82–3), which is closed to the public, was built in the early 13th century and later added to by Brunelleschi and Vasari. The leaders of the Guelph faction raised this fortified building

in 1265, taking up land and houses that had been confiscated from the Ghibellines.

Piazza della Signoria

The hub of the city's political life throughout the centuries and surrounded by some of its most celebrated buildings, this piazza resembles an outdoor sculpture gallery.

Over the centuries, whenever Florence entered one of its innumerable political crises, the people would be called here as a *parlamento* (people's plebiscite) to rubberstamp decisions that frequently meant ruin for some ruling families and victory for others. Scenes of great pomp and circumstance alternated with those of terrible suffering – it was here that the preacher-leader Savonarola was burned at the stake along with two supporters in 1498. A bronze plaque marks the spot.

Ammannati's huge *Fontana di Nettuno* (Neptune Fountain) spurts beside Palazzo Vecchio. The pin-headed bronze satyrs and divinities frolicking at its edges aren't the prettiest creations, and Il Biancone (The Big White Thing), as locals derisively refer to it, was considered by Michelangelo to be a waste of good marble.

At the entrance to the palace are copies of Michelangelo's *David* (the original is in the Galleria dell'Accademia) and Donatello's *Marzocco*, the heraldic Florentine lion (the original is in the Museo del Bargello). To the right is a 1980 copy of Donatello's bronze *Giuditta e Oloferne* (Judith and Holofernes); the original is inside the palazzo.

A bronze equestrian statue of Cosimo I de' Medici by Giambologna prances in the centre of the piazza.

PALAZZO VECCHIO

Formerly known as Palazzo della Signoria and built by Arnolfo di Cambio between 1298 and 1314, this **palace** (Map pp82-3; ☎ 055 276 82 24; Piazza della Signoria; admission €6; ☑ 9am-7pm Fri-Wed, 9am-2pm Thu) is the traditional seat of Florentine government. Its 94m-high **Torre d'Arnolfo**, with its striking crenellations, is as much a symbol of the city as the Duomo.

Built for the *priori* (city government) that ruled Florence, it came to be known as Palazzo della Signoria as the government took on this name.

In 1540 Cosimo I de' Medici moved from Palazzo Medici into this building, making it the ducal residence and centre of government. Cosimo commissioned Vasari to renovate and decorate the interior, but the ruler's wife, Eleonora de Toledo, turned her nose up at the results and persuaded her consort to buy Palazzo Pitti instead.

It took time to expand and fit out Palazzo Pitti just the way the demanding Eleonora wanted. Ironically, and with a dash of poetic justice, she died before the work was finished, but the Medici family moved in anyway in 1549. From then onwards, the ducal palace has been known as the Palazzo Vecchio (Old Palace). It remains the seat of the city's power, and the mayor keeps his office here.

Coming in from Piazza della Signoria, you arrive first in the courtyard, reworked in early Renaissance style by Michelozzo in 1453. The decoration came more than a century later when Francesco de' Medici married Joanna of Austria. The cities depicted are jewels in the Austrian imperial crown.

A stairway leads up to the magnificent **Salone dei Cinquecento** (16th-Century Room). This was created within the original building in the 1490s to accommodate the Consiglio dei Cinquecento (Council of 500), called into being during the republic under Savonarola. Cosimo I de' Medici later turned the hall into a splendid expression of his own power. In the 1560s the ceiling was raised 7m, and Vasari, aided by his apprentices, added the swirling battle scenes that glorify Florentine victories over archrivals Pisa and Siena. At floor level, the monumental statuary includes a graphic series on the *Labours of Hercules* by Vincenzo de' Rossi, including a painful-looking grapple between Hercules and Diomedes. The star-turn, though, is Michelangelo's sculpture *Genio della Vittoria* (Genius of Victory), destined for Rome and Pope Julius II's tomb, but left unfinished in the artist's studio when he died.

Vasari also designed the intimate yet equally sumptuous little **studiolo** (Francesco I's study), decorated by a team of top Florentine Mannerist artists, that comes off the vast hall.

There follows a series of rooms, each dedicated to a senior member of the Medicis, its décor blaring their glory in a heavy-handed manner. From the Salone dei Cinquecento you enter **Quartiere di Leone X** (Leo X Area), named after the Medici pope and adorned with scenes from his life, again by Vasari.

Upstairs is **Quartiere degli Elementi** (Elements Area), a series of richly decorated rooms and terraces dedicated to classical deities. Verrocchio's bronze *Putto col Delfino* (Cupid with Dolphin), mentioned in Vasari's *Lives of the Artists*, is in Sala di Giunone.

From here a walkway takes you across the top of the Salone dei Cinquecento into the **Quartiere di Eleonora**, the apartments of Cosimo I's fractious wife. The ceiling of the first room, Camera Verde, was painted by Ridolfo del Ghirlandaio and was inspired by designs from Nero's *Domus Aurea* in Rome. The small chapel off to the side contains vibrant frescoes by Bronzino.

Of the succeeding rooms, the most interesting is the **Sala di Gualadra**, decorated by Giovanni Stradano with views of 16th-century Florence, including a scene of a ball game in Piazza di Santa Maria Novella and a jousting match in Piazza di Santa Croce.

You pass through the **Capella dei Priori** (Chapel of the Priors), which houses a lunette of the Annunciation by Ridolfo del Ghirlandaio, before reaching the **Sala dell'Udienza** (Audience Room), where the *priori* administered medieval Florentine justice.

The next room is the **Sala dei Gigli**, named after its frieze of fleur-de-lys, representing the Florentine Republic, that decorates three of the walls. Look at its remarkable coffered ceiling and enjoy Donatello's powerful carving of *Guiditta e Oloferne* (Judith and Holofernes). Domenico Ghirlandaio's fresco on the far wall, depicting figures from Roman history, was meant to be one of a series by other artists including Botticelli. A small study off the hall is the chancery, where Machiavelli plotted for a while. The other room, **Sala delle Carte Geografiche** (Map Room), houses Cosimo I's fascinating collection of 16th-century maps, often rudimentary and of varying degrees of accuracy, charting everywhere in the known world of the time, from the polar regions to the Caribbean.

From here you can climb to the battlements for fine views over the city. Alternatively, by paying a little extra you can join in small guided groups to explore the Percorsi Segreti (Secret Passageways; not open to disabled visitors) or head for the **Museo dei Ragazzi** (Children's Museum).

The former consist of several options, including the possibility of visiting the **Studiolo di Francesco** (Francesco's little study) and the nearby **treasury** of Cosimo I. Another choice takes you into the roof of the Salone dei Cinquecento, or you can also choose to be guided around the artworks by an actor portraying Giorgio Vasari.

In the Museo dei Ragazzi, you can interact with actors dressed up as Cosimo I and Eleonora de Toledo – children are invited to dress up as the ducal offspring (Bia and Garcia) and play with the kinds of toys they would have enjoyed. Other activities include building and taking apart models of Palazzo Vecchio, bridges and the like.

For a standard visit plus one of these options, you pay €8. If you want to add on more of the extras, each one costs an additional €1. You can get family tickets (€16) for two adults and not more than three children. Tickets and information on all these extra activities are available in a room just back from the main ticket area.

LOGGIA DELLA SIGNORIA

Built in the late 14th century as a platform for public ceremonies, this **loggia** (Map pp82–3) eventually became a showcase for sculptures. It also subsequently assumed the alternative name of Loggia dei Lanzi as Cosimo I used to station his Swiss mercenaries, armed with lances, in it to remind people who was in charge.

To the left of the steps stands Benvenuto Cellini's magnificent bronze statue of *Perseus* (1545) brandishing the head of Medusa. To the right is Giambologna's Mannerist *Ratto delle Sabine* (Rape of the Sabine; 1583), his final work. Inside the loggia is another of Giambologna's works, *Ercole col Centauro Nesso* (Hercules with the Centaur Nessus), which originally stood near the southern end of Ponte Vecchio.

Uffizi Gallery & Around

The Palazzo degli Uffizi, designed and built by Vasari in the second half of the 16th century at the request of Cosimo I de' Medici, originally housed the city's administrators, judiciary and guilds. It was, in effect, a government office building (*uffizi* means offices).

Vasari also designed the Corridoio Vasariano (p96), a private corridor that links Palazzo Vecchio and Palazzo Pitti, through the Uffizi and across Ponte Vecchio.

Cosimo's successor, Francesco I, commissioned the architect Buontalenti to modify the upper floor of Palazzo degli Uffizi to house the Medicis' growing art collection. Thus, indirectly, the first steps were taken to turn it into an art gallery.

THE GALLERY

The **Uffizi Gallery** (Galleria degli Uffizi; Map pp82–3; Piazza degli Uffizi) now houses the family's private collection, bequeathed to the city in 1743 by the last of the Medici family, Anna Maria Ludovica, on condition that it never leaves the city. Over the years, sections of the collection have been moved to the Museo del Bargello and the Museo Archeologico. In compensation, other collections have joined the core group. Paintings from Florence's churches have also been moved here. Although by no means the biggest art gallery around, the Uffizi houses the world's single greatest collection of Italian and Florentine art.

Sadly, several artworks were destroyed and others badly damaged when a car bomb planted by the Mafia exploded outside the gallery's west wing in May 1993, killing five people. Documents cataloguing the collection were also destroyed. Partly in response to the bombing, but even more so to the gallery's immense popularity (more than 1.5 million visitors march through every year, compared to a mere trickle of 100,000 annually in the 1950s), restoration and re-organisation will lead to what promoters refer to as the 'Nuovi Uffizi'.

NUOVI UFFIZI

With an investment of €60 million and a planned, perhaps optimistic, completion date in late 2007, the Uffizi is set to double in size over the next few years. So the arrangement of paintings and rooms that we describe may change radically during this book's life span.

While work is in progress, you're likely to find several galleries closed and others newly opened. Check the illuminated signboard by the main entrance for the order of the day. If you read Italian, you might want to visit www.polomuseale.firenze.it/uffizi. Clicking on *collezioni* gives you a room-by-room breakdown of what's currently displayed, though we can't vouch for how regularly the site's updated.

Since there's such a wealth of treasures competing for your attention, investing in an **audio guide** (for 1/2 persons €4.65/6.20) makes sound sense, especially if it's your first visit.

Long queues are common – to avoid the worst of them, arrive in the morning, before the gallery opens, or book ahead (see the boxed text, p87).

VISITING THE GALLERY

The **collection** (☎ 055 238 86 51; Piazza degli Uffizi 6; admission €6.50; ⏲ 8.15am-6.50pm Tue-Sun) begins on the 1st floor with the small **Galleria dei Disegni e delle Stampe** (Drawing and Print Gallery), in which sketches and initial drafts by the great masters are often shown. The display is rotated frequently, as prolonged exposure can damage the drawings.

Upstairs in the gallery proper you pass through two vestibules, the first with singularly unflattering portrait busts of several of the Medici clan, the second with some Roman statuary.

The long corridor has been arranged much as it appeared in the 16th century. Below the frescoed ceilings is a series of small portraits of great and good men, interspersed with larger portraits, often of Medici family members or intimates. Room 1, which holds some archaeological treasures, is closed.

The first accessible rooms feature works by Tuscan masters of the 13th and early 14th centuries. Stars of Room 2 are three paintings of the *Madonna in Maestà* by Duccio di Buoninsegna, Cimabue and Giotto. All three were formerly altarpieces in Florentine churches. Looking at them in this order, you sense the transition from Gothic to the precursor of the Renaissance. Also in the room is Giotto's polyptych *Madonna col Bambino Gesù, Santi e Angeli* (Madonna with Baby Jesus, Saints and Angels).

Room 3 traces the Sienese school of the 14th century. Of particular note are Simone Martini's shimmering *Annunciazione* (Annunciation), considered a masterpiece of the school, and Ambrogio Lorenzetti's triptych, *Madonna col Bambino e Santi* (Madonna with Child and Saints). Room 4 contains Florentine works of the 14th century.

Rooms 5 and 6 house examples of the International Gothic style, among them Lorenzo Monaco's sensitive *Incoronazione della Vergine* (Coronation of the Virgin).

Room 7 features works by painters of the early-15th-century Florentine school, which pioneered the Renaissance. There is one panel (the other two are in the Louvre and London's National Gallery) from Paolo Uccello's striking *La Battaglia di San Romano* (Battle of San Romano). In his efforts to create perspective, he directs the lances, horses and soldiers to a central disappearing point. Other works include Piero della Francesca's famous profile portraits of the Duke and Duchess of Urbino, and a *Madonna col Bambino* (Madonna with Child) painted jointly by Masaccio and Masolino.

In the next room, devoted to a collection of works by Filippo and Filippino Lippi, is Filippo's delightful *Madonna col Bambino e due Angeli* (Madonna with Child and Two Angels).

Room 9 is devoted largely to Antonio de Pollaiolo. His series of six virtues is followed by a seventh, *Fortezza* (Strength) by Botticelli. The clarity of line and light, and the humanity in the face, set it apart from Pollaiolo's work. It's a taster for the Botticelli Rooms, Nos 10 to 14, considered the gallery's most spectacular. Highlights are the ethereal *Nascita di Venere* (Birth of Venus) and the deeply spiritual *Annunciazione*. Contrast these with his *Calunnia* (Calumny): for some, a disturbing reflection of Botticelli's loss of faith in human potential as he aged; for others, a deliberate reining in of his free spirit in order not to invite the attentions of the puritanical Savonarola.

Room 15 features Da Vinci's *Annunciazione*, painted when he was a student of Verrocchio. Quite different in style but equally arresting in its swirling composition is his unfinished *Adorazione dei Magi* (Adoration of the Magi).

Room 16 has mainly 2nd- and 3rd-century Roman funerary sculpture, while the small Room 17, the Sala dell'Ermafrodito, displays a collection of bronze statuettes.

Room 18, known as the Tribuna, houses the celebrated *Medici Venus,* a 1st-century-BC copy of a 4th-century-BC work by the Greek sculptor Praxiteles. The room also contains portraits of various members of the Medici family.

The great Umbrian painter Perugino, who studied under Piero della Francesca and later became Raphael's master, is represented in Room 19, as is Luca Signorelli.

Piero di Cosimo's *Perseo Libera Andromeda* is full of fantastical whimsy, with beasts and flying heroes.

Room 20 features artists of the German Renaissance, including Dürer, with a magnificent *Adorazione dei Magi,* and several canvases by Lucas Cranach.

Room 21, with a heavily Venetian leaning, has works by Giovanni Bellini and his pupil Giorgione, along with a few by Vittorio Carpaccio.

Room 22 is given over to various German and Flemish Renaissance artists, and houses, among others, a small self-portrait by Hans Holbein. The following room concentrates on the Veneto region in Italy's northeast, with paintings by Andrea Mantegna and Correggio. Peek into Room 24 to see the 15th- to 19th-century works in the Miniatures Room, and then cross into the west wing, which houses works of Italian masters dating from the 16th century.

The star of Room 25 is Michelangelo's dazzling *Tondo Doni,* which depicts the Holy Family. The composition is highly unusual, as Joseph gently holds Jesus on his mother's shoulder as she twists round to gaze at him, the colours as vibrant as when they were first applied.

In Room 26 are works by Raphael (1483–1520) and Andrea del Sarto. Room 27 is dominated by the sometimes disquieting works of Florence's two main Mannerist masters, Pontormo and Rosso Fiorentino.

Room 28 boasts 11 Titians, including *Madonna delle Rose* (Madonna of the Roses), a tender study in which the Christ child plays with flowers proffered by the infant John the Baptist, as Mary watches with a hint of amusement on her face. Also here is Titian's portrait of *Pope Sixtus IV.*

Standing out in Rooms 29 and 30, devoted mainly to comparatively minor painters from northern Italy, are three canvases by Parmigianino, while Room 31 has some powerful paintings by Venice's Paolo Veronese, especially his *Sacra Famiglia con Santa Barbara* (Holy Family with St Barbara).

Room 32 is mostly dedicated to Tintoretto, and houses his *Leda e il Cigno* (Leda and the Swan). He is accompanied by a few Jacopo Bassano canvases. Room 33, called the Corridor of the 16th Century, has a mix of lesser-known artists. A trio of pieces by Vasari feature, along with an unexpected

foreign contribution: El Greco's *I Santi San Giovanni Evangelista e San Francesco.* Room 34 has mainly 16th-century works by Lombard painters.

Room 35 comes as a bit of a shock, as you are confronted with the enormous, sumptuous religious canvases of Lodovico Buti (1560–1611) of Florence, and Federico Barocci (1535–1612) of Urbino.

The numbering resumes at Room 41. This room is a showcase of Flemish art, dominated by two colossal tableaux by Rubens sweeping with violence and power: *Enrico IV alla Battaglia di Ivry* and *Ingresso Trionfale di Enrico IV a Parigi,* which represent the French King Henri IV at the Battle of Ivry and his triumphal march into Paris. Also here is a trio of works by Van Dyck.

Room 42, with its exquisite coffered ceiling and splendid dome, is filled with Roman statues. Room 43 is given over to lesser-known Italian and European artists of the 17th century, while Rembrandt and other Dutch masters feature in Room 44.

Room 45 takes us back to Venice, with 18th-century views of the city by Canaletto and Guardi, and Crespi's arresting *Amore e Psiche* (Cupid and Psyche), with its interplay of light and shade. You'll also find a couple of stray portraits by the Spaniard Goya.

Downstairs on the 1st floor, the Sala Caravaggio presents three of his chiaroscuro masterpieces, including the *Sacrificio d'Isacco* (Sacrifice of Isaac), and works by his followers. The theme of Caravaggio's admirers and imitators continues in the following rooms. Work on the bulk of this floor to create the Nuovi Uffizi is still under way.

CORRIDOIO VASARIANO

When the Medicis moved into Palazzo Pitti, they wanted to maintain their link, literally, with what from then on would be known as Palazzo Vecchio. And so Cosimo I commissioned Vasari to build an enclosed **walkway** (Map pp82–3) between the two palaces that would allow the Medicis to wander between each in privacy.

At the time of writing, the passageway was closed to the public. For an update, contact Firenze Musei (p87).

MUSEO DI STORIA DELLA SCIENZA

Telescopes that look more like works of art, complex instruments for the measurement f distance, time and space, and a room full of wax and plastic cutaway models of the various stages of childbirth are among the highlights in the bizarre collection of the **Museum of the History of Science** (Map pp82-3; ☎ 055 26 53 11; Piazza de' Giudici 1; admission €6.50; �9.30am-5pm Mon & Wed-Fri, 9.30am-1pm Tue & Sat). There, too, preserved like a saintly relic, is Galileo's desiccated middle finger, raised skywards, as if a timeless riposte to his Inquisition accusers.

Santa Maria Novella & Around

BASILICA DI SANTA MARIA NOVELLA

Just south of Stazione di Santa Maria Novella, this **church** (Map pp80-1; ☎ 055 21 59 18; Piazza di Santa Maria Novella; admission €2.50; �9am-5pm Mon-Thu & Sat, 1-5pm Fri & Sun) was begun in the late 13th century as the Dominican order's Florentine base. Although it was mostly completed by around 1360, work on the façade and embellishment of the interior continued well into the 15th century. It was here that the Church Council of Florence was held in 1439. The tomb of the Patriarch of Constantinople, who died in the city, is near the **Cappella Rucellai**.

The lower section of the green-and-white marble façade is transitional from Romanesque to Gothic, while the upper section and the main doorway were designed by Alberti and completed around 1470. Halfway along the north aisle, the highlight of the Gothic interior is Masaccio's superb fresco *Trinità* (Trinity; 1428), one of the first artworks to use the then newly discovered techniques of perspective and proportion.

The first chapel to the right of the altar, **Cappella di Filippo Strozzi**, features lively frescoes by Filippino Lippi, depicting the lives of St John the Evangelist and St Philip the Apostle. Domenico Ghirlandaio's series of frescoes behind the main altar was painted with the help of artists who may have included the young Michelangelo. Relating the lives of the Virgin Mary, St John the Baptist and others, the frescoes are notable for their depiction of Florentine life during the Renaissance, and feature portraits of members of the Tornabuoni family, who commissioned them. Brunelleschi's crucifix hangs above the altar in the **Cappella Gondi**, the first chapel left of the choir. Giotto's crucifix (c 1288) hangs above the centre of the nave.

To reach the **Chiostro Verde** (Green Cloister), which takes its name from the green earth base used for its frescoes, go out of the church and follow signs for the *museo*. Three of its four walls are decorated with fading frescoes recounting Genesis. The most interesting artistically, by Paolo Uccello, are those on the party wall with the church. *Il Diluvio Universale* (Great Flood) is outstanding.

Off the next side of the cloister is the **Cappellone degli Spagnoli** (Spanish Chapel), which was set aside for the Spanish retinue that accompanied Eleonora de Toledo, Cosimo I's wife. It contains some well-preserved frescoes by Andrea di Bonaiuto.

On the west side of the cloister is the **museum** (☎ 055 28 21 87; admission €2.70; �9am-5pm Mon-Thu & Sat, 9am-2pm Sun), which contains vestments and other ecclesiastical relics.

CHIESA D'OGNISSANTI

This 13th-century **church** (Map p85; Borgo Ognissanti; �7am-12.30pm & 4-8pm Mon-Sat, 4-8pm Sun) was much altered in the 17th century, when its baroque façade was added. Domenico Ghirlandaio's fresco, above the second altar on the right, is of Madonna della Misericordia, protector of the Vespucci family. Amerigo Vespucci, the Florentine navigator who gave his name to the American continent, is supposed to be the young boy whose head peeks between the Madonna and the old man. Ghirlandaio's masterpiece, *Ultima Cena* (Last Supper), covers most of a wall in the former monastery's refectory, reached via the cloister, while his detailed portrait, *St Jerome*, is in the nave. Opposite is Botticelli's pensive *San Augustin*. All three of these works date from 1480.

LE CASCINE

About 10 minutes' walk westwards along Borgo Ognissanti and Via il Prato brings you to the **Porta al Prato**, part of the walls that were demolished in the late 19th century to make way for the ring of boulevards that still surrounds the city.

A short walk south from here towards the Arno brings you to the eastern tip of Florence's great green lung, the park of **Le Cascine** (pastures; Map pp80-1). The Medici dukes made this a private hunting reserve, but Pietro Leopoldo opened it to the public in 1776, with boulevards, fountains and bird sanctuaries. Nowadays the **Mercato delle Cascine** (Map pp78-9), a big market, is held in the park on Tuesday mornings.

CHIESA DI SAN PANCRAZIO & MUSEO MARINO MARINI

An ecclesiastical building has stood here since the 9th century though the present church dates from the 15th century. Now deconsecrated, it houses the **museum** (Map pp82–3; ☎ 055 21 94 32; Piazza San Pancrazio; admission €4; ☺ 10am-5pm Mon & Wed-Sat Sep-Jul), which was donated to the city of Florence by the sculptor Marino Marini (1901–80). There are around 200 sculptures, portraits and drawings, mostly following the man-and-horse theme. It's unlikely to excite anyone not familiar with his work.

Via de' Tornabuoni & Around

Via de' Tornabuoni is the city's most fashionable and expensive shopping street. It's bordered by Renaissance mansions and classy, stylish shops, including Ferragamo, Gucci and Armani. Often referred to as the 'Salotto di Firenze' (Florence's Drawing Room), it follows the original course of the Mugnone tributary into the Arno.

Head east down Via della Vigna Nuova and turn into Via dei Palchetti; you'll pass the classically inspired **Palazzo Rucellai** (Map pp82–3), designed by Alberti for one of the city's wealthiest families.

Continuing south, you reach Lungarno Corsini on the Arno. **Palazzo Corsini** (Map pp82–3; ☎ 055 21 28 80; www.palazzocorsini.it; Via del Parione 11b; admission free; ☺ 9am-1pm & 4-7pm Mon-Fri), once a grandiose late-baroque edifice, today looks decidedly down at heel. It once belonged to the Medici family, but they sold it in 1640, and work on the exterior wasn't completed until 1735. The most interesting feature inside the building is the spiral staircase known as the *lumaca* (literally 'snail').

Head east for **Ponte Santa Trinità**, a harmonious and charming river crossing. Cosimo I de' Medici put Vasari in charge of the project, and he in turn asked Michelangelo for advice. In the end the job was handed over to Ammannati, who finished it in 1567. The statues of the seasons are by Pietro Francavilla. The bridge was painstakingly restored after being blown up by the Nazis in 1944.

Turning inland, you next arrive at the 14th-century **Chiesa della Santa Trinità** (Map pp82–3; Piazza Santa Trinità; ☺ 8am-noon Mon-Sat, 4-6pm daily). Although rebuilt in the Gothic style and later graced with a Mannerist façade of indifferent taste, you can still get some idea of what the Romanesque original looked like by looking at the façade wall from the inside. The eye-catching frescoes depicting the life of St Francis of Assisi, in the south transept's Cappella Sassetti, are by Domenico Ghirlandaio. Lorenzo Monaco, Fra Angelico's master, painted the altarpiece of the *Annunciation* in the fourth chapel of the south aisle, and also the frescoes on the chapel walls.

Across the road is the looming **Palazzo Spini-Feroni** (Map pp82–3), built in the 13th century for Geri Spini, the pope's banker, and now owned by the Ferragamo shoe empire. The **Museo Salvatore Ferragamo** (Map pp82–3; ☎ 055 336 04 56; Via de' Tornabuoni 2; admission free; ☺ 9am-1pm & 2-6pm Mon-Fri) is on the 2nd floor. The rotating display shows off some of Ferragamo's classic shoes, many worn by Hollywood stars such as Marilyn Monroe, Greta Garbo and Katherine Hepburn, as well as the wooden lasts upon which tailor-made shoes were crafted. The museum has lift access.

Palazzo Buondelmonti (Map pp82–3) also faces Piazza Santa Trinità. The family of the same name was at the heart of the Guelph-Ghibelline feud in Florence. More imposing is **Palazzo Bartolini-Salimbeni** (Map pp82–3), an example of High Renaissance spiced with more than a touch of the classical.

Sneak briefly eastwards along Borgo Santissimi Apostoli to visit the lovely **Chiesa dei Santissimi Apostoli** (Piazza del Limbo 1), a refreshingly – and relatively – sober church, when set against Florence's Renaissance splendour and occasional overstatement. Tucked away in a sunken square that was once the cemetery for unbaptised babies, it's overlooked by most visitors. Most of the 11th-century façade is still intact, and the rounded arches of its Romanesque interior soar heavenwards. Put €0.50 in the slot to the left of the entrance and it bursts into muted light. There's a terracotta tabernacle by Giovanni della Robbia at the end of the north aisle.

Most impressive of the Renaissance mansions that border Via de' Tornabuoni is **Palazzo Strozzi** (Map pp82–3), a great colossus raised by one of the most powerful of the Medici's rival families. Although never completed, its three finished façades in heavy rusticated *pietra forte* (literally 'strong stone', a local sandstone), designed by Benedetto da Maiano, speak naked power. Inside is a grand if somewhat gloomy courtyard. The palazzo is today used for art exhibitions.

Two blocks north stands the baroque façade of **Chiesa di San Gaetano** (Map pp82–3). The church has been around since the 11th century, but the façade dates from 1683. Opposite and a few strides north, **Palazzo Antinori** (Map pp82–3) was built in the 15th century by Giovanni da Maiano.

San Lorenzo Area
BASILICA DI SAN LORENZO
The Medicis commissioned Brunelleschi to rebuild the **Basilica di San Lorenzo** (Map pp82–3; Piazza San Lorenzo; admission €2.50; ☯ 10am-5pm Mon-Sat), on the site of a 4th-century basilica, in 1425. Considered one of the most harmonious examples of Renaissance architecture, it was the Medici family church, and many members are buried here.

Michelangelo prepared a design for the façade that was never executed, which is why this, like so many other Florentine churches, appears unfinished from the outside. The nave is separated from the two aisles by columns made of *pietra serena* (soft grey stone), crowned with Corinthian capitals. The two bronze pulpits, are by Donatello, who died before they were completed. He is buried in the chapel featuring Fra Filippo Lippi's *Annunciation*. Rosso Fiorentino's *Sposalizio della Vergine* (Marriage of the Virgin Mary; 1523) is in the second chapel on the south aisle. To the left of the altar is the **Sagrestia Vecchia** (Old Sacristy), designed by Brunelleschi and decorated in the main by Donatello.

From another entrance off Piazza San Lorenzo you enter the church's peaceful **cloisters**. Off the first cloister, a staircase leads up to the **Biblioteca Laurenziana Medicea**, commissioned by Guilio de' Medici (Pope Clement VII) to house the extensive Medici library and nowadays restricted to researchers burrowing through its 10,000 volumes. The real attraction is Michelangelo's magnificent vestibule and staircase, accessible to all. They are executed in grey *pietra serena*, and the curvaceous steps are a sign of the master's move towards Mannerism from the stricter bounds of Renaissance architecture and design.

Enter the **Cappelle Medicee** (Medicean Chapels; Map pp80–1; ☎ 055 238 86 02; admission €6; ☯ 8.15am-4.50pm Tue-Sat & alternate Sun) via Piazza Madonna degli Aldobrandini. The **Cappella dei Principi** (Princes' Chapel), sumptuously decorated with granite, the most precious marble and semiprecious stones, was the principal burial place of the Medici rulers. Breaking up the colossal splendour of the stone are decorative tableaux made from *pietre dure*. The intention was to place statues of the Medici in the still-empty niches but, apart from bronzes of Ferdinando I and Cosimo II, the project was never completed.

A corridor leads from the Cappella dei Principi to the graceful **Sagrestia Nuova** (New Sacristy), so called to distinguish it from the Sagrestia Vecchia. This, the Medicis' funeral chapel, was Michelangelo's first architectural work. His haunting sculptures *Notte e Giorno* (Night and Day), *Aurora e Crepusculo* (Dawn and Dusk) and *Madonna col Bambino* adorn Medici tombs (1520–34), including that of Lorenzo il Magnifico.

PALAZZO MEDICI-RICCARDI
When Cosimo de' Medici felt fairly sure of his position in Florence, he decided it was time to move house and entrusted Michelozzo with the design in 1444. The result is this **palace** (Map pp80–1; ☎ 055 276 03 40; Via Cavour 3; admission €4; ☯ 9am-7pm Thu-Tue).

Michelozzo's blueprint would continue to influence the construction of Florentine family residences, such as the Palazzo Pitti and Palazzo Strozzi, for years to come. The fortress town houses with their towers that characterised Gothic Florence were no longer necessary, and Cosimo's power was more or less undisputed. Instead, Michelozzo created a self-assured, stout but not inelegant pile on three storeys.

The rusticated façade of the ground floor gives a rather stern aspect to the building, though the upper two storeys are less aggressive, maintaining restrained classical lines – already a feature of the emerging Renaissance canon – and topped with a heavy timber roof whose broad eaves protrude over the street below.

The Medicis stayed here until 1540. A century later its new owners, the Riccardi family, gave it a comprehensive remodelling.

You can wander inside to the courtyard, although much of the building nowadays houses public administration offices.

The highlight is the tiny upstairs **Cappella dei Magi**, which has a series of wonderfully detailed serene frescoes (1459) by Benozzo Gozzoli. His ostensible theme of *Journey of the Magi* is but a slender pretext for portraying members of the Medici clan in their best light.

A couple of hundred years later, the Riccardis built the sumptuously decorated **Galleria**, or **Sala di Luca Giordano**, commissioning the eponymous artist to adorn the ceiling with his complex *Allegory of Divine Wisdom* (1685), another vehicle for showing the Medicis at their best as members of the First Family recline in saintly posture around God, surrounded by lavish, seemingly random scenes from classical mythology. The whole is a rather overblown example of late baroque, dripping with gold leaf and bursting with colour.

Since only seven visitors are allowed in at a time and for a maximum of only seven minutes, it's absolutely essential to reserve your slot in advance – you have to admire the symmetry.

MERCATO CENTRALE

Built in 1874, the city's central produce **market** (Map pp80–1; Piazza del Mercato Centrale; 7am-2pm Mon-Sat) seems to disappear amid the confusion of makeshift stands of the clothes and leather market that fill the surrounding square and streets during the day. The iron and glass architecture was something of a novelty in Florence when the market was first built.

San Marco Area

GALLERIA DELL'ACCADEMIA

No visit to Florence is complete without calling into this **gallery** (Map pp80–1; 055 238 86 09; Via Ricasoli 60; admission Dec-Aug €8, Sep-Nov €6.50; 8.15am-6.50pm Tue-Sun), if only because it contains one of the greatest masterpieces of the Renaissance, Michelangelo's giant *David*.

You first enter the grand **Sala del Colosso**, which is dominated by a plaster model of Giambologna's *Ratto delle Sabine* (Rape of the Sabine). Among the paintings here are a fresco of the *Pietà* by Andrea del Sarto, a couple of pieces by Fra Bartolommeo and a *Deposizione* (Deposition), to which Filippino Lippi and Perugino both contributed.

Immediately to the left off this room, a doorway leads into a long hall, at the end of which is perhaps the most famous sculpture in the world, Michelangelo's *David* (1501–04). Carved from a single block of marble, the 5m-tall, 19-tonne statue originally stood in the Piazza della Signoria (where its left arm fell off one blighted day and killed a passing peasant). It was installed in the gallery in 1882 in a purpose-built niche that hardly does this masterpiece justice. Nearby are Michelangelo's four *Prigioni* ('prisoners' or 'slaves'; 1530) and *San Matteo* (St Matthew; 1503), all unfinished. The four *Prigioni*, who appear to be writhing and struggling to free themselves from the marble, were meant for the tomb of Pope Julius II, itself never completed.

THE GRAND TOUR

The guest book of the now extinct Gabinetto Vieusseux, something of a cultural institution throughout 19th-century Florence, was a veritable who's who of VIPs who passed through the city. Some liked it, some hated it. The American writer Mark Twain veered towards the latter, in particular finding the Arno a poor excuse for a river (after the Mississippi, it must have come as a bit of a letdown).

Stendhal, the French novelist, it is said, discovered 'stendhalismo' in the Basilica di Santa Croce, overwhelmed by the sheer concentration of art in Florence. Judging by his journal notes, he was equally overwhelmed by the need to dispense tips to an unending stream of attendants and urchins to get from one sight to another. His countryman, the Marquis de Sade, found the local women 'tall, impertinent, ugly, dishevelled and gluttonous'.

Percy Shelley composed his 'Ode to the West Wind' in Le Cascine. Percy and pals, such as Lord Byron, the Brownings and Walter Savage Landor, all resided in Florence for a while, maintaining a haughty distance from the locals and indulging their whims.

Dickens, a little more down-to-earth, was fascinated by the city, and Anatole France opined that the 'god who created Florence was an artist'.

Queen Victoria visited three times. Not a great lover of museums or art, she preferred to spend her time in the city's parks and gardens and keep a low profile.

DAVID FRESHLY PAMPERED

In May 2004 David was once again on his pedestal, just in time for the 500th anniversary of his creation, after a beauty treatment that had lasted eight months. It had been controversial from the start. A group of petitioners, fearful for the statue's health, opposed any kind of treatment. Then the chosen restorer walked off in a huff when her method, simply using fine brushes, was rejected. In the event, the lovely boy was given a 'mud pack' of clay and cellulose pulp, then bathed in distilled water.

The process must have been considerably less painful than was last freshen-up, back in 1843, when he was given a working over with hydrochloric acid. Mind you, he's no stranger to trouble; over the centuries he's been struck by lightning, attacked by rioters and, as recently as 1991, had his toes bashed with a hammer.

Off to the left, the **Sala dell'Ottocento** (19th-Century Room) has a collection of plaster models of some of Florence's public statuary, including Bartolini's *Machiavelli* (1846), now in the Uffizi arcade. There are also shelves full of nameless, ghostly busts commissioned by wealthy Victorian 'Grand Tourists' – members of the moneyed middle and upper classes who toured Europe, especially Italy, to soak up the culture and history, and round off their classical education (see opposite).

In the surrounding rooms there is a mixed collection of paintings and sculptures, including works by Botticelli and Taddeo Gaddi.

MUSEO DI SAN MARCO

Piazza San Marco is at the heart of the university area. Flanking it are a now deconsecrated Dominican convent and Chiesa di San Marco, where you'll find the **Museo di San Marco** (Map pp80-1; ☎ 055 238 86 08; Piazza San Marco 1; admission €4; ⏰ 8.15am-1.50pm Tue-Fri, 8.15am-6.50pm Sat, 2nd & 4th Sun & 3rd & 5th Mon of the month).

Dip into the church, founded in 1299, which was rebuilt by Michelozzo in 1437 and again remodelled by Giambologna some years later. It features several paintings, but they pale in comparison with the treasures contained in the adjoining convent.

Famous Florentines who called this convent home include the painters Fra Angelico (c 1400–55) and Fra Bartolommeo (1472–1517). It now serves as a museum of Fra Angelico's works, many of which were moved here in the 1860s.

You first find yourself in the **Chiostro di Sant'Antonio**, designed by Michelozzo in 1440. Turn immediately right to enter the **Sala dell'Ospizio**. Among the better-known works is the *Deposizione di Cristo* (1432), a commission taken on by Fra Angelico after the original artist, Lorenzo Monaco, died after finishing only a small section, in late-Gothic style. Fra Angelico's attention to perspective and the realistic portrayal of nature marked a new development in art, and it has been suggested that this was one of the first true paintings of the Renaissance.

The eastern wing of the cloister, formerly the monks' refectory, is dominated at the far end by Giovanni Antonio Sogliani's fresco *La Providenza dei Domenicani* (The Miraculous Supper of St Domenic; 1536). Just outside you can see Luca della Robbia's colourful *Madonna col Bambino* (c 1460), one of his most expressive terracotta statues. Nearby, in the old kitchen, is a collection of fresco portraits by Fra Bartolommeo.

Next along is the former Chapterhouse, where Fra Angelico's huge *Crucifixion* fresco (1442) is on show, as well as the bronze church bell, known as 'La Pagnona', possibly made by Michelozzo.

The main attractions are upstairs. At the top of the stairs is one of Fra Angelico's most famous works, *Annunciazione* (c 1440), faced on the opposite wall by a *Crocifisso* featuring St Dominic. The artist was invited to decorate the monks' cells with devotional frescoes to guide the friars' meditation. Most were executed by Fra Angelico himself, others by aides under his supervision, including Benozzo Gozzoli. If you're using the museum guide, look carefully for the faded numbers on each door. Among several masterpieces is the magnificent *Madonna delle Ombre* (Virgin of the Shadows), on the external wall between cells No 25 and 26.

Savonarola's cell, which is actually a suite of three small rooms, is at the end of the opposite corridor, and is kept as a kind of shrine to the turbulent priest. It houses a portrait, a few personal items and a grand marble monument erected by admirers in 1873. In a nearby cell you can see the linen banner, painted with a scene of the Crucifixion, which Savonarola carried in processions.

CENACOLO DI SANT'APOLLONIA

Here in the **refectory** (Map pp80–1; Via XXVII Aprile 1; admission free; 8.15am-1.30pm Tue-Sat & alternating Sun & Mon) of what was once a Benedictine convent, restoration work revealed some remarkable frescoes, including a Last Supper in rich shades of red, blue and purple, painted by Andrea del Castagno around 1450. Above it, another three frescoes of his portray Jesus' crucifixion (with a rare example of a beardless Christ figure), burial and resurrection.

PIAZZA DELLA SANTISSIMA ANNUNZIATA

Giambologna's equestrian statue of the Grand Duke Ferdinando I de' Medici commands the scene from the centre of this square, which usually teems with students rather than tourists.

The church that gives the square its name, **Chiesa della Santissima Annunziata** (Map pp80–1; Piazza della Santissima Annunziata; 7.30am-12.30pm & 4-6.30pm), was established in 1250 by the founders of the Servite order, and was rebuilt by Michelozzo and others in the mid-15th century. It is dedicated to the Virgin Mary, and in the ornate tabernacle, to your left as you enter the church from the atrium, is a so-called miraculous painting of the Virgin.

No longer on public view, the canvas is attributed to a 14th-century friar, and legend says it was completed by an angel. Also of note are frescoes by Andrea del Castagno in the first two chapels on the left of the church, a fresco by Perugino in the fifth chapel, and the frescoes in Michelozzo's atrium, particularly the *Nascita della Vergine* (Birth of the Virgin) by Andrea del Sarto and the *Visitazione* (Visitation) by Jacopo Pontormo. The Mannerist Il Rosso Fiorentino (the Redhead from Florence) is also an important contributor to the frescoes. Above the main entrance to the church is a mosaic lunette of the Annunciation by Davide Ghirlandaio, Domenico's little brother. Within the church's official opening hours, you'll need to time it just right in order to squeeze yourself in between each morning's seven masses.

The **Spedale degli Innocenti** (Hospital of the Innocents, Map pp80–1) was founded on the southeastern side of the piazza in 1421 as Europe's first orphanage, hence the 'innocents' in its name.

Brunelleschi designed the portico, which Andrea della Robbia decorated with terracotta medallions of babies in swaddling clothes. At the north end of the portico, the false door surrounded by railings was once a revolving door where unwanted children were left. A good number of people in Florence with surnames such as degli Innocenti, Innocenti and Nocentini can trace their family tree only as far back as the orphanage. Undoubtedly, life inside was hard, but the Spedale's avowed aim was to care for and educate its wards until they turned 18.

A small **gallery** (055 249 17 08; Piazza della Santissima Annunziata 12; admission €2.60; 8.30am-2pm Thu-Tue) on the 2nd floor features works by Florentine artists. The most striking piece is Domenico Ghirlandaio's *Adorazione dei Magi* (1488) at the right end of the hall.

MUSEO ARCHEOLOGICO

About 200m southeast of the piazza is the **Museo Archeologico** (Map pp80–1; 055 23 57 50; Via della Colonna 38; admission €4; 2-7pm Mon, 8.30am-7pm Tue & Thu, 8.30am-2pm Wed & Fri-Sun). Its rich collection of finds, including most of the Medici hoard of antiquities, plunges you deep into the past and offers an alternative to all that Renaissance splendour.

On the 1st floor you can either head left into the ancient Egyptian collection or right for the smaller section on Etruscan and Greco-Roman art.

The former is an extensive, though not well-labelled, collection of stelae inscribed with hieroglyphics, sculptures, painted wooden sarcophagi, and an array of remarkably preserved everyday objects such as textiles and baskets.

The first two rooms of the Etruscan section hold funeral urns. Particularly noteworthy is the marble *Sarcofago delle Amazzoni* (Amazons' Sarcophagus) from Tarquinia. Moving on, you enter a gallery lined with cabinets positively stuffed with bronze statuettes and miniatures, dwarfed by the outstanding, growling 5th-century-BC bronze *Chimera*, lionlike with a supplementary goat and snake head. Found in Arezzo, it's one of the best-known images of Etruscan art

Less allegorical and more literal, yet almost as compelling, is the life-size *Arringatore* (Orator). Dating from the 1st century BC, the figure, draped in a toga, illustrates the extent of Roman influence by this time.

From here you enter an enclosed corridor with displays of ancient jewellery.

The 2nd floor is rich in Greek sculpture and ceramics, and Greek and Roman bronzes. Pause awhile to outstare the magnificent snorting *Medicci Riccardi* stallion's head in Room 1.

Santa Croce Area
PIAZZA DI SANTA CROCE
The Franciscan stands haughty watch over the piazza of the same name, today lined with restaurants and souvenir shops. The square was initially cleared in the Middle Ages, primarily to allow hordes of the faithful to gather when the church itself was full. In Savonarola's day, heretics were executed here.

Such an open space inevitably found other uses, and from the 14th century it was often the colourful scene of jousts, festivals and *calcio storico* matches. This last was like a combination of football and rugby with no rules. Look for the marble stone embedded in the wall below the gaily frescoed façade of **Palazzo dell'Antella** (Map pp82–3), on the south side of the piazza; it marks the halfway line on this, one of the oldest football pitches in the world.

Curiously enough, the Romans used to have fun in much the same area centuries before. The city's 2nd-century amphitheatre took up the area facing the western end of Piazza di Santa Croce. To this day, Piazza de' Peruzzi, Via Bentaccordi and Via Torta mark the oval outline of the north, west and south sides of its course.

BASILICA DI SANTA CROCE
Attributed to Arnolfo di Cambio, **Santa Croce** (Map pp82-3; ☎ 055 246 61 05; admission incl Museo dell'Opera €4; 🕙 9.30am-5.30pm Mon-Sat, 1-5.30pm Sun) was built between 1294 and 1385. The name stems from a splinter of the Holy Cross donated to the Franciscans by King Louis of France in 1258. Today the church is known as much for the celebrities buried here as for its artistic treasures.

The magnificent façade is actually a 19th-century neogothic addition, as indeed is the bell tower. Like the contemporary job done on the Duomo, it's enlivened by the varying shades of coloured marble. A statue of Dante stands to the left of the main entrance.

The church's massive, austere interior is divided into a nave and two aisles by solid octagonal pillars. The ceiling is a fine example of the timber, A-frame style used occasionally in Italy's Gothic churches.

The floor is paved with the tombstones of famous Florentines of the past 500 years, while monuments to the particularly notable were added along the walls from the mid-16th century.

Michelangelo's tomb, designed by Vasari (1570), is along the southern wall between the first and second altars. The three muses below it represent his three principal gifts: sculpture, painting and architecture. Next along is a 19th-century cenotaph to the memory of Dante (whose remains, in fact, are in Ravenna) and, in the same aisle, a monument to Machiavelli.

Beyond the next altar is an extraordinary piece of sculpture of the *Annunciazione* (1430–35) by Donatello. The striking tabernacle, in *pietra serena,* is brightened with a gilded bas-relief. Between the sixth and seventh altars, a doorway leads into the cloister and Brunelleschi's Cappella de' Pazzi.

Continuing, pass the tomb of Giacchino Rossini, then turn right as you approach the transept to enter the **Cappella Castellani** (1385), painted with delightful frescoes by Agnolo Gaddi depicting the life of St Nicholas (later transformed into 'Santa Claus'). Taddeo Gaddi, Agnolo's father, painted the frescoes illustrating the life of the Virgin in the adjacent **Cappella Baroncelli** (1332–38), while Agnolo Gaddi was responsible for the frescoes above the altar. Next, a doorway designed by Michelozzo leads into a corridor off which is the **Sagrestia**, an enchanting 14th-century room dominated on the left by Taddeo Gaddi's fresco of the *Crocifissione*. There are also a few relics of St Francis on show, including his cowl and belt.

Through the next room, which now serves as a bookshop, you can visit the **Scuola del Cuoio** (p112 and p127), a leather school and shop, where you can see the goods being fashioned and also buy the finished products. At the end of the corridor is a Medici chapel with a fine two-tone altarpiece in glazed terracotta by Andrea della Robbia.

Back in the church, the transept is lined by five chapels on either side of the **Cappella Maggiore**. The two chapels nearest the right side of the Cappella Maggiore are decorated with fragmentary frescoes by Giotto; the best preserved, in the **Capella Bardi**, depict scenes from the life of St Francis (1315–20). A second Capella Bardi on the far left houses a wooden Crucifixion (1412) by Donatello. According to Vasari, ever one to gossip, Brunelleschi complained that Donatello's figure of Christ, complete with movable arms, looked like a peasant, so he created his own Crucifixion, housed in Santa Maria Novella, to show the right way to do it.

Returning to the entrance, the first tomb in the left aisle is Galileo Galilei's (1737), featuring a bust of the great scientist holding a telescope and gazing skywards.

Cloisters & Cappella de' Pazzi

Brunelleschi designed the serene **cloisters** just before his death in 1446. His **Cappella de' Pazzi**, at the end of the first cloister, with its harmonious lines and restrained terracotta medallions of the Apostles by Luca della Robbia, is a masterpiece of Renaissance architecture. It was built for, but never used by, the wealthy banking family destroyed in the Pazzi Conspiracy – when papal sympathisers sought to overthrow Lorenzo il Magnifico and the Medici dynasty.

The **Museo dell'Opera di Santa Croce** (Map pp82-3; admission incl Basilica €4; ☺ 9am-7.30pm Mon-Sat, 9am-1.40pm Sun), in the first cloister, features a Crucifixion by Cimabue, restored to the best degree possible after it was severely damaged during the disastrous 1966 flood, when more than 4m of water inundated the Santa Croce area. Other highlights include Donatello's gilded bronze statue *St Louis of Toulouse* (1424), originally placed in a tabernacle on the Orsanmichele façade, a wonderful terracotta bust of St Francis receiving the stigmata by the della Robbia workshop, and frescoes by Giotto, including an *Ultima Cena* (Last Supper; 1333).

MUSEO HORNE

Herbert Percy Horne was one of those eccentric Brits living abroad with cash. He bought this building in the early 1900s and installed his eclectic collection of 14th- and 15th-century Italian paintings, sculptures, ceramics, furniture and other oddments, creating this **museum** (Map pp82-3; ☎ 055 24 46 61; Via de' Benci 6; admission €5; ☺ 9am-1pm Mon-Sat). Horne renovated the house in an effort to re-create a Renaissance ambience. There are a few works by masters such as Giotto, Filippo Lippi and Lorenzetti, though most are by minor artists. Perhaps more interesting than many of the paintings is the furniture, some of which is exquisite.

PONTE ALLE GRAZIE

The first bridge here was built in 1237 by Messer Rubaconte da Mandella, a Milanese *podestà*. It was swept away in 1333 and chapels were built on its replacement. The bridge was called after one of them, the Madonna alle Grazie. The Germans blew up the bridge in 1944, and the present version went up in 1957.

CASA BUONARROTI

Two blocks north of Santa Croce is **Casa Buonarroti** (Map pp82-3; ☎ 055 24 17 52; Via Ghibellina 70; admission €6.50; ☺ 9.30am-2pm Wed-Mon), which Michelangelo owned but never actually lived in. Upon his death, the house passed to his nephew, and eventually became a museum in the 1850s.

Although not uninteresting, the collections are a bit disappointing, given the entry cost. To the right of the ticket window is a small archaeological display of items collected by the Buonarroti family, including some interesting Etruscan pieces. Beyond this room are some paintings done in imitation of Michelangelo's style, plus glazed terracotta pieces by the della Robbia family.

Upstairs, there's a detailed model of Michelangelo's design for the façade of the Basilica di San Lorenzo – as close as the church ever came to getting its façade. Also by Michelangelo are a couple of marble bas-reliefs and a crucifix. Of the reliefs, *Madonna della Scala* (Madonna of the Steps; c 1490) is thought to be his earliest work.

Otherwise, a series of rooms designed by Michelangelo Il Giovane, the genius' great-nephew, are intriguing. The first is full of paintings and frescoes by others that together amount to a kind of apotheosis of the great man.

PIAZZA SANT'AMBROGIO & AROUND

From Casa Buonarroti, turn northwards up Via Michelangelo Buonarroti and continue o Piazza dei Ciompi, these days the venue or a busy flea market (see p128).

The **Loggia del Pesce** (Fish Market; Map pp82-3; ia Pietrapiana) was designed by Vasari for the Mercato Vecchio (Old Market), which was t the heart of what is now Piazza della Repubblica. The loggia was moved to the Convento di San Marco when the Mercato Vecchio and the surrounding area were cleared in the 19th century, and finally re-rected here in 1955.

A block east, the plain **Chiesa di Sant'Am-brogio** (Map pp82-3; Via Pietrapiana) presents an inconspicuous 18th-century façade on the quare of the same name. The first church here was raised in the 10th century, but what you see inside is a mix of 13th-century Gothic and 15th-century refurbishment. The name comes from Sant'Ambrogio (St Ambrose), the powerful 4th-century arch-bishop of Milan, who stayed in an earlier convent on this site when he visited Flor-ence. The church is the last resting place of several artists, including Mino da Fiesole and Verrocchio.

Nearby is the local produce market, the **Mercato di Sant'Ambrogio** (Piazza Ghiberti).

Just north of Piazza Sant'Ambrogio is the **Sinagoga** (Synagogue; Map pp82-3; ☎ 055 234 66 54; Via Farini 6; admission €4; ☑ 10am-6pm Sun-Thu Jun-Aug, o 3pm Apr-May & Sep-Oct, to 2pm Nov-Mar, 10am-2pm Fri ear-round), a fanciful structure with Moorish and neo-Byzantine elements. In the **Museo Ebraico** you can see Jewish ceremonial ob-ects and richly embroidered vestments. A memorial in the garden lists the names of Florentine Jews who died in Nazi concen-tration camps.

Oltrarno
Literally 'Beyond the Arno', the Oltrarno takes in all of Florence south of the river.

PONTE VECCHIO
The first documentation of a stone bridge here, at the narrowest crossing point along the entire length of the Arno, dates from 972. The Arno looks placid enough, but when it gets mean, it gets very mean. Floods in 1177 and 1333 destroyed the bridge, and in 1966 it came close to being destroyed again. Many of the jewellers with shops on the bridge were convinced the floodwaters would sweep away their livelihoods, but this time the bridge held.

They're still here. Indeed, the bridge has twinkled with the glittering wares of jewellers, their trade often passed down from generation to generation, ever since the 16th century, when Ferdinando I de' Medici ordered them here to replace the often malodorous presence of the town butchers, who used to toss unwanted left-overs into the river.

The bridge as it stands was built in 1345 and was the only one saved from destruction by the retreating Germans in 1944; some say on Hitler's express orders, others that the German commander disobeyed those very orders (yet still wreaked havoc by razing the medieval quarters at either end).

At the southern end of the bridge is the medieval **Torre dei Mannelli** (Map pp82–3), which looks rather odd as the Corridoio Vasariano was built around it, not simply straight through it as the Medici would have preferred. Across Via de' Bardi as your eye follows the Corridoio, you can glimpse the **Torre degli Ubriachi** (Map pp82–3), the Drunks' Tower.

CHIESA DI SANTA FELICITÀ
The most captivating thing about the façade of this 18th-century remake of what had been Florence's oldest (4th-century) **church** (Map pp82-3; Piazza Santa Felicità; ☑ 9.30am-12.30pm & 3-6pm Mon-Sat, 9.30am-12.30pm Sun) is the fact that the Corridoio Vasariano passes right across it; the Medicis could stop by and hear Mass without being seen.

Inside, the main interest is in Brunelleschi's small **Cappella Barbadori**, on the right as you enter. Here Jacopo Pontormo (1494–1557) left his mark with a fresco of the *Annuncia-tion* and a *Deposizione*, depicting the taking down of Christ from the Cross in disturb-ingly surreal colours.

PALAZZO PITTI
The wealthy banker Luca Pitti commis-sioned Brunelleschi to build this enormous, forbidding-looking palace in 1457, but by the time it was completed, the family for-tunes were already on the wane, and they were later forced to sell the place to their great rivals, the Medici.

The original nucleus of the **palace** (Map pp82-3; ☎ 055 238 86 14; Piazza de' Pitti) took up the space encompassing the seven sets of win-dows on the second and third storeys.

In 1549 Eleonora de Toledo, wife of Cosimo I de' Medici, acquired the palace from the by then impoverished Pitti family. She launched the extension work, which continued for centuries, and through all that time the original design was respected – today you would be hard-pressed to distinguish the various phases of construction.

After the demise of the Medici dynasty, the palace remained the residence of the city's rulers, the dukes of Lorraine and their Austrian and (briefly) Napoleonic successors.

When Florence was made capital of the nascent Kingdom of Italy in 1865, it became a residence of the Savoy royal family, who presented it to the state in 1919.

Museums

Combined entry to the palace and all galleries and museums costs €10.50 (€7.75 after 4pm) or you can pick and choose; we quote below individual prices for each of the palace's five museums, of which the Galleria Palatina is by far the most significant.

The **Galleria Palatina** (admission €6.50; ☼ 8.15am-6.50pm Tue-Sun) displays paintings from the 16th to 18th centuries, collected mostly by the Medicis and their grand ducal successors and hung in lavishly decorated rooms.

After buying your ticket (which includes entry to the Royal Apartments), you head up a grand staircase to the gallery floor. The first rooms you pass through are a seemingly haphazard mix of paintings and period furniture.

Beyond the resplendent **Sala Bianca** (White Room), with its ornate 18th-century stucco ceiling and crystal chandeliers, are the **Royal Apartments**, a series of rather sickeningly furnished and decorated rooms, where the Medici and their successors lived, slept and received their guests. The style and division of tasks assigned to each room is reminiscent of Spanish royal palaces, all heavily bedecked with drapes, silk and chandeliers. Each room has a colour theme, ranging from aqua green to deep wine red.

The gallery proper starts after the **Sala della Musica** (Music Room). The paintings hanging in the succeeding rooms – all decorated with stunning ceiling frescoes of mythological scenes – are not in any particular order. Among Tuscan masters, you can see work by Filippo Lippi, Botticelli, Vasari and Andrea del Sarto.

The collection also boasts some important works by other Italian and foreign painters. Foremost among them are those by Raphael, whose *Madonna della Seggiola* (Madonna of the Chair; 1515) is particularly intriguing. Caravaggio's *Amore Dormente* (Sleeping Cupid; 1608), Guido Reni's grinning *Bacco Fanciullo* (Young Bacchus; 1620), Guercino's dramatic *San Sebastian* and Tintoretto's *Deposizione* (Deposition) are just a few of the many highlights. Other artists represented include Titian, Veronese, Velasquez, Rubens and Van Dyck. Among the lesser-known works, Dosso Dossi's *Ninfa e Satiro*, featuring a grotesque satyr snarling at a nervous-looking nymph, Lorenzo Lippi's gruesome portrait of *Santa Agata*, and Orazio Rimnaldi's *Amore Artifice* (False Cupid) are worth seeking out.

The palace's other galleries and museums are worth a look if you have plenty of time. The **Galleria d'Arte Moderna** and **Galleria del Costume** (admission €5; ☼ 8.15am-1.50pm Tue-Sat & alternating Sun & Mon) have common opening hours and tariffs. The Modern Art Gallery covers mostly Tuscan works from the 18th to the mid-20th century, while the Costume Gallery has high-fashion apparel from the 18th and 19th centuries.

Giardino di Boboli

Relax in the palace's Renaissance **Boboli Gardens** (Map p85; admission €4; ☼ 8.15am-7.30pm Jun-Aug, 8.15am-6.30pm Mar-May & Sep-Oct, 8.15am-4.30pm Nov-Feb), laid out in the mid-16th century and based on a design by the architect known as Il Tribolo. Within them, the **Grotta del Buontalenti** (Map pp82–3) is a fanciful artificial grotto, designed by the eponymous artist. Within its recesses a fleshy *Venere* (Venus) by Giambologna rises from the waves.

The **Museo degli Argenti** (Silver Museum), entered from the garden courtyard, has a collection of often bizarre and kitsch glassware, silver and jewellery. You may feel that the droll trompe l'oeil frescoes that cover the walls and ceilings are the main attraction. Those in what was once the public audience chamber are particularly fine, displaying high terraces populated with a miscellany of people and animals, including a boy playing with a monkey and an elderly man adjusting his spectacles.

At the upper, southern limit of the gardens, offering great views over the palace complex and Florentine countryside, is the **Museo delle Porcellane** (Porcelain Museum; Map pp82–3). It displays some of the fine porcelain collected by the tenants of Palazzo Pitti. The exhibits include some exquisite Sèvres, Vincennes, Meissen and Wedgewood pieces, including a ceramic portrait of Napoleon, produced by the Sèvres factory.

A combined ticket (€4) gives admission to the gardens and the two museums (which have the same hours as the gardens).

At the top of the hill are the rambling fortifications of the **Forte di Belvedere** (p109), built by Grand Duke Ferdinando I towards the end of the 16th century to protect the Palazzo Pitti. It was closed for renovations when we last visited.

CHIESA DI SAN FELICE

This unprepossessing **church** (Map p85; Piazza San Felice; ☽ 8-11am Mon-Sat) has been made over several times since the Romanesque original was constructed in 1066. Its simple Renaissance façade was designed by Michelozzo, and there's an early-14th-century crucifix by Giotto's workshop inside.

At No 8 on this square is **Casa Guidi** (Map p85; Piazza San Felice), where Robert and Elizabeth Browning once lived.

MUSEO ZOOLOGICO LA SPECOLA

Further down Via Romana from Piazza San Felice, this rather fusty **zoological museum** (Map p85; ☎ 055 228 82 51; Via Romana 17; admission €4; ☽ 9am-1pm Thu-Tue) offers for your delectation, the stuffed-animal collection apart, a collection of wax models of bits of human anatomy in varying states of bad health. An offbeat change from all that art and history!

PORTA ROMANA

Rome-bound pilgrims headed down Via Romana as they left Florence behind them. At the end of the street is the **Porta Romana** (Map p85), an imposing city gate that was part of the outer circle of city walls knocked down in the 19th century. A strip of the wall still stretches north from the gate. If you follow the inside of this wall (the area is now a car park), you soon come across an entrance that allows you to get to the top of the gate.

VIA MAGGIO

In the 16th century this was a rather posh address, as the line-up of fine Renaissance

mansions duly attests. **Palazzo di Bianca Cappello** (Map pp82–3), at No 26, has the most eye-catching façade as it is covered in graffiti designs. It's named after Bianca Cappello, Francesco I de' Medici's lover, who eventually became his wife. Across the street, a series of mansions, more or less following the same Renaissance style, include **Palazzo Ricasoli-Firidolfi** (Map pp82–3) at No 7, **Palazzo Martellini** (Map pp82–3) at No 9, **Palazzo Michelozzi** (Map pp82–3) at No 11, **Palazzo Martelli** (Map pp82–3) at No 13 and **Palazzo di Cosimo Ridolfi** (Map pp82–3) at No 15. All were built and fiddled around with over the 14th, 15th and 16th centuries. Over the road, take a glance too at the squarely imposing **Palazzo Corsini-Suarez** (Map p85) at No 42.

PIAZZA SANTO SPIRITO

From Via Maggio you can turn into Via de' Michelozzi to reach the lively Piazza Santo Spirito. At its northern end, the square is fronted by the flaking façade of the **Basilica di Santo Spirito** (Map p85; ☽ 10am-noon & 4-5.30pm Mon-Sat, 11.30-noon Sun, closed Wed afternoon), one of Brunelleschi's last commissions. Inside, the entire length of the church is lined by a series of semicircular chapels, and the colonnade of grey *pietra forte* Corinthian columns lends an air of severe monumental grandeur.

One of the most noteworthy works of art is Filippino Lippi's *Madonna con il Bambino e Santi* (Madonna with Child and Saints) in the Cappella Nerli in the right transept. Other highlights include Domenico di Zanobi's *Madonna del Soccorso* (Madonna of the Relief; 1485), in the Cappella Velutti, in which the Madonna wards off a little red devil with a club, and Giovanni Baratta's marble and stucco *L'Arcangelo Raffaele e Tobiolo* (The Archangel Raphael and Tobias; 1698), which illustrates an episode from the Apocrypha. The main altar, beneath the central dome, is a voluptuous baroque flourish, rather out of place in the spare setting of Brunelleschi's church. In the sacristy is a poignantly tender wooden crucifix (it's not often you see Christ with a penis) attributed to Michelangelo.

Next door to the church is the refectory, **Cenacolo di Santo Spirito** (Map p85; admission €2.20; ☽ 9am-2pm Tue-Sun Apr-Nov, 10.30am-1.30pm Tue-Sun Dec-Mar). Andrea Orcagna decorated the refectory with a grand fresco depicting the Last Supper and the Crucifixion (c 1370). Also on display is the sculpture collection bequeathed to the city in 1946 by the Neapolitan collector Salvatore Romano. Among its most intriguing pieces are rare pre-Romanesque sculptures and works by Jacopo della Quercia and Donatello.

BASILICA DI SANTA MARIA DEL CARMINE

West of Piazza Santo Spirito, Piazza del Carmine is an old square used as a car park. On its southern flank is the 13th-century **Basilica di Santa Maria del Carmine**, which was all but destroyed by fire in the late 18th century. Fortunately the fire spared the magnificent frescoes in its **Cappella Brancacci** (Map p85; ☎ 055 276 82 24; admission €4; ⏰ 10am-5pm Wed-Sat & Mon, 1-5pm Sun), entered via the cloister to the right of the church. A maximum of 30 visitors are allowed into the chapel at a time. Such is the chapel's popularity that you have to reserve in advance.

This chapel is a treasure of paintings by Masolino da Panicale, Masaccio and Filippino Lippi. Masaccio's fresco cycle, illustrating the life of St Peter, is considered among his greatest works, representing a definitive break with Gothic art and a plunge into new worlds of expression in the early stages of the Renaissance. The *Cacciata dei Progenitori* (Expulsion of Adam and Eve), on the left side of the chapel, is his best-known work. His depiction of Eve's anguish in particular lends the image a human touch hitherto little seen in European painting. Masaccio painted these frescoes in his early 20s, taking over from Masolino, and interrupted the task to go to Rome, where he died, aged only 28. The cycle was completed some 60 years later by Filippino Lippi. Masaccio himself features in his *St Peter Enthroned;* he's the one standing beside the Apostle, staring out at the viewer. The figures around him have been identified as Brunelleschi, Masolino and Alberti. Filippino Lippi also painted himself into the scene of *St Peter's Crucifixion,* along with his teacher, Botticelli.

BORGO SAN FREDIANO

Heading northwards from Piazza del Carmine, you reach Borgo San Frediano. The street and surrounding area retain something of their traditional feel – that of a working-class quarter where artisans have been beavering away for centuries.

At the western end of the street stands the lonely **Porta San Frediano** (Map p85), another of the old city gates left in place when the walls were demolished in the 19th century. Before you reach the gate, you'll notice the unpolished feel of the area neatly reflected in the unadorned brick walls of **Chiesa di San Frediano in Cestello** (Map p85; ⏰ 9-11.30am & 5-6pm Mon-Fri, 5-6pm Sun), its incomplete façade hiding a restrained baroque interior.

BACK TO PONTE VECCHIO

From the front of Chiesa di San Frediano in Cestello, you can follow the river bank as far as Ponte Santa Trinità along Borgo San Jacopo. Along the way you pass several grand family mansions, including the **Palazzo Frescobaldi** (Map pp82–3) on the square of the same name. Two 12th-century towers, the **Torre dei Marsili** and **Torre de' Belfredelli**, still keep watch over the area.

PONTE VECCHIO TO PORTA SAN NICCOLÒ

Continuing east away from Ponte Vecchio, the first stretch of Via de' Bardi shows clear signs of its recent history. This entire area was flattened by German mines in 1944 and hastily rebuilt in questionable taste after the war.

The street spills into Piazza di Santa Maria Soprarno, which takes its name from a church that has long ceased to exist. Follow the narrow Via de' Bardi (the right fork) away from the square and you enter a pleasantly quieter corner of Florence. The powerful Bardi family once owned all the houses along this street, but by the time Cosimo de' Medici married Contessina de' Bardi in 1415, the latter's family was well on the decline.

Via de' Bardi expires in Piazza de' Mozzi, which is also surrounded by the sturdy façades of grand residences belonging to the high and mighty. No 2, at the southern flank of the piazza, is occupied by the **Palazzo dei Mozzi** (Map pp82–3), where Pope Gregory X stayed when brokering peace between the Guelphs and Ghibellines. The western side of the piazza is lined by the 15th-century **Palazzo Lensi-Nencioni, Palazzo Torrigiani-Nasi** (Map pp82–3), with the graffiti ornamentation, and **Palazzo Torrigiani** (Map pp82–3).

Next, turn east down Via dei Renai, past the leafy Piazza Nicola Demidoff, dedicated to the 19th-century Russian philanthropist who lived nearby in Via San Niccolò.

The 16th-century **Palazzo Serristori** (Map pp82–3), at the end of Via dei Renai, was home to Joseph Bonaparte in the last years of his life until his death in 1844; a humble end to the man who, at the height of his career, had been appointed king of Spain by his brother Napoleon.

Turn right and you end up on Via San Niccolò. The bland-looking **Chiesa di San Niccolò Oltrarno** (Map pp82–3) is interesting if for nothing else than the little plaque indicating how high the 1966 flood waters reached – about 4m. If you head east along Via San Niccolò, you emerge at the tower marking the **Porta San Niccolò** (Map pp82–3), all that is left of the city walls hereabouts.

To get an idea of what the walls were once like, walk south from Chiesa di San Niccolò Oltrarno through **Porta San Miniato** (Map pp82–3). The wall extends a short way to the east and for a stretch further west, up a steep hill that leads you to the Forte di Belvedere.

FORTE DI BELVEDERE
Bernardo Buontalenti helped design this rambling **fort** (Map pp82-3; admission free; 9am-dusk) for Grand Duke Ferdinando I towards the end of the 16th century. From this massive bulwark soldiers could keep watch on four fronts, and indeed it was designed with internal security in mind, to protect the Palazzo Pitti, as much as foreign attack. The views are excellent.

The main entrance is near **Porta San Giorgio** (Map pp82–3). You can approach from the east following the walls, or by taking Costa di San Giorgio, up from near Ponte Vecchio. The most usual entry point is via Boboli Gardens. The fort was closed – yet again – for renovations when we last visited.

PIAZZALE MICHELANGELO
The breathtaking panorama from this vast **esplanade** (Map pp78–9) is marred only by the cheap souvenir stalls at your back. It's best approached by a steep 10-minute walk up the wiggly road, paths and steps that climb from the riverside and Piazza Giuseppe Poggi.

An easier but less-rewarding alternative is to hop aboard bus No 13, which sets out from Stazione di Santa Maria Novella, crosses Ponte alle Grazie and passes by the piazzale.

CHIESA DI SAN MINIATO AL MONTE
The real point of your exertions is no more than five minutes further uphill, at this wonderful **Romanesque church** (Map pp78-9; off Viale Galileo Galilei; 8am-7.30pm May-Oct, 8am-noon & 3-6pm Nov-Apr). The church is dedicated to St Minius (San Miniato), an early Christian martyr in Florence who is said to have flown to this spot after his death down in the town (or, if you care to believe an alternative version, to have walked up the hill with his head tucked underneath his arm).

The church was started in the early 11th century. Its typically Tuscan multicoloured marble façade, featuring a mosaic depicting Christ between the Virgin and St Minius, was tacked on a couple of centuries later.

Inside are 13th- to 15th-century frescoes on the south wall, and intricate inlaid marble designs all down the length of the nave, leading to a fine Romanesque crypt. The raised choir and presbytery have an intricate marble pulpit and screen, rich in intricate geometrical designs. The **sacristy**, in the southeast corner, features marvellously bright frescoes depicting the life of St Benedict. The four figures in its cross vault represent the Evangelists.

Slap bang in the middle of the nave is the bijou **Capella del Crocefisso**, to which Michelozzo, Agnolo Gaddi and Luca della Robbia all contributed.

The **Cappella del Cardinale del Portogallo**, beside the north aisle, features a tomb by Antonio Rossellino and a tabernacle ceiling decorated in terracotta by della Robbia.

Come around 4.30pm (in winter) or 5.30pm (in summer) and you can hear the monks' Gregorian chant wafting up from the crypt.

Bus No 13 stops nearby.

North of the Old City
FORTEZZA DA BASSO
This huge defensive **fortress** (Map pp80–1) was built in 1534 on the orders of Alessandro de' Medici. It was a statement of Medici power, aimed at overawing the potentially rebellious Florentines, rather than a defence against invasion. Nowadays it is sometimes used for exhibitions and cultural events.

CHIESA RUSSA ORTODOSSA
A couple of blocks east of Fortezza da Basso, the onion-shaped domes on this Russian

Orthodox **church** (Map pp80–1) are a bit of a giveaway. Built in 1902 for the resident Russian populace, it was designed in the northern-Russian style, with two interior levels decorated in part by Florentine artists but mostly by Russians who were expert in iconography.

MUSEO STIBBERT

Frederick Stibbert was one of the grand wheeler-dealers on the European antiquities market in the 19th century and, unsurprisingly, amassed quite a personal collection. He bought the Villa di Montughi with the intention of creating a **museum** (Map pp78-9; ☎ 055 47 55 20; Via Stibbert 26; adult/child €5/2; ⊙ 10am-2pm Mon-Wed, 10am-6pm Fri-Sun) that would reflect the various countries and periods covered by his collections. The result makes for an intriguing mix.

In the **Sala della Cavalcata** (Parade Room), for example, there are life-sized figures of horses and their riders in all manner of suits of armour from Europe and the Middle East. The exhibits also include clothes, furnishings, tapestries and paintings from the 16th to the 19th centuries.

You can join in on one of the tours (included in the admission price) led by actors portraying either Giovanni delle Bande Nere or the Ottoman sultan Suleiman the Magnificent. One-hour tours for children take place on Saturday or Sunday; if you want English commentary, reserve in advance.

The museum is north of the Fortezza da Basso. Bus No 4 from Stazione di Santa Maria Novella takes you as close as Via Vittorio

---

DO THE DECENT THING

Around central Florence, you'll see large enamel signs bearing the following admonishment in English.

It is forbidden to:

- Lie down, camp or behave in an indecent way

- Leave dogs unleashed or leave dogs droppings uncollected
(*Articles 55 & 117 of the Municipal Police Regulations refer*)

Don't say we didn't warn you…

Emanuele II, from where you have a fairly short walk.

South of the Old City
BELLOSGUARDO

The hill of Bellosguardo (Beautiful View), southwest of the city centre, was a favourite spot for 19th-century landscape painters. A narrow, winding road leads up past a couple of villas from Piazza Torquato Tasso to Piazza Bellosguardo. You can't see anything from here, but if you wander along Via Roti Michelozzi into the grounds of the Albergo Torre di Bellosguardo (p119), you'll see what the fuss was about. The hotel is the latest guise of what was once a 14th-century castle.

CERTOSA DI GALLUZZO

From the Porta Romana at the southern tip of the Oltrarno area, follow Via Senese south about 3km to the village of Galluzzo and its remarkable 14th-century monastery, the **Certosa del Galluzzo** (Map pp78-9; ☎ 055 204 92 26; ⊙ 9am-noon & 3-6pm Tue-Sun Apr-Sep, to 5pm Oct-Mar). Its great cloister is decorated with busts from the della Robbia workshop, and there are frescoes by Pontormo in the Gothic hall of Palazzo degli Studi.

The Certosa can only be visited in a guided group (in Italian). Take bus No 37 from Stazione di Santa Maria Novella.

ACTIVITIES

On those torrid Florentine days in summer when they pull back the movable roof over the Olympic-size pool, **Piscina Bellariva** (Map pp78-9; ☎ 055 67 75 21; Lungarno Aldo Moro 6; adult/child €6.50/4.50, carnet of 10 tickets €50; ⊙ 10am-6pm daily & 8.30pm-11.30pm Tue & Thu Jun-Aug) is a watery haven. Bus No 14 from Piazza dell'Unità and the Duomo passes nearby.

Piscina Le Pavoniere (Map pp78-9; ☎ 055 36 23 33; Viale della Catena 2; adult/child €7.50/4.50; ⊙ 10am-6pm & 8pm-2am Jun–mid-Sep) has a pizzeria and bar. Save that swim for the evening session when admission is free.

From mid-September to June, opening times are considerably more restricted in both pools, so do call ahead for those of the moment.

WALKING TOUR

Florence is best discovered on foot, and this route introduces you to many of the city's brightest highlights.

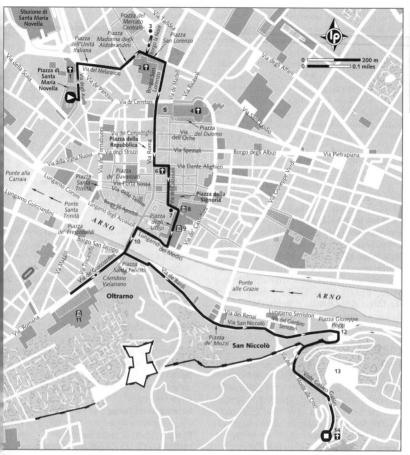

Begin in Piazza di Santa Maria Novella, overlooked by its grand gothic **Basilica di Santa Maria Novella** (**1**; p97). Then take Via degli Avelli north, as far as the busy Piazza dell'Unità Italiana, and continue east on Via del Melarancio, past Piazza Madonna degli Aldobrandini, and on to Piazza San Lorenzo, with its market stalls and Renaissance **Basilica di San Lorenzo** (**2**; p99). From here, slip in a quick detour northwards up Borgo La Noce to enjoy the contemporary bustle of the **Mercato Centrale** (**3**; p100), Florence's premier produce market. Back at the Basilica, walk south along Borgo San Lorenzo until you see the breathtaking **Duomo** (**4**; p87) and **baptistry** (**5**; p89). Take a spin around Piazza del Duomo, then walk southwards along Via Roma, on

WALK FACTS

Distance 5.25km
Duration Two to three hours

into Piazza della Repubblica, an ideal spot for a coffee. Just beyond the square, turn left (east) into Via Orsanmichele, where you'll find the **Chiesa di Orsanmichele** (**6**; p91) with its ornate statuary.

Turn right to follow Via de' Calzaiuoli southwards as far as Piazza della Signoria with its **Loggia della Signoria** (**7**; p94) and the commanding presence of the **Palazzo Vecchio** (**8**; p92), home of Florentine government since the Middle Ages. South just a few steps is the **Uffizi Gallery** (**9**; p94), housing one of the world's most precious collections of primarily Renaissance art. Piazza degli Uffizi leads on to the River Arno.

To the west you will see the **Ponte Vecchio** (**10**; p105), lined with glittering jewellery shops. Cross this bridge, which offers wonderful views up and down stream, and you will be in the Oltrarno district. Continue south along Via de' Guicciardini as far as the brooding hulk of **Palazzo Pitti** (**11**; p105), one-time seat of the Medici dynasty.

Returning to the river and Ponte Vecchio, head upstream along altogether quieter Via de' Bardi as far as Piazza de' Mozzi, surrounded by grand residences, and continue along Via de San Niccolò as far as **Porta San Niccolò** (**12**; p109), one of Florence's few surviving city gates. Behind the gate, a steep, winding footpath leads up to **Piazzale Michelangelo** (**13**; p109) with its breathtaking panorama over the city. From here, barely five minutes more of sturdy uphill work along Viale Galileo Galilei brings you to the **Chiesa di San Miniato al Monte** (**14**; p109), a Romanesque jewel and fitting end to your exertions.

COURSES

Florence has more than 30 schools offering courses in Italian language and culture. Numerous other schools offer courses in art, including painting, drawing, sculpture and art history, and several offer cookery classes. Many will organise accommodation for students on request, either in private apartments or with Italian families.

While Florence is one of the most attractive cities in which to study Italian language or art, it is also one of the more expensive. Many British and American students do come here, so it may not be the best choice if you want to fully immerse yourself in the language and culture.

Non-EU citizens who want to study at a university or language school in Italy must have a study visa (see p357); the school will advise you.

Language

The tourist office on Via Cavour has a list of schools running language courses, including the following well-established institutions.
British Institute of Florence (Map pp82-3; ☎ 055 267 78 200; www.britishinstitute.it; Piazza Strozzi 2) This

much-respected institution has been operating since 1917. It also offers an array of other specialist courses, covering such subjects as opera, art and literature.
Centro Lingua Italiana Calvino (CLIC; Map pp80-1; ☎ 055 28 80 81; www.clicschool.it; Viale Fratelli Rosselli 74)
Centro Lorenzo de' Medici (Map pp80-1; ☎ 055 28 73 60; www.lorenzodemedici.it; Via Faenza 43) This school is popular with American students. It runs a huge variety of supplementary courses including acting, cooking and art history.
Istituto Europeo (Map pp82-3; ☎ 055 238 10 71; www.istitutoeuropeo.it; Piazzale delle Pallottole 1)
Linguaviva (Map pp80-1; ☎ 055 29 43 59; www .linguaviva.it; Via Fiume 17)
Scuola Leonardo da Vinci (Map pp82-3; ☎ 055 26 11 81; www.scuolaleonardo.com; Via Bufalini 3)

Other Courses

Many of the above language schools also offer supplementary courses in areas such as painting, art history, cooking, fashion and music. Some schools specialise in such activities.

Art courses range from one-month workshops to longer-term professional diploma courses. The following are well-regarded places.
Accademia Italiana (Map pp82-3; ☎ 055 28 46 16; www.accademiaitaliana.com; Piazza de' Pitti 15) Offers language, culture and a wide range of design programmes in Italian including graphics, textile and fashion.
Cordon Bleu (Map pp82-3; ☎ 055 234 54 68; www .cordonbleu-it.com; Via di Mezzo 55r) A good choice for gourmet cookery.
Florence Dance Center (Map p85; ☎ 055 28 92 76; www.florencedance.org in Italian; Borgo della Stella 23r) Courses in classical, jazz and modern dance.
Istituto per l'Arte e il Restauro Palazzo Spinelli (Map pp82-3; ☎ 055 24 60 01; www.spinelli.it; Borgo Santa Croce 10) Restoration (anything from paintings to ceramics), interior and graphic design, gilding and marquetry.
La Cucina del Garga (☎ 055 21 13 96; www.garga.it) Hands-on Tuscan cookery courses, from one to eight days, run by the team from Trattoria Garga (p120).
Scuola del Cuoio (Map pp82-3; ☎ 055 24 45 33; www.leatherschool.it; Piazza di Santa Croce 16) Within the Basilica di Santa Croce church, runs a wide variety of leather-working courses, lasting from half a day to a year. Also offers parchment-painting courses.

FLORENCE FOR CHILDREN

As throughout Italy, children are welcome pretty much anywhere, anytime in Florence; you'll see families with young children out in the evenings, strolling with a *gelato* or sitting in a restaurant. That said, Florence isn't the best city to bring very young children; green spaces and playgrounds are scarce and, while some of the pricier hotels can provide baby-sitters, there's no organised service for tourists.

Buy each of the younger kids a copy of *Fun in Florence* by Nancy Shroyer Howard. With do-and-find sections for major sites such as the Duomo and Uffizi courtyard, they can be happily employed while the grown-ups go round gawping at the boring bits.

Older children can get to grips with the city by delving into *Florence, Just Add Water* by Simone Frasca and *Florence: Playing with Art* by Maria Salvia Baldini.

Other books to keep them occupied include *Florence for Kids* from Edizioni Lapis, plus, for older brothers and sisters, *Florence for Teens* and *Florence: a Young Traveller's Guide*.

Younger children can join in the various activities at **Museo dei Ragazzi** (p93), at Palazzo Vecchio, while others might enjoy the weekend guided tours of **Museo Stibbert** (p110), aimed at children, or the **Museo di Storia della Scienza** (p96), where 'Galileo' will talk them through the exhibits. Some, no doubt, will relish the unsettling medical section. Reserve in advance for English commentary.

Mondobimbo (Map pp80–1; ☎ 055 553 29 46; Via Ponte Rosso; admission €5; ☻ 10am-midnight May-Sep, 10am-7pm Oct-Apr) is a well-stocked playground with everything from bouncy castles to a minirailway, aimed at kids aged from two to 10.

Ludoteca Musicale (Map pp82–3; ☎ 055 263 86 00; www.musicarte.it in Italian; Via Pandolfinoi 18; admission free; ☻ 9.30am-12.30pm Mon-Sat) offers children – and their parents – demonstrations of various musical instruments and a chance to join in some hands-on activities and dancing.

The **Giardino di Boboli** (p106) is a pleasant spot for a relaxing day out. Beside the Arno, about 1.2km west of Stazione di Santa Maria Novella, is **Le Cascine** (Map pp80–1), a massive public park with a children's playground that's popular with Florentine families. The **Piscina Bellariva** (p110) swimming pool makes for a fun day out in the steamy Florentine summer.

Lastly and most accessibly, there's a constantly turning vintage merry-go-round (carousel) right in the heart of Piazza dell Repubblica.

TOURS

Bus

CAF Tours (Map pp80–1; ☎ 055 21 06 12; www.caftours.com; Via Sant'Antonino 6r) Does coach tours of the city (€39 to €82) and also trips to the designer-clothes outlet malls (see p127).

CentralSita Viaggi (Map pp80–1; ☎ 055 21 93 83; www.sitabus.it in Italian; Via Santa Caterina da Siena 17) Runs half-day coach tours of Florence (€40) from the SITA Bus Station. It also runs day trips to destinations such as Il Chianti (€39) and Pisa (€38).

Cycling

Accidental Tourist (☎ 055 69 93 76; www.accidentaltourist.com) Does fairly gentle half-day walking (€70) and cycling (€75) tours – plus cookery classes (€80) if your interests are also gastronomic.

Bicycle Tuscany (☎ 055 22 25 80; www.bicycletuscany.com) Also does regular day tours (21km) in the Tuscan countryside (including transport, bike and equipment, lunch and winery visit €60).

Florence by Bike (Map pp80–1; ☎ 055 48 89 92; www.florencebybike.it; Via San Zanobi 120-122r) Does a day tour (32km) of the Chianti area (including bike, equipment and lunch €73.50).

I Bike Italy (☎ 055 234 23 71; www.ibikeitaly.com) Offers a 25km tour around Fiesole or a 50km circuit around Il Chianti (both €70). Both are as much gastronomic as sporty. The price includes bike and gear hire, shuttle bus and lunch.

Walking

Florence Walks & Tours (☎ 800 50 11 72; www.tours-italy.com) Does a three-hour walk (€20, Monday to Saturday). Just turn up at 9.50am outside the Louis Vuitton shop in Piazza Strozzi.

Mercurio Tours (☎ 055 21 33 55; www.mercurio-italy.org) offers a similar range of visits within and beyond the city. Reserve by phone with Mercurio Tours or in person at Amici del Turismo (Map pp80–1; Via Cavour 36r), opposite the main tourist office.

Walking Tours of Florence (Map pp82–3; ☎ 055 264 50 33; www.artviva.com; Piazza Santo Stefano 2) Organises several excellent three-hour walks of the city (€20 to €39) led by historians or art history graduates. It can also plot all sorts of specific walks to suit your personal needs and tastes – at a price – and offer half-day guided cycle tours (€40, 14km).

FESTIVALS & EVENTS

Besides the famous Carnevale in February, there are many other major festivals held in Florence.

Festa delle Rificolone (Festival of the Paper Lanterns) A procession of children carrying lanterns, accompanied by drummers, *sbandieratori* (flag-throwers), musicians and others in medieval dress, winds its way from Piazza di Santa Croce to Piazza SS Annunziata to celebrate the Virgin Mary's birthday on 7 September.

Festa di Anna Maria Medici (Feast of Anna Maria Medici) 18 February, the date of the death in 1743 of the last Medici, Anna Maria, is marked with a costumed parade from Palazzo Vecchio to her tomb in the Cappelle Medicee. Some museums are free on this day.

Festa di San Giovanni (Feast of St John) On 24 June Florence celebrates its patron saint with the almost anything goes *calcio storico* medieval football matches played on Piazza di Santa Croce, ending with a fireworks display over Piazzale Michelangelo.

Internazionale Antiquariato Every two years Florence hosts this major antiques fair, which attracts visitors from across Europe, and is usually held at Palazzo Corsini. The next fair will be in September/October 2007.

Maggio Musicale Fiorentino A major summer music festival (see p126).

Scoppio del Carro (Explosion of the Cart) A cart of fireworks is exploded in front of the cathedral at 11am on Easter Sunday.

SLEEPING

The city has hundreds of hotels in all categories and a good range of alternatives such as hostels and private rooms. Given Florence's popularity, though, rooms are constantly in demand and prices are higher than elsewhere in Tuscany.

The Consorzio ITA office (Informazione Turistiche Alberghiere; Map pp80-1; ☎ 055 28 28 93; fax 055 247 82 32; ⏰ 8.45am-9pm) at Stazione di Santa Maria Novella makes reservations for a small fee.

Tourist offices carry a list of *affittacamere* (rooms in private houses), where you can sometimes find a bedroom for about €30. Most fill with students during the school year (from October to June) but are a good option if you are staying for a week or longer.

We list high-season prices. It's prudent to book ahead at any time of year, but especially then. For those hotels that lift their rates, high season usually starts around 15 April and fizzles out by mid-October (many dip a little in the hot months of July and August). Outside high season, top-end options in particular offer very significant reductions.

If you have trouble finding a room in Florence, consider staying outside the city. Towns such as Arezzo, Prato, Pisa and Montecatini are just a short train trip away and often offer better value, while if you

have your own transport, your options ar clearly even greater.

Accommodation Associations

Such organisations can book you into thei member hotels, but rarely drop below tw stars, and some take their cut from both th client and the hotel.

Florence Promhotels (☎ 055 55 39 41, 800 86 60 22; www.promhotels.it; Viale Volta 72)

Top Quark (☎ 055 33 40 41, 800 60 88 22; www.family hotels.com; Viale Fratelli Rossi 39r)

RENTAL ACCOMMODATION

For an apartment in Florence, start lookin well before you arrive, as apartments ar difficult to come by and can be very expen sive. **Florence & Abroad** (Map pp80-1; ☎ 055 48 7 04; www.florenceandabroad.com; Via San Zanobi 58) specialises in short- and medium-term renta accommodation in Florence and the Fiesol area for those with a liberal budget.

These two bodies specialise in B&Bs, *af fittacamere* and short-stay apartments.

Associazione Bed & Breakfast Affittacamere (AB&BA ☎ 055 654 08 60; www.abbafirenze.it; Via P Mastri 26)

Gente di Toscana (☎ 0575 52 92 75; www.gentedi toscana.it; Via S Michele, Scandicci)

Camping

There are three camping options in and around Florence.

Campeggio Michelangelo (Map pp82-3; ☎ 055 681 19 77; www.ecvacanze.it; Viale Michelangelo 80; car, tent/person €4.50/6/9.50; ⏰ year-round) The closest camp site to the city centre, just off Piazzale Michelangelo, south of the River Arno. Big and comparatively leafy, it's handy for the historic quarter, though the steep walk back may have you panting. Take bus No 13 from Stazione di Santa Maria Novella.

Camping Villa Camerata (Map pp78-9; ☎ 055 60 14 51; fax 055 61 03 00; Viale Augusto Righi 2-4; tent/person €5/6) Beside the HI-affiliated hostel of the same name, and in a green setting. Space for tents is decidedly limited, but more generous for campervans.

See p139 for details of the third camp site, Campeggio Panoramico in the hills near Fiesole.

East of Stazione di Santa Maria Novella

Despite a few fairly seedy joints, most hotels in this area are well run, clean and safe.

BUDGET

Ostello Archi Rossi (Map pp80-1; ☎ 055 29 08 04; www.hostelarchirossi.com; Via Faenza 94r; dm from €18.50, €28.50, all incl breakfast; 💻) This is a well-run private hostel, recently expanded to 144 beds and conveniently close to Stazione di Santa Maria Novella. Decorated with guests' wall paintings and graffiti, it's well equipped and has washing machines, microwaves and six free Internet points. Breakfasts are copious and there's a 2am curfew. You can reserve via the website.

Ostello Spirito Santo (Map pp80-1; ☎ 055 239 82 02; fax 055 239 81 29; Via Nazionale 8; d €42; 🌙 Jul-Oct) This hostel is a reasonable summertime-only option. Run by nuns of the Suore Oblate order and a student hostel in term time, it caters for women and families only. Rooms are all doubles or triples, and the place is predictably quiet…

MIDRANGE

Residenze Johlea I & II (Map pp80-1; ☎ 055 463 32 92; www.johlea.it; Via San Gallo 76 & 80; s €70, d €95-105, all incl breakfast; 🌂) Near neighbours, these two places have a combined capacity of 13 rooms. Each offers tasteful, impeccable, individually decorated rooms with dinky minifridges. For extra space, ask for the suite in No 76 (€115). No 80, which acts as reception for both, has a gorgeous little roof terrace. Reservations are essential between March and November.

Antica Dimora (Map pp80-1; ☎ 055 462 72 96; www.anticadimorafirenze.it; 2nd fl, Via San Gallo 72; s €90-110, d €130-145, all incl breakfast; 🌂) Dimora is the Johleas' recently opened sister B&B, just down the road. Four of its six rooms have sybaritic four-poster beds, and all are large and adorned with reproductions of old black-and-white prints. Wi-fi is available.

Cristina House (Map pp80-1; ☎ 055 48 31 45; www.cristinahouse.it; 2nd fl, Via Leone X 2; d with shower/bathroom incl breakfast €100/120; 🌂) A wonderfully cosy five-room place down a quiet street, just north of busy Viale Spartaco Lavagnini. You can be one of the family as the ever-helpful Cristina's children play beneath postcards sent by satisfied guests from around the globe. Or you can retire to the seclusion of your large room, to which your ample breakfast is delivered with a smile.

Hotel Bellettini (Map pp82-3; ☎ 055 21 35 61; www.hotelbellettini.com; 2nd fl, Via de' Conti 7; s/d/tr €100/140/180; 🅿 🌂 💻) A delightful, welcoming hotel with around 30 bright, well-furnished rooms – try for one with a view of the Basilica di San Lorenzo. The Bellettini has an equally attractive, slightly more expensive annexe nearby. Valet parking is €23 to €27.

Hotel Paris (Map pp82-3; ☎ 055 28 02 81; www.parishotel.it; Via dei Banchi 2; s/d €130/180; 🅿 🌂 💻) Designed by Bernardo Buontalenti in the 15th century, Paris is the place to live and sleep the Renaissance experience. Rooms are large, with high ceilings, and swaths of rich, embroidered drape fall from window pelmets and bed-heads. Some rooms preserve their original ceiling frescoes. On the 1st floor, there's a small, open terrace and a gorgeous breakfast room; don't spill your coffee as your gaze is drawn upwards to the magnificent painted ceiling. For a special treat, go for the presidential suite, with its soft-stone fireplace and fountain. Valet parking is €22 to €27.

Palazzo Benci (Map pp80-1; ☎ 055 21 38 48; www.palazzobenci.com; Piazza Madonna degli Aldobrandini 3; s/d €100/155; 🅿 🌂) Benci occupies a charming 16th-century palazzo that was once the home of one of Florence's leading Renaissance political families. Rooms are comfortable and fully modernised, and there's a quiet internal courtyard. In what are puritanical days for puffers in Italy, there's a smoking lounge where you can actually smoke. Valet parking is €21.

Le Due Fontane (Map pp80-1; ☎ 055 21 01 85; www.leduefontane.it; Piazza della Santissima Annunziata 14; s/d incl breakfast €126/185; 🅿 🌂 💻) This is a grand, fully renovated palazzo on one of Florence's most attractive piazzas, which offers neat, comfortable rooms, some with great views. Both Internet access and phone calls to Europe and the US are free for guests. Hotel parking is €10.

Hotel Accademia (Map pp82-3; ☎ 055 29 34 51; www.accademiahotel.net; Via Faenza 7; s/d/tr with buffet breakfast €85/150/190; 🅿 🌂 💻) Within an 18th-century mansion, Accademia has impressive stained-glass doors, carved wooden ceilings, and a great marble staircase that tempts you to do your best Ginger Rogers or Fred Astaire impersonation. Bedrooms are pleasant and parquet-floored, with bright, sparkling bathrooms. Hotel parking is €25.

Hotel Azzi (Map pp82-3; ☎ 055 21 38 06; www.hotelazzi.it; Via Faenza 56; s/d €60/90, with bathroom €70/110, all incl breakfast) With its attractive terrace, Azzi is popular among artists and visiting musicians and actors. You may be lucky enough to co-incide with one of the hotel's gastronomic and musical soirées. Rooms are comfortable, with freshly upgraded bathrooms; ask for one away from noisy Via Faenza.

Hotel Casci (Map pp80-1; ☎ 055 21 16 86; www .hotelcasci.com; 2nd fl, Via Cavour 13; s/d incl buffet breakfast €110/150; P ✗ 🖳) Casci is a friendly family hotel within a 15th-century mansion where the décor is attractively olive-green. For a relaxing soak, choose a room with one of the recently installed shell-shaped baths. Look up at the fresco as you take breakfast, which includes fresh espresso coffee. Hotel parking is €23 to €27.

Hotel Globus (Map pp80-1; ☎ 055 21 10 62; www .hotelglobus.com; Via Sant'Antonino 24; s/d/tr €70/100/150; P ✗ 🖳) A cosy, stylish hotel, which once belonged to the composer Rossini, Globus comes recommended by several readers. All 23 rooms have a free safe and Internet access via the TV, and some have good views over the city. Showers have hydromassage and the cool-coloured rooms have glass mosaics. Hotel parking costs €21.

Johanna I (Map pp80-1; ☎ 055 48 18 96; Via Bonifacio Lupi 14; s/d €60/95) and **Johanna II** (Map pp80-1; ☎ 055 47 33 77; Via delle Cinque Giornate 12; d €80-95), run by the same consortium as Antica Dimora, are an equally attractive pair of nearby, more modest B&Bs. For more details, consult www.johanna.it.

TOP END

Hotel Il Guelfo Bianco (Map pp80-1; ☎ 055 28 83 30; www.ilguelfobianco.it; Via Cavour 29; s €135, d from €180, all incl breakfast; P ✗ 🖳) This hotel has 40 attractive, comfortable rooms. Room No 124 is a charming double with its own private terrace. Alternatively, Room Nos 42 and 56, on the same level, give great rooftop views. There are some fine antiques and – an original touch for Florence – quality contemporary art adorns the public areas and bedrooms. Valet parking is €24.

Hotel Monna Lisa (Map pp82-3; ☎ 055 247 97 51; www.monnalisa.it; Borgo Pinti 27; s/d/tr incl breakfast €180/290/415; P ✗) The Monna Lisa is in a fine Renaissance palazzo. Most of the furnishings and paintings are of the period, many of them family heirlooms. Nonchalantly on display are works by Giovanni Dupré, the 19th-century sculptor, whose relatives still own the hotel. Some rooms overlook the bijou private garden, bedecked

with flowers, where you can enjoy a buffet breakfast in summer. Hotel parking is €15.

Hotel Loggiato dei Serviti (Map pp80-1; ☎ 055 28 95 92; www.loggiatodeiservitihotel.it; Piazza della Santissima Annunziata 3; s/d €140/205; ✗) Bursting with character, this hotel is within a historic 16th-century building mirroring Brunelleschi's Spedale, right opposite. Rooms are simply but comfortably furnished.

Around Piazza di Santa Maria Novella
BUDGET & MIDRANGE

Hotel Scoti (Map pp82-3; ☎ 055 29 21 28; www.hotel-scoti.com; 2nd fl, Via de' Tornabuoni 7; s/d €65/85) Within a 16th-century palazzo on Florence's smartest shopping strip, Scoti represents exceptional value. With welcoming Italian-Australian owners, its rooms, furnished with antique pieces, are full of character and the common sitting room with its floor-to-ceiling frescoes and chandelier is a little gem.

Hotel Abaco (Map pp82-3; ☎ 055 238 19 19; www .abaco-hotel.it; 2nd fl, Via dei Banchi 1; d €65, with shower €75, with bathroom €90; P ✗ 🖳) Abaco is a simple, well-maintained establishment with just seven rooms, only three with bathrooms. Each room is named after a Renaissance artist and furnished in high-baroque style. In low season you can rent a double for one person (€50 to €65). There's a €5 supplement for air-con. Valet parking is €24.

Pensione Ferretti (Map pp82-3; ☎ 055 238 13 28; www.pensioneferretti.it; Via delle Belle Donne 17; s/d/tr €52/82/110, with bathroom €65/102/130, all incl breakfast; P 🖳) Hidden away on a tiny, quiet intersection, Ferretti is a modest hotel with a friendly, family feel to it. Rooms have ceiling fans, and low-season rates are substantially lower than high season's. Hotel parking is €21.

TOP END

Grand Hotel Baglioni (Map pp80-1; ☎ 055 2 35 80; www.hotelbaglioni.it; Piazza dell'Unità Italiana 6; s €188-270, d €261-375; P ✗ 🖳) This place has a mellow tone, with wooden beams and staircase, and public areas made of *pietra serena*, the soft grey stone typical of many Florentine monuments. The rooftop terrace restaurant and garden have stirring views over the city. Hotel parking is €35 to €40.

Grand Hotel Minerva (Map pp82-3; ☎ 055 2 72 30; www.grandhotelminerva.com; Piazza di Santa Maria Novella 16; s/d €270/340; P ✗ 🖳 ⚲) Stylish and welcoming, this hotel has elegantly furnished rooms. There's a lovely internal garden (you could be several kilometres from the sometimes seedy square outside) and an excellent restaurant, plus wonderful views over the piazza and church from the open-air rooftop swimming pool. The house shiatsu massage service in your room is a delightful original touch, and there are bicycles for guest use (per half/full day €5/10). Valet parking is €27 to €31.

Hotel Aprile (Map pp80-1; ☎ 055 21 62 37; www .hotelaprile.it; Via della Scala 5; s/d incl breakfast €120/180; **P** ✗ ☐) Aprile is a pleasant 15th-century palazzo, just a stone's throw away from the piazza. Its small but comfortable rooms have recently been fully renovated, and the hotel's about to upgrade to four-star status. There's a pleasant walled garden and – an original touch, this – it offers art and history lectures in English for guests three times a week. Hotel parking is €20 to €32.

Between the Duomo & the Arno
BUDGET

Hotel Dalí (Map pp82-3; ☎ 055 234 07 06; www .hoteldali.com; 2nd fl, Via dell'Oriuolo 17; s/d €40/60, d with bathroom €75, extra bed €20; **P**) This is a spruce, simple, warmly recommended hotel, run by a friendly, helpful young couple. Some rooms overlook the serene inner courtyard. One bedroom can squeeze in up to six, so bring the gang. There's free parking, which is rare as icebergs in Florence.

Hotel Cestelli (Map pp82-3; ☎ 055 21 42 13; www .hotelcestelli.com; Borgo SS Apostoli 25; s/d €40/65, d with bathroom €80; **P**) Cestelli has new owners who have whirlwinded through, repainting and refurbishing. Room No 4 (€100 plus €20 per person) is vast (stick your head out and you get a view of the Arno) and can comfortably accommodate up to four. The only things smoking in this friendly place are the joss sticks, beloved of Alessio, its dynamic proprietor. Valet parking is €20.

Hotel Orchidea (Map pp82-3; ☎ 055 248 03 46; www.hotelorchideaflorence.it; 1st fl, Borgo degli Albizi 11; s/d without bathroom €55/75) This is a fine, homely, old-fashioned *pensione* in a grand mansion. Its seven rooms are simple, well maintained and rich in character.

MIDRANGE

Hotels San Giovanni and Perseo, a pair of excellent choices, have the same Italian-Australian owners.

Hotel San Giovanni (Map pp82-3; ☎ 055 28 83 85; www.hotelsangiovanni.com; Via de'Cerretani 2; s/d/tr €55/75/97, d/tr with bathroom €95/120, all incl breakfast; **P**) Once part of the bishop's private residence (see the traces of fresco in several rooms), San Giovanni has charming, often spacious rooms with parquet flooring. Six of the nine rooms have views of the cathedral. Don't be deterred by the rather pokey stairwell up to the 2nd floor. You take breakfast in the Perseo, where you also check in if no one answers here. Valet parking is €24.

Hotel Perseo (Map pp82-3; ☎ 055 21 25 04; www .hotelperseo.it; 3rd fl, Via de'Cerretani 1; d/tr/q incl breakfast €95/120/140; **P** ✗ ☐) Perseo was radically renovated in 2005 and offers greater comfort than its sister, a well-lobbed stone's throw away. The décor is befittingly arty, with original canvases by the owner and one or two by long-forgotten, impecunious students who, in the harsh days after WWII, would leave a painting in lieu of rent. Valet parking is €24.

Hotel Bavaria (Map pp82-3; ☎ 055 234 03 13; www .hotelbavariafirenze.it; Borgo degli Albizi 26; s/d €50/70, d/tr with bathroom €98/113, all incl breakfast) This hotel is within the fine 16th-century Palazzo di Ramirez de Montalvo. Built around a peaceful courtyard, its rooms are furnished with nice antique pieces. With its warm ochre colours, low wooden ceilings and flexible pricing, it makes an excellent choice. Reservations, especially between April and July, are imperative.

Hotel Pendini (Map pp82-3; ☎ 055 21 11 70; www .hotelpendini.net; 4th fl, Via degli Strozzi 2; s €80-110, d €110-150; **P** ✗ ☐) A homely 42-room family-owned place whose rooms are furnished with antiques and reproductions. Some rooms look out over Piazza della Repubblica. Valet parking is €24.

Hotel della Signoria (Map pp82-3; ☎ 055 21 45 30; www.hoteldellasignoria.com; Via delle Terme 1; s/d incl breakfast from €115/175; ✗) A neat little 27-room hotel, right in the heart of things, with smart, tastefully furnished rooms.

TOP END

Relais Uffizi (Map pp82-3; ☎ 055 267 62 39; www.relais uffizi.it; 2nd fl, Chiasso del Buco 16; s/d/tr from €120/180/220; **P** ✗) A stylish small hotel, hidden away down an alley (it's off Chiasso de' Baroncello) in a 16th-century building, a mere pigeon hop from Piazza della Signoria. From its breakfast room, there are unparalleled views of the seething square. The large, tastefully

FLORENCE

AUTHOR'S CHOICE

Gallery Hotel Art (Map pp82-3; ☎ 055 2 72 63; www.lungarnohotels.com; Vicolo dell'Oro 5; s/d incl breakfast from €320/340; P ⊠) This is where you should set yourself up, should your Great Aunt Emily prove generous in her will. It is a very modish place indeed, unique in Florence and the perfect spot to retreat if all that Renaissance begins to overwhelm. Owned by the Ferragamo fashion house, it's strictly 21st-century, minimalist, edgy and soft-hued. It earns the 'gallery' of its title for the contemporary art that decorates corridors and each of its 74 rooms. There's also a changing exhibition in its downstairs lounge/library and Japanese-style Fusion Bar. Valet parking is €32.

---

furnished bedrooms have four-poster beds. Hotel parking is €30.

Hotel La Residenza (Map pp82-3; ☎ 055 21 86 84; www.laresidenzahotel.com; Via de' Tornabuoni 8; s/d €130/220; ⊠) This sits at the heart of Florence's fanciest shopping street. It's a small hotel with large, individually styled rooms, all substantially renovated in 2005, and a pleasant rooftop terrace. Wi-fi is available.

Hotel Helvetia & Bristol (Map pp82-3; ☎ 055 2 66 51; www.royaldemeure.com; Via de Pescioni 2; s/d from €275/440; P ⊠ ⊡) Deservedly five-star, this hotel is distinguished by the elegance of its *belle epoque* setting and the discreet yet warm charm of its staff. Each of its 67 rooms is individually and tastefully furnished in rich fabrics, fine antiques abound, and bathrooms are of Carrara marble. Guests who've savoured its charm include Bertrand Russell, Pirandello and Stravinsky. Hotel parking is €30 to €35.

Santa Croce & East of the Centre

Hotel Dante (Map pp82-3; ☎ 055 24 17 72; www.hotel-dante.it; Via S Cristofano 2; s/d €88/120; P ⊠) Down a quiet street right by the Basilica di Santa Croce, Dante has 14 pleasant yet undramatic rooms. That said, it's popular with visiting theatrical folk, as the photo gallery of smiling faces beside reception attests. Fully 50% of its rooms have a kitchen, which is ideal for families, dining in or rustling up an alternative to the pricey breakfast (€12). Parking is €10 to €15 and wi-fi is available.

Hotel Wanda (Map pp82-3; ☎ 055 234 44 84; www.hotelwanda.it; Via Ghibellina 51; s/d/tr €70/88/119, d/tr with bathroom €119/140, all incl breakfast; ⊠) This is a welcoming, tranquil, higgledy-piggledy place. Its large rooms, many with ceiling frescoes, are much airier and lighter than the dowdy façade would suggest. For a fun night, request Room 13, lined with old mirrors.

Oltrarno
BUDGET
Ostello Santa Monaca (Map p85; ☎ 055 26 83 38; www.ostello.it; Via Santa Monaca 6; dm €17; ⊡) Once a convent, Santa Monaca is warmly recommended. At this friendly hostel, run by a co-operative, there are no meals, but guests get a special deal at a nearby restaurant. Single-sex dorms sleep between four and 20. There's a laundrette, a guests' kitchen (you'll need your own equipment) and free safe deposit at reception. Reservations by email or letter.

Hotel Boboli (Map p85; ☎ 055 229 86 45; www.hotelboboli.com; Via Romana 63; s/d €60/86; ⊠) This is a pleasant, homely and unpretentious little hotel with rooms that are spotless and cosy. The higher you go, the better the views over nearby Boboli Gardens.

MIDRANGE
Hotel Silla (Map pp82-3; ☎ 055 234 28 88; www.hotelsilla.it; Via dei Renai 5; s/d €125/170; P ⊠) Silla, which served briefly as Allied headquarters in 1944, sits in a charming old palazzo in one of the most attractive and leafy parts of Florence. It has pleasant, impeccably maintained rooms, furnished in dark timber. Some have beguiling views across the Arno. Hotel parking is €16.

Hotel La Scaletta (Map pp82-3; ☎ 055 28 30 28; www.hotellascaletta.it; top fl, Via de'Guicciardini 13; s/d incl breakfast €90/140; ⊡ ⊠) This hotel has new owners, who have improved upon what was already a delightful place, full of rambling corridors over three levels, within a 15th-century palazzo. It's worth the room rate simply for the great 360-degree roof terrace view, and you're scarcely 100m from both the Ponte Vecchio and Palazzo Pitti.

TOP END
Residenza Serristori Palace (Map pp82-3; ☎ 055 200 16 23; Lungarno Serristori 13; apt for 2/4/6 from €190/210/295; ⊠) An attractive 19th-century villa and, until recently, a modest hotel, this place has been comprehensively and tastefully renovated.

Apartments are large and fully equipped, and most offer a river view, balcony or both.

Albergo Torre di Bellosguardo (Map p85; ☎ 055 229 81 45; www.torrebellosguardo.com; Via Roti Michelozzi 2; s/d €160/290; P ⊗ ⊑ ☺) This hotel is worth considering if only for its position. Long appreciated as a bucolic escape from the simmering heat of summertime Florence, the Bellosguardo hill, to the southwest of the city centre, offers not only enchanting views, but also enticing accommodation in what started life as a small castle in the 14th century.

Around Florence

Ostello Villa Camerata (Map pp78-9; ☎ 055 60 14 51; florenceaighostel@virgilio.it; Viale Augusto Righi 2-4; dm €18, d/tr/q with bathroom €46/57/70, all incl breakfast; P ⊑) This is an HI-affiliated hostel in a converted 17th-century villa. Surrounded by extensive grounds, it ranks as one of Italy's most beautiful. Take bus No 17, 17B or 17C (€1, 30 minutes, every half-hour) from the southwest of Stazione di Santa Maria Novella.

EATING

Simplicity and quality sum up Tuscany's cuisine, and Florence offers the widest choice. Here, rich green Tuscan olive oil, fresh fruit and vegetables, tender meat and, of course, the classic wine, Chianti, are so often the basics of a good meal.

Meat eaters might want to take on the challenge of the local carnivore's classic, *bistecca alla fiorentina*, a huge slab of prime Florentine steak. It usually costs around €40 per kilo, which is quite adequate for two.

Eating out in Florence, like just about every other activity, tends to be more expensive than elsewhere in Tuscany. Assume that you'll be paying below €25 for a full meal that we classify as 'budget', ranging from sandwich joints (where you might pay around €3 for a filling roll) through to trattorie that serve respectable and good-value set meals (*menù del giorno* – the menu of the day – or *menù turistico*), and upwards into the modest categories of restaurants.

Eating at a good trattoria can be surprisingly economical – a virtue of the competition for customers' attention.

East of Stazione di Santa Maria Novella

BUDGET

Nerbone (Map pp80-1; ☎ 055 21 99 49; Mercato Centrale San Lorenzo; mains €5; ☺ 7am-2pm Mon-Sat) As simple as they come, and just inside the central market's western entrance, Nerbone has been serving steaming lunchtime platters since 1872. The handwritten menu changes daily. Start with the particularly substantial *ribollita* (a rich, chewy vegetable soup) and round off a hearty lunch with *biscotti di Prato* (a crunchy almond biscuit/cookie) served with a shot of *vin santo* (sweet dessert wine). Friday is fish day.

Mario (Map pp80-1; ☎ 055 21 85 50; Via Rosina 2; mains around €6, pasta €3.50-4.50; ☺ lunch Mon-Sat) This place has been in business for more than 50 years. It is a bustling bar and trattoria that attracts a mix of market workers and others in search of a guaranteed cheap,

---

GREAT GELATO

Once you've shivered with pleasure at real Italian *gelato,* you'll never touch the supermarket stuff again. *Gelato* can cost anything from €2 for a *coppetta* (small cup) to around €6 for a *cono* (massive cone). Florentines, like other Italians, prefer to round off the evening with a *gelato* while taking a leisurely stroll around town, and most *gelaterie* stay open late. Here are some of our favourite places.

Carabè (Map pp80-1; Via Ricasoli 60r; ☺ closed Wed) This family-run *gelateria* offers traditional Sicilian *gelato* and *granita* (sorbet).

Festival del Gelato (Map pp82-3; ☎ 055 29 43 86; Via del Corso 75r) Just off Piazza della Repubblica and with more than 70 flavours on offer, it should satisfy even the most demanding child.

Gelateria Vivoli (Map pp82-3; Via dell'Isola delle Stinche 7; ☺ 9am-1am Tue-Sat) People queue outside this place, near Via Ghibellina, to delight in the broad range of creamy *gelati*.

Perchè No? (Map pp82-3; ☎ 055 239 89 69; Via dei Tavolini 19r; ☺ Wed-Sun) In business for around 70 years, this *gelateria* also does excellent ice creams.

Vestri (Map pp82-3; Borgo degli Albizi 11r; ☺ closed Sun) This little place specialises in truly indulgent chocolate *gelato* in a variety of combinations, including cinnamon, orange and pistachio.

filling lunch. It's well worth the wait you'll probably have before lunching elbow to elbow with the person next to you.

Il Vegetariano (Map pp80-1; ☎ 055 47 50 30; Via delle Ruote 30r; meals around €15; ☺ lunch & dinner Tue-Fri, dinner Sat & Sun) One of the few veggie options in town, this has a great selection of fresh food, salads and mains. There's always a vegan option and the chalked-up menu changes regularly, reflecting what's freshest at the market.

MIDRANGE & TOP END

Lobs (Map pp80-1; ☎ 055 21 24 78; Via Faenza 75-77r; mains around €25) A superb fish restaurant that offers fresh, exclusively Mediterranean fish and seafood. The setting has maritime frescoes and, appropriately, salmon-pink walls. At lunchtime it offers a selection of pasta specials (€7). Sluice it all down with the Soave wine from Italy's northeast.

Ì Tozzo di Pane (Map pp80-1; ☎ 055 47 57 53; Via Guelfa 94r; mains €8-15; ☺ closed Sun & lunch Mon) A simple neighbourhood place, run by a young, friendly team, where cool jazz warbles in the background. For starters, go for the *zuppa toscana,* a thick gruel of vegetables and barley. Although not to all tastes, the *trippa alla Fiorentina* (tripe) follows on a treat. The small rear garden is a pleasant retreat from the street in summer.

Trattoria ZàZà (Map pp80-1; ☎ 055 21 54 11; Piazza del Mercato Centrale 26r; lunch menu €13, mains €9-13; ☺ Mon-Sat) This trattoria gets its produce fresh from the covered market, just across the square. It's a great spot for combining outdoor dining and a little people-watching. Watch out too for the pigeons that flutter down in a flash to peck at any crumbs that fall. You can also hunker down in the bare-brick vaulted interior, its walls clad with photos of glitterati who've dined here before you.

Around Piazza di Santa Maria Novella

L'Osteria di Giovanni (Map p85; ☎ 055 28 48 97; Via del Moro 22; mains €8.50-15.50; ☺ closed Tue lunch) This is a very recent addition to Florence's gourmet options, run with flair by a father-and-son team, fresh from years of culinary triumph in Siena. Get along there quickly before the word spreads...

Trattoria dei 13 Gobbi (Map p85; ☎ 055 21 32 04; Via del Porcellana 9r; mains €10-12.50; ☺ Tue-Sun) This is low-ceilinged and snug, its bucolic setting matched by the plant-filled rear courtyard. Beef and pork dishes figure prominently, so prepare to ease out your belt a notch.

Trattoria Sostanza (Map p85; ☎ 055 21 26 91; Via del Porcellana 25r; mains €8.50-12.50; ☺ Mon-Fri) With its simple décor and tiled walls, this is another authentic Tuscan eatery that simmers a mean minestrone. Another favourite of the house is the *petti di pollo al burro* (chicken breasts in butter).

Ostaria dei Centopoveri (Map pp80-1; ☎ 055 21 88 46; Via del Palazzuolo 31r; meals €35-40; ☺ closed Mon & lunch Tue) The 'hostel of the hundred poor people' is far from being a soup kitchen. It's a top-quality dining option and a congenial spot in a not-so-congenial part of town. On offer are creative variations on traditional Tuscan food in a down-to-earth setting.

Trattoria Garga (Map p82-3; ☎ 055 239 88 98; Via del Moro 48r; mains €21-25; ☺ dinner Tue-Sun) With more than 25 successful years in business, Garga offers imaginative, creative fare. It also does cookery courses, where you can learn to make a dish you might just have eaten, and organises gastronomic tours of Tuscany (see p112).

Da il Latini (Map pp82-3; ☎ 055 21 09 16; Via dei Palchetti 6r; mains €10-20; ☺ Tue-Sat) Da il Latini is a popular Florentine favourite – so much so that you may find yourself waiting in line, since they don't take reservations. It's well worth hanging around; the wine list is impressive and the food largely Tuscan, but the dining area speaks of Spain with all those legs of ham dangling from the ceiling.

Il Grillo (Map pp82-3; ☎ 055 28 24 38; Piazza di Santa Maria Novella 32; menu €15, mains €13-15) This is the kind of place where you can limit yourself simply to pasta or pizza if you wish. Its outdoor seating, overlooking the magnificent façade of the Basilica di Santa Maria Novella, can't fail to induce an appetite.

Between the Duomo & the Arno

BUDGET

In addition to the below options, there are also several *pizzerie* tucked away in the streets between the Duomo and the Arno. Many offer a takeaway option – anything from a full round disc to a simple slice (around €1.80).

I Fratellini (Map pp82-3; ☎ 055 239 60 96; Via dei Cimatori 38r; panini €2.10) Established in 1875, I Fratellini is little more than a hole in the wall. But you'll never see *panini*, freshly filled as you order, whipped up so quickly. Just watch the deft backhand pass from maker to wine pourer. There's no seating and etiquette requires that you leave your empty glass on one of the two wooden shelves on the wall outside.

Ristorante Self-Service Leonardo (Map pp82-3; ☎ 055 28 44 46; Via de' Pecori 35r; mains €4-5; ⏰ Sun-Fri) A refectory-style option, this is hard to beat if you're after a full meal while pinching the pennies.

Queen Victoria (Map pp82-3; ☎ 055 29 51 62; Via Por Santa Maria 32r; ⏰ Tue-Sun) A busy place serving filling *panini* and focaccia from €4, and pizzas and salads from around €7. There's an outdoor seating area at the back.

Trattoria da Benvenuto (Map pp82-3; ☎ 055 21 48 33; Via della Mosca 16r; mains €6-13; ⏰ Mon-Sat) This trattoria dishes out reliable, modestly priced fare. Mains include several Florentine favourites, including *lampredotto* (a type of tripe) and *ossobuco alla fiorentina*.

MIDRANGE & TOP END

Trattoria Coco Lezzone (Map pp82-3; ☎ 055 28 71 78; Via Parioncino 26r; mains €9.50-15.50; ⏰ closed Sun) Another cheerful, homely spot. No credit cards, no coffee, just very good food; this tiny place knows its clients believe it's good and doesn't make unnecessary concessions. *Ribollita* is the house speciality, and Friday is fresh-fish day.

La Grotta Guelfa (Map pp82-3; ☎ 055 21 00 42; Via Pellicceria 5r; menus €19-39, mains €8.50-15; ⏰ closed Sun) This place pitches hard at the tourist trade. This said, it serves up hearty Tuscan fare with lots of beef and veal dishes, as well as pasta and salads. For a lunchtime pit stop, settle into the two-course *menu toscana* (€8).

Caffè Concerto Paszkowski and Giubbe Rosse (p123), beside Piazza della Repubblica, are a pair of classic 19th-century cafés where you can also eat well.

Santa Croce & East of the Centre
BUDGET

Antico Noè (Map pp82-3; ☎ 055 234 08 38; Volta di San Piero 6r; panini €3.80-4.50, mains €8-13; ⏰ noon-midnight Mon-Sat) A legendary place, just off Piazza San Pier Maggiore, with two sections: a takeaway sandwich bar with juicy cold cuts and, just next door, a cosy little restaurant where you can enjoy fine cooking and mellow wine with slow jazz and blues tunes.

Il Nilo (Map pp82-3; ☎ 055 24 16 99; Volta di San Piero 9r; ⏰ noon-10pm) Run by Zaki from Cairo, the man with the widest grin in town, Il Nilo does tasty shawarma and felafel sandwiches (€2.50 to €3.50) to take away or munch on the spot.

Koo-cli-Koo (Map pp82-3; ☎ 055 234 22 01; Borgo Pinti 2r, cnr Via dell'Oriuolo; sandwiches €1.50-3, dishes €5; ⏰ noon-10pm, closed Sat dinner & Sun) Koo-cli-koo is one of Italy's rare hole-in-the-wall vegetarian takeaways. Run by a cheerful family, its food, all laid out before you so you can pick and choose, is both wholesome and tasty.

Ramraj (Map pp82-3; ☎ 055 24 09 99; Via Ghibellina 61r; set menu €8; ⏰ Tue-Sun) Ramraj does takeaway tandoori and other Indian specialities that you can also munch at the single bench. The set menu comes in vegetarian and carnivore variants, or you can select from the ample range before your eyes.

Ruth's (Map pp82-3; ☎ 055 248 08 88; Via Luigi Carlo Farini 2a; meals around €12; ⏰ closed dinner Fri & lunch Sat) Beside Florence's synagogue, Ruth's serves tasty dishes, at once kosher and vegetarian. For a variety of savours, try the *gran piatto di Ruth per due* (their English translation, 'big Ruth's dish for two', does the svelte owner a disservice). This filling mixed platter (€18 for two) includes couscous, felafel, filo pie and potato salad.

Sedano Allegro (Map pp82-3; ☎ 055 234 55 05; Borgo della Croce 20r; dishes €5-7; ⏰ Tue-Sun) This is a small, slightly out-of-the-way place that's well worth the walk. It offers a wide range of creative vegetarian options plus a few fish dishes, and there's a pleasant shady courtyard at the rear.

MIDRANGE & TOP END

Osteria de' Benci (Map pp82-3; ☎ 055 234 49 23; Via de' Benci 13r; mains €10-15; ⏰ Mon-Sat) This *osteria*'s menu changes monthly. Dining is a pleasure beneath its vaulted ceiling, and the young team serves up well-prepared fare, including honest slabs of *carbonata di chianina* – even more tender and succulent than the ubiquitous *bistecca alla fiorentina*. The atmosphere is intimate and prices are moderate.

Trattoria Cibrèo (Map pp82-3; ☎ 055 234 11 00; Via de' Macci 122r; starters €5, mains €13; ⏰ Tue-Sat Sep-Jul) An excellent-value little trattoria where dried red peppers dangle like coral necklaces from the ceiling. It uses the same kitchens as its namesake, the much more expensive restaurant next door, and offers the same, though much more restricted, menu. Bring cash and come early; they take neither reservations nor credit cards.

Ristorante Cibrèo (Map pp82-3; ☎ 055 234 11 00; Via de' Macci 118; starters €18, mains €34; ✆ Tue-Sat Sep-Jul) Adjoining the trattoria, this restaurant is justifiably famous in Florence and beyond. The décor and table settings are suitably more elegant, and the menu is imaginative. Reservations are essential.

Ristorante Natalino (Map pp82-3; ☎ 055 28 94 04; Borgo degli Albizi 17r; mains €11-16; ✆ Mon-Sat) In a long-deconsecrated church, Natalino has been around for well over a century. It's a friendly, informal place where you'll eat well, whether in the small dining area beside the bar or the attractive vaulted interior. If it features (the menu changes regularly), savour the fried calves' liver with sage – and leave a corner for the tempting homemade desserts.

La Pentola dell'Oro (Map pp82-3; ☎ 055 24 18 08; Via di Mezzo 24r; meals around €40; ✆ closed Sun) At sub-street level and long a jealously guarded secret among Florentine gourmands, this restaurant has recently started to advertise. Its menu involves all sorts of mixes, such as beef prepared with a black pepper and pear sauce. Up at street level, there's a tiny off-shoot with marble-topped tables, wooden benches and only 25 place settings. It has a delightfully simple, regularly updated menu and equally accessible pricing policy; mains are all €7 and desserts are €3.50.

Oltrarno
BUDGET
Al Tranvai (Map p85; ☎ 055 22 51 97; Piazza Torquato Tasso 14r; mains €8-12; ✆ Mon-Fri) A wonderful, rustic Tuscan eatery where you can eat nudged up with the locals at the interior tables or out on the terrace. Since it's so deservedly popular, you'd be wise to reserve your small space.

Trattoria da Ginone (Map p85; ☎ 055 21 87 58; Via de' Serragli 35r; meals around €15; ✆ Mon-Sat) Established by Big Gino just after WWII and run by his son, this trattoria serves inexpensive wholesome food, including vegetarian options. You can opt for the set menu (€12) or go à la carte. Either way, it's a great deal and is understandably popular with a young student crowd.

L'Brindellone (Map p85; ☎ 055 21 78 79; Piazza Piattellina 10/11r; meals around €12.50; ✆ dinner Thu-Tue)

Weave your way between dangling garlic strands and old Chianti bottles in this truly Tuscan spot with a slightly vegetarian bent. The *stracotto alla fiorentina* (beef stew) will warm you to the core on a cold day, and the house red slips down agreeably.

I Tarocchi (Map pp82-3; ☎ 055 234 39 12; Via de' Renai 12-16r; pizzas & mains €6-8; ✆ Tue-Sun, dinner only Sat & Sun) I Tarocchi is a popular pizzeria and trattoria that serves excellent pizzas. Its first courses alone are enough to satisfy most people's hunger, and the menu changes regularly. Plant yourself on the pavement terrace or snuggle up on one of the inside benches.

Trattoria Casalinga (Map p85; ☎ 055 21 86 24; Via de' Michelozzi 9r; mains around €5; ✆ Mon-Sat) This is a cheerful, family-run place where a filling meal with wine comes in at bargain-basement prices. Don't expect to linger as there's usually a queue of expectant diners eager to take over your table.

MIDRANGE & TOP END
Trattoria Cammillo (Map pp82-3; ☎ 055 21 24 27; Borgo San Jacopo 57r; mains €13-17; ✆ Thu-Mon) A traditional place, Cammillo's walls are crowded with canvases, and its ample menu changes daily. The street may be seething with visitors, but it remains a very Florentine haunt: we were the only *stranieri* the day we dined there. Staff, bow-tied and aproned, offer discreet service with a smile. If it's on, go for the juicy roast pork: the crackling is as stiff as the waiters' starched shirts.

Borgo San Jacopo (Map pp82-3; ☎ 055 28 16 61; Borgo San Jacopo 62r; mains €18-25; ✆ dinner Wed-Mon) A *very* stylish recent arrival, all gleaming glass and stainless steel. It's just as innovative as you'd expect from an offshoot of the equally hip Gallery Hotel Art (p118) and, ultimately, the Ferragamo fashion house.

Osteria Santo Spirito (Map p85; ☎ 055 238 23 83; Piazza Santo Spirito 16r; meals around €30) This *osteria* offers a slightly higher-quality meal than most of the bustling haunts across the square. Built on two floors, it spills onto the piazza in summer. Try the gnocchi with soft cheese *gratiné* and truffle oil (€9).

Trattoria Cavolo Nero (Map p85; ☎ 055 29 47 44; Via dell'Ardiglione 22; mains around €15; ✆ Tue-Sat) The 'Black Cabbage' is a little gem, tucked away down a back street. Try the entrecôte of Angus steak prepared in a grape sauce (€18). And save a cranny for one of Michela's mouthwatering homemade desserts.

FAST FOOD FLORENCE-STYLE

When Florentines feel like a fast snack instead of a sit-down lunch, they might well stop by a *trippaio* (often just a mobile stand) for a nice tripe burger.

On a more sophisticated plain, savouring fine wines is one of the great pleasures of the palate in Florence, and for many there is nothing better than a couple of glasses accompanied by simple local snacks – sausage, cheeses, *ribollita* (vegetable stew) and suchlike. And the good news is that the tradition of the *vinaio* (wine merchant) has won new life in the past few years in Florence. You may never see the word '*vinaio*' on the doorway, but the idea remains the same. The old traditional places still exist – often dark little bars where you can get a bite to eat too. Look out for the signs 'Mescita di Vini' (roughly 'wine outlet') and *enoteca* (wine bar).

Enoteca Baldovino (Map pp82-3; ☎ 055 234 72 00; Via di San Giuseppe 18r; ⏰ closed Mon) This is a big place in a pleasant location, with a street side terrace in the shadow of Santa Croce. You can taste fine wines accompanied by sophisticated snacks and salads.

Enoteca Boccadama (Map pp82-3; ☎ 055 24 36 40; Piazza di Santa Croce 25-26r; dishes from €7.50; ⏰ closed Mon) An excellent wine bar with outdoor seating on the piazza and a cosy lounge and restaurant indoors. The wine list is extensive, and it serves light salads and pasta dishes.

Enoteca Fuori Porta (Map pp82-3; ☎ 055 234 24 83; Via Monte alle Croci 10r; dishes around €5; ⏰ closed Sun) In this fine old *enoteca* the wine list has more than 400 varieties – and an impressive roll call of Scotch whiskies and other liquors too. Pick a plate or two from the limited list of *primi* (first courses) for a pleasant evening meal. The desserts slip down well too.

Il Santo Bevitore (Map p85; ☎ 055 21 12 64; Via di Santo Spirito 64/66r; dishes €6-8; ⏰ closed Sun) This modern, inviting little *enoteca* in Oltrarno is a great place to sample a wide variety of wines, with a selection of light pasta dishes.

Le Barrique (Map p85; ☎ 055 22 41 92; Via del Leone 40r; meals with wine €30; ⏰ closed Mon) Hidden deep in the San Frediano area, this charming little spot offers a limited *menù del giorno* or, for those just stopping in for a quick drink or two, bar snacks. Again, the emphasis is on wine, and there's usually a selection of Tuscan and French cheeses.

Olio & Convivium (Map p85; ☎ 055 265 81 98; Via di Santo Spitito 4; meals around €20; ⏰ closed Sun) It's a small gastronomic restaurant, a well-stocked wine bar and also a shop selling everything from fresh-baked bread to meats, pasta and cheeses.

Vini e Vecchi Sapori (Map pp82-3; ☎ 055 29 30 45; Via dei Magazzini 3r; meals around €16) One of the city centre's last surviving true *osterie* (restaurants offering simple dishes). It's indeed a little den of 'wines and old tastes' where you can eat decently and taste some solid local wines at low prices. It also imports *fragolino*, a strawberry-flavoured wine made in the northeast of Italy.

Ristorante Beccofino (Map p85; ☎ 055 29 00 76; Piazza degli Scarlatti 1r; 1st/2nd courses €10/20 ⏰ Tue-Sun) This is both innovative restaurant and stylish *enoteca* (wine bar) with more than 50 wines on offer by the glass. It's decidedly *nouvelle* chic; the giant terracotta fish skeleton splayed over one wall may induce a shudder, and the stainless steel, floor-lit toilets are far from the least of its charms.

Self-Catering

Mercato Centrale San Lorenzo (Map pp80-1; Piazza del Mercato Centrale; ⏰ 7am-2pm Mon-Sat) Florence's vast central market is a cornucopia of delights for self-caterers and sandwich fillers.

Pasta Fresca Morioni (Map pp80-1; ☎ 055 239 61 73; Via Palazzuolo 56r) A tiny pasta shop where you can see the team turning out the freshest pasta in many different guises.

DRINKING
Cafés

Three classic cafés, rich in character and each speaking its own individual style, flank Piazza della Repubblica.

Caffè Concerto Paszkowski (Map pp82-3; ☎ 055 21 02 36; Piazza della Repubblica 31-35r; mains €13.50-15.50; ⏰ 7am-2am Tue-Sun) More than 150 years old, this café was originally a beer hall and is now a national monument. Snack, sip or dine in the opulent interior, or eat and drink on the terrace.

Giubbe Rosse (Map pp82-3; ☎ 055 21 22 80; Piazza della Repubblica 13-14r; mains around €15; ⏰ 8am-2am) This is where die-hard members of the early-20th-century futurist artistic movement used to drink and debate. Inside, long vaulted halls lined with old photos, sketches and artwork make a great place for coffee over a newspaper – there are some hanging up for the customers' use.

Caffè Gilli (Map pp82-3; ☎ 055 21 38 96; Piazza della Repubblica 39r; ✆ 8am-1am Wed-Mon) Gilli has been serving good coffee since 1733. Elegantly decorated with Art Nouveau ceiling frescoes, it's very reasonably priced if you stand at the bar.

Rinascente (Map pp82-3; Via Speziali 13-23r) For stunning views of the square and Duomo way below, sip a coffee (€3 to €5) at the rooftop café of the department store, just off Piazza della Repubblica.

Bars

Astor Caffè (Map pp82-3; Piazza del Duomo 5r; ✆ 10am-3am daily) Take breakfast here, then return some 12 hours later to mix with the nocturnal crowd who gather around for loud music and cocktails, opposite the solemn walls of the cathedral. Keep an eye on the giant red clock so closing time doesn't sneak up on you…

Mayday (Map pp82-3; Via Dante Alighieri 16r; ✆ 8pm-2am Mon-Sat) This bar is strong on theme nights and often runs art exhibitions. The two *ragazzi* who run the place have an amazing collection of CDs, sometimes supplemented with live music.

Capocaccia (Map pp82-3; Lungarno Corsini 12-14r; ✆ noon-1am) This is where the beautiful people of Florence go, especially on balmy spring and summer evenings, for a riverside nibble and cocktail. Tuesday is sushi night, and the DJ takes over at 11pm each evening. It's also one of the 'in' places for Sunday brunch.

Rex Caffè (Map pp82-3; Via Fiesolana 25r; ✆ 5pm-3am Sep-May) Another top stop on the cocktail circuit, Rex is a hip place to sip your favourite mixed concoction against a background of an illuminated world map. There are DJs on call on the weekends.

Cabiria (Map p85; Piazza Santo Spirito 4r; ✆ 11am-2am Wed-Mon) A popular café by day, Cabiria converts into a busy nocturnal music bar. In summer the buzz extends onto Piazza Santo Spirito, which becomes a stage for an outdoor bar and regular free concerts.

La Dolce Vita (Map p85; Piazza del Carmine 6r; ✆ 5pm-2am Tue-Sun) Just a piazza away from Santo Spirito, La Dolce Vita attracts a very stylish crowd, especially on weekends. At other times it's usually a quiet spot to enjoy a cocktail.

Zoe (Map pp82-3; Via dei Renai 13r; ✆ 8.30am-1am Mon-Sat, 6.30pm-1am Sun) With its innards glowing red and bedecked with art exhibitions that change monthly, Zoe heaves as its squadrons of punters, mostly young locals, spill out onto the street.

Negroni (Map pp82-3; ☎ 055 24 36 47; Via dei Renai 17r; ✆ 8.30am-2am Mon-Sat, 6pm-2am Sun) Just as popular as its near neighbour Zoe, this place is named after one of the several tempting cocktails its bartenders shake up. It too goes in for temporary art exhibitions. Should you drift by in the daytime, it serves a good-value lunchtime buffet (€7).

Cheers Pub (Map pp82-3; ☎ 055 24 58 29; Via de Renai 27) Cheers is a small, usually packed British-style pub whose happy hour lasts from 4pm to 9pm. The TV flickers to all the major football games.

ENTERTAINMENT

Several publications list the city's major festivals as well as theatrical and musical events.

Turismonotizie, nominally €0.50 but often available free, is a bimonthly published by the tourist office. *Informacittà* is a monthly freebie. Check the website www.informacittafirenze.it (in Italian), for the latest updates. *Eventi* is a free monthly flyer listing major events that's compiled by the tourist office, which also produces the annual brochure *Avventimenti*, covering major events in and around the city.

Florence Concierge Information is a more compendious privately published free bimonthly that runs a good what's-on website, www.florence-concierge.it, with plenty of links.

Firenze Spettacolo, the city's definitive entertainment publication, is available monthly for €1.75 at bookstalls.

Box Office (Map pp80-1; ☎ 055 21 08 04; www .boxol.it; Via Luigi Alamanni 39; ✆ 10am-7.30pm Tue-Sat, 3.30-7.30pm Mon) is a handy central ticket outlet. Reserve in person, by phone or online.

You can book tickets for the theatre, football matches and other events online through **Ticket One** (www.ticketone.it in Italian).

Live Music

Some of the bigger venues are well outside the town centre. Depending on who's play-

---

GAY & LESBIAN FLORENCE

Florence, with its unrivalled artistic and creative history, has a long tradition of openness and tolerance. Its gay community is one of the most vibrant and well established in Italy, boasting a number of well-attended bars and clubs. That said, this is no Amsterdam and there are no specifically 'gay areas' – what nightlife exists tends to be relatively low-key.

Azione Gay e Lesbica (Map p85; ☎ 055 22 02 50; www.azionegayelesbica.it in Italian; Via Pisana 32r; ☺ 6-8pm Mon-Thu) is the city's main contact point for all information on the scene. Tourist offices carry a free 'Gay City Map', showing gay clubs, bars and gay-friendly shops and hotels.

At the **Libreria delle Donne** (Map pp82-3; ☎ 055 24 03 84; Via Fiesolana 2/b; ☺ Mon pm & Tue-Fri) bookshop, you can get information to tune you into the lesbian scene in Florence.

Bars and clubs worth checking out:

Crisco (Map pp82-3; ☎ 055 248 05 80; Via Sant'Egidio 43r; ☺ 9pm-3am Sun & Tue-Thu, to 5am Fri & Sat) A strictly men-only club with dark rooms and a leather/jeans dress code.

Du Monde Café (Map pp82-3; ☎ 055 234 49 53; Via San Niccolò 103r; ☺ 7.30pm-4am Tue-Sun) Members-only cocktail bar with weekend drag acts. It also has a restaurant, which is open until 1am.

Piccolo Café (Map pp82-3; ☎ 055 24 17 04; Borgo Santa Croce 23r; ☺ 5pm-1am) A relaxed little place to hang out and get acquainted with the gay and lesbian scene. It hosts occasional art exhibitions.

Tabasco (Map pp82-3; ☎ 055 21 30 00; Piazza di Santa Cecilia 3r; admission free, drinks around €7; ☺ 10pm-4am, disco until 6am Tue, Fri & Sat) Florence's only serious gay club. Here you can dance through the wee hours of the morning and then some. There's a disco, cocktail bar and dark room. Wednesday is leather night.

YAG Bar (Map pp82-3; ☎ 055 246 90 22; Via de' Macci 8r; ☺ 5pm-2am) Barely a stone's throw from the Piccolo Café, this trendy gay bar is another relaxed and mixed location. It claims to be the largest gay bar in Florence, and has regular live music. There are some computer terminals for going online and video games.

---

ing, admission costs from nothing to more than €10 – the drinks will cost you on top of that (at least €5 for a beer). Many places close in high summer.

Jazz Club (Map pp82-3; ☎ 055 247 97 00; Via Nuova de' Caccini 3; compulsory 12-month membership €5, drinks around €7; ☺ 9.30pm-1am Sun-Thu, 9.30pm-2am Fri & Sat, closed mid-Jun–Sep) Florence's tip-top strictly jazz venue stages some quality acts, both local and from wider afield, in an atmospheric vaulted basement.

Tenax (Map pp78-9; ☎ 055 30 81 60; Via Pratese 46; ☺ 10.30pm-4am Tue-Sun, closed May-Sep) Florence's biggest venue for live bands, this is out to the northwest of town. Admission varies according to the act. Take bus No 29 or 30 from Stazione di Santa Maria Novella to get there. You'll need a taxi or a lift to get home.

Auditorium Flog (Map pp78-9; ☎ 055 49 04 37; Via M Mercati 24b; admission free–€12) Another major venue for bands, this is in the Rifredi area, quite a way north of the centre. It's not as big (in any sense) as Tenax but has a reasonable stage and dance area. Catch bus No 8 or 14 from Stazione di Santa Maria Novella.

Clubbing

Central Park (Map pp80-1; ☎ 055 35 35 05; Via Fosso Macinante 2-6; admission incl 1st drink €20; ☺ 11pm-4am

Tue-Sat) This is one of the city's most popular clubs. As you wander from one of the five dance areas to another, you can expect a general range of music from Latin and pop through to house. In summer, dance inside or under the stars.

Meccanò (Map pp80-1; ☎ 055 331 33 71; Viale degli Olmi; admission incl 1st drink €15; ☺ 11pm-4am Tue-Sat) This club has three dance spaces, offering house, funk and mainstream commercial music to appeal to a fairly broad range of tastes. Occasionally it puts on special theme nights.

YAB (Map pp82-3; ☎ 055 21 51 60; Via Sassetti 5r; admission €15; ☺ 9pm-4am Wed-Mon) YAB is one of the city's more established clubs, popular with local students. It plays a variety of styles of music, with a particular fondness for hip-hop.

Classical Music & Opera

Teatro Comunale (Map pp80-1; ☎ 800 11 22 11; Corso Italia 16) This is a venue for concerts, opera and dance, organised by the **Maggio Musicale Fiorentino** (www.maggiofiorentino.com), which also runs an international concert festival at the theatre in May and June.

Teatro Verdi (Map pp82-3; ☎ 055 21 23 20; www.teatroverdifirenze.it in Italian; Via Ghibellina 99) This place hosts drama, opera, concerts and dance from October to April.

Teatro della Pergola (Map pp82-3; ☎ 055 2 26 41; Via della Pergola 18) From here the **Amici della Musica** (☎ 055 60 74 40; www.amicimusica.fi.it in Italian) organises concerts between October and April.

In summer especially, concerts of chamber music are held in churches across the city. The prestigious Orchestra da Camera Fiorentina (Florentine Chamber Orchestra) performance season runs from March to October.

Cinemas

Surprisingly for such a cosmopolitan city, very few cinemas show subtitled films (versione originale).

Odeon Cinehall (Map pp82-3; ☎ 055 21 40 68; Piazza Strozzi) This cinema is the main location with subtitled films, usually screened on Monday, Tuesday and Thursday.

Cinema Fulgor (Map pp80-1; ☎ 055 238 18 81; Via Maso Finiguerra 22r) Screens English-language films on Thursday evenings.

British Institute of Florence library & cultural centre (Map p85; ☎ 055 267 78 270; Lungarno Guicciardini 9) Shows movies in English at 6pm on Wednesdays. Admission for nonmembers is €5. See p112 for more information on the British Institute of Florence.

Yearly, from mid-June to September, several outdoor cinemas show films in Italian. Private ventures include **Chiardiluna** (Map p85; ☎ 055 233 70 42; Via Monte Uliveto 1) and **Cinema Poggetto** (Map pp78-9; ☎ 055 48 12 85; Via M Mercati 24b), while the municipality puts on outdoor screenings at the Palazzo dello Sport (Map pp78–9) in the Campo di Marte and Palazzo dei Congressi (Map pp80–1).

Theatre & Dance

The theatre season kicks off in October and continues into April/May. This doesn't mean that Florence then comes to a cultural standstill. It's just that many of the main stages stay untrodden while more festive arts events take centre billing.

The theatres that feature in the earlier Classical Music & Opera section also frequently put on mainstream drama. In addition, there are a couple of exciting venues for more experimental theatre.

Ex-Stazione Leopolda (Map pp80-1; ☎ 055 247 83 32; Viale Fratelli Rosselli 5) This is a performance space within a former train station. Theatre, most of it of an avant-garde nature, is frequently the star, although occasionally concerts are put on here too.

Teatro della Limonaia (Map pp78-9; ☎ 055 44 08 52; Via Gramsci 426, Sesto Fiorentino) One of Italy's leading avant-garde theatres, this is well north of the centre of Florence (take bus No 28A or 28C).

Sport

Local Serie A side **ACF Fiorentina** (www.acffiorentina.it) hung on to its place in Italy's premier football division by the straps of its boots, just avoiding relegation by winning its last game of the 2004–05 season.

If you want to see a match, get tickets (€20 to €140) from the stadium itself, **Stadio Comunale Artemio Franchi** (Map pp78-9; ☎ 055 262 55 37; Campo di Marte) or at **Chiosco degli Sportivi** (Map pp82-3; ☎ 055 29 23 63; Via Anselmi), a small kiosk just off Piazza della Repubblica. Alternatively, reserve online via www.listicket.it (in Italian).

You can also book tickets through Box Office or Ticket One (see p124).

SHOPPING

Milan, say serious shoppers, has the best clothes, and Rome the best shoes. But Florence, all concur, has the greatest variety of goods. It's where some of the greats of fashion, such as Gucci and Ferragamo, first entered the rag trade.

The main shopping area is between the Duomo and the Arno, with boutiques concentrated along Via Roma, Via de' Calzaiuoli and Via Por Santa Maria, which leads to the goldsmiths lining the Ponte Vecchio.

Designer Goods

Window-shop along Via della Vigna Nuova and Via de' Tornabuoni, where the top designers, including Gucci, Yves Saint-Laurent, Ferragamo, Versace and Valentino, sell their wares.

Gucci (Map pp82-3; ☎ 055 26 40 11; Via de' Tornabuoni 73r) A temple to one of the most successful families in Florentine-born fashion. The soap-opera family saga has put a lot of spice into the name, but the fashion-faddy take little notice and keep on buying.

Ferragamo (Map pp82-3; ☎ 055 29 21 23; Via de' Tornabuoni 16r) Another grand Florentine name, the one-time shoe specialists now turn out a range of clothes and accessories for dedicated followers of fashion. It also has a curious shoe museum – see p98.

House of Florence (Map pp82-3; ☎ 055 650 53 34; Via de' Tornabuoni 6) This snooty boutique peddles a range of conservative handmade hang-ons such as bags, scarves and ties.

Pucci (Map pp82-3; ☎ 055 21 21 72; Via de' Tornabuoni 20/22r) The swirly, psychedelic patterns of Pucci's womenswear have been very popular with the chic, wealthy and want-to-be-noticed since the 1950s.

Loretta Caponi (Map pp82-3; ☎ 055 21 36 68; Piazza Antinori 4r) To dress up your offspring so they stand out at playschool, call by, armed with a platinum credit card.

To locate labels without the snobbery, hunt around what are called 'stockhouses', where designer wear is often on sale for more affordable prices.

Stockhouse Il Giglio (Map pp80-1; ☎ 055 21 75 96; Borgo Ognissanti 86r) Here men's and women's fashion items with name labels can come in at a considerable discount.

Stockhouse One Price (Map pp80-1; ☎ 055 28 46 74; Borgo Ognissanti 74r) More densely stocked in a smaller space this is also well worth a rummage.

Leather Shops

Leather and shoes are well worth hunting out in Florence. Via de'Gondi and Borgo de' Greci are lined with leather shops. You can also try the markets or some of the speciality stores.

Francesco da Firenze (Map p85; ☎ 055 21 24 28; Via di Santo Spirito 62r) If only every shoemaker made shoes this way – hand-stitched leather is the cornerstone of this tiny family business. You can have shoes and sandals made to specification – at a price.

Il Bisonte (Map pp82-3; ☎ 055 21 57 22; Via del Parione 31r) Here they concentrate on accessories, such as handbags, desktop items, leather-bound notebooks, briefcases and the like.

Pusateri (Map pp82-3; ☎ 055 21 41 92; Via de'Calzaiuoli 25r) This wonderful specialist shop sells stylish gloves, and only gloves.

Scuola del Cuoio (see p112) If the day is right, you can watch leatherworkers fashioning goods and buy their finished products. Access to the workshop is either through the Basilica di Santa Croce or via an entrance behind the basilica at Via San Giuseppe 5r.

Specialist Shops

Florence is famous for its beautifully patterned paper, stocked in the many stationery and speciality shops throughout the city and at some markets.

Il Papiro (Map pp82-3; ☎ 055 28 16 28; Piazza del Duomo 24r) One of six branches in Florence selling all manner of pretty paper and stationery.

Pineider (Map pp82-3; ☎ 055 28 46 55; Piazza della Signoria 13r) This purveyor of paper and related products has been in business since 1774. It still sells a range of colourful stationery, but these days its other products, such as leather and glassware, dominate the store.

And there's one other must-call-by, in a category all its own:

Officina Profumo-Farmaceutica di Santa Maria Novella (Map pp80-1; ☎ 055 21 62 76; Via della Scala 16) Follow your nose to this venerable perfumery, established in 1612, which sells a range of high-quality unguents, balms, soaps, scents and lotions. Marvellous, but you may sniff at the prices when you see them…

Factory Outlets

The tourist office has a list of outlet stores, offering discounts of up to 50%, around Florence. Some are single-brand; most bunch up several designers. Biggest by far is **The Mall** (☎ 055 865 77 75; Via Europa 8, Leccio; ⏰ 10am-7pm Mon-Sat, 3-7pm Sun). A bus (€2.60, 9am and 12.30pm Monday to Friday, 9am Saturday) runs from the SITA bus station, returning at noon and 5pm. If you are driving, take the A1 towards Rome, then the Incisa exit, and follow signs for Leccio.

For truly dedicated bargain sniffers, **CAF Tours** (Map pp80-1; ☎ 055 21 06 12; www.caftours.com; Via Sant'Antonino 6r) runs a bus (€19) on Tuesday, Wednesday and Saturday that allows a couple of hours each at the **Prada outlet** (☎ 055 919 05 80; Località Levanella, Montevarchi; ⏰ 9.30am-12.30pm & 1.30-6pm Mon-Fri, 9.30am-7pm Sat, 4-7pm Sun) and the more extensive The Mall.

Markets

Open-air market (9am-7.30pm Tue-Sun) Coming down to earth, in both price and quality, the market that sprawls around Piazza San Lorenzo and up towards the Mercato Centrale peddles leather goods, clothing and jewellery at low prices. Quality varies hugely and can be decidedly duff. Bargaining's on, but not if you want to use a credit card.

Mercato Nuovo (see p92) You can say the same and more for the goods being hawked at this similarly cheap and cheerful market.

Mercato dei Pulci (flea market; Map pp82-3; Piazza dei Ciompi) Just off Borgo Allegri, this is an amazing clutter of junk, bric-a-brac and tat, with the odd antique waiting to be discovered. There's an especially big one that brings in vendors from all around on the last Sunday of the month.

GETTING THERE & AWAY
Air
Amerigo Vespucci (Map pp78-9; ☎ 055 37 34 98; www .aeroporto.firenze.it), 5km northwest of the city centre, caters for domestic and a handful of European flights.

Galileo Galilei (☎ 050 50 07 07; www.pisa-airport .com) is much larger and one of northern Italy's main international and domestic airports. Nearer to Pisa, it's about an hour away by car or regular train service.

Bus
The **SITA bus station** (Map pp80-1; ☎ 800 37 37 60; www.sita-on-line.it in Italian; Via Santa Caterina da Siena 15) is just to the west of Piazza della Stazione. SITA and Tra-in share a direct, rapid service to/from Siena (€6.50, 1¼ hours, at least hourly) or you can change in Poggibonsi (€4.30, 50 minutes, half-hourly), where there are also connecting buses for San Gimignano (€5.90, 1¼ hours, 12 daily). Buses for Siena also run via Poggibonsi and Colle di Val d'Elsa (1¼ hours, hourly), where you change for Volterra (€6.95, 1½ hours, four daily).

Direct buses serve Arezzo, Castellina in Chianti, Faenza, Grosseto, Greve, Redda and other smaller cities throughout Tuscany.

Several bus companies, including **CAP** (Map pp80-1; ☎ 055 21 46 37) and **COPIT** (Map pp80-1; ☎ 800 57 05 30) operate from Largo Alinari, at the station end of Via Nazionale. Services to nearby towns include Prato (€2.40, 45 minutes, every 15 minutes) and Pistoia (€3, 50 minutes, hourly).

Lazzi (Map pp80-1; ☎ 055 35 10 61; www.lazzi .it in Italian; Piazza Adua 1), next to Stazione di Santa Maria Novella, runs buses to/from Prato (€2.40, 45 minutes, hourly), Pistoia (€3, 50 minutes, 10 daily), Lucca (€4.70, 1½ hours, frequent) and Pisa (€6.20, two hours, hourly).

Lazzi forms part of the Eurolines network of international bus services. You can,

for instance, catch a bus to Barcelona, Paris, Prague or London.

Car & Motorcycle
Florence is connected by the A1 northwards to Bologna and Milan, and southwards to Rome and Naples. The Autostrada del Mare (A11) links Florence with Prato, Lucca, Pisa and the coast, and a *superstrada* (no tolls) joins the city to Siena. If approaching from the north on the A1, exit at Firenze Nord and then follow the bulls-eye 'centro' signs. If coming from Rome, exit at Firenze Sud.

The much more picturesque SS67 connects the city with Pisa to the west, and Forli and Ravenna to the east.

Train
The train **information office** (☒ 7am-9pm) is in the southwest corner of the main foyer at Stazione di Santa Maria Novella. Queues for the ticket office (Map pp80-1) can be long. Better to whip out your credit card, accepted for even the shortest journey, and press the buttons on one of the automatic ticket-vending machines. There's a left-luggage office on platform 16.

Florence is on the Rome–Milan line. There are regular trains to/from Rome (€29.50, 1½ to two hours), Bologna (€13.20, one hour), Milan (€28.90, 2¾ to 3¼ hours) and Venice (€26.60, three hours). To get to Genoa (€16.60), change in Pisa (€5, 1¼ hours, 40 daily); for Turin (€34.65), in Milan.

Frequent regional trains run to Prato (€1.60, 25 minutes), Pistoia (€2.60, 40 minutes) and Lucca (€4.60, 1½ hours).

GETTING AROUND
To/From the Airports
Vola in Bus (€4, 20 minutes, every half-hour from 6am to 11pm) is a shuttle-bus service between the SITA bus station and Amerigo Vespucci airport. A taxi costs around €20.

Trains (€5.40, 1½ hours) leave Stazione di Santa Maria Novella for Galileo Galilei airport near Pisa about every hour until 5pm. If there's nothing direct, take a train to Pisa, from where there are more frequent connections.

Bicycle
Cycling around Florence is one way to beat the traffic – though the cobbles may rattle your bones.

Alinari (Map pp80-1; ☎ 055 28 05 00; www.alinari rental.com; Via Guelfa 85r; ☼ daily Mar-Oct, Mon-Sat Nov-Feb) Rents bikes from €7/12/45 per five hours/day/ week. It also hires out scooters (€22/28/140) and motorbikes (per hour/day from €10/55).

Florence by Bike (see p113) Rents bikes from €7.50/13/32 per five hours/day/three days, and scooters from €23/31/81. It also runs a first-class bicycle spares and repairs service. If you're in Florence for some months, consider investing in a new bike within its sell-and-repurchase plan.

Internet Train (Map pp82-3; ☎ 055 263 85 55; Via dei Benci 36r) The Via dei Benci branch rents town bikes (per half/full day €6/12).

Car & Motorcycle

There are several car parks around the city centre fringe. The cheapest options for a longer stay are the car parks in Parterre (Map pp78-9) and, over the river in Oltarno, Piazza della Calza (Map p85). Both cost €1.50 per hour or €15 for a 24-hour period.

If you're unlucky enough to have your car towed away, phone the **Depositeria Comunale** (car pound; Map pp78-9; ☎ 055 78 38 82) at Ponte a Greve, which is some distance west of the city centre. They will charge you around €50 to recover your car, plus whatever fine is imposed.

A bunch of car-rental agencies cluster together in the Borgo Ognissanti area.

Avis (Map pp80-1; ☎ 199 10 01 33; Borgo Ognissanti 128r)

Europcar (Map p85; ☎ 800 82 80 50; Borgo Ognissanti 53-57r)

Hertz (Map pp80-1; ☎ 199 11 22 11; Via Maso Finiguerra 33r)

A couple of local competitors are **Happy Rent** (Map pp80-1; ☎ 055 239 96 96; Borgo Ognissanti 153r), which also rents out motorbikes and scooters, and **Thrifty Rental** (Map pp80-1; ☎ 055 28 71 61; Borgo Ognissanti 134r).

Public Transport

ATAF (Azienda Trasporti Area Fiorentina; Map pp80-1; ☎ 800 42 45 00; www.ataf.net in Italian) buses service the city centre, Fiesole and other areas on the city's periphery.

You'll find the local bus stop (Map pp80-1) for several of the main routes on the west side of Stazione di Santa Maria Novella. Another of the local bus stops is just south of Stazione di Santa Maria Novella on Piazza dell'Unità Italiana (Map pp80-1). Some of the most useful lines operate from a local bus stop (Map pp80-1) that is just outside the station's southeastern exit. These include bus No 7 for Fiesole, No 13 for Piazzale Michelangelo and No 70 for the cathedral and the Uffizi (this is a night bus only).

A network of dinky little electric *bussini* (minibuses) operates around the centre of town from Monday to Saturday. You can get a map of all bus routes, published by ATAF, from tourist offices.

Tickets for buses and *bussini* cost €1, and a handy *biglietto multiplo* (four-journey ticket) is €3.90; a day pass is €4.50. Buy tickets at kiosks and tobacconists or on board the bus (after 9pm only, €1.60) and stamp your ticket in the machine as you get on board.

If you are hanging around Florence longer, you might want to invest in a weekly ticket (€16), or a *mensile* (monthly) at €31.

Taxi

For a taxi you can call ☎ 055 42 42 or ☎ 055 43 90.

SMILE, YOU'RE ON CAMERA

Casual traffic is banned from the heart of Florence and the fines for transgressors are savage. Cyclopean cameras positioned at entry points to the historic centre snap your numberplate as you drive into the zone. If you're staying in a hotel, let the reception desk know the car registration number and the time you crossed into no-cars-land (you have a two-hour window). They then email Authority, which cancels your potential fine. It all sounds heavyweight and bureaucratic, but in fact makes for a much more pleasant city where you can stroll the streets without fear of being run down.

Parking anywhere can induce apoplexy; the only practical advice is to dump your vehicle as soon as you can. Some hotels have their own facilities, while many, including modest establishments, have a special arrangement with private garages nearby. It's expensive: typical fees for 24 hours vary from €15 to more than €50. Valet parking, increasingly on offer, normally costs no more.

AROUND FLORENCE

One of the beauties of Florence, believe it or not, is leaving it behind. Whether it's just to check out less-visited towns to the north and west, to make a delicious lunchtime assault on the nearby towns of Fiesole and Settignano, or to explore the hilly wine region of Il Chianti to the south, there's no shortage of day outings.

PISTOIA

pop 84,200

Pistoia is a pleasant city that sits snugly at the foot of the Apennines. Only 45 minutes northwest of Florence by train, it deserves more attention than it normally gets. Although it has grown well beyond its medieval ramparts – and is now a world centre for the manufacture of trains – its historic centre is well preserved. In the 16th century the city's metalworkers created the pistol, which was named after the city.

On Wednesday and Saturday mornings, Piazza del Duomo and its surrounding streets become a sea of blue awnings and jostling shoppers as Pistoia hosts a lively market.

Orientation

From the train station, head north along Via XX Settembre, eventually turning right into Via Cavour. Via Roma, branching off the northern side of Via Cavour, takes you to the main square, Piazza del Duomo.

Information

Hospital (Ospedale Riuniti; ☎ 0573 35 21) Off Viale Giacomo Matteotti, behind the old Ospedale del Ceppo.
Main post office (Via Roma 5)
Tourist office (☎ 0573 2 16 22; www.pistoia.turismo .toscana.it in Italian; Piazza del Duomo 4; ⏰ 9am-1pm & 3-6pm Mon-Sat) Occupies part of the Antico Palazzo dei Vescovi.

Sights

PIAZZA DEL DUOMO

Much of Pistoia's visual wealth is concentrated on this central square. The Pisan-Romanesque façade of the **cathedral** (⏰ 8.30am-12.30pm & 3.30-7pm) boasts a lunette of the *Madonna col Bambino fra due Angeli* (Madonna and Child between two Angels) by Andrea della Robbia, who also made the terracotta tiles that line the barrel vault of the main porch. Inside

is the remarkable silver **Dossale di San Giacomo** (Altarpiece of St James; adult/child €2/0.50; ⏰ 10am-noon & 4-7.30pm). It was begun in the 13th century, with artisans adding to it over the ensuing two centuries until Brunelleschi contributed the final touch, the two half-figures on the left side. However, it's locked away in the gloomy **Cappella di San Jacopo** off the north aisle. To visit, you'll need to track down a church official.

The venerable building between the cathedral and Via Roma is the **Antico Palazzo dei Vescovi** (admission €3.60; ⏰ 10am-1pm & 3-5pm Tue, Thu & Fri). There are guided tours (in Italian) four times daily through the wealth of artefacts, discovered during restoration work and dating as far back as Etruscan times. Reserve at the tourist office.

Across Via Roma is the **baptistry** (admission free; ⏰ 8am-6pm Tue-Sun). Elegantly banded in green-and-white marble, it was started in 1337 to a design by Andrea Pisano. The bare, red-brick interior is enlivened with an ornate square marble font. Closed for extensive renovations when we last passed, it should again be open to the public.

Dominating the eastern flank of the piazza, the Gothic **Palazzo Comunale** houses the **Museo Civico** (☎ 0573 37 12 96; Piazza del Duomo; adult/child €3.10/1.55; ⏰ 10am-7pm Tue-Sat, 9.30am-12.30pm Sun), with works by Tuscan artists from the 13th to 20th centuries.

AROUND PIAZZA DEL DUOMO

The rich portico of the nearby **Ospedale del Ceppo** (Piazza Giovanni XXIII), with its detailed polychrome terracotta frieze by Giovanni della Robbia, will stop even the monument-weary in their tracks. It depicts the *Sette Opere di Misericordia* (Seven Works of Mercy), while the five medallions represent the *Virtù Teologali* (Theological Virtues), including a quite beautiful Annunciation.

A short walk westwards from the piazza along Via degli Orafi takes you past the striking Art Nouveau façade of the **Galleria Vittorio Emanuele** (Via degli Orafi 54), guarded over by a bronze statue of Mercury. Its lovely external wrought-iron balconies and internal painted ceiling above two-tiered galleries merit more than the uninspiring shops and booths that trade there today.

South of here is a museum-cum-gallery, **Museo Marino Marini** (☎ 0573 3 02 85; Corso Silvano Fedi; admission €3; ⏰ 10am-6pm Mon-Sat), which is

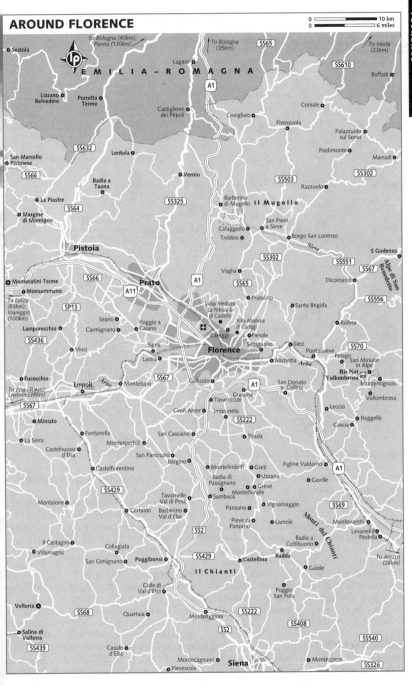

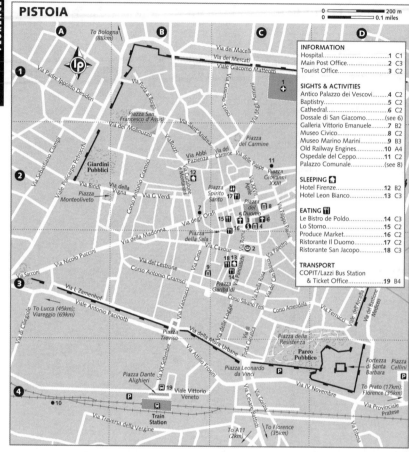

PISTOIA

INFORMATION
Hospital.................................1 C1
Main Post Office....................2 C3
Tourist Office........................3 C3

SIGHTS & ACTIVITIES
Antico Palazzo dei Vescovi.....4 C2
Baptistry................................5 C2
Cathedral..............................6 C2
Dossale di San Giacomo.....(see 6)
Galleria Vittorio Emanuele.......7 B2
Museo Civico.........................8 C2
Museo Marino Marini..............9 B3
Old Railway Engines..............10 A4
Ospedale del Ceppo..............11 C2
Palazzo Comunale............(see 8)

SLEEPING
Hotel Firenze.......................12 B2
Hotel Leon Bianco...............13 C3

EATING
Le Bistro de Poldo................14 C3
Lo Storno.............................15 C3
Produce Market....................16 C2
Ristorante Il Duomo..............17 C3
Ristorante San Jacopo..........18 C3

TRANSPORT
COPIT/Lazzi Bus Station
   & Ticket Office....................19 B4

devoted to Pistoia's most famous modern son, the eponymous sculptor and painter (1901–80).

A TRAINSPOTTERS' DELIGHT

Abandoned, rusting, unattended and un-loved, a sad collection of steam engines and early diesels squats forever on the sidings a little east of the train station. Walk further east and you'll see the very latest locomotives and carriages to have rolled out of Pistoia's workshops, destined for railway networks the world over.

Festivals & Events

Giostra dell'Orso On 25 July, Pistoia holds the Joust of the Bear, a grand medieval equestrian and jousting

festival, held in the Piazza del Duomo in honour of the town's patron saint, San Giacomo.

Pistoia Blues (www.pistoiablues.com) Over a weekend in July (which one varies) this festival pulls in an international selection of artists. The 2005 line-up featured Chuck Berry, BB King and – goodness gracious, great balls of fire! – Jerry Lee Lewis.

Sleeping

Hotel Leon Bianco (☎ 0573 2 66 75; www.hotelleon bianco.it; Via Panciatichi 2; s/d €60/100; P ✗ ▯) This is a friendly, family-owned hotel, by far the most venerable in town, which has operated as an inn since the 15th century. Rooms are spacious and comfortable. Parking is €5.

Hotel Firenze (☎ 0573 2 31 41; www.hotel-firenze .it; Via Curtatone e Montanara 42; s/d incl breakfast €60/80;

FLORENCE

(P X 💻) Here you will find large, simple rooms with fridges. Although a little colourless and glum, the facilities are just fine. Hotel parking is €5.

Eating

If you're looking for a place to eat or to rest your feet with a drink, Via del Lestrone may be barely 50m long, but packed with bars and eateries, it's the one to prowl.

Lo Storno (☎ 0573 2 61 93; Via del Lastrone 8; meals from €20; 🕒 Wed-Sat & lunch Tue) This place has a long pedigree; an *osteria* of one sort or another has existed here for the past 600 years. Today the chef prepares a continually changing array of dishes in full view of the guests, the atmosphere is cheery and bustling, and portions are large.

Ristorante San Jacopo (☎ 0573 2 77 86; Via Crispi 15; meals around €20; 🕒 closed Sun dinner & Mon) This restaurant has new owners, who have respected and retained most of the previous à la carte menu, and continue to serve great Tuscan dishes. House specialities include *baccalà alla Livornese* (salted cod) and *maccheroni alla Pistoiese* (macaroni as you've never tasted it, in a duck sauce).

Ristorante Il Duomo (☎ 0573 3 19 48; Via Bracciolini 5; mains around €5; 🕒 noon-3pm Mon-Sat) This is a cheap, self-service, buffet-style place where your plate can be heaped high with generous portions of pasta and salad. There's also a small selection of main dishes – if you've still a spare cranny.

Le Bistro de Poldo (☎ 0573 2 92 30; Via Panciatichi 4; menu €10, mains €9-14; 🕒 Thu-Tue) Beside a quiet street, this place serves typical local fare plus some more exotic dishes. How about, for example, *risotto delicato scampi curry e champagne* (a prawn and champagne risotto; €7) for starters?

There's a small **produce market** (🕒 Mon-Sat) in Piazza della Sala, west of the cathedral.

Getting There & Around

Buses connect Pistoia with Florence (€3, 50 minutes, hourly) and local towns in Tuscany. The main ticket office and departure point for COPIT and Lazzi buses is opposite the train station.

The city is on the A11 and the SS64 and SS66, which head northeast for Bologna and northwest for Parma respectively. Buses No 10 and 12 connect the train station with the cathedral.

Trains link Pistoia with Florence (€2.80, 45 minutes, half-hourly), Prato (€1.50, 20 minutes, half-hourly), Lucca (€3.20, 45 minutes, more than 20 per day), Pisa (€4.10, 1¼ hours, five daily) and Viareggio (€4.10, one hour, hourly).

If you arrive by car, most hotels can provide a pass entitling you to free street parking, 9pm to 9am, or can arrange private garage parking (around €5).

Leave your vehicle in the car park by Piazza Cellini and you can hop on a shuttle bus (return €1) into the centre of town.

AROUND PISTOIA
Montecatini Terme

The graceful little town of Montecatini Terme, one of Italy's foremost spa resorts, offers a wide range of health and beauty treatments. Verdi and Puccini found inspiration here, while many Hollywood stars, from Audrey Hepburn to Woody Allen, have dropped by to unwind. These days it markets itself as the 'European Capital of Wellness', and is a pleasant place to spend a relaxing weekend or more.

The **tourist office** (☎ 0572 77 22 44; www.turismo .pistoia.it; Viale Verdi 66-68; 🕒 9am-12.30pm & 3-6pm Mon-Sat year-round, 9am-noon Sun Easter-Oct) has a neat little free guide, *Liberty Seasons in Tuscany*, which includes a walking tour of Montecatini's rich Art Nouveau architecture.

For more specific information about the *terme* (hot-spring centres) and the various treatments available, call by the **Terme di Montecatini information office** (☎ 0572 77 81; www.termemontecatini.it; Viale Verdi 41; 🕒 8am-1pm & 2.30-6pm Mon-Fri, 8am-12.30pm Sat).

SIGHTS

Nine separate *terme* operate, many of them housed in grand *belle époque* buildings in and around a lovely central park. Most function between May and October, although services in some go on longer. **Excelsior's Centro di Benessere** (Thermal Well-Being Centre; ☎ 0572 77 85 18; Viale Verdi; 🕒 8am-8pm Mon-Sat, 10am-8pm Sun) is the only one open year-round.

The range of services, treatments and medical tests available is staggering – you could go for the three-day 'wellness reflects' programme and have a body and facial with mud and bath, plus reflexology and hot-stone body massage (€250), or indulge in a week of massages, manicures, face-packs and the like (from €393). Then again, you could just get your eyebrows plucked (€8).

On the same road, the huge Art Nouveau complex of the **Terme Tettuccio** (admission €8) offers laxative waters, if you feel a bit bunged up. It has more than 400 toilets and beautiful gardens.

SLEEPING & EATING
Montecatini has more than 200 hotels, many of which offer half and full board as well as spa packages.

Hotel La Pia (☎ 0572 77 13 82; www.lapiahotel.it; Via Montebello 30; half board from €70 per person; 🍴) This is a friendly, family-run place with an excellent restaurant. It usually requires half board and a minimum stay of three days, and offers a range of special spa packages.

Grand Hotel Plaza (☎ 0572 7 58 31; www.hotel plaza.it; Piazza del Popolo 7; s/d €74/125; P 🍴 🐾) A wonderfully atmospheric *fin-de-siècle* hotel with a great price-quality ratio. Past guests include Verdi, Garibaldi and Rossini. Hotel parking is €10.

Turismo Verde (☎ 0572 6 72 25, 329 743 33 64; nievole@tin.it; Molino delle Galere, Via Renaggio 12, Nievole) Those interested in *agriturismo* (farm-stay accommodation) should contact Turismo Verde. The head honcho, Giuseppe Mazzocchi, is a chef who runs cookery classes (from €90) in an old mill in the nearby village of Nievole. Two- and three-day courses and specialist options, such as cooking with chocolate, are also offered. Large apartments at the mill cost €80 for two people.

Enoteca Giovanni (☎ 0572 7 16 95; Via Garibaldi 25-27; meals €40-50; 🕐 closed Mon & 2nd half Feb & Aug) This is two places in one, both guaranteed to please your palate. Giovanni, a qualified sommelier, is a welcoming host whose teams offer equally knowledgeable, attentive service. His *enoteca*, with more than 900 wines from around the world, serves snacks and nibbles. Next door, the much garlanded restaurant (skim the impressive diplomas and tributes just inside the door) offers refined cuisine, strong on game dishes in season.

La Cascina (☎ 0572 7 84 74; Viale Giuseppe Verdi 43; mains around €15; 🕐 Tue-Sun) Set on the edge of the park opposite the tourist office, there's dining in the stylish interior (precede it with an apéritif in the swanky bar) or on the open terrace.

You shouldn't leave town without some of the delicious local Cialde di Monticatini,

large, round dessert wafers filled with crushed almonds. You're guaranteed the real McCoy at **Bargilli** (☎ 0572 7 94 59; Viale Grocco 2; 🕐 closed Mon), open till midnight in summer.

GETTING THERE & AWAY
Montecatini has a couple of train stations, Montecatini Centro and Montecatini Montsummano, barely a kilometre apart. Trains running between Lucca (€2.60) and Florence (€3.20) stop at both. Regular buses stop beside Montecatini Monsummano train station, and service Florence (€3.10, 50 minutes), Lucca (€2.70), Pescia (€1.40), Monsummano (€1) and other nearby locations.

Montecatini Alto
The late-19th-century **cable car** (funicular railway; one way/return €3/5; 🕐 10am-midnight mid-Apr–Sep, 10am-7.30pm late-Mar–mid-Apr & Oct) hauls itself uphill every 30 minutes to Montecatini Alto, much fought-over, besieged and battered throughout the Middle Ages. This pretty village offers great views of the surrounding countryside. You'll recognise its 12th-century Chiesa di Santa Maria a Ripa by the bizarre, trophy-laden crucifix outside.

If you want to stay up high, try the well-appointed **Hotel Villa Gaia** (☎ 0572 7 86 37; www .villagaia.it; Via Mura P Grocco 11; d incl buffet breakfast €120) and ask for a room with a view. Failing this, you can enjoy the gorgeous panorama from its terrace.

Monsummano
Die-hard lovers of spa complexes could take in Monsummano, a few kilometres away from Montecatini Terme by bus (€1.35). The main attraction is the **Grotta Giusti Terme** (☎ 0572 9 07 71; www.grottagiustispa.com; Via Grotta Giusti; 🕐 9am-1pm & 3-7pm Mon-Sat 21 Mar-8 Jan), just outside town. A vast range of treatments is on offer, from nasal irrigation (€20) to aromatherapy facials (€70) and full programmes of massages and baths, or you can dunk yourself in the naturally heated pool (per day €16). The bus from Montecatini Terme goes right past the complex.

PRATO
pop 174,600
Virtually in Florence's urban and industrial sprawl and a mere 17km to its northwest, Prato is one of Italy's main textile production centres. Tuscany's second-largest town

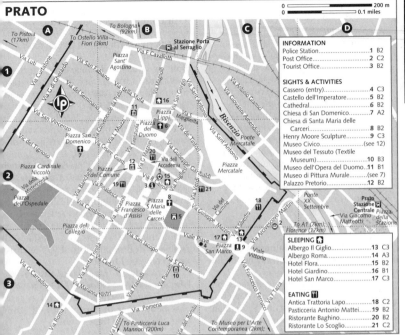

PRATO

after Florence, it has the country's biggest concentration of Chinese immigrants, many now second- or even third-generation Pratese. Founded by the Ligurians, the city fell to the Etruscans, then the Romans. As early as the 11th century it was an important centre for wool production. Continuing a tradition, textiles, together with leather working, are to this day Prato's main industries. It's worth dropping in on your way to the more picturesque cities of Pistoia, Lucca and Pisa or as a half-day trip from Florence.

Orientation

Prato's compact historical heart is girdled by near-intact city walls. Its nucleus is Piazza S Maria delle Carceri. The main train station (Prato Stazione Centrale) lies east of the city centre.

Information

Police Station (☎ 0574 55 55; Via B Cairoli 29)
Tourist office (☎ 0574 2 41 12; www.prato.turismo.toscana.it; Piazza S Maria delle Carceri 15; ☼ 9am-1.30pm & 2.30-6.30pm Mon-Sat Oct-Mar, daily Apr-Sep)

Sights

A combined ticket (€5), bought at any of the three sites, gives entry to the Museo di Pittura Murale, Museo dell'Opera del Duomo and Castello dell'Imperatore.

DUOMO

Head along Via Mazzoni from Piazza del Comune to the 12th-century **Duomo** (cathedral; Piazza del Duomo; ☼ 7.30am-noon & 3.30-7pm). The typical Pisan-Romanesque façade, unadorned except for a terracotta lunette by Andrea della Robbia, is banded in white-and-green Tuscan marble, a pattern you'll keep coming across in Siena, Pistoia and Lucca.

What's unusual about this cathedral is its protruding exterior **Pulpito della Sacra Cintola**, jutting out over the piazza to the right of the western entrance. The original, much-eroded panels of the pulpit, adorned with playful *putti* (winsome cherubs) and designed by Donatello and Michelozzo in the 1430s, are in the **Museo dell'Opera del Duomo** (☎ 0574 2 93 39; Piazza del Duomo 49; admission €3; ☼ 9.30am-12.30pm & 3-6.30pm Mon & Wed-Sat, 9.30am-12.30pm Sun), which

FLORENCE

A GIRDLE FOR A VIRGIN

You don't often see a pulpit on the *outside* of a cathedral. But Prato's is rather special. It was grafted on so that the *sacra cintola* (sacred girdle), believed to be the Virgin Mary's, could be displayed five times a year (Easter, 1 May, 15 August, 8 September and 25 December). The Virgin, so goes the story, gave the girdle (or belt) to St Thomas. Generations later, after the Second Crusade, a soldier brought it to Prato from Jerusalem. In medieval times huge importance was attached to such holy relics. But just how many girdles did Mary have? Another, declared the real thing in 1953 by the Orthodox Patriarch of Antioch, is stored in the Syrian city of Homs.

also has a collection of paintings by masters including Filippo Lippi, Caravaggio, Bellini and Santi di Tito.

Filippo Lippi's magnificent frescoes behind the cathedral's high altar, depicting the lives of John the Baptist and St Stephen, have been under restoration for several years. You can gaze from below or join a guided tour (€8; 10am, 11am, 4pm and 5pm Saturday, 10am and 11am Sunday), up on the scaffolding. Reserve at the tourist office. Agnolo Gaddi's fresco cycle of the *Legend of the Holy Girdle* is in a chapel in the northwest corner of the nave.

MUSEO DEL TESSUTO

Prato's **textile museum** (☎ 0574 61 15 03; Via Santa Chiara 24; adult/child €4/2; ☽ 10am-6pm Mon & Wed-Fri, 10am-2pm Sat, 4-7pm Sun) devotes itself to textiles throughout the ages. It highlights the achievements of the local cloth industry, but you'll also find examples of textiles (some from as early as the 3rd century) from Italy and Europe, and as far afield as India, China and the Americas.

MUSEO DI PITTURA MURALE

This small but impressive **museum** (☎ 0574 44 05 01; Piazza San Domenico; admission €5; ☽ 9am-1pm Mon & Wed-Sat, 3-6pm Fri & Sat), within the **Chiesa di San Domenico**, houses a collection of largely Tuscan paintings. Among artists represented are Filippo Lippi, Paolo Uccello and Bernardo Daddi, with his touchingly naive polyptych of the miracle of the Vir-

gin's girdle (see left). Enjoy too the 14th- t 17th-century frescoes and graffiti.

CHIESA DI SANTA MARIA DELLE CARCERI & AROUND

Built by Giuliano da Sangallo towards th end of the 15th century, the high, graceful interior of this **church** (Piazza Santa Maria dell Carceri; ☽ 7am-noon & 4-7pm) was a prototyp for many a Renaissance church in Tuscany The glazed terracotta frieze and, above it medallions of the Evangelists are by Andre della Robbia and his team.

Found on the same piazza, the **Castell dell'Imperatore** (☎ 0574 3 82 07; Piazza Santa Mari delle Carceri; admission €2; ☽ 9am-1pm Apr-Sep), Pra to's castle, was built in the 13th century by the Holy Roman Emperor Frederick II. It' an interesting enough example of military architecture but, with its bare interior, only really worth dropping into if you're carrying a combined ticket.

Just down the road is the **Cassero** (Vial Piave; admission free; ☽ 10am-1pm & 4-7pm Wed-Mon) a long, much-restored medieval covered passageway that originally allowed access from the castle to the city walls.

CONTEMPORARY ART

Prato's most striking piece of modern art is Henry Moore's **sculpture** *Forma Squadrata con Taglio* (Cleft Square), an eye-catching white monolith smack bang in the middle of Piazza San Marco. South of the city walls is the **Museo per l'Arte Contemporanea** (☎ 0574 53 17; Viale della Repubblica 277 admission €7; ☽ core hr 10am-7pm Wed-Mon). Part of a centre devoted to contemporary art, its permanent collection is complemented by temporary exhibitions and performances throughout the year.

PALAZZO PRETORIO & MUSEO CIVICO

The impressive bulk of the **Palazzo Pretorio**, long undergoing extensive renovation, will one day again house the city's **Museo Civico**.

Festivals & Events

Outside town in Poggio a Caiano and in various locations around Prato itself, they have been celebrating the **Festival delle Colline** (Hills Festival) since 1979. This concert series brings together class acts of world music from late June to late July.

THE MERCHANT OF PRATO

'Fate has so willed that, from the day of my birth, I should never know a whole happy day...' So wrote one of Prato's most celebrated sons, Francesco di Marco Datini, in the 1390s.

Datini, to whom a statue was erected in the shadow of Palazzo Pretorio after his death in August 1410, was neither a war hero nor a great statesman. Nor was he a man of learning or an inventor. Born in 1335 to a poor innkeeper, Datini grew up to become a highly successful international merchant.

Although he never reached the dizzy heights of the great Florentine trading families, Datini carved out a respectable business empire for himself that stretched from Prato and Florence to Avignon, Barcelona and the Balearic Islands. Not bad for a 15-year-old boy who arrived in the papal city of Avignon with 150 florins in his pocket.

Prato was (and remains) a town of shopkeepers and small businesses. Datini rose above this, and by the time he returned from Avignon 33 years later he was the richest man in town. For the people of Prato, this made him something of a hero. Basing himself principally in Florence, he traded in just about anything that looked likely to turn a profit, from cloth and raw materials to slaves and armaments, through his branches and agents in France, Spain, England and Flanders.

Datini knew how to have fun, and there are multiple stories of his sybaritic lifestyle and womanising. On the other hand, he worked like a slave himself, often sleeping no more than four hours a night. Only at the end of his life did he seem to give thought to things other than the accumulation of money. In his will he left all his wealth (after bequests) to a new charitable foundation established in his name in his fine house on Via Rinaldesca.

Nowadays, Datini is not so much known for his financial exploits as for the reworking of his extensive correspondence. He spent long hours every day writing not only to his branches but also to his wife Margherita and friends. He was meticulous about keeping all mail that came to him, and ordered his branch managers to do the same. His charity, the Ceppo di Francesco di Marco, has kept the archive of this correspondence in one piece for more than 500 years. It provides a rare glimpse not only into the business life of a late medieval trader, but also into the daily life of middle-class Tuscans, especially in Prato and Florence.

Iris Origo distilled this wealth of material into a fascinating account of medieval life entitled *The Merchant of Prato* (1957).

Sleeping

Within easy reach of Florence, Prato is worth considering as an alternative base to the big city, especially in high season when prices rise and places can be booked solid.

Hotel Flora (☎ 0574 33 521; www.hotelflora.info; Via B Cairoli 31; s/d incl buffet breakfast €95/150; P ⊠ ▯) An attractive three-star midrange option in the heart of town. All 31 bedrooms have been recently renovated, and the small, enclosed roof terrace offers good views over town. Hotel parking is €10.

Hotel Giardino (☎ 0574 60 65 88; www.giardino hotel.com; Via Magnolfi 2-6; s/d €78/110; P ⊠ ▯) The Garden Hotel has 28 rooms, all agreeably retro in their furnishings, and each with a gleaming, tiled bathroom. Hotel parking is €11.

Albergo Il Giglio (☎ 0574 3 70 49; albergoilgiglio@tin .it; Piazza San Marco 14; s/d €41/60, with bathroom €58/72; ⊠) This hotel is a friendly place with a cosy, could-be-home guest sitting room. The same family (who also own Albergo Roma) have run the place since 1969, so they've clearly got the mix right.

Albergo Roma (☎ 0574 3 17 77; albergoilgiglio@tin .it; Via G Carradori 1; s/d €55/60; ⊠) This hotel is a one-star joint with 12 modest rooms, but they're spruce, clean and excellent value for your euro. Ask for a one at the back, as the hotel overlooks a busy road.

Hotel San Marco (☎ 0574 2 13 21; Piazza San Marco 48; s/d €70/95; P ⊠ ▯) This is a reasonably priced three-star option beside the busy piazza. Rooms are small and neat, with refrigerator, and those overlooking the square have double-glazed windows.

Ostello Villa Fiorelli (☎ 0574 69 76 11; cspsrl@ interfree.it; Parco di Galceti, Via di Galceti 64; dm/d €14.50/35) Prato's HI-affiliated youth hostel, served by bus No 13, is some 3km north of Piazza del Duomo.

Eating

Piazza Mercatale, with its popular restaurants and lively atmosphere, is well worth trawling.

Ristorante Lo Scoglio (☎ 0574 2 27 60; Via Verdi 42; meals around €20, pizzas from €6; ☼ Tue-Sun) This restaurant has a wide-ranging menu offering everything from pizza to fresh fish.

Ristorante Baghino (☎ 0574 2 79 20; Via dell'Accademia 9; meals around €25; ☼ Mon-Sat) In much the same vein as Lo Scoglio, Baghino offers more stylish surroundings and carries a decent wine list.

Antica Trattoria Lapo (☎ 0574 2 37 45; Piazza Mercatale 141; meals from €20) This place has an appealingly relaxed, informal atmosphere and offers plenty of Tuscan dishes. It's popular, so arrive early or reserve.

Pasticceria Antonio Mattei (☎ 0574 2 57 56; Via Ricasoli 20; ☼ Tue-Sat & morning Sun) Pick up a packet of *cantucci,* also called *biscotti di Prato,* a crunchy, rusklike biscuit studded with almonds that you usually dip in wine. This place makes them on the spot.

Pasticceria Luca Mannori (☎ 0574 2 16 28; Via Lazzarini 2; ☼ Wed-Mon) Just outside the city walls, this *pasticceria* serves altogether more subtle cakes and pastries. On two occasions, Signor Mannori has been proclaimed world champion in international confectionery competitions – his *torta sette veli* (tart of the seven veils) is a true *pièce de résistance.*

CAP THIS ONE

The owner of a restaurant in a village near Florence recently found himself €3000 lighter after a customer bit on a human tooth, not his own, as he took a forkful of pizza.

Refusing the chef's offer of a complimentary meal, the client took the restaurant to court, where it was fined for faulty hygiene.

This, despite a spirited argument from the defence lawyer. 'Your honour,' he argued 'my client and his staff observe regulations and always wear a hat or net over their hair. Are they now expected to wear surgical masks as well?'

No-one knows – or no-one is telling – how the offending tooth got into the topping.

Getting There & Around

CAP and Lazzi buses operate regular services to and from Florence (€2.40, 45 minutes, every 15 minutes) departing from Prato Stazione Centrale train station. The train, however, works out quicker and cheaper.

By car, take the A1 from Florence and exit at Calenzano, or the A11 and exit at Prato Est or Ovest. The SS325 connects Prato with Bologna.

Prato is on the Florence–Bologna and Florence–Lucca train lines. Sample fares and destinations include to Florence (€1.50, 25 minutes, every 10 minutes), Bologna (€7.45, one hour, 20 daily), Lucca (€4.10, one hour, 20 daily) and Pistoia (€1.50, 20 minutes, half-hourly).

The local LAM blue bus runs every seven minutes between the train station and the town centre, generally terminating at Piazza San Domenico.

FIESOLE

Perched in hills about 8km northeast of Florence, and wedged between the valleys of the Arno and Mugnone rivers, Fiesole and its scattered villas have attracted the likes of Boccaccio, Marcel Proust, Gertrude Stein and Frank Lloyd Wright. Especially in summer, it continues to entice visitors away from muggy Florence with cooler air, lush olive groves and spectacular views of the plain below.

For long the most important city in northern Etruria, Fiesole was founded in the 7th century BC by the Etruscans. An easy half-day outing from Florence, it's a fabulous spot for a picnic and short walk. Avoid Sunday when half of Florence invades.

The **tourist office** (☎ 055 59 87 20; Via Portigiani 3; ☼ 9am-6pm Mon-Sat, 10am-1pm & 2-6pm Sun Apr-Oct, 9am-5pm Mon-Sat, 10am-4pm Sun Nov-Mar) is just off Piazza Mino da Fiesole, the heart of the village.

Sights

A combined ticket (€6.70) gives you entry to Fiesole's main sights, Museo Bandini and Zona Archeologica.

The tiny **Museo Bandini** (☎ 055 5 94 77; Via Duprè; ☼ 10am-7pm daily Apr-Sep, 10am-5pm Wed-Mon Oct-Mar) has an impressive collection of early Tuscan Renaissance works, including Taddeo Gaddi's *Annunciazione* (Annunciation).

Opposite the museum, **Zona Archeologica** (Via Dupré; 9.30am-7pm daily Apr-Sep, 9.30am-5pm Wed-Mon Oct-Mar) features a 1st-century-BC Roman theatre, that is the venue for the **Estate Fiesolana**, a series of concerts and performances held between June and August. Also in the complex are a small Etruscan temple and Roman baths. Its small archaeological museum, with exhibits from the Bronze Age to the Roman period, is worth a look.

Far in time and style from the Renaissance splendours of the valley below, **Museo Primo Conti** (☎ 055 59 70 95; Via Dupré 18; admission €3; 9am-2pm), about 300m north of the piazza, was the home of the eponymous avant-garde 20th-century artist, and houses more than 60 of his paintings.

The **cathedral** (Piazza Mino da Fiesole; 7.30am-noon & 3-6pm May-Oct, 7.30am-noon & 2-5pm Nov-Apr) overlooks the main square. Begun in the 11th century, it was heavily renovated in the 19th century. Inside, a glazed terracotta statue of San Romolo (St Romulus; 1521) by Giovanni della Robbia sits above the entrance.

For a five-star panorama, head 200m up steep Via S Francesco to a small viewpoint. If you're planning a picnic or just want a refreshing walk, pick up the tourist office brochure *Parco di Montefeceri*, which describes four easy walks from 1.5km to 3.5km.

Sleeping & Eating

Hotel Villa Aurora (☎ 055 5 93 63; www.villaaurora.net; Piazza Mino da Fiesole 39; d €170-210, meals around €45; P) Sitting square on the main piazza, this is a great deal more impressive than the peeling façade might have you believe. Rooms at this welcoming mid-19th-century hotel are smart and spacious, and those at the rear offer a superb sweeping panorama of Florence. Ask for No 31, the largest, with its unencumbered view of the plain below. The hotel also runs a fine restaurant, where you'll eat very well, whether in the lavish indoor dining room or on one of the open-air terraces.

Hotel Villa Bonelli (☎ 055 5 95 13; www.hotel villabonelli.com; Via Poeti 1; s/d €75/124;) This is a friendly, family-run place in a peaceful location. There's a wide terrace, and its 19 large, airy rooms have an agreeably rustic feel.

Campeggio Panoramico (☎ 055 59 90 69; Via Peramonda 1; person/pitch €10.50/15.75;) This is altogether larger and cooler than the cramped options around Florence. It has panoramic views of the city, makes a seductive alternative, and has a bar, restaurant and pool thrown in.

Pizzeria Etrusca (☎ 055 59 94 84; Piazza Mino da Fiesole 2; pizzas around €5.50) A popular spot on the main square for pizza and pasta, Etrusca will again have outdoor seating under the trees, once the extensive roadworks in the square are completed.

Trattoria Le Cave di Maiano (☎ 055 5 91 33; Via Cave di Maiano 16; meals around €30; closed lunch Mon) Alternatively, drop down to this trattoria in Maiano. This favourite with Florentines is a fine spot for traditional meat dishes. There are several intimate, interconnecting dining rooms and, for optimum views, external terraces.

Getting There & Away

Take ATAF bus No 7 from Stazione di Santa Maria Novella in Florence. If you're driving, Fiesole is signed from Florence's Piazza della Libertà, north of the cathedral.

SETTIGNANO

Just 6km east of Fiesole along a delightful, if at times nail-bitingly narrow back-country lane, Settignano offers views of Florence that can equal Fiesole's (but come in the morning in summer; by early afternoon all you can see is glare).

Villa Morghen (☎ 055 69 73 62; Via Feliceto 8; s/d incl breakfast €75/120; P) was comprehensively overhauled in 2001 when the last five monks left this erstwhile monastery. It remains a pleasant, tranquil retreat in the hills. Walls are thick, rooms spacious and ceilings high, all helping to keep the temperature cool in high summer.

La Capponcina (Map pp78-9; ☎ 055 69 70 37; Via San Romano 17r; meals €30-35; closed Mon) is a popular out-of-town gastronomic venue for Florentines. The kitchen is renowned in particular for its *tagliata di manzo*, succulent beef fillets sliced up and served on a bed of rocket. Sitting in the garden is a true pleasure in summer, when you're sure of being several degrees cooler than down in Florence.

Take bus No 10 (or bus No 67 after 9pm) from Florence's Stazione di Santa Maria Novella. La Capponcina is a few steps off central Piazza San Tommaseo, where the bus terminates.

NO TRUFFLING MATTER

In late 2004 a consortium headed by Zafferano, a Michelin-star Italian restaurant in London, shelled out €40,000 at a charity auction for a prized 850g Tuscan white truffle, a mud-clogged, knobbly lump of fungus about the size of a child's brain. 'Earthy, sexy and an aphrodisiac' is how Sr Enzo Cassini, the restaurant manager, described his prize. Earthy, it was, undoubtedly, and rich too in a chemical that's almost identical to a sex hormone secreted by the male pig – so perhaps an aphrodisiac as well to a gentleman or two of your acquaintance.

The head chef reverentially placed this ball of pungent scent, in form not unlike a dinosaur turd, within the restaurant fridge, locked it, pocketed the keys and flew off for four days of holiday. His return left a bitter taste as he discovered within the fridge one sad, seeping and decidedly 'off' truffle. Making the best of a bad bungle, he interred it in his back garden.

But the truffle was still not at peace. This king of its kind merited a more regal burial so it was flown back to its native Tuscany. There, attended by guards in medieval costume and to the throb of a drum, it was solemnly buried in the grounds of the Castello di Cafaggiolo, 25km north of Florence and its final resting place – unless, that is, some feisty sow should come snuffling by…

MEDICI VILLAS

The Medicis built several villas in the countryside around Florence as their wealth and prosperity grew during the 15th and 16th centuries. Most are now enclosed by the city's suburbs and industrial sprawl, and are easily reached by ATAF bus from Stazione di Santa Maria Novella. A combined ticket (€2) gets you in to two of the finest, Villa Medicea La Petraia and Villa Medicea di Castello.

Villa Medicea La Petraia (Map p131; ☎ 055 45 26 91; Via della Petraia 40; ☟ 8.15am-sunset, closed 2nd & 3rd Mon of the month) is about 3.5km north of the city. Commissioned by Cardinal Ferdinando de' Medici in 1576, this former castle was converted by Buontalenti, and features a magnificent garden with a fountain by Giambologna. Take bus No 28.

Villa Medicea di Castello (Map p131; ☎ 055 45 47 91; Via di Castello 47; ☟ 8.15am-sunset, closed 2nd & 3rd Mon of the month), further north, was Lorenzo il Magnifico's summer home. You can only visit the park. Again, take bus No 28.

Villa Medicea di Careggi (Map p131; ☎ 055 427 95 01; Viale Pieraccini 17; admission free; ☟ 9am-6pm Mon-Fri, 9am-noon Sat) is where Lorenzo il Magnifico breathed his last in 1492. Nowadays, it serves as administrative offices for the local hospital, and access is limited, although you're free to visit the gardens. ATAF bus No 14C from Stazione di Santa Maria Novella runs past.

Another Medici getaway was the **Villa di Poggio a Caiano** (☎ 055 87 70 12; Piazza Medici, Poggio a Caiano; villa/grounds €2/free; ☟ tours hourly 8.30am-6.30pm Jun-Aug, 8.30am-dusk Sep-May, closed 2nd & 3rd

Mon of the month). About 15km from Florence on the old road to Pistoia, this mansion is set in magnificent sprawling gardens. Its interior is sumptuously decorated with frescoes and furnished much as it was when it functioned as a royal residence of the Savoys. Take the COPIT bus (€4 return, 30 minutes) running between Florence and Pistoia; it stops right outside.

IL MUGELLO

The area northeast of Florence leading up to the border with Emilia-Romagna is known as Il Mugello. In it are some of Tuscany's most traditional villages, interspersed with elegant second homes for fortunate Florentines. The valley that the River Sieve winds through is one of Tuscany's premier wine areas.

In the town of **Borgo San Lorenzo**, the **Comunità Montana del Mugello** (☎ 055 849 53 46; Via P Togliatti 45), **Associazione Turismo Ambiente** (☎ 055 845 87 93; Piazza Dante 29) and **Borga Informa** (☎ 055 845 62 30; infoborgo@tin.it; Villa Pedori Giraldi) are all useful sources of information about the area. The last two can arrange accommodation and excursions in the area.

The Medici originated from the Mugello, and there are several of their family castles, villas and palaces in the area. Most, however, are closed to the public.

Take the SS65 north from Florence. Near Vaglia, about 5km north of Pratolino, the **Parco della Villa Medici-Demidoff** (☎ 055 40 91 55; admission €2.60; ☟ 10am-8pm Thu-Sun Apr-Sep, 10am-6pm Sun Mar & Oct) is a romantic garden, built around a Medici villa, long ago demolished.

Follow the SS65 for another 13km and turn right for glimpses of another pair of Medici villas: **Trebbio**, then **Cafaggiolo**, further along the same road, originally a fortress and converted into a villa by Michelozzo in 1451. Neither is open to the public.

Il Mugello makes for pleasant walking. Sorgenti Firenze Trekking (SOFT; Florence Springs Trekking) is a network of signed day or half-day trails crisscrossing the area. *Mugello, Alto Mugello, Val di Sieve*, produced by SELCA, is a decent map for hikers at 1:70,000 (its trail No 8 is an easy 3½-hour round-trip walk, starting from the villa at Cafaggiolo and passing by Trebbio).

IL CHIANTI

When many people think of classic Tuscan countryside, the olive groves and gentle vine-and-poppy-speckled hills and valleys between Florence and Siena in the Chianti region usually spring to mind. The region suffered severe economic hardship and depopulation in the postwar period, but from the 1960s, waves of sun-hungry foreigners – mostly British and German – began arriving, snapping up holiday homes or moving in permanently. In some areas, British expats now make up almost a third of the population – no wonder it's sometimes referred to as 'Chiantishire'.

Il Chianti is split between the provinces of Florence (Chianti Fiorentino) and Siena (Chianti Sienese). The lovely Monti del Chianti rising into the Apennines mark the area's eastern boundary.

Apart from beautiful countryside, Il Chianti is also home to some of Italy's best-marketed wines. The oldest and most famous is Chianti Classico. A blend of red grapes with a minimum of 75% Sangiovese, it's sold under the Gallo Nero (Black Cockerel) symbol. The rest of Il Chianti is split into a further six classified wine-growing regions: Colli Fiorentini, Colli Senesi, Colline Pisane, Colli Aretini, Montalbano and Rufina, all with their distinct characteristics. As well as these wines, look out for *vin santo*, a sweet, aged dessert wine akin to sherry, produced by many wineries and often enjoyed with *cantucci* biscuits.

The picturesque SS222, known as the Strada Chiantigiana, runs between Florence and Siena. You can bus-hop, but your own wheels make exploration much easier. Many explore Il Chianti by bicycle, and it's also gentle walking country. Pack a copy of *Chianti Classico: Val di Pesa-Val d'Elsa*, a map at 1:25,000 with hiking trails superimposed. Lonely Planet's *Walking in Italy* describes a three-day classic hike that passes through Greve and Radda.

Budget accommodation is limited, and wherever you stay, it's wise to book well ahead since Il Chianti is a popular tourist destination year-round.

For some useful links, check www.chianti online.com, a commercial, after-your-euro

---

DETOUR: IL CHIANTI

Il Chianti is one of the most attractive and rewarding regions of Tuscany, but to appreciate it fully you need your own transport. From Greve in Chianti, take the SS222 – also known as the Via Chiantigina – southwards for roughly 1km, at which point you will see a local road on your right. Take this road, leading in a southeasterly direction through typical Chianti countryside of olive trees and vines, and after about 2km you will come upon Villa Vignamaggio. Here you can stop for a bite to eat and stock up on some wine. Continue eastwards, and after another 2km the road turns south and passes through the pretty village of Lamole, famous for its *vin santo* (sweet dessert wine). Just over 2km further south, the road meets the SP118; turn eastwards (the road now becomes the SP112) and continue on this road as it turns south to the tiny village of Volpaia, with wonderful views of the surrounding countryside. The winery here is particularly good, and you can take a tour of the cellars and try some of the products.

From here it's a 3km journey south along the SP112, passing vineyards and fields full of poppies along the way, to Lo Spiccio. Take the secondary road to the east, which, after a little over 1km, joins the SS429. If you like, you can then double-back southwestwards for about 500m to visit Radda. Otherwise, continue travelling east on the SS429 for around 6km, at which point you will see a secondary road to the north that soon leads to the remote and beautiful Badia a Coltibuono, which has an excellent restaurant and a shop selling the property's wine.

sort of site. For more details about the region's wines, and Tuscan wines in general, see p63.

Chianti Fiorentino

GREVE

About 20km south of Florence on the SS222, Greve is the first good base for exploring the area. You can get there easily from Florence by SITA bus. Its unusual, triangular Piazza Matteotti, surrounded by porticoes, is an interesting provincial version of a Florentine piazza. At its heart stands a statue of Giovanni da Verrazzano, local-boy-made-good and discoverer of New York harbour. He's commemorated there by the Verrazano Narrows bridge (the good captain lost a 'z' from his name somewhere in the mid-Atlantic), linking Staten Island to Brooklyn and indelibly printed in the soul and on the soles of every runner who's done the New York marathon.

If good wines tickle your palate, hit town for Greve's annual wine fair, held during the first or second week of September.

The **tourist office** (☎ 055 854 62 87; Viale Verrazzano 59; � 9.30am-1pm & 2.30-7pm Mon-Sat Mar-Oct) is on the main street. **Chianti Slow Travel** (☎ 055 854 62 99; www.chiantiechianti.it in Italian; Piazza Ferrante Mori 1) can book accommodation and arrange visits to local wineries.

Greve has a couple of good hotels, both with quality restaurants.

Albergo Giovanni da Verrazzano (☎ 055 85 31 89; www.verrazzano.it; Piazza Matteotti 28; s/d €68/90, with bathroom €86/105; � closed 1st 3 weeks Feb; ☐) is a pleasant three-star family hotel, run by the same family for three generations. Some of its 10 rooms overlook the main square.

Albergo Del Chianti (☎ 055 85 37 63; www.albergo delchianti.it; Piazza Matteotti 86; d incl breakfast €75; � mid-Mar–mid-Nov; ☒ ☒) is another three-star hotel, also sitting on Greve's central piazza. It has a pool, garden and attractive breakfast bar.

Villa Vignamaggio (☎ 055 85 46 61; www.vigna maggio.it; Via Petriolo 5; d €150-350; ☒ ☐ ☒) is an exquisite 15th-century manor house 5km south of Greve. Reputedly the birthplace of Mona Lisa and a location in Kenneth Branagh's film *Much Ado About Nothing*, it also has fully equipped villas and cottages with huge bathrooms and Jacuzzis (€200 to €250). There's a great Italian garden, a pair of outdoor pools and tennis courts. Take

the S222 southwards for 2km, then turn left, following the signs for Lamole.

Macelleria Falorni (☎ 055 85 30 29; Piazza Matteotti 69-71) is a butcher's, renowned throughout Tuscany for its prime quality meat, including the traditional *cinta senese* pork. The two huge chopping tables outside its door give a clue to what is happening inside…

Mangiando Mangiando (☎ 055 854 63 72; Piazza Matteotti 80; mains €9.50-14) is the place to enjoy similar quality, carefully selected meats (notice the gleaming scales and slicer on the counter as you enter). It's an intimate little restaurant with heavy wooden tables and chairs and friendly service. Since capacity's limited, do reserve.

Le Cantine di Greve in Chianti (☎ 055 854 64 04; Piazza delle Cantine; � 10am-7pm) is a vast *enoteca* with more than 1200 varieties of Chianti and other wines on sale. It blends tradition and 21st-century technology: buy yourself a prepaid wine card (from €10), stick it into one of the taps that dispense around 150 different wines, and your tipple trickles out. Follow the signs from Piazza Matteotti.

MONTEFIORALLE

The few houses of this ancient castle-village 2km west of and up from Greve, follow the ovoid shape of the old walls. For a pleasant walk back down, follow a dirt road for a few hundred metres, then turn right to reach the simple **Pieve di San Cresci**, from where you can descend directly to Greve.

BADIA DI PASSIGNANO

In its magnificent setting of olive groves and vineyards, the mighty Badia di Passignano is about 7km west of Montefioralle (the last 3km is along an unmade road). Founded in 1049 by Benedictine monks of the Vallombrosan order, the abbey is a massive, towered castle encircled by cypresses.

The abbey church of **San Michele** was closed for renovations at the time of writing. Inside are early-17th-century frescoes by Passignano (so called because he was born here) and, in the refectory, *Ultima Cena* (Last Supper; 1476) by Domenico and Davide Ghirlandaio.

The excellent **Osteria di Passignano** (☎ 055 80 12 78; www.vignamaggio.it; Via Passignano 31; � Mon-Sat serves a creative menu, made from local ingredients, with three-course menus around €35. There's also an extensive wine list. Tour the wine cellars cost €10, and the *osteria* ins one-day cookery classes for €110.

ANZANO

ravelling south along the Santa Chiangiana, you pass through the quiet medieval illage of Panzano. You get more than your eat at the **Antica Macelleria Cecchini** (☎ 055 5 20 20; Via XX Luglio; ☒ closed Wed), a butcher's in by local celebrity Dario Cecchini, who elcomes his customers with wine, platters f meat and Dante recitals. From here you an continue on to Chianti Senese.

hianti Sienese

ASTELLINA

The huge cylindrical silos at the entry to nis town may make you think you've hit he industrial zone by mistake. In fact, hey're brimming with Chianti Classico, he wine that, together with tourism, brings vealth to this small community, long ago a rontier town between warring Siena and lorence. From the southern car park, take 'ia Ferruccio, then turn right almost imnediately to walk into town beneath the unnel-like Via del Volte. This medieval treet, originally open to the elements, then ncroached upon by shops and houses, is iow a long, vaulted, shady tunnel, particuarly welcome in summer.

Castellina's **tourist office** (☎ 0577 74 13 92; www.essenceoftuscany.it; Via Ferruccio 26; ☒ 10am-1pm & 2-6pm daily Mar-Nov, 10am-1pm & 2-4pm Mon-Sat Dec & Feb), towards the village's northern end, is in enterprising place that rents bikes, books iccommodation and arranges visits to winries. It'll even lay on a cookery class for a mall group.

Albergo Squarcialupi (☎ 0577 74 11 86; www.essen eoftuscany.it; Via Ferruccio 22; d incl breakfast from €110; ☒ mid-Mar–Oct; P ☒ ☐ ☒) has large, airy rooms in a much adapted 15th-century palazzo that's full of character, and there's a mall bar and *enoteca*. Outside is a lovely errace and garden with pool.

La Capannuccia (☎ 0577 74 11 83; d incl breakfast €90-120; ☒), tucked away down a valley at he end of a 1.5km dirt road with no other building in sight, is the ultimate Tuscan getaway. Its five rooms are attractively furnished with antiques, there's a cosy lounge, ind hosts Mario, Daniela and their daughters couldn't be more welcoming. Reserve in the morning for one of Daniela's very

special dinners (around €25). To get there, follow signs from Bar Pietra Fitta (near Km39 on the S222 north of Castellina).

At **Antica Trattoria La Torre** (☎ 0577 74 02 36; Piazza del Comune 15; mains from €6; ☒ closed Fri & 2nd half Feb) the Stiaccini family, now in its fourth generation, continues to rustle up traditional Chianti fare, using prime quality ingredients. Dine in the large, beamed interior or on the ample terrace in the shadow of the fortress.

Pick up a bottle or two of the classic nectar at **Antica Fattoria la Castellina** (☎ 0577 74 04 54; Via Ferruccio 26) or simply browse the dusty collection of vintage wines. It runs a two-hour seminar, including tasting, on the secrets of Chianti Classico.

RADDA

Radda, 11km east of Castellina, makes a good base for a couple of days' walking. The **tourist office** (☎ 0577 73 84 94; Piazza Castello 6; ☒ 10am-1pm & 3-7pm Mon-Sat, 10.30am-12.30pm Sun Mar-Oct, 10.30am-12.30pm & 2.30-6.30pm Mon-Sat Nov-Feb) occupies an ex-convent. It has a couple of route descriptions (in English) of halfday walks, and can advise on winery visits.

ChiantiMania (☎ 0577 73 89 79; www.chiantimania .com; Via Trento e Trieste 12), run by the helpful Alessandra and Lorenzo, offers a wide variety of excursions, wine-tasting tours (from €45) and guided walks (€35), and also arranges accommodation around the region.

The nucleus of the village is Piazza Ferrucci, where the 16th-century **Palazzo del Podestà**, its façade emblazoned with shields and escutcheons, faces the village church. The *Christ in Majesty* over the main portal is now sadly all but effaced by the elements.

Da Giovannino (☎ 0577 73 80 56; giochianti@ katamail.com; Via Roma 6-8; s/d €50/60) is a charming family-run hotel in the centre of town, complete with wood-beamed ceilings and views of the countryside. The cosy bar below does tasty snacks and pasta dishes. There are also a couple of apartments (double room €75).

Palazzo Leopoldo (☎ 0577 73 56 05; www.palazzo leopoldo.it; Via Roma 33; d incl breakfast from €180; ☒ closed Jan; P ☒ ☐ ☒), where Leopold, the Archduke of Tuscany, stayed briefly in 1837 (hence the name), is now a charming hotel with 17 individually furnished and decorated rooms. Buffet breakfast is in the original setting of the palazzo's 18th-century kitchen. Its restaurant, La Perla del Palazzo, has a lovely terrace and garden with staggeringly beautiful views.

Enoteca Toscana (☎ 0577 73 88 45; Via Roma 29) carries a good selection of local wines and olive oil.

From Radda you can explore some of the best wineries in the area, including tiny **Volpaia** (☎ 0577 73 80 66; guided tour & tasting from €11), around 6km to the north, most of whose 44 inhabitants work in the winery. Tours of the cellars and olive-oil facility, and wine tasting are by appointment.

GETTING THERE & AWAY

SITA buses connect Florence and Greve (one hour, half-hourly), one daily continuing to Radda (1½ hours), and one to Castellina (1½ hours).

Florence to the Val d'Elsa

Another route south from Florence might start from the Certosa di Galluzzo (p110). You can choose between the SS2 *superstrada* that connects Florence with Siena, or the more tortuous and winding road that runs alongside it. Following the latter to **Tavarnuzze**, you could make a detour for **Impruneta**, about 8km southeast.

Impruneta is famed for its production of terracotta – from roof tiles to imaginative garden decorations. The centre of town is Piazza Buondelmonti. Not the most fascinating of Chianti towns, it has been around since the 8th century. Its importance historically was due above all to an image of the Madonna dell'Impruneta, supposedly miraculous, now housed in the Basilica di Santa Maria, which looks onto the piazza.

Back at Tavarnuzze, you can head south towards **San Casciano** in Val di Pesa. An important wine centre, the town came under Florentine control in the 13th century and was later equipped with a defensive wall, parts of which remain intact. The town centre itself is not overly interesting, so drink in the views and hit the road again. Before reaching San Casciano, you pass the **US war cemetery** (⊗ 8am-6pm mid-Apr–Sep, 8am-5pm Oct–mid-Apr), where the clean rows of white crosses are a powerful reminder of the carnage of WWII.

Just before Bargino, take the side road east for **Montefiridolfi**. It's one of those charming little detours that takes you winding up onto

a high ridge through vineyards and oliv groves. Along the way you pass the **Castell di Bibbione** (☎ 0545 824 92 31; www.castellodibibbior .com), a picturesque stone manor house onc owned by Niccolò Machiavelli. A night's ac commodation for two here costs from €210

Another 1.5km brings you to a larg Etruscan tomb. Keep going until you hit crossroads. From there turn west for **Tavar nelle Val di Pesa**, from where you can reach the charming little medieval *borgo* of **Bar berino Val d'Elsa**, worth a stop for a brief strol along the main street.

At Tavarnelle you have the option o staying at a modern youth hostel, the **Ostell del Chianti** (☎ 055 805 02 65; Via Roma 137; dm €13.5C d with bathroom €34; ⊗ mid-Mar–Oct).

Heading directly south from Barberinc would take you to Poggibonsi, and then t San Gimignano.

Certaldo

This pretty hill-top town, about 15km wes of Barberino, is well worth the effort of a detour, although this move takes you out o Chianti territory. The upper town (Certaldc Alto) has Etruscan origins, while the lowe town in the valley sprang up in the 13th century, by which time both settlements hac been absorbed into the Florentine republic

The upper town was the seat of the Boc caccio family. Giovanni Boccaccio die and was buried here in 1375. On the mair street – Via Boccaccio, inevitably – yor can visit the largely reconstructed version of his **house** (☎ 0571 66 42 08; Via Boccaccio 18; ad mission €3.10 incl audioguide to museum & upper town ⊗ 10am-7pm Apr-Sep, 10.30am-4.30pm Oct-Mar, closec Tue), which was severely damaged in WWII. The library inside contains several precious copies of Boccaccio's *Decameron*, but there's little else directly linked with him. A couple of doors up, in Chiesa di SS Jacopo e Filippo, there's a bust (1503) of the writer and a marble slab in his honour on the floor of the nave; his remains were disinterred and scattered in 1783 by townspeople who considered his work scandalous.

The upper, walled *borgo* is commanded by the stout figure of the **Palazzo Pretorio** (☎ 0571 66 12 19; admission €3; ⊗ 9.30am-1pm & 2-7.30pm May-Sep, 10.30am-4.30pm Oct-Apr), the seat of power, whose 14th-century façade is richly decor ated with family coats of arms. Frescoec halls lead off the Renaissance courtyard.

FLORENCE

You can avoid the steep climb to the upper town (but do enjoy a jaunty stroll down) by taking the short cable car (single/return €1/1.20, every 15 minutes) that climbs from central Piazza Boccaccio (with its handy car park) in the new town.

Osteria del Vicario (☎ 0571 66 82 28; www.osteria elvicario.it; Via Rivellino 3; s/d/tr incl breakfast €60/90/110), immediately south of the Palazzo Pretorio, is an outstanding choice. Four of its eight rooms, nowadays cosy as can be and rich in antique furnishings, occupy what were once the spartan cells of a 13th-century monastery. The remainder – two with stunning views of the plain below – are in a nearby building of comparable antiquity and just as comfy. There's a tranquil terrace and quite outstanding **restaurant** (mains €20-26; ✆ closed Sun). Half board is an extra €30 per person, and well worth the extra outlay. Reservations are essential between May and September.

If you fail to get in, **Albergo Il Castello** (☎ 0571 6 82 50; www.albergoilcastello.it; Via della Rena 6; s/d incl breakfast €60/100; ✆ closed Nov), beside the upper Certaldo Alto cable-car exit, is an excellent fall-back. It's a charming old mansion with an attractive garden, and the family runs a more-than-decent **restaurant** (mains €8-12).

Lonely Planet's *Walking in Italy* describes a none-too-arduous three-day walk from Certaldo to San Gimignano and on to Volterra.

WEST OF FLORENCE

West of Florence and south of Pistoia lie several towns of secondary interest. If time is on your side you could include them in a scenic loop between Pistoia and Florence that makes a tranquil alternative to a belt down the *autopista*.

A joint €6 ticket gives entry to Museo Leonardiano in Vinci, Empoli's Museo della Collegiata and the Museo Archeologico e della Ceramica in Montelupo.

Vinci & Around

From Pistoia, a lovely, winding country road, the SP13, threads south towards Empoli. After wiggling through the forested high country of Monte Albano, you come across a sign pointing left to the **Casa Natale di Leonardo** (Leonardo's Birthplace; admission free; ✆ 9.30am-7pm Mar-Oct, 9.30am-6pm Nov-Feb), the only building still standing in what was once the thriving hamlet of Anchiano, which is

about 1.5km further up the hill. Here, it's believed, Leonardo da Vinci was born, the bastard child of a Florentine solicitor, Piero (you couldn't trust lawyers, even then), but there isn't a whole lot to see.

Back down on the SP13, you're about 1km short of Vinci itself. The **tourist office** (☎ 0571 56 80 12; Via della Torre 11; ✆ 10am-7pm Mar-Oct, 10am-3pm Mon-Fri, 10am-6pm Sat & Sun Nov-Feb) is near the commanding **Castello dei Conti Guidi**, named after the feudal family that ruled both the town and surrounding area until Florence took control in the 13th century.

Inside the castle is the **Museo Leonardiano** (☎ 0571 5 60 55; adult/child €5/2; ✆ 9.30am-7pm Mar-Oct, 9.30am-6pm Nov-Feb) and, within it, more than 50 models based on Leonardo's far-sighted designs, including a mirror-polishing machine, underwater breathing apparatus and a strikingly modern-looking bicycle.

Down below the castle is the **Museo Ideale Leonardo da Vinci** (☎ 0571 5 62 96; Via Montalbano 2; adult/child €5/3.50; ✆ 10am-1pm & 3-7pm), a private competitor to the official Museo Leonardiano, with a reasonably diverting collection of models, prints and documents.

COPIT buses run between Empoli and Vinci (25 minutes, half-hourly).

The drive from Pistoia is delightful – as indeed is the ride between Poggio a Caiano and Vinci via the wine centre of **Carmignano**, famous for its DOCG wines (see p64), first documented in 1396. The tourist office in Prato has information and maps pinpointing wineries in the area, if you're tempted to fashion yourself a tasting tour.

Empoli

The road south from Vinci brings you to Empoli, a pleasant, sleepy town. The Romanesque white-and-green-marble façade of its **Collegiata di Sant'Andrea** in Piazza Farinata degli Uberti is testimony that the medieval settlement that emerged from a place called Emporium must have been of some importance. Behind it is the **Museo della Collegiata** (☎ 0571 7 62 84; Piazzata San Giovanni 3; adult/child €3/1, audioguide €2; ✆ 9am-noon Tue-Sun & 4-7pm Thu-Sat), with religious works by Tuscan artists from the 14th to 16th centuries, including canvases by Lorenzo Monaco and Masolino.

On the western edge of town rises the somewhat worn profile of the 12th-century **Chiesa di Santa Maria a Ripa**. The original town, documented in the 8th century, lay here.

A half-hourly COPIT bus connects Vinci and Empoli. From Florence take the train (€4.80, 40 minutes), which is quicker and cheaper than the bus.

Montelupo

Montelupo, a market town at the confluence of the Arno and Pesa rivers, has been a well-known centre of Tuscan ceramics production since medieval times. Today there's no shortage of shops ready to accept your money.

Museo Archeologico e della Ceramica (☎ 0571 5 13 52; Via Baccio da Montelupo 43; admission €3, audio guide €2; ☷ 10am-6pm Tue-Sun) is in the 14th-century Palazzo del Podestà, and shares premises with the **tourist office** (☎ 0571 51 89 93; ☷ 10am-6pm Tue-Sun). The ground floor is devoted to archaeology, the 1st and 2nd floors portray local pottery from prehistoric times onwards, while outside the separate garden building devoted to Etruscan ceramics there's a haunting display of impaled and inventive contemporary heads, created by students of Montelupo's school of ceramics. Via Baccio da Montelupo is also called Via Bartolomeo Sinibaldi.

Across the Pesa stream, the Medici villa known as the **Ambrogiana** (which is closed to visitors), built for Ferdinando I, is nowadays a psychiatric hospital.

On the third Sunday of every month, there's a themed market (flowers, health foods, ceramics and more) in the streets of the old quarter, while in the last week of June Montelupo hosts an international pottery fair.

To get to Florence, the best bet is by train (€2.30, 25 minutes).

Northwestern Tuscany

a's seriously disorientated tower apart, tourists tend to ignore northwestern Tuscany en route to the grand-slam sights of Florence and Siena. It's a shame, as there is plenty to capture the imagination here. For example, after you have bought your fluorescent leaning tower, cover the backstreets of this mildly scuffed but seductive old lady. At nearby Lucca, it's love at first sight. This classy city has aged gloriously. Encased by 16th-century walls, butter-coloured buildings form a maze of high, thin streets, Romanesque buildings and gracious piazzas; all within a high-heeled strut of sophisticated shops. If you're still hungry for stylish architecture, the gentle countryside surrounding Lucca has two outstanding villas, both sitting amid lovely gardens. Each is a great spot to take children, who'll love the theme-park fun offered by the Collodi's Parco di Pinocchio, a tribute to Italy's naughtiest fictional boy.

Further inland, up towards the Appenines, the countryside becomes rugged and green, with tortuous roads that snake around the mountain peaks, dramatically descending into thickly forested pine valleys. Picturesque riverside villages like Bagni di Lucca have a quasi-alpine feel, while further north lies Abetone, one of the country's foremost skiing resorts. Due west are the dramatic Apuane Alps, popular with both Italian and foreign walkers.

This is also marble territory, centred above all on the town of Carrara, known worldwide for its exquisite white stone. To this day, sculptors from all over the world seek their raw materials here, just as Michelangelo did five centuries ago.

On the coast, resorts like Viareggio fill up quickly in summertime with local families. There may not be much towel-space on the sand but, like much of the northwest, the atmosphere is intrinsically Italian, with not one 'I love Viareggio' T-shirt in sight.

HIGHLIGHTS

- Visit Piazza dei Miracoli in **Pisa** (p149) at dusk or dawn, when it's free of crowds and vendors of naff trinkets
- Rent a bike and ride **Lucca**'s (p155) intact town walls
- Join in the Rio-style partying at Viareggio's springtime **Carnevale** (p166)
- Poke around the world's most famous marble quarries at **Carrara** (p170)
- Savour the wild beauty of the rural **Garfagnana** (p162) region and its northern neighbour, **Lunigiana** (p172)

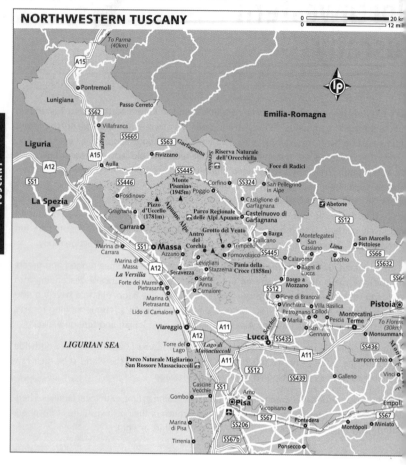

NORTHWESTERN TUSCANY

PISA

pop 89,000

Once, if briefly, a maritime power to rival Genoa and Venice, Pisa now draws its fame from an architectural project gone terribly wrong: its Leaning Tower (Torre Pendente). But the world-famous tower is only one of a trio of Romanesque splendours on the green carpet of the Piazza dei Miracoli, a serious rival to Venice's Piazza San Marco for the title of Italy's most memorable square.

Pisa has a centuries-old tradition as a university town and today swarms with students. Its charms merit more than the usual off-the-coach, take-a-snap, then off again experience of so many visitors.

History

Possibly of Greek origin, Pisa became a important naval base under Rome and re mained a significant port for many cent ries. The city's golden days began late in th 10th century, when it became an independ ent maritime republic and a rival of Gen and Venice. The good times rolled on in the 13th century, by which time Pisa co trolled Corsica, Sardinia and all the Tusca coast. Most of the city's finest buildings da from this period, when the distinctive Pisa Romanesque architectural style flourished

Pisa's support for the Ghibellines durin the tussles between the Holy Roman Emper and the pope brought the city into confli with its mostly Guelph Tuscan neighbour

cluding Siena, Lucca and Florence. The
al blow came when Genoa's fleet inflicted
devastating defeat on Pisa at the Battle of
eloria in 1284. After the city fell to Flor-
ce in 1406, the Medici court encouraged
eat artistic, literary and scientific endeav-
rs and re-established Pisa's university. The
y's most famous son, Galileo Galilei (see
9), later taught at the university.

The medieval city underwent profound
ange under the grand dukes of Tuscany,
ho began a process of demolition to make
ay for wider boulevards to ease traffic
oblems. The single heaviest blow to Pisa
me during WWII, when about 50% of old
sa was destroyed.

ientation

azione Pisa Centrale, the main train sta-
on, is at the southern edge of town. The
ain intercity bus station is on nearby Piazza
nt'Antonio. The medieval centre is about
00m north, across the River Arno. Piazza
ei Miracoli is about another 650m north.

formation

TERNET ACCESS

ernet Planet (☎ 050 83 07 02; Piazza Cavallotti 3-4;
r hr €3.10; ☟ 10am-midnight Mon-Fri, 10am-8pm Sat,
3pm Sun)

COMBINED TICKETS

Pisa's monuments have a staggered pricing system. A single monument or museum
costs €5, while €6 admits you to two. Another ticket (€8.50) – which we recommend
as it can eliminate queuing – gives entry to
four venues (baptistry, Camposanto cemetery and the two museums). A huffing, puff-
ing trip up the Leaning Tower is a hefty €15.
Bring the kids while they're small; under
10s go free everywhere except the tower,
from which under eights are excluded for
safety reasons.

Opening times are of Machiavellian com-
plexity. In some cases there are summer,
autumn and winter times, plus weekday and
weekend variants. We quote here summer
and winter 'extremes'. For the pattern of the
day, call ☎ 050 56 05 47, a number covering
all monuments and museums.

Buy tickets from the ticket office beside
the tourist office on Piazza del Duomo.

Koinè Internet Point (☎ 050 83 07 01; Via dei Mille
3/5; per hr €3; ☟ 10am-midnight Mon-Fri, 1pm-midnight
Sat & Sun)

LAUNDRY
Onda Blu (☎ 800 861 346; Via San Francesco 8a;
☟ 8am-10pm)

MEDICAL SERVICES
Farmacia Nuova Fantoni (Lungarno Mediceo 51;
☟ 24hr)
Hospital (☎ 050 99 21 11; Via Roma 67)

POST
Main post office (Piazza Vittorio Emanuele II)

TOURIST INFORMATION
Tourist office airport (☎ 050 50 37 00; ☟ 10.30am-
4.30pm & 6-10pm); Piazza del Duomo 1 (☎ 050 56 04
64; www.pisa.turismo.toscana.it; ☟ 9am-6pm Mar-Sep,
9.30am-5pm Oct-Feb) Main tourist office just north of
the Leaning Tower, beside the ticket office; Piazza Vittorio
Emanuele II 16 (☎ 050 4 22 91; ☟ 9am-7pm Mon-Fri,
9am-1.30pm Sat)

Sights
PIAZZA DEI MIRACOLI
Piazza dei Miracoli (also known as Piazza del
Duomo) ranks as one of the world's loveli-
est squares. Set among its sprawling lawns
is one of Europe's most extraordinary con-
centrations of Romanesque splendour – the
cathedral, the baptistry and the Leaning
Tower – all financed with the loot and booty
brought back to the city after Pisa whupped
the Arabs in Sicily. The piazza teems with
people – students studying or at play, local
workers eating lunch and tourists, many (a
fun one, this) getting snapped as they extend
their arms tai chi–like so the shot suggests
they're preventing the tower from keeling
over.

You may also care to indulge in one of
the wonderfully kitsch tower souvenirs,
ranging from the inevitable cigarette light-
ers to the infinitely more exciting glowing,
flashing lamps.

CATHEDRAL
Pisa's majestic **cathedral** (admission Mar-Oct €2, free
Nov-Feb; ☟ 10am-5.30pm Mon-Sat, 1-5.45pm Sun Mar-
Oct – to 7.45pm Apr-Sep, 10am-12.30pm & 3-4.45pm Mon-
Sat, 3-4.30pm Sun Nov-Feb) became a model for
Romanesque churches throughout Tuscany
and even on Sardinia. Begun in 1064, it's

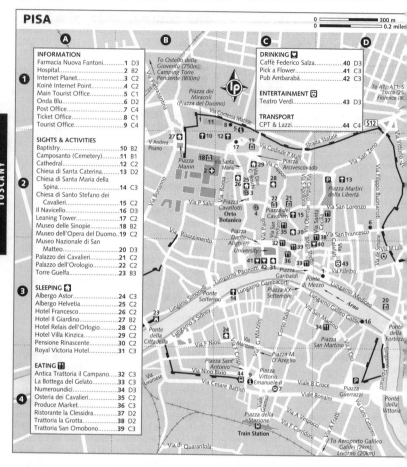

PISA

clad inside and out with alternating bands of the dark green and cream marble that is so characteristic of the Pisan-Romanesque style.

The main façade has four exquisite tiers of columns diminishing skywards. The vast interior has 68 columns in classical style. The bronze doors of the transept, facing the Leaning Tower, are by Bonanno Pisano. The 16th-century bronze doors of the main entrance were designed by the school of Giambologna to replace the wooden originals, destroyed in a fire in 1596, after which the interior was also mostly redecorated. Enjoy the depth of detail that Giovanni Pisano imparted to the vibrant early-14th-century marble pulpit in the north aisle, on which he spent 10 years

of his life. Above the altar, a striking mosa of *Christ in Majesty,* completed by Cimabu in 1302, stares down upon visitors.

LEANING TOWER

No matter how many postcards and holida snaps you've seen of the **Torre Pendente** (ww .opapisa.it/boxoffice; admission €15; 8.30am-8.30p Apr-Sep, 9am-7pm Oct, 9.30am-5pm or 6pm Nov-Mar nothing prepares you for the real thing. It' well, gravity defying (see opposite).

Only a limited number of visitors are al lowed up each day. To be sure you're one o them, reserve well in advance, either onlin or in person. If a view of Pisa by night ap peals, take advantage of the nightly tou until 11pm between mid-June and Augus

BRACE, BRACE, BRACE

When architect Bonanno Pisano undertook construction work on the campanile (bell tower) for the Romanesque cathedral in 1173, he was on shaky ground. Barely 2m above sea level, what lies below the deep green lawns of the Campo dei Miracoli is hardly ideal for a major building. A treacherous sand-and-clay mix sits atop a series of alternate strata of clay and sand to a depth of more than 40m.

Pisano had barely begun to build when the earth below the southern foundations started to give. By the time construction ground to a halt five years later, with only three storeys completed, Pisano's stump of a tower already had a noticeable lean.

A new band of artisans and masons set to work on it again in 1272. They attempted to bolster the foundations, but could not right the tower. Their solution was to keep going, compensating for the lean by gradually building straight up from the lower storeys, creating a slight but definite banana curve. The bell chamber at the top was built in 1370. At some point the process came to a halt and until the 18th century the lean remained stable.

Over the following centuries, the banana solution showed it was no solution, as the tower continued to lean a further 1mm each year. By 1993 it was 4.47m out of plumb, more than five degrees from the vertical.

In addition to the problems down on the ground floor, the structure is itself a little on the dodgy side. The tower is basically a pretty but hollow cylinder, cased on the inside and out with layers of marble. Between those layers is a loosely packed mix of rubble and mortar, very unevenly distributed. Some observers fear that one day the stresses caused by the lean will make the casing crack and crumble.

In 1990 the tower was closed to the public. Two years later the government in Rome assembled a panel of experts to debate a solution. In 1993 engineers placed 1000 tonnes of lead ingots on the northern side in a bid to counteract the subsidence on the southern side. Steel bands were wrapped around the 2nd storey to try to keep it all together. For a while it seemed to have worked, until in 1995 it slipped a whole 2.5mm.

In 1999 a new solution was tried that consisted of slinging steel braces around the 3rd storey of the tower. These were attached to heavy hydraulic A-frame anchors some way from the northern side. The frames were later replaced by steel cables that were attached to neighbouring buildings. The tower thus held in place, engineers began gingerly removing soil from below the northern foundations. After some 70 tonnes of earth had been extracted from the northern side, the tower sank to its 18th century level and, in the process, rectified the lean by 43.8cm. This process was quite a success according to the experts as it guarantees the tower's future (and a fat tourist income) for the next three centuries.

BAPTISTRY

The unusual round **battistero** (🕐 8am-7.30pm Apr-Sep, 9am-5.30pm Mar & Oct, 9am-4.30pm Nov-Feb) was started in 1153 by Diotisalvi, remodelled and continued by Nicola Pisano and son Giovanni more than a century later and finally completed in the 14th century – hence the hybrid architectural styles. The lower level of arcades is in Pisan-Romanesque style, while the pinnacled upper section and dome are Gothic. Inside, Nicola Pisano carved the beautiful pulpit (compare it with the one that Giovanni made for the cathedral), while in 1246 Guido da Como chiselled the octagonal white marble font, as big as a modern-te swimming pool and used in its time for baptism by total immersion. The acoustics beneath the dome are remarkable; risk a low whisper and hear it resound. Climb the stairs to the gallery for a great overview.

CEMETERY

They say that behind the white wall of this exquisite **Camposanto** (🕐 8am-7.30pm Apr-Sep, 9am-5.30pm Mar & Oct, 9am-4.30pm Nov-Feb) is soil shipped from Calvary during the crusades – and reputed to reduce cadavers to skeletons within days. During WWII Allied artillery badly damaged or destroyed many of the cloisters' precious frescoes. Among those saved and displayed in the Fresco Room are the *Triumph of Death* and *Last Judgement*, attributed to an anonymous 14th-century painter known as 'The Master of the Triumph of Death'. Many of the more interesting sarcophagi are of Greco-Roman origin, recycled in the Middle Ages as the last resting place of prominent Pisans.

MUSEO DELLE SINOPIE

This **museum** (Piazza dei Miracoli; ☾ 8am-7.30pm Apr-Sep, 9am-5.30pm Mar & Oct, 9am-4.30pm Nov-Feb) houses vast reddish-brown sketches drawn onto walls as an outline for frescoes – and revealed in the cemetery after the WWII artillery raids. Now restored to the degree possible, these *sinopie* give a fascinating insight into the process of creating a fresco.

MUSEO DELL'OPERA DEL DUOMO

In the line of fire if the tower should ever fall, this **museum** (Piazza dei Miracoli; ☾ 8am-7.30pm Apr-Sep, 9am-5.30pm Mar & Oct, 9am-4.30pm Nov-Feb) has a profusion of artworks from the tower, cathedral and baptistry, including a magnificent ivory carving of the *Madonna and Child* by Giovanni Pisano (Room 11). Another highlight is a bust, known as the *Madonna del Colloquio* (Madonna of the Colloquium), by the same sculptor.

THE CITY

South of Piazza dei Miracoli, the swarms of tourists give way to quiet back alleys and shopping streets where Pisans go about their daily business.

From the piazza, head south along Via Santa Maria and turn left at Piazza Cavallotti for the Piazza dei Cavalieri, the city's centre of temporal power remodelled by Vasari in the 16th century. **Palazzo dell'Orologio**, north of the piazza, occupies the site of a tower where, in 1288, Count Ugolino della Gherardesca, his sons and grandsons were starved to death on suspicion of helping the Genoese enemy at the Battle of Meloria, an incident recorded in Dante's *Inferno*.

The **Palazzo dei Cavalieri**, on the northeastern side of the piazza, was redesigned by Vasari and features remarkable graffiti decoration. The piazza and palace are named after the Knights of St Stephen, a religious and military order founded by Cosimo I de' Medici. Their church, **Chiesa di Santo Stefano dei Cavalieri** (Piazza dei Cavalieri; admission €1.30; ☾ 10am-7pm Mar-Oct, 11am-4.30pm Mon-Sat & 11.30am-5.30pm Sun Nov-Feb), was also designed by Vasari.

The **Chiesa di Santa Caterina** (Piazza Martiri della Libertà; ☾ 10.30am-6.30pm Mon-Sat, 1-6.30pm Sun), a fine example of Pisan-Gothic architectu has works by Nino Pisano.

Wander southwards to the area arou Borgo Stretto, the city's medieval hea East along the waterfront boulevard, Lu garno Mediceo, is the **Museo Nazionale di S Matteo** (☎ 050 54 18 65; Lungarno Mediceo; admissi €4; ☾ 8.30am-7pm Tue-Sat, 8.30am-1pm Sun), a fi gallery featuring works by Giovanni an Nicola Pisano, Masaccio and Donatello.

Cross the Ponte di Mezzo and head we to reach the **Chiesa di Santa Maria della Spi** (Lungarno Gambacorti; admission €1.50; ☾ 10am-1.30p & 2.30-6pm Tue-Fri, 10am-7pm Sat & Sun Mar-Oct, 10a 2pm Tue-Sun Nov-Feb). Built in the early 14th ce tury to house a thorn from Christ's crow this tiny church is refreshingly intimate aft the megaweights of the Piazza dei Miracol

A few paces west again is the **Torre Guel** (☎ 050 214 41; Piazza Tersanaia; admission €2; ☾ 3-7p Fri-Sun Mar-Oct, 2-5pm Sat & Sun Nov-Feb), where haul up 200 steps rewards you with gre views over the city's rooftops.

Activities
BOAT TRIPS
Il Navicello (☎ 050 50 31 08; www.ilnavicello.it Italian) does boat trips that cruise the Arn (adult/child €4/5) and other excursion including fishing trips.

Festivals & Events
Gioco del Ponte (Game of the Bridge) On the last Sunday in June, two groups in medieval costume battle it out over the Ponte di Mezzo.
Luminaria On 16 June, Pisa celebrates the Luminaria, when some 50,000 candles and blazing torches glow, making the night-time city bright with light.
Palio delle Quattro Antiche Repubbliche Marinar (Regatta of the Four Ancient Maritime Republics) This see a procession of boats and a dramatic race between the fou historical maritime rivals – Pisa, Venice, Amalfi and Genoa The event rotates between the four towns: it's Pisa's turn in 2006, then Venice in 2007, Genoa (2008) and Amalfi (2009). Although usually held in June, it has on occasion been delayed as late as September. Ring the tourist office or check the website for exact dates.
Regata Storica di San Ranieri On 17 June, the river Arno comes to life with a rowing competition commemorating the city's patron saint.

Sleeping
BUDGET
Pensione Rinascente (☎ 050 58 04 60; Via dei Casto letto 28; d with/without bathroom €62/51) This friendl

AUTHOR'S CHOICE

Albergo Helvetia (☎ 050 55 30 84; Via Don Gaetano Boschi 31; s/d €35/45, d with bathroom €62) On a quiet street just south of the cathedral, this is a welcoming, family place run by an engagingly enthusiastic young couple. Most bathrooms and all floors of its 29 large, pleasant rooms have recently been freshly and attractively tiled. Some rooms overlook the appealingly quirky, tousled courtyard and garden, where cacti abound, together with the odd, temporarily abandoned child's toy.

ace with a cluttered, homey feel is within a vely old building that has frescoed, vaulted ilings. Rooms are huge and ideal for fames or small groups. There are no single ooms.

Ostello della Gioventù (☎ /fax 050 89 06 22; Via trasantina 15; dm/d €15/42) Cosy enough, this mbling non-HI hostel sits beside a murky ream where mosquitoes breed in summer. ke bus No 3 from the train station or wn centre.

Camping Torre Pendente (☎ 050 56 17 04; www mpingtoscana.it/torrependente; Via delle Cascine 86; car/ nt/person €4.50/6.50/8; ☽ Apr–mid-Oct; ☒) About km northwest of Piazza dei Miracoli, this mpsite isn't Tuscany's most attractive but does boast a supermarket, restaurant and nall pool.

IDRANGE

tel Il Giardino (☎ 050 56 21 01; www.pisaonline.it ardino; Piazza Manin 1; s/d incl breakfast €70/110; P ☒) as sparkling, well-maintained rooms with ts of shiny light wood and a classy cool colur scheme. Enjoy breakfast on the tranquil pstairs terrace with the city walls and dome f the baptistry in full view.

Hotel Villa Kinzica (☎ 050 56 04 19; www.hotel lakinzica.it; Piazza Arcivescovado 2; s/d/tr incl breakfast 8/108/124; P ☒) Once a private villa, this uilding has been tastefully revamped into a racious hotel. Its 34 attractive rooms have ags of character – and some boast views of e Leaning Tower as a bonus.

Royal Victoria Hotel (☎ 050 94 01 11; www.royalvic ia.it; Lungarno Pacinotti 12; s/d incl buffet breakfast €67/77; l/tr with bathroom & incl buffet breakfast €108/128/138; ☒) Offers old-world luxury accompand by warm, attentive service. This doyen

of Pisan hotels, run by the Piegaja family for five generations, represents excellent value for money and has wi-fi. Ecologically friendly, it rents bicycles to guests for €5 per day and whizzy little Smart cars for a mere €15 plus mileage a day. Parking costs €18.

Hotel Francesco (☎ 050 55 41 09; www.hotelfranc esco.com; Via Santa Maria 129; s/d €95/115; ☒ ▢) Set in an ideal location (parking apart!) in the main bar/restaurant drag, is this small, welcoming 13-room hotel that's recently had a total revamp, imparting a slick, modern look. There are views over the nearby botanical garden.

Albergo Astor (☎ 050 445 51; www.hotel-astor.com; Via Manzoni 22; d with/without bathroom €75/60) An easy walk from the train station, this is a good-value, two-star family hotel that has recently been comprehensively redecorated, inside and out.

TOP END

Hotel Relais dell'Orologio (☎ 050 83 03 61; www.hotel relaisorologio.com; Via della Faggiola 12-14; s/d incl breakfast from €200/300; P ☒) Pisa's newest and only five-star hotel, occupies a tastefully restored 14th-century noble tower house, tucked away in a quiet street. Each of the 21 rooms, some with original frescoes, has its individual décor and is elegantly furnished with lashings of white linen and antique mirrors. The large tranquil rear patio is an extra bonus, but parking will cost you €20.

Eating

Being a university town, Pisa has a good range of eating places, especially around Borgo Stretto, Piazza Dante Alighieri and the university – and, increasingly, the popular student area on and around Via San Martino, south of the Arno.

Antica Trattoria il Campano (☎ 050 58 05 85; Via Cavalca 19; mains €10-14; ☽ closed Wed) This stylish trattoria beside Pisa's earthy fruit and veg market has an adventurous Tuscan menu. For starters (though it's almost a complete meal in itself), go for the vast *tagliere del Re* (€12, minimum two people). 'It's a surprise', says the menu but we'll let you in on the secret – you get a wonderfully rich platter of 12 kinds of Tuscan antipasti. Dine downstairs beneath vaulted arches or upstairs under the bare rafters.

Trattoria la Grotta (☎ 050 57 81 05; Via San Francesco 103; mains €13-15; ☽ Mon-Sat) As its name suggests, this trattoria is indeed a cavelike place that serves up good portions of Tuscan fare. The creative menu changes at least monthly, reflecting what's in season. The atmosphere is laid-back and friendly.

Ristorante la Clessidra (☎ 050 54 01 60; Via Santa Cecilia 34; mains €9-12; ✆ dinner Mon-Sat Sep-Jul) Offers excellent value for the quality of its meat and fish dishes; vegetarians may have to content themselves with the *rucola e parmigiano* (rocket and Parmesan) salad, followed by a suitably girth-widening dessert.

Osteria dei Cavalieri (☎ 050 58 08 58; Via San Frediano 16; ✆ Mon-Fri & dinner Sat) Offers a high-speed, one-dish only – but what a dish – lunchtime special (€11). It also carries an enticing choice of dishes, including *carpaccio di pulpo* (octopus carpaccio). Although the size of portions may mean a siesta afterwards, the set meals (€26 to €32) are worth it and the wine list is impressive.

Trattoria San Omobono (☎ 050 54 08 47; Piazza San Omobono 6/7; mains €8-9; ✆ dinner Mon-Sat) This is a family-run place where you can tuck into reliable, unpretentious, traditional fare. There are just a few tables (and one Roman column), and the menu is refreshingly short and sweet. If you're hungry, tuck into a bowl of *minestra di fagiola* (bean soup) for starters. The house wine is very drinkable.

Numeroundici (☎ 050 2 72 82; Via San Martino 47; mains €4-7; ✆ closed Sat lunch & Sun) This is a firm student favourite for its price, quality and quick turnaround. Come prepared to share a table. Self-service and bustling, it offers loads of choice including Indian (pretty rare in these parts), fat slices of *focaccine* (filled bread), grilled steak and superb salads.

La Bottega del Gelato (☎ 050 57 54 67; Piazza Garibaldi 11; ✆ closed Wed) Just north of the river, this is the place for seriously creamy *gelato*. Join the constant queue, winter and summer alike.

There's an animated open-air morning **produce market** (Piazza delle Vettovaglie) off Borgo Stretto.

Drinking

Several stylish bars flank Via Oberdan and Borgo Stretto. Otherwise, head south of the river, where casual student hangouts abound.

Caffè Federico Salza (Borgo Stretto 46; ✆ daily Apr-Oct, Tue-Sun Nov-Mar) Try this long-established café popular with Pisa's shirt-and-tie so-

phisticates, who prop up the amply stocke bar. It also tempts with a tantalising sele tion of cakes, *gelati* and chocolates.

Pick a Flower (Via Serafini Angolo) Here yo find a great moody atmosphere inside wi candlelight, high ceilings, good wines t the glass and tapas. The outside terrace a tracts a lively, chic crowd.

Pub Ambarabà (Vicolo della Croce Rossa 5; ✆ clos Tue; 🖳) This popular bar specialises in sas cocktails and international beer. There a also light veggie snacks and Internet acce on offer.

Entertainment

Teatro Verdi (☎ 050 94 11 11; Via Palestro 40) Regul offerings include opera, dance and theatre

Getting There & Away

AIR

The city's **Aeroporto Galileo Galilei** (☎ 050 07 07; www.pisa-airport.com), about 2km south town, is Tuscany's main international ai port and handles flights to most major E ropean cities.

Other daily destinations include Londc Gatwick (British Airways), London Sta sted (Ryanair), Liverpool (Ryanair), Cover try, Doncaster/Sheffield and Bournemou (all Thomsonfly).

BUS

Lazzi and CPT share a common bookir office on Piazza Sant'Antonio.

Lazzi (☎ 050 4 62 88) operates hourly ser ices to Lucca (€2.20, 45 minutes, 30 dail and Florence (€6.20, two hours, hourly Change at Lucca for services to Prato, Pi toia, Massa and Carrara.

CPT (☎ 050 50 55 11) runs to Volterra (€4.5 two hours, up to 10 daily) and Livorn (€2.30, 45 minutes, half-hourly).

CAR & MOTORCYCLE

Pisa is close to both the A11 and A12. Th SS67 is a toll-free alternative for Florenc while the north–south SS1, the Via Aureli connects the city with La Spezia and Rom

TRAIN

Pisa is connected by rail to Florence ar is also on the Rome–La Spezia train lin Destinations include Florence (€5, 1 hours, 40 daily), Rome (€21.30, three four hours, 20 daily), Livorno (€1.70,

inutes, hourly), Pistoia (€4.10, 1¼ hours,
'e direct daily) and Lucca (€2.10, 25 mines, around 20 daily).

tting Around
or the airport, take a train from Stazione
sa Centrale (€1, five minutes, 15 per day),
CPT bus No 3, which passes through the
:y centre and past the station on its way
the airport.
CPT bus Nos 3 and 4 run between the
in station and cathedral.
Large, paying car parks abound around
e heart of Pisa. There's a huge free one
out 2km north of Piazza dei Miracoli,
th frequent shuttle buses to the cen-
(return €1.60). When we last passed
ough, a cavernous subterranean car park
s being gouged out beneath Piazza Vit-
io Emanuele II and may now be ready to
allow your vehicle.
For a taxi, call ☎ 050 54 16 00.

DETOUR: MONTÓPOLI

If you're travelling the well-trodden SS67
option between Pisa and Florence, take
the 9.5km turn-off east of Pontedera,
signposted to the charming Montópoli in
Val d'Arno. Pass through the nondescript
sprawl of Capanne and, once in Montópoli,
follow the signs to the centre and the
tourist office. The restaurant of Albergo
Quattro Gigli, with its imaginative menu
of traditional Tuscan dishes, is also well
signposted. Grab a table on its delightful
rear terrace, overlooking the greener-than-
green valley, or eat in one of the warren of
small rooms and passages. After your blow
out meal, pick up the *Historical Footpaths*
brochure from the tourist office and work
off those calories by exploring this lovely
old village.

UCCA
p 81,900
icca is simply gorgeous, a beautiful city,
ch in history with more than a hundred
urches and a smattering of excellent res-
urants. Hidden behind imposing Renais-
nce walls, it's an essential stopover on any
uscan tour and also makes a charming
se for exploring the Apuane Alps and the
arfagnana.

Founded by the Etruscans, Lucca became a Roman colony in 180 BC and a free
comune (self-governing city) during the
12th century, when it enjoyed a period of
prosperity based on the silk trade. In 1314 it
briefly fell to Pisa but, under the leadership
of local adventurer Castruccio Castracani
degli Anterminelli, the city regained its independence and began to amass territories
in western Tuscany, including marble-rich
Carrara. Castruccio died in 1325 but Lucca
remained an independent republic for almost 500 years.

Napoleon ended all this in 1805, when he
created the principality of Lucca and placed
one of the seemingly countless members
of his family in need of an Italian fiefdom
(this time his sister Elisa) in control of all of
Tuscany. Twelve years later the city became
a Bourbon duchy before being incorporated
into the Kingdom of Italy.

Lucca remains a strong agricultural centre.
The long periods of peace it has enjoyed explain the almost perfect preservation of the
city walls, which were rarely put to the test.

Orientation
From the train station on Piazza Ricasoli,
just outside the city walls, walk westwards
to Piazza Risorgimento and through Porta
San Pietro. Head north along Via Vittorio
Veneto, over immense Piazza Napoleone
and on to Piazza San Michele, the centre
of town.

Information
EMERGENCY
Police station (☎ 0583 44 27 27; Viale Cavour 38)

INTERNET ACCESS
Armonie Lucchesi (Via del Gocifisso 4; per 15 min incl
drink €3; ☺ 9.30am-1pm & 3.30-8pm)
Copisteria Paolini (Via Catalani 28; per hr €4.80;
☺ 8am-9pm Mon-Fri, 8am-noon Sat)
Mondochiocciola (☎ 0583 44 05 10; Via del Gonfalone
12; per hr €5.50; ☺ 9.30am-1pm & 3.30-8pm Mon-Sat)
Keeps irregular hours.

INTERNET RESOURCES
Two useful portals are www.luccatourist.it
and www.in-lucca.it.

LAUNDRY
Lavanderia Niagara (Via Michele Rosi 26; ☺ 8am-
10pm)

NORTHWESTERN
TUSCANY

LUCCA

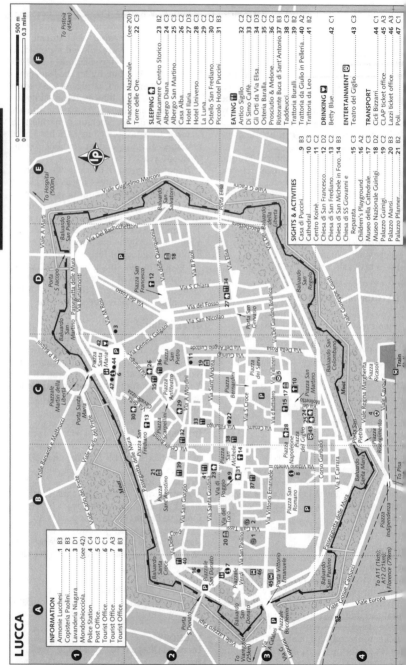

0   500 m
0   0.3 miles

EDICAL SERVICES

ospital (☎ 0583 97 01; Via dell'Ospedale) Beyond the
y walls to the northeast.

OST

ain post office (Via Vallisneri 2)

OURIST INFORMATION

ourist office Piazza Napoleone (☎ 0583 91 99
; 10am-7pm Apr-Oct, 10am-1pm Nov-Mar); Piazza
nta Maria 35 (☎ 0583 91 99 31; 9am-8pm Apr-Oct,
m-1pm & 3-6pm Nov-Mar); Piazzale Verdi (☎ 0583 58
50; 9am-7pm Easter-Oct, 9am-5.30pm Nov-Easter)
nts bicycles and stocks an excellent city audioguide in
glish (1/2 persons €9/14)

ghts & Activities

RD'S-EYE LUCCA

uff and puff your way up the 207 steps
the **Torre delle Ore** (Via Fillungo; admission €3.50;
9am-7pm, to 5pm Oct-Feb), a 13th-century clock
wer whose possession was hotly contested
y rival families in medieval days. Or else
tack the 230 equally steep stairs of the
wer of the **Palazzo Guinigi** (Via Sant'Andrea; adult/
ild €3.50/2.50; 9am-midnight May-Sep, 9am-7.30pm
ar-Apr, 9am-5pm Oct-Feb), where a tiny copse of
olm oak trees offers welcome shade.

Whichever one you choose, the sweeping
verview of the city, once you make the top,
stunning.

ATHEDRAL

ucca's mainly Romanesque **cathedral** (Piazza
n Martino; 9.30am-6.45pm Apr-Sep, 9.30am-4.45pm
t-Mar), dedicated to San Martino, dates from
e 11th century. The exquisite façade was
nstructed in the prevailing Lucca-Pisan
yle and designed to accommodate the pre-
xisting *campanile*. Each of the multitude of
olumns in its upper part is different. The
liefs over the left doorway of the portico
e believed to be by Nicola Pisano.

The interior was rebuilt in the 14th and
5th centuries with a Gothic flourish. Mat-
o Civitali designed the pulpit and, in the
orth aisle, the 15th-century *tempietto*
mall temple) that contains the **Volto Santo**.
egend has it that this simply fashioned
nage of Christ on a wooden crucifix, in
ct dated to the 11th century, was carved
y Nicodemus, who witnessed the cruci-
xion. A major object of pilgrimage, it's
rried in procession through the streets
ch 13 September at dusk.

> ### SO WHO'S THE LADY IN THE TOMB?
>
> Ilaria del Carretto, the young second wife
> of the 15th-century Lord of Lucca, Paolo
> Guinigi, died in childbirth when only 24.
> Distraught, her husband commissioned
> Jacopo della Quercia, perhaps the most
> accomplished sculptor of his day, to carve
> her tomb.
>
> So, for centuries, has gone the story…
>
> But recent research has thrown a dark
> shadow over the image of this loving, griev-
> ing husband. It's been suggested that the
> reclining marble form in fact represents
> Caterina Antelminelli, one of four maidens
> engaged to Paolo – all of whom died before
> their wedding day.
>
> Now *there's* a story that could have given
> the tabloids of the day a feeding frenzy.

In the **sacristy** (admission €2, incl Museo della
Cattedrale €6), the cool marble tomb of Ilaria
del Carretto is a masterpiece of funerary
sculpture.

The cathedral's many other artworks
include a magnificent *Last Supper* by Tintoretto; you'll find it over the third altar of
the south aisle.

The adjacent **Museo della Cattedrale** (☎ 0583
49 05 30; Via Arcivescovado; adult/child €4/2.50; 10am-
6pm Easter-Oct, 10am-2pm Mon-Fri, 10am-5pm Sat & Sun
Nov-Easter) has a well-displayed collection of
mainly 15th- and 16th-century religious
art, sculptures from the cathedral and illuminated manuscripts.

CHIESA DI SAN MICHELE IN FORO

Equally dazzling is this Romanesque **church**
(Piazza San Michele; 9am-noon & 3-6pm, to 5pm Oct-Mar),
built on the site of its 8th-century precursor
over a period of nearly 300 years, beginning
in the 11th century. The exquisite wedding-
cake façade is topped by a figure of the Archangel Michael slaying a dragon. Look for
Andrea della Robbia's *Madonna and Child*
in the first chapel of the south aisle.

CHIESA DI SS GIOVANNI E REPARATA

The 17th-century façade of this **church** (Piazza San Martino; admission €2.50; 10am-6pm), once
Lucca's cathedral, hides over 1000 years of
history. Parts of its archaeological area have
been dated to the 2nd century and there are
traces of Roman construction below floor

level. Today's church is largely the 12th-century remodelling of its early-Christian 5th-century predecessor, of which you can see traces in the present Gothic baptistry.

CASA DI PUCCINI

There Puccini the maestro still sits, languidly lording it over Piazza Cittadella, cast in bronze, a cigarette dangling from his slender fingers, oblivious and in defiance of recent legislation. Just to the north of the piazza is the **Casa di Puccini** (☎ 0583 58 40 28; Corte San Lorenzo 9), the composer's modest house, preserved in much the same way as he left it, his glasses and pen poised on the desk beside the piano where he wrote *Madame Butterfly* and much of his later work. The mildly morbid surprise is the tiny, elaborately marbled chapel, converted from a sitting room to house the composer's tomb. The house was closed for renovations when we last tried to pay our respects.

VIA FILLUNGO

Lucca's busiest street, Via Fillungo, threads its way through the medieval heart of the old city. It's a fascinating mix of smart boutiques and restaurants and buildings of great charm and antiquity – often occupying the same space; just look up, above the street-level bustle.

EAST OF VIA FILLUNGO

The **Piazza Anfiteatro** is a huge oval just east of Via Fillungo. The houses, raised upon the foundations of the one-time Roman amphitheatre, retain the shape of this distant original. Nowadays, pavement cafes and restaurants jostle to accommodate one another around the edges of the square – or, rather, ellipse.

A short walk further east is **Piazza San Francesco** and the attractive 13th-century **Chiesa di San Francesco**. Along Via della Quarquonia is the Villa Guinigi, home to the **Museo Nazionale Guinigi** (☎ 0583 49 60 33; adult/child €4/free; ☺ 8.30am-7.30pm Tue-Sat, 8.30am-1.30pm Sun) and the city's art museum. On display is a collection of paintings, sculptures and archaeological finds.

WEST OF VIA FILLUNGO

The façade of the **Chiesa di San Frediano** (Piazza San Frediano; ☺ 9am-noon & 3-6pm, to 5pm Oct-Mar) has a unique (and much-restored) 13th-century mosaic in a markedly Byzantine style. That's

not the only anomalous feature – pause t check your bearings. Unlike just about eve other church this side of Jerusalem, the ap faces *west*, away from the Holy City.

The main feature of the beautiful basilica interior is the **Fontana Lustrale**, a 12th-centu baptismal font decorated with sculpted r liefs, just to the right as you enter. Behind it *Annunciation* by Andrea della Robbia. No too the fine capitals, many of them recycle from the nearby Roman amphitheatre.

To retreat temporarily from an excess churches and Renaissance splendour, d into the nearby 17th-century **Palazzo Pfann** (☎ 340 9 23 30 85; Via degli Asili 33; adult/child €2.50/1. incl garden €4/3; ☺ 10am-6pm Mar–mid-Nov). A stai case leads to the sumptuously furnished li ing area. In the ornate 18th-century garde the only one of substance within the ci walls, you pass between a guard of honour statues representing Greek and Roman de ties. (Incidentally, the eponymous Felix Pfa ner, may God rest his soul, was an Austria émigré who first brought beer to Italy – an brewed it in the palazzo's cellars.)

The 17th-century **Palazzo Mansi** (Via Galli Ta 43), a wonderful piece of rococo excess (th elaborate, gilded bridal suite must have i spired such high jinks in its time), house the smallish **Pinacoteca Nazionale** (☎ 0583 5 70; admission €4; ☺ 8.30am-7.30pm Tue-Sat, 8.30am 1.30pm Sun) with paintings of the same perio and some lively frescoes.

CITY WALLS

Take time out from monument bashin to walk, jog or cycle all 3km of the ri of the city's walls, raised in the 16th an 17th centuries. You'll be far from alone an you'll get some great Peeping Tom glimpse into the lives of those below. If you're wit children, reward them with a play on th swings and things at the **children's playgroun** near the Baluardo San Donato.

Courses

Centro Koinè (☎ 0583 49 30 40; www.koinecenter.co Via A Mordini 60; 2/4 week courses €390/615) offers Ita ian language and cultural courses.

Festivals & Events

Festa di San Paolino On the third Sunday in July there is a torch-lit procession and crossbow competition.
Luminaria di Santa Croce The 13 September sees another torch-lit procession.

...ccini festival The city that gave birth to both Puccini ...d Boccherini has admirably Catholic musical tastes. For ...re than 50 years the nearby village of Torre del Lago has ...en holding its annual festival, spanning July and August.

...mmer Festival (www.summer-festival.com in Italian) ...ld in July, this pulls in top performers such as Oasis, ...vid Bowie, Jamiroquai, Van Morrison and Elton John. ...ere is an information and ticket office in Piazza ...poleone from early June.

...eeping

...JDGET

...tello San Frediano (☎ 0583 46 99 57; info@ostello ...ca.it; Via della Cavallerizza 12; dm/d €16.50/43; ☐) ...his excellent HI-affiliated hostel with its ...8 beds in voluminous rooms occupies ...vast former schoolhouse. It has a bar, is ...termittently staffed, and has a reasonable ...staurant.

Albergo Diana (☎ 0583 49 22 02; www.albergodiana ...m; Via del Molinetto 11; d with/without bathroom €67/47, ...nexe s/d €75/95; ☐ ☐ ☒) This family-run ...vo-star hotel has nine slightly chintzy but ...tisfying rooms, but parking will cost you ...4. For more comfort, consider the nearby ...nnexe, previously the family home. The ...vo ground floor rooms are handicapped ...quipped and have air-con.

...IDRANGE

...sa Alba (☎ 0583 49 53 61; www.casa-alba.com; 2nd fl, ...a Fillungo 142; s/d incl breakfast €45/55, s/d with bathroom ...incl breakfast €70/80; ☒) Antipodean travellers ...ill feel especially at home here; the delight-...l owner has spent many years in Australia. ...er five rooms, each with a fridge, are small ...ut sunny, washed in pastel colours and ...ecorated with arty prints. Reservations are ...ssential from Easter to October, and winter ...rices are substantially lower.

Affittacamere Centro Storico (☎ 0583 49 07 ...; www.affittacamerecentrostorico.com; Corte Portici 16; ...with/without bathroom incl buffet breakfast €120/80) ...his is a B&B with aspirations. Friendli-...ess itself, it's a great option smack in the ...eart of town. There's no curfew (you get ...our own front-door key) and all rooms ...re equipped with a small fridge and safe. ...ack period rates are significantly cheaper. ...eception is closed from noon to 2.30pm.

Piccolo Hotel Puccini (☎ 0583 5 54 21; www.hotel ...ccini.com; Via di Poggio 9; s/d with bathroom €60/85; ...☎) This is a stylish, friendly three-star with ...glossy marble lobby. Its 14 modern rooms ...ave all the trimmings, including ceiling

fans, and the location is unbeatable, within spitting distance of Piazza San Michele. Go for a room with a street view. Parking will set you back €18.

La Luna (☎ 0583 49 36 34; www.hotellaluna.com; Corte Compagni 12; s €80, d from €95; ☒ closed Jan; ☐ ☒) This is a clean, tidy hotel with a handy pizzeria across the road. Some rooms are old-style with beams and wardrobes, while others are modern but rather bland. Parking at the hotel costs €11.

Albergo San Martino (☎ 0583 46 91 81; www.albergo sanmartino.it; Via della Dogana 9; s/d €80/110; ☐ ☒) In a quiet elbow off grandiose Piazza Napoleone, this upbeat, welcoming hotel has just 10 rooms decorated in warm peachy tones. Extras include fridges, bike rental and special-needs facilities. Parking will set you back €10. From May to October, the buffet breakfast (€10) is compulsory.

TOP END

Hotel Ilaria (☎ 0583 46 92 00; www.hotelilaria.com; Via del Fosso 26; s/d incl buffet breakfast €150/230; ☐ ☒ ☐) This hotel occupies the former stables of the magnificent Villa Bottini (which stages several concerts during the summer festival; something that, depending on your musical tastes, could be a bonus or living hell) next door. It's executive-style slick with plenty of Internet terminals, meeting space for business folk and great park views. Bedrooms are modern and large, with bright marble bathrooms and terraces. Both coffee shop fare and bikes are free for guests.

Hotel Universo (☎ 0583 49 36 78; www.universolucca .com; Piazza del Giglio 1; s €100, d from €140, all incl breakfast) Built in 1857 the hotel sits on an attractive tree-lined square and offers old-fashioned charm with modern service. Each of its 60 rooms offers views of either the equally venerable Teatro del Giglio or the cathedral.

Eating

Trattoria da Leo (☎ 0583 49 22 36; Via Tegrimi 1; mains €8-9.60; ☒ closed Sun) This wonderful, bustling, noisy trattoria has a mixed clientele of students, workers and ladies taking a break from shopping. Save a small corner for their *torta di fichi e noci* (fig and walnut tart). In summer the shaded outside seating comes into its own.

Gli Orti da Via Elisa (☎ 0583 49 12 41; Via Elisa 17; mains €7-9; ☒ dinner Thu-Tue) You'll find locals and transient visitors tucking into pizzas and generous mains or working their way through the regularly changing set menu (€24) at this crowded, popular trattoria and pizzeria.

Di Simo Caffè (☎ 0583 49 62 34; Via Fillungo 58) The grand bar and *gelateria* here was once patronised by Puccini and his coterie (the maestro would tickle the ivories of the piano at the entrance to the dining area). In season, it spoons out some mean ice creams. Year-round, go for the leafy salads and mains (€8), cakes and world-beating coffees. And hey, you'll never come across a more subtly camouflaged toilet door, indistinguishable from the wooden panelling that surrounds it. Take your leave early…

Osteria Baralla (☎ 0583 44 02 40; Via Anfiteatro 5-9; mains €9.50-13; ☯ closed Sun) You'll find pleasing pink-brick vaulting and sotto voce piped jazz at this popular place. Rich in Tuscan specialities, it carries a good range of wines by the glass. Go meat, go red in tooth and claw; the roast lamb for example, is cooked to perfection with all its juices intact. Service is swift and needs to be; Luccheses flock in to savour its rich cuisine.

Ristorante Buca Sant'Antonio (☎ 0583 5 58 81; Via della Cervia 3; mains around €15; ☯ closed Sun dinner & Mon) Founded in 1782, this restaurant is all whitewashed rooms, old beams, tiled floors and copper pots. The dishes seem deliciously innovative but are touted as traditional Luccan cuisine. Savour, for example, the ricotta and leek pie with chickpea sauce.

Trattoria da Giulio in Pelleria (☎ 0583 5 59 48; Via delle Conce 45-47; mains €5-7.50; ☯ dinner Mon-Sat) Don't be put off by the multilingual menu at this earthy, inexpensive restaurant; the food's solidly traditional with barely a chip to chew on. Photos of famous – and not so famous – customers line the walls.

Prosciutto & Melone (☎ 0583 4 88 45; Via Anfiteatro 13/17; ☯ closed Tue) This eatery is in a handy location for a spot of refuelling with plenty of choice. Choose between scrubbed pine surrounds with artwork on the walls, or the outside terrace.

Antico Sigillo (☎ 0583 9 10 42; Via degli Angeli 13; mains €8, menus €9-20; ☯ closed Wed) Tucked into a quiet side street, this place is good for a light lunch with more salads than you can shake a carrot stick at, plus pizzas and pastas at wallet-friendly prices.

Trattoria Buralli (☎ 0583 95 06 11; Piazza Sant'Agostino 9; ☯ Thu-Tue) This intimate local favourite makes few concessions to outsiders. You can play easy and go for the à la carte menu with English translation Better, however, to throw a wild ca. and pluck one of the five different men (around €16). Friday night is veggie nigh when they offer a four-course, meat-fr menu for €18.50.

You shouldn't leave town without sam pling a slice of *buccellato,* a cross betwee a biscuit and a bun, typical of Lucca. Yo won't find it fresher than at **Taddeucci** (Piaz San Michele 34; ☯ closed Thu), a fine *pasticcer* where it's made on the premises.

Drinking

Except during festival time, Lucca tends t turn in early.

Betty Blue (☎ 0583 49 21 66; Via del Gonfalo 16/18) A lively spot with a sixties feel, op a on the walls and plenty of slouching spac

Entertainment

The **Teatro del Giglio** (Piazza del Giglio) is Lucca prime venue for opera and theatre. Mus cal recitals also take place in the Chie di SS Giovanni e Reparata (p157). Pick u *Lucca Musica,* a free monthly, for details what's in store. The local English-langua monthly *Grapevine* (€2), is a bit paris pump and self-congratulatory unless you' an insider but it also carries a useful What On section. Tourist offices carry both.

Getting There & Away

BUS

CLAP (☎ 0583 58 78 97) serves the region, in cluding destinations in the Garfagnan such as Castelnuovo (€3.30, 1½ hours, eigh daily).

Lazzi (☎ 0583 58 48 76) runs hourly buses Florence (€4.70, 1½ hours) and Pisa (€2.2 45 minutes). It has four daily services La Spezia (€5.20, three hours) and six Marina di Carrara (€3.50, two hours) v Marina di Massa. Both companies opera from Piazzale Verdi.

TRAIN

Lucca is on the Florence–Pisa–Viaregg train line and there are also services into th Garfagnana. There are frequent trains t from Pisa (€2.10, 25 minutes) and also Flo ence (€4.60, 1½ hours), via Pistoia (€3.2 45 minutes) and Prato (€4.10, one hour).

R & MOTORCYCLE

ne A11 runs westwards to Pisa and Via-
ggio and eastwards to Florence. The SS12,
en the SS445 from Forno, links the city
ith the Garfagnana.

etting Around

ost cars are banned within the city walls
d you can expect a few hard stares if you
tempt to drive in. This said, most hotels
ll give you a permit entitling you to park
 spaces reserved for residents (indicated
 yellow lines) and you can generally park
r free outside the city walls.

Small CLAP electric buses connect the
ain station, Corso Garibaldi and Piazzale
erdi but it's just as easy and lots more
easurable to walk.

Lucca is a very bike-friendly town. You
n hire cycles from **Poli** (☎ 0583 49 37 87; Piazza
nta Maria 42), nearby **Cicli Bizzarri** (☎ 0583 49 60
; Piazza Santa Maria 32) and the tourist office in
azzale Verdi (p157). Rates are about €2.25
r hour, €11 per day.

For a taxi, call ☎ 0583 95 52 00.

AST OF LUCCA

illas

om the 16th to the 19th centuries, Luccan
usinessmen who had finally arrived built
emselves opulent country residences –
me 300 all told. Today most have crumbled
vay, been abandoned or are inaccessible
it at least a dozen fine examples still stand
oud northeast of Lucca.

Villa Reale (☎ 0583 3 00 09; Via Fraga Alta; admis-
n €6; ⏰ 10am-noon & 3-6pm Tue-Sun Mar-Nov) at
arlia, about 7km from Lucca, is the most
riking. Much of its present appearance
d that of the meticulously planned gar-
ens, is owed to the tastes of Elisa Bona-
arte, Napoleon's sister and a short-lived
ler of Tuscany. Between July and Septem-
er, entry is only by guided tour (there are
x between 10am and 6pm).

Just north in the village of San Pancran-
o is the neoclassical **Villa Grabau** (☎ 0583
60 98; Via di Matraia 269; villa & park €6.50, park only
; ⏰ 10am-1pm & 3-7pm Tue-Sun Easter-Oct), set in
vast nine-hectare parkland with sweep-
g traditional English and Italian gardens,
lashing fountains, more than 100 terra-
otta vases of centenary lemon trees and
e 1700 Casa dei Limoni, still used to store
mons.

To get to the villas, take the SS435 towards Pescia, then turn northwards for
Marlia (signposted 7km east of Lucca).

Collodi

A further 8km along the SS435 brings you
to a turn-off north for **Collodi**.

Alternatively, while heading south towards the SS435 from Villa Torrigiani, you
could take a left-hand turn at the signpost
for the village of **Petrognano**. This road winds
its way uphill through olive groves and affords fantastic views of the valley below. In
Petrognano, follow the signs to **San Gennaro**
where the road starts its decent into Collodi. It is moderately interesting in its own
right, if only for the **Villa Garzoni** (☎ 0572 42 95
90; Piazza della Vittoria; adult/child €7/5; ⏰ 9am-sunset
Mar-Oct), a baroque building, richly frescoed
inside, whose majestic gardens rise from
the entrance on the town's main road. At
the time of writing the villa was closed for
renovations.

The **Parco di Pinocchio** (☎ 0572 42 93 42; adult/
child €9/7; ⏰ 8.30am-sunset), a tribute to Italy's
naughtiest and best-selling fictional character, is in a wood just outside the village of
Collodi. Pinocchio is quite a phenomenon
in Italian literature (and considerably darker
and more meaningful than the Disney version – see p162). His creator, Carlo Lorenzini, who spent time in Collodi when he was
a child, took the hamlet's name as his nom
de plume and the town repaid the compli-
ment with this theme park. With a series of
mosaics recounting the main episodes in
the puppet's life, statues and tableaux, it's as
much a treat for grown-ups as for kids.

Be warned: not many buses between
Lucca and Montecatini Terme stop in Collodi; it's a lot easier by car.

Pescia

pop 18,400

Pescia, split by the course of the river of the
same name, is the self-proclaimed flower
capital of Tuscany, with national and international exports worth around €130 million
annually. Every other September, in even-
numbered years, Pescia hosts the **Biennale
del Fiore**, Europe's largest flower festival.

In season, the fields around Pescia are
spectacular to drive through but the town
itself has little to detain you. At the northern
end of Piazza Mazzini is the 13th-century

THE REAL ADVENTURES OF PINOCCHIO

Pinocchio is one of the best-known children's classics and, no, it isn't a Walt Disney invention. (Roberto Benigni's 2002 version of the film was more faithful to the original story, even if casting himself, when aged 50, as the boy puppet he strained dramatic licence in other ways!)

This timeless tale of a wooden puppet that turns into a boy is one of the most widely read and internationally popular pieces of literature ever to emerge from Italy. In the early 1880s, Carlo Collodi, a Florentine journalist, wrote a series for one of united Italy's first children's periodicals entitled *Storia di un Burattino* (Story of a Puppet). Subsequently renamed *Le Avventure di Pinocchio* (The Adventures of Pinocchio), it would have made Collodi (real name Lorenzini) a multimillionaire had he lived to exploit the film and translation rights.

Collodi did not merely intend to pen an amusing child's tale. Literary critics have been trawling the text for the past century in search of ever more evidence to show that it was as much aimed at adult readers as children.

The character of Pinocchio is a frustrating mix of the likeable and the odious. At his worst he's a wilful, obnoxious, deceitful little monster who deserves just about everything he gets. Humble and blubbering when things go wrong, he has the oh-so-human tendency to resume his wayward behaviour when he thinks he's in the clear. The wooden puppet is a prime example of flesh-and-blood failings. You thought Jiminy Cricket was cute? Pinocchio thought him such a pain, he splattered him against the wall (in the real, not the sanitised Disney, version).

Pinocchio spends a good deal of the tale playing truant and one of Collodi's central messages seems to be that only good, diligent schoolchildren have a hope of getting anywhere or, in this case, of turning into a fine human lad. But Collodi was not merely taking a middle-class swipe at naughty-boyish behaviour. He was convinced that the recently united Italy was in urgent need of a decent education system to help the country out of its poverty and lethargy. His text can be read in part as a criticism of a society as yet incapable of meeting that need.

Indeed the story, weaving between fantasy and reality, is a mine of references, some more veiled than others, to the society of late-19th-century Italy – a troubled country with enormous socioeconomic problems compounded by the general apathy of those in power. Pinocchio waits the length of the story to become a real boy. But, while his persona may provoke laughter, his encounters with poverty, petty crime, skewed justice and just plain bad luck constitute a painful education in the machinations of the 'real' world.

Palazzo del Vicario, these days the Palazzo Comunale (Town Hall). The square itself is fun on Saturday, when it's taken over by the **weekly market**. On other days, it's little more than a car park.

Boutique del Cibo (☎ 0572 47 61 76; Via Libria Andreotti 6; mains €6-13, pizzas €4-7; ⏲ closed Thu) is a friendly restaurant two blocks west of the river. The atmosphere is kitchen-sink informal and there's a terrace for alfresco dining beside a busy street.

CLAP buses connect Pescia with Lucca (€2.60, 45 minutes). Lazzi services run east to Montecatini Terme (€1.20, 20 minutes, half-hourly).

THE GARFAGNANA

At the heart of the Garfagnana is the valley formed by the Serchio river and its tributaries. Historically a region of net migration as villagers packed their bags to lead less harsh lives on the plains, it's now revitalised thanks to tourism and to the paper mills that whir outside most valley town (Diecimo's alone produces over 100,000 tonnes annually, including kilometre upon kilometre of Eco Lucart, the *soi-disant* environmentally friendly toilet paper.)

Most visitors to this relatively undiscovered area of raw beauty are here for the active life, enjoying horse-trekking, hiking and biking. For walkers, it's also a launch pad for treks into the Apuane Alps.

The SS12 sneaks away from the north walls of Lucca (follow the signs for Abetone) along the Serchio river valley (a detour east at **Vinchiana** along a narrow, winding road for a few kilometres brings you to the **Pieve di Brancoli**, a fine 12th-century Romanesque church).

Continuing upstream along the SS12, you hit **Borgo a Mozzano**, with its wacky, asymmetrical

cal Ponte della Maddalena (also known as
onte del Diavolo, or Devil's Bridge). Each
' its five arches is different. Typical of the
a, this medieval bridge rises to a high mid-
oint, then descends to the other side of the
rchio – only the 'midpoint' here is well off
ntre so the whole thing looks like a rearing
och Ness monster in stone.

agni di Lucca
p 6550

he exquisite small town of Bagni di Lucca is
few kilometres further on, where the SS12
arves east, just past the turn-off for Barga.
1 the early-19th century, Bagni was famous
or its thermal waters, enjoyed by both the
entry of Lucca and an international set;
yron, Shelley, Heinrich Heine and Giacomo
uccini were among the celebrity guests to
ke the waters. The dignified neoclassical
uildings still speak of the town's former
»lendour. This spa town had its own casino
id theatre and there was even an atypi-
illy ornate Anglican church (look for the
ucco lion and unicorn motif above each
indow), nowadays the municipal library.
qually trans-cultural are the baroque tombs
1 the small British cemetery.

A couple of **spas** (Apr-Oct) have been revi-
lised and offer a huge range of treatments
id pampering, such as mud baths, gum
assages and irresistible 'endotympanic in-
fflations'. The hale and hearty may want
> open their pores in one of the *grotte a va-
ore* (steam grottoes) after a day's hiking.

There are two distinct areas: the smaller
onte a Serraglio, clustered around a bridge
at crosses the Lima River, and the Villa
own), 2km northwards. As the name sug-
ests, the latter is larger with more shops,
estaurants and hotels. The **tourist office**
 0583 80 57 45; Via del Casinò; 9.30am-12.30pm &
30-6.30pm Mon-Sat, 9.30am-12.30pm Sun mid-Mar–mid-
»p; 9.30am-12.30pm Mon & Wed-Sat mid-Sep–mid-Mar)
 in Ponte a Serraglio.

LEEPING & EATING
otel Roma (0583 8 72 78; albergo.romabagnilucca@
rgilio.it; Viale Umberto I 110; s/d €35/45, d without bath-
om €35; mid-Mar–Oct) Located in Villa, this
otel dates back to 1690 and was later con-
erted to be the summer residence of Elisa
onaparte. Owner Renato (who bears an
ncanny resemblance to Jack Nicholson) is
lovingly restoring the building without

threatening its historical integrity. There
are lovely shady gardens and the attic is
furnished in period style as though Elisa
has just stepped out for a stroll.

Hotel Svizzero (/fax 0583 80 53 15; Via Casalini
30; s/d €40/55) This gracious building in Villa
has a quasi-colonial feel, overlooking the
northwest corner of a small park. Bedrooms
have high ceilings and simple furniture and
the mood is unbeatably welcoming.

Hotel Bernabo (0583 80 52 15; Ponte a Serraglio;
s/d incl breakfast €35/70) Perched high above the
bridge, the hotel has superb views of Bagni's ochre buildings and grey stone church.
Rooms are swing-a-cat size but have all
creature comforts. There's a large sun terrace, and restaurants and bars are within
short strolling distance.

Circolo dei Forestieri (0583 8 60 38; Piazza Jean
Varraud 10; tourist menu €10, mains €6; Wed-Sun & dinner Tue Easter-Oct, Fri-Sun Nov-Easter) With its high
ceilings and chandeliers, the 'foreigners club'
in Villa struts pure *belle époque* and is hugely
recommended. There are fresh flowers on
every table, your meal is punctuated by tasty
extras that arrive unannounced and you can
dine like royalty at paupers' prices. Try the
crêpes ai fungi (mushroom crepes).

Lazzi buses run here from Lucca (€2.50,
50 minutes, nine daily).

The Lima Valley & Abetone
The SS12 continues northeast from the Garfagnana into Pistoia province. If you're going
to the ski slopes, it's the most picturesque
route. Possible minor detours en route are
to **San Cassiano**, with its 12th-century church,
and **Lucchio**, spectacular for its position on
the northeast slope of a wooded ridge.

Abetone, on the Emilia-Romagna border,
has some 30 hotels. It's Tuscany's main ski
resort and also makes a good base for a day
or two of summertime striding. For more
information, click on www.abetone.com (in
Italian) or, for detailed skiing low-down,
flick back to p50.

Ostello Renzo Bizzarri (0573 6 01 17; bucaneve@
abetone.com; Via Brennero 157; dm/d €13/30 all incl breakfast; Dec-Apr & mid-Jun–Sep), Abetone's large,
secluded HI hostel with its enthusiastic
staff, is well equipped for skiers and summer walkers, and its prices are certainly the
most wallet-friendly in town.

Otherwise, half board at the town's hotels
(most will insist on this) starts at around

DETOUR: LUCIGNANO

On the SS445 between Bagni di Lucca and Barga, take a turn right after 9.5km, past Alpine meadows and just beyond Calavorno. It's signposted to the picturesque stone village of Lucignano, perched high above to your right. At 4.7km cross a bridge over the river and watch for the magnificent view of the medieval village of Montefegatesi to your right. At 10km you will enter the village. Conquer the narrow ascent in first gear, squeeze your wing mirrors through the stone gateways and you'll find yourself in a world of leaning passages, cobbled squares and bent but welcoming old women. Park and ponder the magnificent view from the stone wall due north of here, before winding your way back to the main road.

€36 per person. Another dozen or so hotels are strung out in nearby towns.

For those without their own transport, the easiest way up is to catch a bus from Pistoia (see p133).

Barga
pop 10,000

The high point of the steep old town of Barga is quite literally its highest point. Climb to the top of town for panoramic views and look inside the **cathedral**, built between the 10th and 14th centuries. The pulpit in particular is exquisitely carved by the idiosyncratic 13th-century sculptor Guido Bigarelli, and sits on four red marble pillars. The two front ones rest on lions that dominate a dragon and a heretic, while one of the back pillars rests on a disconsolate dwarf. The town, a lovely patchwork of narrow streets, archways, ancient walls and small piazzas, spreads beneath the cathedral.

There's a small **tourist office** (☎ 0583 72 47 45; Via di Mezzo 45).

CLAP buses from Lucca (€3.25, 1¼ hours) run up to 10 times daily, stopping in Piazzale del Fosso by Porta Mancianella, the main gate into the old town. Other buses run to Bagni di Lucca twice daily.

SLEEPING & EATING
La Pergola (☎ 0583 71 12 39; www.hotel-lapergola .com; Via San Antonio 1; s/d €49/66) This is a good-

value hotel in an attractive residential are Rooms (No 43 is especially charming) a prettily floral and several have good view of the village. There's also a 3rd-floor su trap terrace.

Albergo Alpino (☎ 0583 72 33 36; www.bargah day.com; Via Pascoli 41; s/d €45/65; ⊙ closed Nov) In t hands of the Castelvecchi family for nigh a century, this is a 1920s lodge-style ho with a great bar and restaurant. Rooms a tidy, clean and comfortable and the o town's a mere five minute's walk away.

Castelnuovo di Garfagnana
pop 6050

Castelnuovo towers over the confluence the river Serchio and its smaller tributar the Turrite. Apart from the formidab 14th-century **Rocca**, a castle built for the Es dukes of Ferrara, there's little to see. It do make a good base for adventure activities the Garfagnana and Apuane Alps.

The **Centro Visite Parco Alpi Apuane** (☎ 0583 42 42; www.parks.it/parco.alpi.apuane; Piazza delle Erbe ⊙ 9am-1pm & 3-7pm Jun-Sep, to 5.30pm Oct-May) well stocked with maps and brochures abo the Apuane Alps. Its pamphlet *Apuan Alp A World to Get to Know* gives details *rifugi* (mountain huts) and walks.

The **Consorzio Garfagnana Turistica** (☎ 0583 44 73; www.garfagnanaturistica.info; Via della Centrale ⊙ 9am-1pm & 2.30-7pm Mon-Sat), rather less e ficient and with varying hours, can reser accommodation. Its free booklet, *Garfa nana Trekking*, describes a 10-day rou while *Garfagnana a Cavallo* details guide horse treks. *Garfagnana by Bicycle* (€16.5 by Lucia and Bruno Giovannetti comes a handy wallet form and describes over 2 cycle trips for all levels of fitness.

Cartadel Turismo Rurale della Garfa nana e Valle del Serchio, a free map availab from the tourist office, has detailed mult lingual suggestions for hikes and drivin routes in the region. For general readin *Valley Garfagnana & the Serchio Valle* produced by the Lucca tourism authorit is a more substantial volume. For a gener overview, pick up their free booklet *Garfa nana & the Serchio Valley*.

The municipal **tourist office** (☎ 0583 64 07; Via Cavalieri di Vittorio Veneto; ⊙ 9.30am-1pm & 3.3 7pm daily Jun-Sep, to 6.30pm Mon-Sat Oct-May) is the same square as the Centro Visite Parc Alpi Apuane.

EEPING & EATING

Carlino (☎ 0583 64 42 70; www.dacarlino.it in Italian; Garibaldi 15; s/d €45/70) This hotel has comrtable, chintzy rooms with balconies. At restaurant, one of the best in town, trout the speciality – as well as homemade eringues.

Trattoria Marchetti (☎ 0583 63 91 57; Via Testi 10; ins from €6) This earthy, inexpensive lunch ot has warm wooden innards and a busy unter dishing up massive plates of delious local dishes. For starters, dig into eir *zuppa di farro*, a rich soup made from elt, a peculiarly Tuscan cereal.

TTING THERE & AROUND

ere are up to 10 CLAP buses from Lucca weekdays (€3.60, 1½ hours).

You can rent a bike from **Cicli Maggi** (☎ 0583 63 91 66; Via Nicola Fabrizi 49; half/full day '15).

ound Castelnuovo di Garfagnana

veral scenic roads fan out from Castelovo. If you've steady nerves, try the cortina of hairpin bends that lifts you, via astiglione di Garfagnana, to the Foce di adici pass across the Apennines and into nilia-Romagna. The scenery in parts is ite splendid. The minor parallel road to e south leads you to **San Pellegrino in Alpe**, e site of a fine monastery.

Walkers will enjoy the small **Riserva Natule dell'Orecchiella** park on the narrow road a **Corfino**, itself a pleasant village with seval hotels. Seven kilometres further north the park's **tourist office** (☎ 0583 61 90 98; 9am-7pm Jul-mid-Sep, 10am-5pm Sat & Sun Jun & e-Sep) where you can pick up information d maps for walks within the reserve. For e most scenic route to the park, turn west eft) to Villa Collemandine along a tiny ad just beyond Castiglione, then right ong the road for Corfino.

The SS445 follows the Serchio Valley to e east of the Apuane Alps and bores into e Lunigiana region (see p172) at Tuscany's rthern limit. It's a pretty, twisting route at leads you through lush green countryde. About 8km north of Castelnuovo at ggio, there's a turn-off to the pretty, aricial **Lago Vagli** along the Torrente Edron ream. You can do some pleasant short lks in the area, or simply a circular driving ute that brings you back to Castelnuovo.

Hollowed within these hills are an astounding 1300 caves, nearly all requiring a guide and special tackle. The most accessible and spectacular is the **Grotta del Vento** (Wind Cave; ☎ 0583 72 20 24), 9km west of the SS445. Here, the wonders of the underground abysses, lakes and caverns contrast with the bleak landscape above. From April to October, you can take a one-hour guided tour (adult/child €7.50/5, eight times daily), a two-hour option (adult/child €12/8.50, four times daily) or a three-hour full monty (adult/child €17/11.50, at 10am and 2pm). From November to March, only the one-hour tour is on offer. Bring your woollies; it can feel chilly down there, even in high summer.

VIAREGGIO

pop 61,800

Viareggio is the most popular sun-and-sand resort along the Versilia coastal strip. The celebrated Art Nouveau façades beside Via Regina Margherita recall the town's initial heyday, back in the 1920s. Nowadays, Viareggio is equally famous for its flamboyant Carnevale, second only to Venice for party spirit.

Orientation

It's a short walk from the train station to the waterfront and main tourist office. The city is arranged roughly north to south on a grid pattern. South from the Canale Burlamacca, lined with pleasure boats, stretch the enticing woods of the Pineta di Levante. Another smaller wood, the Pineta di Ponente, occupies a large chunk of the northern end of town. Beyond it Viareggio merges seamlessly into the next beach resort of Lido di Camaiore.

Information

EMERGENCY

Police station (☎ 0584 4 27 41; Piazza S. Antonio)

INTERNET ACCESS

Floating Point (☎ 0584 43 30 25; Piazza Dante; per hr €5; ⏱ 9.30am-1pm & 5-8pm Jun-Aug, 4-7.30pm Mon-Sat) Opposite train station.

LAUNDRY

Wash & Dry (Corso Garibaldi 5)

POST

Main post office (Corso Garibaldi)

TOURIST INFORMATION

Main tourist office (☎ 0584 96 22 33; www.versilia
.turismo.toscana.it; Carducci 10; ⏰ 9am-2pm & 3-7.30pm
Mon-Sat, 9.30am-1pm Sun)
Tourist office (⏰ 9.30am-12.30pm Mon-Fri, 9.30am-
12.30pm & 4-6pm Sat & Sun) A smaller office at the train
station.

Sights & Activities

When you tire of the beach, you can stroll
along the tracks in the **Pineta di Levante**, beside the Canale Burlamacca and along Via
Regina Margherita. And if you feel even the
most distant call of the sea, you'll thrill to
the stylish pleasure vessels, big and small,
being constructed or refurbished in the
town's docks and shipyards. Should you
exhaust Viareggio, pick up a copy of the
tourist office's excellent free booklet that
describes in detail 14 graded walks around
the coastal towns and inland mountains.

Literature lovers might like to pass by
Piazza Shelley to pay brief homage. It's
about the only tangible reference to the
romantic poet who drowned in Viareggio;
his body was washed up on the beach and

his comrade-in-arts, Lord Byron, had h
cremated on the spot.

A good deal of the waterfront area as
appears today was built in the 1920s a
'30s. Several of the buildings, such as Pu
cini's favourite, **Gran Caffè Margherita**, reta
something of their ornate stylishness.

The beach costs. It has been divided
into *stabilimenti* – individual lots whe
you can hire cabins, umbrellas, reclin
and the like. Two recliners with umbrel
will set you back about €20 a day.

Festivals & Events

Viareggio's moment of glory lasts a go
three weeks from mid-February to ea
March when the city goes wild at **Carnevale**
a festival of floats, many with giant satiri
effigies of political and other topical figur
plus fireworks and a dusk-to-dawn spirit.

Sleeping

There are half a dozen camp sites in
Pineta di Levante woods between Viareg
and Torre del Lago. Most open from Ap
to September.

Campeggio dei Tigli (☎ 0584 341278; www.camping
gli.com; Viale dei Tigli; person/pitch €9/15; ☙ Apr-
This is one of the biggest camp sites
h a restaurant and disco. Take CLAP bus
1 or 2 from Piazza d'Azeglio.

Viareggio boasts more than 120 hotels of
classes, along with *affittacamere* and vil-
. They jostle for space beside or a couple
blocks inland from the waterfront and
mostly modern, clean – and bland. In
;h summer, especially July, many charge
least *mezza pensione* (half board) and
en *pensione completa* (full board).

Al Piccolo (☎ 0584 5 10 14; alpiccolohotel@cheapnet
Via Duilio 16; s/d €32/65; ▯) Has large rooms
an older building on a quiet residential
eet, and breakfast's a bumper one. It's pos-
le that the owners may be selling up soon
things – and in particular prices – may be
for a shake-up.

American Hotel (☎ 0584 4 70 41; info@american
eggio.com; Piazza Mazzini 6; s/d incl breakfast €110/180;
) This slick modern hotel has lots of
iny marble and coral-coloured fabric.
oms have king-size beds and views of
e piazza, fountain and (with a little neck
ning) the sea.

Grand Hotel Excelsior (☎ 0584 5 07 26; www
celsiorviareggio.it; Viale Carducci 88; s/d €112/194;
▯ ✿) This hotel is the last word in ele-
nce with a glorious feel, the charm of
plush furnished rooms accentuated by
andeliers and antiques.

Peralta (☎ 0584 95 12 30; www.peraltatuscany.com;
om €88, apartments per week from €690, houses from
30; ☙ May-Oct; ▧) High up a side valley,
is wonderful abandoned hamlet, resus-
ated by Anglo-Italian sculptor Fiore De
nriquez has stunning views. It's the per-
ct place to relax though if you'd prefer a
tle self-improvement, there are courses in
inting and cooking, plus hearty hill walk-
g. Check the website since low season
tes can be over 50% cheaper. Bring all you
ed since it's a long, vertiginous haul to the
ops. You'll find it 10km from Viareggio,
;nposted from the village of Camaiore.

ting

you dodge full board in the hotels, there
e plenty of restaurant options, although
e waterfront places tend to be expensive
d uninspiring.

Da Giorgio (☎ 0584 4 44 93; Via G Zanardelli 71; meals
und €35; ☙ Thu-Tue) Run by the same family

for three generations, this is *the* place for
fish – and exclusively fish – of the freshest
kind, succulently cooked. Its walls are plastered with testimonials from satisfied guests
(including, on the left, just as you enter, a
signed photo of Gina Lollobrigida in her
prime). You'll need to make reservations,
especially for dinner.

Brasserie Stuzzichino (☎ 0584 43 30 65; Viale Foscolo
3; salads €6-10, mains €9-12; ☙ closed Tue) This simply
decorated restaurant supplements its sound
menu of familiar pasta dishes and eccentri-
cally titled mains with a jumbo selection of
imaginative and equally plentiful salads.

Sergio (☎ 0584 46 12 56; Piazza del Mercato 130; mains
around €8; ☙ closed Mon) Beneath the arcades on
the south side of Viareggio's market, Sergio
serves quick, nourishing, tasty fare. It's more
of a deli with excellent cheeses and cold
meats, but there are a few tables inside.

L'Oca Bianca (☎ 0584 38 84 77; 1st fl, Via Coppino 409;
menu €45-47; ☙ dinner Wed-Mon) The White Goose
offers a deliciously grand, if expensive, menu
that includes a taste of three wines. Typical
dishes include ravioli with white truffles.

Drinking

Viareggio has a healthy selection of bars
and clubs for those who like to keep the
tempo going after sundown. For listings,
consult the monthly *Note* and the more
comprehensive *Il Mangiarbere*, or *Paspartu*,
which comes out every two weeks. Tourist
offices have a copy and they're available at
hotels and popular bars.

Patchouly (☎ 0368 353 99 00; Viale Foscolo 17;
☙ closed Mon) For cocktails and New Age
music, float into this hip cafe with a glassed-
in terrace and photos of jolly-looking patrons papering the walls.

Agorà Café (☎ 0584 61 04 88; Viale Colombo 666, Lido
di Camaiore) Try this cool, laid-back hang-out
if you like the tempo energetic rather than
frenetic. Later in the evening it converts into
a disco with plenty of space to get jiggy.

Getting There & Around
BOAT

From June to September **Consorzio Marittimo
Turistico** (☎ 0187 73 29 87; Via Minzoni 13, La Spezia)
puts on passenger boats connecting Via-
reggio (and also Marina de Pisa, Forte dei
Marmi, Marina di Carrara and Marina di
Massa) with coastal destinations in Liguria,
such as the Cinque Terre and Portofino.

BUS
Lazzi (☎ 0584 4 62 34) and **CLAP** (☎ 0584 3 09 96) buses run from Piazza d'Azeglio, where both have offices, to destinations around Tuscany, including services running direct or via Lucca to Florence (€6.70, 1½ hours, seven daily).

CLAP has fairly regular buses up the coast to Pietrasanta and Forte dei Marmi, as well as up to 12 daily to Lucca (€2.70) and between three and six services a day to Massa (€2.40). It also runs the town's local buses.

From June to September long-distance buses run to such destinations as Milan (€23.50). Buy tickets at travel agencies or the Lazzi kiosk.

TAXI
Call ☎ 0584 4 70 00 or ☎ 0584 4 54 54.

TRAIN
Local trains run to Livorno (€3.10, one hour), Pisa (€2.10, 20 minutes) and La Spezia (€3.70, one hour) via Massa and Carrara. Regular trains run to Florence (€5.90), via Lucca (€2.10). A couple of Eurostar Italia trains bound for Rome, Genoa and Turin stop by, as do four to five fast trains, bound for Milan and Turin.

SOUTH OF VIAREGGIO
Torre del Lago
A few kilometres south of Viareggio on the other side of the Pineta di Levante, Torre del Lago is a quiet continuation of the seaside theme, but with one important difference. A further couple of kilometres inland spreads the **Lago di Massaciuccoli**, a shallow lagoon within the **Parco Naturale Migliarino San Rossore Massaciuccoli** (right). The lagoon hosts more than 100 species of permanent, migratory and nesting birds, including heron, egret, wild duck and moor buzzard. **Eco-Idea** (☎ 0584 35 02 52; www.laversilia.it/eco-idea/in Italian; adult/child €5/2) runs boat excursions across the lagoon for about an hour from Villa Puccini, with a minimum of 20 people.

The composer Puccini had a **villa** (☎ 0584 34 14 45; adult/child €7/1.50; ☉ 10am-12.30pm & 3-6.30pm Tue-Sun Jun-Oct, to 5.30pm Dec-Mar, to 6pm Apr-May) built here by the lake, where he wrote most of his operas, including *Madame Butterfly* and *Tosca*. In July and August the open-air theatre by the lagoon is one of the main stages for the **Festival Puccini** (www.puccinifestival .it), when his operas are performed.

CLAP bus No 4 runs from the centre Viareggio.

Parco Naturale Migliarino San Rosso Massaciuccoli
Covering around 23,000 hectares and stretc ing from Viareggio in the north to Livor in the south, this park is one of Tuscan rare stretches of protected coastline.

Part swamp, part pine forest, the park host to particularly diverse birdlife, especia during the migratory periods, when spec of falcon, vulture, duck, heron, cormor and other water birds linger or pass throu Deer, wild boar and feral goats are the b gest of the quadruped year-round residen

The **Centro Visite** (Visitors Centre; ☎ 050 53 01 ☉ 9am-1pm & 2.30-6pm Jun-Sep, 9am-1pm & 2-5pm May) in Cascine Vecchie is your best sou of information.

A sliver of coast between the Arno a Livorno is not part of the park, and for P ans the small seaside towns of **Marina di F** and the more attractive **Tirrenia** are weeke beach-action favourites. Beyond the pa the next stop south on the coast is t sprawling port town of Livorno (p175).

LA VERSILIA
The coastal area from Viareggio nor wards to the regional border with Ligu is known as La Versilia. Although popu with local holidaymakers and some foreig ers (mainly Germans, French and Brits) has been blighted by beachfront strip c velopment. It's hugely popular with the g community, over 100,000 of whom desce upon the resort each summer.

THE PINE WOODS OF VERSILIA

The woods of cluster pine (Pinus pinea) that spread through Versilia like stands of open green parasols aren't native habitat, hanging in there as tourist development encroaches. Most were planted by humans, back in the 17th and 18th centuries. The bark was used in dyeing, the resin as an additive in chemical products. Above all, the tiny, tasty nuts were shaken from the cones, collected and sold. Still today, Versilia remains one of Italy's biggest producers of pine nuts, a valued addition to many a local dish and a crunchy treat in its own right.

La Versilia makes a good gateway to the uane Alps (see p173), with roads from the astal towns snaking their way deep into e heart of the mountains and connecting th small villages and walking tracks.

The website www.rivieratoscana.com is a h resource for this stretch of coast, inland nigiana (p172) and the Apuane Alps.

etrasanta & Around

ading up the coast from Viareggio, you ss into **Lido di Camaiore**. The development comes sparser as you press on northwards d the beaches are usually less crowded.

When you reach **Marina di Pietrasanta**, turn and 3.5km for the town of **Pietrasanta** it-f. The centre of the old town is Piazza iomo. If it's open, pop into the Chiesa di nt'Agostino; its rather stark, Gothic façade ay be off-putting but the cloister inside is easant. Also here is a 13th-century cathe-al and the Palazzo Moroni, with a modest chaeological museum.

Seravezza, further inland, has been an im-rtant centre for marble extraction since e 16th century (Michelangelo spent some ne here poking around for raw materials). owadays, it's a gateway to the **Parco Regionale lle Alpi Apuane**. The park **information centre** 0584 7 58 21; info@parcapuane.toscana.it; Via Corrado Greco 11; 9am-1pm & 4-8pm daily summer, 9am-1pm .30-4.30pm Mon-Sat winter), which stocks maps d walking booklets, is co-located with the urist office (0584 75 73 25).

At the confluence of the rivers Serra and ezza and with the Apuane Alps rising be-nd it, Seravezza is a pleasant small town. ie cathedral has some superb works by orentine goldsmiths, including a crucifix, hile about 4.5km north, the Pieve della appella (parish church) in **Azzano** has a autiful rose window nicknamed the 'eye Michelangelo'. The village's Palazzo ediceo was built by Cosimo I de' Medici a summer getaway.

One recommended route is due south-st along the Vezza River to the picturesque imlet of **Stazzema**, high in the hills. The vil-ge entrance is marked by the Romanesque iiesa di Santa Maria Assunta, and it makes great base for walks in the Apuane Alps.

Procinto (0584 77 70 04; Via Novembre 21; d m €44) is a good rural hotel in the heart of azzema, although its management could e a course at charm school. Meals are huge

and well priced. Rumbling tummies should fill up on the delicious *polenta con fungi* (mushroom polenta).

Back down on the coast, **Forte dei Marmi** is the most chic resort on this stretch of coastline (post-Cannes film festival over the border, several of the stars, starlets and satellites retire here to recover). You'll find plenty of places to stay, eat and drink close to the waterfront; the **tourist office** (0584 8 00 91; www.fortedeimarmi.it in Italian; Via Franceschi 8b; 9am-1pm & 3.30-6.30pm Mon-Sat, 10am-noon Sun Jun-Sep, 9am-1pm Mon-Sat & 3-7pm Sat Oct-May) car-ries a list. Time your visit for the town's Wednesday **market** (replicated on Sunday in summer), when you can pick up designer label clothing for a relative snip.

Beyond Forte dei Marmi the seaside is fairly uninspiring, until you reach the bor-der of Liguria and beyond.

Massa
pop 66,900

Massa is the administrative centre of the province of the same name, also known as Massa Carrara. And that's really all there is to say about it.

Little remains of the old core of the town apart from the **cathedral**, itself of slight in-terest. Dominating the town is the **Castello Malaspina** (0585 4 47 74; adult/child €5/3; 9.30am-12.30pm & 5.30-8pm Tue-Sun mid-Jun–mid-Sep). From this high point, the Malaspina family could keep watch on the surrounding territory.

The main **tourist office** (0585 24 00 63; www .aptmassacarrara.it in Italian; Viale Vespucci 24) is on the coast in Marina di Massa.

There are only two hotels in Massa, should you want to stay. Marina di Massa, down on the coast, is a lively, fun place with loads of restaurants and bars. To its north are plenty of camping grounds.

Hotel Caprice (0585 86 80 28; www.hotelcaprice .net; Via delle Pinete 3, Marina di Massa; d from €60; P) This hotel sits within lovely, mature shaded gardens. Rooms are a little threadbare but comfortable enough and the English-Italian owners are cheery and helpful with info on the area.

GETTING AROUND

Buses for a good number of destinations around the northwest of Tuscany leave from the train station in Massa itself. Buses to Lucca run five times a day (€3.50, 1½ hours).

Carrara

pop 64,900

Just look at the snow-capped mountains dominating Carrara (even in high summer), at the foothills of the Apuane Alps – but it's all illusion. It is really marble, field upon field of it, in vast quarries that eat into the hills. The texture and purity of Carrara's white marble is unrivalled. Michelangelo selected blocks from here for many of his masterpieces. More recently, Henry Moore picked his way through the jumble of rocks and cut-offs in search of the perfect piece.

Carrara, about 7km northwest of Massa, is the world capital of both the extraction and working of white marble. The marble quarries were already being worked in Roman times. It's hard, dangerous work and, in Piazza XXVII Aprile, the town has erected a monument to workers who have lost their lives in the quarries. These tough men formed the backbone of a strong leftist and anarchist tradition in Carrara, something that won them no friends among the Fascists or, later, the occupying German forces. Nowadays, environmentalists oppose the continual massive quantity of marble that is hauled from the hillside, while quarry owners fight back in their interest and that of their 14,000 or so employees.

The gracious little old centre of Carrara is tucked away in the northwestern corner of the town, almost 10km inland from its coastal counterpart, Marina di Carrara, and nuzzling up to the scarred foothills of the Apuane Alps.

INFORMATION

There's a **tourist office** (☎ 0585 63 25 19; Via Garib 41/d; ☀ core hr 9am-1pm Tue-Sat, 3-6pm Tue & Thu) Marina di Carrara. If you are interested visiting the *laboratori*, or marble worksho they can provide you with a map.

Carrara Point (☎ 0585 77 96 36; Via Ulivi 19; pe €4) provides Internet access.

SIGHTS

The **cathedral** (Piazza Duomo; ☀ 7am-noon & 3. 7pm), at the heart of the old town, is one of 𝟭 earliest medieval buildings to have been co structed entirely of Apuane marble. Buildi began in the 11th century and dragged for two centuries. The façade – Romanesq below and elaborately fretted Gothic abov was largely inspired by Pisan models.

The partly colonnaded 15th-centu Piazza Alberica with its festively pain houses deserves a dawdle. On the west si is the exuberant 18th-century **Palazzo Medico**, erected to speak power by the mo powerful quarry owners of the time. Che out the cherubs below each window, le ing gargoyles above and the family coat arms sitting over the central window, all, course, in Carrara marble.

The much modified castle on Piaz Gramsci started life as a fortified resider of the Malaspina clan and is now the **Pala dell'Accademia di Belle Arti**, Carrara's fine a school.

Museo del Marmo (☎ 0585 84 57 46; Viale XX Sette bre; adult/child €4.50/2.50; ☀ 10am-6pm Mon-Sat M Jun, Sep, 10am-8pm Mon-Sat Jul-Aug, 9am-5pm Oct-A

CARRARA'S MARBLE

For centuries, marble (derived from the Greek *marmaros,* meaning shining stone) has been hewn and shaped as a luxury material for sculpture and prestige construction. And Carrara has long been the world's largest extractor.

It's amazing that there's any mountain left. The Romans first hacked into the hillside (look for these early quarrymen's initials, chiselled into the rock to indicate stakes and claims). Their tools and extraction techniques remained largely unchanged until the 19th century, when gunpowder was introduced.

Wasteful and destructive, gunpowder was eventually replaced by the helicoidal thread, a thick hawser that ground its way through the rock like a cheese wire paring off Parmesan. Nowadays, towering cranes operate diamond-cutting chains that slice off huge cubes that litter the mountain like some giant kid's building blocks.

The workshops of Carrara still turn out their share of *putti* (winsome cherubs), Madonnas and the like, but most marble nowadays is shipped abroad in huge blocks, to be worked elsewhere. Then again, several international sculptors we won't name have had a chip knocked off the old block and a corner or two rounded in order to fashion their next oeuvre into rough shape.

To Colonnata
& Cava di
Fantiscritti (6km)

Via Carriona

Carrione

Piazza
Duomo

Piazza
Alberica

Piazza
Manzoni

Via Loris Giorgi

Via S. Maria

Via del Plebiscito

Piazza
Gramsci

Via Tacca

Via Apuana

Piazza
Accademia

Corso Fratelli Rossi

Via UNI

Via Verdi

Via Cavour

Piazza
XXVII
Aprile

Via Roma

Via Mazini

Via VII Luglio

Via di Cavatore

Piazza
Matteotti

Piazza
Don
Minzoni

Aronte

To Museo del Marmo (3km);
Train Station (4km); Marina di
Carrara & Tourist Office (6.5km)

opposite the stadium, halfway between
[Ca]rrara and Marina di Carrara. With de-
[sc]riptive panels in English, it has more mar-
[bl]e in more varieties than you'll ever have
[se]en before and describes extraction from
[ch]isel-and-hammer days to the 21st cen-
[tu]ry's high-powered industrial quarrying.

Colonnata and the **Cava di Fantiscritti**, around
[6k]m north of town, are the two major quar-
[ri]es. Follow the *cava* (quarry) signs. At the
[la]tter, the guy who runs the souvenir shop
[ha]s a small private **marble museum** (☎ 0585 7
[...]81; admission free; 9am-7pm). Cross the Ponti
[di] Vara, a viaduct built in the 19th century
[fo]r the railways and a monument in its own
[ri]ght; at the time it was considered one of
[th]e great feats of modern engineering.

You can visit some of the marble *laboratori*, such as **Studi di Scultura Nicoli** on Piazza
XXVII Aprile. To get an idea of the hard
grind, poke your nose into the dust-filled air
of the workshops on either side of the square.
Commissions range from the banal to the
bizarre. Artists frequently instruct the **workshops** on how they want a piece executed –
or at least begun – thus cleverly avoiding the
hard and dusty work themselves.

Over the summer, there's a special hop-
on hop-off bus service that runs from the
coast, passing many of the *laboratori* and
the museum, then on to Colonnata. Ask at
the tourist office for the current schedule.

SLEEPING & EATING

Ostello Apuano (☎ 0585 78 00 34; ostelloapuano@hot
mail.com; Viale delle Pinete 237, Marina di Massa; dm €10;
 mid-Mar–Sep) This attractive HI-affiliated
youth hostel is right on the seafront at Partac-
cia, just north of Marina di Massa. From Carrara train station catch bus No 53, marked
Via Avenza Mare.

Hotel Michelangelo (☎ 0585 77 71 61; fax 0585 7
45 45; Corso Fratelli Rossi 3; s without/with shower €30/60
d/tr with bathroom €85/100; P) This hotel is past
its best but rooms are still comfortable and
filled with some lovely old furniture. Parking costs €5 to €10.

Da Roberto (☎ 0585 7 06 34; fax 0585 7 06 34; Via
Apuana 3f; s/d €31/46.50) Family run, pristine and
good value, the location of this hotel, overlooking the small river Carrione and the
junction of two busy roads, may mean you
need to sleep with the window closed.

There are several worthwhile bars and
restaurants around Piazza Alberica.

Ristorante Roma (☎ 0585 7 06 32; Piazza Cesare
Battisti 1; mains €7-10) Just off the square, this
restaurant offers smiley, speedy service and
the menu changes regularly according to
the season. Try the seafood risotto followed
by a simple yet memorable vanilla *gelato*.

GETTING THERE & AWAY

The bus station is on Piazza Don Minzoni.
CAT buses (☎ 0585 8 53 11) serve the surrounding area, including Massa to the south and,
in the Lunigiana area, Fivizzano, Aulla and
Pontremoli.

Trains along the coastal line (from La
Spezia, Genoa, Rome, Viareggio and so on)
stop nearer Marina di Carrara, from where
local buses shuttle into Carrara itself.

LUNIGIANA

Inland and north is one of Tuscany's wildest and least-known pockets: the Lunigiana. This landlocked enclave of Tuscan territory is bordered to the north and east by Emilia-Romagna, to the west by Liguria and to the south by the Apuane Alps. Pontremoli, charming in its own right, makes a great base for exploring this relatively unexplored, rugged territory.

The medieval Via Francigena, a vital route connecting northern and central Italy in Roman days and later a key access for armies and Rome-bound pilgrims alike, roughly follows the modern A15 autostrada from into Cisa pass south to Sarzana, just over into Liguria and on the coast.

Our favourite driving route is one of several options.

From Carrara take SP446 northwards, following signs to **Fosdinovo** and its formidable **castle** (☎ 0187 6 88 91; adult/child €5/3; ☼ tours five times daily Wed-Mon). Owned by the Malaspina clan since 1340 (still today, it belongs to a branch of the family), its defensive walls and towers were gradually modified from the 16th century when the family converted it into a residence. A charming legend has it that a young princess died of a broken heart within the castle walls and at full moon her shadow can be seen drifting from window to window.

From Fosdinovo, follow the SS446 until a T-junction with the SS63. Heading right (eastwards) will bring you to **Fivizzano**, a largely modern farming centre, from where a wonderfully pretty mountain road runs northwards over the Apennines and deep into Emilia-Romagna.

Heading in the opposite direction, southwest from Fivizzano, you hit **Aulla**, a fairly drab town with a 16th-century fortress as its only draw.

North of Aulla is **Villafranca**, altogether more interesting, a one-time waystation on the Via Francigena and, according to the stories, quite a medieval tourist trap. Here, so they reckon, the difference between local tax collectors and plain old thieves was decidedly vague. At the village's northern end is what was once a thriving mill. Within is the small, yet fascinating **Museo Etnografico della Lunigiana** (Via Antico Molino; ☼ 9am-noon & 4-7pm summer, 9am-noon & 3-6pm winter), overlooking a footbridge that spans the river Magra.

Albergo Manganelli (☎ /fax 0187 49 30 62; Pi San Niccolò 5; s/d €36/42, with bath €40/46), ochre-c oured and inviting, is a true bargain. Roo are big and airy and there's a great popu restaurant downstairs. It's beside the finger of a ruined tower on the south s of town.

Pontremoli

pop 8100

A primary halting place along the (Francigena, the original old town is a lc sliver stretching north to south betwe the Magra and Verde Rivers. These wat courses served as natural defensive barri in what was a key position for the contro traffic between northern and central Ita In the 17th century the town enjoyec boom and most of the fine residences d back to those times.

The town's charm resides in its sm piazzas surrounded by colonnaded arc that give shade to enticing bars and ca Its shops are a mix of the old-fashion and idiosyncratic next to the stylish a sophisticated.

The **tourist office** (☎ 0187 83 37 01; www. nigiana.it in Italian; Piazza della Repubblica 6; ☼ 9 12.30pm & 3-6pm Mon-Fri, 9.30am-12.30pm Sat) op ates on weekends from a different off within the town hall on the opposite si of the square.

From central Piazza della Republ and adjacent Piazza del Duomo (the l ter flanked by the 17th-century cathed with its neoclassical façade), a steep, win ing way takes you to the **Castello del Piagn** (☎ 0187 83 14 39; admission €2.50; ☼ 9am-noo 2-5pm Tue-Sun). Although originally rais in the 9th century, what you see today largely the result of 14th- and 15th-centu reconstruction. The views across town a enchanting and inside is a small museu its treasure a number of striking primit *stele* found nearby.

Golf Hotel (☎ 0187 83 15 73; www.golfho .it; 1 Via della Pineta 32; s/d incl buffet breakfast €62 P 🖳 🕿) This is a puzzling name (w back, a golf course was planned but nev even got seeded) for an attractive hotel w a grand marble lobby leading to bright, sp cious rooms and a lovely terrace restaura Some 2km west of and above the town, i a bracing place with an open-air pool a free bike hire for guests.

Take a coffee break at the delightful **Caffè
li Svizzeri** (Piazza della Repubblica 21-22; ☺ Tue-
. As a notice entreats, refrain from lean-
your elbows on the marble-topped
les which, like the cafe itself, all in pan-
d wood, are well over 100 years old. In
iter, you can huddle around the ceramic
ve in the intimate inner room.

At **Trattoria Da Bussè** (☎ 0187 83 13 71; Piazza del
mo 32; mains €8-12; ☺ lunch Mon-Thu, lunch & dinner
& Sun) you can dine on excellent local spe-
lities in the shadow of the cathedral.

CAT (☎ 800 22 30 10) buses run regularly south
Aulla and other destinations around the
nigiana and you can also get to La Spezia.
ntremoli also sits on the Parma–La Spezia
in line.

uane Alps

is mountain range rears up between the
astal Versilia Riviera and, inland, the vast
ley of the Garfagnana. Altitudes are rela-
ely low – the highest peak, Monte Pis-
ino, is 1945m high – compared to the real
ps further north, but the Apuane Alps

offer great walking possibilities (see p45),
often with spectacular views of the coastline
and Ligurian Sea. Lonely Planet's *Walking
in Italy* describes a couple of enjoyable
multiday routes and *The Alps of Tuscany*
by Francesco Greco presents many more.

You'll find a good network of marked
walking trails and *rifugi*. To guide your
steps, pick up *Alpi Apuane Settentrionali*,
published by the Massa and Carrara tourist
offices with trails and *rifugi* marked up, or
Alpi Apuane, produced by Edizione Multigraphic of Florence. Both are at 1:25,000.

The other main attraction of the area is
its caves – over 1300 of them. Of these, the
most accessible and spectacular is the **Grotta
del Vento** (p165).

Antro del Corchia (☎ 0584 77 84 05; admission
€12; ☺ 9am-6pm daily Jul-Aug, shorter hr, Sat & Sun
only mid-Mar–Jun & Sep–mid-Nov), to the north of
Seravezza near Levigliani, is a part of Italy's deepest and longest cave. Tours leave
hourly and last two hours. Bring something
warm to wear as the caves maintain a chilly
7.6°C year-round.

Central Coast & Elba

The Central Coast and its hinterland are a hotchpotch of mundane working cities, intriguing medieval towns and well-preserved Etruscan sites. It's stimulating for travellers in its diversity and also because eye-catching places like the ancient villages of Suvereto and Campiglia Marittima have remained largely untainted by tourism. The area offers a cooler, enticing alternative from the sweltering, summertime coast and is best explored by car.

The port city of Livorno has never been on the tourist trail and yet there's a gritty individuality about the place that some may find appealing. For those interested in Etruscan civilisation, the Parco Archeologico di Baratti e Populonia, together with minuscule medieval Populonia Alta nearby, also make for an absorbing diversion. Livorno and Piombino are departure points for ferries to the breezy Tuscan islands of Capraia and Gorgona, and for those going deeper into the Mediterranean, to Sardinia and Sicily too.

Much of the coast south of Livorno, known as the Maremma Pisana, was once unpleasantly damp and malarial. But these days, thanks to an intricate network of drainage ditches, the swamps are dry and cattle and semiwild horses crop the rich, tufted grass.

Today another obvious plus of the Central Coast is its beach scene. Several strands are well worth exploring, especially on the southern Golfo di Baratti. Those seriously into sand and sea, however, should hop on a ferry to Elba, which, although best enjoyed out of season, has all the classic appeal of a typical Mediterranean island without a single high-rise fronting the beach. Take in too the rugged interior that demands to be tramped.

HIGHLIGHTS

- Tuck into a generous helping of **cacciucco** (p178), a delicious and traditional seafood stew, down by Livorno's harbour

- Combine a beach flop at **Golfo di Baratti** (p183) with an exploration of Etruscan tombs at the **Parco Archeologico di Baratti e Populonia** (p183)

- Catch a ferry to unspoilt **Capraia** (p179) – great for diving, walking or simply sunbaking

- Exercise your calf muscles on the tortuously steep streets of little **Suvereto** (p182)

- Lace up those walking boots or saddle up a mountain bike to explore the western heights of the island of Elba around **Monte Capanne** (p190)

CENTRAL COAST & ELBA

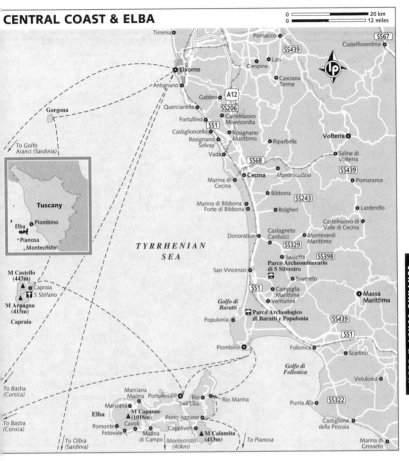

LIVORNO

pop 156,200

Livorno, Tuscany's second-largest city, is still occasionally called by its bizarre anglicised name, Leghorn. The place was heavily bombed during WWII (it was one of Fascist Italy's main naval bases) and there's something mildly melancholic about the centre of town. The post-war rebuilding program may be charitably described as unimaginative. On the plus side, the un-Tuscan absence of wonderful old churches and buildings means you can concentrate on other things – such as the seafood, reputedly the best on the Tyrrhenian coast. Be sure to tuck into a *cacciucco*, a remarkable mixed seafood stew.

The earliest references to Livorno date from 1017. The port was in the hands of Pisa and then Genoa for centuries, until Florence took control in 1421. It was still tiny – by the 1550s it boasted a grand total of 480 permanent residents. All that changed under Cosimo I de' Medici, who converted the scrawny settlement into a heavily fortified coastal bastion.

By the end of the 18th century, around 80,000 people lived in this busy port; it had become one of the main staging posts for British and Dutch merchants who were then operating between Western Europe and the Middle East. In the following century it was declared a free port, stimulating further growth and prosperity.

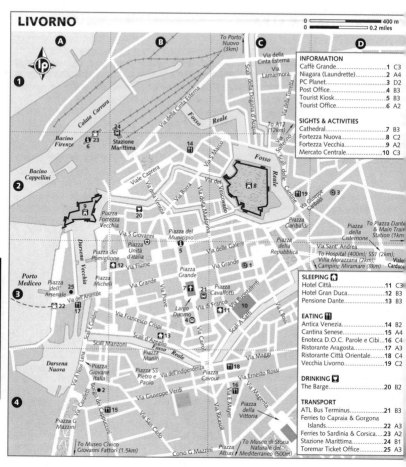

LIVORNO

Orientation

From the main train station on Piazza Dante walk westwards along Viale Carducci, Via de Larderel, then Via Grande into central Piazza Grande, Livorno's main square.

Information
INTERNET ACCESS

Caffè Grande (Via Grande 59; per hr €5; 7am-11pm daily Jun-Sep, 7am-11pm Wed-Mon Oct-May) Has four machines upstairs.

PC Planet (0586 82 95 16; Via Giuseppe Garibaldi 110; per hr €4.15; 9.30am-1pm & 3.30-8pm Mon-Sat)

LAUNDRY

Niagara (Borgo dei Cappuccini 13)

MEDICAL SERVICES

Hospital (0586 22 31 11; Viale Alfieri 36)

POST

Post office (Via Cairoli 46)

TOURIST INFORMATION

Tourist kiosk (0586 20 46 11; www.costadegli etruschi.it; Piazza del Municipio; 10am-1pm & 3-6pm Mon-Sat Apr-Oct, 9am-5pm Mon-Sat Nov-Mar)
Tourist office (0586 89 53 20; Jun-Sep) Near the main ferry terminal at Stazione Marittima.

Sights

The **Fortezza Nuova** (New Fort; admission free), in the area known as Piccola Venezia because of its small canals, was built, using Vene-

an methods of reclaiming land from the
ea, for the Medici court in the late 16th
entury. Laced with canals, what this area
cks in gondolas and tourists, it makes up
or with a certain shabby charm: waterways
re flanked by faded, peeling apartments
rightly decorated with strings of washing.
'he interior of the fort is now a park and
ttle remains except the sturdy outer walls.

Close to the waterfront is the city's other
ort, the **Fortezza Vecchia** (Old Fort), con-
tructed 60 years earlier on the site of an
1th-century building. With huge vertical
racks and bits crumbling away, it looks as
hough it might give up and slide into the
ea at any moment.

The **Mercato Centrale** (Via Buontalenti), Livor-
o's magnificent late-19th-century 95m
ong neoclassical food market, miraculously
urvived Allied WWII bombing intact. For
s, it's the finest site in town, both architec-
urally and gastronomically (see p179).

Livorno's **Museo di Storia Naturale del Medi-**
erraneo (☎ 0586 26 67 11; Via Roma 234; adult/child
10/5; ☺ 9am-1pm Tue-Sat, 3-7.30pm Tue, Thu & Sun)
has recently undergone a huge facelift and
s now much more friendly and hands on.
The star of the show remains the 20m-long
skeleton of 'Annie', a common whale.

The **Museo Civico Giovanni Fattori** (☎ 0586
30 80 01; Via San Jacopo in Acquaviva 65; admission €4;
☺ 10am-1pm & 4-7pm Tue-Sun), in a pretty park,
features works by the Livorno-based, 19th-
century Italian impressionist Macchiaioli

school, led by Giovanni Fattori. It often
hosts temporary exhibitions.

The city's unspectacular **cathedral** is just
off Piazza Grande.

The Etruscan Coast (Costa degli Etruschi)
begins south of Livorno. The town's beaches
stretch for some way southwards but they
are pebbly and generally nothing special.
Overlooking a few are some grand old seaside villas that merit more than a glance.
Bus No 1 from the main train station heads
down the coast road, passing via the town
centre and Porto Mediceo.

Sleeping

Villa Morazzana (☎ 0586 50 00 76; www.villamorazzana
.it; Via Curiel 110; hostel dm/d €18/44, hotel s/d/tr €50/75/
100, all with breakfast; ⓟ ▣) A HI-affiliated
youth hostel, friendly informal hotel and
quality restaurant, are all packed into this
attractive 18th-century villa with a huge
rear garden. The hotel's 11 spacious, bright
rooms are each individually decorated with
great flair. Choose room 201 with its sylvan
scene and you could almost be sleeping al
fresco in your garden. Its Ristorante Lavilla
(open for dinner from Thursday to Sunday)
offers gourmet cuisine and keeps a great cellar of wines and whiskies. Bus No 3 runs
hourly from Piazza Grande. Driving, take
the Montanero exit from the A12.

Hotel Gran Duca (☎ 0586 89 10 24; www.granduca
.it in Italian; Piazza Micheli 16; s/d incl breakfast €86/124;
ⓟ ✄) Built into the old protective walls

CENTRAL COAST & ELBA

PARCO NAZIONALE DELL'ARCIPELAGO TOSCANO

A local legend tells, when Venus rose from the waves, seven precious stones fell from her tiara,
creating seven islands off the Tuscan coast. They range in size from the 530 sq km of Elba,
the largest, to tiny Montecristo, at just over 1000 hectares. All except Montecristo, nowadays
a closed marine biological reserve, live mainly from the income of tourism. So this national
park, established in 1996, was created to protect the delicate ecosystems of the islands. But not
only the land – the 60,000 hectares of sea that washes around them make up Europe's largest
marine protected area. Here, typical Mediterranean fish abound and rare species, such as the
wonderfully named Neptune's shaving brush seaweed, unique to the archipelago, cling on to
life. And the monk-seal, driven from the other islands by human presence, still gambols in the
deep underwater ravines off Montecristo.

The islands, an essential rest stop for birds migrating between Europe and Africa, are a treat
for birdwatchers year-round. The shy red partridge survives on Elba and Pianosa and the archipelago supports over a third of the world's population of the equally uncommon Corsican seagull,
adopted as the national park's symbol.

For more information, go to www.islepark.it or www.isoleditoscana.it (both lead to the same
site. It's informative if you read Italian; the English section is fairly feeble, but they're working on
it…) or contact Info Park Are@ (p186), the park information office on the island of Elba.

AMEDEO DOES PARIS

Modigliani's portraits of women with their long necks, faces like African masks and tilted oblong heads are among the most readily recognisable of all of modern art.

Born in Livorno in 1884, Amedeo Modigliani showed talent as an artist at an early age and trained under the influence of the former Macchiaioli artists who had shaken up the Florentine, and indeed Italian, art scene in the years before and after Italian unity (see p61). Livorno's own Giovanni Fattori had been a leading light among the Macchiaioli.

Modigliani was soon drawn away from his home town. His early influences were the Renaissance masters, so he headed first to Florence, then on to Venice. From Venice, he made the move to Paris in 1906, which by then was the epicentre of the art world, and where he was influenced by Cézanne, Picasso and Cocteau.

Modigliani returned to Italy briefly in 1909 but, from then until the end of his short life in 1920, continued to live in the fertile artistic environment of Montparnasse in Paris. For the next five years he turned to sculpture, rapidly accelerating the process of simplification and emphasising the contours. This period was then reflected in his subsequent paintings – the long faces typical of his later work are a result of his venture into sculpture. In 1914 and 1915 he concentrated on portraiture and then, in the last years of his life, produced the series of nudes that figure among his best-known works and display a classical and serene eroticism.

His work, like that of so many artists, only began to receive wide critical acclaim after his death, particularly in the wake of an exhibition of his paintings at the Venice Biennale in 1930. Nowadays, his canvases are prominent features of art galleries the world over.

of the port, rooms are fully equipped. For fitness freaks, there's the added bonus of a Jacuzzi, Turkish bath and fitness centre. It's right opposite the port and has a decent restaurant (mains are €12 to €14).

Hotel Città (☎ 0586 88 34 95; www.hotelcitta.it; Via di Franco 32; s/d €83/108; P ☒ ☐) Family owned and friendly, this is an even more tempting three-star option in the heart of town. It looks unprepossessing from the outside but rooms, though smallish, are just fine and come equipped with fridge and safe. Parking will set you back €13.

Pensione Dante (☎ 0586 89 34 61; 1st fl, Scali d'Azeglio 28; s/d €35/40) Overlooking a canal and run by a cheerful old couple, this place has eight large, simply furnished rooms with corridor bathrooms. It has a friendly, rough-and-tumble family feel about it and is not a bad option if you're euro-economising.

Camping Miramare (☎ 0586 58 04 02; www.camping miramare.com; Via del Littorale 220; person €11, pitch €10-40; ☒ year-round; ☒) This is a shady place with its own restaurant and pizzeria, right beside the beach in Antignano, about 8km south of town.

Eating

Ristorante Aragosta (☎ 0586 89 53 95; Piazza dell'Arsenale 6; mains €8-12; ☒ Mon-Sat) Right on

the waterfront, this is the place for seafood Here too, a nondescript exterior mask inner pleasures, mainly of a fishy kind.

Cantina Senese (☎ 0586 89 02 39; Borgo dei Cappu cini 95; meals from €25; ☒ Mon-Sat) Also fabulou for seafood, this popular, unpretentiou local eatery is just a little inland. Squeez onto one of the long wooden tables and, you pass by on a Friday, try the Livornes speciality *cacciucco di pesce*, a rich fish sou served with garlic bread.

Enoteca D.O.C. Parole e Cibi (☎ 0586 88 75 83; V Goldoni 40-44; menus from €25; ☒ closed Mon) Change its menu weekly; you can enjoy fresh past dishes and good *carpaccio*, as well as snack The wines are excellent; it styles itself a an *enoteca*, *olioteca* (oil) and whiskyteca s you can be confident of getting top qualit lubricants, whatever your preference.

Vecchia Livorno (☎ 0586 88 40 48; Scali del Cantine 34; mains €9-13; ☒ closed Tue) Facing th Fortezza Nuova, this small, intimate famil restaurant has a buzzy neighbourhood fee Expect hearty, filling food; stick with th excellent fresh fish.

Antica Venezia (☎ 0586 88 73 53; Piazza dei Do menicani; mains around €15; ☒ closed Sun) Attract a smart clientele with its imaginative men of catch-of-the-day specials prepared wit an innovative twist. The atmosphere is at tractively upbeat. Book ahead.

Ristorante Città Orientale (☎ 0586 88 82 66; Via nori 23; mains €3-6) For a change, this Chinese estaurant offers a wide selection of dishes vithout the usual migraine-inducing décor. he set menus are great value.

Load up with fresh produce for the boat t Livorno's magnificent Mercato Centrale.

rinking

he area around Piazza XX Settembre is the lace for bars and cafés.

Barge (☎ 0586 88 83 20; Scali Delle Ancore 6; ☼ 8pm-2am Tue-Sun) Join the effortlessly hip oung crowd inside this approximation of n English pub or enjoy the breeze on one f the trio of boat-shaped waterfront teraces. It also functions as a piano bar and estaurant (mains €15).

Getting There & Away
BOAT

Livorno is a major port. Regular departures or Sardinia and Corsica leave from Calata Carrara, beside the Stazione Marittima. Ferries to Capraia and Gorgona depart rom Porto Mediceo, a smaller terminal near Piazza dell'Arsenale, and some services to Sardinia and ferries to Sicily depart rom Porto Nuovo, about 3km north of the ity along Via Sant'Orlando.

Ferry companies operating from Livorno are listed below.

Porto Mediceo
Toremar (☎ 199 12 31 99; www.toremar.it in Italian) Daily services to Isola di Capraia (€10.50, 2½ hours).

Porto Nuovo
Grandi Navi Veloci (☎ 0586 40 98 04; www.grimaldi it) Three departures a week to Palermo, Sicily (deck class €80, 17 hours).

Lloyd Sardegna (☎ 0565 22 23 00; www.lloyd sardegna.it) Daily ferries to Sardinia (Olbia; €26, 11 hours).

Stazione Marittima
Corsica Ferries/Sardinia Ferries (☎ 019 21 55 11; www.corsicaferries.com, www.sardiniaferries.com; Stazione Marittima) Offers two or three services per week (daily in summer) to Bastia, Corsica (deck-class €25 to €32, four hours), and four services per week (daily in summer) to Golfo Aranci, Sardinia (deck-class €25 to €37, six hours express, nine hours regular).

Moby (☎ 199 30 30 40; www.moby.it) Has services to Bastia, Corsica (€15 to €29, three to four hours) and Olbia, Sardinia (€20 to €49, eight to 12 hours).

BUS
ATL (☎ 0586 88 42 62) buses depart from Largo Duomo for Cecina (€2.90, one hour, halfhourly), Piombino (€6.20, 2¼ hours, six daily) and Pisa (€2.30, 45 minutes, halfhourly).

CAR & MOTORCYCLE
The A12 runs past the city and the SS1 connects Livorno with Rome. There are several car parks near the waterfront.

TRAIN
Livorno is on the Rome–La Spezia line and is also connected to Florence and Pisa. Sample destinations and fares include Rome (€14.30 to €24.70, three to four hours, 12 daily), Florence (€5.90, 1½ hours, 16 daily) and Pisa (€1.70, 15 minutes, hourly).

Trains are a lot less frequent to Stazione Marittima, the station for the ports, but buses to/from the main station run quite regularly.

Getting Around
ATL bus No 1 runs from the main train station to Porto Mediceo. To reach Stazione Marittima, take bus No 7 or electric bus Nos PB1, PB2 or PB3. All pass through Piazza Grande.

AROUND LIVORNO
Capraia & Gorgona
Toremar (left) operates boats to the islands of Capraia and Gorgona from Livorno. Along with Elba, and four other islands further south still (Pianosa, Montecristo, Giglio and Giannutri), they form the Parco Nazionale dell'Arcipelago Toscano (p177).

The elliptical, volcanic island of **Capraia**, 8km long by 4km wide, lies 65km from Livorno. Its highest point is Monte Castello at 447m and is covered mainly in *macchia*, or scrubland. Tuscany's third-largest island after Elba and Giglio, it has changed hands several times over the course of its history, belonging to Genoa, Sardinia, the Saracens from North Africa and Napoleon.

You can join boat trips (€12) around the coastline or trek across the island. The most popular walk is to the Stagnone, a small lake in the south. There are also seven popular dive sites off the coast; contact **Capraia Diving** (☎ 0586 90 51 37; www.capraiadiving.it; Via Assunzione 72). The only beach worthy of the name is

Cala della Mortola, a few kilometres north of **Capraia** town.

The tiny island of **Gorgona** is the greenest and northernmost of the islands. At just 2.23 sq km, there's not much to it. Its two towers were built respectively by the Pisans and the Medicis of Florence. Part of the island is off-limits as a low-security prison. You can effectively only visit the island on Tuesday, when the 8.30am Toremar ferry from Livorno stops there on the way to/from Capraia, giving you about five hours from the arrival time at 10am.

INFORMATION

Agenzia Viaggi e Turismo Parco (☎ 0586 90 50 71; www.isoladicapraia.it in Italian; Capraia) Shares the same space as the tourist office and can advise on activities, such as trekking and boat trips.

Tourist office (☎ 0586 90 51 38; Via Assunzione 42; ⓧ 9am-12.30pm & 4.30-7pm Fri-Wed Apr-Sep)

SLEEPING & EATING

Accommodation on Capraia is tight, and there are no places to stay on Gorgona.

Da Beppone (☎ 0586 90 50 01; Via della Assunzione 78; s/d €45/75) A very friendly and reliable choice. Rooms are smallish but pleasant and the bar and restaurant are a bonus.

Il Saracino (☎ 0586 90 50 18; Via Cibo 30; s/d incl breakfast €110/220) Down near the beach, this place has bright modern rooms with plenty of wood and white paint. There's a snazzy rooftop bar for a nightcap under the stars.

Relais La Mandola (☎ 0586 90 51 19; www.lamandola .it; Via della Mandola 1; half-board per person from €120; Ⓟ ⓧ ⓡ) A seriously swish hotel with private beach (and its own beach bar). Rooms have balconies, sea views and all mod cons. Prices drop dramatically out of season.

GETTING THERE & AWAY

A daily Toremar boat to Capraia sails from Livorno (see p179). On most days there is also a return trip but triple-check before you go. The one-way fare costs €10.50, whether you go to Capraia or Gorgona. In summer, there are also excursions from Elba to Capraia.

THE ETRUSCAN COAST

The province of Livorno stretches down the coast to just beyond Piombino and the ferry to the island of Elba.

Overall, Tuscany's beaches are basic bucket-and-spade, though some have pebbles rather than sand. Watch out for the price you can fork out plenty for the privilege of sun bed and brolly.

Several attractive small towns are scattered within the hilly hinterland, while the slender plain between coast and hills offers the possibility of discovering some of Tuscany's lesser known, but often very good wines.

Livorno to Piombino

You can chug down the coast from Livorno by train or bus, but your own transport will give you greater freedom to explore.

There's a good small beach a couple of kilometres short of **Querciancella**. Heading south from Livorno, keep a watch out for a tower and castle atop a promontory. The beach is at the head of an inlet directly north of this. As you round a curve into the inlet, a small sign indicates a path down to the beach. There is limited parking.

In leafy Querciancella you'll find a couple of little grey-stone beaches. At the northern end of town, surfers gather even when an adverse wind is up. After another 5km or so watch for the **Parco Comunale di Fortullino** sign. If you can find a place to park, walk down to the water's edge. The park is pleasant and a bar operates in summer. The beach, by contrast, is disappointing and rocky.

CASTIGLIONCELLO

This small seaside resort is agreeably unpretentious. In the late 19th century Digo Martelli, the Italian critic and patron of the arts gave court here. He would play host to the Florentine Impressionist artists of the period, giving birth to the artistic movement known as La Scuola di Castiglioncello.

The small sandy beaches on the north side of town are the best, although sun-bed rental is expensive (from €8). At the heart of this straggling town is Piazza della Vittoria and the vast terrace of Caffè Ginori (opposite).

Information

Within the train station, there's a small **tourist office** (☎ 0586 75 48 90; Via Aurelia 632; ⓧ 9.30am-12.30pm & 4-6pm).

Sleeping & Eating

Pensione Bartoli (☎ 0586 75 20 51; Via Martelli 9; s/d €48/58; ⓧ Easter-Oct; Ⓟ) Rich in character, this offers unbeatable value. It's an old-fashioned 'let's stay with grandma' kind of place with well-dusted, large rooms, lace curtains and venerable family furniture. Room 19, the largest, also has the best sea view.

Villa Parisi (☎ 0586 75 16 98; www.emmeti.it/Villa Parisi; Via Romolo Monti 10; s/d €219/372; ☺ Apr-Sep; P ☻ ☂) This is a special-occasion hotel, perched on a headland. Rooms are stylish and good-sized and most have a seamless sea view. There's a pool and large sun terrace, plus private access to the beach. Prices are over 10% cheaper outside high season.

Caffè Ginori (☎ 0586 75 90 55; Piazza della Vittoria; ☺ daily Mar-Oct, Fri-Wed Nov-Feb) With its large, shaded terrace and redolent of the best of the 1950s, this is where locals drop by to jaw at the bar. You can see why it was a favourite hangout of Italian heart-throb Marcello Mastroianni, who had a summer villa in town.

Getting There & Away

There are frequent trains to/from Livorno (€2.10, 25 minutes).

AROUND CASTIGLIONCELLO

Rosignano Marittimo perches high up a hill. Already a small settlement in Lombard times, Rosignano was one of Lorenzo il Magnifico's preferred bases for hunting. Although there has been a castle here since the 8th century, the fortifications date from the days of Cosimo I de' Medici.

Back down on the coast, **Vada** is a fairly characterless seaside spot but at least the beaches have sand. Another 8km south of Vada and you reach **Marina di Cecina**, where there is plenty of life, as well as hotels and restaurants that mainly front a beach. Children and the young at heart will enjoy splashing around **Acqua** (Via Tevere 25; ☺ Jun-Aug), a family-friendly water park.

About halfway between the sea and the modern centre of **Cecina**, the **Villa Guerrazzi**, also called La Cinquantina, houses a couple of small museums: the small **Museo Archeologico Comunale** (☎ 0586 26 08 37; adult/child €4/2.50; ☺ 4-7.30pm Tue-Sun Jul-Aug, 3.30-7pm Sat & Sun Sep-Jun) in the grounds, the recently established **Museo della Vita e del Lavoro**, a small folk museum with a collection of vintage agricultural machinery and bicycles from boneshakers to modern racers. It observes similar hours.

You can train or bus it to Cecina from Livorno. The train (€5, 30 minutes) is more convenient; the ATL bus (€2.90, one hour, every half-hour) is the better deal.

MONTESCUDIAO

From Cecina you could follow the SS1 or minor coast roads south. Better still, head inland. The province of Livorno has developed a Strada del Vino (wine route), with a map and list of vineyards between Cecina and Montescudaio. It makes for a pretty drive, compared to the relatively drab coastal flats.

MARINA DI BIBBONA

Head south from Montescudaio to Bibbona, a medieval hill town that dominates the plain running beside the coast. A little further south and on the coast is Marina di Bibbona, south of which stretches a narrow strip of sandy beach backed by *macchia* and pine woods.

There's plenty of accommodation to choose from.

Hotel Paradiso Verde (☎ /fax 0586 60 00 22; Via del Forte 9; s/d incl breakfast €60/93; ☺ Easter-Oct) is a small 15-room hotel located a Frisbee throw from the beach, with spick-and-span rooms and a small bar/restaurant out the front. You pay more for a balcony and sea view.

A short way south of Marina di Bibbona is the small but important **Rifugio Palustre di Bolgheri** (☎ reservations 0565 22 43 61; entrance just west off the SS1; adult/child €5/3; ☺ visits 9am & 2pm Sat, 9am Sun Oct-May). This nature reserve is a key stop for migratory birds, and the best time for seeing them is in December and January. Two-hour visits are severely limited and must be arranged in advance. The entrance to the park is through a narrow tunnel that passes under the *superstrada*, just south of the cypress-lined, arrow-straight road that leads eastwards to the village of Bolgheri.

BOLGHERI

In Bolgheri, the castle that takes in the city gate and Romanesque Chiesa di SS Giacomo e Cristoro was restructured towards the end of the 19th century. Although very pretty, the village has been over-heritaged, with pricey restaurants and shops. Have a quick look around, take a few photos and move on.

CASTAGNETO CARDUCCI

The next stretch of the Strada del Vino takes you through dense woodland along a minor road south of Bolgheri. The route rolls between vineyards and olive groves, then climbs up into the hills to reach Castagneto Carducci.

Behind its town walls lies a web of steep, narrow lanes crowded in by brooding houses and dominated by the castle (turned into a mansion in the 18th century) of the Gherardesca clan that once controlled the surrounding area. The 19th-century poet Giosuè Carducci spent much of his childhood here.

Traditional old recipes have been resurrected at the lovely **Ristorante Glorione** (☎ 0565 76 33 22; Via Carducci 6; mains €11-15; dinner Wed-Mon Jun-Sep, Sat & Sun Oct-May), with its swish chandelier-lit dining room. There is a palm-shaded courtyard for atmospheric, soothing summertime dining.

Pick up some locally produced olive oil and liqueurs, distilled on the spot, at the 100-year-old **L'Elixir** (☎ 0565 76 60 17; Via Garibaldi 7).

SASSETTA

Next stop on the winding, forested hill road is the tiny hamlet of Sassetta. Approaching from Castagneto, the houses here seem to be hanging on to their perches for dear life. There is a large map at the village entrance showing the main treks in the area.

Albergo La Selva (☎ 0565 79 42 39; hotel.selva@tiscalinet.it; Via Fornaci 32; s/d incl breakfast €40/80) has squeaky-clean large plain rooms with a choice of bath or shower. All have balconies and there's a large terrace with positively swoony valley views. The restaurant (mains €6 to €8) does an excellent six-course dinner (€20).

SUVERETO

Nearby Suvereto, with its tortuous streets and steep stairways, has been a busy little centre since well before the year 1000. For a while it was the seat of a bishopric, only incorporated into the Tuscan grand duchy in 1815. Nowadays, it's a well tended place where flowers and plants contrast with the soft tones of brick and stone.

The **tourist office** (☎ 0565 82 93 04; 10am-12.30pm & 5-10pm Mon-Sat, 5-10pm Sun Jun-Sep) is on Piazza Gramsci.

On the terrace of **Ristorante Enoliteca Ombrone** (☎ 0565 82 82 94; Piazza dei Giudici 1; mains €15-22; closed Mon) you can enjoy fine traditional cuisine with the attractive façade of Suvereto's mainly 13th-century Palazzo Comunale looming before you.

Enoteca dei Difficili (☎ 0565 82 80 18; Via San Leonardo; mains €5-8; closed Mon) is an atmospheric brick-and-beam spot for a drink, snack or full meal. Alongside an array of delightful snacks, salads and main courses, you can take a pick from the blockbuster selection of wines.

Mid-August sees the traditional **Corsa delle Botte**, when townsfolk race each other, pushing huge tumbling wine barrels along the town's cobbled lanes. In December they tuck into their **Sagra del Cinghiale** (Wild Boar Festival), with plenty of eating, drinking and a show of crossbow skills.

CAMPIGLIA MARITTIMA

From Suvereto, drop down onto the plains along the SS398, signed Piombino, for about 5km, then turn off right to head back into the hills. Aim for the dun-coloured stone houses of Campiglia Marittima, another near-intact medieval town, with its roots in Etruscan times.

The one building of special interest is the **Palazzo Pretorio**, up steep Via Cavour, which is these days also a wine information centre. Long the seat of government, its main façade, plastered with an assortment of coats of arms, resembles the bulky bemedalled chest of some banana-republic general.

The **Parco Archeominerario di San Silvestro** (☎ 0565 83 86 80; admission €8.50; 10am-7pm Tue-Sun Jun-Sep, 10am-6pm Sat & Sun Mar-May & Oct, 10am-4pm Sun Nov-Feb) is just 1.25km northwest on the road to San Vincenzo. Around 50m before the turn-off to the park entrance, a sunken lane on the right, signed *forni fusori*, leads to the remains of some Etruscan smelting ovens, once used for copper production.

The park tells the story of the area's 3000-year mining history. The highlight for most is **Rocca di San Silvestro**, a medieval mining town abandoned in the 14th century. The surrounding Temperino mines produced copper and lead, some used for the mints of Lucca and later Pisa.

There are two guided tours, one of Rocca di San Silvestro, the other to the Temperino mine and museum. The mine and museum (the latter is in the same building as the ticket office) are near the entrance, while Rocca di San Silvestro is about a half-hour walk away (or take the park shuttle). Each tour leaves approximately every hour.

SAN VINCENZO

Back on the road leading away from Campiglia, continue westwards to the moderately

---

DETOUR: SAN VINCENZO TO PIOMBINO

From the San Vincenzo tourist office on Via B Alliata, take the coast road flanked by pine trees and dense woodland towards Piombino. Look for *tavoli* (picnic area) signs if you fancy stopping for a picnic with the luxury of tables and benches. After about 11km you'll see an old water tower to your left: park by the side and cross the road to a pleasant beach backed by wild brush and poppies (in season). Continue on to more good sandy stretches at Golfo di Baratti (below) or follow the road to Piombino.

---

attractive seaside town of San Vincenzo, popular in summer with Italian visitors. There is a small **tourist office** (☎ 0565 70 15 33; Via B Alliata) here. Yachties can park their vessels in the marina, but there's not much to do after that. Sandy beaches stretch to the north and south of town; to the south beaches are backed by *macchia* and pine plantations. Although there are quite a few hotels, getting a room in summer is challenging and so are the prices. There's only one campsite.

Ristorante La Barcaccina (☎ 0565 70 19 11; Via Tridentina; mains €13-15; closed Wed) serves fine seafood that matches this glassed-in restaurant's location on a great stretch of pale golden sand. Decidedly on the smart side, it's not the kind of place where you stroll in wearing your beachwear. From the coast road (not the SS1), follow signs to the parking area near the Parco Comunale.

GOLFO DI BARATTI

Thirteen kilometres south of San Vincenzo, a minor road leads off the SP23 and heads southwest for 5km to the Golfo di Baratti. This must be one of the Tuscan coast's prettiest mainland beaches, although, as the weird and wonderful postures of the trees attest, it's often windy – and so a favourite with windsurfers.

Inland from here is the **Parco Archeologico di Baratti e Populonia** (☎ 0565 2 90 02; Populonia; whole park adult/child €12/9, 1 sector adult/child €5/2.50, family €28; 10am-7pm daily Jul & Aug, 10am-6pm Tue-Sun Mar-Jun & Sep-Oct, 10am-4pm Sat & Sun Nov-Feb) where several Etruscan tombs have been unearthed. Most interesting are the circular tombs in the Necropoli di San Cerbone, between the

coast road and the visitors centre, which sells an excellent guidebook in English (€7.75). The Via delle Cave is a signed trail through shady woodland that passes by the quarries from which the soft ochre sandstone was extracted, and into which tombs were later cut. Allow two hours, and wear trainers and a sun hat. Between March and October, there are guided tours (included within the admission fee) for each area or you can wander at will.

POPULONIA

Where the road ends, 2km beyond the park, is **Populonia Alta**, a three-street hamlet still owned by a single family. Walled in and protected by its 15th-century castle, the settlement grew up on the site of a Pisan watchtower. Its small, privately owned **Etruscan Museum** (adult/child €1.50/1) has a few local finds; opening times are sporadic. For superb views south along the coast, climb the **Torre di Populonia** (adult/child €2/1; 9.30am-noon & 2.30-7pm), north of the museum. Among several craft workshops along the main street, the gallery at No 19 has a permanent exhibition of glass sculptures and creative lamps by artist Laura Pescae and her daughter.

Next to the car park is the **Etruscan acropolis** (9am-7pm) of ancient Populonia. If your Italian is up to it, join a guided tour (every half-hour). The digs have revealed the foundations of an Etruscan temple dating to the 2nd century BC, along with its adjacent buildings.

Piombino

pop 33,850

Poor old Piombino, it really gets a lot of lousy press. The smoke stacks to the south of town are dismal and only urge you to hop on the next ferry to Elba – which is probably why you are here in the first place. A Roman-era port, and from the late 19th century a centre of steel production, the city was heavily damaged during WWII and precious little remains of the walled historical centre.

The new **Museo Archeologico del Territorio di Populonia** (☎ 0565 22 16 46; Piazza Cittadella 8; adult/child €6/4; 5-11pm Jul-Aug, 10am-1pm & 3-7pm Tue-Sun Jun-Sep, 10am-1pm & 3-5pm Sat & Sun Oct-May), in the western suburbs, complements and displays many of the artefacts from the Parco Archeologico di Baratti e Populonia (left), plus other sites in and around the Maremma.

If you have time, the town centre, whose focal point is the 15th-century **Torrione Rivellino**, and fishing port are not without a little charm.

Should you need, for whatever emergency, to stay, **Hotel Roma** (☎ 0565 3 43 41; www.htroma.it; Via San Francesco 43; s/d €40/60) is a reasonable, albeit monastically spartan, central choice two minutes' walk from the ATM bus stop.

GETTING THERE & AWAY

Piombino-based **ATM** (☎ 0565 260 11 18) buses running between Piombino and Cecina (€3, 1½ hours) usually stop at Castagneto Carducci, Sassetta, San Vincenzo and Golfo di Baratti. Another bus line serves Suvereto (€2.20, 40 minutes) on a regular basis on its way to Monterotondo. Yet another connects Piombino with Campiglia Marittima. ATM buses also run to Massa Marittima. All leave from Via Leonardo da Vinci 13 in the centre of town.

There are also six buses daily to Livorno (€6.20, 2¼ hours).

For coastal destinations such as San Vincenzo, the train is a better bet, but the hill towns are generally a considerable hike from the nearest train station.

Piombino is on the Rome–Genoa train line and there are fairly regular connections to Florence too.

For Elba ferry information, see p186.

ELBA

pop 30,100

Napoleon should have considered himself lucky to have been exiled to such a pretty spot as the Isola d'Elba. Arriving in May 1814, he escaped within the year and went on to meet his Waterloo. Nowadays tourism has firmly supplanted iron-ore mining, for centuries Elba's main earner. Over a million visitors a year willingly allow themselves to be marooned here. They come to swim in Elba's glorious blue waters, lie on the beaches and eat fine food. Others are drawn by Elba's mountainous terrain, which offers challenging treks and staggering views.

Although Elba is the largest, most visited and most heavily populated island of the Tuscan Archipelago, it measures just 28km long and 19km across at its widest point. The island, 15km southwest of the ferry port in Piombino, is well equipped for visitors, with plenty of hotels and campsites. The main towns are Portoferraio on the north side and Marina di Campo in the south.

If you can, avoid August when the island gets unpleasantly crowded and reservations are essential.

History

Elba has been inhabited since the Iron Age and the extraction of iron ore and metallurgy were the island's principal sources of economic wellbeing until well into the second half of the 20th century. You can still fossick around to your heart's content in museums dedicated to rocks.

Ligurian tribes people were the island's first inhabitants, followed by Etruscans and Greeks from Magna Graecia. The iron business was well established by then, making the island doubly attractive to wealthier Romans, who built holiday villas here.

Centuries of peace under the Pax Romana gave way to more uncertain times during the barbarian invasions, when Elba became a refuge for those fleeing mainland marauders. By the 11th century, Pisa (and later Piombino) was in control and built fortresses to help ward off attacks by Muslim raiders and pirates operating out of North Africa.

In the 16th century, Cosimo I de' Medici grabbed territory in the north of the island, where he founded the port town of Cosmopolis (today's Portoferraio). At the same time, the Spanish took control of the southeastern strip of the island.

In the 18th century, Grand Duke Pietro Leopoldo II encouraged land reform, the drainage of swamps and greater agricultural production on the island. Nevertheless, iron remained the major industry. In 1917 some 840,000 tonnes were produced, but in WWII the Allies bombed the industry to bits and by the beginning of the 1980s production was down to 100,000 tonnes. The writing was on the wall: tourism had arrived to take the place of mining and smelting.

Getting There & Away

AIR

Most folk opt for the ferry but there's a small **airport** (☎ 0565 97 60 11) at La Pila, just outside Marina di Campo. **Elbafly** (☎ 0565 9 19 61; www.elbafly.it) flies to and from Pisa and Milan (Malpensa), mid-June to mid-September.

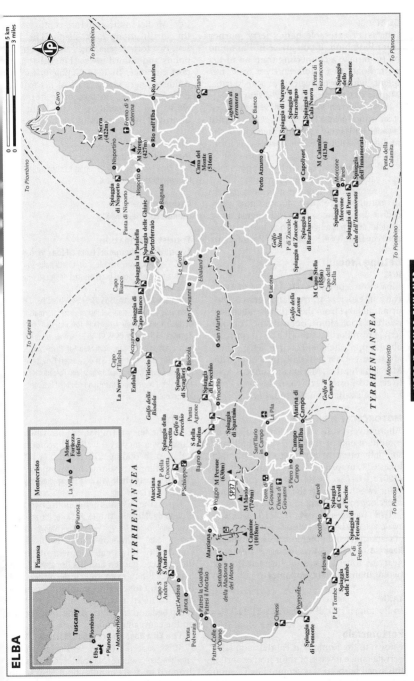

ELBA

CENTRAL COAST & ELBA

BOAT

Elba is an agreeable hour's ferry journey from Piombino. If you arrive in Piombino by train, take a connecting train on to the port. Boats to Portoferraio are most frequent, while some call in at Rio Marina, Marina di Campo and Porto Azzurro.

Boats are run by **Moby** (☎ 199 30 30 40; www .moby.it) and **Toremar** (☎ 199 12 31 99; www.toremar.it in Italian). Unless it's a summer weekend or the middle of August, when queues can form, simply buy a ticket at the port. Fares (€6 to €9.50 per person, €20.70 to €49 per small car) vary according to season.

Toremar also operates a passenger-only hydrofoil service (€10, 40 minutes) year-round, and, between June and August, a fast vehicle and passenger service (two passengers/car from €69.20 return) to Portoferraio.

Getting Around

BUS

Elba's bus company, **ATL** (☎ 0565 91 43 92), runs an efficient trans-island service. Pick up a timetable from the main **bus station** (Viale Elba, Portoferraio), almost opposite the Toremar jetty. From Portoferraio (the bus terminal is almost opposite the Toremar jetty), there are at least seven runs daily (all €2) to/from Marciana Marina, Marina di Campo, Capoliveri and Porto Azzurro. A day pass costs €7 and a six-day run-around, €19.

MOTORCYCLE & BICYCLE

Alternatively, you can steam around Elba by mountain bike or scooter. Typical high season daily rates are city bikes €15, mountain bikes €24, mopeds (50cc) €30, and scooters (100cc to 125cc) €40. You can hire small vehicles – just don't; the roads are already overclogged with cars in summer.

TWN (Two Wheels Network; ☎ 0565 91 46 66; www .twn-rent.it; Viale Elba 32, Portoferraio), with branches at Capoliveri and other locations, and **Happy Rent** (☎ 0565 91 46 65; www.renthappy.it; Viale Elba 7), near the tourist office in Portoferraio, are two of many rental companies.

TAXI

In Portoferraio, call ☎ 0565 91 51 12.

Portoferraio

Known to the Romans as Fabricia and later Ferraia (since it was a port for iron exports), this small harbour was acquired by Cosimo I de' Medici in the mid-16th century, when the fortifications took shape. The walls link two forts (Stella and Falcone) on high points and a third tower (Linguella) at the port entrance. In 1814 Napoleon took up residence here at the start of his exile on Elba (see the boxed text, opposite). Steelworks began operating in 1902 but were destroyed by the Allies in 1943.

INFORMATION
Internet resources
Elba Link (www.elbalink.it) Carries lots of detailed information about the island.

Laundry
Laundrette (Viale Elba 51)

Tourist Information
Associazione Albergatori Isola d'Elba (☎ 0565 91 55 55; www.albergatorielbani.it; Calata Italia 20) The island's professional hotel association, it can reserve accommodation.
Info Park Are@ (☎ 0565 91 94 94; Viale Elba; ☺ 8am-8pm daily summer, Mon-Sat rest of year) Information office of the Parco Nazionale Arcipelago Toscano.
Tourist office (☎ 0565 91 46 71; www.aptelba.it; Calata Italia 43; ☺ 8am-8pm Mon-Sat, 8am-2pm Sun Easter-Oct, 8am-6pm Mon-Sat Oct-Easter) Called the Agenzia per il Turismo dell'Archipelago Toscano. Near the ferry port it has a list of the island's limited Internet log-on options.

SIGHTS
From the ferry terminal, the old town, enclosed by a medieval wall and protected by a pair of brooding fortresses, is a bit less than a kilometre along the foreshore. You can visit **Forte Stella** (Via della Stella; admission €1.30; ☺ 9am-7pm Easter-Sep).

Up on the bastions between the two forts, is **Villa dei Mulini** (☎ 0565 91 58 46; Piazzale Napoleone; adult/child €3/free; ☺ 9am-7pm Mon & Wed-Sat, 9am-1pm Sun), Napoleon's home while he was emperor of this small isle, with its splendid terraced garden and his library. During his brief Elban exile, the emperor certainly didn't want for creature comforts – contrast his Elba lifestyle with the simplicity of his camp bed and travelling trunk when he was on the campaign trail.

The **Villa Napoleonica di San Martino** (☎ 0565 91 46 88; adult/child €3/free; ☺ 9am-7pm Wed-Sat, 9am-1pm Sun), where Napoleon occasionally dropped in, is set in hills about 5km south-

THE EMPEROR NAPOLEON TAKES EARLY RETIREMENT

At precisely 6pm on 3 May 1814, the English frigate *Undaunted* dropped anchor in the harbour of Portoferraio on the island of Elba. It bore an unusual cargo. Under the Treaty of Fontainebleau, the emperor Napoleon, who had held all Europe in his thrall since the turn of the century, was exiled to this seemingly safe open prison, some 30km from the Tuscan coast.

It could have been so much worse for the emperor, but the irony for someone who hailed from Corsica, just over the water, must have been bitter. Napoleon, the conqueror who had stridden across all Europe and taken Egypt, was awarded this little island as his private fiefdom, to hold until the end of his days.

His arrival was greeted with considerable pomp. The guns of Portoferraio shot off a 100-round salute, to which the English frigate replied. That, at least, is French author Alexandre Dumas' take. Other sources reckon the guns were actually firing *at* the frigate.

Whatever the case, Elba would never be quite the same again. Napoleon, ever hyperactive, threw himself into frenetic activity in his new, humbler domain. After touring the island, he prescribed a mass of public works, such as improving operations in the island's iron-ore mines (whose revenue, it's pertinent to note, now went his way), boosting agriculture, initiating a road-building program, draining marshes and overhauling the legal and education systems. Quite often, he would order some of the 500 members of his faithful guard to pitch in.

A great deal of ink has been spilled over the diminutive emperor's dictatorial style and seemingly impossible ambitions, but he can't have been all bad. To this day, they still say a Mass each May for his soul at the island's Chiesa della Misericordia.

Napoleon installed himself in the bastions of the city wall, in what became known as the Residenza dei Mulini. He'd drop into his so-called country or summer home, outside town in San Martino, for an occasional stopover on excursions but he never slept there. Some weeks after his arrival, his mother Letizia and sister Paolina rolled up. But he remained separated from his wife, Maria Luisa, and was visited for just two no doubt hectic days by his lover, Maria Walewska.

At the Congress of Vienna, the new regime in France called for Napoleon's removal to a more distant location. Austria, too, was nervous. Some participants favoured a shift to Malta, but Britain objected and suggested the remote South Atlantic islet of St Helena. The Congress broke up with no agreed decision.

Napoleon was well aware of the debate. Under no circumstances would he allow himself to be shipped off to some rocky speck in the furthest reaches of the Atlantic Ocean. A lifelong risk taker, he decided to have another roll of the dice. For months he had sent out on 'routine' trips around the Mediterranean a couple of vessels flying the flag of his little empire, Elba. When one, the *Incostante,* set sail early in the morning of 26 February 1815, no-one suspected that the conqueror of Europe was stowed away on board. Sir Neil Campbell, his English jail warden, had returned to Livorno the previous day, confident that Napoleon was, as ever, fully immersed in the business of the island.

Elba lost its emperor and Napoleon, his little gilded cage. He made his way to France, reassumed power and embarked on the Hundred Days, the last of his expansionist campaigns that would culminate in defeat at Waterloo – after which he got his Atlantic exile after all, dying there in 1821, from arsenic poisoning, according to the most accepted contemporary theory, probably from the hair tonic he applied to keep that famous quiff glistening.

west of town. Modest by Napoleonic standards, it's dominated by the overbearing mid-19th-century gallery built to house his memorabilia. A combined ticket for both villas costs €5.

The Linguella fortifications, near the port, house the modest **Museo Civico Archeologico** (☎ 0565 91 73 38; adult/child €2/1.50; 9.30am-2.30pm & 6pm-midnight mid-Jun–mid-Sep, 9am-8.30pm mid-Sep–Oct, 10am-1pm & 3.30pm-7.30pm Apr–mid-Jun), with a collection generally focussed on ancient seafarers.

ACTIVITIES

If you're here for an active time, pick up the multilingual tourist office leaflet *Lo Sport Emerge del Mare*. It has a useful map and lists walking and cycling trails plus where to sign on for scuba diving, windsurfing and other watery activities.

Isola d'Elba, 1:25,000 and published by Edizione Multigraphic, and *Isola d'Elba*, 1:35,000 from Vivaldi Editori, both feature recommended routes for walkers and cyclists. *Isola d'Elba: Itinerari tra Storia e Natura* at 1:25,000 has a multilingual key and a stimulating range of walks superimposed. The Vivaldi Editori edition has descriptions in English of 10 walks and six mountain bike routes around the island. **Il Libraio** (☎ 0565 91 71 35; Calata Mazzini 10), on the waterfront beside the old town, stocks them.

You can spend a more sedentary but nonetheless enjoyable two hours on a glass-bottom boat with **Aquavision** (☎ 328-709 54 70; Portoferraio harbour; adult/child €15/8).

SLEEPING

In the height of summer many hotels operate a compulsory half-board policy.

Albergo Ape Elbana (☎ 0565 91 42 45; apelbana@ elba2000.it; Salita de' Medici 2; s €40-60, d €55-95; P ⊠) In the old town, this hotel overlooks Piazza della Repubblica (where guests can park for free). This butter-coloured building is the island's oldest hotel, where guests of Napoleon are reputed to have stayed. The position is its best feature as rooms, while large, are a little soulless. Ask for one of the larger ones looking onto the piazza.

Villa Ombrosa (☎ 0565 91 43 63; www.villaombrosa .it; Via De Gasperi 3; s/d incl buffet breakfast €91/182; P) Another of the very few hotels on the island that is open year round. With a great location overlooking the sea and Spiaggia delle Ghiaie, it also has its own small private beach. Half-board, considerably more creative than many hotels' bland buffet fare, is obligatory in summer.

Hotel Acquamarina (☎ 0565 91 40 57; www.hotel acquamarina.it; Località Paduella; s/d €73/146) Just 400m away and under the same ownership as Villa Ombrosa, Acquamarina is a knockout hotel, also within strolling distance of Portoferraio. Rooms are sunny and bright with large balconies overlooking the naturally wild gardens. A path leads down to a small cove.

Acquaviva (☎ 0565 91 91 03; www.campingacqua viva.it; person/tent/car €12/13/3; ☾ mid-Mar–mid-Oct) About 4km west of town is Portoferraio's nearest campsite. A great choice for sunsets over the sea, it's about as close as you can get to the beach without getting your feet wet.

EATING

Trattoria da Zucchetta (☎ 0565 91 53 31; Piazza della Repubblica 40; mains €8-10; ☾ closed Wed lunch) This Neapolitan eatery dates back to 1891 and has a huge menu offering the full range of pasta and more than 40 pizza toppings. It enjoys a great people-watching position tucked in the corner of the piazza. Service, however, can be slow, unsmiling and decidedly un-Neapolitan.

Stella Marina (☎ 0565 91 59 83; Banchina Alto Fondale; meals €23-35) This is a justifiably popular fish and seafood restaurant. Stuck in a car park beside the Toremar ferry jetty and unpromising from the exterior, its cuisine is fine and imaginative though drinks are overpriced.

Trattoria La Barca (☎ 0565 91 80 36; Via Guerrazzi 60-62; mains €10-13; ☾ closed Wed) A good place to slurp a plate of *cacciucco*. The place is popular with locals in the know, so there's not much elbow space between tables. Go for the terrace if there's room.

DRINKING

Sir William's Irish Bar (☎ 0565 91 92 88; Via Mangana-naro 28) The very name tells you the Celtic connection is tenuous, but this is the place for a wee dram o' whisky or a pint of bitter. It generally doesn't start jumping till at least midnight and pulls in all sorts, from local punters to the casually hip.

L'Inferno (☎ 0565 91 87 83; Le Foci 2) Locals pile into their cars and head to this lively bar with dancing about 5km west of town on the road to Marciana Marina.

West to Capo d'Enfola

Several modest beaches spread west from Portoferraio. Quite nice, although narrow and shelly, are **Spiaggia la Padulella** and its counterpart just west of Capo Bianco, **Spiaggia di Capo Bianco**. A couple of similar beaches dot the coast along the 7km stretch out to **Capo d'Enfola**. You can have a dip here or head south down the coast a few kilometres to **Viticcio**, with its handful of restaurants and hotels, where the road ends. From here you can walk to the beaches of the **Golfo della Biodola**.

SLEEPING & EATING

Hotel Scoglio Bianco (☎ 0565 93 90 36; www.scoglio bianco.it; Viticcio; half-board per person from €70) This hotel has bright, spacious rooms set around a central patio decorated with deckchairs and cats. The downstairs Pizzeria da Gi-acomino has a terrace over the sea.

Hotel Paraiso (☎ 0565 93 90 34; www.elbaturistica .it; Viticcio; half-board per person €90; ☯ mid-Apr-Oct; Ⓟ ☒ ☒) Owned by a British-Italian couple, Paraiso has expansive sea views. Many rooms have good-sized balconies. Set high above the road, there is a vast outdoor bar, pool, tennis court and private beach access.

Emanuel (☎ 0565 93 90 03; Enfola; menus €18-27, mains €14-17; ☯ Easter-Nov) At road's end on Capo d'Enfola, Emanuel offers splendid views over the water. Enjoy a lingering dinner on its beachfront terrace, shaded by a magnificent fig tree. The cuisine is consistently good. Fish and seafood predominate but there are always a couple of inventive meat dishes and a vegetarian option.

West to Marciana Marina

From Portoferraio, a provincial road heads south and then forks westwards along the coast to Marciana Marina, via Procchio.

The pick of the beaches are the sandy strands lining the **Golfo della Biodola.**

Hermitage (☎ 0565 93 69 11; www.hotelhermitage .it; La Biodola; half-board per person from €185; Ⓟ ☒ ☒) is pure Beverly Hills. One of the island's truly luxurious hotels, it's a gorgeous retreat complete with infinity pool overlooking the sea and a golf course just over the fence.

PROCCHIO

In season, Procchio is a small bustling place with the added bonus of sandy beaches.

Osteria del Piano (☎ 0565 90 72 92; Via Provinciale 24; mains €12-15; ☯ Apr-Oct) is an unassuming restaurant on the Procchio side of the junction where the road peels away towards Marciana Marina. The open-plan kitchen means you can watch the creative energy behind such innovative dishes as black-and-white spaghetti in crab sauce.

West from Procchio, the road hugs the cliffs, offering fine views all along the winding coast. If you can manage to park, **Spiaggia di Spartaia** and **Spiaggia della Paolina** are part of a series of beautiful little beaches, all requiring a steep clamber down.

Marciana Marina

Almost 20km west of Portoferraio, Marciana Marina, unlike so many brash, modern marinas, is a place with roots and character. Fronted by some pleasant pebble beaches, it makes a fine base for attacking the island's best walking trails.

Hotel Marinella (☎ 0565 9 90 18; www.elbahotel marinella.it; Viale Margherita 38; s/d €75/154; ☯ Easter-Sep) A well-aged classic beside the sea front. Rooms in the annexe overlook the garden but the best are those in the main building with balconies and sea views.

Casa Lupi (☎ /fax 0565 9 91 43; Località Ontanelli 35; s/d €30/70; ☯ closed Jan-early Mar) This is about half a kilometre inland on the road to Marciana. Beside a vineyard, with a garden of peach trees and rose bushes, it's a small hotel in peaceful surroundings. Rooms are no-frills basic but comfortable and clean.

Ristorante Loris (☎ 0565 9 94 96; Via XX Settembre 29; pizzas €4.70-7.70, mains €8.50-15; ☯ closed Mon) This is a promising fish and seafood venue where all pastas and desserts are homemade. Try, for something special, their *ravioli all'astice* (lobster ravioli in a pepper and Parmesan sauce).

Poggio & the Interior

A twisting 4km ascent into the mountains from Marciana Marina brings you to the attractive inland village of Poggio, famous for its spring water. It's an enchanting little place with steep, cobblestone alleys and stunning views of Marciana Marina and the coast.

Albergo Monte Capanne (☎ /fax 0565 9 90 83; Via dei Pini 13; s/d €26/46, d with bathroom €55; ☯ Apr-Oct) is a great little mountain retreat where you're assured of a robust, cheery welcome. If it gets too warm for you on the coast, chill out here in the hinterland. The terrace is large and ivy-clad, and rooms, with swoony views of the coast way below, are cosy.

Publius (☎ 0565 9 92 08; mains €9-18; ☯ closed Mon), at the northern entrance to the village, is the place to spill money on a great meal. The plunging views down to the coast should keep your mind off the commensurately steep prices.

From Poggio you can choose from two options: either proceed west to **Marciana** then head around the coast (see p190), or opt for the narrow, spectacular SP37. Heading towards Marina di Campo, it winds through some of the highest, most densely wooded and tourist-free countryside on the island.

Following the SP37, park at the picnic site at the foot of **Monte Perone** (630m) – you can't miss it. To the left (east) you can wander up to the mountain, with spectacular views across much of the island. To the right (west) you can scramble fairly quickly to a height that affords broad vistas down to Poggio, Marciana and Marciana Marina. From there you could press on to **Monte Maolo** (749m).

The road then descends into the southern flank of the island. On the way, you pass the granite shell of the Romanesque **Chiesa di San Giovanni** and, shortly after, a ruined tower, the **Torre di San Giovanni**.

The two small hamlets here, **Sant'Ilario in Campo** and **San Piero in Campo**, are short on sights but still pleasant enough and little affected by tourism.

Albergo La Rosa (☎ /fax 0565 98 31 91; Piazza Maggiore Gadani 17, San Piero; s/d €55/80) is a quiet, old-fashioned hotel in a side street with large but rather dark rooms. The restaurant is popular, specialising in enormous plates of pasta at rock-bottom prices.

Marciana & the West Coast

From Poggio, it is possible is to continue west to Marciana (355m), the most engaging of the western interior towns. Once an important defensive position under Pisan rule, it subsequently passed to Piombino, the French and finally to the grand duchy of Tuscany.

The much knocked about **Fortezza Pisana** (☉ Apr-Sep), above the village, is a reminder of the old medieval days. Down a cobbled lane below it is a modest **Museo Archeologico** (☎ 0565 90 12 15; Via del Pretorio; admission €2; ☉ closed Tue). A 40-minute or so walk west out of town brings you to the **Santuario della Madonna del Monte**, the most important object of pilgrimage on the island. A much-altered 11th-century church houses a stone upon which a divine hand is said to have painted an image of the Virgin.

Some 750m south of Marciana, a **cable lift** (☎ 0565 90 10 20; one way/return €9/13) with open, barred cabins like parrot cages operates in summer and whisks you almost to the summit of **Monte Capanne** (1018m), the island's highest point with views as far as Corsica on a clear day.

The road west out of Marciana pursues a course around the island, maintaining a prudent distance and altitude from the often precipitous coastline.

Sant'Andrea is a popular new resort with a concentration of a dozen or so hotels winding back up the hill to the main road.

Hotel Barsalini (☎ 0565 90 80 13; www.hotel barsalini.com; Sant'Andrea; s/d incl half board €95/190; ☉ Easter-late Oct), just 20m from the beach, has been designed with a lot of TLC. Rooms are spacious, bright and comfortable and the aquarium-flanked restaurant has an excellent and varied menu.

Following the road round to the south side of the island, you pass several small beaches. **Chiessi** and **Pomonte** have pebbly beaches, but the water is beautiful. Sandy **Spiaggia delle Tombe** is one of the few spots on the island with a nude-bathing scene.

At **Fetovaia**, **Seccheto** and **Cavoli** you will find further protected sandy beaches, accommodation and restaurants. West of Seccheto, **Le Piscine** is another mostly nudist stretch.

Marina di Campo

Marina di Campo, on the south side of the island, is Elba's second-largest town. Curling around a picturesque bay, its small fishing harbour adds character to what is otherwise very much a holiday town. Its beach of bright, white sand pulls in holidaymakers by the thousands; coves further west, though less spectacular, are more tranquil.

Campsites abound along this stretch of coast and the place gets ridiculously packed in the height of summer. But this is where some of the island's action can be found too; several discos help keep the brat-pack happy through the hot months.

There is a seasonal **tourist office** (☎ 0565 97 79 69; Piazza dei Granatieri; ☉ Jun-Sep) in town.

Just northeast of town in the Lacona/Porto Azzurro direction, over 150 Mediterranean species swim, crawl and wave about in the **Acquario dell'Elba** (☎ 0565 97 78 85; adult/child €8/6; ☉ 9am-11.30pm Jun–mid-Sep, 9am-7.30pm mid-Mar–May & mid-Sep–Nov).

Montecristo (☎ 0565 97 68 61; www.elbalink.it /hotel/montecristo; Viale Nomelini; s/d from €90/180; ☎) is a pleasantly posh hotel on the beach, with flower-framed balconies and a bar and pool overlooking the sea. The large sunny rooms have Scandinavian-style light furnishings and king-size beds.

Albergo Thomas (☎ 0565 97 77 32; www.elbathomas hotel.com; Viale degli Etruschi 32; per person incl breakfast €32-59; ☉ mid-Mar–Oct; P), barely 100m away, is a three-star hotel, attractively set among pine trees. Popular with scuba divers, it's only a short walk from the beach and is one of the more affordable options in the town itself.

Il Tinello (☎ 0565 97 66 45; Località Casina), on the outskirts, is a heaving drinking and dancing dive, especially on summer nights.

Capoliveri & the Southeast

High up on a ridgeback in the southeastern pocket of the island, this is an enchanting village, all steep, narrow alleys with houses sardined together. At the height of summer it is jammed with tourists (at least one Italian newspaper writer has remarked tartly that one may as well hoist the German flag at Capoliveri). Come out of season and you can rediscover some of the peace of this hamlet, which used to live off iron-ore mining.

EATING

Il Chiasso (☎ 0565 96 87 09; Via Cavour 32; mains €15-18; ☽ closed Tue) One of the best restaurants in town, with a classy set menu. The décor is a savvy combination of traditional and trendy and there's an excellent wine list.

Freccia Azzurra (☎ 0565 96 89 68; Via Verdi 4; mains €7-12) This is a bustling, popular restaurant in season. There's not much squeeze-by space in the dining room but its terrace on Capoliveri's main square is vast. Try the *penne gamberetti e rucola* (shrimp and rocket penne) for a real tastebud treat.

DRINKING

Fandango (☎ 0565 93 54 24; Via Cardenti 1; drinks from €4; ☽ closed Mon) Right beneath the main square, here you can taste fine Tuscan wines in pleasant surroundings.

Velvet Underground (Vicolo Lungo 14) This is only a short stumble from the main square. It's a pub-style bar that feels like a real local.

ENTERTAINMENT

Sugar Reef (☎ 0338 917 90 26; Località La Trappola) *The* place on the island for a little hip-swinging salsa, both live and DJ-mixed. It's about 1km south of Capoliveri on the road to Morcone.

Around Capoliveri

Directly west of Capoliveri (take the Portoferraio road and watch for signs) are the beaches of **Spiaggia di Zuccale** and **Spiaggia di Barabarca**. You end up on a dirt track – leave your vehicle in the car park and walk the final stretch.

If you take the road heading south from Capoliveri, another three charming sandy little coves – **Morcone**, **Pareti** and **Innamorata** – come in quick succession.

East of Capoliveri, you have two choices. One road takes you to the comparatively long stretch of beach at **Naregno**, fronted by a series of discreet hotels.

The more adventurous should follow signs for **Stracoligno**, one of the first in a series of beaches running down the east coast. The road at this point becomes a dirt track and, if you don't mind dusting up your vehicle, you can push on to a couple of less-frequented beaches. **Cala Nuova** is a nice enough little beach with a good restaurant.

Ristorante Calanova (☎ 0565 96 89 58; mains €16-18; ☽ summer only, closed Tue) is a table-for-two kind of place, wonderfully secluded with only the gently lapping sea for company. As you'd expect, the menu is based on seafood.

Another 4km or 5km and you reach a path down to the **Spiaggia dello Stagnone**, which even in summer should not be too crowded, if only because of the effort required to rattle down this far.

Porto Azzurro

Overlooked by its fort, built in 1603 by Philip III of Spain and now a prison, Porto Azzurro is a pleasant resort town, close to some good beaches.

Albergo Villa Italia (☎ 0565 9 51 19; villaitalia@infoelba.it; Viale Italia 41; d/tr/q incl breakfast €80/90/105; ☽ mid-Mar–Oct; P) is a friendly, family-run place. Their 12 clean bedrooms are small but spruce and about the cheapest in town. It's on a fairly noisy road yet scarcely 200m from the beach.

Hotel Belmare (☎ 0565 9 50 12; www.elba-hotel belmare.it; Banchina IV Novembre; s/d incl breakfast €60/100; ☽ year-round) has an enviable location on the main promenade. This traditional green-shuttered hotel is nothing fancy but rooms are comfy enough, and there's a small bar and TV room for post-beach R&R.

Ristorante Cutty Sark (☎ 0565 95 78 21; Piazza del Mercato 25; meals €25-35; ☽ closed Tue) has a mainly fish menu with a couple of concessions to carnivores. Savour their *raviolini all'Ammiraglia*, large ravioli filled with courgettes (zucchini) and shrimp meat and bathed in a shrimp and tomato sauce.

La Lanterna Magica (☎ 0565 95 83 94; Lungomare Vitaliani 5; mains €9-13), one of a trio of fish restaurants protruding into the harbour, is the place to sample local specialities from the sea. Try, for example, their *zerri mari-nati* (a kind of pickled fish) or *stoccafisso all'Elbana* (dried cod and potato bathed in an olive and tomato sauce).

The Northeast

If, on leaving Portoferraio, you swing around to the east and head for Rio nell'Elba and beyond, you will experience the least-visited part of the island, with lovely, albeit pebbly, beaches and glorious views.

The road hugs the coast on its way around to **Bagnaia**, the first worthwhile stop. En route you will scoot past **San Giovanni**, home to a rather expensive and dull mud spa, and **Le Grotte**, where a few stones still managing to stand on top of each other are all that remain of a Roman villa. At the Porto Azzurro and Bagnaia fork is **Elbaland** (☎ 335 819 46 80; Località Fonte Murato; adult/child €6/3; 11am-midnight Jul-Aug, 10am-9pm Jun & Sep, 10am-7pm Apr-May), a low-key amusement park that is more like an oversized park with swings and minor attractions.

From Elbaland head north to Bagnaia, a lush, green part of the island with an attractive beach and some accommodation, including a campsite.

Pizzeria Sunset (☎ 0565 93 07 86; Bagnaia; pizzas from €5; May-Oct) offers great views across the gulf to Portoferraio, a hang-out beach-bum atmosphere, happy hour and sangria in addition to good pizza. At night, there's a head-thumping disco that spills out onto the beach.

From Bagnaia you can follow the 3km dirt road to **Nisporto** and then on to **Nisportino** with spectacular views along the way. Both have a small beach and, in summer, snack stands and one or two restaurants. From Nisportino, head back a few kilometres to the junction with the road that links Nisporto and Rio nell'Elba. About halfway along this road, stop for a short stroll to what is left of the **Eremo di Santa Caterina**, a tiny stone hermitage, and more good views.

The road plunges down to the inland bastion of **Rio nell'Elba**, the heart of the island's iron-mining operations. It's a little gloomy, but the simple fact that it caters little to tourism has its appeal. The **Museo della Gente di Rio** (☎ 0565 93 91 82; Passo della Pietà; admission €2.75; 10am-1pm & 4-7.30pm Tue-Sun mid-Apr–Sep) has 200 rare mineral specimens from the east of the island and Monte Capanne.

Next, take the short run downhill to Rio nell'Elba's coastal outlet, **Rio Marina**, with yet another mineral museum. This apart, not a lot will hold you up.

Hotel Rio (☎ 0565 92 42 25; hotelriomarina.it; Via Palestro 31; s/d €40/70; Apr-Oct) is a well-worn hotel with family-size rooms, some with a sea view, plus TV room, garden, lots of paintings of dubious quality and an overall homey, retro-1970s feel.

Da Oreste La Strega (☎ 0565 96 22 11; Via Vittorio Emanuele 6; mains €10; closed Tue) is an attractive seafood restaurant, with large windows overlooking the harbour and an excellent wine list.

THE COUNT OF MONTECRISTO

This feel-good swashbuckling tale was born from author Alexandre Dumas' acquaintance with Jérome Bonaparte, Napoleon Bonaparte's brother, whom he accompanied on a trip to Elba. Dumas became aware of another island, the deserted Montecristo, deeper in the Mediterranean, and determined to write a novel in remembrance of the trip. In the person of the swashbuckling Dantes, Dumas takes a dig at the corruption of the bourgeois world. The dashing officer is imprisoned for a crime he hasn't committed and vows to get even. He escapes and, after a tip-off, searches for treasure on the island of Montecristo where, after much adventure and jolly japes, our man wins all the prizes – getting rich, becoming the Count of Montecristo and exacting a full measure of revenge on those who framed him.

Of course, it's all a tall tale (and no-one has ever found any treasure on Montecristo) but this particular yarn has made a lot of loot for a lot of people. At least 25 film and TV versions of the story have been made, with greater or lesser skill. Among the better ones are the oldies: Rowland Lee's 1935 film and the 1943 version by Robert Vernay were equally good celluloid yarns. In Italy, Andrea Giordana had women swooning at their TV sets in the 1966 series by Edmo Fenoglio. Richard Chamberlain had a go at the lead role in David Greene's 1975 *The Count of Montecristo*, as, more recently, did Gérard Depardieu in *Montecristo* (1997).

The best beach hereabouts is a little further down at **Ortano**. To get there, go back a couple of kilometres towards Rio nell'Elba and swing southwards. It's a nice location but, once again, the beach is that part-sand, part-pebble mix.

MINOR ISLANDS

Seven islands, including the island of Elba, form part of the Parco Nazionale dell'Arcipelago Toscano (see the boxed text, p177). Two out of the park's seven islands, Capraia and Gorgona (see p179), are in the central coast area and the islands of Giglio (p248) and Giannutri (p248) are further south. The remaining two are Pianosa and Montecristo.

Pianosa, 14km west of Elba, is a flat, triangular affair measuring about 5.8km by 4.6km. From 1858 until as late as the mid-1990s it was a penal colony. Day trips (return €25) to the island leave from Porto Ferraio and Marina di Campo during summer.

There are no ferry services to **Montecristo**, 40km south of Elba, which was also briefly a prison island. Since 1979 it has been a marine biological reserve and can be seen only as part of an organised visit; you need special permission from the **Ufficio Forestale in Follónica** (☎ 0566 4 06 11) on the Italian mainland.

Central Tuscany

Buildings the colour of ripe corn, hills with gentle curves and folds, scored here and there by steep ravines, as scarred and eroded as any cowboy badlands; here in the central Tuscan countryside, especially around Le Crete with its impressionist-style landscape, beats the heart of rural Tuscany. Lofty cypresses form a dramatic border to fields speckled with sheep and, if you pass by in spring, you have the additional treat of brilliant red poppy fields, sweeping to the sun-hazed green horizon. Gentle on the eye and feet, the region is ideal family walking country – and do get a first overview on the scenic Treno Natura, if your visit coincides with one of the summer days when it's running.

There are a few outstanding abbeys for lovers of ecclesiastical architecture and several spas too, capturing the sweet, restorative waters that flow from deep within the region's hills.

Some of Tuscany's most attractive towns poke up hereabouts: steep, straggling Montepulciano and the one-time defensive bulwark of Monteriggioni with its 14 defensive towers, the pilgrim-route bastion of San Gimignano, with still more medieval towers, and Volterra, the ancient brooding successor to an Etruscan settlement, standing aloof and watching over the lunar expanses to the south.

Siena with its magnificent piazza, cobbled streets and alleys and haunting black-and-white striped cathedral is the only true city. The hottest frontier in medieval Tuscany was the line separating Florence and its possessions from the county of Siena, its rival over the centuries. This proud Gothic city, although long ago swallowed up by Florence and ingested, in its day, into the grand duchy of Tuscany, even now sustains a separate identity. In some respects the Sienese have neither forgiven nor forgotten.

CENTRAL TUSCANY

HIGHLIGHTS

- Climb the 400 steps of Siena's **Torre del Mangia** (p199) for glorious views, then enjoy a cold beer outside in the **Piazza del Campo** (p198) below
- Visit Siena's **cathedral** (p199), Italy's most elaborate Gothic place of worship
- Explore the pastureland of **Le Crete** (p216), calling by the imposing abbeys of Sant'Antimo and Monte Oliveto Maggiore
- Feel small beneath the medieval towers of **San Gimignano** (p219)
- Linger in the *enoteca* within Montalcino's **fortezza** (p228), sipping local Brunello wine
- Puff your way up the steep streets of the pretty historical hill town of **Montepulciano** (p234)

CENTRAL TUSCANY

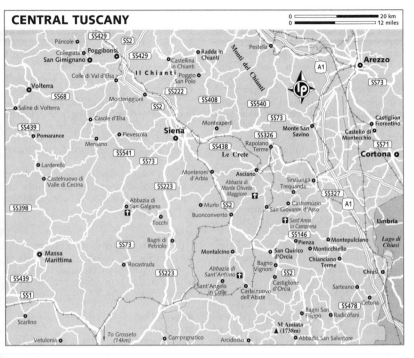

0　　　　20 km
0　　　　12 miles

SIENA

pop 52,800

Siena is one of Italy's most enchanting cities. While Florence, its historical rival, saw its greatest flourishing during the Renaissance, Siena's artistic glories are largely Gothic.

The medieval centre bristles with majestic buildings, such as the Palazzo Comunale on Piazza del Campo, the main square, while its profusion of churches and small museums harbour a wealth of artwork. Budget in a couple of days to savour the city and its rich treasures. Or make it more than two; Siena also makes a great base for exploring central Tuscany – especially the five-star medieval towns of San Gimignano and Volterra.

History

According to legend Siena was founded by Senius, son of Remus; the symbol of the wolf feeding the twins Romulus and Remus is as ubiquitous in Siena as it is in Rome. In reality, the city was probably of Etruscan origin, although it wasn't until the 1st century BC, when the Romans established a military

colony here called Sena Julia, that it began to grow into a proper town. Even so, it remained a minor outpost until the arrival of the Lombards in the 6th century AD. Under them, Siena became a key point along the main route from northern Italy to Rome, the Via Francigena. The medieval town was an amalgamation of three areas (Città, Camollia and San Martino) that would come to be known as the *terzi* (thirds). The city was next under the control of local bishops before power passed to locally elected administrators, the *consoli* (consuls).

By the 13th century, Siena had become a wealthy trading city, producing textiles, saffron, wine, spices and wax and its traders and bankers did deals all over western Europe. Its rivalry with neighbouring Florence also grew proportionately, leading to numerous wars between Guelph Florence and Ghibelline Siena, each intent upon controlling ever more Tuscan territory. In 1230 Florence besieged Siena and catapulted dung and donkeys over its walls. Siena's revenge came at the Battle of Montaperti in 1260 but victory was short-lived. Nine years later the Tuscan Ghibellines were defeated by Charles of Anjou and, for almost a century, Siena was obliged to toe the Florentine line in international affairs, becoming a member of the Tuscan Guelph League (supporters of the pope).

Siena reached its peak under the republican rule of the Consiglio dei Nove (Council of Nine), an elected executive dominated by the rising mercantile class. Many of the finest buildings in the Sienese Gothic style were constructed during this period, including the cathedral, the Palazzo Comunale and the Piazza del Campo. The Sienese school of painting (p58) was born at this time, with Guido da Siena, and flowered in the early 14th century, when artists such as Duccio di Buoninsegna and Ambrogio Lorenzetti were at work.

A plague outbreak in 1348 killed two-thirds of the city's 100,000 inhabitants and led to a period of decline.

At the end of the 14th century, Siena came under the control of Milan's Visconti family, followed in the next century by the autocratic patrician Pandolfo Petrucci. Under Petrucci the city's fortunes improved until the Holy Roman Emperor Charles V conquered it in 1555 after a two-year siege that left thousands dead. He handed the city over to Cosimo I de' Medici who barred the inhabitants from operating banks, thus severely curtailing Siena's power.

Siena was home to St Catherine (Santa Caterina), one of Italy's most venerated saints. But saints don't make money. Siena today relies for its prosperity on tourism and the success of its Monte dei Paschi di Siena bank, founded in 1472 and now one of the city's largest employers.

That Siena has remained largely intact as a Gothic city is the silver lining in what was, for the people of this city, a particularly dark and long-lingering cloud. Its decline in the wake of the Medici takeover was so complete that no-one gave thought to demolition or new construction. As the population began to grow again in the years after WWII (it had dropped to 16,000 in the latter half of the 18th century), Siena was the first European city to banish motor traffic from its heart (in 1966). To stroll its arteries, unclogged by carbon monoxide and unthreatened by speeding vehicles, is not the least of the town's pleasures.

Orientation

Historic Siena, still largely surrounded by its medieval walls, is small and easily tackled on foot, although the way in which streets swirl in semicircles around the city's heart, Piazza del Campo (also known as 'Il Campo'), may confuse you.

The names of two of Siena's main central streets, Banchi di Sopra and Banchi di Sotto, recall its once thriving banking activity. Another artery is Via di Città, which joins the others just behind Piazza del Campo.

From Piazza Gramsci, where most buses call, walk south along Via dei Montanini, which turns into Banchi di Sopra and leads to Piazza del Campo.

MAPS

If the rather cramped tourist office map isn't adequate for you, invest in *Siena* (€5.50) by Litografia Artistica Cartografia; at a scale of 1:7000, this map comes complete with a street index.

Information

BOOKSHOP

Libreria Senese (☎ 0577 28 08 45; Via di Città 62-6) Has a good stock of English, Dutch and German books. Also sells international newspapers.

EMERGENCY

Police station (☎ 0577 20 11 11; Via del Castoro)

INTERNET ACCESS

Internet Train Via di Città 121; Via di Pantaneto 57 (per hr €6; ☽ 8am-8pm Sun-Fri) A popular cafe with wi-fi.
Meg@web (☎ 0577 4 49 46; Via Pantaneto 132; per hr €6; ☽ 10am-11pm Mon-Sat, 3-9pm Sun)

LAUNDRY

Onda Blu (Via del Casato di Sotto 17; ☽ 8am-10pm)
Wash & Dry (Via di Pantaneto 38; ☽ 8am-10pm)

MEDICAL SERVICES

Hospital (☎ 0577 58 51 11; Viale Bracci) Just north of Siena at Le Scotte.

POST

Post office (Piazza Matteotti 1)

TELEPHONE

Telecom office (Via dei Rossi 86) The office is unstaffed, as are the other Telecom offices at Via di Città 113 and Via di Pantaneto 44.

SIENA

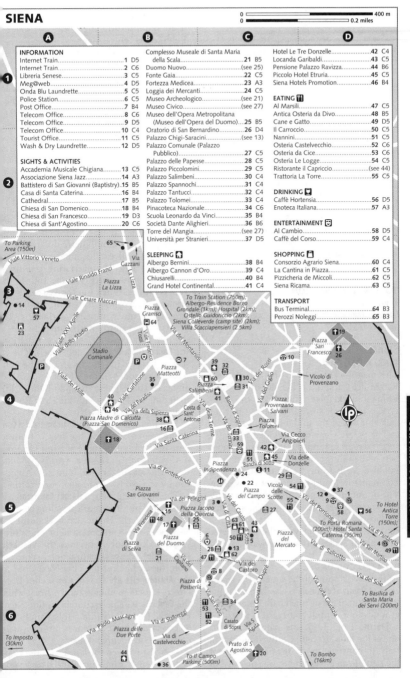

INFORMATION
Internet Train.....................1 D5
Internet Train.....................2 C6
Libreria Senese...................3 C5
Meg@web..........................4 C5
Onda Blu Laundrette............5 C5
Police Station.....................6 C5
Post Office.........................7 B4
Telecom Office....................8 C6
Telecom Office....................9 D5
Telecom Office..................10 C4
Tourist Office....................11 C5
Wash & Dry Laundrette........12 D5

SIGHTS & ACTIVITIES
Accademia Musicale Chigiana...13 C5
Associazione Siena Jazz.........14 A3
Battistero di San Giovanni (Baptistry)...15 B5
Casa di Santa Caterina..........16 B4
Cathedral..........................17 B5
Chiesa di San Domenico........18 B4
Chiesa di San Francesco........19 D3
Chiesa di Sant'Agostino........20 C6
Complesso Museale di Santa Maria della Scala...21 B5
Duomo Nuovo..................(see 25)
Fonte Gaia........................22 C5
Fortezza Medicea................23 A3
Loggia dei Mercanti.............24 C5
Museo Archeologico............(see 21)
Museo Civico....................(see 27)
Museo dell'Opera Metropolitana (Museo dell'Opera del Duomo)...25 B5
Oratorio di San Bernardino.....26 D4
Palazzo Chigi-Saracini.........(see 13)
Palazzo Comunale (Palazzo Pubblico)...27 C5
Palazzo delle Papesse..........28 C5
Palazzo Piccolomini.............29 C5
Palazzo Salimbeni...............30 C4
Palazzo Spannochi..............31 C4
Palazzo Tantucci.................32 C4
Palazzo Tolomei.................33 C4
Pinacoteca Nazionale...........34 C6
Scuola Leonardo da Vinci.......35 B4
Società Dante Alighieri.........36 B6
Torre del Mangia...............(see 27)
Università per Stranieri........37 D5

SLEEPING
Albergo Bernini.................38 B4
Albergo Cannon d'Oro.........39 C4
Chiusarelli.......................40 B4
Grand Hotel Continental........41 C4

Hotel Le Tre Donzelle...........42 C4
Locanda Garibaldi...............43 C5
Pensione Palazzo Ravizza.......44 B6
Piccolo Hotel Etruria...........45 C5
Siena Hotels Promotion........46 B4

EATING
Al Marsili........................47 C5
Antica Osteria da Divo.........48 B5
Cane e Gatto....................49 D5
Il Carroccio......................50 C5
Nannini...........................51 C5
Osteria Castelvecchio...........52 C6
Osteria da Cice..................53 C6
Osteria Le Logge................54 C5
Ristorante il Capriccio.........(see 44)
Trattoria La Torre...............55 C5

DRINKING
Caffè Hortensia.................56 D5
Enoteca Italiana.................57 A3

ENTERTAINMENT
Al Cambio........................58 D5
Caffè del Corso..................59 C4

SHOPPING
Consorzio Agrario Siena.........60 C5
La Cantina in Piazza............61 C5
Pizzicheria di Miccoli..........62 C5
Siena Ricama.....................63 C5

TRANSPORT
Bus Terminal.....................64 B3
Perozzi Noleggi..................65 B3

SAFE COMBINATIONS

Siena has a bewildering permutation of combined tickets. The distribution when we last visited was as follows:

- Museo Civico and Torre del Mangia (€10)
- Museo Civico, Santa Maria della Scala and Palazzo Papesse (€10, valid for two days)
- Museo dell'Opera Metropolitana, Oratorio di San Bernardino and Battistero di San Giovanni (€10, valid for three days)
- Museo Civico, Santa Maria della Scala, Palazzo Papesse, Museo dell'Opera Metropolitana, Battistero di San Giovanni and Oratorio di San Bernardino – the bumper bundle though not including Torre del Mangia (€16, valid for seven days)

TOURIST INFORMATION

Tourist office (☎ 0577 28 05 51; www.terresiena.it; Piazza del Campo 56; ⏰ 9am-7pm) Can help reserve accommodation.

Sights

PIAZZA DEL CAMPO

The magnificent, scallop-shaped, slanting Piazza del Campo, on the site of a former Roman marketplace, has been the city's civic centre ever since the Council of Nine staked it out in the mid-14th century.

The piazza's paving is divided into nine sectors, representing the number of members of the ruling council. In 1346 water first bubbled forth from the **Fonte Gaia** (Happy Fountain) in the upper part of the square. The fountain's panels are reproductions; the severely weathered originals, sculpted by Jacopo della Quercia in the early 15th century, are on display in the Complesso Museale di Santa Maria della Scala (p209).

PALAZZO COMUNALE

At the lowest point of the square, the spare, elegant **Palazzo Comunale** is also known as the Palazzo Pubblico, or town hall. Entry to the ground-floor central courtyard is free.

Dating from 1297, the palazzo itself is one of the most graceful Gothic buildings in Italy. Its construction, as the nerve centre of the republican government, was planned to be an integral part of the piazza. The resu is an amphitheatre effect with the Palazz Pubblico as central stage.

The Council of Nine wanted to unite th offices of government and courts in on central building, thus further removing th instruments of power, symbolically and ac tually, from the hands of the feudal noble

Inside is the **Museo Civico** (☎ 0577 29 22 6 adult/student €7/4.50; ⏰ 10am-7pm mid-Mar–Oct, 10am 5.30 or 6.30pm Nov–mid-Mar), a series of rooms o an upper floor of the palazzo with fresco by artists of the distinctive Sienese scho (p58). Here, as in other great buildings c Siena and elsewhere in the province (fc example the Palazzo del Popolo and Col legiata in San Gimignano), the decoratio often with a foundation of deep-blue hue on the ceiling, tends to be rich and ful leaving scarcely a millimetre uncovered.

Upstairs are five rather nondescript room filled with equally unarresting painting mostly by Sienese artists of the 16th to th 18th centuries. Check out the **Sala del Risorg mento** to your left with its more impressiv late-19th-century frescoes serialising ke events in the campaign to unite Italy.

From here, cross the central corridor int the **Sala di Balia** (or Sala dei Priori). The 1! scenes depicted in frescoes around the wall recount episodes in the life of Pope Alex ander III (the Sienese Rolando Bandinelli) including his clashes with the Holy Roma Emperor Frederick Barbarossa.

You then pass into the **Anticamera del Con cistoro**, remarkable for the fresco (move here in the 19th century) of *Santi Caterine d'Alessandria, Giovanni e Agostino* (Saint Catherine of Alexandria, John and Augus tine), executed by Ambrogio Lorenzetti.

The following hall, **Sala del Concistoro**, i dominated by the allegorical ceiling frescoe of the Mannerist Domenico Beccafumi.

Back in the Anticamera del Concistoro you pass to your right into the **Vestibol** (Vestibule), whose star attraction is a bronze wolf, the symbol of the city. Next door ir the **Anticappella** are frescoes of scenes from Greco-Roman mythology and history, whil the **Cappella** (Chapel), contains a fine *Sacr Famiglia e San Leonardo* (Holy Family and St Leonardo) by Il Sodoma and intricately carved wooden choir stalls.

The best is saved for last. From the Cap pella, you emerge into the **Sala del Mappamondo** where you can admire the masterpiece of the ntire building – Simone Martini's powerful nd striking *Maestà* (Virgin Mary in Majsty) fresco, his earliest known work and one of the most important works of the Sienese chool. Other large frescoes along the inside ong wall depict famous Sienese victories.

In the next room, the **Sala dei Nove** (or Sala lella Pace) are Ambrogio Lorenzetti's didactic frescoes depicting the *Effetti del Buon del Cattivo Governo* (Allegories of Good nd Bad Government), contrasting the harmony of good government with the – las, much deteriorated and maybe there's a message there – privations and trials of hose subject to bad rule. On the party wall with the Sala del Mappamondo are scenes of a charming serenity that lend a little insight nto everyday life in medieval Siena and its countryside. This sunlit idyll is the result of good and wise government, symbolised by the figures on the narrow inner wall. Turning to the next long wall you see the symbolic figures of all the nasty vices that can come to rule the hearts of princes and lead to the misery depicted next to them.

Finish the visit by climbing the stairs to the **loggia** which looks southeast over Piazza del Mercato and the countryside.

TORRE DEL MANGIA

Climb all 400 steps of this graceful **bell tower** (admission €6; ⏰ 10am-7pm mid-Mar–Oct, 10am-4pm Nov–mid-Mar) for splendid views across the city. The ticket office closes 45 minutes before the tower shuts and only 30 people are allowed up at any time.

CATHEDRAL

Siena's **cathedral** (Piazza del Duomo; admission €3; ⏰ 10.30am-7.30pm Mon-Sat, 1.30-6.30pm Sun Mar-Oct, 10.30am-6.30pm Mon-Sat, 1.30-5.30pm Sun Nov-Feb) is one of Italy's great Gothic structures. Begun in 1196, it was largely completed by 1215, although work continued on features such as the apse and dome well into the 13th century.

Exterior

After the cathedral's completion, work began on changing, enlarging and embellishing the structure. The magnificent façade of white, green and red polychrome marble was begun by Giovanni Pisano – who completed only the lower section before his death – and was finished towards the end of the 14th century. The mosaics in the gables were added in the 19th century. The statues of philosophers and prophets by Giovanni Pisano, above the lower section, are copies; the originals are preserved in the adjacent Museo dell'Opera Metropolitana.

In 1339 the city's leaders launched a plan to enlarge the cathedral and create one of Italy's largest places of worship. Known as the **Duomo Nuovo** (New Cathedral), the

---

QUENCHING THE THIRST

In 1556 Emperor Charles V apparently claimed that 'Siena is as beautiful under the ground as it is above it'. As he had spent the two previous years plundering the city and slaughtering most of its inhabitants, this observation did not go down well at the time. Yet his seemingly wacky observation had an element of truth.

Beneath Siena lies an incredible 15-mile network of underground tunnels and interconnecting passages dating back to the 13th century. Back then, Siena was the main city on the much-travelled route through northern Italy to Rome. As the city prospered, the shortage of water became critical.

The resulting underground tunnels were an incredible feat of engineering. Two teams of workers started from opposite directions: one some 16km away at the source of the water in the hills, the other underneath Siena. There was no communication and the only instruments the medieval builders had were plumb lines and pick axes. They also worked in the dark, apart from the flickering light of oil lamps. The tunnels were built with absolute precision, at a very low, constant gradient that kept the water flowing at a regular rate. More than 700 years later, the network of tunnels is still working, flowing into many of Siena's fountains. Water from the main tunnel is also used to cool the fridge of Nannini (see p214), the famous ice cream and pastry shop; a fitting example of how Siena's history lives on, complementing the medieval with the modern.

remains of this unrealised project are on Piazza Jacopo della Quercia, at the eastern side of the main cathedral. The daring plan, to build an immense new nave with the present cathedral becoming the transept, was scotched by the plague of 1348.

Interior

The cathedral's interior is truly stunning. Walls and pillars continue the black-and-white-stripe theme of the exterior, while the vaults are painted blue with gold stars. High along the walls of the nave is a long series of papal busts.

After looking up, look down…and you'll see the cathedral's most precious feature – the inlaid-marble floor, decorated with 56 glorious panels depicting historical and biblical subjects. The earliest ones are graffiti designs in black-and-white marble, dating from the mid-14th century. The latest panels, in coloured marble, are from the 16th century. The most valuable are kept covered and revealed only from 7 to 22 August each year but a few are uncovered and fenced off.

Seek out the exquisit 13th-century marble and porphyry pulpit by Nicola Pisano, who was aided by his equally talented son, Giovanni. Intricately carved with vigorous, realistic crowd scenes, it's one of the masterpieces of Gothic sculpture. You can't inch as close as you might like as barriers keep you at a respectful distance. To shed a little light on the subject, stick coins into the machine (€0.50 gets you a generous minute of illumination).

Other significant artworks include a bronze statue of St John the Baptist by Donatello in a chapel off the north transept.

Libreria Piccolomini

Off the north aisle, the **Libreria Piccolomini** is another of the cathedral's great treasures. Pope Pius III built this compact hall to house the books of his uncle, Enea Silvio Piccolomini, who was Pope Pius II; only a series of huge choral tomes remains on display.

The walls of the hall have vividly coloured narrative frescoes by Bernardino Pinturicchio. They depict events in the life of Piccolomini, starting from his early days as a secretary to an Italian bishop on a mission to Basle, through to his ordination as pope and eventually his death in Ancona while trying to mount a crusade against the Turks.

In the centre of the hall is a group of statues known as the *Tre Grazie* (Three Graces), a 3rd-century Roman copy of an earlier Hellenistic work.

MUSEO DELL'OPERA METROPOLITANA

This **museum** (☎ 0577 28 30 48; Piazza del Duomo 8; admission €6; ⊙ 9am-7.30pm mid-Mar–Sep, 9am-6pm Oct 9am-1.30pm Nov–mid-Mar), also known as Museo dell'Opera del Duomo, is next to the cathedral, in what would have been the southern aisle of the nave of the Duomo Nuovo. Among its great artworks, which formerly adorned the cathedral, are the 12 statues of prophets and philosophers by Giovanni Pisano that decorated the façade. Their creator designed them to be viewed from ground level, which is why they look so distorted as they crane uncomfortably forward.

On the 1st floor is Duccio di Buoninsegna's striking early-14th-century *Maestà* (Majesty), painted on both sides as a screen for the cathedral's high altar. The front and back have now been separated and the panels depicting the Story of Christ's Passion hang opposite the *Maestà*. Duccio's narrative genius is impressive. Take the lower half of the bottom big middle panel. In one 'shot', three scenes take place: Christ preaches to the Apostles in the Garden of Gethsemane; he then asks them to wait up for him; and then is portrayed while in prayer. In the half-panel above, he is kissed by Judas while Peter lops off a soldier's ear and the remaining Apostles flee.

To the right of the *Maestà*, a door leads into a back room with statues by Jacopo della Quercia, while on the left is a room with 19th-century illustrations of the entire collection of marble floor panels in the cathedral.

On the upper floors other artists represented include Ambrogio Lorenzetti, Simone Martini and Taddeo di Bartolo, and there's also a rich collection of tapestries and manuscripts.

For a great panoramic view – and a touch of physical exertion to counterbalance so much aesthetic exercise – haul yourself up the 131 steps that lead, via a very narrow, corkscrew stairway, to the **Panorama del Facciatone**, at the top of the façade of the putative Nuovo Duomo.

(Continued on page 209)

Sculpture in Boboli Gardens (p106), Florence

Fresco by Vasari and Zuccari on the ceiling of Florence's Duomo (p87)

Ponte Vecchio (p105), Florence

DAMIEN SIMONIS

Palazzo dei Cavalieri (p152), Pisa

Old centre of Suvereto (p182)

DAMIEN SIMONIS

Marble quarry, Apuane Alps (p173)

ROBIN CHAPMAN

Trees above beach at Populonia (p183)

Boats moored at Elba (p184)

WAYNE WALTON

DAMIEN SIMONIS

Bas-reliefs, columns and entablature on the Duomo (p170) in Carrara

DAVID TOMLINSON

Hot-spring pool on hillside, Bagno Vignoni (p232)

Etruscan cellar in Montepulciano (p234)

ALAN BENSON

Standard bearers of the Selva *contrada* (town district) at Il Palio (p212)

DAVID

Natural bastion town, Pitigliano (p250)

Via Cava di San Rocco in Sorano (p252)

Thermal waters of Terme di Saturnia (p249)

Porto Santo Stefano (p247) on the Monte Argentario peninsula

Palazzo del Bargello (p296),
Gubbio

Local ceramics, Gubbio (p296)

Chiesa di Santa Margherita (p263), Cortona

Tempio di Minerva (p285), Assisi

The cathedral (p269) in Perugia

Interior of a *norcineria*, Norcia (p318)

Outdoor restaurant, Orvieto (p338)

Tempio di San Fortunato (p323), Todi

Continued from page 200)

BATTISTERO DI SAN GIOVANNI

Just north of the cathedral and down a flight of steps is the **baptistry** (Baptistry of St John; Piazza San Giovanni; admission €3; ☺ 9am-7.30pm mid-Mar–Sep, 9am-6pm Oct, 10.30am-1pm & 2-5pm Nov–mid-Mar). Its Gothic façade, although unfinished on the upper levels, is quite a remarkable extravagance in marble.

Inside, the ceiling and vaults are lavishly decorated with frescoes. The life of Jesus is portrayed in the apse of this oddly shaped rectangular baptistry. The one on the right showing Christ carrying the cross is of particular interest. If you look at the city from which it appears he and the crowd have come, it is hard to escape the feeling that among the imaginary buildings have been illustrated Brunelleschi's dome and Giotto's Campanile in Florence. Could this be a nasty little anti-Florentine dig suggesting Siena's rival as the source of Christ's tribulations?

The centrepiece, literally and figuratively, is a marble font by Jacopo della Quercia, decorated with bronze panels in relief depicting the life of St John the Baptist. The panels, executed by several top-notch artists, include Lorenzo Ghiberti's *Baptism of Christ* and *St John in Prison* and Donatello's *Herod's Feast*.

SANTA MARIA DELLA SCALA

Originally a hospice for pilgrims and until quite recently a working hospital with almost a millennium of history the **Complesso Museale di Santa Maria della Scala** (☎ 0577 22 48 11; Piazza del Duomo 2; admission €6; ☺ 10.30am-6.30pm Apr-Oct, 10.30am-4.30pm Nov-Mar) has as its main attraction the vivid, secular frescoes (quite a relief after so much spirituality all around town) by Domenico di Bartolo, lauding the good works of the hospital and its patrons.

Before entering the hospital proper, pass by the **Chiesa della Santissima Annunziata**, a 13th-century church remodelled two centuries later.

Turn right into the **Cappella del Manto**, decorated with frescoes; the most striking is by Beccafumi (1514) and portrays the *Meeting of St Joaquim and St Anna,* the supposed parents of the Virgin Mary.

You will pass into a long hall where, to the left, is the remarkable 14th-century **Sala del Pellegrinaio**, the pilgrim hall and subsequently

the hospital's main ward. The bulk of its fresco series was done by Domenico di Bartolo in the 1440s. The first panel, by Il Vecchietta, depicts *gettatelli* (orphans) ascending to heaven. Taking in orphans was frequently one of the tasks of hospitals throughout Tuscany. Later panels show *balie* (wet-nurses) suckling orphans and other needy children. One jolly panel depicts a doctor nodding off as his patient describes his symptoms.

Downstairs is the **Fienile**, once storage space for the hospital. The original panelling of the Fonte Gaia (and a few replicas) is now housed here. Through the Fienile is the **Oratorio di Santa Caterina della Notte** (Oratory of St Catherine of the Night), a gloomy little chapel for sending up a prayer or two for the unwell upstairs.

MUSEO ARCHEOLOGICO

This **museum** (☺ 10.30am-6.30pm Apr-Oct, 10.30am-4.30pm Nov-Mar) is within Santa Maria della Scala. Most of the collection consists of pieces found near Siena, ranging from elaborate Etruscan alabaster funerary urns to gold Roman coins. In between you'll see some statuary, much of it Etruscan, a variety of household items, votive statuettes in bronze and even a pair of playing dice. The collection is well presented, and the surroundings – twisting, arched tunnels – perfectly complement it and are a cool blessing on stifling-hot summer days.

Admission to the museum is included in the price for Santa Maria della Scala.

PALAZZO DELLE PAPESSE

Change eras with a visit to this contemporary **art gallery** (☎ 0577 2 20 71; Via di Città 126; adult/child €5/free; ☺ noon-7pm Tue-Sun) if you've had your fill of medieval religious art. The gallery houses a number of permanent pieces from the likes of Micha Ullman and Botto and Bruno, mixed in with ever-changing exhibitions. The rooftop terrace has stunning views.

PALAZZO CHIGO-SARACINI

The magnificent curving Gothic façade of the **Palazzo Chigi-Saracini** (Via di Città) is in part a travesty, the result of 'restoration' in the 18th and 19th centuries to re-create the medieval feel. From the tower, which is the genuine article apart from its brick crenellations, they say a young boy with particularly good eyesight watched the Battle of Montaperti in

1260 and shouted down details of the home side's progress against the Florentines to eager crowds in the streets below.

The palazzo is the headquarters of Accademia Musicale Chigiana (see opposite).

PINACOTECA NAZIONALE

This **gallery** (☎ 0577 28 11 61; Via San Pietro 29; adult/child €4/free; ☒ 8.15am-7.50pm Tue-Sat, 8.15am-1.15pm Sun, 8.30am- 1.30pm Mon), within the 14th-century Palazzo Buonsignori, displays the world's greatest concentration of Gothic masterpieces from the Sienese school. But the collection also demonstrates the subsequent gulf cleaved between artistic life in Siena and Florence in the 15th century. While the Renaissance flourished 70km to the north, Siena's masters and their patrons remained firmly rooted in the Byzantine and Gothic precepts that had stood them in such good stead from the early 13th century. Stock religious images and episodes predominate, typically pasted lavishly with gold and generally lacking any of the advances in painting, such as perspective, emotion or movement, that artists in Florence were exploring.

Start your tour on the 2nd floor where, in the first two rooms, you can see some of the earliest surviving pre-Gothic works from the Sienese school, including pieces by Guido da Siena. Rooms 3 and 4 are given over to a few works by Duccio di Buoninsegna and his followers. The most striking exhibits in Room 3 are Simone Martini's *Madonna della Misericordia* (Madonna of Mercy), in which the Virgin Mary seems to take the whole of society protectively under her wing, and his *Madonna col Bambino* (Madonna and Child).

The two brothers Pietro and Ambrogio Lorenzetti feature in Rooms 7 and 8, while the following three rooms contain works by several artists from the early 15th century.

Rooms 12 and 13 are mostly devoted to Giovanni di Paolo; a couple of his paintings show refreshing signs of a break from strict tradition. His two versions of the *Presentazione nel Tempio* (Presentation of Jesus in the Temple) have virtually no gold and introduce new architectural themes, a hint of perspective and a discernible trace of human emotion in the characters depicted.

Down on the 1st floor, the Sienese rollcall continues and, although there are some exceptions, the interest starts to fade. Rooms

meriting a visit include Nos 27 to 32 and 37 which are dominated by works of the Mannerist Domenico Beccafumi and Il Sodoma Particularly striking is Il Sodoma's *Cristo alla Colonna* (Christ Tied to the Pillar) in Room 31, where, in a particularly human touch, tears trickle down Jesus' cheeks.

CHIESA DI SANT'AGOSTINO

This 13th-century **church** (☎ 0577 38 57 86; Prato di San Agostino; admission €2; ☒ 10.30am-1.30pm & 3-5.30pm mid-Mar–Oct), a few streets south of the Pinacoteca Nazionale, was originally designed by the Dutch Vanvitelli, chief architect to the King of Naples. Its richly rococo interior dates from the 18th century, after the church had been gutted by fire. The second altar on the south aisle has a superb *Adoration of the Crucifix* by Perugino while the Piccolomini chapel's jewel is Il Sodoma's *Adoration of the Magi*.

CHIESA DI SAN DOMENICO

This imposing 13th-century Gothic **church** (Piazza San Domenico; ☒ 7.30am-1pm & 3-6.30pm) has been altered time and time again over the centuries.

The bare, barnlike interior is in keeping with the Dominican order's ascetic spirit. Near the entrance is the raised **Cappella delle Volte**, where Santa Caterina di Siena took her vows and, according to tradition, performed some of her miracles. In the chapel is a portrait of the saint painted during her lifetime.

In the **Cappella di Santa Caterina**, off the south aisle, are frescoes by Sodoma depicting events in Santa Caterina's life – and her head, in a 15th-century tabernacle above the altar. She died in Rome, where most of her body is preserved, but, in keeping with the bizarre practice of collecting relics of dead saints, her head was returned to Siena.

Another bit that managed to find its way here is her desiccated thumb, on grisly display in a small window box to the right of the chapel. Also on show is a nasty-looking chain whip with which she would apply a good flogging to herself every now and then for the well-being of the souls of the faithful.

CASA DI SANTA CATERINA

For more of Santa Caterina – figuratively speaking – visit **Casa di Santa Caterina** (☎ 0577 28 08 01; Costa di Sant'Antonio 6; admission free; ☒ 9am-12.30pm & 3-6pm), where the saint was born and lived with her parents plus, says legend, 24 siblings. The rooms, converted into small chapels in the 15th century, are decorated with frescoes of her life and paintings by Sienese artists, including Il Sodoma.

FORTEZZA MEDICEA
Just northwest of the Chiesa di San Domenico, this **fortress**, also known as the Forte di Santa Barbara, is typical of those built in the early years of the grand duchy. The Sienese could not have been given a more obvious reminder of who was in charge than this huge Medici bastion, raised on the orders of Cosimo I de' Medici in 1560.

OTHER CHURCHES & PALAZZI
The 15th-century triple-arched balcony **Loggia dei Mercanti**, where merchants used to plot deals, is just northwest of Il Campo. From here, strike east along Banchi di Sotto to pass **Palazzo Piccolomini**, a Renaissance palazzo housing the city's archives. Further east are the 13th-century **Basilica di Santa Maria dei Servi**, with frescoes by Pietro Lorenzetti in a chapel off the north transept, and the 14th-century **Porta Romana**.

North of Loggia dei Mercanti on Banchi di Sopra, the 13th-century **Palazzo Tolomei** dominates Piazza Tolomei. Further north, Piazza Salimbeni is bounded by **Palazzo Tantucci**, Gothic **Palazzo Salimbeni** (prestigious head office of Monte dei Paschi di Siena bank), and the Renaissance **Palazzo Spannocchi**, from where 29 finely carved busts stare down at you from beneath the eaves.

Northeast of here, along Via dei Rossi, is **Chiesa di San Francesco**, with its vast single nave. It's suffered over the years – from a devastating 17th-century fire and use as army barracks – and was being further disturbed by massive works in the square that spreads before it when we last passed by. Beside the church is the 15th-century **Oratorio di San Bernardino** (☎ 0577 28 30 48; Piazza San Francesco 9; admission €3; ☼ 10.30am-1.30pm & 3-5.30pm mid-Mar–Oct), notable for its frescoes by Il Sodoma and Beccafumi, plus a small museum of religious art.

Courses
LANGUAGE & CULTURE
Scuola Leonardo da Vinci (☎ 0577 24 90 97; www .scuolaleonardo.com; Via del Paradiso 16) A reputable Italian-language school that offers supplementary cultural – and even culinary – options.

Società Dante Alighieri (☎ 0577 4 95 33; www .dantealighieri.com; Via Tommaso Pendola 37) Offers courses in Italian language and culture.
Università per Stranieri (University for Foreigners; ☎ 0577 24 01 15; www.unistrasi.it; Via di Pantaneto 45) Offers various courses in Italian language and culture.

MUSIC
Accademia Musicale Chigiana (☎ 0577 2 20 91; www.chigiana.it; Via di Città 89) Offers classical music courses every summer as well as seminars and concerts performed by visiting musicians, teachers and students as part of the Settimana Musicale Senese (below).
Associazione Siena Jazz (☎ 0577 27 14 01; www .sienajazz.it; Piazza Libertà) Within the Fortezza Medicea. One of Europe's foremost institutions of its type, it offers courses in jazz.

Tours
Ecco Siena (☎ 0577 4 32 73) Runs city tours for groups and individuals. Group tours (€15, Monday to Saturday between March and October) take around two hours and leave from outside the San Domenico Church at 3pm. Reserve at Siena Hotels Promotion (p212).
Treno Natura (☎ 0577 20 74 13; www.ferrovie turistiche.it; ☼ May, early Jun, Sep & Oct) A great way to see the stunning scenery of the Crete Senese, south of Siena. The line dates back to the 19th century but trains now run exclusively for tourists and staffed by volunteers. The route loops from Siena, through Asciano, across to the Val d'Orcia and Stazione di Monte Antico and back to Siena. Trains stop at Asciano and Monte Antico and connect with the service from Florence. They only run for about 20 days a year so check the website or ask at the tourist office. Round-trip tickets cost €15 if you go by diesel, €25 if it's a steam train.

Festivals & Events
Estate Musicale Chigiana The Accademia Musicale Chigiana (above) mounts this event in July, August and September. Concerts in the series are frequently held in the magnificent settings of the Abbazia di San Galgano (p217), about 20km southwest of the city and Abbazia di Sant'Antimo (p230), near Montalcino. For information, call ☎ 0577 2 20 91.
Festa di Santa Cecilia In November a series of concerts and exhibitions takes place to honour Cecilia, patron saint of musicians.
Il Palio (see p212) The most spectacular event on the Sienese calendar, held in July and August each year.
Settimana Musicale Senese Held in July and also run by the Accademia Musicale Chigiana.
Siena Jazz In July and August the city hosts this international festival promoted by the Associazione Siena Jazz (above) with concerts at the Fortezza Medicea and various sites throughout the city.

CENTRAL TUSCANY

IL PALIO

This spectacular event, held twice yearly on 2 July and 16 August in honour of the Virgin Mary, dates back to the Middle Ages and features a series of colourful pageants, a wild horse race around Piazza del Campo and much eating, drinking and celebrating in the streets.

Il Palio is one of very few major medieval spectacles of its type in Italy that has survived through the sheer tenacity of Sienese traditionalism. Most other displays of medieval folk tradition have in fact been brought back to life in the 20th century out of a combination of nostalgia and the urge to earn a few more tourist bucks. The Sienese place incredible demands on the national TV network, RAI, for rights to televise the event.

Ten of Siena's 17 town districts, or *contrade,* compete for the coveted *palio,* a silk banner. Each has its own traditions, symbol and colours, and its own church and *palio* museum. As you wander the streets you'll notice the various flags and plaques delineating these quarters, each with a name and symbol relating to an animal. On the downside, competition is so fierce that fist fights sometimes break out between *contrade* and Il Palio jockeys often live in fear from rival *contrade.* Scheming rivals have been known to ambush jockeys and even drug their horses.

On festival days Piazza del Campo becomes a racetrack, with a ring of packed dirt around its perimeter. From about 5pm, representatives of each *contrada* parade in historical costume, each bearing their individual banners.

The race is run at 7.45pm in July and 7pm in August. For not much more than one exhilarating minute, the 10 horses and their bareback riders tear three times around Piazza del Campo with a speed and violence that makes your hair stand on end.

Even if a horse loses its rider it is still eligible to win and, since many riders fall each year, it is the horses in the end who are the focus of the event. There is only one rule: riders mustn't interfere with the reins of other horses.

Book well in advance for a room and join the crowds in the centre of Piazza del Campo at least four hours before the start for a good view. Surrounding streets are closed off well before the race begins, except for Via Giovanni Dupré, which stays open right up until the flag drops. If you arrive late you can try your luck reaching the Piazza via this street – but don't count on it as everyone else has the same idea. If you prefer a more comfortable seat overlooking the race from one of the buildings lining the piazza, ask in the cafés and shops. They're as rare as hen's teeth but, if you do manage to find one, expect to pay around €220 for the privilege. If you can't find a good vantage point, don't despair – the race is televised live and then repeated throughout the evening on TV.

If you happen to be in town in the few days immediately preceding the race, you may get to see the jockeys and horses trying out in Piazza del Campo – almost as good as the real thing.

Sleeping

The tourist office has lists of accommodation and will also make reservations free of charge for *affittacamere* (rooms for rent) and hotels of three stars and above. You can also book in person (€2 administration charge) or online through **Siena Hotels Promotion** (☎ 0577 28 80 84; www.hotelsiena.com; Piazza San Domenico 5; ☽ 9am-8pm Mon-Sat Mar-Oct, 9am-7pm Mon-Sat Nov-Feb), near the San Domenico church

Accommodation can be difficult to find in summer – and is nearly impossible during the famous twice-yearly festival, Il Palio.

BUDGET

Hotel Le Tre Donzelle (☎ /fax 0577 22 39 33; Via delle Donzelle 5; s/d €33/46, d with bathroom €60) Central,

friendly and popular, this hotel was originally constructed as a tavern in the 13th century. Rooms are clean and simple and the shared bathrooms are spotless.

Ostello Guidoriccio (☎ 0577 5 22 12; Via Fiorentina 89, Località Stellino; per person €13.50) All rooms are doubles at Siena's HI-affiliated youth hostel, about 2km northwest of the city centre. Take bus No 10, 15 or 35 from Piazza Gramsci, or No 4 or 77 from the train station.

Siena Colleverde (☎ 0577 28 00 44; Via Scacciapensieri 47; per person/pitch €7.75/7.75; ☽ mid-Apr–mid-Oct; ☒) This is a good camp site 2km north of the historical centre. To get there take bus No 3 or No 8 from Piazza Gramsci or Viale Tozzi.

MIDRANGE

Locanda Garibaldi (☎ 0577 28 42 04; Via Giovanni Dupré 18; d €75, menu €20, mains €7-9) This place is brilliantly located, just south of Piazza del Campo. Its seven rooms are big, bright and furnished with flair; the whole place has an individual, funky feel. The twinkly eyed, jovial host and his wife also run the well-patronised ground-floor restaurant (closed Saturday).

Albergo Bernini (☎ 0577 28 90 47; www.albergo bernini.com; Via della Sapienza 15; s with bathroom €78, d with/without bathroom €82/62) This is a welcoming, family-run hotel (owner Mauro is a professional accordion player who often squeezes his box for guests). Its tiny terrace has views across to the cathedral and the Chiesa di San Domenico. For space and views, choose room No 11. Reservations are essential from April to October.

Piccolo Hotel Etruria (☎ 0577 28 80 88; www.hotel etruria.com; Via delle Donzelle 3; s/d/tr €50/80/105; ✖) Another equally welcoming family hotel, just off Il Campo. The air-con whooshing into its large, pleasant, rooms is a plus in summer and there's a central light, airy sitting area.

Albergo Cannon d'Oro (☎ 0577 4 43 21; www.can nondoro.com; Via dei Montanini 28; s/d €75/95; P ✖) Trim, attractive and excellent value. Don't be deterred by the golden cannon (the very one that gave the place its name) trained upon you as you debouch from a narrow alley to face the otherwise amicable reception desk. A few rooms have air-con and parking costs €15.

Hotel Antica Torre (☎ 0577 22 22 55; anticatorre@ email.it; Via Fieravecchia 7; d €113; ✖) With only eight rooms you'll need to reserve weeks in advance. Bathrooms are scarcely large enough to swing a flannel, but this snug place, all exposed beams and brickwork, tucked into a 16th-century tower and hidden down a side street, is a jewel. Haul yourself to the top floor for the best views.

Albergo-Residence Borgo Grondaie (☎ 0577 33 25 39; www.borgogrondaie.com; Via delle Grondaie 15; s/d incl breakfast €100/140, 6-person apartments €209; P ✖ ⚐) A couple of kilometres north of the centre, is a former farm that still produces olive oil. Rooms are simple and tasteful, with lots of terracotta and earthy colours. The exquisite apartments are in the former stables. There is a special-needs unit, saltwater pool and free bicycles for guests.

Chiusarelli (☎ 0577 28 05 62; www.chiusarelli.com; Viale Curtatone 15; s/d incl breakfast €80/120; P ✖ ⚐) Functioning continuously since its construction in 1870, this hotel has a pleasant, spacious breakfast room and bedrooms are attractive. The rear ones are for lovers of quiet and lucky football fans – they overlook the stadium where Siena, regularly propping up Serie A, play home matches, on alternate Sundays in season. It has a vast, popular restaurant where you'll be dodging elbows to find a seat among the locals.

TOP END

Grand Hotel Continental (☎ 0577 5 60 11; www.royal demeure.com; Banchi de Sopra 85; s/d from €215/360) Siena's only five-star hotel has recently taken over the gloriously ornate, richly frescoed Palazzo Gori Pannilini. If nothing else, poke your nose into the magnificent 1st floor reception room and award yourself a drink in the stylish ground-floor wine bar, open to all comers.

Hotel Santa Caterina (☎ 0577 22 11 05; www.hsc siena.it; Via Piccolomini 7; s/d incl breakfast up to €105/155; P ✖) This renovated 18th-century elegant villa, just outside the city walls, is a stone's throw beyond the Porta Romana. It's a tranquil haven: rooms are tastefully furnished, the breakfast room is light and airy and there's a lovely garden with open views to the surrounding hills. Parking is €12.

Villa Scacciapensieri (☎ 0577 4 14 41; www.villa scacciapensieri.it; Via Scacciapensieri 10; s/d incl breakfast from €116/185; P ✖ ⚐) Around 2.5km north of Siena is a 19th-century villa with carved wooden ceilings, oil paintings, antiques, formal gardens and an old family chapel. There are tennis courts and bicycles to rent.

AUTHOR'S CHOICE

Pensione Palazzo Ravizza (☎ 0577 28 04 62; www.palazzoravizza.it; Pian dei Mantellini 34; s/d/ tr incl breakfast from €130/160/220; P ✖ ⚐) *Pensione* is far too modest a title for this intimate, tranquil, truly sumptuous place. An easy walk from the heart of the action, it occupies a delightful Renaissance palazzo with frescoed ceilings and carefully selected antique furniture. Service is courteous and efficient, there's a small, leafy garden and their Ristorante il Capriccio is worth crossing town for.

Eating

According to the Sienese, most Tuscan cuisine has its origins here, though Tuscans elsewhere may well dispute such boasting. Among many traditional dishes are *ribollita* (a rich vegetable soup), *panzanella* (summer salad of soaked bread, basil, onion and tomatoes), *pappardelle con sugo di lepre* (ribbon pasta moistened with hare ragù) and the juicy charcoal-grilled beef steaks of the Chianina. *Panforte* (literally, strong bread) is a rich cake of almonds, honey and candied fruit, originally created as sustenance for Crusaders to the Holy Land.

BUDGET

Trattoria La Torre (☎ 0577 28 75 48; Via di Salicotto 7-9; mains €6.50-10, menu turistico €20; ☺ closed Thu) This intimate family-run place with only 10 tables and a vaulted cellar is just off Il Campo. The food is rustled up in full view of diners. There's fresh, homemade pasta and portions in general are formidable; keep space for one of the delightful homemade desserts.

Il Carroccio (☎ 0577 4 11 65; Via del Casato di Sotto 32; pasta €6.50-7, mains €12-15; ☺ closed Tue dinner & Wed) This restaurant does exceptional pasta. Try the *pici*, a kind of thick spaghetti typical of Siena, followed by the *tegamate di maiale* (pork with fennel seeds) and select something a little special from the long and carefully nurtured wine list. The restaurant is a member of the Slow Food movement (see p62) – always a good sign.

Osteria da Cice (☎ 0577 28 80 26; Via San Pietro 32; mains €7-11.50, tourist menu €12; ☺ Tue-Sun) In the hands of a friendly team, reflecting its mainly youthful clientele, this is the place for an informal, relaxed meal. The menu has plenty of vegetarian options among its *primi piatti*.

Nannini (Banchi di Sopra 22) Always crowded, this is something of a Sienese institution, baking its finest cakes and serving good coffee with speed and panache.

MIDRANGE

Osteria Le Logge (☎ 0577 4 80 13; Via dei Porrione 33; mains €15-18; ☺ Mon-Sat) This place changes its menu of creative Tuscan cuisine almost daily. In the downstairs dining room, once a pharmacy, bottles are arrayed in cases, floor to ceiling, like books in a library (there are over 18,000 more in the cellars so you won't go thirsty); there's also a large street side terrace.

Ristorante il Capriccio (☎ 0577 28 17 57; Pian de Mantellini 32; mains €9-16; ☺ Thu-Tue) The restaurant of Pensione Palazzo Ravizza (p213) offers fine cuisine and the chance to eat in its wood-panelled dining room or outside in the wonderful garden.

Osteria Castelvecchio (☎ 0577 4 95 86; Via di Castelvecchio 65; mains €9.50, menu €25; ☺ Mon-Sat) Highly regarded by locals, this eatery has a couple of attractive bare-brick rooms. Rumbling tummies should opt for the constantly changing *menù degustazione* (€25). It's also a good spot for veggies, with at least four meatless dishes normally on offer.

Al Marsili (☎ 0577 4 71 54; Via del Castoro 3; mains €11-17; ☺ Tue-Sun) One of the city's classiest restaurants, here you'll find white-smocked waiters dishing up traditional Sienese cuisine like *pici alla casareccia* (fresh Sienese pasta, like thick spaghetti, with a meat and mushroom sauce). The restaurant also offers more innovative dishes such as gnocchi in a duck sauce.

Antica Osteria da Divo (☎ 0577 28 43 81; Via Franciosa 29; mains €16-19; ☺ Sun-Fri) Here you'll find background jazz that's as smooth as the walls are rough-hewn. At the lower, cellar level you're dining amid Etruscan tombs. The inventive menu includes dishes like tarragon-scented lamb followed by girth-widening goodies such as vanilla and pistachio pie with raspberry sauce.

TOP END

Cane e Gatto (☎ 0577 28 75 45; Via Pagliaresi 6; menu €65; ☺ dinner only Fri-Wed) The name Dog & Cat might suggest that you're in for a pub lunch. Far from it. It's one of Siena's finest restaurants, with prices that reflect its quality. Avoid decision making by rolling with their regularly changing five-course menu or just pick a selection from it.

Drinking

Enoteca Italiana (☎ 0577 28 84 97; Fortezza Medicea; ☺ noon-1am Tue-Sat, noon-8pm Sun) Within the fortress walls, the former munition cellars have been artfully transformed into a classy *enoteca* that carries over 1500 labels. The Italian wine display includes some dusty *reservas*, the oldest dating back to 1944.

Among several pleasantly poky bars along Via di Pantaneto, **Caffè Hortensia** at No 95 is small, crowded and much favoured by students, both local and visiting.

Entertainment

As elsewhere in Italy, the big dance venues are generally well outside town.

Caffè del Corso (Bianchi di Sopra 25; 🖳) During the day, this is the place for an espresso and croissant. At night the action moves upstairs to the moody plum-coloured music bar.

Al Cambio (☎ 0577 22 05 81; Via di Pantaneto 48; ☻ closed Mon) One of the few dance spots in Siena where you can indulge in a little frenetic all-night air-punching.

Bombo (☎ 333 605 63 45; admission plus 1st drink €13) A popular *discoteca* in Monteroni d'Arbia, about 15km southeast of Siena on the SS2, that sometimes has live music at weekends.

Shopping

Via di Città is a chic shopping street where you can buy ceramics, food items, antiques, jewellery and so on. If you're after clothes, go window-shopping along Banchi di Sopra with its stylish boutiques and designer emporia.

Pizzicheria de Miccoli (☎ 0577 28 91 84; Via di Città 93-5) Richly scented, this is a great place to stock up on picnic fodder. Its windows are festooned with sausages, piled-up cheeses and porcini mushrooms by the sackful.

La Cantina in Piazza (Via del Casato di Sotto 24; ☻ closed afternoon Wed) This is a particularly well endowed wine shop, ideal for a special picnic or a case to lug home or have freighted.

Consorzio Agrario Siena (Via Pianagini 13) A rich emporium of local food and wines.

Siena Ricama (☎ 0577 28 83 38; Via di Città 61) Promotes the crafts of Siena, in particular embroidery.

Siena's **Wednesday market** (☻ 7.30am-1pm) spreads all around Fortezza Medicea and seeps towards the Stadio Comunale. One of Tuscany's largest, it's great for foodstuffs and cheap clothing, or just aimless browsing.

Getting There & Away
BUS

The hub for buses is Piazza Gramsci. Tra-in and SITA express buses race up to Florence (€6.50, 1¼ hours, up to 30 daily). Other regional Tra-in destinations include San Gimignano (€5.20, 1¼ hours, 10 daily either direct or changing in Poggibonsi), Montalcino (€3.25, 1½ hours, six daily), Poggibonsi (€3.60, one hour, up to 10 daily), Montepulciano (€4.45, 1¾ hours) and Colle di Val d'Elsa (€2.50, 30 minutes,

hourly), with connections for Volterra. Other destinations in the Crete Senese and Chianti area include San Quirico d'Orcia (€3), Pienza (€3.40) and Grosseto (€5.60).

SENA buses run to/from Rome (€17.50, three hours, eight daily) and Milan (€25, 4¼ hours, three daily) and there are seven buses daily to Arezzo (€5, 1½ hours).

Both **Tra-in** (☎ 0577 20 42 46) and **Sena** (☎ 0577 28 32 03; www.sena.it) have ticket offices underneath the piazza, where there's also a left-luggage office.

CAR & MOTORCYCLE

For Florence take the SS2, the *superstrada*, or the more attractive SS222, also known as the Chiantigiana, which meanders its way through the hills of Chianti.

TRAIN

Siena isn't on a major train line and buses are generally a better alternative. By train, change at Chiusi for Rome and at Empoli for Florence. Trains arrive at Piazza F Rosselli, north of the city centre.

Getting Around
BICYCLE & SCOOTER

Perozzi Noleggi (☎ 0577 28 83 87; Via dei Gazzani 16-18) rents mountain bikes (per day/week €10/50) and 50cc scooters (per day/week €26/150). If there's no one in the showroom, pop round the corner to Via del Romitorio 5.

BUS

Tra-in operates city bus services (€0.90). Bus Nos 8, 9 and 10 run between the train station and Piazza Gramsci.

CAR & MOTORCYCLE

Cars are banned from the town centre, though visitors can drop off luggage at their hotel, then get out. Don't park illegally inside the city walls or around its gates; you'll be towed away quicker than you can yell 'Where the *&@!'s my car?'. There are large car parks at the Stadio Comunale and around the Fortezza Medicea, both just north of Piazza San Domenico. There's also another big one at Il Campo, south of the centre.

TAXI

For a taxi, call ☎ 0577 4 92 22.

CENTRAL TUSCANY

AROUND SIENA
Le Crete

Southeast of Siena, this area of rolling clay hills scored by steep ravines is a feast of classic Tuscan images – bare ridges topped by a solitary cypress tree and hills silhouetted one against another as they fade into the misty distance. The area of Le Crete changes colour according to the season – from the creamy violet of ploughed clay to the green of young wheat, which then turns to gold.

Hire a car or bike in Florence or Siena and spend a few days pottering around Le Crete, a word in the Tuscan dialect meaning clay. And should your visit coincide, book your passage on the spectacular Treno Natura (p211), which runs on certain days in summer.

ASCIANO

This pretty little hamlet has a trio of small museums dedicated to Sienese art and Etruscan finds in the area. It's most easily reached along the scenic SP438 road running southeast from Siena; the occasional slow local train from Siena also passes through. Asciano is at the heart of Le Crete, so the journey there and beyond (such as south to the Abbazia di Monte Oliveto Maggiore) is a treat in itself. There's a small **tourist office** (☎ 0577 71 88 11; Corso Matteotti 78; ⊙ core hr 10am-1pm & 4-6pm Tue-Sat, 10am-1pm Sun Apr-Oct, 10am-1pm & 3-6pm Fri, Sat, 10am-1pm Sun Nov-Mar).

ABBAZIA DI MONTE OLIVETO MAGGIORE

This 14th-century **monastery** (☎ 0577 70 76 11; admission free; ⊙ 9.15am-noon & 3.15-6pm Apr-Oct, to 5pm Nov-Mar) is still a retreat for around 40 monks. It's famous for the frescoes in its Great Cloister by Signorelli and Il Sodoma, illustrating events in the life of the ascetic St Benedict.

The fresco cycle begins with Il Sodoma's work on the west wall, to the right of the entrance, and continues along the south wall of the cloisters. The nine frescoes by Signorelli line the east side and Il Sodoma picks up again on the northern wall. The decorations on the pillars between some of Il Sodoma's frescoes are among the earliest examples of 'grotesque' art, copied from decorations found in the then newly excavated Domus Aurea of Nero in Rome.

The baroque interior of the **church** adjoining the cloister is a pleasingly sober play of

perspective and shape. It has further works by Il Sodoma and some wonderfully intricate marquetry choir stalls.

From the monastery, head for **San Giovanni d'Asso**, where there's an interesting 11th-century church with a Lombardic-Tuscan façade, and a picturesque hamlet with the remains of a castle. Continue on to Montisi and the pretty village of **Castelmuzio**, its entrance lined with chestnut trees, to take a look at the 16th-century **Chiesa di Santa Maria** with its Romanesque Gothic façade. Along a side road just outside Castelmuzio is the abandoned **Pieve di Santo Stefano in Cennano**, a 13th-century church.

Opened in 2001, **La Locanda della Moscadella** (☎ 0577 66 53 10; www.lamoscadella.it; Castelmuzio; d from €95) is a former 16th-century farmhouse that has been artfully resurrected as a secluded hotel, restaurant and wine bar with sublime views.

Around 2km past Castelmuzio on the road to Pienza is the 14th-century monastery of **Sant'Anna in Camprena** (☎ 0578 74 80 37), one of the settings for the film *The English Patient*, with some lovely frescoes by Il Sodoma in the **refectory** (admission free; ⊙ 9.30am-12.30pm & 3-6pm mid-Mar–Oct).

The route from Monte Oliveto Maggiore to Pienza runs almost entirely along a high ridge, offering great views of Le Crete.

BUONCONVENTO

On first approaching Buonconvento down the SS2 highway, you could be forgiven for thinking it a large roadside rest stop. Lying perfectly flat in a rare stretch of plain, the low-slung fortified walls of this farming centre hide a quiet little town of medieval origins. One of its historical moments came when the Holy Roman Emperor Henry VII, having shortly before captured the town, died here in August 1313 and so put an end to any hopes the Empire might have had of reasserting direct control over Tuscany.

The **Museo della Mezzadria Senese** (☎ 0577 80 90 75; Via Tinaia del Taja; ⊙ 10am-6pm Tue-Sun), with its lifesize figures and antique farm tools and machinery, offers a multimedia presentation of what life was like living off the land until quite recently.

You might want to slip into the local **Museo d'Arte Sacra** (☎ 0577 80 71 90; Via Soccini 18; adult/child €3.50/free; ⊙ 10am-1pm & 2.30-6pm

CENTRAL TUSCANY

Tue-Sun Apr-Sep, 10am-1pm & 3-5pm Sat & Sun Oct-Mar). It contains religious art collected in the town and from neighbouring churches and hamlets.

Abbazia di San Galgano & Around

ABBAZIA DI SAN GALGANO

About 20km southwest of Siena on the SS73 is the ruined 13th-century **San Galgano abbey** (☎ 0577 75 67 00; admission free; ⏰ 8am-7.30pm), one of the country's finest Gothic buildings in its day and now a ruin that still speaks strongly of its past. The monks of this former Cistercian abbey were among Tuscany's most powerful, forming the judiciary and acting as accountants for the *comuni* of Volterra and Siena. They presided over disputes between the cities, played a significant role in the construction of the cathedral in Siena and built themselves an opulent church.

As early as the 14th century, Sir John Hawkwood, the feared English mercenary, sacked the abbey on at least two occasions. By the 16th century the monks' wealth and importance had declined and the church had deteriorated to the point of ruin, and in 1786 the bell tower simply collapsed, as did the ceiling vaults a few years later.

The great, roofless, stone and brick monolith stands silent in the fields. Come on a rainy winter's day and you feel more like you are in France or England, surrounded by glistening green fields and confronted by this grey ruin, its style strongly reminiscent of French Gothic architecture.

Next door to the church are what remain of the monastery buildings, as well as a brief stretch of cloister housing a small **tourist office** (☎ 0577 75 67 38; ⏰ 10.30am-7pm Easter-Oct).

The Accademia Musicale Chigiana in Siena sponsors concerts at the abbey during summer (see p211).

On a hill overlooking the abbey is the tiny, round Romanesque **Cappella di Monte Siepi**. This is the site of the original Cistercian settlement – from it came the impulse to build the great abbey below. Inside the chapel are badly preserved frescoes by Ambrogio Lorenzetti depicting the life of local soldier and saint, San Galgano, who had a vision of St Michael on this site and lived his last years here as a hermit. A real-life 'sword in the stone' is under glass in the floor of the chapel, plunged there, legend has it, by San Galgano to indicate his renunciation of worldly life.

The bus service between Siena and Massa Marittima passes nearby.

BAGNI DI PETRIOLO

About halfway along the SS223 highway between Siena and Grosseto, a side road leads down to the hot sulphur springs of **Bagni di Petriolo**. Steaming spring water cascades into a few small natural basins. Anyone can come and sit in them, and there's usually a motley assortment of permanent campers making use of the natural shower.

Val d'Elsa

MONTERIGGIONI

This famous walled medieval stronghold is just off the SS2, about 12km north of Siena.

First raised in 1203 as a forward defensive position against Florence, the walls and towers today are the most complete example of such a fortified bastion in Tuscany. Seven of the 14 towers were reconstructed in the 20th century but you have to peer pretty closely to make out which ones. According to descriptions by Dante – a writer not averse to a little hyperbole – they were considerably higher when the Florentines had reason to fear them and their Sienese defenders.

Monteriggioni has real charm but it's in danger of being over-heritaged to appeal to the tsunami of tourists that flows in each summer day.

Hotel Monteriggioni (☎ 0577 30 50 09; www.hotel monteriggioni.net; Via Primo Maggio 4; s/d €110/220; P ⚹ ⚹) was originally two stone houses, now fused together. The interior is lavishly decorated with antiques, and all rooms have picture-postcard views. There's the added perk of a small pool within the lovely gardens, bordered by the original city walls. The hotel is open between March and December.

Ristorante Il Pozzo (☎ 0577 30 41 27; Piazza Roma 2; menu around €35; ⏰ closed Sun dinner & Mon) is on the main square and passed daily by invading hordes but 'The Well' retains its individuality and character, offering delicious food, including homemade desserts and its legendary crêpes Suzette. There's a pleasant patio for dining alfresco.

COLLE DI VAL D'ELSA

pop 19,800

All that most visitors do here is change buses for Volterra. That's a shame because Colle has long been Italy's major centre for fine

---

NAILING THE NAIL

There are some 30 reputedly authentic nails from the one true cross around Tuscany. But Colle di Val d'Elsa's has a special distinction. Brought back from the Holy Land during the Crusades, so the story goes, it was given to a local priest, who placed it in the town's otherwise quite unremarkable cathedral. It disappeared or was stolen several times (on one occasion washed downstream by spring floods) but always made its independent way back.

Nowadays it undergoes a degree of protection worthy of Fort Knox. Under lock and key – actually four locks with four differing keys held by four different citizens – it's only allowed out of the cathedral once a year, on the second Sunday of September, when it's taken in procession around Colle Alta in, appropriately, a finely wrought crystal vessel.

---

glass and crystal production and, unburdened by any notable church, museum or work of art, the place has kept its character as a rural market town. The old one-street town up on its hill is fun for its own sake and for the views. Down below, the **Friday market** in and around Piazza Arnolfo is a vast bustling affair selling everything from great wheels of cheese to frilly knickers.

The larger of its two **tourist offices** (☎ 0577 92 13 34; Piazza Arnolfo 9; ❧ 11am-5pm) is in the main square of **Colle Bassa**, the lower town. Between March and October, it offers a **crystal tour** (€20) with visits to glass blowing, shaping, cutting and engraving workshops and crystal showrooms.

The most engaging part of town is historic **Colle Alta**, perched up on a ridge. From Piazza Arnolfo, it's a 10-minute uphill walk on Via San Sebastiano. Alternatively, park near Porta Nova at the western end of town. It's still a 10-minute walk, but a flat one.

At the eastern end of Via del Castello, the only real street, there's a medieval *casa torre* (tower house; No 63), birthplace of Arnolfo di Cambio, architect of Florence's Palazzo Vecchio. Piazza del Duomo, overshadowed by the cathedral's bell tower with its giant clock, is about halfway along.

Nearby are three small museums. Admission to each costs €3 or you can buy a combined ticket (€6). The **Museo Archeologic** (☎ 0577 92 29 54; Piazza Duomo 42; ❧ 10.30am-12.30pr & 4.30-7.30pm Tue-Sun May-Oct, 3.30-6.30pm Tue-Sur 10am-noon Sat & Sun Nov-Apr) is on the square. Th **Museo Civico** and **Museo d'Arte Sacra** (☎ 0577 9 38 88; Via del Castello 31; ❧ 10.30am-12.30pm & 4.30 7.30pm Tue-Sun May-Oct, 3.30-6.30pm Tue-Sun, 10am-noo Sat & Sun Nov-Apr) share premises. Most interesting is the Museo d'Arte Sacra, with some worthwhile paintings by Sienese masters.

In Colle Bassa you'll find the **Museo de Cristallo** (☎ 0577 92 41 35; Via dei Fossi 8a; admissio €3; ❧ 10.30am-12.30pm & 4.30-7.30pm Tue-Sun May Oct, 3.30-6.30pm Tue-Sun, 10am-noon Sat & Sun Nov-Apr) which illustrates the history and production of crystal and displays some stunning pieces (leave your toddler at home).

Hotel Arnolfo (☎ 0577 92 20 20; www.hotelarnolfo .it; Via Campana 8; s/d €53/75) is the only hotel in the historic part of town and has 10 comfortable, sizable rooms. The hotel is closed in February.

La Vecchia Cartiera (☎ 0577 92 11 07; Via Oberdan 5-9; s/d incl buffet breakfast €91/109; P ✸) was once just that. But The Old Papermill has been so comprehensively overhauled that you'd scarcely guess it. This hotel has all the extras and is well situated for an overview of the town's Friday market. The multilingual owner is a charmer and the breakfast buffet more lavish than most. Parking costs €7.

Hourly buses run to/from Siena (€2.50, 30 minutes) and Florence (€4.70, 1¼ hours) Up to four CPT connecting buses head west to Volterra daily, except Sunday.

CASOLE D'ELSA & AROUND

Casole d'Elsa, a quiet fortified backwater, was a key part of Siena's western defences against Volterra and Florence during the Middle Ages. Little remains to detain you but those with romantic tastes and a Swiss bank account could stick to the tiny road that winds south out of town, call by pretty hilltop **Mensano**, then swing east to **Pievescola**.

Relais La Suvera (☎ 0577 96 03 00; www.lasuvera .it; Pievescola; d €360-560, ste €480-880; ❧ mid-Apr–Oct; P ✸) is a 12th-century former fortress and palace, still run by the Marchese Ricci family. The décor is heavily brocaded opulence with tapestries, dark and enormous oil paintings, rococo mirrors and four-poster beds. There is a brand-new health centre with a Jacuzzi bubbling out of the palace's original well.

Il Colombaio (☎ 0577 94 90 02; Località Il Colombaio; mains around €18; ✷ closed Tue lunch & Mon), opposite vineyards with a distant view of Casole, is an elegant place with stained glass and paintings. It also takes its wines seriously – 1400 varieties at last count, including Japanese, Israeli and a Bodegas Vega Sicilia '90 for €500. The menu includes such goodies as quail salad and *pecorino* cheese soufflé with pear slices in chestnut honey sauce. They also have apartments to rent.

POGGIBONSI
pop 27,500
WWII managed to take care of what little was interesting about Poggibonsi, which takes line honours as one of the ugliest places in central Tuscany. If you're travelling by bus between Florence (€4.30, 50 minutes, half-hourly) or Siena (€3.60, one hour, up to 10 daily), heading for San Gimignano or Volterra, you can't avoid the place.

Ambassador Hotel (☎ 0577 98 29 22; www.toscana -ambassador.it; s/d €120/160; ⓟ ✷) is a glossy, fairly bland hotel, well placed for a quick getaway, that has all the extras, including satellite TV and shoe polish.

SAN GIMIGNANO
pop 7150
As you crest the hill coming from the east, the 14 towers of this walled town look like a medieval Manhattan. And when you arrive you might well feel that half of Manhattan's population has moved in. Within easy reach of both Siena and Florence, San Gimignano is a tourist magnet. Come in winter or early spring to indulge your imagination a little; in summer you'll spend your time dodging fellow visitors. Even then though, you'll discover a different, almost peaceful San Gimignano, once the last bus has pulled out.

There's good reason for such popularity. The towers, which once numbered 72, were symbols of the power and wealth of the city's medieval families. San Gimignano delle Belle Torri (meaning 'of the Fine Towers' – though they're actually almost devoid of design and rather dull unless sheer height impresses you) is surrounded by lush, productive land and the setting is altogether enchanting.

History
Originally an Etruscan village, the town was named after the bishop of Modena, San Gimignano, who is said to have saved the city from Attila the Hun. It became a *comune* in 1199, but fought frequently with neighbouring Volterra. Internal battles between Ardinghelli (Guelph) and Salvucci (Ghibelline) families over the next two centuries caused deep divisions. Most towers were built during this period – in the 13th century, one *podestà* (town chief) forbade the building of towers higher than his own 51m pile.

In 1348 plague wiped out much of the population and weakened the nobles' power, leading to the town's submission to Florence in 1353. Today, not even the plague would deter the summer swarms.

Orientation
Piazzale dei Martiri di Montemaggio, at the southern end of the town, lies just outside the medieval wall and next to the main gate, the Porta San Giovanni. Via San Giovanni heads northwards to central Piazza della Cisterna and the connecting Piazza del Duomo. From here the other major thoroughfare, Via San Matteo, extends to the principal northern gate, Porta San Matteo.

Information
Post office (Piazza delle Erbe 8)
Tam Tam (☎ 0577 90 71 00; Via XX Settembre 4b; per hr €6; ✷ 10am-7pm Apr-Oct, 2-7pm Nov-Feb)
Tourist office (☎ 0577 94 00 08; www.sangimignano .com in Italian; Piazza del Duomo 1; ✷ 9am-1pm & 3-7pm Mar-Oct, 9am-1pm & 2-6pm Nov-Feb) Hires out audioguides of town (€5).

Sights
Start in triangular Piazza della Cisterna, named after the 13th-century cistern at its centre. The square is lined with houses and towers from the 13th and 14th centuries. In the Piazza del Duomo, the Collegiata (cathedral) looks across to the late-13th-century

---

MONEYSAVERS
If you're an assiduous sightseer, two combined tickets may be worth your while. One (adult/child €7.50/5.50) gives admission to the Palazzo Comunale and its Museo Civico, the archaeological museum, Torre Grossa and some secondary sights. The other (adult/child €5.50/2.50) gets you into the Collegiata and nearby Museo d'Arte Sacra.

Palazzo del Podestà and its tower, the **Torre della Rognosa**. The Palazzo Comunale, right of the cathedral, is the town hall.

COLLEGIATA

Access to the town's Romanesque **cathedral** (adult/child €3.50/1.50; ⌚ 9.30am-7.30pm Mon-Sat, 12.30-5pm Sun Apr-Oct, 9.30am-5pm Mon-Sat, 12.30-5pm Sun Nov–mid-Jan & Mar) is up a flight of steps from Piazza del Duomo. Its bare façade belies the remarkable 14th-century frescoes that stripe the interior walls like some vast medieval comic strip, stretching amid the black-and-white striped arches and columns that separate the three naves.

A fresco by Taddeo di Bartolo covers the upper half of the rear wall and depicts the Last Judgment, while the lower half is dominated by Benozzo Gozzoli's rendering of the martyrdom of St Sebastian. Frescoes extend into the interior of the church, on the right side depicting *Paradiso* (Heaven) and on the left *Inferno* (Hell). Both are by Taddeo di Bartolo, who seems to have taken particular delight in presenting the horrors of the underworld. Remember that many of the faithful in those times would have taken such images pretty much at face value.

Along the left (north) wall are scenes from Genesis and the Old Testament by Bartolo di Fredi, dating from around 1367. The top row runs from the creation of the world through to the forbidden fruit scene. This in turn leads to the next level and

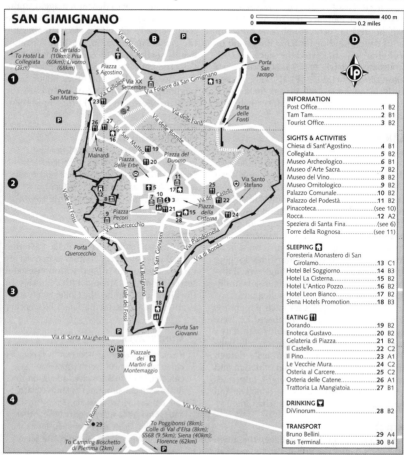

fresco, the expulsion of Adam and Eve from the Garden of Eden. Further scenes include Cain killing Abel, the story of Noah's ark and Joseph's coat. The last level picks up this story with the tale of Moses leading the Jews out of Egypt, and the story of Job.

On the right (south) wall are scenes from the New Testament by Barna da Siena, completed in 1381. Again, the frescoes are spread over three levels, starting in the six lunettes at the top. Commencing with the Annunciation, the panels proceed through episodes such as the Epiphany, the presentation of Christ in the temple and the massacre of the innocents on Herod's orders. The subsequent panels on the lower levels summarise the life and death of Christ, the Resurrection and so on. Some are in poor condition.

The **Cappella di Santa Fina**, off to the right, has a pair of naive and touching frescoes by Domenico Ghirlandaio depicting events in the life of the saint and a quite superb alabaster and marble altar picked out in gold.

MUSEO D'ARTE SACRA
Across the square, the **Museo d'Arte Sacra** (☎ 0577 94 03 16; Piazza Pecori 1; adult/child €3/1.50; ⊙ 9.30am-7.30pm Mon-Sat, 12.30-5pm Sun Apr-Oct, 9.30am-5pm Mon-Sat, 12.30-5pm Sun Nov–mid-Jan & Mar) has some fine works of religious art, in particular a collection of medieval painted wooden statues, culled, in the main, from the town's churches. One curiosity is Sebastiano Mainardi's *Il Volto Santo Adorato* on the ground floor, where two hooded figures, looking suspiciously like KKK members, kneel at the feet of a smartly-dressed Jesus on the cross.

PALAZZO COMUNALE
San Gimignano's other principal sight is this seat of secular power, founded in 1288, expanded in the 14th century and with a neogothic façade tacked on in the late 19th century.

From the internal courtyard climb the stairs to the **Pinacoteca** (☎ 0577 99 03 12; Piazza del Duomo; adult/child museum & tower €5/4; ⊙ 9.30am-7pm Mar-Oct, 10am-5pm Nov-Feb).

In the main room, the **Sala di Dante**, the great poet addressed the town's council, imploring it to join a Florentine-led Guelph League. You can't miss the *Maestà*, a masterful 1317 fresco by Lippo Memmi depicting the enthroned Virgin Mary and Christ child with angels and saints. Other frescoes

portray jousts, hunting scenes, castles and other medieval goings-on.

Upstairs, the collection of medieval religious works includes a Crucifix by Coppo di Marcovaldo and a pair of remarkable *tondi* (circular paintings) by Filippino Lippi.

Also on this level, there's a small frescoed room. Opinion is divided on what these frescoes, showing wedding scenes, are all about. It all looks like great fun, with the newlyweds taking a bath together and then hopping into the sack.

Climb up the palazzo's **Torre Grossa** for a spectacular view of the town and surrounding countryside.

MUSEO DEL VINO
At San Gimignano's recently opened **wine museum** (☎ 0577 94 12 67; Parco della Rocca; admission free; ⊙ 11am-7pm Thu-Mon, 3-7pm Wed Mar-Oct), just outside the town's fortress, a sommelier is on hand to lead an informed – and paying – tasting of some of the choice local white wines.

MUSEO ARCHEOLOGICO & SPEZIERA DI SANTA FINA
There are actually two **museums** (☎ 0577 94 03 48; Via Folgore da San Gimignano 11; adult/child both museums €3.50/2.50; ⊙ 11am-5.30pm mid-Mar–Dec) and a gallery in this complex. The Speziera section includes ceramic and glass storage vessels from the 16th-century Speziera di Santa Fina, a reconstructed 16th-century

---

VERNACCIA DI SAN GIMIGNANO
'It kisses, licks, bites, thrusts and stings.' That's how Michelangelo, clearly drawing upon the purple end of his palate, described San Gimignano's Vernaccia white wine. Smooth and aromatic with a slightly bitter aftertaste and pale golden yellow in colour, it was Italy's first DOC wine (see p64) and only the second white to be awarded DOCG status.

But these are only its most recent accolades. It's been around, though scarcely unsung, for centuries. Dante in his Divine Comedy banished Pope Martin IV to purgatory because of it, Boccaccio fantasised about flowing streams of cool Vernaccia, Pope Paul III reputedly bathed in it and the ever-demure Santa Caterina of Siena used it as medicine.

pharmacy and herb garden. Many are beautifully painted and still contain curative concoctions. Follow your nose to the second room, called 'the kitchen', which is filled with herbs and spices used for elixirs.

Beyond is a small archaeological museum divided into Etruscan/Roman and medieval sections with exhibits found locally.

The museum also houses a good modern art gallery that in itself merits a visit. Permanent works include the distinctive swirly abstracts of Renato Guttuso and some excellent oils on canvas by Raffaele de Grada.

OTHER SIGHTS

Just west of the Piazza del Duomo, the **Rocca** is the crumbling shell of the town's fortress with great views across the valley, a small playground – and not much else.

Due south of the fort is the **Museo Ornitologico** (☎ 0577 94 13 88; Via Quercecchio; adult/child €1.50/1; ☿ 11am-5.30pm Apr-Sep). Its mournful collection of stuffed birds dates back to 1886 and looks it.

At the northern end of the town is the **Chiesa di Sant'Agostino** (Piazza Sant'Agostino; ☿ 7am-noon & 3-7pm Apr-Oct, 7am-noon & 3-6pm Nov-Mar) with a Benozzo Gozzoli fresco cycle in the apse depicting the life of St Augustine.

Tours

If you'd prefer to sip your Vernaccia di San Gimignano on the spot, the tourist office organises vineyard visits (€26). Two-hour tours leave at 11am on Tuesday and 5pm on Thursday from June to October. Advance reservations are essential.

Sleeping

In high summer San Gimignano can be as unpromising for accommodation as Christmas Eve in Bethlehem. But a couple of organisations will help to find you a roof.

Siena Hotels Promotion (☎ 0577 94 08 09; www .hotelsiena.com; Via San Giovanni 125; ☿ closed Sun) will book hotels and some *affittacamere* via their website or for callers-in (€2 surcharge for the latter). The tourist office, for its part, will reserve a wider range of *affittacamere* and also *agriturismi* if you call by in person.

BUDGET

Camping Boschetto di Piemma (☎ 0577 94 03 52; www.boschettodipiemma.it; per car/tent/person €3/6.50/7.20;

☿ year-round) Located at Santa Lucia, 2km south of town, this is the nearest camp site. Buses stop right outside.

Foresteria Monastero di San Girolamo (☎ 0577 94 05 73; Via Folgore da San Gimignano 26-32; per person €25; [P]) Run by friendly Benedictine nuns, this is an excellent budget choice with basic but spacious, comfortable rooms, all sleeping two to five people and with a bathroom. If you don't have a reservation, arrive between 9.30am and 12.30pm or between 3.30pm and 5.30pm and ring the monastery bell (not the Foresteria one, which is never answered).

MIDRANGE

Hotel Bel Soggiorno (☎ 0577 94 03 75; www.hotelbel soggiorno.it; Via San Giovanni 91; d incl breakfast €95-120) With an upbeat décor, every room here is different, but each has lots of colour. Try to go for one with a countryside view. The restaurant has received rave reviews from readers. The hotel is closed in January and February.

Two highly recommended hotels flank Piazza della Cisterna, the main square. In both, you pay a little more for superb views.

Hotel La Cisterna (☎ 0577 94 03 28; www.hotel cisterna.it; Piazza della Cisterna 24; s/d/tr incl breakfast from €75/95/125; ☒ ☐) Located in a splendid 14th-century building with vaulted ceilings and chandeliers. A view of the square? Or vistas across the valley? You can take your pick. Nearly 100 years in business, it offers truly 21st-century comfort in quiet, spacious, comfortable rooms.

Hotel Leon Bianco (☎ 0577 94 12 94; www.leon bianco.com; Piazza della Cisterna 13; s/d/tr incl breakfast from €75/105/145; ☒ ☐) Faces Hotel La Cisterna across the square and also occupies a 14th-century mansion. This smoothly run hotel is equally welcoming and friendly with a pretty inner courtyard and breakfast patio.

Hotel L'Antico Pozzo (☎ 0577 94 20 14; www .anticopozzo.com; Via San Matteo 87; s/d/tr incl breakfast from €100/135/165; ☒ ☐) Named after the old softly illuminated *pozzo* (well), just off the lobby. Each room has its own personality, with thick stone walls, high ceilings, wrought-iron beds, frescoes, antique prints and peach-coloured walls. No 20 has a magnificent domed ceiling. The hotel is closed the first two weeks of November.

TOP END

Hotel La Collegiata (☎ 0577 94 32 01; www.lacollegiata
.it; Località Strada 27; s/d from €200/340; Ⓟ Ⓧ Ⓡ)
A serious money-no-object place, to get
here you'll need a car as it's outside town. A
former Franciscan convent, its formal gardens are magnificent and are surrounded
by parkland, while the rooms are conservative yet elegant.

Eating
BUDGET

Osteria al Carcere (☎ 0577 94 19 05; Via del Castello 5;
soup €6.20; Ⓨ closed Thu lunch & Wed) A fine *osteria* that offers great food at moderate prices.
The reassuringly brief menu has a half-dozen
soups, including *zuppa di farro e fagioli* (local
grain and white bean soup), a meal in itself.

Gelateria di Piazza (☎ 0577 94 22 44; Piazza della
Cisterna 4; Ⓨ Mar–mid-Nov) Looks modest but,
as the pictures around the wall attest, many
celebrities have closed their lips around one
of Gelateria di Piazza's rich ice creams ('all
the family thought the ice cream was delicious' attested one Tony Blair). Master
Sergio uses only the choicest ingredients:
pistachios from Sicily and cocoa from Vene-
zuela. There's a variant based on Vernaccia,
the local wine, and, if you want to be more
adventurous, saffron cream.

Each Thursday morning there's a **produce
market** (Piazza della Cisterna & Piazza del Duomo).

MIDRANGE

Trattoria La Mangiatoia (☎ 0577 94 15 28; Via Mainardi 5; mains €15; Ⓨ Wed-Mon Feb-Oct) A highly regarded trattoria serving tempting, regional
fare. With candles flickering and classical
music in the background, share it with that
special someone. Or hold hands after dark
on their delightful summer patio.

Le Vecchie Mura (☎ 0577 94 02 70; Via Piandornella
15; meals €25-30; Ⓨ dinner Wed-Mon) This is a wonderful spot, especially if you snap up a terrace table on a warm summer's night. The
food competes with the phenomenal view of
rolling green hills and the wine list has over
a dozen varieties of Vernaccia di San Gimignano. Choose from a delicious selection of
primi piatti such as *gnocchi con tartufo e formaggio* (gnocchi with truffles and cheese).
Book ahead to guarantee that panorama.

Enoteca Gustavo (☎ 0577 94 00 57; Via San Matteo 29; snacks & wine from €2.10; Ⓨ Sat-Thu) There
isn't much elbow space inside, so go for

one of the outside tables if you can. Snacks
include fat focaccias and a plate of cheese
with honey to go with your choice from
their impressive selection of wines.

Il Castello (☎ 0577 94 08 78; Via del Castello 20; mains
€11-15; Ⓨ Mar–mid-Jan) Both wine bar and restaurant, this place has a delightful patio with
views. Most dishes are macho-meaty, like
bistecca alla fiorentina (grilled T-bone steak)
and *cinghiale alla sangimignanese con polenta*
(wild boar with polenta and tomato salad).

Osteria delle Catenae (☎ 0577 94 19 66; Via Mainardi
18; menù degustazione €20, mains €15; Ⓨ closed Wed &
mid-Dec–Feb) This isn't what you'd term a modest little restaurant (windows are plastered
with the guidebook accolades its received).
But it's justified in having attitude. The brick-
barrelled interior is softly lit while the menu is
short, stylish and also heavy on strong meats –
hare, boar, duck and rabbit. Alongside many
Tuscan stalwarts, it also experiments – for
instance using saffron, a common spice in
medieval times, in *zuppa medievale*. The carrot and leek soufflé is sublime.

Il Pino (☎ 0577 94 04 15; Via Cellolese 8-10; mains
€14-16; Ⓨ Fri-Wed) The atmosphere here is
spruce, vaulted and airy, with fresh flowers on each table. Service is friendly and
attentive and the menu, including several
truffle-based specialities, can rival any in
town. The desserts, all confectioned on the
premises, are dinner's final temptation.

Dorando (☎ 0577 94 18 62; Vicolo dell'Oro 2; mains
€15-20; Ⓨ daily Easter-Oct, Tue-Sun Oct-Easter) Recognised by the Slow Food Movement (see
p62), Dorando runs a classic five-course

DETOUR: SAN GIMIGNANO TO VOLTERRA

Instead of driving the heavily trafficked
SS68 between San Gimignano and Volterra,
choose this back route that passes through
some stunning countryside and potential
picnic areas. Turn left out of the San Gimignano car park (just outside Porta San Giovanni). At 2.3km, just past the Hotel San
Michele, turn left again at the signpost to
Páncole and Castelfalfe. Carry on along this
road through green rolling valleys, wooded
areas and vineyards. At 6.8km beyond the
first turn, take a left (signed 'Volterra 15km').
After around 10km turn right for the final
stretch into town.

menu with dishes based on authentic Etruscan recipes like carrot dumplings with zucchini, and *pecorino* blue cheese with a puree of shallots. The atmosphere is swanky yet cool, with intimate corners and art work.

Drinking

DiVinorum (Piazza della Cisterna 30; 11am-midnight daily Mar-Oct, Fri-Sun Nov-Feb) Housed in cavernous former stables, is this cool wine bar run by local lads. In summer, sip your drink on the tiny outdoor terrace with stunning valley views.

Getting There & Around

BUS

Buses arrive in Piazzale dei Martiri di Montemaggio, beside Porta San Giovanni. Services run to/from Florence (€5.90, 1¼ hours, 12 daily) and Siena (€5.20, one to 1½ hours, 10 daily). A few are direct but most require a change at Poggibonsi. The tourist office carries timetables.

For Volterra (€4.30, 1½ hours, four daily except Sunday), you need to change in Colle di Val d'Elsa, and maybe also in Poggibonsi, which has the closest train station.

CAR & MOTORCYCLE

From Florence or Siena, take the SS2 to Poggibonsi, then the SS68 via Colle di Val d'Elsa. From Volterra, take the SS68 east and follow the turn-off signs north to San Gimignano.

There are car parks (per hour €2) outside the city walls, and beside and below Porta San Giovanni. There's free parking in the new parts of town, just northwest of the old centre.

Bruno Bellini (0577 94 02 01; Via Roma 41) rents mountain bikes (per day €15) and scooters (from per day €31).

VOLTERRA

pop 11,400

Straggling high on a rocky plateau, 29km southwest of San Gimignano, Volterra's well-preserved medieval ramparts give the windswept town a proud, forbidding air, while the gentle Tuscan countryside for miles around provides the perfect contrast.

History

The Etruscan settlement of Velathri was an important trading centre and senior partner of the Dodecapolis. It is believed that as many as 25,000 people lived here in its Etruscan heyday. Partly because of the surrounding inhospitable terrain, the city was among the last to succumb to Rome – it was absorbed into the Roman confederation around 260 BC and renamed Volaterrae.

The bulk of the old city was raised in the 12th and 13th centuries under a fiercely independent free *comune*. The city first entered into Florence's orbit in 1361, but it was some time before Florence took full control. When this domination was first threatened, Lorenzo il Magnifico made one of his few big mistakes and created lasting enemies in the people of Volterra; in 1472 he marched in and ruthlessly snuffed out every vestige of potential opposition to direct Florentine rule.

Since Etruscan times, Volterra has been a centre of alabaster extraction and workmanship. During the Middle Ages, its quarries lay fallow for several centuries until their soft, semitransparent, easily worked stone again became a popular material for sculpture during the Renaissance. To this day the city maintains a strong alabaster industry.

Orientation

Whichever of the four main gates you use to enter Volterra, the road will lead you to central Piazza dei Priori.

Information

Post office (Piazza dei Priori)

Tourist office (0588 8 72 57; www.volterratur.it; Piazza dei Priori 19-20; 9am-1pm & 2-7pm Apr-Oct, 10am-1pm & 2-6pm Nov-Mar) Offers a free hotel booking service and rents out a good town audioguide (1/2-4 persons €7/10).

Web & Wine (see p227) Web access costs €4 per hour.

Sights

PIAZZA DEI PRIORI & AROUND

Piazza dei Priori is ringed by austere medieval mansions. The 13th-century **Palazzo dei**

COMBINED TICKETS

An €8 ticket, valid for a year, covers visits to the Museo Etrusco Guarnacci, the Pinacoteca Comunale and the Museo Diocesano di Arte Sacra. A similar €2 ticket allows entry to both the Roman theatre and the seriously dilapidated Etruscan necropolis within the Parco Archeologico.

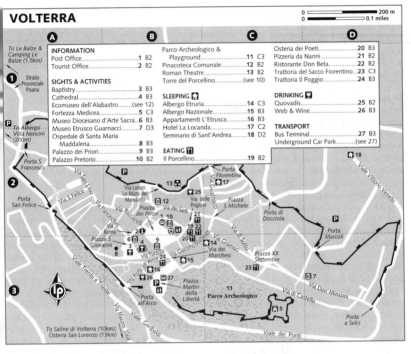

VOLTERRA

0 ———— 200 m
0 ———— 0.1 miles

INFORMATION
Post Office..................................1 B2
Tourist Office............................2 B2

SIGHTS & ACTIVITIES
Baptistry...................................3 B3
Cathedral...................................4 B3
Ecomuseo dell'Alabastro........(see 12)
Fortezza Medicea.......................5 C3
Museo Diocesano d'Arte Sacra..6 B3
Museo Etrusco Guarnacci.........7 D3
Ospedale di Santa Maria
   Maddalena.............................8 B3
Palazzo dei Priori.......................9 B3
Palazzo Pretorio........................10 B2

Parco Archeologico &
   Playground...........................11 C3
Pinacoteca Comunale...............12 B2
Roman Theatre..........................13 B2
Torre del Porcellino.............(see 10)

SLEEPING
Albergo Etruria.........................14 C3
Albergo Nazionale.....................15 B3
Appartamenti L'Etrusca.............16 B3
Hotel La Locanda......................17 C2
Seminario di Sant'Andrea..........18 D2

EATING
Il Porcellino.............................19 B2

Osteria dei Poeti......................20 B3
Pizzeria da Nanni......................21 B2
Ristorante Don Beta..................22 B2
Trattoria del Sacco Fiorentino...23 C3
Trattoria Il Poggio....................24 B3

DRINKING
Quovadis..................................25 B2
Web & Wine.............................26 B3

TRANSPORT
Bus Terminal............................27 B3
Underground Car Park..........(see 27)

Priori (Piazza dei Priori; admission €1; 10.30am-5.30pm daily mid-Mar–Oct, 10am-5pm Sat & Sun Nov–mid-Mar), the oldest seat of local government in Tuscany, is believed to have been a model for Florence's Palazzo Vecchio. Highlights are a fresco of the Crucifixion by Piero Francesco Fiorentino on the staircase, the magnificent cross-vaulted council hall and a small antechamber on the 1st floor giving a bird's-eye view of the piazza below.

The **Palazzo Pretorio** is from the same era. From it thrusts the **Torre del Porcellino** (Piglet's Tower), so named because of the wild boar protruding from its upper section.

The **cathedral** (Piazza San Giovanni; 8am-12.30pm & 3-6pm) was built in the 12th and 13th centuries. Highlights include a small fresco, the *Procession of the Magi* by Benozzo Gozzoli, behind a terracotta nativity group tucked away in the oratory at the beginning of the north aisle. An exquisite 15th-century tabernacle by Mino da Fiesole rises above the high altar. Laterally and overhead, the black-and-white marble banding and Renaissance coffered ceiling, gilded and gleaming, both make their mark.

Just west of the cathedral is the 13th-century **baptistry** with a small marble font by Andrea Sansovino. On the west side of Piazza San Giovanni the porticoed **Ospedale di Santa Maria Maddalena** was once a foundlings hospital. Nearby, the **Museo Diocesano d'Arte Sacra** (0588 8 62 90; Via Roma 1; 9am-1pm & 3-6pm mid-Mar–Oct, 9am-1pm Nov–mid-Mar) merits a peek for its collection of ecclesiastical vestments, gold reliquaries and works by Andrea della Robbia and Rosso Fiorentino.

The **Pinacoteca Comunale** (0588 8 75 80; Via dei Sarti 1; 9am-7pm mid-Mar–Oct, 8.30am-1.45pm Nov–mid-Mar), in the Palazzo Minucci Solaini, houses a modest collection of local, Sienese and Florentine art.

ECOMUSEO DELL'ALABASTRO

As befits a town that has hewn the precious rock from nearby quarries since Etruscan times, Volterra has its own **alabaster museum** (075 98 73 06; Via dei Sarti 1; admission €3; 11am-5pm daily mid-Mar–Oct, 9am-1.30pm Sat & Sun Nov–mid-Mar), which shares the same building as the Pinacoteca. On the ground floor are contemporary creations, including a finely chiselled mandolin and a bizarre fried egg, while on the two upper floors are choice examples from Etruscan times onwards and a re-created artisan's workshop. From the top floor windows, there are gorgeous views of the surrounding countryside.

MUSEO ETRUSCO GUARNACCI

In terms of content, this is one of Italy's finest **Etruscan museums** (☎ 0588 8 63 47; Via Don Minzoni 15; ⏱ 9am-7pm mid-Mar–Oct, 8.30am-1.45pm Nov–mid-Mar). Sadly, it's still very much old-style didactic in tone, badly labelled and stuffy. You really need to invest an extra €3 in the multilingual audioguide.

All exhibits were unearthed locally. They include a vast collection of some 600 funerary urns carved mainly from alabaster and tufa and displayed according to subject and period. Be selective; they all start to look the same after a while. The best examples (those dating from later periods) are on the 2nd and 3rd floors.

Original touches are the Ombra della Sera bronze *ex voto*, a strange, elongated nude figure that would fit harmoniously in any museum of modern art, and the urn of the Sposi, a terracotta rendering of an elderly couple, their wrinkled features depicted in portrait fashion rather than the usual stylised manner.

FORTEZZA MEDICEA & PARCO ARCHEOLOGICO

The 14th-century **Fortezza Medicea**, later altered by Lorenzo il Magnifico, is nowadays a prison (you can't enter unless you plan to stay for a while).

To its west is the pleasant **Parco Archeologico** (⏱ 8.30am-8pm May-Sep, 8.30am-5pm Oct-Apr), site of the ancient Acropolis. Little of archaeological interest has survived, apart from a few battered Etruscan tombs, but the park has swings and things for kids, and it's a good place for a picnic.

OTHER SIGHTS

On the city's northern edge is a **Roman theatre** (⏱ 10.30am-5.30pm daily mid-Mar–Oct, 10am-4pm Sat & Sun Nov–mid-Mar), a well-preserved complex, complete with a Roman bath house.

Le Balze, a deep, eroded limestone ravine about 2km northwest of the city centre, has claimed several churches since the Middle Ages as the buildings tumbled into its deep gullies. A 14th-century **monastery**, perched near the precipice, seems perilously close to continuing the tradition. To get there head out through Porta San Francesco, the city's northwestern gate, along Via San Lino and follow its continuation, Borgo Santo Stefano, then Borgo San Giusto.

Festivals & Events

On the third and fourth Sundays of August, the citizens of Volterra roll back the calendar some 600 years, take to the streets in period costume and celebrate **Volterra A.D. 1398** with gusto and all the fun of a medieval fayre.

Sleeping

Seminario di Sant'Andrea (☎ 0588 8 60 28; fax 0588 9 07 91; Viale Vittorio Veneto 2; d with/without bathroom €36/28; **P**) Still an active church retreat, this is a peaceful, if a mite dilapidated place with vaulted ceilings and 60 large, clean rooms. Open to all comers, it's a mere 600m or so from Piazza dei Priori, has free parking and makes an excellent budget choice.

Albergo Etruria (☎ 0588 87377; www.albergoetruria .it; Via Giacomo Matteotti 32; s/d €60/80) This is a pleasant, cosy hotel, recently taken over by two ladies with grand plans. Bathrooms have been freshly tiled and refurbished. Look for the remains of an Etruscan wall upstairs and savour the fine views from the roof garden – a genuine garden with lawns and bushes. The hotel is closed in January.

Albergo Nazionale (☎ 0588 8 62 84; www.albergo nazionalevolterra.it; Via dei Marchesi 11; s/d/tr €50/69/80) DH Lawrence once stayed in this late-19th-century hotel. Rooms vary in size and style and some have balconies; No 403, with a pair of them, is your best option. Meals in its summertime restaurant are simple, solid and uncomplicated; the reception desk betrays the same qualities.

Albergo Villa Nencini (☎ 0588 8 63 86; www.villa nencini.it; Borgo Santo Stefano 55; s/d incl breakfast €60/83; **P** 🖳 🖳) This is a tranquil family hotel, a mere 200m beyond Porta S Francesco yet a world away from the town's summer bustle. Choose the original 17th-century mansion or the recently constructed new wing. The grounds are shady, the views across the valley are magnificent and, with access to its restaurant and impressive collection of wines, you're fully self-sufficient.

Appartamenti l'Etrusca (☎ 0588 8 40 73; letrusca@ libero.it; Via Porta all'Arco 37-41; apartments for 1/2/3 persons

€40/70/80) Unlike most such rental companies, this place is happy to take you in for even a single night. The exterior of this late Renaissance building gives no hint of all the mod cons within.

Hotel La Locanda (☎ 0588 8 15 47; www.hotel-la locanda.com; Via Guarnacci 24-28; s/d €92/115; ❄) This is well worth flexing your credit card for. In a former nunnery, there is nothing austere about its classy rooms, most with a choice of massage shower or whirlpool. A suite with sauna will cost you a cool €250 and a handicapped-equipped double, €105.

Camping le Balze (☎ 0588 8 78 80; Via di Mandringa 15; per car/tent/person €2/4/6; ❄ Easter-Oct; ⚑) The closest camp site to town, has a pool and sits right on Le Balze.

Eating

Ristorante Don Beta (☎ 0588 8 67 30; Via Giacomo Matteotti 39; mains €10-12, menus €13-18; ❄ closed Mon) With four truffle-based *primi piatti* and five *secondi* enhanced by their fragrance, this is the place to sample the prized fungus, which abounds – in so far as it abounds anywhere – in the woods around Volterra. Do check on the price first. Or else, choose the local *ciandoli alle noci*, little, spring-shaped whorls of curly pasta in a walnut sauce. The only downside is the flickering, if sotto voce, TV in the corner.

Trattoria del Sacco Fiorentino (☎ 0588 8 85 37; Piazza XX Settembre 18; mains €8-14; ❄ closed Wed) A great little vaulted trattoria that serves up imaginative dishes with a happy selection of local wines. Try the *coniglio in salsa di aglio e vin santo* (rabbit cooked in a garlic dessert-wine sauce) or the mouthwatering gnocchi with baby veg.

Trattoria il Poggio (☎ 0588 8 52 57; Via Porta all'Arco 7; meals around €20; ❄ closed Tue) A popular restaurant where the cheery waitresses bustle around and find time to chat with the regulars while the electric dumbwaiter merely raises your food from the subterranean kitchen. There's a good set menu, an outdoor terrace and rich dishes such as risotto with clams, scampi and rocket, plus at least three different lasagnes.

Osteria dei Poeti (☎ 0588 8 60 29; Via Giacomo Matteotti 55; mains €8-16, tourist menu €12; ❄ Fri-Wed) Extremely popular with locals, this is another typical Tuscan rustic restaurant, all pleasing mellow brickwork and golden arches. The cuisine, however, is delightfully

out of the ordinary. For starters, opt for the *antipasto del poeta*, a rich assortment of canapés, cheeses and cold cuts.

Il Porcellino (☎ 0588 8 63 92; Via delle Prigioni; mains around €10; ❄ closed Tue) This is a local favourite with old-fashioned attentive, if gruff, service. The menu includes game dishes, seafood and some surprises – like roast pigeon and boar with olives.

Pizzeria da Nanni (☎ 0588 8 40 47; Via delle Pregioni 40; pizzas €5.25-6.25; ❄ Mon-Sat) This is a hole-in-the-wall-plus – the plus being the excellent pizzas that Nanni spatulas from his oven, while sustaining a vivid line of backchat, notably with his long-suffering wife.

Osteria San Lorenzo (☎ 0588 4 41 60; Via Massetana, San Lorenzo; mains €8-12; ❄ closed Tue) Around 15km out of town, you can get superb, home-style cooking at this rustic restaurant. Take the SS439 road south, heading towards Pomarance. About 3km beyond Saline di Volterra you enter San Lorenzo; the *osteria* is the highlight of this tiny village.

Drinking

Web & Wine (☎ 0588 8 15 31; Via Porta all'Arco 11-13; ❄ 7am-1am daily Mar-Oct, closed Tue Nov-Feb) This is one of those splendid places that defy guidebook characterisation. It's at once internet point (web access per hour €4), a stylish *enoteca* (with a good selection of tipples), a snack stop and a hip designer café (it's not everyday you step across a glass floor, revealing under-lit Etruscan remains and a 5m-deep Renaissance grain silo). Surf your way through a creamy cappuccino while checking your inbox.

Quovadis (☎ 0588 8 00 33; Via Lungo Le Mura del Mandorlo 18) If you can't survive without a shot of the dark nectar, this is the only place for miles around where you can get draught Guinness. The garden is pleasant on hot summer nights and rumour has it there's even an Irish owner somewhere in the background.

Getting There & Away

The tourist office carries bus and train timetables.

BUS

The bus terminal is on Piazza Martiri della Libertà. **CPT** (☎ 0588 8 61 86) buses connect the town with Saline (€1.55, 20 minutes, frequent) and its train station. From Saline,

9km southwest, there are bus connections for Pisa (€5.05, two hours) and Cecina (€3.20), to where there's also a train link.

For San Gimignano (€4.30, 1½ hours), Siena (€4.45, 1½ hours) and Florence (€6.95, two hours), change at Colle di Val d'Elsa (€2.25, 50 minutes), to where there are four runs daily from Volterra, except on Sunday.

Other buses head south in the direction of Massa Marittima but only go as far as Pomarance (€2.25, 12 daily) and Castelnuovo di Valle di Cecina (€3.35, 10 daily).

CAR & MOTORCYCLE
By car, take the SS68, which runs between Cecina and Colle di Val d'Elsa. A couple of back routes to San Gimignano are signposted north off the SS68.

Driving and parking inside the walled town are more or less prohibited. Park in one of the designated parking areas around the circumference, most of which are free. There's a four-level paying underground car park beneath Piazza Martiri della Libertà.

TRAIN
From the small train station in Saline, you can catch a train to Cecina on the coast and change to the Rome–Pisa line.

SOUTH OF VOLTERRA
If you have a car and want to head for Massa Marittima (a worthwhile objective – see p243), the ride south from Volterra is very scenic.

The SS68 drops away to the southwest from Volterra towards Cecina. At Saline di Volterra, the SS439 intersects the SS68 on its way from Lucca, south towards Massa Marittima. **Saline di Volterra** takes its name from the nearby salt mines; a source of wealth in the 19th century.

The lunar-landscape ride south passes through **Pomarance**, an industrial town. To the south, take the hilly road for **Larderello**, Italy's most important boric acid producer. The road out of here winds its way south to Massa.

SOUTH OF SIENA
You may already have had a taste of the gentle, seductively undulating countryside of Le Crete (p216). For a while, similar countryside persists as you roam south

amid the classic Tuscan landscape of rolling hills of hay topped with a huddle of cypress trees. Gradually the landscape gives way to more unruly territory. This part of the province offers everything: the haughty hilltop medieval wine centres of Montalcino and Montepulciano; hot sulphurous baths in spa towns such as Bagno Vignoni; the Romanesque splendour of the Abbazia di Sant'Antimo; and the Renaissance grace of Pienza, an early example of idealised town planning.

Montalcino
pop 5100
A pretty town perched high above the Orcia valley, Montalcino is best known for its wine, Brunello. Produced only in the surrounding vineyards and one of Italy's best reds, it has gained considerable international renown. You can also savour unpedigreed, more modest but very palatable local reds such as Rosso di Montalcino.

Plenty of *enoteche* around town allow you to taste and buy Brunello (a bottle costs a minimum of €20; we did say it was special!). Top names in excellent years come with price tags well over the €105 mark, or break the bank with a bottle from the 1940s – a snip at €5000. Price alone is not necessarily an indication of the wine's quality as all Brunello is made to strict standards.

INFORMATION
Essepi Informatica (☎ 0577 84 61 05; Via Mazzini 30; per hr €6) Head here for Internet access.
Tourist Office (☎ 0577 84 93 31; www.prolocomontalcino.it in Italian; Costa del Municipio 1; ☼ 10am-1pm & 2-5.40pm daily Apr-Oct, closed Mon Nov-Mar)

SIGHTS & ACTIVITIES
A combined ticket (€6) gives entry to Montalcino's principal sights, the *fortezza* and the Museo Civico e Diocesano d'Arte Sacra.

The **fortezza** (☎ 0577 84 92 11; Piazzale Fortezza; courtyard free, ramparts adult/child €3.50/1.50; ☼ 9am-8pm Apr-Oct, 9am-6pm Nov-Mar), an imposing 14th-century fortress that was later expanded under the Medici dukes, dominates the town from a high point at its southern end. You can sample and buy local wines in the *enoteca* (p230) inside and also climb up to the fort's ramparts (though the view is almost as magnificent from the courtyard). Buy a ticket at the bar.

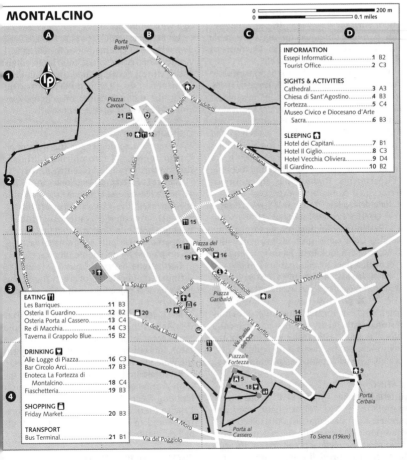

MONTALCINO

INFORMATION
Essepi Informatica....................1 B2
Tourist Office...........................2 C3

SIGHTS & ACTIVITIES
Cathedral.................................3 A3
Chiesa di Sant'Agostino............4 B3
Fortezza..................................5 C4
Museo Civico e Diocesano d'Arte
  Sacra..................................6 B3

SLEEPING
Hotel dei Capitani....................7 B1
Hotel Il Giglio.........................8 C3
Hotel Vecchia Oliviera..............9 D4
Il Giardino.............................10 B2

EATING
Les Barriques........................11 B3
Osteria Il Guardino..................12 B2
Osteria Porta al Cassero...........13 C4
Re di Macchia.........................14 C3
Taverna il Grappolo Blue.........15 B2

DRINKING
Alle Logge di Piazza................16 C3
Bar Circolo Arci.....................17 B3
Enoteca La Fortezza di
  Montalcino........................18 C4
Fiaschetteria..........................19 B3

SHOPPING
Friday Market........................20 B3

TRANSPORT
Bus Terminal.........................21 B1

The **Museo Civico e Diocesano d'Arte Sacra** (☎ 0577 84 60 14; Via Ricasoli 31; adult/child €4.50/3; 10am-1pm & 2-5.50pm Tue-Sun), in the former convent of the neighbouring **Chiesa di Sant'Agostino**, contains an important collection of religious art from the town and surrounding region. Jewels include a triptych by Duccio di Buoninsegna and a *Madonna with Child* by Simone Martini. Other artists represented include the Lorenzetti brothers, Giovanni di Paolo and Sano di Pietro and the museum has a fine collection of painted wooden sculptures by the Sienese school.

The **cathedral**, alas, is an ugly 19th-century neoclassical travesty of what was once a fine Romanesque church.

If you want to visit **vineyards** in the Montalcino area, the tourist office can provide you with a list of 183 producers (many smaller ones have little more than a hectare or two of land). It can also advise on which vineyards are open to the public and those that have an English speaker to help you.

If you're a jazz-loving oenophile, you'll savour the annual **Jazz & Wine festival**, held in the second and third weeks of July and attracting national and international acts.

There's a vigorous **Friday market** on and around Via della Libertà.

SLEEPING

Both Il Giardino and Il Giglio have restaurants that are well worth a visit.

Il Giardino (☎ /fax 0577 84 82 57; Piazza Cavour 4; s/d €45/53) An excellent value, friendly, family-run, two-star hotel. Occupying a venerable building overlooking Piazza Cavour, its décor has a distinct 1970s feel.

Hotel Il Giglio (☎ 0577 84 81 67; www.gigliohotel .com; Via S Saloni 5; s/d/tr €60/90/105, annexe s/d €48/65, apt 2-4 people €70-90; **P**) Montalcino's oldest hotel, recently and substantially renovated, is another family concern. Rooms have comfortable wrought-iron beds – each gilded with a painted *giglio* (lily) – and all doubles have panoramic views. Il Giglio also has a small annexe just up the street and a couple of apartments. Room 1 has an enormous terrace that comes at no extra cost.

Hotel dei Capitani (☎ 0577 84 72 27; www.deicapitani .it; Via Lapini 6; s/d incl breakfast €88/103; 🖳 🖭) Set in a 15th-century building, rooms vary greatly, ranging from super spacious to small with a view, so take a look first. There's a pretty terrace with a pool to splash around in.

Hotel Vecchia Oliviera (☎ 0577 84 60 28; www .vecchiaoliviera.com; Angolo Via Landi 1; d incl breakfast from €150; **P** 🖳 🖭) Just beside the Porta Cerbaia, this a former olive mill, tastefully restored with earthy colours and terracotta tiles. Tranquil – it's at the very limit of the town – each of its rooms is individually decorated. The back patio has stunning views.

EATING

Osteria Il Giardino (☎ 0577 84 90 76; Piazza Cavour 1; mains €8-12; 🕙 closed Wed) All light wood and arches, this place has a good selection of traditional dishes, including *risotto al radicchio rosso, Brunello e pecorino* (risotto with red chicory, Brunello wine and *pecorino* cheese) and wild boar.

Re di Macchia (☎ 0577 84 61 16; Via Soccorso Saloni 21; mains €10-13, menu €19; 🕙 closed Thu) This is a very agreeable small restaurant run by an enterprising young couple. Roberta selects the freshest of ingredients and the wine cellar is impressive; to sample a variety, try Antonio's personal selection of four wines (€14), each to accompany a course.

Taverna Il Grappolo Blu (☎ 0577 84 71 50; Scale di Via Moglio 1; meals €17-25) Does ingenious things with local ingredients – try the juicy *coniglio al Brunello* (rabbit cooked in Brunello wine).

Osteria Porta al Cassero (☎ 0577 84 71 96; Via Ricasoli 32; mains €7; 🕙 closed Wed) A simple place selling hearty peasant-style fare like bean and vegetable soup, and Tuscan pork saus age with white beans.

Les Barriques (☎ 0577 84 84 11; Piazza del Popolo 20-22; mains €6.50-15) Lined floor to ceiling with bottles, this is the place to sample robust local wines accompanied by something light and tasty. If you don't fancy a full meal, the menu includes bruschetta, *crostini* and at least five different salads.

DRINKING

We make no apologies for the disproportionate number of recommended drinking dens in this very wine-oriented town!

Enoteca La Fortezza di Montalcino (☎ 0577 84 92 11; Piazzale Fortezza; wine by the glass from €4) Within the fort itself, this *enoteca* is perfect for trying out one of countless varieties of Brunello, buying a bottle and/or climbing up onto the ramparts. It also puts on informal tastings, accompanied by delectable nibbles.

Fiaschetteria (Piazza del Popolo 6; 🕙 closed Thu) A fine tiled old cafe full of crusty locals, this is the perfect place for putting the world to rights over a bottle of wine.

Alle Logge di Piazza (Piazza del Populo 1; 🕙 closed Wed) Across the square, this is brighter and more consciously modern. It can shake a mean cocktail; the choice is almost as long as the wine list. Happy hour is 7pm to 9pm.

Bar Circolo Arci (Via Ricasoli 2) A contrast to the more formal *enoteche*, this bar is an unpretentious cheerful place within 16th-century Palazzo Pieri. It has a lovely cobbled courtyard – and an impressive collection of football pennants and flags behind the bar.

GETTING THERE & AWAY

The **bus terminal** is on Piazza Cavour. Regular Tra-in buses run to/from Siena (€3, 1½ hours, six daily).

Abbazia di Sant'Antimo

This beautiful isolated Romanesque **church** (☎ 0577 83 56 59; Castelnuovo dell'Abate; admission free; 🕙 10.30am-12.30pm & 3-6.30pm Mon-Sat, 9am-10.30am & 3-6pm Sun) is best visited in the morning, when the sun, streaming through the east windows, creates an almost surreal atmosphere. At night too, it's impressive, lit up like a beacon. Set in a broad valley, just below the village of **Castelnuovo dell'Abate**, its architecture is clearly influenced by northern European versions of Romanesque architecture, especially that of the Cistercians.

Tradition tells that Charlemagne founded the original monastery here in 781. In subsequent centuries, the Benedictine monks became among the most powerful feudal landlords in southern Tuscany, until they came into conflict with Siena in the 13th century. Until the mid-1990s, the church and abbey lay pretty much abandoned. Then a body of monks moved in and supervised restoration work. There are regular daily prayers and Mass in the church, which are open to the public. This is a worthwhile exercise as the monks sing Gregorian chants. If you can't make it, they can sell you the CD.

The exterior, built in pale travertine stone, is simple but for the stone carvings, which include various fantastical animals, set in the bell tower and apsidal chapels. Inside study the capitals of the columns lining the nave, especially the one representing Daniel in the lion's den (second on the right as you enter). Below it is a particularly intense polychrome 13th-century Madonna and Child and there's a haunting 12th-century Christ on the Cross above the main altar.

Concerts are sometimes held here as part of Siena's Estate Musicale Chigiana (see p211).

Locanda Sant'Antimo (☎ 0577 83 56 15; www .locandasantantimo.it; Via Bassomondo 8; mains €6-9; Ⓧ closed Tue & Nov–mid-Dec), less than 1km away at Castelnuovo dell'Abate, serves solid traditional cooking. Should you wish to catch the early morning light over the abbey, they have four rooms (single/double €30/60).

Agriturismo Aiole (☎ 0577 88 74 54; www.agritur ismo-aiole.com; Strada Provinciale 22 della Grossola; d/tr incl breakfast €65/80; Ⓧ closed mid-Jan–mid-Feb; ⓐ), 8km southeast of the abbey and 900m down a signed dirt road, is a fabulous place to stop for one day – or five. Family-friendly, it's in a restored 19th-century farmhouse with knockout views, a pool and a children's playground. There's a kitchen available for groups or save yourself the bother and enjoy your hostess's dinner (€20, reserve in advance).

Three buses a day run from Montalcino (€1.10) to Castelnuovo dell'Abate, from where it's a short walk to the church.

You may want to consider an alternative lunch or dinner excursion west from Castelnuovo dell'Abate along a dirt road to **Sant'Angelo in Colle**. The views from the village

are wonderful. You can eat excellent home-cooked food at **Trattoria Il Pozzo** (☎ 0577 84 40 15; meals from €17; Ⓧ closed Tue), in the middle of Sant'Angelo, just off the square.

San Quirico d'Orcia

San Quirico, a fortified medieval town and one-time pilgrim stopover on the Via Francigena, is just off the SS2 at a crossroads between Montalcino and Pienza. Its Romanesque **Collegiata** is notable for its unusual three doorways, decorated with bizarre stone carvings. Inside is a triptych by Sano di Pietro.

Just off Piazza della Libertà, the main square, the **Horti Leononi** are lovely formal Italian Renaissance gardens with clipped and cropped geometrical boxwood hedges.

The **tourist office** (☎ 0577 89 72 11; www .comunesanquirico.it in Italian; Via Dante Alighieri 33a; Ⓧ 10am-1pm & 3.30-6.30pm Thu-Tue Easter-Dec) also acts as the information office for the Parco Artistico Naturale e Culturale della Val d'Orcia.

The harmonious Val d'Orcia, a land of flat, chalky plains and gentle conical hills, is the latest Italian area to be declared a Unesco World Heritage site. The equally recent **Parco Artistico Naturale e Culturale della Val d'Orcia** (www.parcodellavaldorcia.com), with its headquarters in San Quirico d'Orcia, protects this legacy.

Affittacamere L'Orcia (☎ 0577 89 76 77; Via Dante Alighieri 49; s/d €30/50), right in the centre of town, has a pleasantly old-fashioned no-frills feel about it, complete with drapes and religious pictures.

Trattoria Al Vecchio Forno (☎ 0577 89 73 80; Via Piazzola 8; mains €9-12; Ⓧ closed Wed) is a few steps away from Via Dante Alighieri, the main street. Enjoy the intimate dining room with its mellow brick arches or savour the lovely mature garden. Famed for its roasts and grills, it also simmers a mean *pollo al Brunello* (chicken in a Brunello wine sauce).

Inside **Bar Centrale** (Piazza della Libertà 6) the local menfolk play cards and knock back grappa, while the outside terrace is more popular with the younger ice-cream-and-cola set.

There's a magnificent small **cheese shop** (Via Dante Alighieri 113b), an outlet for the Fattoria Pianporcino cheesemakers, where you can pick up the renowned *pecorino di Pienza* and other richly aromaed delights.

CENTRAL TUSCANY

Bagno Vignoni

About 5km from San Quirico along the SS2 towards Rome, this tiny spa town dates back to Roman times and was later a popular overnight stop for pilgrims eager to soothe weary limbs. The hot sulphurous water bubbles up into a picturesque pool, built by the Medici and surrounded by mellow stone buildings. Some 36 springs cook at up to 51°C and collect in the pool, although in winter the water is considerably cooler.

You can't dunk yourself in the pool. To take the waters, dive into nearby Hotel Posta Marcucci's open-air **Piscina del Sole** (day ticket adult/child €10/7, half-day adult/child €7/5; closed Thu evening).

Alternatively, you can dangle your feet in the hot water streams in Il Parco dei Mulini di Bagno Vignoni, just above the entrance to the hotel, where the two vast cubes hewn into the rock were once holding tanks for water-driven windmills below.

Albergo Le Terme (☎ 0577 88 71 50; www.albergo leterme.it; s/d €62/110; Dec; P ⚇ 🖳 🖳) is sumptuous, with lots of shiny wood and plush fabrics. This 15th-century building (the top floors were added in the mid-20th century) was built by Rossellino for Pope Pius II, who used it as a summerhouse. Ask for a room at the front with views of the pool.

Osteria del Leone (☎ 0577 88 73 00; Piazza del Moretto 28; mains €11-13; closed Mon) is a pleasantly lit rustic building with a heavy-beamed ceiling, back a block from the pool. You can eat solid Tuscan country fare, such as *faraona al vin santo* (pheasant cooked in sweet wine).

Bagni San Filippo

Those who prefer free hot-water frolics could press on about 15km south along the SS2 to Bagni San Filippo. Just uphill from Hotel le Terme, the village's only hotel, follow a sign, 'Fosso Bianco', down a lane for about 150m to a bridge and a set of hot tumbling **cascades** where you can enjoy a relaxing soak. It's a pleasant if slightly whiffy spot for a picnic – and best in winter, when the hotel's closed and the water pressure greater.

Pienza

pop 2200

Pienza, too often dismissed as Montepulciano's little sister, is well worth visiting for its own sake.

Renaissance town-planning concepts wer first put into practice here when Pope Piu II decided to transform the look of his birth place. To rebuild the little town, he chose th architect Bernardo Rossellino, who applie the principles of his mentor, Leon Battist Alberti. This new vision of urban space wa realised in the superb Piazza Pio II and th surrounding buildings. The only questio today is, where do locals go to buy a loa of normal bread? Shops here are geared to wards the gourmet tourist – cheese, meat and preserves.

Information

Internet Point (Via della Madonnina 4; per hr €4; 9.30am-12.30pm, 2.30-7.45pm & 9-11.30pm) At rear of San Gregoro Residence.

Tourist office (☎ 0578 74 90 71; Piazza Pio II; 9.30am-1pm & 3-6.30pm) Within the Palazzo Comunale, it rents a 50-minute audioguide of the town (1/2 persons €5/8).

SIGHTS

Stand in Piazza Pio II and spin 360 degrees You have just taken in Pienza's major monuments. Gems of the Renaissance and all constructed in a mere three years between 1459 and 1462, they're all grouped around Piazza Pio II.

The square was designed by Roberto Rossellino, who left nothing to chance. The space available to him was limited so, to increase the sense of perspective and dignity of the great edifices that would grace the square, he set the Palazzo Borgia and Palazzo Piccolomini off at angles to the cathedral.

The **cathedral** (8.30am-1pm & 2.15-7pm) was built on the site of the Romanesque Chiesa di Santa Maria, of which little remains. The Renaissance façade, in travertine stone, is of clear Albertian inspiration.

The interior of the building, a strange mix of Gothic and Renaissance, contains a collection of five altarpieces painted by Sienese artists of the period, as well as a superb marble tabernacle by Rossellino.

Perhaps the most bizarre aspect of the building is the state of collapse of the transept and apse. Built on dodgy ground, the top end of the church seems to be breaking off. The huge cracks in the wall and floor are matched by the crazy downwards slant of this part of the church floor. Various attempts to prop it all up have failed to

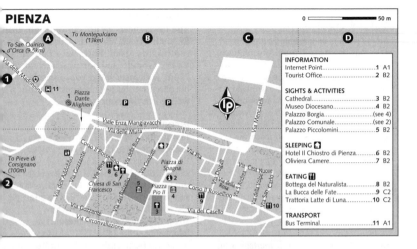

PIENZA

olve the problem, as is quite clear from the major cracking in the walls and floor.

The **Palazzo Piccolomini** (☎ 0578 74 85 03; adult/ child 30-min guided tour €3.50/2.50; 10am-12.30pm & -6pm Tue-Sun), to your right as you face the athedral, was the pope's residence and is considered Rossellino's masterpiece. Built on the site of former Piccolomini family houses, the building demonstrates some indebtedness on Rossellino's part to Alberti, whose Palazzo Rucellai in Florence it appears in part to emulate.

Inside is a fine courtyard, from where stairs lead you up into the papal apartments, now filled with an assortment of period furnishings, minor art and the like. To the rear, a three-level loggia offers a spectacular panorama over the Val d'Orcia below.

To the left of the cathedral is the **Palazzo Borgia** (also known as Palazzo Vescovle), built by Cardinal Borgia, later Pope Alexander VI, and containing the **Museo Diocesano** (☎ 0578 74 99 05; Corso il Rossellino 30; adult/child €4.10/2.60; 10am-1pm & 3-6.30pm Wed-Mon mid-Mar-Oct, Sat & Sun only Nov-mid-Mar), which has an intriguing miscellany of artworks, illuminated manuscripts, tapestries and miniatures.

Make time to visit the Romanesque **Pieve di Corsignano**, leaving Pienza by taking Via Fonti from Piazza Dante Alighieri. This church dates from the 10th century and boasts a strange circular bell tower. There are no fixed visiting times but it is usually open between Easter and November.

SLEEPING & EATING

Oliviera Camere (☎ 0578 74 82 74; www.nautilus -mp.com/oliviera; Via Condotti 4b; s/d €30/50, apt d/q €60/70) Once an olive oil mill and squeezed into a side street, this place represents excellent value. Its four rooms are fresh, modern and attractive and there are also three larger studio apartments.

Hotel Il Chiostro di Pienza (☎ 0578 74 84 00; www.relaisilchiostrodipienza.com; Corso il Rossellino 26; r incl breakfast from €160; closed Jan–mid-Mar;) Come here to wallow in luxury – and history; it occupies the former convent and cloister of the adjacent Chiesa di San Francesco. The décor is refreshingly unfussy and the manicured gardens have views and definite romantic appeal.

La Buca delle Fate (☎ 0578 74 84 48; Corso il Rosselino 38a; mains €7-10; closed Mon & 15-30 Jun) Despite its dress-for-dinner appearance, this eatery is one for euro-economisers. There are no surprises on the menu but the standard is high. Save room for the dessert trolley.

Trattoria Latte di Luna (☎ 0578 74 86 06; Via San Carlo 6; mains €7-10; closed Tue) On a kind of squarette where the street splits off from Corso il Rossellino, this trattoria has a lovely terrace with plenty of shady umbrellas. Try the *anatra arrosto alle olive* (roast duck with olives) topped off with homemade hazelnut ice cream.

Almost a monument in its own right, the pungent **Bottega del Naturalista** (Corso Rossellino 16) has a truly mouthwatering choice of cheeses, from fresh to well-aged and smelly,

CENTRAL TUSCANY

DETOUR: MONTICCHIELLO

From Pienza main junction (northern gate) take the minor road south out of town signposted to San Lorenzo Nuovo and Monticchiello. Follow this road as it wiggles through green valleys and farmland. At 6.2km, just after you cross a small bridge, take the left turn signposted to Monticchiello. At the 11km junction, turn right and continue for 500m until you reach the car park. Take an hour or so to wander around this pretty medieval village, stopping for an ice cream at Bar La Guardiola's outdoor terrace. When you leave, turn left and follow the signs to Montepulciano, passing a natural park with picnic tables on your left.

from the classic *pecorino di Pienza* to ones lightly infused with peppers or truffles.

GETTING THERE & AWAY

Up to six buses run on weekdays between Siena and Pienza (€3.40, 1¼ hours) and nine to/from Montepulciano. The bus terminal is just off Piazza Dante Alighieri.

Montepulciano
pop 13,900

Set atop a narrow ridge of volcanic rock, Montepulciano looks down upon the superb countryside of the Valdichiana. '*Montepulciano, di ogni vino il re*' (Montepulciano, of every wine the king), wrote the 17th-century poet and physician Francesco Redi. Producer to this day of some of the region's finest wines, including the highly reputed Vino Nobile, it's the perfect place to spend a quiet day or two.

A late Etruscan fort was the first in a series of settlements here. During the Middle Ages, it was a constant bone of contention between Florence and Siena, until in 1404 Florence won the day. And so the Marzocco, or lion of Florence, came to replace the she-wolf of Siena as the city's symbol, atop a column just off Piazza Savonarola. The new administration introduced a fresh architectural style as Michelozzo, Sangallo il Vecchio and others were invited in to do some innovative spring cleaning, imparting a fresh wind of Renaissance vigour to this Gothic stronghold. That mix alone makes the town an intriguing place for a stopover.

ORIENTATION

The town sheers off to left and right from the main street, which rises equally steeply southwards from Porta al Prato to the Piazza Grande and fortress beyond. The 750m walk may leave you breathless but bordered by the town's finest buildings, i well worth the exercise.

INFORMATION

Tourist office (☎ 0578 75 73 41; www.proloco montepulciano.it; Piazza Don Minzoni; 9.30am-12.30pm & 3-8pm Easter-Jul & Sep-Oct, 9.30am-8pm Aug, 9.30am-12.30pm Mon-Sat & 3-6pm Sun Nov-Easter) Can reserve accommodation without charge, has a couple of Internet points (per hr €4) and sells local bus tickets, plus train tickets for destinations throughout Italy.

Strada del Vino Nobile di Montepulciano Information Office (☎ 0578 71 74 84; www.strada vinonobile.it; Piazza Grande 7; 10am-1pm & 3-7pm Mon-Sat Mar-Oct, to 6.30pm Nov-Feb) Can also book accommodation. Among other activities, it arranges wine tours and tastings and leads an unstrenuous country walk, culminating in lunch.

SIGHTS & ACTIVITIES

Most of the main sights are clustered around Piazza Grande, although the town's street harbour a wealth of palazzi, fine building and churches.

The **Chiesa di Sant'Agnese** with its beelik banding around the façade lies just outside the city walls. The original church was buil in the early 14th century but this version was the result of a remake by Antonio d Sangallo il Vecchio in 1511. He may also have restructured the medieval gate leading into the city proper, the **Porta al Prato**.

From the gate, walk southwards along Via di Gracciano nel Corso. At the upper end of Piazza Savonarola is the **Colonna de Marzocca**, erected in 1511 to confirm Montepulciano's allegiance to Florence. The splendid stone lion, squat as a pussycat atop this column is, in fact, a copy; the original is in the town's Museo Civico.

The late-Renaissance **Palazzo Avignonesi b** Giacomo da Vignola is at No 91. Several **man sions** line Via di Gracciano nel Corso, includ ing the **Palazzo di Bucelli** at No 73, the lowe courses of whose façade are recycled Etrusca and Latin inscriptions and reliefs. Sangall also designed **Palazzo Cocconi** at No 70.

Continuing up Via di Gracciano ne Corso, you'll find Michelozzo's **Chiesa d**

CENTRAL TUSCANY

Sant'Agostino (Piazza Michelozzo; ☽ 9am-noon & 3-6pm) with its lunette above the entrance holding a terracotta Madonna and Child, John the Baptist and St Augustine. Opposite **Torre di Pulcinella**, a medieval tower house, is topped by the town clock and the hunched figure of Pulcinella (Punch of Punch and Judy fame), which strikes the hours.

Keep ascending the hill and turn right at the **Loggia di Mercato**, first left into Via del Poggiolo, then left again into Via Ricci. In the Renaissance **Palazzo Ricci** is Cantina del Redi (p237), a cavernous warren of ancient wine cellars that you can wander through, ending up at the wine-tasting room and shop.

The town's **Museo Civico** (☎ 0578 71 73 00; Via Ricci 10; adult/child €4.15/2.60; ☽ 10am-7pm Tue-Sun Aug, 10am-1pm & 3-6pm Tue-Sun Sep-Jul) is opposite in the Gothic Palazzo Neri-Orselli. The small collection features terracotta reliefs by the della Robbia family and some Gothic and Renaissance paintings.

Overlooking Piazza Grande, the town's highest point, is the **Palazzo Comunale** (admission free; ☽ 9am-1.30pm Mon-Sat). Built in the 13th-century Gothic style and remodelled in the 15th century by Michelozzo, it still functions as the town hall. From the top of its **tower** (entry on 2nd fl; admission €1.55; ☽ Apr-Oct) on a clear day, you can see as far as the Monti Sibillini to the east and the Gran Sasso to the southeast.

Opposite is the **Palazzo Contucci**, and its extensive wine cellar, Cantine Contucci, open for visiting and sampling (see p237).

MONTEPULCIANO

CENTRAL TUSCANY

Palazzo Tarugi, attributed to Giacomo da Vignola, is beside a well, surmounted by a particularly genial pair of lions.

The nice 16th-century **cathedral** (Piazza Grande; 🕑 9am-noon & 4-6pm) has an unfinished façade. Above the high altar is a lovely triptych by Taddeo da Bartolo depicting the Assumption.

If you take the low road from Piazza Michelozzi and follow Via di Voltaia nel Corso, you pass first, on your left at No 21, the Renaissance **Palazzo Cervini**, built for Cardinal Marcello Cervini, the future Pope Marcellus II. The unusual U-shape at the front – most palazzi have austere, straight fronts – also incorporates a courtyard into the façade design and appears to have been another Sangallo creation. A few blocks further along on the left, is the **Chiesa del Gesù**, bleak brick outside and elaborately Baroque within.

To the west and prominent in the valley below is domed **Chiesa di San Biagio** (Via di San Biagio; 🕑 9am-12.30pm & 3-7pm, to 6pm winter), a fine Renaissance church built by Antonio da Sangallo the Elder. Its highlight is an impressive marble altar piece.

COURSES

Il Sasso (☎ 0578 75 83 11; www.ilsasso.com; Via di Gracciano nel Corso 2) offers Italian language courses for non-native speakers.

FESTIVALS & EVENTS

Bravio delle Botti takes place on the last Sunday in August, when the eight rival *contrade* (districts) of Montepulciano engage in needle-keen competition, rolling vast barrels through the streets, accompanied by lots of flag waving and general merriment.

SLEEPING

Meublé Il Riccio (☎ 0578 75 77 13; www.ilriccio.net; Via Talosa 21; s/d €75/85; **P** 💱 🖳) This gorgeous tiny hotel, with only six bedrooms, occupies a Renaissance palazzo just off Piazza Grande. It has large rooms, antiques, a solarium, a porticoed courtyard and a terrace bar for your glass of *vino* with a view.

Albergo Il Marzocco (☎ 0578 75 72 62; www.albergoilmarzocco.it; Piazza Savonarola 18; s/d incl breakfast €60/95) This place has been run as a hotel by the same family for over a century. Rooms in the fabulous 16th-century building are large, comfortable and well furnished. Those with a balcony and views come at no extra cost.

Albergo Il Borghetto (☎ 0578 75 75 35; www.ilborghetto.it; Via Borgo Buio 7; s/d €93/105) It may look like every other 15th-century building on this street but once inside, this place i a gem, packed with antiques – includin Napoleonic-era beds. There's even a tunnel leading to the house across the street. The hotel is normally closed from mid-January to February.

Bellavista (☎ 0578 75 73 48, ☎ 0347 823 23 1 bellavista@bccmp.com; Via Ricci 25; d €50-65) At the budget end, this is an excellent choice where nearly all of its 10 double rooms have fantastic views. No-one else lives here so phone ahead in order to be met and given a key (if you've omitted this stage, there' a phone in the entrance lobby from where you can call).

EATING

La Grotta (☎ 0578 75 74 79; Via San Biagio 2; meal €45-55; 🕑 Thu-Tue) Opposite the church of Sar Bagio, La Grotta is Montepulciano's fines restaurant. Inside this 15th-century build ing the dining is appropriately elegant while the tables in the garden are tempting for a summer lunch.

Osteria dell'Acquacheta (☎ 0578 75 84 43; Vi del Teatro 22; mains €5-6; 🕑 closed Tue) This is a small eatery with the look and feel of a country trattoria. The food is excellent and mainly meaty, ranging from *misto di salam Toscani* (a variety of Tuscan sausages and salamis) to huge steaks.

Trattoria Diva e Maceo (☎ 0578 71 69 51; Via di Gracciano nel Corso 90; meals €20-28; 🕑 closed Tue An uncomplicated place, Trattoria Diva e Maceo is popular with the locals and carries a good selection of local wines. You can feast on Tuscan cuisine like *tagliatell al tartufo* (tagliatella with truffles) in simple surroundings.

Borgo Buio (☎ 0578 71 74 97; Via Borgo Buio 10 meals €30-40; 🕑 closed Fri) This place has a menu that could scarcely be shorter. But then the quality of the cuisine could hardly be higher at this rustic, low-lit restaurant that also functions as an *enoteca*.

Caffè Poliziano (☎ 0578 75 86 15; Via di Voltaia nel Corso 27) Established as a cafe in 1868 Poliziano has had a chequered past – at times café-cabaret, minicinema, grocery store and, once again since 1990, an elegant café, lovingly restored to its original form by the current owners.

DRINKING

There are plenty of places including several long-established cantinas, where you can whet your palate on the local red, Vino Nobile.

Cantina del Redi (Via Ricci 19; ☉ 10.30am-1pm & 3-7pm) This place doubles as a wine cellar that you can wander around. 'No smoking, No microphones, Do not shout out, No dogs, No trash, Do not touch the casks' is the notice that welcomes you. 'No way,' we muttered, preferring to sample Montepulciano's fine wines somewhere more congenial…

Cantine Contucci (☎ 0578 75 70 06; Palazzo Contucci, Piazza Grande; ☉ 8am-12.30pm & 2.30-6.30pm) Vintners since Renaissance times, this is another active cellar where you can sample a drop of the local wine. The owner is a great character and will give you a personal tour, tasting and photo session – if he likes the look of you.

GETTING THERE & AROUND

Tra-in runs five buses daily between Montepulciano and Siena (€4.45, 1¾ hours) via Pienza. Regular LFI buses connect with Chiusi (€2, 50 minutes, half-hourly) and continue to Chiusi–Chianciano Terme train station.

There are three services daily to/from Florence and two to/from Arezzo (change at Bettolle). Buses leave from the **terminal** shared with car park No 5, outside the Porta al Prato at the northern end of town.

Chiusi-Chianciano Terme, 18km southeast and on the main Rome–Florence line, is the most convenient train station (rather than Stazione di Montepulciano, which has very infrequent services).

By car, take the Chianciano Terme exit from the A1 and follow the SS146. Cars are banned from the town centre. There are car parks near the Porta al Prato, from where minibuses weave their way to Piazza Grande.

Chianciano Terme

pop 7000

You could skip Chianciano Terme, a short trip south from Montepulciano, unless you think a local spa-water treatment for your liver is in order. The town has a small medieval core, which seems to recoil at all the surrounding development. Given its proximity to Montepulciano, however, it could make a good base with its some 250 hotels catering to spa guests. Most are fairly bland and modern, yet reasonable. However, be prepared for half or full board as, strangely, there are precious few bars and restaurants in town.

Chiusi

pop 8600

One of the most important of the 12 cities of the Etruscan League, Chiusi was once powerful enough to attack Rome, under the leadership of the Etruscan king Porsenna. These days it's a fairly sleepy country town but well worth dropping into. The **tourist office** (☎ 0578 22 76 67; prolocochiusi@bcc.tin.it; ☉ 10am-12.30pm & 3.30-6.30pm Jun-Aug, 10am-12.30pm Sep-May) is on central Piazza Carlo Baldini.

SIGHTS

Chiusi's main attractions are the **Etruscan tombs** dotted around the surrounding countryside. Unfortunately, almost all are in such a serious state of disrepair that they are closed. Guided visits (€2, 11am and 4pm March to October, 11am and 2.30pm November to February) to the two accessible tombs, Tomba della Scimmia (the best) and Tomba del Leone, about 3km from town, leave from the **Museo Archeologico Nazionale** (☎ 0578 2 01 77; Via Porsenna 93; adult/child €4/free; ☉ 9am-8pm). You'll need your own transport. The museum itself has a small collection of artefacts from local tombs that are well displayed and documented in English.

The Romanesque **cathedral**, reworked in the 19th century, holds little interest, although the adjacent **Museo della Cattedrale** (☎ 0578 22 64 90; Piazza Duomo; adult/child €2/0.50; ☉ 9.30am-12.45pm & 4.30-7pm Jun–mid-Oct, 9.30am-12.45pm Mon-Sat, 10am-12.45pm & 4.30-7pm Sun mid-Oct–May) has an important collection of psalm books.

Beneath the Piazza del Duomo is the **Labirinto di Porsenna**, a series of tunnels dating back to Etruscan times that formed part of the town's water-supply system. A section can be visited with a guide (€3; buy your ticket at the Museo della Cattedrale).

A combined ticket giving entry to both the cathedral and Labirinto di Porsenna costs €4 and there are guide sheets in English.

You can also visit several Christian **catacombs** (admission €5; ☉ guided tours 11am & 5pm daily Jun–mid-Oct, 11am Mon-Sat, 11am & 4pm Sun mid-Oct–May), 2km from Chiusi. Tours leave from the Museo della Cattedrale, where you buy your ticket.

CENTRAL TUSCANY

SLEEPING & EATING

Albergo La Sfinge (☎ 0578 2 01 57; www.albergolas finge.com; Via Marconi 2; s/d €50/74; ☒ closed Feb; ☒) Just within the confines of Chiusi's historical centre, the clean, attractive rooms here have wrought-iron bedsteads. Some rooms come with a balcony and a few have great views. No 12 manages both.

La Solita Zuppa (☎ 0578 2 10 06; Via Porsenna 21; mains €12-15; ☒ closed Tue) A predominantly Tuscan-based menu with a wide range of soup options is this restaurant's forte. The food is wholesome and cooked to perfection, and the owners make you feel like a long-lost friend.

GETTING THERE & AWAY

Chiusi is just off the A1. Its train station, in the valley below the town, is on the main Rome–Florence line.

DETOUR: LAGO DI CHIUSI

Stock up on stale bread and exit Chiusi in the direction of Castiglione del Lago, passing the petrol station to your left. After 2km, just past a church on your right, turn left at the signpost marked 'Lago di Chiusi'. At the 2.6km fork, turn right to the lake, following the road to the right. Look for the 'Restaurant da Gino' sign and turn right along an avenue of pine trees. Park by the quay and stroll down to the lake to feed the ducks. Retrace your route until you reach the restaurant sign where, instead of turning left to Chiusi, carry on straight towards Montepulciano and Chianciano Terme. At 5.2km turn right to Chianciano. Just before you reach the town, take the left fork towards Sarteano (approximately 10km) and Cetona.

Sarteano & Cetona

Heading into this quiet rural territory, you sense that you have left the last of the tour buses well and truly behind. Sarteano and Cetona, delightful little medieval towns amid gentle countryside, are well worth a wander, perhaps extending to a hike up Monte Cetona (1145m), which overlooks Cetona. Pick up Touring Club Italiano's detailed walking map *Cetona* (€1) at 1:15,000 from the town's **tourist office** (☎ 0578 23 91 43; www.cetona.org; ☒ 10am-noon & 5-7pm daily mid-Jun–mid-Sep, 9am-12.30pm Sat mid-Sep–mid-Jun) on Cetona's Piazza Garibaldi.

Four buses a day go to both towns from Montepulciano and seven from Chiusi.

CETONA

Just off Piazza Garibaldi, the main square cavelike **Cantina la Frasca** (Via Roma 13; ☒ closed Wed) sells its own oil, wine and *pecorino* cheese, straight from the farm, and is a pleasant spot for a snack.

La Frateria di Padre Eligio (☎ 0578 23 82 61; www.lafrateria.it; Via di San Francesco; s/d incl breakfast €140/220; meals excl wine €88; ☒ restaurant Wed-Mon closed Jan–mid-Feb) is for those seeking a special retreat. Up a signed lane 1km from Cetona on the road to Sarteano, this former convent dating from 1212 has been lovingly restored and converted into a top-class seven-room hotel and gourmet restaurant where you can expect an eight-course dining experience of world-class standing.

More modestly, you'll sleep like a top after a day's walking at **La Cocciara** (☎ 0578 23 79 31; www.ostellocetona.it in Italian; Via San Sebastiano 18; dm/d €12/26; ☒ year-round), Cetona's smart new HI-affiliated youth hostel, and eat well on one of the two floors of **Osteria Vecchia** (☎ 0578 23 90 40; Via Cherubini 11; mains €9-15; ☒ closed Tue), just off Piazza Garibaldi. The *spaghetti dell'osteria* is a spicy little number and the meat dishes, such as roast pork and Chianina steak, are cooked to perfection.

SARTEANO

Sarteano, topped by a brooding castle, recently made international headlines (see the boxed text, opposite). Its **tourist office** (☎ 0578 26 92 04; pro-loco.sarteano@libero.it; ☒ 9.30am-12.30pm & 3.30-7.30pm daily Aug–mid-Sep, 10am-noon Wed-Mon Jun-Jul, 10am-noon Thu-Sun mid-Sep–May) is at Corso Garibaldi 9.

At the well-equipped camp site of **Parco Campeggio delle Piscine** (☎ 0578 2 69 71; www.parco dellepiscine.it; Via Campo dei Fiori 30; per person/tent/car €12.50/12.50/6; ☒ Apr-Sep; ☒) guests can luxuriate in the naturally warm mineral waters of three pools including the large Piscina Bagno Santo, which is also open to non-campers (€6 to €10).

Abbadia San Salvatore & Around

On your travels in this part of Tuscany you'd have to be short-sighted not to no-

THE TOMB OF THE INFERNAL CHARIOT

Recently, archaeologists excavating an intact 4th-century-BC tomb in the necropolis of Pianacce, just outside Sarteano, discovered a unique fresco, its colours still as bright as the day they were applied. On the walls surrounding the alabaster sarcophagus, a demonic figure with wild flowing russet hair drives a chariot pulled by a pair of lions and two griffins. Fabulous monsters – a three-headed snake, and a huge seahorse – rear up and an unknown Etruscan nobleman and his wife engage in tender embrace.

The deceased had chosen his last resting place well, with its commanding views over the Val di Chiana, and it's worth the short diversion for the panorama alone. Closed for further research at the time of writing, the tomb should now be open to visitors. Ask at Sarteano's small tourist office.

ice the village of **Radicófani**, 17km southwest of Sarteano on the SS478, – or, more precisely, its **rocca** (☎ 338 816 61 05; adult/child 4/2.50; ⌚ 10am-8pm daily May-Oct, 10am-5pm Fri-Sun Nov-Apr). Built high on a blancmange-shaped ill, it's an impressive sight from any approach, and the views from its ramparts are stunning. It now houses a small **museum** devoted to medieval times.

La Torre (☎ 0578 5 59 43; Via G. Matteotti 7; d incl breakfast €60) is the only place to stay in town. Don't be put off by the bland red-brick exterior. The rooms, with balconies, are good value and the restaurant is always full of locals here for the appetising homemade fare.

Eighteen kilometres further southwest is **Abbadia San Salvatore**, a largely ugly mining own that grew rapidly and tastelessly from the late 19th century. It does have a couple of saving graces, however. The old town, a sombre stone affair entered off Piazzale XX Settembre, is curious enough, although perhaps not really worth an excursion on its own. Its small **tourist office** (☎ 0577 77 58 11; ⌚ 9am-1pm & 4-7pm Mon-Sat) operates from Via Adua 25.

The **Abbazia di San Salvatore** (☎ 0577 77 80 83; Piazzale Michelangelo 8; ⌚ 7am-6pm Mon-Sat, 10.30am-5pm Sun Apr-Oct, 7am-5pm Mon-Sat, 10.30am-5pm Sun Nov-Mar) was founded in 743 by the Lombard Erfo. It eventually passed into the hands of Cistercian monks, who still occupy it today. Little remains of the monastery, but the church more than compensates. Built in the 11th century and Romanesque in style, it was reconstructed in the late 16th century, when the whole area from the transept to the apse was raised and adorned with broad, frescoed arches that give the impression of walking into a tunnel. Best of all, however, is the 8th-century Lombard crypt, a remarkable stone forest of 36 columns.

The town lies in the shadow of **Monte Amiata** (1738m) and serves as a base for local holidaymakers getting in a little skiing, snow permitting, in winter or some walking in summer. You can, for instance, walk right around the mountain following a 30km-trail known as the **Anello della Montagna**. The path is signposted and the tourist office has maps that also cover other walks in the surrounding area. There are hotels aplenty in Abbadia San Salvatore and several others in towns dotted about the broad expanse of the mountain, so you should not have too much trouble finding a place to stay.

From Siena, two RAMA buses (€4.50, 1¾ hours) call by the abbey daily.

CENTRAL TUSCANY

Southern Tuscany

The south of Tuscany, bordering the neighbouring region of Lazio, is a land of lush rumpled hills, distant smoky mountains and ancient hill-top villages. Inland are several of Tuscany's most important Etruscan sites, including the enigmatic *vie cave,* or sunken roads, over whose significance archaeologists still puzzle. For pure drama, the medieval town of Pitigliano is inimitable, looming above a mountainous cliff face pitted with the caves of former Etruscan tombs. Sovana too, just along the road, is rich in Etruscan remains. When you've had your fill, you can dunk yourself in the hot natural pools of Saturnia, only a short drive away.

Grosseto's old town provides an atmospheric setting for the *passeggiata* (traditional evening stroll), while Massa Marittima, the only other inland town of any size, has an equally small, equally charming old quarter and a couple of worthwhile mining museums.

Back on the coast, the Monte Argentario peninsula has smart marinas, good beaches, shady pine groves ideal for a picnic, and a craggy interior, beckoning cyclists and walkers to enjoy a strenuous day out. To its north, the quiet Parco Regionale della Maremma embraces the most varied and attractive stretch of the Tuscan coastline, protected at its rear by the Monti dell'Uccellina range. The park is threaded with signed walking trails or you can hire a mountain bike. You can even join a guided canoe trip along its quiet backwaters. Then again, you could just flop on one of its long, sandy beaches.

Tuscany's southern tip has a couple of delights. The saltwater Lago di Burano teems with birdlife, especially in winter. Nearby, and all the more extraordinary for being implanted in such a natural setting, the Giardino dei Tarocchi (Tarot Garden) is an astounding sculpture park on the grand scale, created over the years by Franco-American artist Niki de Saint Phalle.

HIGHLIGHTS

- Explore the extraordinary town of **Pitigliano** (p250), rising dramatically from a rocky outcrop, and its tiny Jewish quarter
- Follow in the footsteps of the Etruscans in the necropolises around **Sovana** (p251) and the *vie cave* (sunken roads)
- Bathe in the natural hot springs of **Saturnia** (p249)
- Join a guided walk in the rugged, unspoiled surroundings of the **Parco Regionale della Maremma** (p245)
- Enjoy a special seafood moment at one of the waterfront restaurants in picturesque **Porto Santo Stefano** (p247)

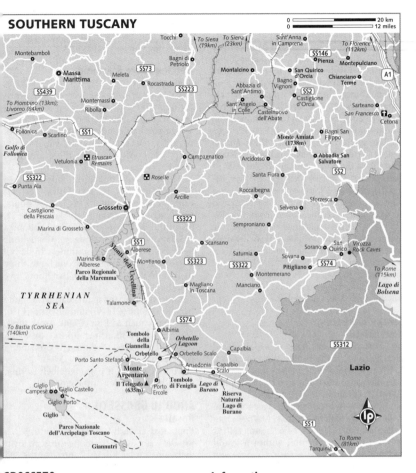

SOUTHERN TUSCANY

GROSSETO

pop 71,400

Poor Grosseto generally and unfairly gets a lousy press, but do give it a chance. Ignore the modern sprawl and head straight for the old walls, raised in 1559 and still forming a near-perfect hexagon. Within, where relatively few tourists penetrate, the historic old town has plenty of unpretentious charm. It's also one of the rare places in Tuscany where the oft-proclaimed 'no car zone' means almost that.

Grosseto was the last Siena-dominated town to fall into Medici hands in 1559. Once in control, Florence had the walls, bastions and fortress raised in order to protect what was then an important grain and salt depot for the grand duchy.

Information

Caffè Ricasoli (☎ 0564 2 62 20; Via Ricasoli 20; per hr €4; ☼ 7am-9.30pm Mon-Sat) Internet access.

Seasonal tourist office (☎ 0564 46 26 11; Via Gramschi; ☼ 8.30am-6.30pm Mon-Fri, 8.30am-1.30pm Sat) At the entrance to the old town.

Tourist office (☎ 0564 46 26 11; www.lamaremma .info; Via Monte Rosa 206; ☼ 8.30am-6.30pm Mon-Fri, 8.30am-1.30pm Sat) Outside the old quarter, it's well informed about the town and region, including the Parco Regionale della Maremma.

Sights

Within the city walls, Grosseto's **cathedral** (☼ 7.30am-noon & 3.30-7pm), begun in the late 13th century, has a distinctive Sienese air. It has been added to and much of the façade was renewed along neo-Romanesque lines during the 19th century. Within, the choc-ice painted white-and-brown bands are an assault on the eyes, but to make up for it there is a lovely tabernacle altar and an elaborate sculpted font. Next door, on Piazza Dante, the Palazzo della Provincia seems Sienese Gothic, which is exactly what its early-20th-century architects hoped you might think.

Sharing common premises, **Museo Archeologico e d'Arte della Maremma** and smaller **Museo d'Arte Della Diocesi di Grosseto** (☎ 0564 48 87 50; Piazza Baccarini 3; admission free; ⊗ 9am-7.30pm Tue-Sat, 9.30am-1pm & 4.30-7pm Sun) are well worth a visit. On the ground floor are Etruscan and Roman artefacts unearthed from Roselle. Room 11 in particular has some imposing statues and fragments, ingeniously jigsawed together. The next floor displays items recovered from Vetulonia and other Maremma sites, while the top storey is mainly devoted to Grosseto's rich ecclesiastical heritage. Ask for the guide sheet in English.

Sleeping & Eating

Hotel Mulinacci (☎ 0564 2 84 19; Via Mazzini 78; s/d incl breakfast €40/80; ✖) This is a well-priced choice, right in the heart of the old town. With traditional green shutters and a friendly welcome, it has small but adequate rooms. Its ground-floor Ristorante l'Italiana is popular with locals – always a good sign.

Bastiani Grand Hotel (☎ 0564 2 00 47; www.hotel bastiani.com; Piazza Gioberti 64; s/d incl breakfast €84/146; **P** ✖ 🖳) A smart hotel within a grand old building, complete with a *Gone with the Wind*–type, dance-me-down staircase. Rooms are elegant, and bathrooms, mostly with a bathtub, are tiled and gleaming.

Ristorante il Canto del Gallo (☎ 0564 41 45 89; Via Mazzini 29; mains €10-13; ⊗ closed Sun & lunch Mon) This is a long, thin tunnel of a place. The Cock Crow is decorated with every possible variant upon the cockerel (rooster) theme, even down to the stoppers used on the rich choice of grappas. The genial, beaming chef emerges from her kitchen, clucks an order or two, greets her guests, then retires to prepare another delicious platter, while the sole waiter darts up and down like an Olympic sprint finalist.

Danubio Blu (☎ 0564 2 22 16; Via Cavour 6; mains €7-9) This is a hugely popular, noisy restaurant with cheery, frazzled staff and a dizzy

choice of dishes, including the traditional polenta and risotto – and occasional surprises like chichen (sic) curry.

Getting There & Around

Rama (☎ 0564 2 52 15; www.griforama.it in Italian; Piazza Marconi) buses cover destinations throughout the province of Grosseto. Most leave from the train station. Buses for Siena, where you can connect with either Tra-in or SITA buses to Florence, run roughly every hour. Alternatively, there are three direct services.

There is only one direct bus a day to Massa Marittima (€3.05). Other destinations include Piombino (€4.70, 1¼ hours, three daily), Magliano in Toscana (€2, 50 minutes, two to five daily), Follonica (€3.05, one hour, three daily), Castiglione della Pescaia (€4.15, 50 minutes, 15 daily), Porto Santo Stefano (€3.05, one hour, three daily) and Pitigliano (€5.50, two hours, five daily).

Grosseto is on the main coastal train line between Rome (€14.80) and Livorno (€10). For places such as Pisa (€7.90, two hours), Florence (€11.30, three hours) or Siena (€5.90, 1½ hours), the train is probably a smarter bet.

There's plenty of parking, albeit paying, beneath the exterior of the city walls.

AROUND GROSSETO
Roselle

Populated as early as the 7th century BC, Roselle was a middle-ranking Etruscan town that came under Roman control in the 3rd century BC.

Although no great monuments are left standing, the extensive **historic site** (☎ 0564 40 30 67; admission €4; ⊗ 9am-sunset) retains Roman defensive walls, an oddly elliptical amphitheatre, traces of houses, the forum and streets. You'll also find remains of an abandoned medieval village. There are wonderful views down to the plains and out to sea.

Vetulonia

This windswept mountain village seems to rise out of nothing from the surrounding plains. It retains elements of the ancient surrounding wall and has a small **Museo Archeologico** (☎ 0564 94 80 58; Piazza de Vetulonia; adult/child €4.15/3; ⊗ core hr 10am-1pm & 3-5pm Tue-Sat, to 9pm Jun-Sep) with a rich display of artefacts revealed by excavations at the two nearby **Etruscan sites** (☎ 0564 94 95 87; admission free; ☽ 9am-sunset). The more extensive area, known as **Scavi Città** (Town Excavations), is just below the village as you leave by the only road.

More interesting are four unearthed **Etruscan tombs** (Via dei Sepolcri; ☽ 9am-sunset), a couple of kilometres further downhill and along a turn-off to the right. Best is the last, about 1km down a rough dirt track.

A daily bus runs to/from both Grosseto and Castiglione della Pescaia.

MASSA MARITTIMA
pop 8800

Massa is a compelling place with a pristine medieval centre. Briefly under Pisan domination, it thrived on the local metal mining industry, even becoming an independent *comune* in 1225, only to be swallowed up by Siena a century later. The plague in 1348, and the end of mining 50 years later, reduced the city almost to extinction. Not until the 18th century, with the draining of marshes and re-establishment of mining, did Massa Marittima finally come back to life.

Information
Tourist office (☎ 0566 90 27 56; www.altamaremma turismo.it; Via Todini 3/5; ☽ 9am-1pm & 4-8pm Mon-Sat, 9.30am-12.30pm Sun Easter-Sep, 9am-1pm Mon-Sat, 3-7pm Mon, Wed, Fri Nov-Mar) Down a side street, beneath the Museo Archeologico.

Sights
The heart of medieval Massa is Piazza Garibaldi, watched over by the imposing bulk of the **cathedral** (☽ 8am-noon & 3-5pm), in Pisan Romanesque style. Probably designed by Giovanni Pisano, its interior is graced with substantial remnants of frescoes and several paintings, including a *Madonna delle Grazie* attributed to Siena's Duccio di Buoninsegna. There's also a fine 14th-century total immersion baptismal font.

Opposite is the **Palazzo Comunale**, the city's historic seat of government. The proud coat of arms of Florence's Medicis doesn't quite outweigh that earlier symbol of rival Siena's one-time ascendancy here – the wolf with Romulus and Remus.

The 13th-century **Palazzo del Podestà** houses the **Museo Archeologico** (☎ 0566 90 22 89; Piazza

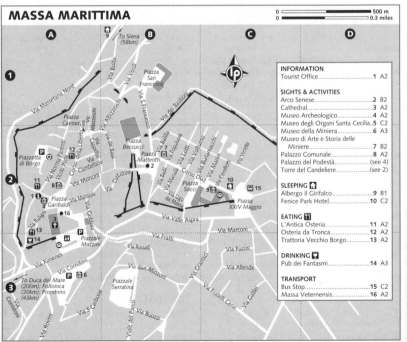

MASSA MARITTIMA

0   500 m
0   0.3 miles

Garibaldi 1; adult/child €3/1.50; ⏱ 10am-12.30pm & 3.30-7pm Tue-Sun Apr-Oct, to 5pm Nov-Mar), visited above all for Ambrogio Lorenzetti's magnificent *Maestà* (Majesty). Paling into comparative insignificance is a modest collection of ancient Roman and Etruscan artefacts recovered from around town.

Up in the Città Nuova (New Town) is the **Torre del Candeliere** (Piazza Matteotti; adult/child €2.50/1.50; ⏱ 10am-1pm & 3-6pm Tue-Sun Apr-Oct, 11am-1pm & 2.30-4.30pm Tue-Sun Nov-Mar). The tower is linked to defensive bastions in the wall by the vast sweep of the so-called **Arco Senese** (Sienese Arch). You can enter the tower and walk across the arch for stupendous views over the Città Vecchia (Old Town).

Music-lovers will enjoy the recently inaugurated **Museo degli Organi Santa Cecilia** (☎ 0566 94 02 82; Corso Diaz 28; adult/child €4/2; ⏱ 10am-1pm & 4-8pm Apr-Oct, 10.30am-12.30pm & 3-6pm Tue-Sun Nov-Mar) with its collection of antique organs, harpsichords and clavichords, which, if you strike lucky, the curator will play for you.

Museo della Miniera (☎ 0566 90 22 89; Via Corridoni; adult/child €5/3; ⏱ guided visits hourly 10am-12.45pm & 3.30-5.45pm Apr-Oct, 10am-12.45pm & 3-4.30pm Tue-Sun Nov-Mar) relates the city's long mining history. The display includes a replica of a length of mine. Guided tours in Italian and optional English last around 45 minutes.

The smaller **Museo di Arte e Storia delle Miniere** (☎ 0566 90 22 89; Piazza Matteotti 4; adult/child €1.50/1; ⏱ 3-5.30pm Tue-Sun Apr-Oct) has more mining material and a strong photographic collection.

Festivals & Events
In the first two weeks of July, the **Toscana Foto Festival** (www.toscanafotofestival.com in Italian) attracts international professional photographers, whose works are displayed all over town until mid-August.

Sleeping & Eating
Many hotels and restaurants in Massa take a long winter break between January and March.

Duca del Mare (☎ 0566 90 22 84; www.ducadelmare.it; Piazza Dante Alighieri 1/2; s/d incl buffet breakfast €60/95; Ⓟ 🐾 🖧) Duca del Mare is about a 10-minute walk from the historic centre. This modern, sunny hotel is a friendly place. It has a Scandinavian air with lots of shiny light wood and Ikea-style furnishings.

La Fenice Park Hotel (☎ 0566 90 39 41; www.lafeniceparkhotel.it; Corso Diaz 63; s/d €77.50/155; 🐾 🖧) This is a seductive marble-clad hotel (bathrooms are a sensual delight) where all rooms have a minikitchen. The junior suites (€180) are essentially roomy, fully equipped apartments, and there's a croquet-quality lawn.

Albergo Il Girifalco (☎ 0566 90 21 77; www.cometanet.it/girifalco; Via Massetana Nord 25; s/d €45/72) is a low-key place just outside the walls. It's family friendly, with a playground and picnic area. Rooms are clean and bright, and many have sweeping views.

Trattoria Vecchio Borgo (☎ 0566 90 39 50; Via Norma Parenti 12; mains around €9; ⏱ closed Mon) A brick-clad restaurant with a cavernous barrel-vaulted interior where a welcoming fire roars away in winter. There's an economically priced set menu and a good variety of dishes, and its *gnocchi al pomodoro* (gnocchi in a tomato sauce) is hard to beat.

L'Antica Osteria (☎ 0566 90 26 44; Via Norma Parenti 19; mains around €9) This *osteria* (trattoria-style restaurant with a bar) is also great value, offering several lip-smacking vegetarian options like cheese-filled ravioli with mushrooms.

Osteria da Tronca (☎ 0566 90 19 91; Vicolo Porte 5; mains €9; ⏱ closed Mon) Squeezed into a side street, da Tronca is another intimate stone-walled restaurant. There's lots of antipasto (€2.50) to choose from. For mains, try anything with *cinghiale* (wild boar).

Drinking
Pub dei Fantasmi (☎ 0566 94 02 75; Via Norma Parenti 2/4; ⏱ 9.30pm-2am or 3am Thu-Tue) This is the place to head if you're feeling frisky after dinner; it's about the only place in town big enough to hold a crowd. There's occasional live jazz.

Getting There & Away
There are two daily buses to Siena (€4.30) at 7.05am and 4.40pm, and around four to Volterra (changing at Monterotondo). The nearest train station is Massa-Follonica, served by a regular shuttle bus (€1.80). All buses call at the stop on Piazza XXIV Maggio. **Massa Veternensis** (☎ 0566 902 20 16; Piazza Garibaldi 18) sells both bus and train tickets.

THE COAST
There are no great swaths of sand as you cruise the coast south from Piombino, where occasional stretches of pine-backed

beach are pleasant without being breathtaking. What does deserve a detour along this southern stretch of mainland Tuscan coast is the Parco Regionale della Maremma.

Golfo di Follonica

Maintaining an industrial tradition that dates back to Etruscan times, the gulf these days is mostly chimney stacks and factories – all necessary, to be sure, but no reason to hang about. Heading south, the first town you will reach is **Follonica**, with its cheap and scruffy high-rises. The outlook improves a few kilometres further around the gulf with a pleasant pinewood backdrop to the beaches; look for the turn-off signs inland for **Scarlino**.

Some sadistic committee in **Punta Ala** succeeded in devising the most Kafkaesque road system for this leafy but rather fake getaway for the seriously moneyed. On the plus side, the promontory is green and sparingly brutalised by building development, and, along the northern flank, there is a pleasant pine-backed sandy beach.

Castiglione della Pescaia
pop 7300

The modern sprawl around the foot of the hill on which this medieval stone village sits lives harmoniously enough with its more venerable antecedent.

The walled old town has no specific monuments of interest, but is pleasant to stroll through – and the views out to sea are majestic.

The **tourist office** (☎ 0564 93 36 78; www.castiglionepescaia.com; Piazza Garibaldi 6; ☎ 9am-1pm & 4-8pm Mon-Sat, 10am-1pm Sun) is in the main square of the lower town.

SLEEPING & EATING

Hotel Bologna (☎ /fax 0564 93 37 46; Piazza Garibaldi 8; s/d €28/52, with bathroom €34/65; ✱) This is a no-frills small hotel whose rooms are comfortable, even if the furniture's dated and retro-plastic. By contrast, the location is five-star superb – across from the harbour, with great views from the corner breakfast room and some bedrooms.

Hotel Lucerna (☎ 0564 93 36 20; Via IV Novembre 27; s/d incl breakfast €65/95; **P** ✱) An attractive traditional hotel that's been run by the same family for three generations. Rooms are cheerful and large, and have balconies with sea or old-town views. The adjacent

restaurant and pizzeria is handy for staving off hunger pangs.

Ristorante La Fortezza (☎ 0564 93 61 00; Via del Recinto 1/3; mains €9-12; ☎ daily Mar-Oct, Tue-Sun Nov-Feb) La Fortezza is just beyond the massive gate leading to the old town. You can dine outside or within the cavelike interior and savour typical dishes of the Maremma, including pasta with lobster.

GETTING THERE & AWAY

Rama buses run to/from Grosseto (€4.15, 50 minutes, 15 daily) and connect with other places on the coast, such as Marina di Grosseto (€2.10).

Marina di Grosseto

The beach is broad and sandy, but the resort is modern, with slapped-together housing and an anonymous gridlike street system. At least it's predominantly low-rise and well camouflaged by the umbrella pines typical of the Maremma coast. It's a favoured spot for locals to come and splash in the sea, but there are more interesting places close by.

Parco Regionale della Maremma

The Maremma extends along the Tuscan coast from just north of Grosseto to the southern border with Lazio, embracing the Parco Regionale della Maremma and Monte Argentario. Fronting the coast, it's an area of long, sandy beaches and reclaimed marshland, crisscrossed by dykes and drainage ditches. This **nature park** (admission €6-8) protects its most spectacular parts and incorporates the **Monti dell'Uccellina**, which drop to a magnificent stretch of unspoiled coastline. Native animals include wild boar, wild cats and porcupines.

The park's main **visitors centre** (☎ 0564 40 70 98; www.parcomaremma.it in Italian; ☎ 7.30am-6.30pm Jul-Sep, 8.30am-1.30pm Oct–mid-Mar, 8.30am-4pm mid-Mar–Jun) is in Alberese, at the park's northern edge. There's a small **seasonal centre** (☎ 7.30am-6.30pm Jul-Sep, 8.30am-4pm mid-Mar–Jun) at the park's southern extremity, 400m up a dirt lane about 1km before Talamone. Talamone itself is a little coastal village, surmounted by a plain, functional blockhouse of a fortress, from whose base there's a great sea view.

Entry to the park is limited and cars must be left in designated areas. Walking is the best way to explore its riches, and 11 signed

COWBOY CULTURE

The fascination Europe held for the cowboy culture of the American West was never more apparent than in the late 1800s when Colonel William Cody (alias Buffalo Bill) took his fabulously successful Wild West show on two grand European tours.

Buffalo Bill brought the show to Italy, complete with the sharp-shooting Annie Oakley and bands of real Sioux warriors, many the very same braves who had fought Custer at the Battle of Little Big Horn. The troupe was invited to the Vatican to attend the celebration of the 10th anniversary of the coronation of Pope Leo XIII. Then, in Verona, Cody fulfilled his ambition of exhibiting his Wild West in the ancient Roman amphitheatre, where the high point was a bronco-busting challenge match between Buffalo Bill's cowboys and the *butteri*. These were Tuscany's legendary cowboys, who survived the harsh conditions of the Maremma, its swampland a breeding ground for malarial mosquitoes. The Maremma was divided between landowners of vast estates where the *butteri* tended herds of Cajetan horses, one of the most unmanageable and wild breeds in Europe. In front of a crowd of some 20,000 spectators, the *butteri* challenged the American cowboys to break the Cajetans. The Rome correspondent of the *New York Herald* wrote: 'The brutes made springs into the air, darted hither and thither in all directions, and bent themselves into all sorts of shapes, but all in vain. In five minutes the cowboys [*butteri*] had caught the wild horses with the lasso, saddled, subdued and bestrode them. Then the cowboys rode them around the arena while the dense crowds applauded with delight.'

Today, longhorn cattle and horses still graze free in the Maremma, the swamps have all been drained, the grass is lush, and malaria a menace of the past. On the first Sunday in August, the *butteri* gather and brand the cattle. The **Equinus Association** (☎ 0564 24988; www.cavallomaremmano .it) organises *butteri* shows and equestrian tourism, and even provides information on buying – presumably tamed – Maremma horses. There is also an official organisation, **Butteri di Alta Maremma** (www.butteri-altamaremma.com), which protects and promotes the remaining *butteri* and also arranges rodeo-style events.

walking trails, varying from 2.5km to 12km, have been marked out within its borders. Entry (by ticket bought at one of the visitors centres) varies according to whether a minibus transports you to your chosen route. Depending upon your trail, you stand a chance of spotting deer, wild boar, foxes and hawks.

The **Centro Turismo Equestre Il Rialto** (☎ 0564 40 71 02), 600m north of the main visitors centre, offers guided canoe outings (adult/child €16/8; three hours) and horse-riding trips (€33), and rents mountain bikes (per hour/day €3/8). If you're an experienced horse rider, you might be lucky enough to ride with the legendary *butteri*, cowboys who still work the area in and around the park – see above. Check at one of the visitors centres.

Between July and September, when the park gets very crowded, a couple of routes are closed and two others can only be undertaken in a guided group because of the high risk of forest fire. There are no shelters within the park, so make sure you wear sunblock and carry water.

To restore energy after a walk, there are a couple of simple, good-value eating op-

tions. **Il Mangiapane** (☎ 0564 40 72 63; mains €7-9), beside the Centro Turismo Equestre Il Rialto, has a shaded wooden terrace where you can munch a snack or something more substantial, including homemade pasta.

Osteria la Nuova Dispensa (☎ 0564 40 73 21; Via Aurelia Vecchia 11; mains €6.50-9; ☒ closed Wed), recently opened, occupies the old village store and offers local specialities such as *acquacotta* (literally 'cooked water', a hearty vegetable and egg soup). If you like your food spicy, fire up on the *peposo*, a peppery stewed beef dish with vegetables and Tuscany's answer to a vindaloo. The restaurant's 4.5km south of Alberese, just before the junction with the SS1.

MONTE ARGENTARIO
pop 12,400

Once an island, this rugged promontory came to be linked to the mainland by an accumulation of sand that is now the isthmus of Orbetello. Further sandy bulwarks form the Tombolo della Giannella and the Tombolo di Feniglia to the north and south. They enclose a lagoon that is now a protected nature reserve. Intense building has spoiled the northern side of the promontory, but the south and centre have been left in peace (forest fires aside). It's a favourite summer weekend getaway for Romans, when it gets packed to the gunwales.

GETTING THERE & AROUND

Frequent **Rama** (☎ 0564 85 00 00) buses connect most towns on Monte Argentario with downtown Orbetello (€1.50, 20 minutes) and continue to the train station. They also run to Grosseto (€3.40, one hour, up to four daily).

By car, follow signs for Monte Argentario from the SS1, which connects Grosseto with Rome.

Orbetello

pop 14,750

Sitting among three isthmuses, Orbetello speaks of Mediterranean lands further west. The main attraction is its **cathedral** (Piazza della Repubblica; ⊙ 9am-noon & 3-6pm), which has retained its 14th-century Gothic façade despite being remodelled in the Spanish style in the 16th century. Other reminders of the Spanish garrison that was stationed in the city for nearly 150 years include the Viceroy's residence on Piazza Eroe dei Due Mondi, the fort and the city walls, parts of which are the original Etruscan fortification.

The **tourist office** (☎ 0564 86 04 47; ⊙ 9.30am-1pm & 4-7pm Apr-Sep, to 8pm Jul-Aug, 9am-12.30pm & 4-7pm Oct-Mar) is opposite the cathedral.

The best place for observing birdlife (as many as 140 species have been identified) on Orbetello's lagoon is out along the Tombolo della Feniglia, the southern strip of land linking Monte Argentario to the mainland. It is blocked to traffic, but you can park your car near the campsite and continue on foot or bicycle. The beach on the seaward side is one of the best on the peninsula.

SLEEPING & EATING

Hotel I Presidi (☎ 0564 86 76 01; Via Mura di Levante 4; s/d incl breakfast €110/160; P ✗ ⬚) This is an airy, thoroughly modern hotel, wedged between the lagoon-side road and the old quarter. The striped wallpaper in the rooms is offset by a floral frieze and flowery coverlets. Those on the 4th floor have a small balcony, and there's a peaceful interior patio.

Osteria del Lupacante (☎ 0564 86 76 18; Corso Italia 103; mains €9-13; menu turistico €20; ⊙ closed Tue) This *osteria* is run by a Sicilian family. You really

must begin with one of the splendid soups, which is almost a meal in itself. The *spaghetti alla messinese* (Messina style, with swordfish, tomato, peppers, sunflower seeds and spices) is only one of the imaginative creations.

Osteria il Nocchino (☎ 0564 86 03 29; Via Furio Lenzi 64; mains €10-12; ⊙ Thu-Tue Mar-Oct, Fri-Sun Nov-Feb) Another excellent choice, albeit with about as much seating capacity as a glorified matchbox (supplemented in summer by outdoor seating). Prices are moderate and the food is like mamma used to make.

Porto Santo Stefano

Porto Santo Stefano is a small, fashionable resort town, where you can expect to see a few Ferraris and G-strings.

INFORMATION

Il Galeone (Lungomare dei Navigatori 40; per hr €5; ⊙ 8am-midnight) A bar with a couple of Internet points.

Tourist office (☎ 0564 81 42 08; www.lamaremma .info; Piazzale Sant'Andrea; ⊙ 9am-1pm & 3-5pm Mon-Sat) At the eastern end of the port.

SIGHTS & ACTIVITIES

Acquario Mediterraneo (☎ 0564 81 59 33; Lungomare dei Navigatori 44/48; adult/child €4.50/1; ⊙ 10.30am-12.30pm & 5pm-midnight Jul-Aug, 10.30am-12.30pm & 4-8pm Jun & Sep, 3-5pm Tue-Sun, 10.30am-12.30pm Sat & Sun Oct-May), on the waterfront, has a fun collection of marine life.

Fortezza Spagnola (☎ 0564 81 06 81; Piazza del Governatore; adult/child €3/2; ⊙ 6pm-midnight daily Jun-Sep, Sat & Sun only Oct-May) houses a small collection of underwater archaeological finds, and gives breathtaking views of Porto Santo Stefano – if you've any breath left after the steep ascent.

If you've wheels, follow signs for the **Via Panoramica**, a circular route offering great coastal views over the water to the hazy whaleback of the Isola de Giglio. For another spectacular drive, take a right turn 6km east of Porto Santo Stefano, up the signed road leading to **Convento dei Frati Passionisti**, a convent with sensational views across to the mainland.

There are several good beaches, mainly of the pebbly variety.

SLEEPING & EATING

Pensione Weekend (☎ /fax 0564 81 25 80; Via Martiri d'Ungheria 3; d with bathroom from €55) This *pensione* is a true gem. It was undergoing extensive renovation when we last visited, so prices may have risen. The friendly, polyglot owner can give you a voucher entitling you to a 20% reduction at Lo Sfizio restaurant.

Hotel La Caletta (☎ 0564 81 29 39; www.hotelcal etta.it; Via del Fortino 51; s/d €85/104; **P** **⊠**) This is a three-star hotel whose private beach is a welcome perk. The floral and white décor may be a bit girly for some, but overall this is a fair-priced place (outside August, when half board is compulsory) in a choice location.

Hotel Torre di Cala Piccola (☎ 0564 82 51 11; www.torredicalapiccola.com; Cala Piccola; s/d/tr incl breakfast €270/356/420; ⌚ Apr-Oct; **P** **⊠** **⊡** **⊠**) This hotel is a self-contained complex in splendid isolation, built around an old Spanish watchtower, 8km southwest along the Via Panoramica. There are spectacular seascapes from the balcony of the luxury bungalows, and the dining setting in the gardens is particularly glorious on a sunny day. A minibus transports you down the hillside to the hotel's private beach.

Albergo Belvedere (☎ /fax 0564 81 26 34; Via del Fortino 51; s/d incl breakfast €60/100; ⌚ May-Oct) This is a luxury complex 1km east of the harbour. Overlooking the water, it too has its own private beach.

Il Veliero (☎ 0564 81 22 26; Via Panoramica 149-151; meals €30-35; ⌚ Tue-Sun Feb-Dec) An excellent restaurant, high above the port, that serves the freshest of fare from the sea – the owner's father runs a fish shop in town. It's a steep climb (head up the steps, guarded by a terracotta lion, just above Pensione Weekend) but well worth the exertion, especially if you've reserved a table on the small terrace with its plunging view. The *scampi flambati al cognac* (prawns flambé) comes highly recommended.

Il Moletto (☎ 0564 81 36 36; Via del Molo 52; ⌚ closed Wed) Among several enticing quayside seafood restaurants, this place wins for its location. At this wooden cabin, set apart from the rest at the end of a mole, you can dine beside a picture window or on the jetty as the evening breeze cools your pasta.

Trattoria Da Siro (☎ 0564 81 25 38; Corso Umberto 100; meals €30-35; ⌚ Tue-Sun) Overlooking the waterfront, this trattoria also manages a good mix of well-prepared fish and seafood, spiced with an impressive seascape.

Lo Sfizio (☎ 0564 81 25 92; Lungomare dei Navigatori 26; pizzas from €5.50, meals €22-30; ⌚ daily Apr-Oct, Tue-Sun Nov-Mar) Its corny fish-theme décor and

bar of blinking lights looks unpromising, but what draws in diners is the very reasonably priced fish and seafood dishes and the friendly informality of its youthful staff.

For a great view without paying panoramic prices, grab a pizza from **Pizzeria da Gigetto** (☎ 0564 81 44 95; Via del Molo 9) and munch it on the waterfront terrace, then finish off with an ice cream from Bar Gelateria Chioda, right next door.

Porto Ercole

Porto Ercole, in a picturesque position between two Spanish forts, still manages to retain some of its fishing village character. The beach is serviced, so it's clean but cluttered with deck chairs and umbrellas. Further away, it becomes less crowded but, as with most public beaches in Italy, also dirtier.

SLEEPING & EATING

Camping Feniglia (☎ 0564 83 10 90; camping.feni glia@virgilio.it; per person/pitch €9/12; ⌚ year-round) In Feniglia, about 1.5km north of Porto Ercole, this camp site is just 50m from the sea. Trouble is, most of it is occupied by permanently planted caravans and family tents.

Gatto e la Volpe (☎ 0564 83 52 05; Via dei Cannoni 3; mains around €20; ⌚ closed Wed) This is a brakesqualing stop on the right as you sweep down the road to the harbour. The views are wonderful. Try the speciality *linguine all'astice* (lobster linguine), leaving room for the homemade desserts.

THE ISLANDS

More than a few locals skip Monte Argentario altogether and choose to head off on excursions to one of two islands off the coast. The islands of Giglio and Giannutri are both part of the Parco Nazionale dell'Arcipelago Toscano.

Giannutri

This tiny island, just 5km long, has a grand old ruin of a Roman Villa (1st century AD) but not much else, aside from a pleasant shady bay, Cala Spalmatoio, on the eastern side.

Giglio

The hilly island of Giglio is Tuscany's second largest after Elba. Some 14km off Monte Argentario, its pristine waters are increasingly popular with divers. Regular boat services from Porto Santo Stefano make getting to this pretty little spot easy. You arrive at colourful Giglio Porto, once a Roman port and now the best spot to find accommodation. A local bus service will take you 6km to the inland fastness of Giglio Castello, dominated by a Pisan castle.

Aside from a couple of patches of sand the size of a beach towel, the only beaches are on the western side of the island, in and around the modern resort of Giglio Campese, built around the old watch tower.

Toremar (☎ 0564 81 08 03) and **Maregiglio** (☎ 0564 81 29 20; www.maregiglio.it) run several daily ferries (adult/child return €10.60/5.40) between Porto Santo Stefano and the island.

LAGO DI BURANO & AROUND

Little more than 10km further east along the coast, this saltwater flat is a nature reserve, **Riserva Naturale Lago di Burano** (☎ 0564 89 88 29; Capalbio Scalo; admission €5.25; 🕙 guided visits 10am & 2.30pm Sun Sep-Apr), run by the World Wide Fund for Nature (WWF). Covering 410 hectares and stopping about 5km short of the regional frontier with Lazio, it is typical of the Maremma in its flora, but interesting above all for its migratory birdlife. Tens of thousands of birds of many species winter here, including several kinds of duck and even falcons. Among the animals, the most precious is the beaver. A path with seven observation points winds its way through the park.

About 8km south of the lake turn-off, you can see the terraces of **Il Giardino dei Tarocchi** (☎ 0564 89 51 22; www.nikidesaintphalle.com; Località Garavicchio-Capalbio; adult/child €10.50/6; 🕙 2.30-7.30pm May–mid-Oct) tumbling down the hillside. Here Franco-American artist Niki de Saint Phalle (1930–2002) sculpted on the grand scale in mosaic, shards of glass, splinters of tile and sculpted rock. Strongly influenced by the Catalan artist Antoni Gaudí, her giant sculptures illustrate the main players from the tarot card pack, such as the Moon, the Fool, the High Priest of Feminine Intuitive Power – and the Empress, within whose innards she lived for months on end.

For both, take the Capalbio Scalo exit from the SS1.

INLAND & ETRUSCAN SITES

The deep south of Tuscany is home to thermal springs, medieval hill towns and Etruscan archaeological finds.

Magliano & Scansano

From **Albinia**, at the northern tip of the Orbetello Lagoon, take the SS74 in the direction of Manciano and make a detour left (north) up the SS323.

The first stop is **Magliano in Toscana**, impressive above all for its largely intact city walls. Some date from the 14th century, while most were raised by Siena in the 16th century. The town is a little scrappy on the inside.

Lunch at **Antica Trattoria Aurora** (☎ 0564 59 20 30; Via Chiasso Lavagnini 12/14; mains €12; 🕙 closed Wed) is a good idea, and there's a pretty sheltered garden, open for dinner. Cutting-edge menu concepts include *cinghiale al finocchio selvatico* (wild boar tortellini with wild fennel).

Next, continue up to **Scansano**. Although there are no monuments of great importance, the old centre, all narrow lanes and archways, is a pleasure to wander around and offers some great views over the surrounding countryside.

Montemerano, Saturnia & Manciano

Continuing from Scansano towards Manciano along the SS322, you first hit the small walled medieval town of **Montemerano**. Pick up a bottle of the excellent local Morellino di Scansano wine at **La Vecchia Dispensa** (Via Italia 31), a richly scented delicatessen that presses its own olive oil, then drop into **Chiesa di San Giorgio**, decorated with 15th-century frescoes of the Sienese school. Finally, stroll up to harmonious, oh-so-photogenic Piazza del Castello.

Le Fontanelle (☎ 0564 60 27 62; s/d €47/75), 1.2km down a turn-off 2.5km south of Montemerano, is a wonderful rustic place with cabinlike accommodation, a duck pond, plenty of shady trees, geese, goats, deer – and the venerable Gina, a 30-year-old donkey. Daughter Daniella is a sparkling hostess for dinner (€20), taken alfresco with other guests around a large communal table.

From here it's 6km to **Saturnia**, with its Etruscan remains, including part of the town wall. A tomb at **Sede di Carlo**, just northeast of the town, is one of the area's best preserved.

The sulphurous spring and thermal baths at **Terme di Saturnia** (☎ 0564 60 01 11; www.termedi saturnia.it; day admission €16, after 2pm €12; 🕙 9.30am-7.30pm Apr-Sep, 9.30am-5.30pm Oct-Mar; 🅿) are 2.5km south of the village. You can happily spend a whole day dunking yourself in the hot pools and signing on for some of the

---

DETOUR: MONTE ARGENTARIO TO MANCIANO

Travelling from Monte Argentario to Manciano, turn right after 18.8km at the Vallerana sign. Turn left after 1.4km, in the direction of Pitardi. You'll pass vineyards on your left as the road continues through seamless rolling countryside, with the town of Manciano straddled on a hill top in the distance. After 3.2km, turn into the farm on your left (look for the *vendita vino-olio* sign) and ask for Renalto, the farmer, who has excellent olive oil, and red and white wine for sale. After you have made your purchases, turn left out of the gate and continue past a pastoral scene of fields of cows and sheep. Turn left at 3.9km then, at 8.3km, rejoin the main road to Manciano happily weighed down with *vino*.

---

ancillary activities such as the alluring 'four-hand massage shower' or, for that light-as-air feeling, the 'infiltration of gaseous oxygen to reduce excess fat'. Parking here costs €3.

On the other hand, if you just fancy a quick dip, head left down a dirt lane 700m south of the Terme turn-off and frolic for free in the warm waters that cascade down a gentle waterfall, where the temperature remains a constant 37.5°C.

Manciano is another former Sienese fortress. Apart from the much-interfered with Rocca (the Fortress), there is not much to keep you.

Pitigliano
pop 4150

From Manciano head east along the SS74 for Pitigliano, a hill-top fastness that seems to grow organically from the high volcanic rocky outcrop that towers over the surrounding country. The gorges that surround the town on three sides constitute a natural bastion, completed to the east by the manmade fort.

Originally built by the Etruscans, Pitigliano remained beyond the orbit of the great Tuscan city-states, such as Florence and Siena, until it was finally absorbed into the grand duchy under Cosimo I de' Medici.

In the course of the 15th century, a Jewish community settled here, increasing notably when Pope Pius IV banned Jews from Rome in 1569. They moved into a tiny ghetto, where they remained until 1772. From then until well into the following century, the local community of 400 flourished and Pitigliano was dubbed Little Jerusalem. By the time the Fascists introduced the race laws in 1938, most Jews had moved away (only 80 or so were left and precious few survived the war).

INFORMATION
Tourist office (☎ 0564 6 71 11; Piazza Garibaldi 10.20am-1pm & 3-7pm Tue-Sun Apr-Oct, 10.20am-1pm & 2-6pm Tue-Sun Nov-Mar).

SIGHTS
The first glimpse of Pitigliano from the Manciano approach road (arrive at night and you see it lit up) is breathtaking. Within the town, twisting stairways disappear around corners, cobbled alleys bend out of sight beneath arches and the stone houses seem to have been piled up higgledy-piggledy by some giant child playing with building blocks.

The main sights are within a stone's throw of Piazza Garibaldi. Just off the square is an imposing 16th-century **viaduct** and, keeping watch over interlinked Piazza Garibaldi and Piazza Petruccioli, the 13th-century **Palazzo Orsini** (☎ 0564 61 44 19; adult/child €2.50/1.50; 10am-1pm & 3-7pm Tue-Sun, to 5pm Oct-Mar). Eighteen of its rooms are open to the public and decked out with a cluttered collection of ecclesiastical objects, assembled, you get the feeling, as much to fill the vast empty space as for any aesthetic merit.

Opposite is the altogether more organised **Museo Archeologico** (☎ 0564 61 40 67; Piazza della Fortezza; adult/child €2.60/1.55; 10am-1pm & 4-7pm Tue-Sun Apr-Sep, 10am-1pm & 3-6pm Tue-Sun Oct-Mar) with a rich display of finds from local Etruscan sites. They're well displayed, but descriptive panels are in Italian only.

Only the tall bell tower remains as a reminder of the Romanesque original of Pitigliano's **cathedral**, with its baroque façade and unexceptional interior.

The town's medieval lanes and steep alleys are a delight to wander, particularly around the small **Ghetto** quarter. Head down Via Zuccarelli and turn left at a sign indicating **La Piccola Gerusalemme** (☎ 0564 61 60 06; Vicolo Manin 30; adult/child €2.50/1.50; 10am-12.30pm & 4-7pm Sun-Fri May-Oct, 10am-12.30pm & 3-5.30pm

Sun-Fri Nov-Apr). The area fell into disrepair with the demise of Pitigliano's Jewish community at the end of WWII, and was practically rebuilt from scratch in 1995. A visit includes the tiny, richly adorned synagogue and a small museum of Jewish culture, including the old bakery, kosher butcher's and dyeing workshops.

There are some spectacular walks around Pitigliano. The base of the rocky outcrop is stippled with Etruscan tomb caves carved into the soft tufa, many of them recycled as storage cellars. From there, you can follow a signed trail (about 6km) to Sovana.

SLEEPING & EATING

Albergo Guastini (☎ 0564 61 60 65; www.albergoguas tini.it; Piazza Petruccioli 16; s/d/tr €36/62/80; ⏰ closed mid-Jan–mid-Feb) Pitigliano's only hotel is friendly and welcoming. Perched on the edge of the cliff face, many of its rooms have marvellous views. Its highly regarded restaurant (meals around €25) also merits a visit.

Hotel Valle Orientina (☎ 0564 61 66 11; www.valle orientina.it; Località Valle Orientina; s/d €70/120; Ⓟ Ⓡ) In lovely pastoral surroundings about 3km from town, this is a relaxing spot with its very own 7th-century thermal baths and the potential for gentle or more strenuous walking in the surrounding countryside.

Osteria Il Tufo Allegro (☎ 0564 61 61 92; Vico della Costituzione 2; mains €13-17.50; ⏰ closed Wed lunch & all Tue) This *osteria* is just off Via Zuccarelli. The aromas emanating from its kitchen should be enough to draw you into the cavernous chamber, carved out of the tufa foundations.

Pick up a stick or two of *sfratto*, a gorgeously sticky local confection of honey and walnuts, from **Il Forno** (Via Roma 16). Counterbalance the sweetness with a glass of the town's lively dryish Bianco di Pitigliano wine from one of the shops lining Via San Chiara, off Piazza Petruccioli.

DRINKING

Jerry Lee Bar (☎ 0564 61 40 99; Via Roma 28; ⏰ closed Mon; ▯) This place has a young vibe and occasional live music. Internet access is €6 per hour.

Il Ghetto (Via Zuccarelli 47) A smart new flagstone and brick wine bar, Il Ghetto has cheese and salami snacks to accompany that favourite tipple.

GETTING THERE & AWAY

Rama (☎ 0564 61 60 40) buses leave from the train station at Grosseto for Pitigliano (€5.50, two hours, four daily). They also connect Pitigliano with Sorano (€2.45, 15 minutes, seven daily) and Sovana (€2.45, 20 minutes, one daily). For Saturnia, change at Manciano.

Sovana

Sovana is really little more than a one-street village of butterscotch-coloured sandstone – but, gosh, it's pretty and has some fine Etruscan sites nearby. The **tourist office** (☎ 0564 61 40 74; ⏰ 10am-1pm & 3-7pm Tue-Sun Mar-Nov, Fri-Sun only Dec-Feb) is in the Palazzo Pretorio.

VIE CAVE

There are at least 15 rock-sculpted passages spreading out in every direction from the valleys below Pitigliano. These sunken roads (vie cave) are enormous, up to 20m deep and 3m wide, and are believed to be sacred routes linking the *necropoli* and other sites associated with the Etruscan religious cult. A less popular, more mundane explanation is that these strange megalithic corridors were used to move livestock or as some kind of defence, allowing people to move from village to village unseen. Whatever the reason, every spring on the night of the equinox (19 March) there is a torch-lit procession down the Via Cava di Giuseppe, which culminates in a huge bonfire in Pitigliano's Piazza Garibaldi. It serves as a symbol of purification and renewal marking the end of winter.

The countryside around Pitigliano, Sovana and Sorano is riddled with *vie cave*. Two particularly good examples, 500m west of Pitigliano on the road to Sovana, are Via Cava di Fratenuti, with its high vertical walls and Etruscan graffiti, and Via Cava di San Giuseppe, which passes the Fontana dell'Olmo, carved out of solid rock. From this fountain stares the sculpted head of Bacchus, the mythological god of fruitfulness, as the water flows from his mouth. Via Cava San Rocco, near Sorano, is another fine example. It winds its way through the hills for 2km between the town and the Necropoli di San Rocco.

If you plan to visit most of the archaeological sites in and around Sovana and Sorano, invest in a €7 combined ticket. It gives entry to Tomba della Sirena, Tomba di Ildebranda, Fortezza Orsini in Sorano, Necropoli di San Rocco, and the Vitozza rock caves outside San Quirico. Buy a ticket at any of the sites.

The **Chiesa di Santa Maria** (Piazza del Pretorio; 9am-6pm), opposite the tourist office, is a starkly simple Romanesque church (although it was interfered with in parts in later centuries) with some rich Renaissance frescoes and, over the altar, a magnificent 9th-century ciborium, or canopy, in white marble, one of the last remaining pre-Romanesque works left in Tuscany.

Walk west along Via del Duomo to reach the imposing Gothic-Romanesque **cathedral** (10am-1pm & 3-7pm Mar-Nov, to 6pm Dec-Feb). Although largely rebuilt in the 12th and 13th centuries, the original construction dates back to the 9th century. The striking portal on the north wall is pieced together from fragments of this earlier building – or, as some would maintain, from a pagan temple.

Sovana was the birthplace of Pope Gregory VII; at the eastern end of the village are a cluster of medieval mansions and the remains of a fortress that belonged to his family.

Within the **Necropoli di Sovana** (admission €5; 9am-7pm Mar-Nov, 10am-5pm Fri-Sun only Dec-Feb), 1.5km south of the village, are Tuscany's most significant Etruscan tombs. Look for the yellow sign on the left for the **Tomba della Sirena**, where you follow a trail running alongside a rank of tomb façades cut from the rock face, as well as walk along a *via cava*.

About 300m beyond is the **Tomba di Ildebranda**, by far the grandest of Etruscan mausoleums and the only surviving temple-style tomb, which still preserves traces of its columns and stairs.

Due east of the village, just outside the tiny hamlet of San Quirico and signposted from the main square, are the **Vitozza rock dwellings** (admission €2; 10am-1pm & 3-6pm Tue-Sun Mar-Oct, 9am-6pm Fri-Sun only Nov-Feb), more than 200 of them, peppering a high rock ridge. One of the largest troglodyte dwellings in Italy, the complex was first inhabited in prehistoric times.

SLEEPING & EATING
Taverna Etrusca (0564 61 61 83; www.sovanahotel.it; Piazza Pretorio 16; s/d €60/80, mains €10-12; closed Jan) This is a three-star hotel whose simple

but attractive rooms have stripped wooden floors. Its restaurant (closed Wednesdays), in the hands of a new and vastly experienced cook, serves mainly Tuscan specialities and always has at least one vegetarian option.

Albergo Scilla (0564 61 65 31; www.scilla-sovana.it; Via R Siviero 1-3; d incl breakfast €92, meals around €35; P) Scilla has eight terracotta-and-white rooms with marshmallow-soft pillows and attractive wrought-iron beds, mosaic bathrooms and a quiet garden. Across the road you can enjoy fine fare at its glassed-in restaurant, Ristorante dei Merli (open Tuesday to Sunday), which has vegetarian options.

Sorano
pop 3850

Retrace your route from Sovana, pass the turn-off for Pitigliano and continue northeast to Sorano. Two kilometres before the village are the **Necropoli di San Rocco** (admission €2; 11am-6pm Tue-Sun Mar-Oct, Fri-Sun only Nov-Feb), another Etruscan burial site. From here it's possible to walk to Sorano along a *via cava*.

Sorano is something of a poor relation of the three hill towns. High on a rocky spur, its houses, many unoccupied and forlorn, seem to huddle together in an effort not to shove one another off the precarious perch.

There's a small **tourist office** (0546 63 30 99) on Piazza Busati.

The town's main attraction is the partly renovated **Fortezza Orsini** (0564 63 37 67; Piazza Cairoli; admission €2; 10am-1pm & 3-7pm mid-Mar–Oct Tue-Sun), with its medieval museum and underground passageways, visited by separate guided tour (€3, 11am and 3pm).

You could also climb up **Masso Leopoldino** (admission €2; 10am-1pm & 3-7pm Apr-Nov), a large platform at the top of the village, for spectacular views of the surrounding countryside.

SLEEPING & EATING
Hotel della Fortezza (0564 63 20 10; www.fortezzahotel.it; Piazza Cairoli 5; s/d €90/150; Mar-Dec) A 14-room hotel within the fortress, this has a heady historical feel with wood-beamed ceilings, tapestries and antique furnishings, plus fantastic views and a decent restaurant.

Talismano (0564 63 32 81; Via San Marco 29; mains €5-7; closed Tue) This is a cavernous place highly popular with locals. The menu has an excellent selection of pizzas and Tuscan dishes, so you'll be hard-pressed not to find something to your liking.

Eastern Tuscany

An easy train ride from Florence puts the capital of this region, Arezzo, within tempting reach even of many fleeting tourists in Tuscany, but relatively few get beyond this former Etruscan city. In the old centre, at its heart the severely sloping Piazza Grande, is the Pieve di Santa Maria, one of the most inspiring examples of Tuscan Romanesque construction. Arezzo has more than enough to warrant a day trip or weekend stopover, while the city also makes an excellent base for exploring the surrounding countryside.

Another popular destination is Cortona, the steep, spectacularly located hill-top eyrie that offers soul-stirring views out over the surrounding Tuscan and Umbrian plains and beyond to Lago di Trasimeno.

The cineworld has recently found both towns to be ideal locations. Roberto Benigni filmed much of the Oscar-winning film *Life Is Beautiful* in Arezzo, while Audrey Wells chose Cortona for some scenes from *Under the Tuscan Sun,* her film of the book by Frances Mayes.

Art-lovers will be attracted by the Piero della Francesca trail. His fresco cycle of the *Legend of the True Cross,* in Arezzo's Chiesa di San Francesco, is unmissable. Then you can head out in search of his other masterpieces in towns such as Monterchi and Sansepolcro.

Beyond the towns, one of the least-visited corners of Tuscany is the hill country of the Casentino, on the frontier with the region of Emilia-Romagna, a lush forested landscape dotted with castles and a couple of fine monasteries.

HIGHLIGHTS

- Join in the medieval fun of the Giostra del Saracino in Arezzo's **Piazza Grande** (p256)

- Gaze in awe at Piero della Francesca's magnificent fresco cycle in the **Chiesa di San Francesco** (p254) in Arezzo

- Explore the back roads of the little-visited **Casentino** (p260) region

- Follow the **Piero della Francesca trail** (p259) from Arezzo to Sansepolcro

- Discover the Etruscan heritage of **Cortona** (p262) and enjoy the splendid views across the Tuscan and Umbrian countryside

★ Casentino

★ Sansepolcro

Arezzo ★

★ Cortona

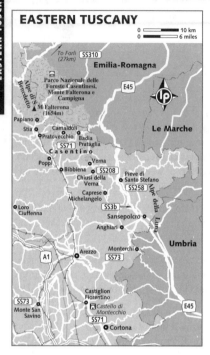

EASTERN TUSCANY

painter and architect who contributed so much to Renaissance Florence.

Another illustrious son, born in a nearby village, is comic actor and director Roberto Benigni, who created and starred in an Oscar-winning film, *Life Is Beautiful*. Locations used in the film are marked throughout Arezzo by signs featuring stills and dialogue in Italian and English.

Orientation
From the train station on the southern edge of the city, pedestrianised, shop-lined Corso Italia, the town's main promenade, leads to the Piazza Grande, Arezzo's nucleus.

Information
Centro di Accoglienza Turistico (☎ 0575 40 35 74; Via Ricasoli; ⊗ 9.30am-5.30pm Apr-Sep, 9.30am-7pm Jul-Aug, 10am-5pm Oct-Mar) An alternative tourist office. Hires out audioguides to Arezzo (adult/child €5/3 per day) with an accompanying map.
Eutelia (Via Guido Monaco 61; per hr €1.50; ⊗ 9am-9pm) Offers Internet access and cheap international phone calls.
Nuovo Ospedale San Donato (☎ 0575 25 50 01; Via A de Gasperi) Hospital outside the city walls.
Police station (☎ 0575 31 81; Via Fra Guittone 3)
Post office (Via Guido Monaco 34)
Tourist office (☎ 0575 2 08 39; www.apt.arezzo .it; Piazza della Repubblica 28; ⊗ 9am-1pm & 3-7pm Mon-Sat, 9am-1pm Sun Apr-Sep, 9am-1pm & 3-6.30pm Mon-Sat Oct-Mar) Can reserve accommodation for personal callers (fee €3).

Sights
CHIESA DI SAN FRANCESCO
Gracing the apse of this 14th-century **church** (Piazza San Francesco; ⊗ 8.30am-noon & 2-6.30pm) is one of the greatest works of Italian art, Piero della Francesca's fresco cycle of the *Legend of the True Cross*. Painted between 1452 and 1466, it relates in 10 episodes the story of the cross on which Christ was crucified.

The illustration of this medieval legend, as entertaining as it is inconceivable, begins in the top right-hand corner and follows the story of the tree that Seth plants on the grave of his father, Adam, and from which, eventually, the True Cross is made. A scene on the opposite wall shows the long-lost cross being rediscovered by Helena, mother of the emperor Constantine; behind her, the city of Jerusalem is represented by a medieval view of Arezzo. Even Khosrow, the Persian emperor accused of making

AREZZO
pop 92,450
Heavily bombed during WWII, Arezzo isn't one of Tuscany's prettiest cities. This said, it's well worth a visit, whether for an overnight stay or as a day trip from Florence. Its small medieval centre retains real character and a number of rewarding highlights. Best known is the five-star fresco cycle by Piero della Francesca in the Chiesa di San Francesco, while the sloping Piazza Grande and the Pieve di Santa Maria, a Romanesque jewel, are also worth seeking out.

Arezzo, in its time an important Etruscan town, was absorbed into the Roman Empire, where it continued to be a flourishing centre of trade. A free republic as early as the 10th century, it supported the Ghibelline cause in the prolonged and bloody conflict between pope and emperor. Arezzo eventually lost its independence in 1384, when it was effectively bought by Guelph Florence.

It's the birthplace of the Renaissance poet Petrarch, who popularised the sonnet format, penning his verses in both Latin and Italian, and Giorgio Vasari, the prolific

off with the cross, features, ignominiously. Rarely will you get a better sense of medieval frescoes as strip cartoon, telling a tale with such vigour and sheer beauty.

You can get some sense of the frescoes from beyond the cordon in front of the altar, but to really appreciate them up close you need to plan ahead for a **visit with audio guide** (☎ 0575 35 27 27; www.pierodellafrancesca.it; admission €6; ☼ 9am-6.30pm Mon-Sat, 1-5pm Sun Apr-Oct, 9am-5.30pm Mon-Sat, 1-5pm Sun Nov-Mar). Since only 25 people are allowed in every half-hour, it's essential to prebook, either by phone or at any of the sights that participate in the combined ticket scheme. The ticket office is at Piazza San Francesco 4, to the right of the church's main entrance.

PIEVE DI SANTA MARIA & AROUND

This 12th-century **church** (Corso Italia 7; ☼ 8am-1pm & 3-7pm May-Sep, 8am-noon & 3-6pm Oct-Apr) has a magnificent Romanesque arcaded façade – reminiscent of the cathedral at Pisa writ small, yet without the glorious marble facing – where each column is different. Over the central doorway are carved reliefs representing the months of the year. The 14th-century bell tower with its 40 apertures is something of an emblem for the city. The monochrome of the interior's warm stone is relieved by Pietro Lorenzetti's fine polyptych *Madonna and Saints*, beneath the semidome of the apse.

Below the altar is a 14th-century silver bust reliquary of the city's patron saint, San Donato. Other treasures on display include

AREZZO

0   200 m
0   0.1 miles

> ## COMBINED TICKET
>
> You can buy a combined ticket (€14) giving entry to the Piero della Francesca frescoes in the Chiesa di San Francesco, plus Museo Archeologico, Museo Statale d'Arte Medievale e Moderna and Museo di Casa Vasari, at any of the four venues.

a 13th-century Crucifix by Margherito di Arezzo and a carved marble bas-relief of the *Adoration of the Magi*.

Opposite the church is the **Casa Museo di Ivan Bruschi** (☎ 0575 35 41 26; Corso Italia 14; admission €3; ☑ 10am-1pm & 3-7pm Tue-Sun Apr-Sep, 10am-1pm & 2-6pm Tue-Sun Oct-Mar), where you can cast an eye over the varied collection of art and antiques amassed by the man who founded the Arezzo antiques fair.

PIAZZA GRANDE & AROUND
This cobbled piazza, the venue for the Giostra del Saracino (opposite), is overlooked at its upper end by the porticoes of the **Palazzo delle Logge Vasariane**, completed in 1573. The **Palazzo della Fraternità dei Laici** with its churchlike façade, in the northwest corner, was started in 1375 in the Gothic style and finished after the onset of the Renaissance.

Via dei Pileati leads to **Casa di Petrarca**, the poet's former home, which contains a small museum and the Accademia Petrarca, a library and research institute devoted primarily to Petrarch. Visits are by appointment and really only for serious Petrarch fans. Enquire at the tourist office for more details.

CATHEDRAL & AROUND
Arezzo's **cathedral** (Piazza Duomo; ☑ 6.30am-12.30pm & 3-6.30pm), at the top of the hill, was started in the 13th century, yet was not completed until well into the 15th century. In the northeast corner, to the left of the bulky, intricately carved main altar, there's an exquisite fresco of *Mary Magdalene* by Piero della Francesca, itself dwarfed in size but not beauty by the rich marble reliefs of the adjoining tomb of Bishop Guido Tarlati.

Off the north aisle, the Capella della Madonna del Conforto has a pair of fine glazed terracotta images from the della Robbia workshop. On the right as you enter is the tomb of Pope Gregory X, who died in Arezzo in 1276.

Up high to the southeast of the cathedral, across the peaceful gardens of the **Passeggio del Prato**, rears the **Fortezza Medicea** (admission free; ☑ 7am-8pm Apr-Oct, 7.30am-6pm Nov-Mar), completed in 1560 and offering grand views of the town and surrounding countryside.

CHIESA DI SAN DOMENICO & AROUND
The short detour to the **Chiesa di San Domenico** (Piazza San Domenico 7; ☑ 8.30am-7pm), with its unusual, asymmetrical façade, is a must. Above the main altar rears a haunting *Crucifixion*, one of Cimabue's earliest works, painted around 1265. Note too the pair of well-preserved frescoes by Spinello Aretino (1350–1410) at the western end, and, in the south aisle, a statue by the della Robbia school of San Pietro Martire with a sword cleaving his skull.

To the west, the **Casa di Vasari** (☎ 0575 40 90 40; Via XX Settembre 55; adult/child €2/1; ☑ 8am-7.30pm Mon & Wed-Sat, 8.30am-1pm Sun) was built and sumptuously decorated (overwhelmingly so in the case of the Sala del Camino, the Fireplace Room) by the architect himself – ring the bell if the door's closed.

Further west again, the **Museo Statale d'Arte Medievale e Moderna** (☎ 0575 40 90 50; Via San Lorentino 8; admission €4; ☑ 8.30am-7.30pm Tue-Sun) primarily houses works by local artists. The two small rooms on the ground floor mostly contain sculptures from local churches, while on the next floor is a display of medieval paintings, including works by Bartolomeo della Gatta and Domenico Pecori, a collection of glazed terracotta pieces by the della Robbia family, and colourful majolica plates. Upstairs, in addition to works by Luca Signorelli and several canvases on the grand scale by Vasari, the chronology continues into the 19th century.

MUSEO ARCHEOLOGICO & ROMAN AMPHITHEATRE
The **Museo Archeologico** (☎ 0575 2 08 82; Via Margaritone 10; admission €4; ☑ 8.30am-7.30pm) is in a former convent overlooking the remains of the **Roman amphitheatre** (admission free; ☑ 7.30am-8pm Apr-Oct, to 6pm Nov-Mar), which once seated up to 10,000 spectators. Inside, there's a sizable collection of Etruscan and Roman artefacts, including locally produced ceramics and bronzes. Among the highlights is the Cratere di Euphronios, a large 6th-century-BC Etruscan vase, decorated with vivid scenes

showing Hercules in battle, and, upstairs, an exquisite tiny portrait of a bearded man executed on glass in the 3rd century AD.

Activities

Alessandro Madiai (☎ 338 6491481; torrequebrada@ virgilio.it) A passionate cyclist, runs two five-hour bicycle tours, plus overnighters, around the enchanting southern Tuscany countryside within reach of Arezzo.

Centro di Accoglienza Turistico (p254) Projects *Arezzo da Vedere*, a 15-minute audiovisual show (adult/child €2/1.50) that gives a vivid overview of the city.

Festivals & Events

Antiques Fair Arezzo stages a huge and highly reputed antiques fair that pulls in over 500 exhibitors and spreads over the Piazza Grande and surrounding streets on the first Saturday and Sunday of every month.

Arezzo Wave (www.arezzowave.com in Italian) Over five or six days in late June/early July, the town hosts this music festival featuring artists and bands from Italy and abroad. It occasionally includes some top international acts (Motorhead topped the bill in 2005).

Giostra del Saracino (below) Takes place on the second-last Sunday of June, and on the first Sunday of September.

Sleeping

Villa Severi (☎ 0575 29 90 47; www.peterpan.it; Via F Redi 13; dm/d €15/35; ⌚ year-round) A non-HI youth hostel, Severi is out of town in a wonderfully restored and spacious villa overlooking the countryside. Take bus No 4 from Piazza Guido Monaco.

La Terrazza (☎ 0575 2 83 87; laterrazza@lycos.it; 5th fl, Via Guido Monaco 25; s/d incl breakfast €35/50) This place, with shared bathrooms, is welcoming and good value. Essentially a couple of stylish apartments on two floors, its five rooms are large and light, there's a kitchen for guest use and the landlady bakes the tastiest of cakes. Go down the passage beside Blockbuster.

Hotel Patio (☎ 0575 40 19 62; www.hotelpatio.it; Via Cavour 23; s/d/ste from €130/176/224; P ✖) This is Arezzo's most characterful hotel, with seven themed rooms, each dedicated to one of Bruce Chatwin's travel books. Each has original furnishings from the various countries represented, including Australia, Morocco and China. Valet parking is €18.

Hotel I Portici (☎ 0575 40 31 32; www.hoteliportici .com; Via Roma 18; r incl breakfast from €130; ✖) This is an elegant four-star place with just eight rooms on the 4th floor of a city-centre apartment block. It offers luxurious, individually designed rooms with large bathrooms. All have power showers and a couple come with Jacuzzis. Much of the furniture includes family heirlooms, and Room 28 (€185) has a terrace with a sweeping view of the town. It's where Bruno Beatrice, ex-Fiorentina and Italy football star, invested his money, converting the family home into a hotel.

Hotel Continentale (☎ 0575 2 02 51; www.hotelconti nentale.com; Piazza Guido Monaco 7; s/d €67/98; P ✖ ▢) A modern, central, three-star hotel option, with comfy, spotless rooms. There's individual

---

GIOSTRA DEL SARACINO

With its origins back in the time of the Crusades, the 'Joust of the Saracen' is one of those grand, noisy affairs involving extravagant fancy dress and neighbourhood rivalry that Italians delight in. Like many such Tuscan folk spectacles, the tournament was revived in its present form in 1931 after long neglect. The day begins with a herald reading a proclamation, followed by a procession of precisely 311 people in 14th-century dress and 31 horses. The jousters are then blessed on the steps of the cathedral by the Bishop of Arezzo. It's the highlight of the year for the city's four Quartieri (Quarters), each of which puts forward a team of knights armed with lances. In the Piazza Grande, the 'knights' try their hand jousting at a wooden effigy, known as the 'Buratto', representing a Saracen warrior. In one hand the Buratto holds a shield, etched with various point-scores, which the knights aim for while trying to avoid being belted with the *mazzafrustro* – basically three heavy leather balls on ropes – which dangle from the Buratto's other hand. The winning team takes home the coveted Golden Lance, bringing glory to their Quartiere.

Arezzo's division into Quartieri dates back to at least the 11th century, and there's still a strong sense of neighbourhood pride and loyalty, with heraldic flags fluttering from shops and homes, and communal events taking place throughout the year. The Quartieri are named after the four gates of the city, and each has its own distinctive colours. They are the centre of social and cultural life for their inhabitants, throwing dinners, running excursions and generally fostering community spirit.

EASTERN TUSCANY

Internet access in every room, a bar that tempts you to linger and a roof terrace with fine views. Valet parking is €15.

Cavaliere Palace Hotel (☎ 0575 2 68 36; www .cavalierehotels.com; Via della Madonna del Prato 83; s/d incl breakfast €93/135; P ☒) This is a reliable four-star choice, barely 200m from the station, that offers a friendly welcome. Rooms, while unexciting, are snug, well sound-proofed and more than adequate. Hotel parking is €13.

La Toscana (☎/fax 0575 2 16 92; Via M Perennio 56; s/d €37/48) A little away from the action, La Toscana is another good budget choice. Rooms are bright and clean as a new pin, and there's a small garden at the rear.

Camping Le Ginestre (☎ 0575 36 35 66; www.camp ingleginestre.it; Via Ruscello 100; person/pitch €8/13; ☒ year-round) This is the nearest camp site. Take LFI bus No S2 in the direction of Viciomaggio.

Eating

Torre di Gnicche (☎ 0575 35 20 35; Piaggia San Martino 8; mains around €9; ☒ closed Wed) Just off the Piazza Grande, this is a fine old traditional restaurant that offers a rich variety of anti-pasti. Choose from the ample range of local *pecorino* cheeses, accompanied by a choice red from its extensive wine list.

Lancia d'Oro (☎ 0575 2 10 33; Piazza Grande 18-19; mains €11-13; ☒ closed Sun evening & Mon) A sophis-ticated place with fresh flowers on the ta-bles where your order is supplemented by excellent snacks and titbits that arrive un-announced. There's a jolly, waggish waiter, while the interior, painted with swags and green-and-white stripes, is like dining in a marquee. It is run by two brothers who also run Logge Vasari, and has a terrace under the loggia that looks down over Piazza Grande.

Ristorante Logge Vasari (☎ 0575 30 03 33; Via Vasari 19; mains €12-14; ☒ closed Tue) This restau-rant has two pleasant interior rooms and serves equally delectable cuisine. You'll leave satisfied and satiated if you treat yourself to the innovative *menu degustazione* (€36). Like Lancia d'Oro it also has a terrace over-looking Piazza Grande.

Antica Trattoria da Guido (☎ 0575 2 37 60; Via della Madonna del Prato 85; meals from €18; ☒ closed Sun) Wood-panelled and with ochre walls, this is an economical family-run trattoria that serves up excellent, home-style food. Its short, handwritten menu changes regularly, according to what's best in the market.

Trattoria Il Saraceno (☎ 0575 2 76 44; Via G Mazzini 3a; mains €7-11; ☒ closed Wed) With 60 years in business, this trattoria serves quality, varied Tuscan fare at very reasonable prices. The impressive wine collection, to suit all pal-ates and pockets, is arrayed around every wall, and it also does pizzas (from €5).

Buca di San Francesco (☎ 0575 2 32 71; Via San Francesco 1; mains €8-10; ☒ closed Mon dinner & Tue) Arched and vaulted, this is all soft angles, its walls decorated with frescoes. Mains are good value and it does three set menus (€13, €16 and €19), styled *frate, abate* and *priore* (friar, abbot and prior), as befits a restaurant that's beside the Chiesa di San Francesco.

I Tre Bicchieri (☎ 0575 2 65 57; Piazzetta Sopra I Ponti 3-5; mains €18; ☒ closed Wed) An upscale restaurant in a little square off Corso Italia, serving, among a range of innovative op-tions, dishes such as roast quail in Chianti and creative fresh pasta options.

La Tua Piadina (☎ 0575 2 32 40; Via de' Cenci 18) A justifiably popular takeaway place hidden away down a side street, where you can get a range of hot, tasty *piadine*, the Emilia ver-sion of the wrap, from around €3.

Piazza Sant'Agostino comes alive each Tuesday, Thursday and Saturday with the city's produce market.

Drinking

Compagni di Merende (☎ 0575 1 82 23 68; Logge Vasari 16) A friendly, unassuming little wine bar with an unparalleled position, tucked under the loggia overlooking Piazza Grande. Enjoy a plate of cheese or cold cuts, or sim-ply a restorative glass of wine.

Vita Bella (☎ 0575 35 37 96; Piazza San Francesco 22) Opposite the Chiesa di San Francesco, Vita Bella is an agreeable place with wrought-iron chairs where you can sip a Negroni and watch the world go by.

Crispi's (☎ 0575 2 28 73; Via Francesco Crispi 10/12) This is a restaurant (pizzas from around €5.50) that, from 10.30pm, converts into a pub, where you can have an evening tipple among a primarily young crowd.

Getting There & Away

Services from the bus station at Piazza della Repubblica include Cortona (€2.60, one hour, more than 10 daily), Sansepolcro (€3, one hour, seven daily) and Siena (€5, 1½ hours, seven daily). For Florence, you're better off hopping on the train.

Arezzo is on the Florence–Rome train line, with frequent services to Rome (€20.70, two hours) and Florence (€10.10, 1½ hours). Trains call by Cortona (€2.10, 20 minutes, hourly).

Arezzo is a few kilometres east of the A1, and the SS73 heads east to Sansepolcro.

NORTHEAST OF AREZZO

The art-lover's trail in search of masterpieces by Piero della Francesca leads northeast of Arezzo to the towns of Monterchi and Sansepolcro, both easy day trips from Arezzo.

Monterchi & Anghiari

Visit Monterchi to see Piero della Francesca's fresco **Madonna del Parto** (☎ 0575 7 07 13; Via della Reglia 1; adult/child €3.10/free; ⊙ 9am-1pm & 2-7pm Tue-Sun Apr-Sep, to 6pm Oct-Mar). The Pregnant Madonna is considered one of the key works of 15th-century Italian art and the only such representation known from the period. A sensitive touch: pregnant women get free admission and there are also free medieval music recitals at 9pm on Wednesdays from June to August. Parking can be a problem since there's no special provision.

A few kilometres north of Monterchi and the SS73 lies the pretty medieval village of Anghiari, which is worth a brief stop-off to meander along its narrow twisting lanes.

Some 17km north of Anghiari is **Caprese Michelangelo**, birthplace of the great artist. Within the town's castle is the **Museo Michelangelo** (☎ 0575 79 37 76; Via Capuolog 1; adult/child €4/3; ⊙ 10am-7pm Jun-Sep, 10am-6pm Mon-Fri Oct-May), a rather lacklustre affair devoted to the man and his works.

Sansepolcro
pop 15,750

Sansepolcro is best known as the birthplace of Piero della Francesca (c1420–92), though the artist left town when he was quite young, and returned only when he was in his 70s to work on his treatises, including the seminal *On Perspective in Painting*. Today, while the surrounding light-industrial sprawl doesn't make for a picturesque frame, the town's medieval heart remains pleasant.

There's a small **tourist office** (☎ 0575 74 05 36; infosansepolcro@apt.arezzo.it; Via Matteotti 8; ⊙ 9am-1pm & 3.30-6.30pm Apr-Sep, 9.30am-12.30pm & 3.30-5.30pm Mon-Sat, 9.30am-12.30pm Sun Oct-Mar) in town.

In the former town hall, just outside the main city gate and around the corner from the tourist office, the **Museo Civico** (☎ 0575 73 22 18; Via Aggiunti 65; adult/child €6.20/3; ⊙ 9am-1.30pm & 2.30-7.30pm Jun-Sep, 9.30am-1pm & 2.30-6pm Oct-May) features a couple of Piero della Francesca's masterpieces. In the *Resurrezione* (Resurrection), the newly risen Christ stares out at the viewer, banner in hand like a triumphant warrior, while his guards slumber. In the splendid *Madonna della Misericordia* polyptych, the Virgin spreads her protective cloak over the painting's benefactors.

There are also works by another local artist, Santi di Tito, whose *Riposo Durante la Fuga in Egitto* (Rest During the Flight into Egypt) portrays the Holy Family in a tender and humanistic light.

Upstairs there's a display of 14th- and 15th-century frescoes, including a haunting portrait of St Sebastian, while the basement holds a small gathering of archaeological finds and ecclesiastical knick-knackery.

DETOUR: PIERO DELLA FRANCESCA TRAIL

The so-called Piero della Francesca trail makes for a pleasant day trip, taking in the Valtiberina (High Tiber Valley). From Arezzo take the SS71 north for about 4km, as far as Ponte alla Chiassa. Turn east, through the hilly countryside of the Alpe di Catenaia, passing through the village of Chiaveretto. Continue on to the well-preserved medieval village of Anghiari, which makes a rewarding short stopover. From here it's a straight, though not particularly scenic, 6km drive northeast to Sansepolcro, where a number of the great artist's works are on show.

Head southwest from Sansepolcro along the SS73. After roughly 12km you will see a sign for the *Madonna del Parto* (Pregnant Madonna); take the minor road that leads east for 3km, and then turn south for about 500m and you'll be in Monterchi, the home of della Francesca's *Madonna del Parto*. Retrace your route back to the SS73 and zoom down the four-lane highway back to Arezzo.

John Pope-Hennessy's book *The Piero della Francesca Trail* (1993) is an interesting source of information on the painter and the region.

About 150m eastwards is the **Aboca museum** (☎ 0575 73 35 89; Via Aggiunti 75; adult/child €8/4; 10am-1pm & 3-7pm Tue-Sun Apr-Sep, 10am-1pm & 2.30-6pm Oct-Mar), dedicated to the history of pharmacy and herbal medicine, with a re-creation of a 17th-century laboratory. Given the high ticket price, it's likely to appeal only to those with a specialist interest in things alternative and pharmaceutical.

Just south of the tourist office is the **cathedral**, closed for extensive renovation at the time of writing. Its most celebrated treasure is the *Volto Santo* (Holy Visage), a striking wooden crucifix with a wide-eyed Christ, dating back to at least the 12th century.

On the second Sunday in September, the **Palio della Balestra**, a crossbow contest, pits costumed archers from Gubbio against Sansepolcro's best.

Locanda Giglio (☎ 0575 74 20 33; Via L Pacioli 60; s/d/tr incl buffet breakfast €45/70/95; P) and **Ristorante Fiorentino** (meals €20-25) are exceptionally friendly and have been in the same family for four generations. The four hotel rooms, with their oak floors, underfloor lighting and period furniture recovered from the family loft, have been imaginatively renovated by Alessia, an architect and youngest of the family (ask for La Torre with a lovely low bed and the best of the views, while Dad, Alessio, still runs the restaurant with panache. The pasta's homemade, and the imaginative menu changes with the seasons (Alessio tells you with pride that there'll never be a freezer in *his* kitchen).

Orfeo (☎ 0575 74 20 61; fax 0575 74 22 87; Viale Armando Diaz 12; s/d €35/55) is a decent budget option just outside the old town's western gate though you may find the wall-to-wall pink décor a bit overwhelming.

SITA buses link Sansepolcro with Arezzo (€3, one hour, seven daily) and several trains leave daily to Perugia (€4.40, 1¾ hours).

THE CASENTINO REGION

A tour through the remote forest and farming region of Casentino takes you through a little-visited area that boasts a couple of still active monasteries and some wonderful walking in the Parco Nazionale delle Foreste Casentinesi, Monte Falterona e Campigna.

La Ferroviaria Italiana (LFI; ☎ 0575 3 98 81), a private train line, runs from Arezzo, following the upper reaches of the River Arno, and serves towns and villages as far as Stia.

The rest of the region is only practically accessible with your own transport, for which we describe a one-day circuit.

Parco Nazionale delle Foreste Casentinesi, Monte Falterona e Campigna

This **national park** (www.parcoforestecasentinesi.it) goes over both sides of the Tuscany-Emilia-Romagna border, taking in some of the most scenic stretches of the Apennines. The Tuscan part is gentler than the Emilian side.

One of the highest peaks, **Monte Falterona** (1654m), marks the source of the Arno. Apart from the human population, including the inhabitants of two monasteries, the park is also home to a rich assortment of wildlife, including foxes, wolves, deer and wild boar, plus nearly 100 bird species. The dense forests are a cool summer refuge, ideal for walking and also escaping the madding crowds. The Grande Escursione Appenninica (GEA) trekking trail passes through here, and myriad walking paths crisscross the park.

From Arezzo take the SS71 northwards through Bibbiena and on up to **Badia Prataglia**, a pleasant little mountain village in the Alpe di Serra, near the border with Emilia-Romagna. Its **visitors centre** (☎ 0575 55 94 47; www.orostoscana.com in Italian; 9am-12.30pm & 3.30-6pm Tue-Sun Jun-Sep, 9am-12.30pm Tue-Sat, 9am-12.30pm & 3.30-6pm Sun Oct-May) carries a wealth of information about the park, including two useful titles in English: *The National Park of the Casentine Forests: Where the Trees Touch the Sky* (€12) and *The National Park of the Forests of Casentin, Monte Falterona and Campigna* (€7.50). There's a free leaflet in Italian detailing nine short, signed nature walks within the park. For more strenuous hiking, pick up the *Carta Escursionista, Parco Nazionale delle Foreste Casentinesi, Monte Falterona e Campigna* map (€8.25) at 1:25,000, which features more than 800km of trails.

Camaldoli

From Badia Prataglia, go back along the SS71, then turn right after 3.5km to head for Camaldoli and its **monastery** (☎ 0575 55 60 12; 8.30am-12.30pm & 2.30-6.30pm). The monks managed the forests that still stand around the monastery, and developed all sorts of medicinal and herbal products. You're free to wander about the place and visit the **Antica Farmacia** (9am-12.30pm & 2.30-6pm Thu-Tue). The monks still make all manner of products, including liqueurs, honey, perfumes and chocolate. If the monastery's closed, the bar of the Albergo Camaldoli opposite sells some of its products, which are also available in other towns in the region, including Arezzo.

Continue for a further 1.5km, then turn right and follow signs to the more interesting **Eremo di Camaldoli**. Apparantly, Conte Maldolo gave the land for this isolated retreat to St Romualdo in 1012. From the name of the count came that of the location, and around 1023 Romualdo set about building the monastery that became home to the Camaldolesi, an ascetic branch of the Benedictines and a powerful force in medieval Tuscany. You can visit his wood-panelled cell, the model for 20 small, tiled houses that are the cells of today's resident Benedictine monks.

Retrace your route for 600m, then turn right, signed Pratovecchio, which is reached after 16km. The drive itself is a delight, the lush forest and superb views easily compensating for the energy exerted coping with the bends.

Pratovecchio & Around

Pratovecchio itself is of little interest apart from its porticoed Piazza Garibaldi. The LFI private train line runs through here, with regular trains connecting Arezzo (via Bibbiena and Poppi) with Stia.

Just west of town you can make a detour to follow signs to the attractively sited Romanesque **Pieve di Romena**, then on between the fields to **Castello di Romena.** This crumbling, mainly 13th-century castle, closed for safety reasons when we last called by and looking likely to stay that way, has known better days. Erected around AD 1000 on the site of an Etruscan settlement, it was in its heyday an enormous complex surrounded by three sets of defensive walls. Dante, says legend, got his inspiration for the Circles of Hell from observing the castle's prison tower at the heart of its concentric defensive walls.

Take the SS310 down the valley to Poppi, then on to Bibbiena.

Poppi & Bibbiena

The most striking town of the Casentino region is Poppi, perched on a hill in the Arno plain. It's topped by the gaunt commanding presence of the **Castello dei Conti Guidi** (☎ 0575 52 05 16; Piazza Repubblica 1; adult/child incl audioguide

€4/3; ☒ core hr 10am-6pm Jul-Oct), built by the same counts who raised the Castello di Romena.

Its main attraction is the chapel on the 2nd floor, with frescoes by Taddeo Gaddi. The scene of *Herod's Feast* shows Salome apparently clicking her fingers as she dances, accompanied by a lute player, while John the Baptist's headless corpse lies slumped in the corner. Also of interest is the Sala della Feste, with its restored medieval frescoes.

Bibbiena has reasonable transport links to the national park. There are four buses daily to both Camaldoli (€1.60) and Verna (€2.10), each taking around 45 minutes.

Santuario di San Francesco (Verna)

This Franciscan monastic complex is 23km east of Bibbiena in Verna. Of more interest than the Camaldoli monastery to many modern pilgrims, it's where St Francis of Assisi is said to have received the stigmata, and, in a sense, it's closer to the essence of the saint than Assisi itself.

When you enter, follow signs for the **sanctuary** (☎ 0575 5341; ☒ 6.30am-8.30pm). The Chiesa Maggiore (also known as the Basilica) has some remarkable glazed ceramics by Andrea della Robbia. There are also reliquaries containing items associated with the saint, including his clothing stained with blood from stigmatic wounds and the whip with which he'd impose a little self-discipline.

Beside the Basilica entrance is the **Cappella della Pietà**. From it, the **Corridoio delle Stimmate**, painted with frescoes recounting the saint's life, leads to a cluster of chapels. At the core of the sanctuary, is the **Cappella delle Stimmate**, beautifully decorated with terracotta works by Luca and Andrea della Robbia.

SOUTH OF AREZZO
Castiglion Fiorentino

This commanding hillside village merits a quick stop off on the route between Arezzo and Cortona. Fought over throughout the Middle Ages for its strategic position, it finally fell to Florentine rule in 1384.

Above the main Piazza del Municipio and at the highest point of the old town, is the **Pinacoteca** (☎ 0575 65 74 66; Via del Cassero; adult/child €3/2; ☒ 10am-12.30pm & 4-6.30pm Tue-Sun), whose paintings include works by Taddeo Gaddi. Nearby, the **Museo Archeologico** (☎ 0575 65 94 57; Via del Tribunale 8; admission €3; ☒ 10am-12.30pm & 4-6.30pm Tue-Sun Apr-Oct, 10am-12.30pm & 3.30-6pm

Sat & Sun only Nov-Mar) has a small collection of local finds. A combined ticket giving access to both costs €5/3 per adult/child.

A few kilometres further south along the road to Cortona, you can't miss the **Castello di Montecchio**, a formidable redoubt that Florence gave to the English mercenary Sir John Hawkwood (c1320–94) in return for his military services. You can see the knight's portrait in the Duomo (see p87) in Florence. The privately owned castle is presently closed to visitors.

Cortona

pop 22,300

Set high on a hillside cloaked in olive groves, Cortona offers stunning views across the Tuscan countryside. A small settlement when the Etruscans moved in during the 8th century BC, it later became a Roman town. In the late 14th century Fra Angelico lived and worked here, and fellow artists Luca Signorelli (1450–1523) and Pietro da Cortona (1596–1669) were both born within its walls.

Large chunks of *Under the Tuscan Sun*, the soap-in-the-sun film of the book by Frances Mayes, were shot in Cortona. (You'll look in vain, though, for the fountain in which the eccentric Englishwoman cavorts; it was built specially for the occasion and only flowed during shooting.)

The town is small, easily seen in a few hours, and well worth visiting for the sensational views over Val de Chiana and as far as Lago di Trasimeno.

ORIENTATION

Piazza Garibaldi, on the southern edge of the walled city, is where buses arrive. From it, there are sensational views across the plain to Lago di Trasimeno. From the piazzale, walk straight up Via Nazionale – about the only flat street in the whole town – to Piazza della Repubblica, the main square.

INFORMATION

Pensieri Grandi e Piccoli (Via Guelfa 36; per hr €5; ☾ 10am-1pm & 2-6pm Mon-Sat) An eccentric souvenir shop with a couple of Internet terminals.
Tourist office (☎ 0575 63 03 52; Via Nazionale 42; ☾ 9am-1pm & 3-7pm Mon-Sat, 9am-1pm Sun May-Sep, 9am-1pm & 3-6pm Mon-Fri, 9am-1pm Sat Oct-Apr)

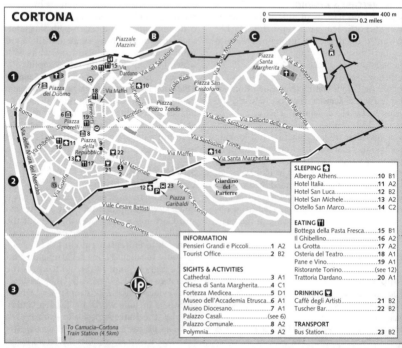

CORTONA

INFORMATION	
Pensieri Grandi e Piccoli	1 A2
Tourist Office	2 B2

SIGHTS & ACTIVITIES	
Cathedral	3 A1
Chiesa di Santa Margherita	4 C1
Fortezza Medicea	5 D1
Museo dell'Accademia Etrusca	6 A1
Museo Diocesano	7 A1
Palazzo Casali	(see 6)
Palazzo Comunale	8 A2
Polymnia	9 A2

SLEEPING	
Albergo Athens	10 B1
Hotel Italia	11 A2
Hotel San Luca	12 B2
Hotel San Michele	13 A2
Ostello San Marco	14 C2

EATING	
Bottega della Pasta Fresca	15 B1
Il Ghibellino	16 A2
La Grotta	17 A2
Osteria del Teatro	18 A1
Pane e Vino	19 A1
Ristorante Tonino	(see 12)
Trattoria Dardano	20 A1

DRINKING	
Caffè degli Artisti	21 B2
Tuscher Bar	22 B2

TRANSPORT	
Bus Station	23 B2

To Camucia–Cortona Train Station (4.5km)

SIGHTS

Brooding over lopsided Piazza della Repubblica is the **Palazzo Comunale**, built in the 13th century, renovated in the 16th, and once again in the 19th. To the north is attractive Piazza Signorelli and, on its north side, 13th-century **Palazzo Casali**, whose rather plain façade was added in the 17th century.

Inside the palace is the **Museo dell'Accademia Etrusca** (☎ 0575 63 04 15; Piazza Signorelli 9; adult/child €4.20/1.50; ☾ 10am-7pm daily Apr-Oct, 10am-5pm Tue-Sun Nov-Mar), with an eclectic array of art and antiquities, including Etruscan bronzes, medieval paintings and 18th-century furniture. One of the most intriguing pieces is an elaborate 2nd-century-BC bronze Etruscan oil lamp, decorated with satyrs, sirens and a Gorgon's head, and weighing in at a hefty 55kg. The Egyptian collection includes a couple of mummies. In the Medici Room are a pair of early-18th-century globes of heaven and earth, where the creative cartographer shows the Isola di California floating free from the western coast of America. Upstairs you can see material recently excavated from local Etruscan tombs. Book in advance for a guided tour of the museum in English (€5, 10.30am, minimum five people) and of three Etruscan tombs (adult/child €10.50/7.75 with guide) in the surrounding countryside. Combined tours of both cost €13/9.50.

Little is left of the original Romanesque character of the **cathedral** (Piazza del Duomo), northwest of Piazza Signorelli. It was completely rebuilt late in the Renaissance and again, indifferently, in the 18th century. Its true wealth lies in the riches within the **Museo Diocesano** (☎ 0575 6 28 30; Piazza del Duomo 1; adult/child €5/1; ☾ 10am-7pm daily Apr-Oct, 10am-5pm Tue-Sun Nov-Mar) in the former church of Gesù.

Room 1 has a remarkable Roman sarcophagus decorated with a frenzied battle scene between Dionysus and the Amazons. Here and continuing into the adjoining Room 4 are paintings by Luca Signorelli, including his *Compianto sul Cristo Morto* (Grief over the Dead Christ; 1502) a masterpiece of colour, composition and pathos. In Room 3 there's a moving *Crucifixion* by Pietro Lorenzetti, the star work of the collection: Fra Angelico's *Annunciazione* (Annunciation; 1436), one of the most recognisable images of Renaissance art that by its sheer luminosity leaves all the surrounding works in the shade. Also by Fra Angelico and almost as moving is his exquisite *Madonna*. Downstairs the Oratorio is decorated with biblical frescoes by Vasari's workshop.

Walk up through a sleepy warren of steep, cobbled lanes in the eastern part of town to the largely 19th-century **Chiesa di Santa Margherita** (Piazza Santa Margherita; ☾ 7.30am-noon & 3-7pm Apr-Oct, 8.30am-noon & 3-6pm Oct-Apr). Within is the ornate 14th-century tomb of Cortona's patron saint, Margherita, whose remains are within the coffin above the main altar. It's a stiff climb, but it's worth pushing even further uphill to the end of Via di Fortezza and the forbidding **Fortezza Medicea** (☎ 0575 63 04 15; adult/child €3/1.50; ☾ 10am-6pm Apr-Oct). This is Cortona's highest point, with stupendous views over the surrounding countryside.

ACTIVITIES

Cortona Wellness (☎ 0575 60 31 36; www.cortona wellness.it in Italian) organises guided four- to five-hour hikes (about €15 per person) in the spectacular countryside around Cortona.

COURSES

Polymnia (☎ 0575 61 25 82; www.polymnia.net; Vicolo Boni 18) offers Italian language courses and related cultural and social activities for non-native speakers.

FESTIVALS & EVENTS

Giostra dell'Archidado A full week of merriment in May or June (the date varies to coincide with Ascension day), with trumpeting, parading and neighbourhood rivalry, culminates ina crossbow competition first held in the Middle Ages. Among other festivities, contestants from the city's traditional neighbourhoods dress up in medieval garb to compete for the *verretta d'oro* (golden arrow).

Mostra Antiquaria Every year for about a week from late August into the first days of September, Cortona hosts one of Italy's main antique fairs.

Sagra del Fungo Porcino Held in mid-August this is a similar celebration to the Steak Festival, honouring this delectable variety of mushroom.

Sagra della Bistecca (Steak Festival) Held on 14 and 15 August this is a gastronomic celebration, when Giardino del Parterre becomes one vast open-air grill.

SLEEPING

Hotel San Michele (☎ 0575 60 43 48; www.hotel sanmichele.net; Via Guelfa 15; s/d incl breakfast from €83/134; ☾ closed Jan–mid-Mar; ℗ ﹩) This is Cortona's finest hotel. Primarily Renaissance, but with elements dating from the 12th century and modifications over subsequent centuries, it's like a little history of Cortona in stone. Rooms are airy, spacious and exquisitely furnished. Parking is €11.

Hotel Italia (☎ 0575 63 02 54; www.planhotel.com /hitalia; Via Ghibellina 5/7; s/d/tr incl breakfast €75/100/125; ✸) Recently taken over and extensively renovated by the new owners, Italia is in a 17th-century palazzo just off Piazza della Repubblica. Rooms have traditional crossbeamed ceilings and are decorated in warm orange and ochre colours. Views are breathtaking from the roof-level breakfast room.

Hotel San Luca (☎ 0575 63 04 60; www.sanlucacortona.com; Piazza Garibaldi 2; s/d €70/100; ✸ 🖳) This is a modern hotel, handy for the bus stop. Uniquely for Cortona, it has public parking in front, and also a great restaurant, Torino. Rooms in general are fairly small but many have magnificent panoramic views.

Albergo Athens (☎ 0575 63 05 08; fax 0575 60 44 57; Via Sant'Antonio 12; s/d/tr/q without bathroom €24/37/45/52; ✷ closed Dec-Jan & Aug) This is a pleasant option with simple rooms, some with commanding views. You can often squeeze in, though most rooms are occupied by US students during the academic year, when their professors pamper themselves in Room 2, the only one with a bathroom.

Ostello San Marco (☎ 0575 60 13 92; ostellocortona@ libero.it; Via Maffei 57; dm/d incl breakfast €12/32) An HI-affiliated youth hostel a short, steep walk east of Piazza Garibaldi, this is a run-down, ill-cared-for place (we got bed bugs here), despite its impressive premises.

EATING

Osteria del Teatro (☎ 0575 63 05 56; Via Maffei 2; mains €8-15; ✷ Thu-Tue) This place has friendly service and fresh flowers on every table. Featuring in nearly every Italian gastronomic guide, its walls are clad with photos of actors who have dined here. In summer try the *ravioli ai fiori di zucca* (pumpkin-flower ravioli). Downsides are the over-obtrusive music and the staple of *soi-disant* Italian restaurants outside Italy – a giant phallus of a pepperpot that the waiter handles with difficulty.

Ristorante Tonino (☎ 0575 63 05 00; Piazza Garibaldi 1; meals about €30-35; ✷ closed Mon dinner & Tue) Tonino has magnificent views as far as Lago di Trasimeno from its summer terrace, and specialises in antipasti. Try the *ravioli al tartufo e pecorino* (ravioli with truffles and *pecorino*).

Pane e Vino (☎ 0575 63 10 10; Piazza Signorelli 27; ✷ Tue-Sun) This is a hugely popular dining hall, in the centre of town. For a quick snack of regional specialities, go for the *piatto del cacciatore*, the hunter's platter of wild boar, deer, goose and turkey. There are more than 500 wines to choose from and most of the pasta (€5.20 to €6) is homemade.

La Grotta (☎ 0575 63 02 71; Piazzetta Baldly 3; mains €8-15; ✷ closed Tue) At the end of a blind alley just off Piazza della Repubblica, this is a rock-reliable choice, though the service can be a little haphazard. Twin-roomed and intimate, it has all the virtues of a traditional trattoria. If you go for strong flavours, begin with the melted *scrota* smoked cheese with either porcini mushrooms or black truffles.

Il Ghibellina (☎ 0575 63 02 54; Via Ghibellina 9; mains from €6.20) In the barrel-vaulted cellar of a 17th-century palazzo, this place serves up typical Tuscan fare and has a good choice of wines.

Trattoria Dardano (☎ 0575 60 19 44; Via Dardano 24; meals €15-20; ✷ Thu-Tue) Dardano is just one of half a dozen reliable, no-nonsense trattorie that line Via Dardano.

Self-caterers should stock up at **Bottega della Pasta Fresca** (Via Dardano 29), a glorious little hole-in-the-wall shop that makes its own pasta. There's a Saturday market, including farmers' products, in Piazza Signorelli.

DRINKING

Tuscher Bar (☎ 0575 6 20 53; Via Nazionale 43; ✷ closed Mon) This is a stylish place to enjoy a coffee or cocktail, and also does good light lunches.

Caffè degli Artisti (☎ 0575 60 12 37; Via Nazionale 18) Across the road and in the same vein, this place also serves great snacks throughout the day and pours a decent pint of Guinness.

GETTING THERE & AROUND

From the bus station at Piazza Garibaldi, LFI buses connect the town with Arezzo (€2.60, one hour, more than 10 daily), via Castiglion Fiorentino.

Shuttle buses (€1, 15 minutes) run at least hourly to Camucia-Cortona train station, on the main Rome–Florence line. Destinations include Arezzo (€2.10, 20 minutes, hourly), Florence (€6.50, 1½ hours, hourly), Rome (€8.90, 2¼ hours, every two hours) and Perugia (€2.70, 40 minutes, over 12 daily).

The tourist office has timetables and sells both bus and train tickets.

By car, the city is on the north–south SS71 that runs to Arezzo. It's also close to the SS75 that connects Perugia to the A1.

Umbria

DAVID TOMLINSON

Northern Umbria

Italy has a green heart: Umbria.

The tourist slogan rings true. Umbria is Italy's most rural region, and the only province that borders neither the ocean nor another country. Umbria has a vast collection of medieval hill towns, sloping farmlands and Etruscan ruins. But Umbria also has a feral geography scattered with jagged rock formations and snowcapped peaks. It has an ethereal feel, and this, along with the indefatigable spirit of its people, makes a visit to Umbria a magical experience.

Much of Umbria looks as it did hundreds of years ago. Assisi's most popular attraction is the Basilica di San Francesco, where pilgrims and visitors congregate to pay homage to St Francis. Winding paths allow ample space for meditative exploration through this hill town, whose pink stone buildings glow at sunset. Perugia's range of restaurants, cultural events, museums and churches gives it a cosmopolitan yet historic air, but the heart of northern Umbria can be found in the smaller towns and countless tiny villages where one could get lost for days.

The best way to see northern Umbria is to wander off on side roads to search for ancient abbeys and fields of brilliant wildflowers. You'll no doubt come across a historic treasure or magnificent event, especially in the summer and autumn – Umbria hosts more festivals, medieval tournaments, outdoor movies, concerts, parades, antique fairs and organic markets than any other place on the planet. Plus, the outdoor activities and walking trails can't be beat.

If that's not enough, there are always epicurean indulgences. Wine buffs from around the world come to Bevagna and Montefalco to spend days tasting Sagrantino and Rosso Riserva. And, of course, there's the food – simple and rich, but always delicious.

HIGHLIGHTS

- Envelop yourself in music during the **Umbria Jazz** (p273) festival in Perugia
- Marvel at the legacy of St Francis at his eponymous **Basilica** (p283) in Assisi
- Attend festivals celebrating everything from history and dance to chocolate, gnocchi and snails, including the **Festival of the Gaite** (p307) in Bevagna
- Wander through fields of sunflowers and olive trees while staying at a villa or on a semi-private island at **Lago di Trasimeno** (p288)
- Eat *cinghiale* (boar) and *tartufi* (truffles) washed down with locally produced wine in a **Montefalco** (p307) or **Bevagna** (p307) restaurant

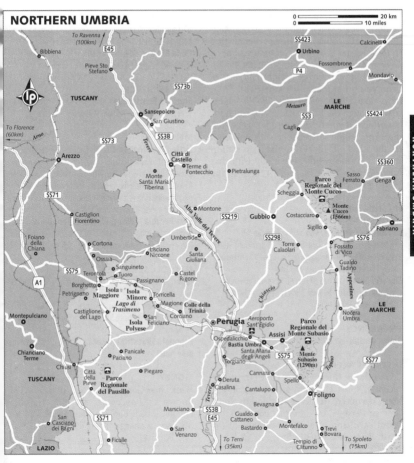

NORTHERN UMBRIA

PERUGIA

pop 149,125

One of Italy's best-preserved medieval hill towns, Perugia is also a hip student town with a never-ending stream of museums, churches, cultural events and concerts.

The Umbrii tribe once inhabited the surrounding area and controlled land stretching from present-day Tuscany into Le Marche, but it was the Etruscans who founded the city, which reached its zenith in the 6th century BC. It fell to the Romans in 310 BC and was given the name Perusia. During the Middle Ages the city was racked by the internal feuding of the Baglioni and Oddi families. In 1538 the city was incorporated into the Papal States under Pope Paul III, remaining under papal control for almost three centuries. It was during this time as a Guelph city that it warred against many of its neighbouring towns.

Perugia has a strong artistic and cultural tradition. In the 15th century it was home to fresco painters Bernardino Pinturicchio and his master Pietro Vannucci (known as Perugino), who was to teach Raphael. Today, the Università per Stranieri, established in 1925, offers courses in Italian and attracts thousands of students from all over the world.

Orientation

Old Perugia's main strip, Corso Vannucci (named after hometown artist Pietro Vannucci), runs south to north from Piazza

Italia to the heart of the city, Piazza IV Novembre, where you'll find the Fontana Maggiore and the cathedral. Almost every listing in this chapter is within a kilometre of here. *Urbano* (city) buses originate from Piazza Italia while *extraurbano* (intercity) buses drop you off at Piazza dei Partigiani. From here, take a few sets of *scale mobili* (elevators) through the Rocca Paolina to reach Piazza Italia. If you have heavy luggage, watch out: *scale mobili* interchange with staircases up the steep hillside. From the train station it's an enormous hike, especially with that luggage, or a quick bus ride, 1.5km up the hill to Piazza Italia.

Information

BOOKSHOPS
La Libreria (☎ 075 573 50 57; Via Oberdan 52; ☻ 9am-8pm Mon-Sat, 9am-1pm & 4.30-8pm Sun) Stocks a selection of English-language books, as well as maps and Lonely Planet guides in Italian and English.
Libreria Betti (☎ 075 573 16 67; librbetti@libero.it; Corso Vannucci 107; ☻ 9am-8pm, closed Sun) Sells English-language books.

EMERGENCY
Police station (☎ 075 572 32 32; Palazzo dei Priori)

INTERNET ACCESS
Over a dozen Internet cafés have popped up recently, most charging around €1.50 per hour. If you are thinking of spending some time in Perugia, buy an *abbonamento* discount card from the café you frequent the most. They will usually buy you 10 hours for €12.
InformaGiovani (☎ 075 572 06 46; www.comune .perugia.it/informagiovani in Italian; Via Idalia 1; free access for clients; ☻ 10am-1.30pm Mon-Fri, 3.30-5pm Mon-Wed) Assists young people to access information on health care, activities etc. Off Via Pinturicchio.
InfoUmbria (☎ 075 57 57; www.infoumbria.com in Italian; Piazza dei Partigiani Intercity bus station, Largo Cacciatori degli Alpi 3; per 30 min €1; ☻ 9am-1.30pm & 2.30-6.30pm Mon-Fri, 9am-1pm Sat)
Tempo Reale (☎ 075 573 55 33; Via del Forno 17; ☻ 10am-11pm) Central and friendly with high-speed connection and ample opening hours.

INTERNET RESOURCES
Perugia (www.perugia.it) Handy information on the area surrounding Perugia, including Lago di Trasimeno.
Perugia Online (www.perugiaonline.com) Offers info on accommodation, restaurants, history, activities and sights.

LAUNDRY
67 Laundry (Via Pinturicchio; ☻ 8am-10pm) Same price as Onda Blu; sells single serves of detergent.
Onda Blu (Corso dei Bersaglieri 4; ☻ 9am-10pm) Incredibly pricey at €3 to wash and €3 to dry.

LEFT LUGGAGE
Stazione Fontivegge (per bag €3 for 1st 12hr, €2 every 12hr thereafter; ☻ 6.30am-7.30pm)

MEDIA
Little Blue What-to-Do This English-language booklet is a must-have for students or anyone staying longer than a few hours. Known as the 'little blue book', it's available free at many locations, including Teatro del Pavone and newsstands. Find restaurants, housing suggestions, side trips and a description of local characters.
Viva Perugia – What, Where, When The comune di Perugia's monthly publication (€0.80 from newsstands) lists events and public transportation schedules.

MEDICAL SERVICES
Emergency doctor (☎ 075 3 40 24; ☻ weekends & nights)
Farmacia San Martino (pharmacy; Piazza Matteotti 26) This pharmacy has a list of all the pharmacies open 24 hours.
Ospedale Silvestrini (hospital; ☎ 075 57 81; S Andrea delle Frate)

MONEY
Banks line Corso Vannucci. All have ATMs, known as *bancomats*. Cashing travellers' cheques inside banks usually garners a 2% to 5% service charge. There's an ATM at Stazione Fontivegge.

POST
Mail Boxes Etc Via D'Andreotto 71 (☎ 075 50 17 98); Via della Pallotta 2B/5 (☎ 075 36 080) Both outlets are between Stazione Fontivegge and town. Instead of lugging a heavy suitcase, send your packages home with FedEx, Airborne Express or DHL.
Main post office (Piazza Matteotti; ☻ 8am-6.30pm Mon-Sat)

TELEPHONE
Centro Omnitel (☎ 075 572 37 78; Piazza Danti 17) Buy your indispensable Italian *telefonino* (mobile phone) here, or if you already have a GSM-compatible phone, purchase an Italian SIM card to pop into your own phone. You can then purchase *ricariche* (charge cards) here or in many *tabacchi* (tobacconists) for more talk-time.
Tempo Reale (☎ 075 573 55 33; Via del Forno 17; ☻ 10am-11pm) Phone calls from the booths here cost

€0.11 per minute to Australia, Canada, the USA, the UK and most places in Europe, and €0.16 to South Africa.

TOILETS
A drug problem has led to a deficiency in public toilet cleanliness. Try to find a bar or restaurant so that you don't have to steer clear of syringes.

TOURIST INFORMATION
ARCI Gay (☎ 075 572 31 75; Via A Fratti 18) Information on gay and lesbian events.

Il Periscopio (☎ 075 573 08 08; Via del Sole 6) A privately run tourist information service. It books courses in cooking, Italian language, painting and ceramics.

InformaGiovani (☎ 075 572 06 46; www.comune perugia.it/informagiovani; Via Idalia 1; ☷ 10am-1.30pm Mon-Fri, 3.30-5pm Mon-Wed; ☐) Assists young travellers and students living in Perugia with information on Italian culture, work opportunities, education and travelling abroad. Come here just to gaze at the flyers offering apartments for rent, band gigs etc.

InfoUmbria (☎ 075 57 57; www.infoumbria.com in Italian; Piazza dei Partigiani Intercity bus station, Largo Cacciatori delle Alpi 3; ☷ 9am-1.30pm & 2.30-6.30pm Mon-Fri, 9am-1pm Sat; ☐) Private InfoUmbria, also known as InfoTourist, offers information on all of Umbria, and is a fantastic resource for *agriturismi* (farm-stay or country inn accommodation), festivals, sights, hotels and general information.

Tourist office (☎ 075 573 64 58; info@iat.perugia.it; Palazzo dei Priori, Piazza IV Novembre 3; ☷ 8.30am-1.30pm & 3.30-6.30pm Mon-Sat, 9am-1pm Sun) As in most tourist offices in Umbria, most employees here don't speak English. The helpful cadre of maps, tour itineraries, booklets and accommodation guides are kept behind the desk, so this is a good time to practise your Italian.

TRAVEL AGENCIES
CTS (☎ 075 572 70 50; Via del Roscetto 21) Specialises in budget and student travel and sells International Student Identity Cards (ISIC) to students studying at the university.

Il Periscopio (☎ 075 573 08 08; Via del Sole 6) Arranges excursions, escorted tours and trips within Italy or abroad. The owner speaks fluent English and French.

Sights

CORSO VANNUCCI
The centre of Perugia – and therefore the centre of Umbria – is Piazza IV Novembre. For thousands of years, it was the meeting point for the ancient Etruscan and Roman civilisations. In the medieval period, it was the political centre of Perugia. Now students and tourists gather here to eat *gelato*.

On the north end of the piazza is the **Cathedral of San Lorenzo** (☎ 075 572 38 32; Piazza IV Novembre). Although a church has been on this land since the 900s, the version you see was begun in 1345 from designs created by Fra Bevignate in 1300. Building of the cathedral continued until 1587, and the doorway was built in the late 1700s; however, the main façade was never completed. Inside you'll find dramatic Gothic architecture, an altarpiece by Signorelli and sculptures by Duccio. The steps in front of the pink façade is where seemingly all of Perugia congregates.

In the very centre of the piazza stands the **Fontana Maggiore** (Great Fountain). It was designed by Fra Bevignate, and father-son team Nicola and Giovanni Pisano built the fountain between 1275 and 1278. Along the edge are bas-relief statues representing scenes from the Old Testament, the founding of Rome, the 'liberal arts', and a griffin and lion. Look for the griffin all over Perugia – it's the city's symbol. The lion is the symbol for the Guelphs, the Middle Ages faction that favoured rule by the papacy over rule by the Holy Roman Empire.

The **Palazzo dei Priori** houses some of the best museums in Perugia. The foremost art gallery in Umbria is the stunning **Galleria Nazionale dell'Umbria** (National Gallery of Umbria; ☎/fax 075 574 14 00; Palazzo dei Priori, Corso Vannucci 1; adult/concession €6.50/3.50; ☷ 8.30am-7.30pm, closed 1st Mon of each month), entered from Corso Vannucci. It's an art historian's dream, with 30 rooms of artwork dating back to Byzantine-like art from the 13th century, as well as rooms dedicated to works from hometown heroes Pinturicchio and Perugino.

Some of the other museums in the Palazzo dei Priori include the gilded **Collegio del Cambio** (Exchange Guild; ☎ 075 572 85 99; Corso Vannucci 25; ☷ core hrs 9am-12.30pm & 3-7pm Mon-Sat summer, often closed afternoon winter), which has three rooms: the Sala dei Legisti (Legist Chamber), with wooden stalls carved by Zuccari in the 17th century; the Sala dell'Udienza (Audience Chamber), with frescoes by Perugino; and the Chapel of San Giovanni Battista, painted by a student of Perugino's, Giannicola di Paolo. The **Collegio della Mercanzia** (Merchant's Guild; ☎ 075 573 03 66; Corso Vannucci 15; ☷ core hrs 9am-12.30pm & 3-7pm Mon-Sat summer, often closed afternoon winter) highlights an older audience chamber, from the 13th century, covered in wood panelling by northern craftsmen.

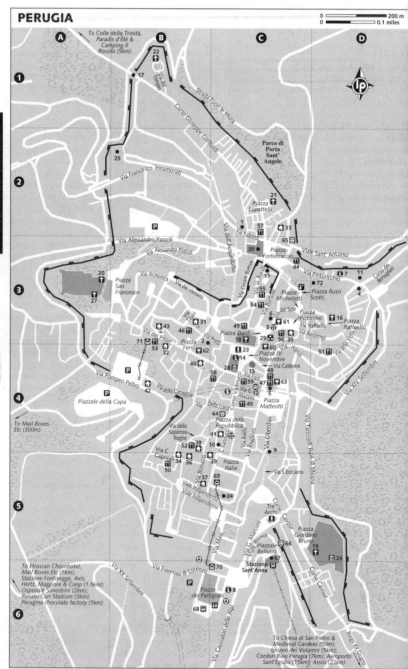

PERUGIA

0 ————————— 200 m
0 ————————— 0.1 miles

To Colle della Trinità,
Paradis d'Été &
Camping Il
Rocolo (5km)

Strada Fuori le Mura

Corso Giuseppe Garibaldi

Via del Tempo

Via Francesco Innamorati

Parco di
Porta
Sant'
Angelo

Piazza
Lupattelli

Via Alessandro Pascoli

Via Alessandro Pascoli

Via dell'Acquedotto

Via Fabretti

Piazza
Fortebraccio

Viale Sant' Antonio

Via Pinturicchio

Corso dei Bersaglieri

Via Armonica

Via del Verzaro

Via Cesare Battisti

Via U. Rocchi

Via Battisti

Piazza
San
Francesco

Piazza
Michelotti

Via del Sole

Piazza
Piccinino

Via Raffaello

Via Bontempi

Piazza
Russi
Scotti

Piazza
Raffaello

Via dei Priori

Via Fratta

Piazza
Danti

Piazza IV
Novembre

Via Alessi

Via Calderini

Piazza
Ferri

Via Pompeo Pellini

Via della Canapina

Via Fani

Via G
Mazzini

Piazza
Matteotti

Via XIV Settembre

Via della Volte

Piazzale della Cupa

To Mail Boxes
Etc (300m)

Della Luna

Corso Vannucci

Piazza della
Repubblica

Via Baldo

Via dei Baglioni

Via Oberdan

Via Tancredi Ripa di Meana

Via della
Sapienza-
Reghe

Via C.
Caporali

Via Mazzini

Via Bonazzi

Piazza
Italia

Via S Ercolano

Viale Indipendenza

Viale Indipendenza

Tre
Archi

Corso Cavour

Piazza
Giordano
Bruno

To Etruscan Chocohotel,
Mail Boxes Etc (1km);
Stazione Fontivegge, Avis,
Hertz, Maggiore & Coop (1.5km);
Ospedale Silvestrini (2km);
Renato Curi Stadium (3km);
Perugina chocolate factory (5km)

Via XX Settembre

Via Masi

Via Fiorenzo di Lorenzo

Viale Roma

Via G. Marconi

Piazzale
Bellucci

Stazione
Sant'Anna

Corso Cavour

Borgo XX Giugno

Piazza
dei Partigiani

Via Cacciatori delle Alpi

To Chiesa di San Pietro &
Medieval Gardens (50m);
Ipogeo dei Volumni (5km);
Cordon Bleu Perugia (7km); Aeroporto
Sant'Egidio (15km); Assisi (23km)

A combined ticket for both *collegi* is adult/concession €4/3. The **Sala dei Notari** (Notaries' Hall; ☎ 075 574 12 74; admission free) was built from 1293 to 1297 and is where the nobility met. The arches supporting the vaults are Romanesque, covered with frescoes depicting biblical scenes and Aesop's fables. To reach the hall, walk up the steps from the Piazza IV Novembre.

At the southern end of Corso Vannucci is the tiny **Giardini Carducci**, which has lovely views of the countryside. This is where the antiques market takes place on the third weekend of each month. The gardens stand atop a once-massive 16th-century fortress, now known as the **Rocca Paolina** – the fortress was built by Pope Paul III in the 1540s and stands over a medieval quarter formerly inhabited by some of the city's most powerful families. Destroyed by the citizens of Perugia after Italian unification, the ruins remain a symbol of defiance against oppression. A series of *scale mobili* runs through the Rocca and you can wander around inside the ruins, which are often used for art exhibitions.

CHURCHES & MUSEUMS
You can buy a combined ticket called the **Perugia City Museum Circuit** (adult/child/senior €2.50/1/2) at any of the three following sights; the ticket is valid for one week. First, you can venture down into the 3rd-century-BC

Pozzo Etrusco (Etruscan Well; ☎ 075 573 36 69; Piazza Danti 18; ◷ 10.30am-1.30pm & 2.30-6.30pm Apr-Oct, 10.30am-1.30pm & 2.30-5pm Nov-Mar, closed Tue year-round). The 36m-deep well was the main water reservoir of the Etruscan town, and, more recently, the source of water during WWII bombing raids. The second stop is the **Cappella di San Severo** (☎ 075 573 38 64; Piazza Raffaello; ◷ 10.30am-1.30pm & 2.30-6.30pm Apr-Oct, 10.30am-1.30pm & 2.30-5pm Nov-Mar, closed Tue year-round), decorated with Raphael's *Trinity with Saints* (thought by many to be his first fresco) and frescoes by Perugino. The third museum included is the **Cassero di Porta Sant'Angelo** (Panoramic Tower; ☎ 075 573 36 69; Porta Sant'Angelo; ◷ 11am-1.30pm & 3-6.30pm Apr-Oct, 11am-1.30pm & 3-5pm Nov-Mar, closed Tue year-round). The panoramic view facing back on to Perugia is the main reason to come out here, plus it offers a historical briefing of the three city walls.

Walking from the Cassero di Porta Sant'Angelo down towards the Università per Stranieri takes you on either side of the two Arco d'Augusto, the ancient city gates. The lower section of the **Arco d'Etrusco** is Etruscan, dating from the 3rd century BC; the upper part is Roman and bears the inscription 'Augusta Perusia'. The loggia on top dates from the Renaissance.

North along Corso Giuseppe Garibaldi is the **Chiesa di Sant'Agostino** (Piazza Lupattelli; ◷ 8am-noon & 4pm-sunset), a church with a beautiful

NORTHERN UMBRIA

A WALK BACK IN TIME

For a thorough self-guided archaeological tour from Etruscan to Renaissance Perugia, pick up the *Archaeological Itineraries* booklet at the Perugia tourist office. Plan on it taking about three or four hours, and wear comfortable shoes.

16th-century choir by sculptor and architect Baccio d'Agnolo. Small signs forlornly mark the places where artworks once hung before they were carried off to France by Napoleon and his men. Further north along the same thoroughfare, Via del Tempio branches off to the Romanesque **Chiesa di Sant'Angelo** (☎ 075 57 22 64; Via Sant'Angelo; ☺ 10am-noon & 4-6pm), which is said to stand on the site of an ancient temple. The columns found inside the round church were taken from earlier buildings.

Built in the 13th century and home to Franciscan monks in the 14th century, **Chiesa di San Francesco al Prato** is now the headquarters for the **Giuditta Brozzetti fabric company** (☎ 075 4 02 36; fax 500 24 92; www.brozzetti.com; Via T Berardi 5/6; ☺ 9am-1pm & 3-6pm Mon-Fri), in operation since 1921. You can buy handwoven linens produced using traditional techniques dating back 1000 years, or take classes in hand-weaving, embroidery and lace-making. Next door is the **Oratorio di San Bernardino** (☎ 075 573 39 57; ☺ mass 5.30pm daily, & noon Sun & holidays), whose polychromatic design surrounding the immense doorway is considered the most important Renaissance work in Perugia.

The cities largest church, the early-14th-century **Chiesa di San Domenico** (☎ 075 573 15 68; Piazza Giordano Bruno; ☺ 8am-noon & 4pm-sunset) is along Corso Cavour. Its Romanesque interior, lightened by the immense stained-glass windows, was replaced by austere Gothic fittings in the 16th century. Pope Benedict XI, who died after eating poisoned figs in 1325, lies buried here. The adjoining convent is home to the **Museo Archeologico Nazionale dell'Umbria** (☎ 075 572 71 41; Piazza Giordano Bruno 10; adult/concession €2/1; ☺ 8.30am-7.30pm Tue-Sun, 2.30-7.30pm Mon), which has an excellent collection of Etruscan pieces and a section on prehistory. The most important item in the collection is the *Cippo Perugino*, (Perugian Memorial Stone), a travertine stone

with one of the longest Etruscan language engravings.

OUT OF TOWN

A fabulous way to while away the afternoo is to stroll or picnic at the **Medieval Garden** (☎ 075 585 64 32; Borgo XX Giugno 74; admission fre ☺ 8am-6.30pm), behind the Chiesa di San Pi etro, 300m southeast of the city. During th medieval period, monasteries often create gardens reminiscent of the Garden of Ede and biblical stories, with plants that sym bolised myths and sacred stories.

Numbered locations through this garde include:

3 the Cosmic Tree, symbolising the forefather of all trees;
6 the Tree of Light and Knowledge;
7 the Tree of Good and Evil;
11 & 12 medicinal and edible plants used for centuries;
16 remnants from an ancient fish pond;
20 the Cosmogonic Ovulation Spring (a lily-pad pond); and
24 the exit of the Medieval Gardens, symbolising the elevation of man from the natural plane.

Be sure to check out the groovy alchemist studio tucked into the corner near numbe 20, the Yggdrasil Incline.

In front of the Medieval Gardens is th medieval 10th-century **Chiesa di San Pietr** (☎ 075 3 47 70; Borgo XX Giugno; ☺ 8am-noon & 4pm sunset), entered through a frescoed door way in the first courtyard. The interior i an incredible mix of gilt and marble an contains a *pietà* (a sculpture, drawing o painting of the dead Christ supported b the Madonna) by Perugino. Many of th paintings in this church feature depiction of biblical women.

About 5km southeast of the city is th **Ipogeo dei Volumni** (☎ 075 39 33 29; Via Assisana adult/child/concession €3/free/1.50; ☺ 9am-1pm & 3.3 6.30pm Sep-Jun, 9am-12.30pm & 4.30-7pm Jul & Aug a 2nd-century-BC Etruscan burial site An underground chamber contains a se ries of recesses holding the funerary urn of the Volumnio family. The surroundin grounds are a massive expanse of partiall unearthed burial chambers with severa buildings housing artefacts that haven been stolen over the years. Take a train o APM bus 3 from Piazza Italia to Ponte Sa Giovanni and walk west from there. By car take the Bonanzano exit heading south o the E45.

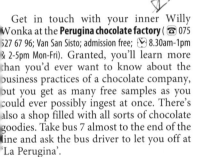

Get in touch with your inner Willy Wonka at the **Perugina chocolate factory** (☎ 075 527 67 96; Van San Sisto; admission free; ⏰ 8.30am-1pm & 2-5pm Mon-Fri). Granted, you'll learn more than you'd ever want to know about the business practices of a chocolate company, but you get as many free samples as you could ever possibly ingest at once. There's also a shop filled with all sorts of chocolate goodies. Take bus 7 almost to the end of the line and ask the bus driver to let you off at 'La Perugina'.

Courses

The list of courses available to locals and foreigners in and around Perugia could constitute a book in itself. You can learn Italian, take up ceramics, study music or spend a month cooking. The tourist office has details of all courses.

Cordon Bleu Perugia (☎ 075 592 50 12 in Italian, 333 981 36 95 in English; www.cordonbleuperugia.com; Via dei Lilla 3, Casaglia) Come for a three-hour beginners' class or a week-long professional chef course on Italian cuisine. Day courses run from 10am to 1pm Wednesday to Saturday from March to October and cost around €75 for instruction in making bread and pasta, and in Umbrian cuisine. Week-long courses cost €350 to €600.

Università per Stranieri (☎ 075 5 74 61; www .unistrapg.it; Palazzo Gallenga, Piazza Fortebraccio 4) This is Italy's foremost academic institution for foreigners, offering courses in language, literature, history, art, music, opera and architecture, to name a few. In addition, it also offers a one-month refresher course for teachers of Italian abroad for €233. A series of degree courses is available, as well as one-, two- and three-month intensive language courses and semester-long accredited programs for students.

Festivals & Events

Perugia – and Umbria in general – has no less than 80 gazillion events, festivals, concerts, summer outdoor movies and *sagre* (traditional festivals)! Not surprisingly, most festivals are held during the warmer weather, between May and October, but tourist offices have a list of all the festivals held throughout the year.

Eurochocolate This is one of the most over-hyped festivals in Italy, held from mid- to late October each year. For one week the streets are lined with hundreds of booths associated with chocolate. The city gets so crowded that most locals lock up or take off for the week. If you must, plan your hotel stay months in advance and don't even think of driving.

Sagra Musicale Umbra (Holy Music Festival; ☎ 075 572 13 74; fax 075 572 76 14; www.sagramusicaleumbra .com in Italian) One of the oldest music festivals in Europe. Begun in 1937, it's held in Perugia from mid- to late September and features world-renowned conductors and musicians.

Umbria Jazz (☎ 075 572 86 85/77; www.umbriajazz .com in Italian) This attracts top-notch international performers for 10 days each July, usually around the middle of the month. In the past, the festival has featured performances by hundreds of jazz greats, including Sonny Rollins, the Buena Vista Social Club, Chick Corea and Al Jarreau. Single tickets cost €10 to €100, but you can also buy passes: full-week passes cost from €100 to €310 and weekend passes cost from €50 to €150. Check with the tourist office for details on where to buy tickets. You can also enjoy free concerts in Piazza IV Novembre and Giardini Carducci between 11am and midnight.

Sleeping

Perugia has a fine array of hotels and *pensioni*, and is a good place to stay if you're visiting Umbria by train or bus, as many towns can be visited on day trips from Perugia. There's no reason to stay outside the historic centre: it's noisier, less charming and not much cheaper.

High-season rates are listed here, but almost every hotel offers a discount during the low season (which varies from place to place but is usually January to March, November to early December and possibly August).

RENTAL ACCOMMODATION

Be warned that some apartment services in Perugia have a reputation of ripping people off; see p345 for more information.

Atena Service (☎ 075 573 29 92; www.atenaservice .com; Via del Bulagaio 38) can arrange accommodation from €200 per month for a shared room in an apartment, and from €550 per month for a one-bedroom apartment.

Il Periscopio (see p269) is a full-service travel agent that arranges local day trips as well as accommodation for students, business travellers and long-term visitors.

There are several ways to investigate rental accommodation yourself:
- ask at the tourist office, which can help with pricier weekly accommodation;
- check any newsstand on Wednesday and Saturday for *Cerco e Trovo* (I search and I find, €1.50) for apartment listings. Be sure to call before noon, as rooms go quick; or

■ check posted flyers at the Università per Stranieri (p273) or at InformaGiovani (p269).

BUDGET
Camping & Hostels

The city has two camp sites, both in Colle della Trinità, 5km northwest of the city, reached by taking bus 9 from Piazza Italia. Ask the driver to drop you off at the Superal supermarket, from where it's a 300m walk to the camp sites.

Paradis d'Été (☎ 075 517 31 21; www.emmeti.it /Welcome/Umbria/Perugia/Alberghi/Paradis/; Via del Mercato 29/A, Str Fontana, Colle della Trinità; per person/car/tent €6.20/2.84/4.65; ☉ year-round; ☒) This camp site has 50 well-shaded sites in a parklike setting with good facilities and a swimming pool. If you're tentless, you can rent a bungalow for up to six people from €41 to €96.

Camping Il Rocolo (☎ /fax 075 517 85 50; www .ilrocolo.it; Str Fontana 1/n, Loc. Colle della Trinità; per person/car/tent €6/2.50/5; ☉ mid-Apr–end Sep) There are over 100 sites here, with a bit of shade and all the standard facilities, including an on-site restaurant, minimarket, bocce and playground. It's 6km from Perugia's city centre, near highway E45. A minibus makes the journey back and forth several times a day.

Centro Internazionale per la Gioventù (☎ /fax 075 572 28 80; www.ostello.perugia.it; Via Bontempi 13; dm €12, sheets €1.50; ▢) If the 9.30am to 4pm lockout and the midnight curfew (*no exceptions*) don't scare you off, then you'll appreciate the sweeping countryside view and wafting sounds of church bells from the hostel's terrace, where guests often gather after making dinner in the well-stocked kitchen. Enjoy the 16th-century frescoed ceilings.

B&Bs & Hotels

Casa Spagnoli Bed & Breakfast (☎ 075 573 51 27, 340 350 38 93; www.perugiaonline.com/bbspagnoli; Via Caporali 17; s/d/tr incl breakfast with shared bathroom €37/56/68) The motto here is *semplice* – simplicity. Join in the Wednesday night yoga class or talk politics with the international Spagnolis, who speak Italian, Spanish, French and English. It offers a small weekly discount and it's perfectly located near Piazza Italia, making it an ideal base for exploring Umbria by public transport. If you stay two days or more, they'll even do your laundry for free!

Albergo Morlacchi (☎ 075 572 03 19; www.hotel morlacchi.it; Via Tiberi 2; s/d/tr €56/70/91, s without bathroom €40; ℗) This friendly, family-run two-star hotel is a popular choice. Rooms are furnished with telephones and simple but comfortable antique furnishings, and a few even have fireplaces. There's a good discount in the low season.

Pensione Paola (☎ 075 572 38 16; Via della Canapina 5; s/d €33/52) It's a great bet if you want use of your own kitchen but don't want the lockout of the hostel. It has eight simply furnished rooms. Take bus 6 or 7 heading towards Piazza Italia and get off at the Pellini car park. Signs will guide you up the steps to the right. From the city centre, walk down Via dei Priori.

Hotel Eden (☎ 075 572 81 02; fax 075 572 03 42; Via C Caporali 9; s/d/tr €40/60/77, breakfast €5) There isn't much else in this hotel's favour other than being cheap and central.

Pensione Anna (☎ /fax 075 573 63 04; annahotel@ hotmail.com; Via dei Priori 48; s/d from €40/62, without bathroom €30/48; ℗) On the 4th floor with no elevator, this eclectic place is great if you want central and fairly quiet, but don't have a lot of heavy luggage.

MIDRANGE

Primavera Minihotel (☎ 075 572 16 57; www.pri maveraminihotel.com; Via Vincioli 8; s/d/tr €48/70/90) This central and quiet hotel run by a dedicated English- and French-speaking mother-daughter team is a fabulous find, quietly tucked in a corner. The magnificent views complement the bright and airy rooms and common areas. All rooms come with private bath, telephone and TV. Great value.

Hotel Fortuna (☎ 075 572 28 45; www.umbria hotels.com; Via Bonazzi 9; s/d/ste incl breakfast €86/124/147; ☒ ▢) In a location both quiet and central, this spotless hotel is partially housed in a building dating back to the 1300s. Ancient stone, frescoes, and Venetian plaster walls gracefully accompany comfortable new furnishings, new parquet floors and (thankfully) modern bathrooms.

Hotel Priori (☎ 075 572 91 55; www.hotelpriori .it in Italian; Via dei Priori; s/d incl breakfast €66/95; ℗) Not the most exciting rooms, but the garage parking (€15 or €25, depending on car size) and full buffet breakfast may make it worth it. Have breakfast on the stunning rooftop terrace.

Etruscan Chocohotel (☎ 075 583 73 14; www .chocohotel.it; Via Campo di Marte 134; s/d €73/120; P ✗ ☐ ☎) The first hotel in the world dedicated to chocolate. Try items from the restaurant's 'chocomenu', shop at the 'choc-ostore' or swim in the rooftop pool (sadly, filled with water). It's just east of Stazione Fontivegge – you can walk, or take buses 2 or 13d.

Hotel la Rosetta (☎ /fax 075 572 08 41; www.perugia online.com/larosetta; Piazza Italia 19; s/d/tr incl breakfast €79/120/161; P ✗ ☐) You'll be so close to the centre of Perugia that you can prac-tically crawl to most sights. Although the building is hundreds of years old, the décor is from the 19th century and 1920s. Up-dated with computer outlets, Sky TV and modern showers, and offering conference space and meeting rooms, the Rosetta is a business hotel where leisure travellers are just as comfortable. The hotel has a few free parking spaces; otherwise it'll cost you €20 in a nearby parking garage.

TOP END

Hotel Brufani Palace (☎ 075 573 25 41; www.sinahotels .com; Piazza Italia 12; s/d €215/320, ste €440-850; P ✗ ☎) Not only is Brufani one of the few five-star hotels in Umbria – it's a five-star-plus. Spe-cial touches include frescoed main rooms, impeccably decorated bedrooms and suites, a garden terrace in which to dine during sum-mer, and a helpful trilingual staff. The only place in the city centre with its own park-ing facilities, this hotel has all the amenities, but the real gem is the fitness centre, with a sauna, Turkish bath and a subterranean pool situated over Etruscan ruins. It also has a 24-hour concierge, wi-fi access and is wheelchair accessible.

Locanda della Posta (☎ 075 572 89 25; novelber@tin .it; Corso Vannucci 97; s/d incl breakfast €108/170; ✗) The service is less than friendly and the amenities are scarce, but this centrally lo-cated, well-advertised hotel is very popular. You could save money by staying at the almost-as-centrally located Hotel la Rosetta or Hotel Fortuna, or upgrade for an experi-ence of a lifetime at Brufani Palace.

Eating

Because of the great number of students and tourists, the amount of places at which to eat in Perugia is staggering. A pizzeria is around every corner, and there are dozens of mid-range restaurants, but you'll often find the best Umbrian dining outside Perugia in the smaller towns or on country roads. A few excellent restaurants stand out for their food, value or location, or all three.

BUDGET

Ristorante dal Mi'Cocco (☎ 075 573 25 11; Corso Giuseppe Garibaldi 12; set meals €13.50; ✗ closed Mon) Adventurous taste buds will be rewarded at this most traditional of Perugian establish-ments. Don't ask for a menu because there isn't one. Diners receive a set menu of a starter, main course, side dish and dessert. You may receive asparagus risotto in May, or tagliatelle (long, ribbon-shaped pasta) with peas and ham in November. It gets very crowded, so it's best to call ahead.

La Cambusa (☎ 075 572 13 83; Via dei Priori 82; mains €5-12.50; ✗ closed Tue) This good-value and reliable restaurant is mostly populated by locals. It specialises in seafood dishes, including a swordfish *carpaccio* (thinly sliced meat, marinated and eaten raw), and reputedly has the best *calamari fritti* (fried calamari) in Perugia.

Ristorante Il Bacio (☎ 075 572 09 09; Via Boncampi 6; meals around €11; ✗ to 12.30am Thu-Tue) This rather cavernous *ristorante* and pizzeria sells good, cheap meals and also sets up a decent out-door café on Corso Vannucci, but its selling point is that it's one of the only late-night restaurants in the historic centre.

Pizzeria Mediterranea (☎ 075 572 13 22; Piazza Piccinino 11/12; pizza from €4.60; ✗ closed Tue) Very trendy and in a good location, Mediterra-nea is the most well-known spot for pizza. It has a lovely open brick oven and con-vivial atmosphere, but it can get fairly busy at times, so be prepared to queue.

Pizzeria Etrusca (☎ 075 572 07 62; Via Ulisse Rocchi 31; pizza from €3.50) Etrusca is a popular student haunt. It's busy and cheap, a great place to meet other students, and the pizza's pretty decent.

For the best *gelato* in town try Augusta Perusia Cioccolato (p277).

MIDRANGE

Osteria del Bartolo (☎ 075 571 60 27; Via Bartolo 30; mains €7-16; ✗ closed Sun) The first clue that you're in for something special is the flam-ing torches lighting the entrance. You de-scend a staircase into a hobbitlike burrow that's surrounded by walls of wine bottles and a handful of cosy tables underneath a low brick ceiling. Dishes mix Mediterranean classics with new twists: herbed lamb in a hazelnut pastry or beef stew marinated in Sangiovese wine.

Il Falchetto (☎ 075 573 17 75; Via Bartolo 20; mains around €15; ☻ closed Mon) In a great location just behind the cathedral, this restaurant (named 'the eagle') is one of Perugia's oldest stand-bys; a great place to take parents. Try its house speciality, *falchetto verde,* a spinach and gnocchi dish served bubbling in a hot casserole dish.

Il Ghiottone (☎ 075 572 77 88; Via C Caporali 12; mains €6.20-10.50; ☻ closed Tue) The owner, Aldo, has run this restaurant for 27 years, and his family has been producing olive oil in the same Trevi orchard for 200 years. Luckily for us, Aldo uses this oil liberally in all of his dishes. Try the *lenticchie* (lentil) soup, made with Castelluccio lentils, or the local handmade pasta – *umbricelli* (handmade Umbrian thick spaghetti) or *strangozzi* (the Umbrian square-shaped version of spaghetti). For €12, he'll even pour you a litre of olive oil.

Il Segreto di Pulcinella (☎ 075 573 62 84; Via Larga 8; ☻ closed Mon) The only 'real' Neapolitan pizza in Perugia. A dazzling array of pizzas range from the simplest *margherita* (mozzarella, tomato sauce and oregano) to the piles of olives, artichokes, meat or even chips. It also features Perugia's best selection of salads (from €2.70 to €6.20), with ingredients like mascarpone and pears, and loads of pasta dishes, including the rich *caramelle al zafferano* (€8.50) – noodles in a creamy, sweet saffron sauce.

Il Gufo (☎ 075 573 41 26; Via della Viola 18; ☻ 8pm-1am, closed Sun & Mon) The owner/chef gathers ingredients from local markets and cooks up whatever is fresh and in season. Try dishes such as *cinghiale* with fennel (€9) or *riso nero* (black rice) with grilled vegetables and brie (€9). There is always a good selection of salads for €5.

CAFÉS

Many of the restaurants that line Corso Vannucci open up pavement cafés in the warmer months. Don't expect the food to be top-notch, as you're paying for atmosphere.

Sandri (☎ 075 572 41 12; Corso Vannucci 32; ☻ 10am-8pm) Just try to walk by this café, a Perugian staple, without having your mouth water at the sight of chocolate cakes

and candied fruit. They wrap all take-home purchases, no matter how small, in beautiful red paper with a ribbon bow.

Caffè Morlacchi (☎ 075 572 17 60; Piazza Morlacchi 6/8; ☻ 8am-1am Mon-Sat) Bring your bongo drums and leftist rhetoric to this most hip of establishments. It serves international light fare and drinks to students, professors and foreigners.

Caffè di Perugia (☎ 075 573 18 63; Via Mazzini 10; ☻ noon-3pm & 7pm-midnight, closed Tue) This is the fanciest sit-down café in town and it makes delectable desserts. It also serves a fine choice of basic pasta and meat dishes and offers outdoor seating in summer and a smoking room indoors.

SELF-CATERING

Coop (Piazza Matteotti; ☻ 9am-8pm Mon-Sat) The largest grocery store in the historic centre. You can buy all sorts of pasta, vegetables and staples here, as well as prepared food from the deli.

Covered market (☻ 7am-1.30pm Mon-Sat) Found below Coop, you can buy fresh produce, bread, cheese and meat from this market. From Piazza Matteotti, head down the stairs of the arched doorway labelled #18A.

Coop (☎ 075 501 65 04; Piazza Vittorio Veneto; ☻ 9am-7.45pm, closed Sun) Across from the train station, this super-sized Coop has rows of groceries, deli items and toiletries.

Drinking

Cinastik (☎ 075 572 09 99; Via dei Priori 36; ☻ 6.30pm-2.30am, closed Sun) Feel very much like you're on the Continent in this swanky hot spot. The downstairs is pumping with sultry music and the mixed drinks are flowing. The upstairs is a little quieter (make sure you check out the coolest bathrooms in Perugia).

Botega di Vino (☎ /fax 075 571 61 81; Via del Sole 1; ☻ wine bar 6pm-1am, wine shop 9am-1pm & 4-8pm, closed Sun) This is a fantastic place to take in the atmosphere. Flaming torches light the way and a fire burns on the terrace. Inside, live jazz and hundreds of bottles of wine lining the walls add to the romance of the setting. You can taste dozens of Umbrian wines, which you can purchase with the help of sommelier-like experts.

Shamrock Pub (☎ 075 573 66 25; Piazza Danti 18; ☻ 6pm-2am) For late-night drinks, sample a Guinness at the Shamrock, down an appropriately dank but atmospheric alley off

Piazza Danti. The place is decorated in a mix of ancient Etruscan and modern Irish pub. The Irish lass who runs the place often has English football on the telly. All drinks are €3 from 6pm to 9pm.

La Terrazza (Via Matteotti 18a; ☼ summer only) Should you sit in the park and enjoy the view of the sun setting over the Umbrian hillside, or head into a darkened pub for a drink? Well, you can come here for both. On the back terrace of the building that houses the Coop and covered markets is this open-air bar, perfect for an evening apéritif.

Bar Centrale (Piazza IV Novembre 35; ☼ 7am-11pm) A popular meeting place for students with outdoor tables under umbrellas where you can sit with a *panini* and watch the students on the cathedral steps.

Entertainment

Much of Perugia's nightlife parades outside the cathedral and around Fontana Maggiore. Hundreds of local and foreign students congregate here practically every night, playing guitars and drums and chatting with friends. Tourists mix in easily, slurping *gelati* and enjoying this fascinating version of outdoor theatre. When the student population grows, some of the clubs on the outskirts of town run a bus to Palazzo Gallenga, starting just before midnight. Students get paid to hand out flyers on Corso Vannucci, so check with them or ask at the steps. Most clubs don't really get going until around midnight.

Cinema Teatro del Pavone (☎ 075 572 49 11; Corso Vannucci 67) It's worth the film price alone just to see this grand theatre, now used exclusively for movies. On Monday night, the theatre shows films in their original languages, usually English, for €4 (students €3.50). Come early to grab a box seat. During the summer, the owners run outdoor movies; check at the cinema for schedules and directions.

Contrappunto (☎ 075 573 36 67; Via Scortica 4/a; ☼ evenings until late, closed Mon) What was a jazz club now opens its doors to all sorts of music. Jazz jams are just on Wednesday now, but try live rock on Thursday, disco on Friday and world-famous DJs on Saturdays (until 5am). Food is available; try the huge antipasto plate for two to four people for €16.

Velvet (☎ 075 572 13 21; Viale Roma 20) Come to where the beautiful people play. It doesn't open until after midnight, but the well-dressed party here until the wee hours.

ARCI Gay (☎ 075 572 31 75; Via A Fratti 18) There's a nightclub scene here from Wednesday to Saturday nights that's popular with both gays and straights.

Perugia football team (☎ 075 500 66 41; www.peru giacalcio.it; Renato Curi Stadium, Via Piccolpasso 48; tickets €2-40) It's not terribly difficult to get tickets for this team, known as Il Grifo (The Griffin) because they've been dropped from the world-class Serie A to second-fiddle Serie B. Take buses 9, 11, or 13 to the stadium.

Shopping

If you're lucky enough to be in Perugia on the last Sunday of the month, spend a few hours in the antiques market around the Piazza Italia and in the Giardini Carducci. It's a great place to pick up old prints, frames, furniture, jewellery, postcards and stamps.

The second week of January sees steep sales in all the clothing stores in Perugia (and Italy, for that matter), with prices reduced by as much as 75%.

On the first Sunday of the month, check out the **Umbria Terraviva** (organic market; ☎ 075 835 50 62; Piazza Piccinino) located along the side of the Duomo heading towards Via Bonanzi. You'll find all sorts of organic fruits, vegetables and fabulous canned or packaged items to take home as gifts.

Augusta Perusia Cioccolato (☎ 075 573 45 77; www.cioccolatoaugustaperusia.it in Italian; Via Pinturicchio 2; ☼ 10.30am-8pm Mon-Sat) Giordano worked for Perugino for 25 years. In 2000, he opened his own shop, creating delectables from the old tradition, including *baci* (hazelnut 'kisses' covered in chocolate) from the original Perugian recipe. Handmade chocolate bars come in boxes with old paintings of Perugia – great for gifts. The shop serves wonderful homemade *gelato*, including flavours such as mascarpone, *baci*, *pinoli* (pine nut), cinnamon and, of course, chocolate.

Getting There & Away

AIR

Aeroporto Sant'Egidio (☎ 075 59 21 41; www.airport .umbria.it), 13km east of the city, offers flights to Milan all year, plus summer flights to Denmark, Sardinia and Mallorca. A one-way or round-trip taxi to Sant'Egidio costs €25.

Sulga (☎ 800 099 661; www.sulga.it in Italian) buses (€2.58) coincide with the three daily year-round Alitalia Milan flights. The buses leave Piazza Italia at 5.20am, 10.20am and 4.10pm (stopping at the train station five minutes later, and the airport 25 minutes after that). It's a tight connection with the outgoing flights, but Alitalia makes allowances for this. Coming back, they leave the airport at 11.34am, 4.55pm and 10.40pm.

BUS

To most towns, it doesn't pay to take the long-distance buses (*interurbano,* as opposed to local, or *urbano,* buses) in terms of time or price, but several towns, such as Panicale, Torgiano and Deruta, are more easily reached by bus than by train. Buses rarely run on Sunday.

Intercity buses leave from Piazza dei Partigiani (take the *scale mobili* from Piazza Italia). Sulga buses head from Partigiani to Rome (€14.50, three hours, five daily) and on to Fiumicino airport (€19.20, 3¾ hours, departs Partigiani 6.33am, 7.30am, 8.30am or 9am, 2.30pm and 5.30pm). Heading to Perugia from Fiumicino, go across the street from international terminal C. Buses leave the airport at 12.30pm, 2.30pm, 4.30pm and 5pm. Sulga also offers a Perugia–Florence service (€9.80, 2½ hours) that runs once daily, except Sunday, leaving Perugia at 7.30am and Florence at 6pm (from Piazza Adua at Santa Maria Novella).

APM (☎ 800 51 21 41, 075 573 17 07 from mobile; www.apmperugia.com in Italian) and **SSIT** (☎ 074 267 07 46) buses leave from Piazza dei Partigiani for Deruta (€2.40, 25 minutes, nine daily), Torgiano (€1.60, 25 minutes, six daily), Assisi (€2.80, 55 minutes, 10 daily), Todi (€4.40, one hour and 20 minutes, four daily), Gubbio (€4, one hour and 10 minutes, eight daily), Gualdo Tadino (€4.80, one hour and 25 minutes, six daily), Lago di Trasimeno towns (€2.40 to €4.40, 30 minutes to one hour and 10 minutes, six to eight daily) and Norcia (€6.80, 2½ hours, 2pm). To get to Narni or Amelia, take an ATC Terni bus from Piazza dei Partigiani or preferably the train to Terni (€6.40, one hour and 15 minutes, 2pm & 1.15pm Monday to Friday and 6.20pm on Saturday) and switch there. Check the TV monitors above the terminals. It's best to take the train to Spello, Foligno, Spoleto, Orvieto or Assisi.

Current train and bus routes, company details and timetables are listed in the monthly booklet *Viva Perugia* (€0.80) available at *tabacchi* everywhere.

CAR & MOTORCYCLE

From Rome, leave the A1 at the Orte exit and follow the signs for Terni. Once there take the SS3bis/E45 for Perugia. From the north, exit the A1 at Valdichiana and take dual carriageway SS75 for Perugia. The SS75 to the east connects the city with Assisi.

You'll find three car-rental companies at the main train station. All are open from 8.30am to 1pm and 3.30pm to 7pm Monday to Friday, and from 8.30am to 1pm Saturday.

Avis (☎ /fax 075 500 03 95; alvalrent@hotmail.com) is run by an English-speaking family or their third generation of Avis employees. Rates cost about €233 per week for a manual transmission (about €400 for an automatic). Ask for Pino.

Hertz (☎ 075 500 24 39; hertzperugia@tiscali.it)

Maggiore (☎ 075 500 74 99; www.maggiore.it in Italian)

Give **Scootyrent** (☎ 075 572 07 10, 333 102 65 05; www.scootyrent.com; Via Pinturicchio 76) a call for scooter hire. For about €20 a day, you can feel like a real Italian, transporting yourself and taking your life in your hands, all at the same time.

TRAIN

Although Perugia's main train station is named 'Stazione Fontivegge', the sign at the station simply reads 'Perugia'. It is on Piazza Vittorio Veneto, a few kilometres west of the city centre and easily accessible by frequent buses from Piazza Italia. The ticket office is open from 6.30am to 8.10pm, but you can buy tickets at the automated machines at any time of day with a credit card or cash. For train information, call Tren Italia ☎ 89 20 21.

There are seven direct services to Rome daily (€10.12 to €18.45, 2¼ to three hours). Even if your ticket doesn't indicate a change, ask whether there is one, as you mostly have to change in Terontola or Foligno. Trains to Florence run about every two hours, more so in the morning (€7.90 to €12.50, two hours). Other destinations and fares include Assisi (€1.65, 25 minutes, hourly), Gubbio (€4.30, 1½ hours, seven daily, change in Foligno), Spello (€2.05, 30 minutes, hourly) and Arezzo

€4.50, one hour and 10 minutes, every two hours).

About half of the tourist destinations in Umbria require a ride on the **Ferrovia Central Umbra** (FCU; ☎ 075 57 54 01; www.fcu.it in Italian; Stazione Sant'Anna, Piazzale Bellucci). These adorable graffitied 'Thomas the Tank Engine' trains also head to Rome (switch in Terni). You must validate your ticket on board, not before boarding as with all other Italian trains.

Take the FCU south to Deruta (€1.25, 20 minutes, 14 daily), Fratta Todina for Monte Castello di Vibio (€2.05, 40 minutes, 18 daily), Todi (€2.55, 50 minutes, 18 daily) or Terni (€4.40, 1½ hours, 17 daily). The Sansepolcro line heads north to Umbertide (€2.05, 45 minutes, 19 daily) and Città di Castello (€3.05, one hour and 10 minutes, 16 daily).

Getting Around

The best way to see Umbria is to take the train or buses to Assisi, Spoleto, Perugia, Orvieto or Gubbio and then to rent a car for a week and wander throughout the countryside.

It's a steep climb uphill from Perugia's train station, so a bus is highly recommended, especially for those with luggage. The city bus costs €0.80 (€0.65 for seniors) and takes you as far as Piazza Italia in the historic centre. Be sure to validate your ticket upon boarding or you will be fined on the spot. If you haven't bought a ticket, you can buy one on the bus for €1.50. Buses 6 and 7 are the most immediate, but buses 11, 13 and 15d will also get you to Piazza Italia. Buy your bus ticket from the small green bus kiosk in front of the train station (or in Piazza Italia, or at many *tabacchi* throughout the city). If you're going to stick around for a while, buy a 10-ticket pass for €7.20. A light rail system was supposed to have been finished by 2003, so expect it to be running by 2012 or so.

An airbus connects Piazza Italia with Aeroporto Sant'Egidio.

CAR & MOTORCYCLE

If you arrive in Perugia by car, following the Centro signs along the winding roads up the hill will bring you to Piazza Italia. Driving and parking in Perugia is expensive. Most of the city centre is largely closed to normal, nonresidential traffic, although tourists may drive to their hotels to drop off luggage. Rumour has it that parking police are more lenient on tourist cars, but if you park illegally for too long you run the risk of getting towed. Perugia has six fee-charging car parks: Piazza Partigiani (the most central and convenient), Viale Pellini, Mercato Coperto, Briglie di Braccio, Viale Sant'Antonio and Piazzale Europa. The free car park is located at Piazza Cupa. *Scale mobili* or *ascensori* (lifts) lead from each car park towards the city centre, but take note: they don't operate 24 hours a day, and they usually stop between about midnight or 1am and 6am or 7am.

Parking fees cost €0.80 to €1.05 per hour, 24 hours a day. If you intend to use a car park a lot, buy a tourist *abbonamento* (unlimited parking ticket pass) from the ticket office at the car park for about €7.75 for the first day and €5.20 for each successive day. If you're just parking for a while, try the Coop (see p276) by the train station, where you can park free for two hours with any purchase. For general parking information, call ☎ 800 017 603.

Call the **Deposito Veicoli Rimossi** (☎ 075 577 53 75) if your car has been towed, but be prepared to pay around €105 to retrieve it.

Your best bet is simply to rent a car on your way out of Perugia.

TAXI

Taxi services are available from 6am to 2am (24 hours a day in July and August) – call ☎ 075 500 48 88 to arrange pick-up.

A ride from the city centre to the main train station, Stazione Fontivegge, will cost about €10. Tack on €1 for each suitcase.

AROUND PERUGIA
Torgiano
pop 5406

Torgiano doesn't offer much in the way of sights or activities except for its great wine museum, several *enoteche*, and ancient wine-making history. Then again, isn't that enough? The most famous export from Torgiano is its Rosso Riserva, awarded with the DOCG (Controlled and Guaranteed Designation of Origin) label (see p64 for more information on wine classification).

The **Museo del Vino** (☎ 075 988 02 00; www .lungarotti.it; Corso Vittorio Emanuele 31; adult/student €4/2.50; ⏰ 9am-1pm & 3-7pm summer, 9am-1pm & 3-6pm winter) is a wine museum sponsored by the Lungarotti Foundation (prolific vintners in Umbria). It has several well-documented collections in 20 rooms, including information on everything to do with wine drinking, wine making and wine tasting. It displays wine-related archaeological finds, ceramics, books, artwork and ethnography, with information in Italian and English.

In the same vein, the **Museo dell'Olivo e dell'Olio** (Olive Oil Museum; ☎ 075 988 03 00; Via Garibaldi 10; adult/concession €4/2.50; ☺ 10am-1pm & 3-7pm Mon-Sat summer, 10am-1pm & 3-6pm winter) displays everything you had no idea you needed to know about olive oil. Combined tickets to both museums cost €7 for adults and €4 for students.

After visiting the museums, stop in at the **Osteria del Museo** (☎ 075 988 00 69; osteriadelmuseo@tele2.it; Corso Vittorio Emanuele 33; ☺ 8am-1pm & 2.30-7.30pm summer, 8am-1pm & 2.30-6.30pm winter), where you can taste (and buy) Lungarotti wines. There are several tasting menus with snacks priced from €4 to €10. You can sample just one or, if you're not driving, each one.

Newly refurbished and opened in 2004, **Al Grappolo d'Oro** (☎ 075 98 22 53; www.algrappolodoro.net; Via Principe Umberto 22/24; s/d incl breakfast €45/70; **P** ⊠ ⓦ) is one of the best hotel deals in all of Umbria. The toiletries are practically worth the price alone, as is the outdoor pool backing onto an expansive vineyard vista. The building has touches of time past as a 19th-century residence, but the 15 smartly furnished bedrooms come with all modern amenities – DSL connection, satellite TV, DVD player, minibar, hairdryer, towel warmer…and even great water pressure in the shower, an Umbrian luxury.

Al Grappolo d'Oro's sister restaurant, **Siro** (☎ 075 988 00 35; Via G Bruno 16; mains €6.50-12), is also an *albergo* (hotel), but it's the food you'll come here for. It's populated by locals who spend leisurely lunches with friends and colleagues. The *menù gastronomica* for €20 is enough for two people and filled with samples of its best plates. For a healthy snack, try the *salata della nonna* – rocket (arugula), pear, pine nuts and Parmesan (€5).

Umbria's most exclusive restaurant is found in Torgiano. **Le Melograne** (☎ 075 988 04 47; www.3vaselle.it; Via Garibaldi 48; fixed price meals around €45), at the luxury five-star hotel Le Tre Vaselle, is owned by the famous wine-producing Lungarotti family (who own many vineyards and the wine museum). It serves deluxe Umbrian cuisine amid luxurious furnishings and beautiful brick floors. Dishes include veal *carpaccio* topped with black truffles, and risotto

---

THE PASSEGGIATA

One of the very best things to take advantage of in Umbria is the *passeggiata* (traditional evening stroll). No matter how big or small a town, locals and visitors of all ages take to the streets with friends or family, by themselves or, these days, attached to a mobile phone. Most towns in Umbria are built concentrically around a main square that might have started out as a Roman forum or medieval gathering place. Best of all, *un passeggio* is free, doesn't require any preplanning and practically forces you to eat a double *gelato*. Think of it as improvised urban street theatre. In Perugia, watch as the students preen and flirt, jostling their way towards adulthood. In Orvieto, sit around the cathedral with older locals, who come to deliver Italian lessons to unsuspecting visitors. In Castelluccio, your *passeggiata* will most likely be shared with the town's herd of goats.

---

cooked with Rubesco red wine produced by, of course, the Lungarottis.

Deruta
pop 8082

Just south of Perugia along the SS3bis/E45, Deruta is a mildly interesting hill town that would hardly be visited if it wasn't considered to be Umbria's (and, according to some, Italy's) centre of ceramics. Derutans have been creating *majolica* ceramics (ceramics that originated in the Middle East) here for more than 600 years. Some shops are still in the walled medieval historical centre, but for serious shopping, try the main road leading from the highway, Via Tiberina.

Museo Regionale Della Ceramica (☎ 075 971 10 00; adult/concession €4/3; ☺ 10.30am-1pm & 2.30-5pm Wed-Mon Oct-Mar, 10.30am-1pm & 3-6pm Apr-Jun, 10am-1pm & 3.30-7pm Jul-Sep), a ceramics museum in the majestic town-hall building, lists all information in Italian and English. Although the museum has over 6000 ceramic pieces, its showcases include archaeological restoration, and ceramic works in each stage of production and Etruscan pottery.

At **Maioliche Nulli** (☎ /fax 075 97 23 84; Via Tiberina 142), Rolando Nulli creates each ceramic item by hand while his brother Goffredo finishes them with intricate paintings, specialising in reproductions of classic medieval designs. The brothers have been creating traditional Derutan ceramics by hand since they were teenagers; now Rolando's teenage son sells his work in the shop, and their sister runs a shop just two doors away. They ship all over the world. If the shop isn't packed, be sure to ask Rolando for a lesson on the wheel downstairs. Bring your camera!

Maioliche CAMA Deruta (☎ 075 971 11 82; www .camaderuta.com; Via Tiberina 112) is a bigger operation than Maioliche Nulli, but is one of the most respected in Deruta. You can order most of its products online.

At **Scuola d'Arte Ceramica** (☎ 075 97 23 83; www .scuoladarteceramica.com in Italian; Via Tiberina Sud 330), intermediate and expert ceramicists will get a thorough lesson in Derutan techniques over several days or even weeks. Courses are usually taught in Italian but some popular summer courses have an English translator.

For a great and cheap meal, try **Hotel Ristorante Asso di Coppe** (☎ 075 971 02 05; SS3bis/E45, Km 73,400), a place populated by locals and serving basic but delicious Umbrian cuisine.

Just south of Deruta in the village of Casalina is **Ristorante & Country House L'Antico Forziere** (☎ 075 972 43 14; www.anticoforziere.com; Via della Rocca 2, Loc. Casalina di Deruta; s/d incl breakfast €100/150; mains €7.50-15; ⊗ restaurant closed Mon; P ✖ ⊠), a charming country house with several well-decorated rooms and an absolutely superb restaurant. The family-run operation has been featured in fine magazines all over the world, but still retains a simple atmosphere. Meals are as inventive as they are delicious – brandy-infused quail, turnip pasta with leek and poppy seeds, and Marsala-braised pork with pineapple, cinnamon and radicchio. Children stay for free!

ASSISI

pop 25,304

Assisi is the quintessentially perfect Italian hill town. It's so perfect, in fact, that millions upon millions of visitors come here, turning it into the most crowded spot in Umbria.

There is perhaps no other place on earth that is as tied to its famous son as Assisi is with St Francis, who was born here in 1182. St Francis renounced his father's wealth in his late teens to pursue a life of chastity and poverty. After his renunciation of worldly goods he founded the order of mendicant friars known as the Frati Minori (Friars Minors; they eventually became known as the Franciscans), which attracted a huge following in Europe. With one of his disciples, St Clare (Santa Chiara), St Francis cofounded the Franciscans' female Ordine delle Clarisse (Order of the Poor Clares). St Francis became the patron saint of Italy in 1939.

Since Roman times, its inhabitants have been aware of the visual impact of their city, perched halfway up Monte Subasio (1290m). From the valley, its pink and white marble buildings shimmer in the sunlight.

ST FRANCIS THE REVOLUTIONARY

Born the wealthy son of a cloth merchant in 1182, Francis (Francesco in Italian) filled his younger years with wild parties and daydreams about becoming a great knight. In his mid-20s, he headed off into battle against Perugia, but a gradual religious awakening was to steer him to a different noble calling.

At the ancient church of San Damiano, 1.5km outside of Assisi, he heard the voice of Jesus on the crucifix: 'Francis, repair my church'. He took cloth from his father's shop to sell for the repairs. When his father dragged him in front of the bishop for punishment, Francis stripped off his clothes and renounced his former life.

He walked the countryside, wearing simple robes and preaching the virtues of poverty and equal respect for popes and lepers alike. He had a special affinity with animals and it's said he once preached to a flock of birds who stayed completely still until he said they could fly off. Many were attracted to Francis' lifestyle and within a few years, he developed the first order of Frati Minori (Friars Minors), which, after his death, became known as the Franciscans.

Francis spent his remaining years living out what would become the Franciscans' vows of poverty, chastity and obedience. In 1224, he received the stigmata, realising a dream to truly feel Jesus' suffering. Two years later, he died lying on the floor of a mud hut with his beloved Lady Poverty.

www.lonelyplanet.com

NORTHERN UMBRIA

ASSISI

The Basilica di San Francesco is the most popular tourist spot in all of Umbria. Crowds can be overwhelming around religious celebrations and holidays, but even in the height of summer, there is the possibility of wandering side streets alone.

Orientation
Piazza del Comune is the centre of Assisi. At the northwestern edge of this square, Via San Paolo and Via Portica both eventually lead to the Basilica di San Francesco. Via Portica also leads to the Porta San Pietro and the Piazzale dell'Unità d'Italia, where most intercity buses stop, although APM buses from smaller towns in the area terminate at Piazza Matteotti. Train riders arrive at Piazza Matteotti by shuttle bus (€0.80) from Santa Maria degli Angeli.

Information
EMERGENCY
Police station (☎ 075 81 28 20; Piazza del Comune)

INTERNET ACCESS
Sabatini Sandro (Via Portica 29/b; per 30 min €3; ☺ 8am-8pm)

INTERNET RESOURCES
Assisi (www.assisi.com) A good website for tourist information.
Assisi Accessibile (www.assisiaccessibile.it) Travellers and pilgrims with physical disabilities heading to Assisi will appreciate this comprehensive site that's stocked with tips on where to stay and eat and how to get around.

LAUNDRY
Acquazzura (☎ 075 804 09 27; Via San Bernardino da Siena 6, Santa Maria degli Angeli; ☺ 8am-10pm) A self-service laundromat near Basilica di Santa Maria degli Angeli.

MEDICAL SERVICES
Ospedale di Assisi (☎ 075 813 92 27) About 1km southeast of Porta Nuova in Fuori Porta.

MONEY
Banks are a dime a dozen in Assisi. Many congregate around the Piazza del Comune and all offer ATMs.

POST
Post office (☺ 8.10am-6.25pm Mon-Fri, 8.10am-1pm Sat & Sun) Just inside Porta San Pietro and next to Porta Nuova.

TOURIST INFORMATION
Tourist office Main tourist office (☎ 075 81 25 34; info@iat.assisi.pg.it; Piazza del Comune 22; ☺ 8am-6.30pm Mon-Sat, 10am-1pm & 2-5pm summer, 8am-2pm & 3-6pm Mon-Sat, 9am-1pm Sun winter); Tourist office branch (☎ 075 81 67 66; ☺ Easter-Nov) The branch office is located just outside Porta Nuova.

Sights
BASILICA DI SAN FRANCESCO
The **Basilica di San Francesco** (☎ 075 81 90 01; Piazza di San Francesco; ☺ 9am-noon & 2-5pm) is the main attraction in Umbria, and one of the most visited religious sites in the world. People come here on pilgrimages from all corners of the planet. It has its own **information office** (☎ 075 819 00 84; www.sanfrancescoassisi.org in Italian; ☺ 9am-noon & 2-5pm) across from the entrance to the lower church. An **audio tour guide** (☎ 075 81 28 50; acoustiguide@yahoo.com; guide €5) is available from an office in the Piazza Inferiore. Or you can call the office a day or two in advance (or drop in) to see if there's an English-language tour you can pay to hitch on to. They're usually led by resident African, English or North American Franciscan friars.

The basilica saw heavy damage during a series of earthquakes on 26 September 1997. Two friars and two Italian governmental inspectors died during a second major earthquake when the vaulted ceiling of the upper church they were inspecting collapsed.

At the end of 1999, after two years of restoration work, the reopening of the basilica was celebrated with a mass of rededication. New technology was used to make the basilica as earthquake-proof as possible. Since the frescoes are being restored, you can buy one of the guidebooks to the basilica (in the bookshop or at the information centre) for photographs of the intact paintings.

St Francis gained a lot of fame and quite a following during his lifetime. When he died in 1226 at age 44, his followers knew they had to hide his body as soon as possible, since the long-held Roman belief in the area was that God was on the side of whoever possessed the corpse of a holy person. Ghibelline Assisi was warring with Guelph Perugia at the time, so they had to build quickly. Construction of the lower church began almost immediately, and Pope Gregory IX himself laid the first stone in 1228. St Francis' body was hidden so well under this church that it wasn't found again until 1818.

The basilica was built on a hill known as Colle d'Inferno (Hell Hill). People were executed at the gallows here until the 13th century. St Francis asked his followers to bury him here in keeping with Jesus, who had died on the cross among criminals and outcasts. The area is now known as Paradise Hill.

The **lower church** (6.30am-6.50pm Easter-Nov, 6.30am-6pm Nov-Easter, 6.30am-7.15pm public holidays) was built between 1228 and 1230. The stained-glass windows are the work of master craftsmen brought in from Germany, England and Flanders during the 13th century, and were quite an architectural feat at that time.

In the centre of the lower church, above the main altar, are four frescoes attributed to Maestro delle Vele, a pupil of Ghiotto, that represent what St Francis called 'the four greatest allegories'. The first was the victory of Francis over evil, and the other three were the precepts on which his order was based: obedience, poverty and chastity.

Lorenzetti's triptych in the left transept ends with his most famous and controversial, *Madonna Who Celebrates Francis*. Mary is seen holding the baby Jesus and indicating with her thumb towards St Francis. On the other side of Mary is the apostle John, whom we're assuming is being unfavourably compared with Francis. In 1234 Pope Gregory IX decided that the image was not heretical because John had written the gospel, but Francis had lived it.

Cimabue was the most historically important painter because he had personally known St Francis. In the *Madonna in Majesty*, in the right transept, much has been tampered with, but Cimabue's intact depiction of St Francis is considered the most accurate, as he painted it from eyewitness accounts from St Francis' two nephews. Francis appears peaceful and calm in this painting. The first biographer of St Francis, Thomas of Celano, wrote in the middle of the 13th century that Francis was an eloquent man, of cheerful countenance and of a kindly aspect.

The basilica's **Sala delle Reliquie** (Relics Hall; 9am-6pm daily, 1-4.30pm public holidays) contains items from St Francis' life, including his simple tunic and sandals and fragments of his celebrated *Canticle of the Creatures*. The most important relic here is the Franciscan Rule parchment, the *Book of Life* composed by Francis.

The **upper church** (8.30am-6.50pm Easter-Nov, 8.30am-6pm Nov-Easter, 8.30am-7.15pm public holidays) was built between 1230 and 1253. It contains a 28-part fresco cycle detailing St Francis' life, as well as corresponding images from the Bible. The frescoes in the basilica revolutionised art in the Western world, on several levels. They were painted by all of the most famous painters of the time – Cimabue and Giotto from the Florentine school were the most prolific, but also Cavalini, Rusuti, and artists from the Tuscan and Sienese schools. The frescoes represented a shift in art style: from the majestic *Divine Judge* Jesus of the Byzantine and Romanesque art to a *Minore* Christ, suffering and humbled. Instead of gold backgrounds symbolising heaven, the basilica artists painted natural backgrounds, with the stars, sky and clouds. This was in keeping with Francis' idea that the human body was 'brother' and the earth around him mother and sister. Some of these frescoes were the first paintings to ever depict third-class citizens, such as shepherds. At the time, the only people who could afford to commission paintings of themselves were noblemen and the very wealthy, so before the basilica was built no one had ever bothered to paint anyone but religious icons or powerful figures.

These fresco painters were the storytellers of their day, turning biblical passages into *Bibliae Pauperum* – open public Bibles for the poor, who were mostly illiterate. Cimabue painted a good number of what is displayed in the upper church, including the Marian scenes in the apse and lower section of the apse, the *Apocalypse* and the *Acts of the Apostles* in the left and right transepts, and the *Crucifixion* in the left transept – an example of both the Minore Christ and what can happen when a lead-white fresco oxidises (it has become a negative of its former image).

Giotto, trained under Cimabue, was responsible for most of the 28-part fresco cycle. Francis appears in concordance with images from both the Old and New Testaments. His life is depicted on the lower portion of the church while the biblical themes are on top: on the right, stories from Genesis, and on the left, stories from the life of Jesus. The upper paintings were done by a host of great artists, including Giotto and Cimabue. In the central nave vault Francis appears, glorified as the convergence of both Testaments.

This symbolism was another way the paintings were used to translate stories of the Bible. The scenes in St Francis' life were tied to the biblical scenes as a way of translating the Bible through images. For instance, the fifth fresco shows St Francis renouncing his father, while the corresponding biblical fresco shows the disobedient Adam and Eve in the Garden of Eden.

Please adhere to the no-flash photography rule – over the years, some of the paintings have been damaged by chemical interactions due to human interference.

OTHER SIGHTS

Basilica di Santa Chiara (☎ 075 812 282; Piazza Santa Chiara; ✆ 6am-noon & 2-7pm summer, 6am-noon & 2-6pm winter) is 13th-century Romanesque, with steep ramparts and a striking façade. The white-and-pink stone that makes up the exterior here (the same stone that makes many buildings in Assisi look like they glow in the sunlight) came from nearby Subasio. The daughter of an Assisian nobleman, St Clare was a spiritual contemporary of St Francis and founded the Order of the Poor Ladies, now known as the Poor Clares. She's buried in the church's crypt. The Byzantine cross that is said to have spoken to St Francis is also housed here.

Northeast of the Basilica di Santa Chiara, the 13th-century Romanesque **Duomo di San Rufino** (☎ 075 81 60 16; Piazza San Rufino; ✆ 7am-noon & 2-7pm), remodelled by Galeazzo Alessi in the 16th century, contains the fountain where St Francis and St Clare were baptised. The façade is festooned with grotesque figures and fantastic animals.

The **Chiesa Nuova** (☎ 075 81 23 39; fax 075 815 50 50; Piazza Chiesa Nuova; ✆ 6.30am-noon & 2.30-6pm summer, 6.30am-noon & 2-6pm winter) was built by King Philip III of Spain in the 1600s on the spot reputed to be the house of St Francis' family. Mass is said at 7am, with an extra service on holidays at 10am.

Piazza del Comune was once the site of a partially excavated **Foro Romano** (Roman Forum; ☎ 075 81 30 53; entrance Via Portica; adult/child plus Pinacoteca €3/2; ✆ 10.30am-1.30pm & 2-6pm, to 5pm winter). The **Tempio di Minerva** (facing Piazza del Comune and **Palazzo dei Priori**) is now a church but retains its impressive pillared façade. Wander into some of the shops on the piazza, which open their basements to reveal Roman ruins. The city's **Pinacoteca**

Comunale (☎ 075 81 20 33; Palazzo Vallemani, Via San Francesco 10; adult/child plus Foro Romano €3/2; ✆ 10am-1pm & 3-6pm 16 Mar-15 Oct, 10am-1pm & 3-5pm 16 Oct-15 Mar) displays Umbrian Renaissance art and frescoes from Giotto's school.

Dominating the city is the massive 14th-century **Rocca Maggiore** (☎ 075 81 30 53; Via della Rocca; admission €2; ✆ 10am-sunset), a hill fortress offering fabulous views over the valley and across to Perugia. The fortress is being turned into an enormous art gallery.

OUT OF TOWN

In the valley southwest of the city, look for the imposing blue dome of the **Basilica di Santa Maria degli Angeli** (☎ 075 8 05 11; Santa Maria degli Angeli; ✆ 6.15am-7.45pm & 9-11pm summer, 6.15am-12.30pm & 2-7.45pm winter), the enormous church built around the first Franciscan monastery. One of the most important Franciscan sites was the Cappella del Transito, now enveloped in the larger basilica, where St Francis and his followers resided for years. St Francis died here on 3 October 1226 (see p281).

About 4km east of the city, reached via the Porta Cappuccini, is **Eremo delle Carceri** (☎ 075 81 23 01; admission free; ✆ 6.30am-7.15pm Easter-Nov, 6.30am-sunset Nov-Easter), the hermitage that St Francis retreated to after hearing the word of God. The *carceri* (prisons) are the caves that functioned as hermits' retreats for St Francis and his followers. St Francis was known to spend time here and to preach sermons to the local animals (the ilex tree where the bird audience sat is still alive). Apart from a few fences and tourist paths, everything remains as it was in St Francis' time, and a few Franciscans live here. Eremo delle Carceri is a great jumping-off point for walks through Monte Subasio.

About 1.5km south from Porta Nuova, the **Santuario di San Damiano** (☎ 075 812 273; admission free; ✆ 10am-noon & 2-6pm summer, 10am-noon & 2-4.30pm winter, vespers 7pm summer & 5pm winter) was built on the spot where St Francis first heard the voice of Jesus and where he wrote his *Canticle of the Creatures*. You can visit the original convent founded by St Clare in 1212, as well as its cloisters and refectory.

Activities

Fans of nature and of St Francis will appreciate the plethora of strolls, day walks and overnight pilgrimage walks leading into and out of Assisi. The tourist office has several maps for those on such a peregrination, including following in St Francis' footsteps to Gubbio (18km).

A popular spot for walkers is nearby Monte Subasio. Local bookstores sell all sorts of walking and mountain biking guides and maps of the area, and the tourist office can help with brochures and maps.

In Santa Maria degli Angeli, you can rent bikes at **Angelucci Andrea Cicli Riparazione Noleggio** (☎ 075 804 25 50; Via Becchetti 31) or **Bartolucci Bruno** (☎ 368 431 758; train station) or at Ostello della Pace (see right).

Courses

Accademia Lingua Italiana Assisi (☎ /fax 075 815 281; www.aliassisi.it; Via San Paolo 36) runs a variety of courses, including Italian language, culture, singing, painting and cooking. It also offers free preparation for the CILS (Italian teacher abroad) course. Classes have a maximum of 12 students and start at €280 for two weeks of instruction.

Festivals & Events

Ars Nova Musica This festival, held from late August to mid-September, features local and national performers.
Festa di Calendimaggio Celebrates spring in medieval fashion and is normally held over several days at the end of the first week of May.
Festa di San Francesco Falls on 3 and 4 October and is the main religious event in the city.
Marcia per la Pace (March for Peace; www.tavoladella pace.it in Italian) The multidenominational walk has been bringing together thousands of marchers from around the world each June to walk from Assisi to Perugia in a show of solidarity for peace.
Settimana Santa (Easter week) Celebrated with processions and performances.

Sleeping

Assisi has a phenomenal number of rooms for rent but in peak periods, such as Easter, August and September, and the period around Festa di San Francesco, you will need to book accommodation well in advance. The tourist office has a complete list of private rooms, religious institutions (of which there are 17), flats and *agriturismi* options in and around Assisi and can assist with bookings in a pinch. Otherwise, keep an eye out for *camere* signs as you wander the streets.

AUTHOR'S CHOICE

St Anthony's Guesthouse (☎ 075 812 542; atoneassisi@tiscalinet.it; Via Galeazzo Alessi 10; s/d/tr incl breakfast €35/55/75; **P**) Look for the iron statue of St Francis feeding the birds and you've found your Assisian oasis. Rooms are austere but welcoming and several have balconies with take-your-breath-away views. Gardens, ample parking, an 800-year-old breakfast salon and an ancient Door of Death make this a heavenly choice. Like most religious accommodations, it has a two-night minimum and an 11pm curfew (there's also a suggested donation for parking of €3). To hear the most delightful Canadian-Italian accent ever, ask for Sister Sue.

BUDGET

Grotta Antica (☎ 075 813 467; www.bellaumbria.net /hotel-grottaantica; Via Macelli Vecchi 1; s/d €30/40) The price is not a mistake. Perfectly located on a tiny side street less than 30m from the Piazza del Comune, it's a wonder these rooms are also clean and hospitable. Abele speaks fluent English and Spanish and takes care of the seven simple rooms and the restaurant of the same name.

Ostello della Pace (☎ 075 816 767; www.assisi hostel.com; Via Valecchie 177; dm incl breakfast €15, half board €24.50, full board €33.50; ♡ closed 10 Jan-1 Mar; **P** 🖳) Assisi's HI youth hostel is lovingly run by a family in a beautiful and quiet location – and it has great pillows. It's on the shuttle-bus route between Santa Maria degli Angeli and Assisi. There's also a laundry room for guests.

Istituto Suore del Giglio Case Religiose di Ospitalitá (☎ /fax 075 81 22 67; Via San Francesco 13; s/d €27/42) There's well over a dozen religious institutions that offer rooms, but this one is centrally located, has an incredibly friendly staff (including several English-speaking Zambian nuns) and a terrace with a view calming enough to inspire a religious experience. Two rooms even have their own balconies, and there are several family rooms that have up to five beds. Look for the sign that reads: Casa di Ospitalitá 'Maria Immacolata'. Curfew is 10.30pm.

Hotel Sole (☎ 075 81 23 73/81 29 22; www.assisi hotelsole.com; Corso Mazzini 35; s/d/tr with bathroom €42/62/83, s/d without bathroom €24/42) This comfortable little hotel has 35 rooms in renovated 15th-century buildings, now on both sides of the street. There are direct-dial phones in every room, a TV room, lounge, restaurant, lift and bar.

Hotel La Rocca (☎ 075 81 22 84; www.hotelarocca .it; Via Porta Perlici 27; s/d/tr/q €39/46/65/73; 🐾) At some point in our lives we all may ask ourselves: What do I value more in life – a hairdryer and the possibility of a good view or a guaranteed quiet night's sleep? If the former, ask for *'una camera con una panorama'* and wear earplugs if the downstairs restaurant and bar is hopping.

Albergo Il Duomo (☎ 075 81 27 42; www.hotelsan rufino.it; Viccolo San Lorenzo; s/d €33/44, d without bathroom €38) Owned by the same folks who run the two-star San Rufino, this is a lovely one-star choice on a quiet alleyway just a stone's throw from the Piazza del Comune. For this price, there aren't too many extras, but the nine rooms are understandably popular, so book ahead.

MIDRANGE

Hotel Il Palazzo (☎ 075 81 68 41; www.hotelilpalazzo .it; Via San Francesco 8; s/d €90/135; 🕒 closed Nov, Jan, Feb) The rooms in this lovely 15th-century palazzo have been restored in the simple elegance that Italians are famous for – white walls, terracotta floors, a few pieces of fine old furniture in splendidly carved wood, and beautiful carpets. Half of the rooms are occupied by the owners (descendants of the original occupants). Despite its central position, the hotel is also very quiet and filled with light. The only disadvantage is that there are a lot of stairs to negotiate.

Agriturismo alla Madonna del Piatto (☎ 075 819 90 50; www.incampagna.com; Pieve San Nicolo 18; d incl breakfast €80-90, holidays €90-115; 🅿) This B&B/ *agriturismo* has seen many upgrades since its inception as a shepherd's outpost some 700 years ago. It's now a refurbished stone farmhouse with heated terracotta floors, six double rooms, an open fireplace and a working farm and olive orchard. Set in verdant hills, it's not unusual to see wild boar or pheasants pass by. The multilingual family often arranges visits to local markets and cooking classes. On the way here, about 7km northeast of Assisi, there's a spectacular view of the basilica. Make sure you rent a hardy car.

La Fortezza (☎ 075 81 24 18; www.lafortezzahotel .com; Vicolo della Fortezza 19/b; r incl breakfast €65, with-

out breakfast €52) This place has seven decent midpriced rooms that aren't as charming as the associated wonderful restaurant, of the same name, around the corner.

Hotel San Rufino (☎ 075 81 28 03; www.hotelsan rufino.it; Via Porta Perlici 7; s/d/tr €42/52/66, breakfast €5) A small hotel owned by the same family as Albergo Il Duomo, this is around the corner and just as quiet. Sweetly decorated rooms all come with direct-dial phones and TVs, and cradles can be provided for babies.

Hotel Pallotta (☎ 075 812 649; www.pallottaassisi.it; Vicolo della Volta Pinta; s/d/tr €35/55/65) The restaurant is legendary but the hotel is nothing to sneeze at, either. Decent rooms come at even better prices. Rooms are as modern as they are ancient; medieval walls and shuttered windows coexist with tile showers and wall-mounted televisions. Be sure to check out the view on the top floor, as well as the restaurant.

TOP END

Hotel San Francesco (☎ 075 81 22 81; www.hotelsan francescoassisi.it; Via San Francesco 48; s/d incl breakfast €100/130; 🐾) For travellers who are looking for a serious view of the basilica, you have a postcard shot just outside most rooms. Amenities include satellite TV (with BBC, CNN, France 2), minibar, elevator, hairdryer, double windows and a hotel shuttle service that will come and collect you at any of the car parks (you can also drive in and drop off your luggage first). Its enormous breakfast buffet is included in the price, and is the perfect way to start a day of travelling. There are also discounts in the low season and for children.

Eating & Drinking

Assisi offers a good selection of traditional Italian and Umbrian delicacies. In a twist, most of Assisi's better restaurants (even the inexpensive ones) are part of hotels.

Ristorante Pallotta (☎ 075 812 649; Vicolo della Volta Pinta; mains €6.80-15; 🕒 closed Tue) Head through the Volta Pinta (Painted Vault) off Piazza del Comune, be careful not to bump into anyone as you gaze at the 16th-century frescoes above you, into this gorgeous setting of vaulted brick walls and wood-beamed ceilings. Staff cook all the Umbrian classics here – rabbit, homemade *strangozzi*, even pigeon. The two-star hotel of the same name is a good bet, and guests get 10% off meals.

Grotta Antica (☎ 075 81 34 67; Vicolo Buscatti 6; mains €5-8.50) Attorney/hotel proprietor/chef Abele is from Liguria, so you can rest assured that although there are only a handful of dishes, you needn't look past the pesto dishes for a delicious, cheap and filling main course. His wine prices can't be beaten anywhere in Assisi.

Buca di San Francesco (☎ 075 81 22 04; Via Brizi 1; mains €14; closed Mon) Sample traditional Umbrian dishes and specialities of the house in a medieval setting. Choose bruschetta, local sausage, *spaghetti alla buca* (spaghetti with roasted mushrooms), gnocchi and home-made desserts.

Medio Evo (☎ 075 81 30 68; Via Arco dei Priori 4; mains around €12; closed Wed) Here, traditional Umbrian dishes are served in fabulous vaulted 13th-century surroundings. The early 6.45pm opening time is geared for, and highly appreciated by, non-Italian tourists.

Ristorante il Duomo (☎ 075 81 27 42; Viccolo San Lorenzo; pizza €3-7.50, mains €4.50-9) Pizza is the stronghold here. Several pages on the menu are dedicated to all toppings and varieties.

La Fortezza (☎ 075 812 418; Vicolo della Fortezza 2/b; mains around €9; closed Thu) Run by a chef-owner and his wife and two sons, this wonderful little restaurant just up the Vicolo della Fortezza stairway serves dishes featuring black truffles and game meats. Has a good selection of local wines.

Dal Carro (☎ 075 81 52 49; Vicolo dei Nepis 2; pizza from €5) Off Corso Mazzini, Dal Carro is a good bet – the *strangozzi alla norcina* (pasta with a black truffle sauce) is a marvel and so is the homemade tiramisu (a dessert of sponge cake soaked in coffee and arranged in layers with mascarpone, then sprinkled with cocoa). Watch as your meal is cooked over an open fire.

Otello (☎ 075 81 32 25; Vicolo San Antonio 1; pizza €7) This restaurant is a local favourite. It serves simple but good pizza, and a wide selection of pasta dishes.

Gran Caffe (☎ 075 815 51 44; Corso Mazzini 16; 8am-midnight) This elegant place has the most fabulous *gelati* and mouthwatering pastries and cakes and a great selection of drinks. Try the *tè freddo alla pesca* (iced tea with peach) on a hot day, or choose from a selection of delicious hot chocolates and coffee when the weather is cool. Remember that it costs much more to sit down.

Shopping

Assisi is a good town for shopping as many shops stay open during siesta. The closer you get to the basilica, the tackier the souvenirs – Franciscan friar shot glasses and nuns playing poker – but meander off the beaten path for leather, ceramics and clothing. Open-air markets are in Piazza Matteotti on Saturday and Santa Maria degli Angeli on Monday.

Getting There & Around

Assisi's train station is 4km west in Santa Maria degli Angeli, but it's the better option as it's cheaper and more frequent than the bus. A constant shuttle (€0.80) runs between the train station and Piazza Matteotti (tickets available in the *tabacchi* at the station and in town). Assisi is on the Foligno–Terontola line with regular services to Perugia (€1.65, 30 minutes, hourly). You can change at Terontola for Florence (€8.99, 1¾ hours to 2¾ hours, 10 daily) and at Foligno for Rome (€8.99 to €14.26, two to 2½ hours, hourly).

Buses run to Perugia (€2.80, 50 minutes, eight daily) and Gubbio (€4.80, one hour and 10 minutes, 11 daily). Take Sulga to Florence (€11, 2½ hours, one daily at 7am, from Florence at 6pm) and Rome's Stazione Tiburtina (€14.50, 3¼ hours, three daily).

To reach Assisi from Perugia by road, take the SS75, exit at Ospedalicchio and follow the signs.

Normal traffic is subject to restrictions in the city centre and daytime parking is all but banned. Six car parks dot the city walls (connected to the centre by orange shuttle buses), or head for Via della Rocca where, for the price of a short but fairly steep walk, you'll find free parking.

For a taxi, dial ☎ 075 813 100.

LAGO DI TRASIMENO

A plethora of outdoor activities and natural beauty is Lago di Trasimeno's main attraction, but it offers an equal amount of cultural and architectural history as well. Walking is a popular pastime in the area, which features the fourth-largest lake in Italy. During spring, flowers blanket the area. Sunflowers are grown for their oil, which is used for frying because it's less expensive than olive oil. Historically, the area bounced back and forth between various factions, but has come to appreciate its location, at the crossroads of Tuscany and Umbria.

The region known as Lago di Trasimeno is made up of eight different *comuni* (municipalities): Castiglione del Lago, Città della Pieve, Magione, Paciano, Panicale, Passignano, Piegaro and Tuoro. Castiglione del Lago and Panicale are the most pleasant places in which to spend a day or two, while Città della Pieve is a farther drive but chock-full of artwork for the connoisseur.

The communities that surround Lago di Trasimeno have banded together with governmental organisations to create a sustainable plan for maintaining the area's ecological purity. Many of the lake's activities involve environmentally friendly water sports, such as kayaking and windsurfing, and the water is tested every few months for quality. Isola Polvese is a living environmental lab housing a sustainable hostel.

Orientation

Tourist offices can provide you with foldout maps such as *Le Mappe di Airone per il Trekking* or *Le Mappe di Airone per il Cicloturismo*. The walking guide has 13 maps and the *cicloturismo* (cycle tourism) guide has six maps. The Kompas Lago Trasimeno map (€6.95) is extremely thorough for both sightseers and walkers.

If you're using public transport, your best bet is to stay in Passignano or Castiglione del Lago or one of the camp sites, where you can rent bicycles. If you have a car, try any of the towns or *agriturismi*. Two major highways (well, major for Umbria) run to the west and north sides of the lake: the SS71 goes from Chiusi in the south to Arezzo in the north; and the SS75bis connects in Tuscany with the A1 (which connects Florence and Rome) and meets up with Perugia in the east.

Information

INTERNET RESOURCES

Trasimeno 2005 (www.lagotrasimeno.net) The area's best website with restaurants, hotels, itineraries and history.

MEDICAL SERVICES

Emergency First-aid Castiglione del Lago (☎ 075 9 52 61); Passignano & Tuoro (☎ 075 829 87 51)

POST

Post office (☉ 8.10am-1.20pm Mon-Fri, 8.10am-12.30pm Sat) Castiglione del Lago (Via F Ili Rosselli);

Città della Pieve (**Via Veneto 6**); Passignano (**Via Rinascita 2**); Tuoro (**Via Baroncino 1**)

TOURIST INFORMATION

You can buy a **percorso museale** (museum ticket; adult/child €6.20/4.15) from any tourist office if you're planning on visiting the entire lake area, including Città della Pieve.
Città della Pieve tourist office (☎ 075 829 93 75; ☉ 10.30am-12.30pm & 3.30-6pm summer, 10am-2.30pm & 3.30-6pm winter)
Panicale tourist office (☎ 075 837 8017; Piazza Umberto I; ☉ 10am-12.30pm & 3.30-7.30pm Easter-Oct, closed Sun winter) Offers tours of the town's major sites at 10.10am, 11.30am, 3.40pm, 5pm and 6.10pm in summer.
Pro Loco Passignano (☎ 075 82 76 35; Piazza Trento e Trieste 6, Passignano; ☉ 10.30am-12.30pm & 4-7pm Mon-Sat, 10.30am-12.30pm Sun)
Trasimeno Area/Castiglione del Lago Tourist Office (☎ 075 965 24 84; www.castiglionedellago.it; Piazza Mazzini 10, Castiglione del Lago; ☉ 8.30am-1pm & 3.30-7pm Mon-Sat, 9am-1pm Sun) This office advises on *agriturismi*, as well as walking and biking trails and water sports.

Sights

PANICALE

Perched on a hill with an expansive view of the lake, the entire town of Panicale is one giant fortress. In the **Church of St Sebastian** is Perugino's *Martyrdom of St Sebastian*, painted by the master in 1505. In the background of the painting is a landscape of the lake as it looked in Perugino's day. If you look closely, especially at the bottom of the painting, you'll see what's known as the *tratteggio* restoration technique, where artists create tiny vertical brushstrokes to fill in damaged artwork. The result is seamless from far away but art historians can tell what is original and what has been restored.

The **Museum of the Madonna della Sbarra** (admission free; ☉ 9am-12.30pm & 3-5.30pm), in the church of the same name, offers an up-close view of church vestments, statues and altar regalia from the past five centuries. Of particularly creepy note are the relic boxes filled with the bones of saints.

Craft fans will appreciate the **lace museum** (☎ 075 83 78 07; Chiesa Sant'Agostino; ☉ 10am-12.30pm & 3.30-7pm Jun-Sep, Fri-Sun winter & by appt), with examples of traditional lace and tulle from the area, housed in a deconsecrated frescoed church. If you want to buy lace, head to San Michael Square No 2 and ring

NORTHERN UMBRIA

SOLDIERS OF FORTUNE

In the 13th century, Italy's burgeoning city-states were in a bit of a bind: they had active govern-ments and prosperous citizens, but not much in the way of armies. So, they outsourced to the medieval Italian cross between a cocaine cartel warlord and a rock star: independent contractors known as the *capitani di ventura* (captains of fortune or luck) or *condottieri* (leaders of mercenary soldiers). These fickle mercenaries' allegiances were so easy to gain with promises of riches and fame that they were known to switch sides *during* battle. Umbria gave birth to many *condottieri*: Erasmo di Narni (1370–1443), known as Gattamelata), who served Florence, Venice and the pope before becoming dictator of Padua; Boldrino da Panicale (1331–91), who fought for Florence against Pisa, for Pisa against Florence and was sometimes paid a salary to stay away from a city; and Bartolomeo d'Alviano (1455–1515), whose adventures you can follow at the Museo Storico Multimediale Bartolomeo d'Alviano e i Capitani di Ventura (see p333) outside of Amelia and find out how he led his troops into battle even after his death.

---

the doorbell. If she's home, Fede Boldrino, who jokes she is the wife of Boldrino da Panicale (see above) and is nearly the right age, still creates lacework by hand.

The Teatro Cesare Caporali runs concerts all summer. During the summer, there's a free concert every Thursday in the main square at 9pm.

CASTIGLIONE DEL LAGO

Castiglione del Lago's history dates back to an Etruscan settlement and is now a popular (but not overwhelmingly so) tourist destina-tion. In the 7th century, the town became an important defensive promontory for the Byzantine Perugia. It was fought over and traded between the papacy, the emperor and various territories for about 1000 years.

An ancient ducal palace, **Palazzo della Corgna** (☎ 075 965 82 10; Piazza Gramsci; admission incl Rocca del Leone adult/concession €3/2; ☉ 10am-1pm & 4-7.30pm summer, 9.30am-4.30pm Sat & Sun winter) houses an important series of 16th-century frescoes by Giovanni Antonio Pandolfi and Salvio Savini. It was built in the 16th cen-tury by Jacopo Barozzi, who incorporated parts of ancient houses once owned by the feudal Baglioni family from Perugia.

A covered passageway connects the pal-ace with the 13th-century **Rocca del Leone**, (Fortress of the Lion), a pentagon-shaped fortress built in 1247 and an excellent ex-ample of medieval military architecture. Seen from the lake, rearing up on a rocky promontory, it cuts a striking pose.

ISOLA POLVESE

There's not much to do in Isola Polvese, which, to those who seek out its tranquillity,

is its charm. The main attraction is that the entire island is a scientific and educational park. Many school groups come here to use the environmental labs that are devoted to teaching preservation of biodiversity and sustainable technologies. Make sure you visit the **Garden of Aquatic Plants**, to see biodiversity at work. Also of interest are the **Monastery of San Secondo** and the **Church of St Julian**. There are also remains of a 14th-century castle. The only inhabited building is the Fattoria il Pog-gio hostel (see p293).

CITTÀ DELLA PIEVE

Città della Pieve is culturally and geograph-ically considered part of Lago di Trasimeno, but it's about 20km to the south.

Although he became known as 'Il Peru-gino' (the Perugian), the famous Renaissance painter Pietro Vannucci was born here in 1445 and his paintings are all over the town. The **Cattedrale di San Gervasio e Protasio** houses Perugino works and was developed from the ancient baptismal church (known as a *pieve*). Perhaps Perugino's most famous work in his hometown is *Adoration of the Magi*, on view at the **Oratory of Santa Maria dei Bianchi**.

The head of the della Corgna family was appointed as governor of the town by his uncle, Pope Julius III, and subsequently commissioned artists to paint works for the town, known then as Castel della Pieve (it was elevated to a city in 1600). The frescoes in the statuesque **Palazzo della Corgna** include ones by Il Pomarancio and Salvio Savini.

ISOLA MAGGIORE

The lake's main inhabited island, Isola Maggiore, near Passignano, was reputedly a favourite with St Francis. The hill-top **Chiesa di San Michele Arcangelo** contains a Crucifixion by master painter Bartolomeo Caporali. The island is famed for its lace and embroidery production and you can see examples in the **Museo del Merlotto** (Lace Museum; ☎ 075 825 42 33; Via Gugliemi, near the port, Isola Maggiore; admission €3; ☑ 10am-1pm & 2.30-6pm).

SAN FELICIANO
This working town still sees fishermen leave to trawl for fish in the morning (see p292 to join them). Although primarily a strip of hotels catering to northern Europeans on a sunny holiday, San Feliciano does have a few worthwhile stops. One of these is the **Fishing Museum** (☎ 075 847 92 61; www.museodellapesca.it in Italian; Via Lungolago della Pace e del Lavoro 20; adult/child/concession €3/1/2; ☑ 10.30am-1pm & 3.30-7pm summer & 9-11pm Jul & Aug), which showcases fishing techniques from ancient times to modern day.

PASSIGNANO
Passignano is the most holiday-ish of the Trasimeno towns, with many restaurants, hotels, *gelato* joints and souvenir shops. The medieval castle on the top of the hill is closed to visitors, but the view from in front of it is as good as it gets. Check out the 16th-century **Chiesa della Madonna dell'Uliveto** (☎ 075 82 71 24; ☑ 5-7pm Wed & Thu, 4-8pm Fri & Sat, 10am-noon & 5-7pm Sun) on the road to Tuoro. Inside, the sanctuary features a Madonna by Bartolomeo Caporali and a decorated holy water trough. A must-see for anyone stopping here on the last Sunday of July is the **Palio delle Barche** (Boat Race), when groups of neighbourhood men carry a heavy boat to the castle on the top of the hill.

TUORO
During the second Punic War between Rome and Carthage, Lago di Trasimeno was the site of one of the deadliest battles in all of Roman history. Roman troops led by Consul Caius Flaminius were set up around the area that is now Tuoro. Quite the wartime strategist, Carthaginian general Hannibal made it look as though he was just passing by on his way to Rome, as nonchalantly as one can with 50,000 troops, 9000 horses and 37 elephants. Hannibal's men even lit a series of torches far from the lake, leading Flaminius' forces to believe the Carthaginians were too far away to be a threat. Under

the cover of the lake's typical misty morning, Hannibal ambushed so expediently that the Romans hardly had time to suit up, killing over three-fifths of Flaminius' 25,000-strong army. A local stream ran with the blood of Flaminius and his soldiers for three straight days, earning the new name *Sanguineto* (the bloody). You can visit the **Permanent Documentation Centre** (☎ 075 82 52 20) and tour the battlegrounds. Pick up the *I Luoghi della Battaglia* brochure from one of the tourist offices for a self-guided tour of the battleground.

Also visit **Field of the Sun** (Campo del Sole), a group of 28 contemporary sand sculptures made by celebrated artists and looking like a modern-day Stonehenge. You'll find it near Loc. Navaccia Lido, close to the lake's edge.

MAGIONE
You may end up here if you suddenly realise that you need a heap of groceries or a mosaic table. It's the commercial centre of the lake and, as such, not terribly interesting. However, the train stops here and it does have a fascinating castle. Originally constructed between 1160 and 1170, the Templars used Magione's fortified abbey as a hospital for crusaders going back and forth to fight in the crusades in Jerusalem. The Knights of Malta took the abbey from the Templars and, to this day, still own it. You can drive up to the **Castle of the Knights of Malta** (☎ 075 84 38 59; admission free), which is open in summer only.

Activities
Walking, riding, swimming, eating, drinking…it can all be done at the lake.

Horse-riding centres include the **Maneggio Oasi** (☎ 0337 65 37 95; Loc. Orto, Castiglione del Lago); and the **Poggio del Belveduto** (☎ 075 82 90 76; www.poggiodelbelveduto.it; Via San Donato 65, Loc. Campori di Sopra, Passignano), which also has archery, if you're feeling particularly medieval.

Canoe, windsurfing and sailboat rentals can be found in Castiglione del Lago at **La Merangola** (☎ 075 965 24 45; Loc. Lido Arezzo) or in Tuoro at **Belneazione Tuoro** (☎ 328 454 97 66; Loc. Punta Navaccia). La Merangola also has a small beach and restaurant, and turns into a *discoteca* at night.

You can hire bicycles at most camp sites, the hostel or at **Cicli Valentini** (☎ /fax 075 95 16 63; Via Firenze 68/b, Castiglione del Lago), which also rents out children's bikes, or **Marinelli Ferrettini Fabio**

(☎ /fax 075 95 31 26; Via B Buozzi 26, Castiglione del Lago), which also rents out scooters. In Passignano, try **Eta Beta Modellismo** (☎ 075 82 94 01; Via della Vittoria 58).

The locals are very proud of their excellent produce – most notably their high-quality DOC wines (see p64) and DOP (Denominazione d'Origine Protetta) olive oils. If you are interested in following the Strada del Vino (Wine Route; see p68) of the Colli del Trasimeno (Trasimeno Hill district), the **Associazione Strada del Vino Colli del Trasimeno** (☎ 075 58 29 41; www.montitrasimeno .umbria.it in Italian) produces a brochure with suggested itineraries. It lists open cellars, which means you can stop by and try wine, but you almost always need to call ahead. You can also pick up this brochure at the tourist office in Castiglione del Lago. Look out, too, for the guide to local restaurants, *Trasimeno a Tavola*, which includes sample menus and price guides, also available from the tourist office.

Do as the locals do, with a day of **fishing** (☎ 075 847 60 05; www.albatrasimeno.it in Italian; Via Alicata 19, San Feliciano; fishing per person €55) out on the lake. Two people at a time can join locals for a four-hour angling or early morning fishing trip. After reeling in your catches at dawn, the fisherman can guide you to restaurants that will cook up your fish using traditional recipes. Book at least one day in advance. Nature trips (for up to 10 people €90) are also available.

For a fun cultural and gastronomic experience, don't miss the **weekly markets**, which have all sorts of fresh local produce and basic goods. They take place from 8.30am to 1pm at the following locations: Castiglione del Lago (Wednesday), Magione (Thursday), Tuoro (Friday) and Passignano (Saturday). Ask at each town's tourist office for more information.

Festivals & Events

As with the rest of festival-happy Umbria, Lago di Trasimeno hosts countless events throughout the year. The region has its share of unique festivals, though.

Art and Culture festival In Città della Pieve over the first weekend in June.

Palio dei Terzieri This showcases the town's Renaissance past with some serious revelry, including acrobatics, fire-eating and archery. Held in mid-August.

Palio delle Barche See p291.

Sleeping

The Lago di Trasimeno area is filled with every type of lodging imaginable, from an environmental hostel on Isola Polvese to your own private rental villa in Lisciano Niccone, where you can take classes in fresco painting or Italian cooking. There are no less than 151 *agriturismi*.

For a full list of places to stay in this area, pick up a brochure from the local tourist office, check www.umbria2000.it or consult the *Umbria Infotourist Map*. The map is available from **InfoUmbria** (☎ 075 57 57; www .infoumbria.com in Italian; Piazza dei Partigiani Intercity bus station, Largo Cacciatori delle Alpi 3, Perugia; ☾ 9am-1.30pm & 2.30-6.30pm Mon-Fri, 9am-1pm Sat), where staff will also help you make reservations.

WEEKLY ACCOMMODATION

The following accommodations are all tucked into the hills above the lake, guaranteeing agreeable weather all year-round.

Casa San Martino (☎ 075 84 42 88; www.tuscany vacation.com; San Martino 19, Lisciano Niccone; r €145, per week for up to 8 people €2000-3000; P ☒) Come with one or seven of your best friends to this farmhouse in the hills north of the lake. The main building is impeccably decorated with terracotta tile floors, wood-beamed ceilings and an open-hearth fireplace, and comes with a completely stocked kitchen, washer and dryer, and four bedrooms (three with bathroom). Outside is a pool facing an expansive countryside view (with a few castles thrown in) and a stone barbecue grill. The building is often rented out weekly during the summer (a three-night minimum booking applies otherwise), but in the low season it opens as a B&B offering cooking and fresco painting classes.

Agriturismo Locanda del Galluzzo (☎ 075 84 53 52; www.locandadelgalluzzo.it; Castel Rigone; r incl breakfast €65, per week 2-/3-/4-person apt €420/470/490; P ☒) This *agriturismo* on the hills above the lake is in a beautiful setting. It has a fantastic restaurant that cooks with delicious ingredients, many grown on site (or hunted nearby). There's a pool, a view of the lake, mountain bikes and a playground for children.

Villa dei Monti (☎ 075 965 90 97; www.badiaccia .com; per week low/medium/high season for up to 10 people €2200/2600/2880; P ☒ ☒) A luxurious hillside house filled with everything 10 very relaxed people could possibly want in an Italian getaway – two indoor kitchens and one poolside kitchenette, pool, tennis court, five bedrooms, six bathrooms, wrap-around balcony, Ping-Pong table, and walking trails leading from the property. The owner stocks the kitchens with local products before you arrive and can arrange a traditional meal and cooking lesson (with a translator). He also owns Camping Badiaccia, so you have free access to everything at the camp site.

BUDGET

Fattoria il Poggio (☎ 075 965 95 50; www.fattoria isolapolvese.com; Isola Polvese; per person dm/f incl breakfast €15/17, meals €10; ⌚ 1 Mar-30 Oct or off-season for groups or by appt, reception closed 3-7pm; ⌨) Besides being impeccably run, you would hardly ever know you're staying in a HI youth hostel. Dorm rooms mingle with doubles and family rooms, all with views of the surrounding lake. It takes some planning, but those who don't mind catching a ferry back by 7pm will be rewarded handsomely with a family-style meal in an environmentally equipped former barn on their own private island. After dinner, enjoy a drink with new friends over the sunset or a game of Ping-Pong. Kayaks, private beaches, games, TV with DVDs, laundry room, Internet (15 minutes for free), 14th-century ruins and a nearby environmental lab are just a part of the offerings.

Il Torrione (☎ 075 953 236; www.trasinet.com /iltorrione; Via delle Mura 4/8, Castiglione del Lago; r €55-65) This tranquil setting near the heart of Castiglione del Lago is a sweet little oasis. Each room and the public areas are decorated with beautiful artwork painted by the owner. The rooms are tastefully furnished and have their own bathroom and shower. A private garden overlooks the lake, complete with chaise lounges from which to watch the sunset.

Camping Badiaccia (☎ 075 965 90 97; www.badiaccia .com; Via Trasimeno I 91, Bivia Borghetto, camp site per person/car/dog/tent €6.50/2/2/6, bungalow 3-6 people €35-93; ⌚ Easter-Sep; ⓟ ⌨ ⛱) Practise your Dutch, Italian or German words while playing tennis, Ping Pong or bocce, eating at the surprisingly good *ristorante*/pizzeria, or swimming in one of three pools. The camp site is paradise for families, but the child-free will equally enjoy renting a kayak, bicycle or paddleboat, working out in the fitness room, availing themselves of the laundry facilities and soaking up the beachfront location. Internet access is also

available, for €5 per hour. Bungalows allow those without camping equipment to stay cheaply, and have a kitchen. There are also free hot showers. For a small fee, staff will pick you up at the Terontola train station, but if travelling by car, the site is just south of the SS75 on the SS71.

Paola's B&B (☎ 075 573 08 08, 335 624 72 40; Città della Pieve; per person €30-50) For an authentic Italian experience, stay in Paola's home. She rents out two rooms in her 17th-century flat (be sure to ask for a peek at the frescoes in her daughter's bedroom). Paola also offers cooking and Italian lessons (usually at the same time) in addition to B&B. During winter, she cooks in her open-hearth fireplace. Paolo speaks French and a bit of English.

MIDRANGE

Hotel La Torre (☎ 075 95 16 66; www.trasinet.com/ latorre; Via Emanuele 50, Castiglione del Lago; s/d €50/75, breakfast €5; ⓟ ⛱) The price is right at this central three-star renovated palace. The rooms are a tad sterile but fully outfitted with TV, minibar and telephone. The breakfast is worth it, as the hotel owners run their own bakery downstairs. They'll pick you up at the train station for a small fee.

Hotel Da Sauro (☎ 075 82 61 68; fax 075 82 51 30; Via Guglielmi 1, Isola Maggiore; r €80) This family-run establishment has just 10 rooms in a rustic stone building. It's found at the northern end of the main village on the island, not far from a private beach. The restaurant downstairs is very popular so expect a lot of noise at mealtimes. This is a great place to try local fish.

Hotel Miralago (☎ 075 95 11 57; www.hotelmiralago .com; Piazza Mazzini 6, Castiglione del Lago; s/d/tr incl breakfast €76/93/113; ⛱) The Miralago is central, and top-floor rooms have magnificent lake views. It's rather austere (besides the plush fabrics), but it has amenities such as satellite TV and room service. There's also a good restaurant downstairs – La Fontana (a perennial favourite).

TOP END

Relais La Fattoria (☎ 075 84 53 22; www.relaislafattoria .com; Castel Rigone; s/d/ste incl breakfast €85/132/188; ⓟ ⛱) This impeccably furnished castle on the hills above the lake offers a spectacular setting for a holiday. The 17th-century building has been outfitted with satellite TV, outdoor swimming pool and beautiful antiques, and has a fantastic restaurant. There are lots of great walking trails nearby. Call ahead and staff will pick you up at the train station.

Eating

The main specialities of the Trasimeno area are *fagiolina* (little white beans), olive oil and wine. In addition, you'll find many fish dishes such as carp *in porchetta* – cooked in a wood oven with garlic, fennel and herb – and *tegamaccio,* a kind of soupy stew of the best varieties of local fish, cooked in olive oil, white wine and herbs.

La Cantina (☎ 075 965 24 32; Via Emanuele 93, Castiglione del Lago; mains €6.60-13.20; ﹇﹈closed Mon winter) Not only is this well-priced restaurant fabulous – it has a stately interior with a lovely outdoor terrace for summer dining – but there's also an adjacent *magazzino* (shop) where you can sample and buy the area's best wine, olive oil and treats. Try the delicious trout with local *fagiolina* (€8.20).

Da Settimio (☎ 075 847 60 00; Via Lungolago Alicata, San Feliciano; mains €6-21.50; ﹇﹈closed Thu & Nov-Dec; P ﹇﹈) If you stay on Isola Polvese, you'll most likely pass by this restaurant near the ferry terminal in San Feliciano. It doesn't look like much, but locals know it as the best fish restaurant in the area, handed down from father to son for four generations. Try the *risotto alla pescatora* (fisherman's risotto) or the appetiser of 'fried little fishies'.

L'Acquario (☎ 075 965 24 32; Via Vittoria Emanuele 69, Castiglione del Lago; set menu €25; ﹇﹈closed winter & Wed summer) This rather refined restaurant is a great place to try out the local carp *in porchetta* fresh from the lake, or have an appetiser of eel in *tegamaccio*.

Ristorante La Corte (☎ 075 84 53 22; Via Rigone 1, Castel Rigone; mains €8.50-23) Relais la Fattoria's restaurant is one of the most upscale in the lake region, serving inventive dishes using ingredients from the area. Its appetisers are the best part of the meal; try the bruschetta, the swordfish *carpaccio* or the sweet lentil soup. It also serves a delectable tagliatelle with black Norcia truffles and freshly made *strangozzi* with porcini.

Lido (☎ 075 82 84 72; Via Roma 3, Passignano; mains €5.50-14; ﹇﹈Mar-Oct) One of the oldest restaurants in Passignano, Lido is located right on the water, facing Isola Maggiore. It serves local cuisine, including specialities such as *crostini* (toasted bread cut thinner than bruschetta and sometimes topped with sauces

or vegetables) with carp eggs and *taglierini al profumo di lago* (which translates, very roughly, as 'pasta with lake perfume').

Getting There & Around

You can travel from Perugia in the direction of Terontola/Florence to Magione (€1.65, 20 minutes, nine daily), Passignano (€2.05, 30 minutes, eight daily) and Tuoro (€2.30, 35 minutes, eight daily). To get to Castiglione del Lago, switch in Terontola (€3.05, one hour, 15 daily, seven daily direct connections).

APM (☎ 075 82 71 57) buses head from Piazza Partigiani in Perugia to Passignano (€2.80, one hour, five daily) via Magione and San Feliciano. Get off in San Feliciano for the Isola Polvese ferry. A separate bus runs to Castiglione del Lago (€4.40, one hour and 20 minutes, eight daily), also through Magione.

APM operates the lake's ferry service. Ferries run about every 1½ hours from Easter until the end of September, and hourly in July and August. For the timetable, check at the docks or pick up the booklet *Intorno al Trasimeno,* free at any tourist office within 20km of the lake. From Passignano, head to either Isola Maggiore (€3.40) or Castiglione del Lago (€3.90). Isola Polvese connects with San Feliciano (€2.80) and on to Passignano (€3.90). Ferries stop running at 7pm or 8pm.

GUBBIO

pop 31,616

Hitched onto the steep slopes of Monte Ingino and overlooking a picturesque valley, the centuries-old palazzi of Gubbio exude a warm ochre glow in the late afternoon sunlight. You don't need to stretch your imagination much to feel that you have stepped back into the Middle Ages as you meander along the town's quiet, treeless lanes and peer into some of the city's many fine ceramic shops.

Gubbio is famous for its Eugubian Tables, which date from 300–100 BC and constitute the best existing example of ancient Umbrian script. In 295 BC Gubbio was the site of an important battle, where the Romans fought the Umbri, Etruscans and Gauls. Because Gubbio didn't participate, Rome elevated its status and the town became Romanised. It was fought over many times, given to the church, and entered into the Battle of Mon-

GUBBIO

INFORMATION		
Easy Gubbio	1	B3
Ospedale Civile (Hospital)	2	B2
Police Station	3	D3
Post Office	4	B3
Tourist Office	5	C3

SIGHTS & ACTIVITIES		
Basilica di Sant'Ubaldo	6	D1
Cathedral	7	C2
Chiesa di San Francesco	8	B3

Chiostro della Pace	9	B3
Fontana dei Pazzi	(see 13)	
Funivia Colle Eletto	10	D3
Museo Civico	(see 12)	
Museo della Ceramica a Lustro		
e Torre Medioevale di Porta		
Romana	11	D3
Palazzo dei Consoli	12	B2
Palazzo del Bargello	13	B2
Palazzo del Podestá	14	C2
Palazzo Ducale	15	C2
Teatro Romano	16	A3

SLEEPING		
Albergo La Locanda del Duca	17	B2
Grotta dell'Angelo	18	C3
Hotel Bosone Palace	19	C2
Relais Ducale	20	C2
Residenza Le Logge	21	B2

EATING		
Alla Fornace di Mastro Giorgio	22	C2
Il Campanone	23	B2
Ristorante Fabiani	24	B2
Taverna del Lupo	25	C2
Trattoria La Lanterna	26	B3

SHOPPING		
Leo Grilli Arte	27	B2

TRANSPORT		
APM bus station	28	B3

taperti between the Guelphs and the Ghibellines. In the 14th century it fell into the hands of the Montefeltro family of Urbino and was later reincorporated into the Papal States in the late 1500s. It didn't gain its independence until 1831, and quickly saw Italian unification in the 1860s.

Gubbio now has a thriving tourist industry. One of the most famous festivals in all of Italy, Corsa dei Ceri, is here on 15 May. Gubbio can be overcrowded at times, especially on summer weekends. But it's possible, even in August, to venture further afield and find your own serene cobblestoned street flanked by grey limestone buildings.

Orientation

The city is small and easy to explore. The immense traffic circle known as Piazza Quaranta Martiri, at the base of the hill, is where buses to the city terminate, and it also has a large car park. The square was named in honour of 40 local people who were killed by the Nazis in 1944 in reprisal for partisan activities. From here it

is a short, if somewhat steep, walk up Via della Repubblica to the main square, Piazza Grande, also known as the Piazza della Signoria. Or, you can take the lift from the Palazzo del Podestà to the Palazzo Ducale and the cathedral. Corso Garibaldi and Piazza Oderisi are to your right as you head up the hill.

Information

EMERGENCY
Police station (☎ 075 927 37 70; Via XX Settembre 97)

INTERNET RESOURCES
Bella Umbria (www.bellaumbria.net/gubbio) The Umbria-wide private tourist website has an excellent section on Gubbio's sites and accommodation. In Italian, English, German, French and Spanish.

MEDICAL SERVICES
Ospedale Civile (☎ 075 923 91; Piazza Quaranta Martiri)

POST
Post office (☎ 075 927 37 73; Via Cairoli 11; ☑ 8.10am-5pm Mon-Sat)

TOURIST INFORMATION

Easy Gubbio (☎ 075 922 00 66; Via della Repubblica 13) Provides travel assistance.

Tourist office (☎ 075 922 06 93; www.gubbio -altochiascio.umbria2000.it; Piazza Oderisi; ☻ 8.30am-1pm & 3-6pm Mon-Sat, 9.30am-12.30pm Sun)

Sights

Gubbio's most impressive buildings look out over Piazza Grande, where the heart of the Corsa dei Ceri takes place. The piazza is dominated by the 14th-century **Palazzo dei Consoli**, attributed to Gattapone. The crenellated façade and tower can be seen from all over the town. The building houses the **Museo Civico** (☎ 075 927 42 98; Piazza Grande; adult/concession incl gallery €4/2.50; ☻ 10am-1pm & 3-6pm Apr-Oct, 10am-1pm & 2-5pm Nov-Mar), which displays the Eugubian Tables, discovered in 1444. The seven bronze tablets are the main source for research into the ancient Umbrian language. Upstairs is a picture gallery featuring works from the Gubbian school. Across the square is the **Palazzo del Podestá**, also known as the Palazzo Pretorio, built along similar lines to its grander counterpart. It's now the city's active town hall – ask nicely and you can take a peek inside to see the impressive vaulted ceilings.

FUNIVIA COLLE ELETTO

The **Basilica di Sant'Ubaldo**, where you'll find the body of the 12th-century bishop of Gubbio, St Ubaldo, is a perfectly lovely church. But the adventure is in the getting there. Take the **Funivia Colle Eletto** (☎ 075 922 11 99; return trip adult/child €5/4; ☻ 10am-1.15pm & 2.30-5pm Thu-Tue Nov-Feb, 9.30am-1.15pm & 2.30-5.30/7pm Mar-Jun & Oct, 9am-7.30pm Jul-Sep), where your first rule is to believe the man when he tells you to stand on the dot. He will then throw you into a moving metal contraption that looks somewhat like a ski lift for open-topped, human-sized birdcages. You're whisked instantly away, dangling dozens of metres precariously above a rocky hill (bring a camera, but hold tight). The ride up is as frightening as it is utterly beautiful. There's a restaurant on top of the hill and the aforementioned church, but the nicest way to spend the day is to bring a picnic and have a wander.

CATHEDRAL & PALAZZO DUCALE

Via Ducale leads up to the 12th-century pink **cathedral** (Via Federico da Montefeltro; ☻ 9am-5pm Mon-Sat, 9am-1pm Sun), with a fine 13th-century stained-glass window and a fresco attributed to Bernardino Pinturicchio. Opposite, the 15th-century **Palazzo Ducale** (☎ 075 927 58 72; Via Federico da Montefeltro; adult/concession €2/1; ☻ 8.30am-7pm Mon & Wed-Fri, 9am-10.30pm Sat & Sun) was built by famed Florentine architect Francesco Giorgio Martino, hired by the Montefeltro family to create a scaled-down version of their grand palazzo in Urbino; its walls hide an impressive Renaissance courtyard.

MUSEUMS, CHURCHES & PALAZZI

Just below the cable car is the **Museo della Ceramica a Lustro e Torre Medioevale di Porta Romana** (☎ 075 922 11 99; Via Dante 24; admission €2.50; ☻ 9am-1pm & 3.30-7pm). Il lustro ceramics came from the Arab influence in Spain in the 11th century. On the 2nd floor, ceramics from prehistoric times sit next to medieval and Renaissance pieces. There's also a collection of crossbows from the 18th century, some of which have a target range as far as 50m. Check out the really un-fun-looking chastity belt on the 4th floor and appreciate that you're alive today instead of 300 years ago.

Perugia's Fra Bevignate is said to have designed the **Chiesa di San Francesco** (Piazza Quaranta Martiri; ☻ 7.15am-noon & 3.30-7.30pm). It features impressive frescoes by a local artist, Ottaviano Nelli. Built in a simple Gothic style in the 13th century, it has an impressive rose window. Wander into the **Chiostro della Pace** (Cloister of Peace) in the adjoining convent to view some ancient mosaics and wander around the peaceful garden.

In the western end of the city's medieval section is the 13th-century **Palazzo del Bargello**, the medieval police station and prison. In front of it is the **Fontana dei Pazzi** (Fountain of Lunatics), so named because of a belief that if you walk around it three times, you will go mad. On summer weekends the number of tourists carrying out this ritual is indeed cause for concern about their collective sanity.

ROMAN GUBBIO

Southwest of Piazza Quaranta Martiri, off Viale del Teatro Romano, is the overgrown remains of the 1st-century-AD **Teatro Romano** (☎ 075 922 09 22; admission free; ☻ 8.30am-7.30pm Apr-Sep, 8am-1.30pm Oct-Mar). In the summer, check with the tourist office about outdoor concerts held here.

Festivals & Events

Corsa dei Ceri (Candles Race) The centuries-old race is held each year on 15 May to commemorate the city's patron saint, St Ubaldo. The event starts at 5.30am and involves three teams, each carrying a *cero* (these 'candles' are massive wooden pillars weighing about 400kg, each bearing a statue of a 'rival' saint) and racing through the city's streets. This is one of Italy's liveliest festivals and warrants inclusion in your itinerary, but those on the shorter side or those susceptible to panic attacks should be careful to not get lost in the pushing crowds.

Palio della Balestra Held on the last Sunday in May, this is an annual archery competition involving medieval crossbows, in which Gubbio competes with its neighbour Borgo San Sepolchro. Every tourist store in Gubbio sells some sort of miniature crossbow (although, those travelling home on airplanes may have a difficult time explaining this purchase to security!).

Sleeping

BUDGET

Many locals rent out rooms to tourists, so ask at the tourist office about *affittacamere*. You can also get a brochure there that lists hotels, camp sites and restaurants in the area, with current prices.

Città di Gubbio & Villa Ortoguidone (☎ 075 927 20 37; fax 075 92 76 20; Loc. Ortoguidone; camp site per person/tent €8.50/9, 2-person apt €40-83, 4-person apt €80-166; ☼ Easter-Sep; 🅿 🐾) For camping, try this site in Ortoguidone, a southern suburb of Gubbio, less than 3km south of Piazza Quaranta Martiri along the SS298 (Via Perugina). There are also stunning apartments in an old stone manor house (Villa Ortoguidone) with TVs, beautiful wood

AUTHOR'S CHOICE

Residenza Le Logge (☎ 075 927 75 74; www .paginegialle.it/residenzalelogge in Italian; Via Piccardi 7-9; s/d/tr incl breakfast €47/70/80) This is one of those rare perfect locations, where you'll either appreciate the great value or feel luxurious on a tight budget. Decorated with homey antiques and comfortable beds, it's quiet, tranquil and central. Three rooms feature garden views – try to get one of these, but the view of Gubbio is also beautiful. During summer, you can take your breakfast in the garden. Ask for the room with the gracious blue-and-white porcelain-and-ceramic bathtub that's big enough to park a Fiat in.

furnishings and private bathrooms. July and August visits require a one-week stay.

Albergo La Locanda del Duca (☎ /fax 075 927 77 53; www.umbriatravel.com/delduca/locandadelducaeng .htm; Via Piccardi 1; s/d/tr/q €42/57/67/77) One of the cheapest hotels in town, Locanda del Duca has just seven rooms, all with pleasant polished-wood interiors and grand wooden doors. Some rooms have views of the Palazzo dei Consoli or the river. Enquire about a room at Ristorante La Cantina.

MIDRANGE

Hotel Bosone Palace (☎ 075 922 06 88; www.mencarel ligroup.com; Via XX Settembre 22; s/d incl breakfast €77/110, ste incl breakfast €165-195; 🅿 🐾) If you're going to stay at a palace while in Umbria, this isn't a bad choice. Take your breakfast under a gold-leafed fresco, or sleep under one in your suite or room. The rooms are spacious and decorated with almost campily over-the-top antique reproductions, but it somehow works perfectly.

Grotta dell'Angelo (☎ 075 927 17 47; grottadell angelo@jumpy.it; Via Gioia 47; s/d/tr €52/75/90; ☼ closed part of Jan) While it's mostly a popular restaurant with all sorts of truffle dishes and a beautiful garden, the Grotta dell'Angelo also serves up a few basic rooms for rent.

TOP END

Relais Ducale (☎ 075 922 01 57; www.mencarelligroup .com; Via Galeotti 19; s/d/ste incl breakfast €119/163/253; 🅿 🐾) Owned by the same savvy group that runs the Bosone Palace, the Relais is a step up – literally, as it's several stories straight up from the Piazza Grande – and lavishly, as it's a fully outfitted, grand four-star hotel. Smallish rooms are detailed with the finest additions – satellite TV and towel warmers, and sheets so warm and snugly that you'd better set an alarm, as you're liable to sleep through the decked-out buffet breakfast. The junior suite dates back to the 15th century, with a balcony that may drive one to look for boiling oil to pour. Near this suite is where you'll find the secret stone passageway that was used by guests of the Duke of Montefeltro – it helped them avoid the above-ground riffraff as they made their way to the palace.

Eating

Taverna del Lupo (☎ 075 927 43 68; Via Ansidei 21; mains about €16; ☼ closed Mon) Il Lupo was the wolf that St Francis domesticated, a wolf that supposedly came back to this restaurant to dine. He made an excellent choice. The atmosphere is sophisticated, if a bit stiff, and diners would feel more comfortable if smartly dressed. Most of what it served is locally produced in the surrounding Apennines, including its cheese, truffles and olive oil. Set aside at least two hours for a meal.

Il Campanone (☎ 075 927 60 11; Via Piccardi 21; mains €7-14.50; ✆ closed Wed) In a cavernous vaulted restaurant just a few blocks from Piazza Grande, the meals are as rich as they are delicious – decidedly popular is the veal with pear and truffle appetiser (€9) and for a main course, puff pastry with beef, local cheese and tomatoes, and basil (€13).

Ristorante Fabiani (☎ 075 927 46 39; Piazza Quaranta Martiri 26; mains €6.80-16.50; ✆ closed Tue) A fabulous spot at which to sit on the back patio and enjoy the garden for a few hours. The selection here is vast, and it offers a rotating €15 tourist menu or a €20 *menù gastronomico* of whatever is in season. Stop in on Thursday or Friday for its fish specials.

Alla Fornace di Mastro Giorgio (☎ 075 922 18 36; Via Mastro Giorgio 2; mains around €14; ✆ closed Tue) One of the better restaurants in town, this is also one of the more expensive, with dining in elegant surroundings. It specialises in local pasta and sumptuous desserts.

Trattoria La Lanterna (☎ 075 927 66 94; Via Gioia 23; mains around €8; ✆ closed Thu) Many of the local specialities feature delicious *tartufi*. Tables are surrounded by ancient stone walls and a low beamed ceiling.

Shopping

Leo Grilli Arte (☎ 075 922 22 72; Via dei Consoli 78; ✆ 9.30am-1pm & 3-7pm, closed Mon) In the Middle Ages, ceramics were one of Gubbio's main sources of income, and there are some fabulous contemporary samples on display in this crumbly 15th-century mansion. Artist/owner Leo Grilli works here almost every day, as he has for decades. You can watch him work at a ministudio in the shop.

Getting There & Around

APM buses run to Perugia (€4, one hour and 10 minutes, eight daily), Gualdo Tadino (€2.40, 50 minutes, 10 daily) and Umbertide (€2.80, 50 minutes, three daily). Buses depart from Piazza Quaranta Martiri.

The closest train station is at Fossato di Vico, about 20km southeast of the city. Hourly APM buses connect the station with Gubbio (€2.20, 30 minutes), although they don't coincide with the train arrival times. From Fossato di Vico, hourly trains take about 30 minutes to Foligno (€2.55), where you can switch for other cities.

By car or motorcycle, take the SS298 from Perugia and follow the signs. Parking in the large car park in Piazza Quaranta Martiri costs €0.50 per hour.

Walking is the best way to get around, but APM buses connect Piazza Quaranta Martiri with the cable car station and most main sights.

AROUND GUBBIO

South on the SS3, on the way from Parco Regionale del Monte Cucco, **Gualdo Tadino** is a fairly industrial town. Although it doesn't offer much in the way of tourist attractions, it does have the best-named site: the 13th-century **Rocca Flea**. One of the town's major industrial outputs is ceramics; in August

---

TOP FIVE PLACES IN UMBRIA TO VISIT BY CAR

Castelluccio (p321) There are only two buses to this town: one Thursday morning and the second Thursday afternoon, so driving is your best bet. It shouldn't be missed, especially in May and June when the Piano Grande is abloom with wildflowers.

La Scarzuola (p320) A hike from just about anywhere listed in this guide, the beautiful drive here will set you in the mood to appreciate the stunning mystery of this combination garden/architectural monument/Franciscan monastery/concert theatre.

Lago di Trasimeno (p288) It's possible to get here and around using the train and bus, but a car will allow you to meander through fields of sunflowers and olive trees.

Monte Castello di Vibio (p325) Many establishments will pick up guests at the Fratta Todina train station, but a car will get you out to Fattoria di Vibio *agriturismo* for a lunch that makes it worth renting wheels.

Wine region (p306) Wineries are just starting to open tasting rooms to the public in the rolling hills surrounding Bevagna and Montefalco. Just make sure you have a designated driver!

it celebrates a month-long exhibition of ceramics. Slightly more enticing than its neighbour Gualdo Tadino, **Nocera Umbra** is mostly known for its spring water, and still has a few vestiges from the past. Its most notable monument is the **Torre dei Trinci**, a medieval tower built by the *signiory* (feudal lordship) Trinci family.

PARCO REGIONALE DEL MONTE CUCCO

East of Gubbio, this park is a haven for outdoor activities and is dotted with caves, many of which can be explored. It is well set up for walkers, rock climbers and horse riders, and has many hotels and *rifugi* (mountain huts). **Costacciaro**, accessible by bus from Gubbio (€1.95, 30 minutes) via Scheggia or Fossato di Vico, is a good base for exploring the area and is the starting point for a walk to the summit of Monte Cucco (1566m).

Monte Cucco is a fantastic place to go caving or spelunking. The Monte Cucco karst system is the largest in Italy and the fifth-deepest in the world (922m). Sinkholes, wells and dolines create unique geological formations and lush habitats for various species of birds and plants.

Club Alpino Italiano (CAI) produces a walking map *Carta dei Sentieri Massiccio del Monte Cucco* (€12), for sale in local bookshops and newsagents. The free *Monte Cucco Park: Country Walks through History* booklet is available in English at *rifugi* and tourist offices throughout Umbria. Use this as a guide to the best of Umbria's nature and history. The booklet describes in detail 11 walks in the area that take you through some of Umbria's most picturesque terrain, more alpine-like than the typical rolling hillside. The guides detail the estimated time needed while walking at a good pace, presence of water sources on the trail and a thorough map of each route (most take at least four hours and are far from civilisation, so take lots of water and emergency supplies). If you don't have your walking gear, Tour #6 is a 62km driving route through ancient abbeys and monasteries in the region.

The **Centro Escursionistico Naturalistico Speleologico** (☎ 075 917 04 00; www.cens.it in Italian; Via Calcinaro 7A, Costacciaro) can help with information about exploring local caves, walking and mountain-bike routes. You can also get information at the **park office** (☎ 075 917 73 26; parco.montecucco@libero.it; Via Matteotti 52, Villa Anita,

TOP FIVE TOWNS IN UMBRIA TO VISIT BY TRAIN

- Perugia (p267)
- Assisi (via Santa Maria degli Angeli; p281)
- Spoleto (p311)
- Città di Castello (p300)
- Orvieto (p333)

Sigillo). Online, look for information at www.parks.it/parco.monte.cucco.

The **Camping Rio Verde** (☎ 075 917 01 38; www.campingrioverde.it in Italian; per adult/car/child/tent €5/2.50/3/4.50) camp site, 3km west of Costacciaro, offers horse riding (€13 per hour, during the summer), rock climbing and speleology. Many *agriturismo* establishments in the area can also arrange horse riding. Don't even consider coming here on a weekend in August – the rates more than quintuple. A good mountain inn is the **Rifugio Escursionistico Dal Lepre** (☎ /fax 075 917 77 33; Pian del Monte, Sigillo, Montecucco; per person incl breakfast €15), which also features a decent restaurant.

It is possible to hire mountain bikes at the **Coop Arte e Natura** (☎ 075 917 07 40; Via Stazione 2) in the village of Fossato di Vico, about 8km southeast of Costacciaro.

ALTA VALLE DEL TEVERE

The northernmost reaches of Umbria, clamped in between Tuscany and Le Marche and known as the Alta Valle del Tevere (Upper Tiber Valley), is regarded as Museum Valley for its extraordinary collection of art and history, especially in the town of Città di Castello.

The area's more interesting spots are Città di Castello, which was a powerful centre during the Renaissance; Umbertide, with a couple of castles and dominated by a 14th-century fortress; tiny Monte Santa Maria Tiberina, where there's a great camp site and an imposing castle; and Montone, a vertical medieval town where Braccio Fortebracci was born. The area is connected with Perugia by the private Ferrovia Centrale Umbra railway and several buses. SITA buses also connect the valley with nearby Arezzo in Tuscany and travels on to Florence.

NORTHERN UMBRIA

Città di Castello

pop 37,889

Città di Castello is surrounded by some
pretty awful suburbs, but if you can look
past this, it has a beautiful historic centre,
many grand buildings and the second-most
important art museum in Umbria after the
Galleria Nazionale dell'Umbria (p269) in
Perugia. Known as Tifernum Tiberium in
the Roman era, Castrum Felicitatis (Town
of Happiness) in the medieval period and
Città di Castello today, it doesn't have a
castle, nor is it much of a city. The town was
economically depressed until the 1960s, but
is now known for its thriving paper, book,
ironworks and furniture industries. The
town's favourite son is Alberto Burri, and
two galleries proudly display much of his
lifetime's work. (The town's current favourite daughter is actress Monica Bellucci.)

Note: Don't come to Città di Castello on
a Monday. Most museums are closed, as are
many restaurants.

ORIENTATION

The entire town, including its historic centre, is within a valley, so it's almost all on
flat ground and easily walkable (a rarity in
Umbrian towns). People using wheelchairs
should have few problems getting around
here, although cobblestones may cause a
few jolts.

From the train station, walk straight
ahead for 200m. Turn right under Porta
Santa Maria Maggiore and take Corso Vittorio Emanuele to Piazza Matteotti, the centre
of town. Driving is mostly forbidden in the
walled city, but there's plenty of free parking just outside the walls, much of it around
Porta San Giacomo and Piazza Garibaldi.

INFORMATION
Bookshops
Libreria Paci (☎ 075 855 43 41; Piazza Matteotti
2; ◷ 9am-1pm & 4.30-8pm, closed Sun & Mon) Has
English- and German-language books as well as a growing
collection of maps and Lonely Planets.

Emergency
Police station (☎ 075 852 92 22; Piazza Garibaldi)

Internet Access
Internet Point (☎ 348 398 55 753; Via Mazzini 8; per
hr €1.50; ◷ 8am-11pm;) Phone calls to the US, UK or
Australia cost €0.15 per minute, €0.25 to mobile phones.

Internet Resources
cdcnet (www.cdcnet.net) The official comune site, with
English-language sections on history and art.

Medical Services
Hospital (☎ 075 8 50 91; Via Angelini)

Money
Cassi di Risparmio (Piazza Matteotti 3a) This bank's
ATM is the most convenient, to the left of the tourist office.

Post
Post office (☎ 075 855 3529; Via Gramsci;
◷ 8.15-5pm)

Tourist Information
Tourist office (☎ 075 855 49 22; info@iat.citta-di
-castello.pg.it; Logge Bufalini, Piazza Matteotti; ◷ 9am-
1.30pm & 3.30-6.30pm Mon-Sat, 9.30am-12.30pm Sun)

SIGHTS

The collection at the **Pinacoteca Comunale**
(☎ 075 855 42 02; Via della Cannoniera; adult/child/con-
cession €5/1.50/3; ◷ 10am-1pm & 2.30-6.30pm, closed
Sun), in the imposing 15th-century **Palazzo
Vitelli alla Cannoniera**, is filled with paintings
from the masters who lived here when Città
di Castello was the second most important
artistic centre in Umbria, behind Perugia.
Luca Signorelli painted his *Martyrdom of
Saint Sebastian* here in 1498. Raphael also
painted in Città; two of his works still stand
in the pinacoteca. Ask for the information
booklet in English, which will guide you
through the paintings, giving explanations
and context to the more prominent works.
A cool astrological fresco cycle graces the
staircase, with depictions of Apollo and the
muses, erudites and emperors, seahorses
and winged cherubs. The halls include wall
frescoes from Cristoforo Gherardi, depicting historical subjects such as Hannibal,
Caesar and Alexander the Great.

Collezione Burri (☎ 075 855 46 49; Palazzo Albizzini,
Via Albizzini 1; secondary exhibit at Ex Seccatoi del Tabacco, Via
Pierucci; adult/child/concession €5/2/3; ◷ 9am-12.30pm &
2.30-6pm Tue-Sat, 10.30am-12.30pm & 3-6pm Sun) houses
Alberto Burri's main collection. The artist
began his art career in 1946 after a stint as a
prisoner of war in Texas. His contemporary
work with paint and physical materials has
been immensely popular throughout the
world. His early work influenced the New
Dada and Pop Art movements, and artists
such as Rauschenberg, Christo and Jasper

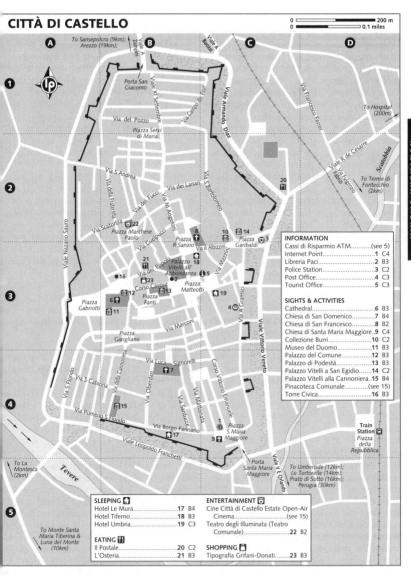

CITTÀ DI CASTELLO

To Sansepolcro (9km); Arezzo (19km);

To Hospital (200m)

To Terme di Fontecchio (2km)

Porta San Giacomo

Piazza Servi di Maria

To Umbertide (12km); Le Tortorelle (14km); Prato di Sotto (16km); Perugia (30km)

To La Montesca (2km)

To Monte Santa Maria Tiberina & Luna del Monte (10km)

Train Station

Piazza della Repubblica

Porta Santa Maria Maggiore

INFORMATION
Cassi di Risparmio ATM	(see 5)
Internet Point	**1** C4
Libreria Paci	**2** B3
Police Station	**3** C2
Post Office	**4** C3
Tourist Office	**5** C3

SIGHTS & ACTIVITIES
Cathedral	**6** B3
Chiesa di San Domenico	**7** B4
Chiesa di San Francesco	**8** B2
Chiesa di Santa Maria Maggiore	**9** C4
Collezione Burri	**10** C2
Museo del Duomo	**11** B3
Palazzo del Comune	**12** B3
Palazzo di Podestá	**13** B3
Palazzo Vitelli a San Egidio	**14** C2
Palazzo Vitelli alla Cannoniera	**15** B4
Pinacoteca Comunale	(see 15)
Torre Civica	**16** B3

SLEEPING
Hotel Le Mura	**17** B4
Hotel Tiferno	**18** B3
Hotel Umbria	**19** C3

EATING
Il Postale	**20** C2
L'Osteria	**21** B3

ENTERTAINMENT
Cine Città di Castello Estate Open-Air Cinema	(see 15)
Teatro degli Illuminata (Teatro Comunale)	**22** B2

SHOPPING
Tipografia Grifani-Donati	**23** B3

NORTHERN UMBRIA

Johns credit him as an inspiration. A secondary exhibit of mostly larger pieces is housed in an old tobacco-drying warehouse – a site in itself to see – and is closed from November to March, except by special requests made three days in advance.

Not much remains of the original Romanesque **cathedral**, but the building houses some treasures. **Museo del Duomo** (Museo Capitolare; ☎ 075 855 47 05; Piazza Gabriotti 3\a; adult/child/concession €5/2/3; ⏰ 9.30am-1pm & 2.30-7pm Tue-Sun summer, 10am-1pm & 2.30-6.30pm Tue-Sun winter) holds the most impressive collection of sacred artefacts in all of Umbria. In the same building is the **Palazzo del Comune**, the governmental seat of the Alte Valle del Tevere for the past few centuries. Also take a look at the statuesque **Torre Civica** (Piazza Gabriotti; temporarily closed for renovation), the city's bell tower that dates back to medieval times.

Città di Castello also has many other impressive buildings. Facing the main square, Piazza Matteotti, is the **Palazzo di Podestá**, with a façade by Nicola Barbioni. The **Chiesa di San Francesco** dates back to 1291; there's a copy here of Raphael's *The Marriage of the Virgin*, which he painted in Città when he was quite young. The painting was a forced gift to one of Napoleon's generals, who moved it to Milan. **Chiesa di Santa Maria Maggiore** dates from the 1400s and also has some fine frescoes. The **Palazzo Vitelli a San Egidio** is a stately home, dating from the 1500s, built by the Vitelli family. The ceilings feature frescoes in the grotesque style. **Chiesa di San Domenico** was built in 1271 by Domenican friars and features an impressive display of frescoes by painters in the Umbria school.

FESTIVALS & EVENTS

During the first week in November, the town plays host to the **Mostra Mercato Tartufo e Prodotti del Bosco**, a festival dedicated to the area's ubiquitous white truffle. Farmers and growers bring every type of truffle product imaginable to this epicurean trade show, as well as honey, mushrooms and many other local delicacies.

SLEEPING
Budget

La Montesca (☎ 075 855 85 66; Loc. Montesca; per person/tent/car €8/6.50/3; May-Sep; P) This fully-stocked camping ground has its own restaurant and swimming pool, and is surrounded by the verdant hills of the Alta Valle del Tevere. It is wheelchair accessible and dogs are allowed.

Luna del Monte (☎ /fax 075 857 00 54; camping@tline.net; Voc S Pietro 10, Monte Santa Maria Tiberina; adult/car/child/tent €6/2/3.50/5; Jun–mid-Sep; P) A bit further afield but worth it for the fantastic hill setting. The camp site has a swimming pool, children's playground and bocce.

Hotel Umbria (☎ 075 855 49 25; www.hotelumbria.net in Italian; Via S Antonio 6; s/d incl breakfast €35/55) The least expensive hotel within the city walls, Hotel Umbria is a fairly charming place to spend the night and is well located. All rooms have bathrooms with showers, satel-

AUTHOR'S CHOICE

Agriturismo/B&B Le Tortorelle (☎ 075 941 09 49, 347 975 4467 for the English-speaking daughter; www.letortorelle.it in Italian; Loc. Molino Vitelli 180, Umbertide; per person incl breakfast €30; P) It means 'the turtle doves', and you will most certainly find peace here. The iron gates will lead you to this small family-run farm specialising in the production of wheat, aloe, herbs and organic salves. You can either volunteer in exchange for room and board as part of the WWOOF (Worldwide Opportunities on Organic Farms – see www.wwoof.org) programme or chill out as a guest. Learn to make organic pasta, wine or cheese, or luck out by arriving in time for a pizza from the outdoor wood-fired brick oven. Teresa and Aldo will pick you up at the train station in Umbertide, on the Sansepolcro line between Perugia and Città di Castello.

lite TV and IDD telephone. Phone ahead, as it sometimes hosts raucous school groups.

Midrange

Terme di Fontecchio (☎ 075 852 06 14; www.termedifontecchio.it; Loc. Fontecchio 4; hotel s/d €54/84, hermitage s/d incl breakfast €150/175; P) This spa resort has a well-priced hotel on its expansive park grounds, two restaurants, a pizzeria and a seven-room hermitage-cum-hotel, all within a few kilometres of Città di Castello. The hotel has 90 modern rooms with Internet hook-up, Sky TV, minibars and firm mattresses. The hermitage feels a world way, as ancient stone walls coexist with elegant antiques and low oak-beamed ceilings. The 'well-being centre' offers single-session treatments or day- or week-long curative retreats filled with shiatsu massage, therapeutic mud baths and thermal pool gymnastics. There's a two-night minimum booking, with a one-week minimum in August.

Hotel Le Mura (☎ 075 852 10 70; www.hotellemura.it; Via Borgo Farinario 24; s/d incl breakfast €48/80;) Located along the ancient city walls, this modernist hotel isn't the most charming, as it caters to both business and leisure travellers. It does offer an array of comforts – satellite TV, Internet access (€0.50 for 30 minutes), minibar, hairdryers, king-sized beds and a rather good restaurant.

op End

otel Tiferno (☎ 075 855 03 31; www.hoteltiferno.it Italian; Piazza R Sanzio 13; s/d €132/152; **P** 🔲 🖳))pened in 1985, this is one of Città di Cas-:llo's top hotels. The building was a monas-:ry for the nearby Chiesa di San Francesco, ien became a palace in the 17th century nd is now a four-star hotel. Rooms still iclude period details of the building's past ves but have been modernized with art-'ork by Burri. Each room has a hairdryer, iinibar and satellite TV and has been oundproofed. Room service is offered.

Veekly

rato di Sotto (☎ 075 941 73 83; www.umbriaholidays om; Santa Giuliana; 2 people low season weekly €700, people high season weekly €2750; **P** 🖳) Stay at this :rene weekly rental with two, eight or up o 16 people, around 16km south of Città i Castello. Set far back among forested ills with an 11th-century ruin as one of s nearest neighbours, Prato di Sotto is less ian an hour from most towns in Umbria. classically furnished stone farmhouse with :rracotta-tiled floors and international an-iques, Prato di Sotto practically forces you o relax. Outside, each building has a terrace, 'y-covered trellis or barbecue, and the four partments share a pool. The owners can rrange sailing on their sailboat at Lago di 'rasimeno or itineraries in Umbria and Tus-any. Kitchens come fully stocked. Check its 'ebsite for last-minute cancellations.

ATING

Postale (☎ 075 852 13 56; Via Raffaele 8; 3-course ienu €30-40; 🕒 Tue-Fri & Sun, closed lunch Sat) If here's such a thing as *nouvelle* Umbrian uisine, this is the place to try it. Il Postale erves dishes such as duck with fennel com-•ote, or carp with hazelnuts. Specialities are ts lentil dishes and, of course, truffles.

L'Osteria (☎ 075 855 69 95; Via Borgo di Sotto; mains 5.50-13.50) Nothing fancy, but good typical Jmbrian food. Friday features fish speciali-ies. Try the asparagus when it's in season late spring to early summer).

NTERTAINMENT

eatro degli Illuminata (☎ 075 855 50 91; Via dei ucci) This civic theatre features musicals and ll kinds of live-arts performances.

Cine Città di Castello Estate (☎ 075 852 92 49; adult/ hild €5/4) During the summer, the pinacoteca's lawn is the perfect place to take in an open-air film. All genres of movies are shown – from Harry Potter to art-house Italian films. Movies are usually screened on Fri-day and Saturday at 9.15pm from July to the end of August.

SHOPPING

On the third weekend of every month the town hosts the **Retro Antiques & Old Things Market**, in Piazza Matteotti. It's not as big as the one in Perugia, but it's still a great place to get a hands-on history lesson (and to purchase unique gifts not found any-where else).

Tipografia Grifani-Donati (☎ 075 855 43 49; Corso Cavour 4; 🕒 8.30am-12.30pm & 3-7pm, closed Sun) sells paper and artwork using the same printing techniques as when it opened in 1799. It has a small museum on the 2nd floor.

GETTING THERE & AWAY

Città di Castello is just east of the E45. The Ferrovia Centrale Umbra railway connects Città di Castello with Perugia (€3.05, one hour and 10 minutes, 16 daily) and onto Todi (€4, 1¾ hours, 10 daily).

SPELLO

pop 8304

Sometimes it seems like there's no way any town you visit could be more beautiful than the last. But Spello, an often passed-by little town between Assisi and Foligno, is a lovely place in which to spend a day or two. The town is surrounded by so many blooming flowers that the entire town actually smells good, especially during spring and autumn. It's located at the foothills of Monte Suba-sio, so there are many good walking trails in the area. Emperor Augustus developed much of the land in the valley, and there is still a smattering of Roman ruins in the area, as well as some spectacular paintings by Pinturicchio, among others. But Spel-lo's main attraction is wandering its nar-row cobblestone streets under a plethora of stone archways.

Orientation

Spello is extremely easy to reach, as the train station is less than a kilometre from the city centre. The town meanders up an incline towards Porta Montanara, the northeast city gate and gateway to Monte Subasio.

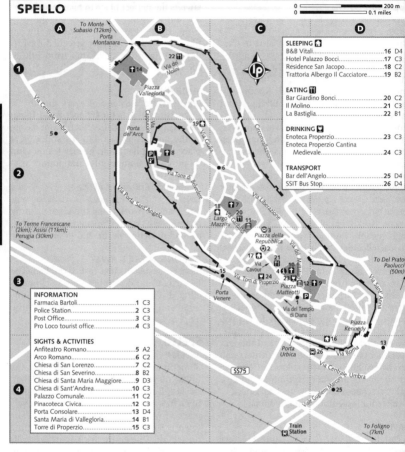

SPELLO

SLEEPING
B&B Vitali	16	D4
Hotel Palazzo Bocci	17	C3
Residence San Jacopo	18	C2
Trattoria Albergo Il Cacciatore	19	B2

EATING
Bar Giardino Bonci	20	C2
Il Molino	21	C3
La Bastiglia	22	B1

DRINKING
| Enoteca Properzio | 23 | C3 |
| Enoteca Properzio Cantina Medievale | 24 | C3 |

TRANSPORT
| Bar dell'Angelo | 25 | D4 |
| SSIT Bus Stop | 26 | D4 |

INFORMATION
Farmacia Bartoli	1	C3
Police Station	2	C3
Post Office	3	C3
Pro Loco tourist office	4	C3

SIGHTS & ACTIVITIES
Anfiteatro Romano	5	A2
Arco Romano	6	C2
Chiesa di San Lorenzo	7	C2
Chiesa di San Severino	8	B2
Chiesa di Santa Maria Maggiore	9	D3
Chiesa di Sant'Andrea	10	C3
Palazzo Comunale	11	C2
Pinacoteca Civica	12	C3
Porta Consolare	13	D4
Santa Maria di Vallegloria	14	B1
Torre di Properzio	15	C3

Information

EMERGENCY
Police station (☎ 0742 65 11 15; Piazza della Repubblica)

INTERNET RESOURCES
Bella Umbria (www.bellaumbria.net/spello) A private tourist website with information on accommodation, history and events.

MEDICAL SERVICES
Doctor (☎ 0742 30 20 16) Can locate a local doctor.
Farmacia Bartoli (☎ 0742 30 14 88; Via Cavour 63; ☼ closed Sat morning)

POST
Post office (☎ 0742 3 00 81; Piazza della Repubblica; ☼ 8am-6.30pm Mon-Fri, 8am-12.30pm Sat)

TOURIST INFORMATION
Pro Loco tourist office (☎ /fax 0742 30 10 09; prospello@libero.it; Piazza Matteotti 3; ☼ 9.30am-12.30pm & 3.30-5.30pm) Can provide you with a list of accommodation and restaurants and offer sightseeing advice. It has many walking maps of the area, including an 8km walk across the hills to Assisi. Purchase a city map here for €0.50.

Sights

Perhaps the best sight in all of Spello is to head up to the **Arco Romano**. From here you can get the best view of the **anfiteatro Romano** (closed to the public) and the surrounding countryside. Nearby is the **Chiesa di San Severino**, an active Cappuccin monastery with a Romanesque façade.

As you enter Spello, you'll come across Piazza Kennedy, the main entrance to the town, with a partially Roman gate, **Porta Consolare**. Further into town, Piazza Matteotti features two enormous churches: the austere **Chiesa di Sant'Andrea** (🕑 8am-7pm), where you can admire *Madonna with Child and Saints* by Bernardino Pinturicchio, and a few doors down, the 12th-century **Chiesa di Santa Maria Maggiore** (🕑 8.30am-12.30pm & 3-7pm summer, to 6pm winter). You'll also find the town's real treat, Pinturicchio's beautiful frescoes, in the **Cappella Baglioni**. The fresco is in the right-hand corner as you enter, behind glass, but be aware that you need to pay to illuminate the fresco. This is done not just to make money; constant light damages the paint. Also of note is the Cappella's exquisite floor (dating from 1566) made of tiles from Deruta. The **Pinacoteca Civica** (☎ 0742 30 14 97; Palazzo dei Cannonica, Piazza Matteotti; adult/concession €4/3; 🕑 10.30am-1pm & 3-6.30pm Tue-Sun Apr-Sep, 10.30am-12.30pm & 3-5pm Tue-Sun Oct-Mar) shows off Spello's artistic, religious and architectural past.

Continuing through to town, you'll reach Piazza della Repubblica. Further along, in the same piazza as the **Palazzo Comunale**, is the **Chiesa di San Lorenzo** (🕑 8.30am-12.30pm & 3-7pm summer, to 6pm winter), with a collection of sacred works. At the far north of town is yet another imposing church, **Santa Maria di Vallegloria**, built in the 1320s in Gothic style with frescoes by Spacca. The **Torre di Properzio** (Porta Venere) stands guard over the western Roman walls. Named for the Roman poet Propertius, the gate and its towers are a hodgepodge of Roman, medieval and 20th-century reconstructionist architecture.

Activities

The Pro Loco (and the tourist office in Assisi) has a badly drawn map called the *Passeggiata Tra Gli Ulivi*, a walking trail between Spello and Assisi down the Via degli Ulivi (Road of Olives). Give yourself several hours. It's not a long walk (8km) and is fairly flat, considering the rest of the region's terrain. If you like flowers, ancient gnarled olive trees and breathtakingly beautiful scenery, you won't be disappointed.

Festivals & Events

Spello, like nearby towns, has no shortage of festivals. The most beautiful – and best smelling – is **L'Infiorata del Corpus Domini**, which happens on Corpus Domini, the Sunday 60 days after Easter. Those familiar with Semana Santa in Guatemala and other Latin American countries will recognise the similar *alfombras* (flower carpets) that decorate the streets in colourful artistic displays. If you want to enjoy it, come on the Saturday evening before to see the floral fantasies being laid out (from about 8.30pm) and participate in the festive atmosphere. On the festival day, the Corpus procession begins at 11am, and can be extremely crowded. Make sure you have a hotel reservation, or just come for the day from Assisi or Perugia.

Sleeping

BUDGET

Residence San Jacopo (☎ 0742 30 12 60; www.residencesanjacopo.it in Italian; Via Borgo di via Giulia 1; 2-/3-r apt from €62/93) This vacation house saw its first incarnation in 1296 as the hospice of San Jacopo, a way station for pilgrims heading to Compostella in Galicia. Much has been rebuilt over the last eight centuries and San Jacopo is as comfortable as it is charming. Seven mini-apartments feature a kitchenette, bathroom and TV, and are furnished with rustic antiques. Vanya, the owner, also runs a nearby *enoteca*, and knows everything about local wine and delicacies.

Del Prato Paolucci (☎ 0742 30 10 18; Via Brodolini; s/d €45/62; 🅿) Paolucci is just outside the main town centre. Rooms aren't anything special, but it's the best-priced accommodation in Spello. The incredibly friendly owners are a hoot. Call ahead and they'll pick you up at the train station. At the time of research, plans were underway to build a pool. (These plans have been underway for the last two editions of this guide. Expect to be swimming in about 10 years' time.)

B&B Vitali (☎ 0742 30 19 47, 339 451 62 31; Via Povera Vita 20; 2/4 people €60/80) Although the address means 'the street of the poor life', this charming one-bedroom apartment next door to the Vitali private home is comfortable, complete with stocked kitchen, bathroom and a fold-out couch for children or extra guests. Discounts are available for three or more nights.

MIDRANGE

Terme Francescane (☎ 0742 30 11 86; www.termefrancescane.com; Via Delle Acque; s/d €70/90; 🅿 ❄ 🖥) After a few weary weeks on the road, a spa

NORTHERN UMBRIA

may be just what you need. A few kilometres from town, it's set in beautiful grounds. There is an entire spa 'village', complete with hotel, restaurant, treatment centre, sports facilities and two outdoor pools.

Trattoria Albergo Il Cacciatore (☎ 0742 65 11 41; fax 0742 30 16 03; Via Giulia 42; s/d/tr €55/85/100) This place has a great restaurant (closed Monday) with a large terrace that's perfect for a summer lunch amidst a panoramic view. Twenty-one rooms over three floors are large and modern, and plainly furnished in business casual, some with a small sitting area.

TOP END

Hotel Palazzo Bocci (☎ 0742 30 10 21; fax 0742 30 14 64; www.palazzobocci.com; Via Cavour 17; s/d €100/160, ste €220-270; P ⛶) This 18th-century hotel is in the Abitare La Storia association of grand hotels and is truly exquisite, with an elegant entryway, fine furnishings and well-appointed, soundproofed rooms and grand suites. Benvenuto Cripoldi frescoes appear in many bedrooms and public spaces. An outdoor terrace begs to host a romantic breakfast.

Eating

Il Molino (☎ 0742 65 13 05; Piazza Matteotti 6/7; mains €9-15; ☿ closed Tue) Owned by the Hotel Palazzo Bocci, the Molino is set in a 700-year-old building. It specialises in truffles, legumes, winter game meats, wild asparagus and cooking with local mountain-grown herbs.

La Bastiglia (☎ 0742 65 12 77; Via dei Molini 17; tasting menu around €50; ☿ closed Wed, Thu morning) The hotel feels a little too exclusive for some tastes, but its restaurant is worth the attitude. Connoisseurs come from all over the world to dine here. The food is beyond outstanding and a rare example of Umbrian *nouvelle* cuisine. If you've been too scared to try pigeon before, try the burned pigeon breast in cherry sauce in a potato puff pastry.

Bar Giardino Bonci (Via Garibaldi 10; mains around €6; ☿ 7am-10pm, to midnight summer, closed Thu) This simple bar has decent light meals and *gelati*, but the best thing is the back veranda, where you could while away hours admiring the view.

Drinking

Enoteca Properzio (☎ 0742 30 15 21; www.enoteche .it; Palazzo dei Canonici, Piazza Matteotti 8/10) Wine lovers need not go anywhere else. This epicurean metropolis sells just about every wine produced in Umbria, plus a substantial collection of Italian and foreign bottles. For €30, you can try five Umbrian wines – two whites and three reds – while snacking on the equally satisfying bruschetta, cheese and Norcia prosciutto.

The more intimate **Enoteca Properzio Cantina Medievale** (☎ 0742 30 16 88; Via Torri di Properzio 8a) around the corner is set in a medieval vault and sells many edibles.

Both places will ship goods home for you, but it's pricey to ship wine home from Italy, up to €146 per case when we visited (see p354 for more information on shipping wine).

Getting There & Away

Spello is directly on the train line between Perugia and Foligno, so trains run at least every hour to Perugia (€2.05, 30 minutes), Assisi (€1.15, 10 minutes) and Foligno (€0.80, 15 minutes). Spello is on the SS75. The station is often unstaffed, so make sure you have coins to buy your tickets at the self-service ticket machine. Or you can buy them at **Bar dell'Angelo** around the corner on Viale Guglielmi Marconi.

Spoletina buses head from Spello to Perugia (€3.60, 50 minutes, four daily) every day. They also pass through a few of the small towns nearby, but the train is much more convenient for travellers.

WINE REGION NEAR SPELLO

The area around Spello is picture perfect: hillsides covered in wildflowers, fields of sunflowers in June and stone villas quietly placed among the natural terrain. Wine is the major attraction of this region – the most well-known is the *sangrantino* from Montefalco. The area is quite upscale, as most travellers are here to taste wine and enjoy the good life, but there are many good camp sites and rooms to let, and some inexpensive hotels.

Buses travel between Montefalco and Bevagna (€2.20, 20 minutes, three daily), Foligno (€4.80, one hour and 10 minutes, nine daily) and Perugia (€5.20, 1½ hours, three daily), as well as between Bevagna and Foligno (€4.40, one hour, 10 daily) and Bevagna and Perugia (€5, one hour and 20 minutes, four daily).

Montefalco

pop 5640

The main reason to come to Montefalco is for the wine. Umbria doesn't have the tasting setup at the vineyards as you would find in Tuscany, or in California's Napa Valley or Australia's Hunter Valley. Most of the tasting that travellers are likely to do is at places with names such as *enoteca* or *degustazione*. An excellent recent innovation in the area is olive-oil tasting, which is becoming quite popular. This is one of the main olive-growing regions in Umbria, and tasting is a fun way for nondrinkers and children to join in the fun. You can play along with the big kids by saying things like 'this extra virgin has a bitter aftertaste' or 'lots of artichoke with overtones of oak'.

The **Museo Civico San Francesco** (☎ 0742 37 95 98; Via Ringhiera Umbra 6; ⏰ 10.30am-1pm & 2.30-5pm Nov-Feb, 2-6pm Mar-May, Sep & Oct, 3-7pm Jun & Jul, 3-7.30pm Aug, closed Mon winter) is housed in the deconsecrated St Francis Church, with a moving fresco cycle about the life and works of St Francis, as well as other important artwork and archaeological finds.

Villa Pambuffetti (☎ 0742 37 94 17; www.villa pambuffetti.com; Viale della Vittoria 20; s/d from €105/140; P ⊠ ⿻), a stone hotel with wood-beamed ceilings, is 'an oasis within an oasis'. It has all the four-star amenities, plus extras such as soundproofed rooms and an excellent restaurant.

The basic **Hotel Ristorante Ringhiera Umbra** (☎ 0742 37 91 66; verziere@tiscali.it; Via Mameli 20; s/d €47/60) has a fantastic, inexpensive restaurant located in a cosy stone-and-brick cave, and serves excellent *strangozzi* with truffles and a *sagrantino* sauce.

On the road out of Bevagna heading towards Spoleto, stop by the **Paolo Bea winery** (☎ 0742 37 81 28; www.paolobea.com; Loc. Cerrete 8; ⏰ Sun summer) for a true tasting experience. The family creates four special wines, which you can taste for €18 along with homemade bruschetta and *crostini*. They also sell their own olive oil and Parmesan cheese. During the summer, a harp player entertains visitors on Sunday. The winery is also open when the owners are home and not busy.

Bevagna

pop 4799

Bevagna began first as an Umbrian settlement, then became Etruscan and eventually a Roman municipium on the Via Flaminia. The town was recently voted the most beautiful village by census takers, who appreciate the safe atmosphere where children play in the streets and everyone can walk to work. For visitors, Romanesque churches, wine bars and a dearth of tourists add to the charm. The heart of Bevagna is in the Piazza Silvestre, where you'll find a Roman column of San Rocco. The nearby asymmetrical Piazza Silvestri is a marvel of medieval urban planning.

The **Pro Loco tourist office** (☎ 0742 36 16 67; pbevagna@bcsnet.it; Piazza Silvestri 1; ⏰ 9.30am-1pm & 2.30-7pm) can help with accommodation and wine-tasting. The **post office** (☎ 0742 36 15 68; Piazza Matteotti; ⏰ 8.10am-1.25pm Mon-Sat) is on the next square. Parking just outside the city centre is free.

The **Pinacoteca Comunale** (☎ 0742 36 00 31; Corso Matteotti 70; adult/concession €3.50/2; ⏰ 10.30am-1pm & 3-7pm summer, 10.30am-1pm & 3-5.30/6pm Tue-Sun winter) features a rudimentary exhibit on local archaeology and ceramics.

The ticket price for the pinacoteca also includes entrance into the **Roman Mosaic Museum of Antiquities** (☎ 075 572 71 41; Via di Porta Guelfa), a well-preserved tile floor from ancient Roman baths. There are also the remains of an old Roman theatre, and a Roman and medieval wall.

At the end of June, Bevagna goes medieval with the **Festival of the Gaite**. For two days, the town goes back in time a few hundred years, selling all sorts of medieval-inspired handicrafts and food.

If you happen upon the area during the last third of August and feel that slime is lacking in your diet, the little town of Cantalupo di Bevagna celebrates its **Sagra della Lumaca** (Festival of the Snail) with snail dishes cooked in every way imaginable (and unimaginable), as well as exhibits, dancing and general slug-related merriment.

SLEEPING & EATING

Enoteca Piazza Onofri (☎ 0742 36 19 20, 335 718 89 03; www.enotecaonofri.it; Piazza Onofri; ⏰ closed Wed) For one-stop shopping, Assù runs a delicious restaurant behind the *cantina* and good-value hotel (2-/4-person apartment €80/100) in addition to her wine shop.

Agriturismo/Camping Pian di Boccio (☎ 0742 36 01 64; www.piandiboccio.com; per person/car/child/tent €6.50/2.50/3.25/6; 2/6-person apt €57/140; P ⿻) This multifaceted camp site has archery, a swimming pool and a pizzeria, and nine rustic but comfortable apartments that come with firewood, fully-equipped kitchens and TV. Kids will love summer evenings, where they can dance, bowl or gather at special events with new international friends. The *agriturismo* produces its own olive oil, jam and tinned goods, and raises barnyard animals. You'll find it 4km southeast of Bevagna.

Ristorante Hotel L'Orto Degli Angeli (☎ 0742 36 09 67; www.ortoangeli.it; Via Dante Aligheri 1; r, ste & apt €220-350; ☺ restaurant closed Wed; 🅿 🞨 🞩) Try to peek at the hanging gardens of this prestigious residence and not want to spend a week. The hotel has had one of the most stunning historical renovations. The higher the room price, the more lavish the details: antique-laden sitting rooms, gold-trimmed canopies, stone or marble fireplaces, grotesque frescoed ceilings. The restaurant menu changes weekly, but you're guaranteed it will be Umbrian dishes made with local produce. The homemade *strangozzi* is excellent.

For your chance to try *sangrantino* wine flavoured *gelato*, head to **La Farfalla** (Corso Matteotti 62; ☺ 8.30am-1pm & 3pm-midnight, closed Tue), where you can also try *cacio e pera* (sheep's cheese and pear) and *cannoli* (a type of pastry), all homemade by a Sicilian family.

FOLIGNO

pop 51,130

Foligno was one of the major centres of power in medieval Umbria, but has lost most of its history and charm to industry. Still, if you decide to stay (or get stuck here due to public-transport mishaps), there are some worthwhile activities, including good shopping, a few interesting monuments and an excellent youth hostel.

At the unhelpful **tourist office** (☎ 0742 35 44 59; www.comune.foligno.pg.it/cultura/servizioturistico in Italian; Corso Cavour 126; ☺ 9am-1pm & 4-7pm Mon-Sat, 9am-1pm Sun), no-one speaks English, but there's information behind the desk for Foligno, as well as for the surrounding towns of Bevagna, Gualdo Cattaneo, Montefalco, Spello and Trevi. It's located near the Porta Romana. Pass up the smaller, equally unhelpful **tourist office** (☺ 10am-1pm & 3-7pm Wed-Sun) at the train station.

The **cathedral** is in Piazza della Repubblica, in which St Feliciano is buried. The building dates from the 12th century and is

a hodgepodge of many architectural styles, from Roman-Gothic to 16th-century Renaissance additions. There are some stunning 16th-century Vespasiano Strada frescoes. In the same square is the worthwhile **Palazzo Trinci** (☎ 0742 35 07 34; admission free; ☺ 10am-7pm Tue-Sun), which has some paintings and frescoes from the 15th century.

The Trinci family was part of the feudal lordship, also known as the *seigniories,* which ruled over much of papal-controlled Umbria in the later medieval period. (You'll notice buildings all over Umbria named after these families: the Baglionis in Perugia or the Vitellis in Città di Castello.) The Trincis paid Ottaviano Nelli to decorate their palace – although they didn't score like the Vitellis in Città di Castello, with Raphael and Giorgio Vasari. There's a small museum (descriptions in Italian only) in the palazzo, which features some of the historic costumes you'd find at the Quintana festival.

If you're in the area during the beginning of June or in September, the main festival is **La Giostra della Quintana** (☎ 0742 35 40 00; www .quintana.it), a medieval equestrian tournament reinvented from the 1400s. Ten neighbourhoods vie against each other in a friendly jousting competition complete with elaborate velvet-and-lace traditional costumes, and dishes from the 15th century.

Ostello Pierantoni (☎ 0742 34 25 66; www.os tellionline.com in Italian; Via Pierantoni 23; dm/f/s incl breakfast €15/17/22; ☺ reception 7am-noon & 2pm-midnight), only 500m from the station, is a full-service hostel with 199 beds, washer/dryer, Internet facilities, an outdoor garden, bike rental, access for people with disabilities and a restaurant. It feels like a palace with its frescoed, echo-high ceilings, but it was actually a monastery for some extremely comfortable monks.

Il Barbablu (☎ 0742 35 46 97; Via Umberto I 46; pizza slice €1) On the way to the hostel is this fantastic cheap pizza place. Try the corn or zucchini.

Getting There & Away

Many public transport users will go through Foligno at some point. If you arrive by train and are switching to a bus, head out of the train station down Viale Mezzetti. The main bus terminal is about 50m to your left. To get to Trevi, head about 40m further to the grandiose Porta Romana. You can

---

DETOUR: OLIVO DI SAN EMILIANO

In the town of Bovara you can see the oldest olive tree in the region. Take the road through Bovara to the highway. Across from the La Foccaccia restaurant on the left is a side road. Turn right and just 50m down the road you'll find the Olivo di San Emiliano, a grandfatherly tree that's 9m in diameter, 5m tall and estimated to be over 1700 years old.

---

buy tickets for either location at the Blu Bar, next to the petrol station at the bus terminal. There are hourly trains to Perugia (€2.30, 30 minutes), and Assisi (€1.55, 20 minutes). Buses head to Bevagna (€4.40, one hour, five daily), Montefalco (€4.80, one hour and 10 minutes, five daily) and Trevi (€2.80, 30 minutes, five daily).

TREVI
pop 7773

Trevi has miraculously avoided any sort of bowing to Umbria's burgeoning tourist industry, and would feel downright foreign to anyone just coming from San Gimignano or Siena. Trevi allied itself with Perugia against Spoleto during the papal rule – it was a papal state until the Unification of Italy. It witnessed several exciting firsts: the first press association and the first pawn shop. Nowadays, you can actually hear the z-z-z-zip as it rolls itself up for siesta, and nary a local soul ventures out between 1pm and 4pm. The town calls itself a 'Slow City' (see p340), and residents pride themselves on its utter mellowness. Greenish-grey olive trees swathe every inch of hillside around Trevi, and the olive oil here is reputedly some of the best in Italy.

The **Pro Loco office** (☎ /fax 0742 78 11 50; www .protrevi.com; Piazza Mazzini 5; ☻ 9am-1pm & 3.30-7.30pm) has an interactive computer display out the front, so if it's closed, you can still get information from its website.

Trevi was a theatre town, all the way back to Roman times. The **Teatro Clitunno** (☎ 0742 38 17 68; Piazza del Teatro) remains the town's most important gathering point. The **Flash Art Museum** (☎ 0742 38 19 78; Palazzo Luncarini; adult/ concession €4/2.50; ☻ 3-7pm Wed-Sun) has a funky collection of modern art. Remnants of concentric rings of a **Mura Romana** (Roman Wall) and a **Mura Medievali** (Medieval Wall) still encircle the historic centre of the town. The **Museo della Civiltá dell' Ulivo** (Olive Museum; ☎ 0742 33 22 22; ☻ 10.30am-1pm & 3-6pm Tue-Sun summer, closed Tue-Thu winter) is a must-see while in the area, as it details the history of olive-oil production in Umbria for millennia.

Antica Dimora alla Rocca (☎ 0742 38 54 01; www .hotelallarocca.it; Piazza della Rocca 1; s €95, d €105-350, all incl breakfast; P ☒ ☐) is a breathtakingly decorated hotel, with palatial furnishings and frescoed hallways. It feels palatial for a reason: the hotel was actually built in the 1500s as a prince's palace. Check the website to get a 20% (or more) midweek discount.

Albergo Ristorante Il Terziere (☎ 0742 78 359; www.ilterziere.com; Via Coste 1; s/d incl breakfast €52/70; ☻ restaurant closed Wed; P), a beautiful hotel and restaurant outside the city centre, is just behind the parking area in Piazza Garibaldi (up the one-way road going the wrong way – really). The views are better than the rather austere rooms, but with a stunning garden and terrace, you won't want to spend much time inside. Try the gnocchi in *sagrantino* sauce at the restaurant.

Named after its location as the old post office, **La Vecchia Posta** (☎ 0742 38 54 01; rooms 333 392 4737; Piazza Mazzini 14; ☻ closed Thu) is a charming restaurant with a few rooms to let. The menu is small, but the *strangozzi* and truffles or chicken in porcini cream should satisfy just about any taste. The candied pear dessert with mint and chocolate sauce is legendary.

Maggiolini (☎ 0742 38 15 34; Via San Francesco 20; mains €5.80-11.40), a beautiful restaurant, is best in summer when you can dine alfresco on several reasonably priced truffle dishes and homemade pasta.

Bus services to Trevi are spotty, so take the train, as it is conveniently located along the main line to Perugia (€2.80, 45 minutes, hourly), Assisi (€1.65, 30 minutes, hourly) and Spoleto (€1.45, 15 minutes, hourly).

Southern Umbria

Southern Umbria isn't as well travelled as its northern counterpart, but it's equally as beautiful and historically significant. The biggest tourist draw is Orvieto, known for its magnificent cathedral. But the area has some quintessentially perfect hill towns: Spoleto, famous for its Festival di Due Mondi; Norcia, a meat-lover's paradise; Narni, charming but undiscovered; Amelia, unassumingly friendly; and Todi, whose popularity has been increasing ever since it was named 'the most livable city in the world'.

Most of southern Umbria is sleepy, slow and laid-back. Everything closes from 12.30pm or 1pm to 3.30pm or 4pm. Locals pride themselves on this relaxed atmosphere and – as there is virtually nothing to do for three hours every day but eat a tenth of your body weight in pasta and then stroll it off – tourists begin to adapt to this lifestyle as well.

History, art and culture dominate the sights and attractions in the area. Near Orvieto lies an Etruscan necropolis dating from the 6th century BC. Carsulae, outside of the south's industrial capital of Terni, is a well-preserved Roman town, once a major stopping-off point on the Roman Via Flaminia. You won't find the artistic masterpieces of Perugia or Città di Castello, but each town has several galleries and historically important artwork in its churches and cathedrals.

If you need to get your adrenaline fix, southern Umbria offers activities and sports of all kinds. Outdoor enthusiasts can indulge in just about any sport they desire. Fancy hanggliding? Try Castelluccio, near the Piano Grande. Rafting? Several places along the Nera and Corno rivers offer white-water rafting, kayaking or canoeing. You can rent bikes outside of Orvieto, rock climb in Ferentillo or go spelunking (caving) in the Valnerina.

HIGHLIGHTS

- Picnic in fields of flowers flanked by snow-capped peaks in the **Piano Grande** (p321)
- Experience the majesty of the black-and-white marble of Orvieto's **cathedral** (p335)
- Take in a concert or performance at the **Spoleto Festival** (p314)
- Take an active and unique day trip through the **Valnerina** (p317) to raft, rock climb, dine in an ancient abbey or even to see dead people
- Savour the view from the top of **La Rocca Albornoz** (p329) in Narni

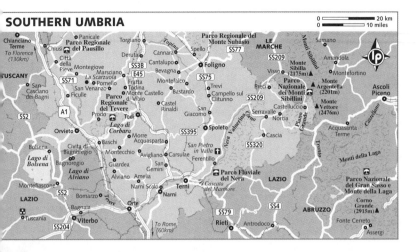

SOUTHERN UMBRIA

SPOLETO

pop 37,918

Spoleto was one of those sleepy Umbrian hill towns until, in 1958, Italian-American composer Giancarlo Menotti changed everything. For a while, Spoleto saw its tourist season peak for only 10 days from the end of June to the beginning of July during its immensely popular Spoleto Festival (p314). During the festival this quiet town takes centre stage for an international parade of drama, music, opera and dance.

Now so many people have discovered the town via the festival that it's become a popular destination for most of the year (although as in the rest of Umbria, you'll have the town mostly to yourself in winter). Even outside the festival season, Spoleto has enough museums, Roman ruins, wanderable streets and vistas to keep you busy for a day or two.

The surrounding Umbra Valley is a masterpiece of well over 2000 years of agricultural practice. From the original Umbrian tribes to the Romans and farmers in the medieval period, the Vale di Spoleto, as it was known then, has been drained using an intricate system of hydraulics and agricultural techniques.

Umbria was first divided in half between the Etruscans and Umbrians. After Rome fell, it was divided again: Byzantines on the east of the Tiber river, Lombards to the west. Spoleto, which was just to the west of the Tiber, became the capital of the Lombardy duchy. Although much of its pre-Lombard artwork has been lost, you'll see many of the signature religious buildings and hermitages in the area.

If you plan to visit during the Spoleto Festival, book accommodation and the most popular performances at least two or three months in advance.

Orientation

The old part of the city is about 1km south of the main train station – take the orange shuttle bus (€0.80) marked A–E for Piazza della Libertà in the city centre, where you'll find the tourist office and the Teatro Romano. Piazza del Mercato, a short walk northeast of Piazza della Libertà, marks the engaging heart of old Spoleto. Between here and Piazza del Duomo you'll find the bulk of the city's monuments and some fine shops.

Information

BOOKSHOPS

Il Libro (☎ 0743 466 78; Corso Mazzini 63) A wide selection of maps, cookbooks, guidebooks and novels in English.

EMERGENCY

Police station (☎ 0743 232 41; Viale Trento e Trieste) A block south of the main train station.

INTERNET ACCESS

A Tuta Birra (Via di Fontesecca 7; ☺ noon-11pm Wed-Mon) There's an Internet terminal at this pub.
Pizzeria Zeppelin (p315; per hr €3)

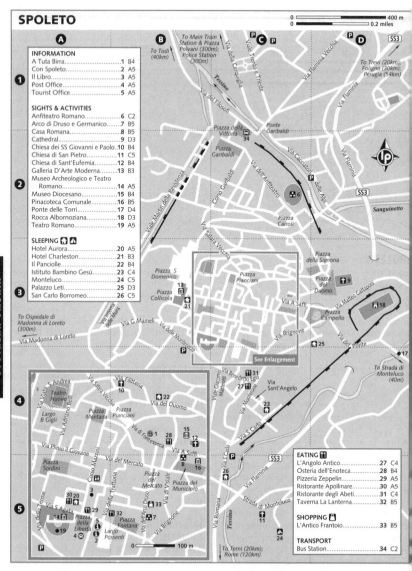

SPOLETO

MEDICAL SERVICES
Ospedale di Madonna di Loreto (Hospital; ☎ 0743 21 01; Via Madonna di Loreto)

POST
Post office (☎ 0743 20 15 20; Viale Giacomo Matteotti; ⏱ 8am-6.30pm Mon-Fri, 8am-12.30pm Sat) The entrance is off Viale Giacomo Matteotti.

TOURIST INFORMATION
Con Spoleto (☎ 0743 22 07 73; www.conspoleto.com; Piazza della Libertà 7) A privately owned service that can book accommodation.
Tourist office (☎ 0743 23 89 20/21; info@iat.spoleto .pg.it; Piazza della Libertà 7; ⏱ 9am-1pm & 4-7pm Mon-Sat & 10am-1pm Sun summer, 9am-1pm & 3.30-6.30pm Mon-Sat winter) English-speaking Umbrian tourist authority.

Sights
ROMAN SPOLETO
Make your first stop the **Museo Archeologico e Teatro Romano** (☎ 0743 22 32 77; www.archeopg.arti .beniculturali.it/musei/spoleto.htm in Italian; Via S Agata; adult/concession/child €4/2/free; ⏱ 8.30am-7.30pm) on the western edge of Piazza della Libertà. Since 1985, this former Benedictine monastery and prison has been used as a museum. Exhibited are many artefacts from ancient and Roman Spoleto, including two marble sculptures of Augustus and possibly Caesar. You can also walk through the 1st-century-AD Roman theatre and, during the Spoleto Festival, watch a performance or ballet staged on the selfsame theatre.

East of Piazza della Libertà, around Piazza Fontana, are more Roman remains, including the **Arco di Druso e Germanico** (Arch of Drusus and Germanicus; sons of the Emperor Tiberius). The grandiose archway marks the entrance to what was the Roman forum. The excavated **Casa Romana** (Roman house; ☎ /fax 0743 464 34; Via di Visiale; adult/child €2/1; ⏱ 10am-1pm & 3-6pm wed-Mon 16 Oct-15 Mar, 10am-8pm daily 16 Mar-15 Oct) dates from the 1st century. It's a good example of a typical Roman house from this time, and still has vestiges of mosaic and painting decoration. The city boasts an **Anfiteatro Romano** (Roman Amphitheatre), one of the country's largest. Unfortunately it is within military barracks and closed to the public. Wander along Via dell'Anfiteatro, off Piazza Garibaldi, in search of a glimpse.

MUSEUMS & CHURCHES
The **cathedral** (Santa Maria Assunta; ☎ 0743 443 07; Piazza del Duomo; ⏱ 7.30am-12.30pm & 3-6pm summer, 7.30am-12.30pm & 3-5pm winter) in Spoleto was consecrated in 1198 and remodelled in the 17th century. The Romanesque façade is fronted by a striking Renaissance porch. In the 11th century, huge blocks of stone salvaged from Roman buildings were put to good use in the construction of the rather sombre bell tower. The mosaic floors are from a 12th-century reconstruction effort. Inside, the first chapel to the right of the nave (Chapel of Bishop Constantino Eroli) was decorated by Bernardino Pinturicchio, and Annibale Carracci completed an impressive fresco in the right transept.

Check out the apse's fresco *Life of the Virgin Mary,* done by Filippo Lippi and his assistants, Fra Diamante and Piero Mat-teo d'Amelia (who painted a starry sky on the Sistine Chapel ceiling 20 years before Michelangelo covered it up). Lippi died during the commission. Lorenzo de' Medici travelled to Spoleto from Florence and ordered Lippi's son, Filippino, to build a mausoleum for the artist. This now stands in the cathedral's right transept. The spectacular closing concert of the Spoleto Festival is held on the piazza, in front of the cathedral.

Dominating the city is the **Rocca Albornoziana** (☎ 0743 437 07; Piazza Campello; adult/concession €5/3; ⏱ core hr 10am-8pm summer, 10am-1pm & 3-6pm Mon-Fri, 10am-5pm Sat & Sun winter), an example of an Albornoz-built fortress from the mid-14th century. Cardinal Albornoz led Pope Innocent VI's forces in the fight to take back control of Umbria. He fostered the building of many of the *rocche* (fortresses) in the area, including the one still standing in Narni (p329), the ruins of one in Orvieto (p336), and one in Perugia (p271) that was destroyed in an uprising against the Pope just three years after it was built. For hundreds of years, until as recently as 1982, Spoleto's *rocca* was used as a high-security prison housing such notables as Pope John Paul II's attempted assassin, Ali Agca. It's now used as a museum and to host open-air theatre performances.

Inside the town hall on Piazza del Municipio is the **Pinacoteca Comunale** (☎ 0743 21 82 70; Via A Saffi; adult/child €2.05/1; ⏱ 10.30am-1pm & 2.30-5pm winter, 10.30am-1pm & 3-6.30pm summer). Accessible by guided tour only, the pinacoteca is a sumptuous building, with some impressive works by Umbrian artists. To check out more modern artwork – in particular the works of Umbrian sculptor Leoncillo Leonardi – head towards the **Galleria D'Arte Moderna** (☎ 0743 464 34; Piazza Collicola; ⏱ 10.30am-1pm & 3-6.30pm winter, 10am-8pm summer) in the Palazzo Collicola.

On Via Filitteria, you'll come across the tiny and ancient **Chiesa di SS Giovanni e Paolo** (⏱ 10am-1pm & 3-8pm Jun-Sep, sporadically in winter), an example of a pre-Romanesque church, built with Roman ruins above an older church, and consecrated in 1174. If it's open, check out the earliest depiction of the Archbishop of Canterbury Sir Thomas Becket's martyrdom. If it's closed, you can still see the 13th-century fresco of Our Mary with Saints above the door.

An hour-long stroll or an all-day hike on a sunny day along the Via del Ponte will get you to the **Ponte delle Torri**, erected in the 14th century on the foundations of a Roman aqueduct. The bridge is 80m high and 230m across, built in an imposing set of 10 arches. Cross the bridge and follow the lower path, Strada di Monteluco, to reach the **Chiesa di San Pietro** (☎ 0743 448 82; Loc San Pietro; ⏱ 9.30-11am & 3.30-6.30pm). The 13th-century façade, the church's main attraction, is liberally bedecked with sculpted animals.

The 12th-century **Chiesa di Sant'Eufemia** (☎ 0743 23 10 22; Via A Saffi; adult/child €3.10/1.55; ⏱ 10am-12.30pm & 3.30-7pm summer, 10am-12.30pm & 3.30-6pm winter) is within the grounds of the Archbishop's palazzo. It is notable for its *matronei* – galleries set high above the main body of the church to segregate the female congregation. The admission price is for the attached Museo Diocesano.

Festivals & Events

The Italian-American composer Giancarlo Menotti conceived the Festival dei Due Mondi (Festival of the Two Worlds) in 1958. Now known simply as the **Spoleto Festival** (☎ 800 56 56 00; www.spoletofestival.it) it has given the city a worldwide reputation and spawned a sister festival in Charleston, South Carolina. During the three weeks from late June to mid-July, all sorts of performances take place, from opera and theatre to ballet and art exhibitions in the Rocca Albornoziana, the Teatro Nuovo and the cathedral, among other places. A special Spoleto Cinema component showcases old and new films. A fairly new but inventive performance tradition has been to re-enact either famous or historical court proceedings.

Tickets range from €5 to €200 but most are between €20 and €30. The most famous performances sell out as early as March or April, but you can still buy tickets that week for many shows. There are usually several free concerts in various churches.

Sleeping

The city is well served by cheap hotels, *affittacamere*, hostels and camp sites. Expect significantly higher prices during the festival.

BUDGET

Monteluco (☎/fax 0743 22 03 58; www.geocities .com/monteluco2002; Loc San Pietro; per person/tent €5/6; ⏱ Apr-Sep) This leafy, quiet camp site is just behind the Chiesa di San Pietro. It's an easy 15 to 20 minute walk from the town centre and less than a kilometre from the aqueduct and several good hiking trails. The restaurant at the camp site is good enough to bring locals out.

Istituto Bambino Gesù (☎ 0743 402 32; Via Sant'Angelo 4; s/d incl breakfast €28/50) The combined age of these enterprising nun/B&B proprietors might be older than the 16th-century convent itself. Get in touch with your monastic side in these barebones cells, no more than a bed, dresser and postage-stamp-sized bathroom. But the price is right, the views are amazing and the dead silent, pitch black nights will guarantee a good night's sleep.

Il Panciolle (☎ /fax 0743 456 77; Via del Duomo 3; s/d with bathroom from €45/60; Ⓟ) Comfortable enough for those used to nicer hotels and a deserving splurge for hostellers, this Spoleto mainstay is in a good position between the cathedral and the Piazza del Mercato. The rooms facing the street can be a tad loud. There are hairdryers, TVs and comfortable bedding in all rooms. Ask for a parking pass.

San Carlo Borromeo (☎ 0743 22 53 20; www.geo cities.com/sancarloborromeo; Via San Carlo; s/d/tr incl breakfast €35/52/72; Ⓟ ⚒ ▢) The least atmospheric of the hotels listed, the convenience, price and free car park make it a safe bet. The back rooms are quieter and have a view of Monteluco, but all are clean, functional and spacious. There is disability access and small pets are welcome.

MIDRANGE

Hotel Charleston (☎ 0743 22 00 52; www.hotelchar leston.it; Piazza Collicola 10; s/d/tr/ste incl breakfast €59/79/110/149; Ⓟ ⚒ ▢) With a sauna, fireplace and an outdoor terrace, the Charleston is an enticing location in both winter and summer. Named after Charleston, South Carolina (home of a sister Spoleto Festival), the hotel is covered in distinguished modern art and provides wine tastings or apéritifs every evening. The 17th-century building has been thoroughly renovated with double-paned windows and some rooms come with VCRs or bathtubs. Internet access (€6 per hour) is also available. The wood-beamed attic suite is worth the splurge. Parking costs €10.

Hotel Aurora (☎ 0743 22 03 15; www.hotelaurora spoleto.it; Via Apollinaire 3; s/d incl breakfast €50/80; ▢) Just off Piazza della Libertà, the Aurora is very central and fabulous value. Staff are friendly and will help you plan your Spoleto

---

TOP FIVE GREAT VALUE PLACES TO SLEEP IN UMBRIA

For the top bang for your buck, try these hotels:

Al Grappolo d'Oro (p280) With an outdoor pool, inclusive breakfast, in-room DSL connection and breathtaking vista, you'll feel like you should be paying double.

Fattoria il Poggio (p293) Yes, it's a hostel, but you wouldn't know it when you gaze at the view of the lake through the old farmhouse windows of your private bedroom.

Residenza La Loggia (p297) Start your day off with breakfast in the quiet garden along the river in this sweet and romantic home-away-from-home.

Romantica Pucci (p340) This place has enough added touches – bedside cookies, bottled water, homemade marmalade for breakfast and four-poster beds – to justify staying in Bagnoregio rather than Civita.

Hotel dei Priori (p330) Perfectly central with an excellent restaurant and a mix of modern and historic rooms, most with a view, is reason enough to venture into the undiscovered hamlet of Narni.

---

itinerary. Some rooms have pleasant balconies and breakfast is excellent.

TOP END

Palazzo Leti (☎ 0743 22 49 30; www.palazzoleti.com; Via degli Eremiti 10; s/d/ste incl breakfast €150/200/260-320; P 🛠) In the southeast part of town facing the hills, this former noble palace exudes romance and charm down to the last detail, from the delicate breakfast china to the historical oak and wrought-iron furnishings. With the view and perfect silence, you'll feel like you're staying in the country, but you're a three-minute walk from the centre of Spoleto. Parking will set you back €13 the first night, and €7 subsequent nights.

Eating

Spoleto is one of Umbria's main centres for the *tartufo nero* (black truffle), which you'll often find shaved over pasta. On Via dell'Arco Druso is a gathering of five shops selling meat, bread, sauces and wine, perfect to pick up supplies for a picnic.

Ristorante Apollinare (☎ 0743 22 32 56; Via Sant' Agata 14; tasting menu €30-35; closed Mon & Tue) A delight for the senses, Apollinare is an extraordinary culinary experience set amid ancient 12th-century walls and low oak beam ceilings lit by flickering candlelight. You can choose to go with one of its tasting menus – vegetarian, truffle or traditional – or choose from its *nouvelle* menu. Seasonal menus include such creations as squid ink pasta with pesto and crayfish or rabbit in black olive sauce. Save room for dessert.

Osteria dell'Enoteca (☎ 0743 22 04 84; Via A Saffi 7; tourist menu €15; closed Tue) Extremely fit waiters carry dishes up and down a curving iron staircase into this 12th-century tavern. Diners sit on dark wood benches under a high stone ceiling surrounded by rows and rows of local wines from which to choose. Dishes are typical of the area – *strangozzi alla spoletina* ('shoelace' pasta in a tomato, garlic and chilli sauce, €6.20), truffle omelette (€6.20) – and priced to allow at least one or two meals while in town.

Ristorante degli Abeti (☎ 0743 22 00 25; Via Benedetto Egio 3/5; mains €6.50-17; closed Tue) Not for dieters or vegetarians, the menu offers sinfully rich piles of artery-thickeners – try *pappardelle con cinghiale e tartufo* (pasta with wild boar and truffles) and *prosciutto di cinghiale* (wild boar prosciutto).

Taverna la Lanterna (☎ 0743 4 98 15; Via della Trattoria 6; tasting menus around €15; closed Wed) A great place with extremely reasonable prices in the town centre, La Lanterna serves a variety of Umbrian pasta dishes. Tasting menus include vegetarian offerings for €11, regular for €13, and *porcini* and *tartufo* for €15.

L'Angolo Antico (☎ 0743 49066; Via Monterone 109; mains €8-14; closed Mon) In a neighbourhood restaurant just outside the main city is this family-run *ristorante* and pizzeria, with a few suits of armour thrown in for good measure. Nothing fancy on the menu, just good filling *strangozzi alla spoletina* and *scallopine al limone* (pork in a lemon sauce).

Pizzeria Zeppelin (☎ 0743 47 767; Corso Mazzini 81; pizza & snacks €0.80-3; 10.30am-9.30pm) A meeting point in town, you can get a filling slice of pizza here for less than €1, plus check your email (€3 per hour).

Shopping

Gathered along Via dell'Arco Druso are several shops that sell locally produced meats,

SOUTHERN UMBRIA

OUTDOOR ADVENTURES IN UMBRIA

Umbria has plenty of outdoor activities to keep you busy for months.

The **Club Alpino Italiano** (Italian Alpine Club; ☎ 075 914 22 13; www.cai.it in Italian) is an authority on all things mountainous in the region, but its website is in Italian only.

Every tourist office carries a brochure entitled *Sport and Environment*. All sports and activities are listed, along with companies, outfitters and contact information in the back of the brochure.

Here's just a sample of the outdoor activities you can try in Umbria (and the best locations to experience them):

Hang-gliding & Paragliding With vertical cliffs and soft rolling hills, Umbria is a great place to learn how to do either, or get in a little practice if you're already certified. The hang-gliding capital of Italy – Castelluccio (p321) – has two popular hang-gliding schools, which also teach paragliding. You can take a five-day course (or longer) or take a tandem ride with a trained instructor.

Rafting/Canoeing The Nera, Tiber and Corno rivers (opposite) offer wild rides in beautiful settings for those who want a leisurely canoe ride or a white-water thrill.

Horse Riding Many places around Lago di Trasimeno (p291) in the north of Umbria lead walks or rent horses by the hour. Some of these places also offer archery lessons.

Spelunking/Caving Monte Cucco (p299) in the north of Umbria has an extensive karst system of caverns to explore.

Rock Climbing Ferentillo (opposite) and the Valnerina are the climbing hotspots.

Hiking & Walking One of the most popular Umbrian pastimes for locals and tourists alike is trekking, hiking or simply strolling in the outdoors. Italy's national park system is a well-maintained consortium, with marked trails, outdoor activities and a system of *rifugi* (mountain huts). Check www.parks.it, at any tourist office in Umbria or p45 for more information.

---

wines or delicacies. **L'Antico Frantoio** (☎ 0743 49 893; Via dell'Arco Druso 8) sells plenty of pasta, *lenticchie* (typical Castelluccian minilentils), wine, oil and cheese for a great gift or picnic. Each town in Umbria has several of these gourmet goods store but here, the fiery owner, Sandra, makes many of her own sauces. Try anything with *tartufi*, olive or *carciofi* (artichokes). She will carefully package and FedEx any purchases you make to anywhere in the world.

Getting There & Around

BUS

The main bus terminal is just north of town, towards the train station. From the train station, take city buses A-E for €0.80 (make sure the bus reads 'Centro'), the company is **Società Spoletina di Imprese Trasporti** (SSIT; ☎ 0743 21 22 08; www.spoletina.com). Long-distance buses are rare as the train is so convenient, but you'll need a bus to get to Norcia and the Valnerina (€4.40, one hour, six daily) or Cascia (€4.40, one hour and 10 minutes, six daily). Buses run to the camp site in Monteluco in summer only (€0.80, 15 minutes, hourly).

TRAIN

Trains from the main **station** (☎ 0743 485 16; Piazza Polvani) connect with Rome (€6.82 to €11.57, one to 2½ hours, hourly), Ancona (€7.90-13.16, two hours, 10 daily), Perugia (€3.50, one hour, seven daily) or Assisi (€2.55, 40 minutes, hourly). If you wind up on a Eurostar train, even to Assisi or Perugia, you'll pay over double to arrive about five minutes earlier.

CAMPELLO SUL CLITUNNO

If you're heading between Foligno and Spoleto, a pleasant place for a stroll is the Campello sul Clitunno, where you'll find the **Fonti del Clitunno** (☎ 0743 52 11 41; Loc. Pissignano; admission €2; ☼ 10am-12.30pm & 2.30-5.30pm winter, 9am-8pm summer), the source for the Clitunno river. This Zen-like garden proffers crystal clear springs, a tranquil lake and exquisitely lush foliage. In ancient times, it was a popular site for religious pilgrimages. Caligula was known to come here to consult the god of the Clitunno river and it was also used for theatre performances, feasts and gladiator matches. While you can't witness gladiator matches, you can stroll the lovely grounds.

In the same area is the **Tempietto del Clitunno** (☎ 0743 27 50 85; Via Flaminia, Km 139; ☼ 9am-8pm Apr-Oct, 8am-6pm Nov-Mar). This Paleo-Christian building was first thought to be an ancient Roman ruin, but artefacts have shown that it was built sometime between the 5th and 8th centuries AD. It has many of the classic Roman features, such as Corinthian columns and neo-Augustan inscriptions (in big block lettering).

VALNERINA

The Valnerina offers the best untouched natural scenery in Umbria. The ancient flow of the Nera river created the striking fluvial geography. Instead of rolling hillsides and vineyards, jagged cliffs rise straight up from the riverbed floor and forests full of beech trees hide the Apennine wolves, wild boar and golden eagles that thrive here. This is the place to go hiking, biking, rock climbing or rafting.

The Valnerina is easily accessed as a day trip from Spoleto, Terni or Norcia, and is only a little over an hour from Trevi, Foligno, Narni or Todi. The SS395 from Spoleto and the SS209 from Terni join with the SS320 and then the SS396, which passes through Norcia. The best way to see the area is to take a day trip along the SS209, starting at Cascata del Marmore (below) in the morning, visiting Ferentillo and its Mummy Museum (right) by its 2.30pm afternoon opening time and ending up at San Pietro in Valle (p318) for a memorable dinner.

The Valnerina is brimming with outdoor activities.

Associazione Gaia (☎ 338 767 83 08; www.asgaia.it; Via Cristoforo Colombo 1/a, Foligno) specialises in rafting trips, but they also offer environmental education, mountain biking, horseback riding and free climbing. Before rafting trips, they offer a small introductory course on the natural surroundings of the Corno River.

Rafting Umbria (☎ 0742 231 46, 348 3511798; www.raftingumbria.it; Via Santi Brinati 2, Foligno) is a full-service outdoor activity centre offering much more than rafting. Activities include canoeing, kayaking, horseback riding, free climbing, mountain biking, white-water rafting, orienteering and survival skills. Based out of Foligno this outfit arranges rafting trips in the Valnerina on the Corno and Nera rivers, bicycling in Monti Sibillini and free climbing in Ferentillo.

Cascata del Marmore

Don't let the tourist trap entrance scare you off (except on weekends in August – then you should run screaming). These waterfalls,

the highest in Europe, are a sight to see. The Romans created them in 290 BC when they diverted the Velino river into the Nera river. These days, the waterfall provides hydroelectric power. If you're without a car, it's worth catching a bus to see it, particularly to witness the arrival of the water after it has been switched on. Local bus No 7 runs from Terni to the falls.

Whenever the waterfalls are operational, the SS209 (connecting Terni and Perugia to Norcia and Ferentillo) and the SS79 (connecting Terni and Perugia to Piediluco and Rieti) come to a virtual standstill. There are four car parks throughout the area. Plan on staying a while, as the area surrounding the falls is equally attractive.

The falls operate on a bizarrely complex schedule that probably isn't even accurate. Just about any tourist office in Umbria will have the schedule for the waterfall, but the local tourist offices – Terni, Narni, Spoleto, Norcia and Perugia – are most likely to know the correct data, or you can call ☎ 0744 629 82. The falls are completely closed in December, January and February. The best time to see them is between 10am and noon, or 3pm or 4pm up until 9pm or 10pm in the summer, during holidays and on Sundays. Opening hours are even more restricted on Saturdays and weekdays.

The skittish and the completely insane are both welcome at **Centro Canoe e Rafting 'Le Marmore'** (☎ 330 75 34 20; www.raftingmarmore.com; Via Carlo Neri, Terni), based in Terni. One can try 'hydrospeeding' – the white-water equivalent of bobsledding – or take what is called a 'Soft Rafting' excursion down the Nera, more appropriate for all ages and skill levels.

Ferentillo

As you head from the waterfalls north up the SS209 you'll see a set of medieval walls placed precariously over a hill above this quiet town set in the midst of the fluvial Valnerina. Horror film fans will have a murderously good time at the **Museo delle Mummie** (Museum of the Mummies; ☎ 0743 543 95; Via delle Torre; adult/concession €3/2; ✆ 9am-12.30pm & 2.30-7.30pm Apr-Sep, 10am-12.30pm & 2.30-6pm Oct & Mar, 10am-12.30pm & 2.30-5pm Nov-Feb), reached through an eerie subterranean 4th-century crypt. You'll find a collection of ancient Ferentillian corpses in various stages of decay, mummified naturally with a process of salt, ammonia and mushrooms. Dozens of mummies sit, stand or lie down, some still clothed, others with a full set of teeth or hair, a mother and child, and the ever-popular display of disembodied heads.

The second thing Ferentillo is known for is its rock climbing. You can contact certified rock climbing guide Kathleen Scheda at **Duka Duka Outdoors** (☎ 0765 6 32 02; dukadukaoutdoors@libero.it) to arrange climbing expeditions. Kathleen's family owns a B&B just across the border in Lazio called **La Torretta** (☎ /fax 0765 6 32 02; www.latorrettabandb.com; Casperia, Lazio; s/d/f €60/80/140). It's in a medieval town about an hour from Rome and close to the best climbing spots in Lazio and Umbria. The B&B has a two-night minimum and offers one-week rock-climbing trips, as well as cooking courses and hiking excursions.

Ostello Il Tiglio (☎ 0744 38 91 04; www.ostellionline.org; Via Abruzzo; dm €13.50, per person f €15.50; P) is perfectly situated to reach many different parts of the Valnerina, Norcia and La Cascata delle Marmore for river rafting and rock climbing. It's a small hostel with just 25 beds, but has self-catering facilities and serves breakfast for €1.50.

Le Due Querce (☎ 0744 781 441; www.bellaumbria.net/agriturismo-Leduequerce; Via del Piano 5; s/d/t €42/60/75, camping person/tent €5.50/1.50; P) is a full-service *agriturismo* (farm-stay), camp site and horse riding stables just next to the Nera river. They produce eggs, honey, olive oil, cheese and truffles and can set you up to do every outdoor sport in the Valnerina.

San Pietro in Valle

There is some serious history going on at **San Pietro in Valle** (St Peter Abbey) in the town of Valle, just 6km north of Ferentillo. Evidence suggests it was a pagan temple before two wandering Syrian hermits happened upon it in the 5th century. The interior of the abbey has pre-Giotto frescoes from the Roman and Lombard epochs.

The **Residenza d'Epoca Abbazia San Pietro in Valle** (☎ 0744 780 129; www.sanpietroinvalle.com; SS209 Valnerina, km 20; s/d incl breakfast €120/135; open Mar-Nov; P), also known as a hotel, is a special place, away from the crowds. Rooms have been upgraded quite a bit since their days as medieval nunnery cells. A few have stone fireplaces or breathtaking views over the cloisters and the surrounding valley; ask for any last-minute discounts. The hotel own-ers can give you trekking maps of the area and set you up with all sorts of adventurous activities. It serves an enormous breakfast of freshly baked bread and homemade preserves on the abbey's outdoor patio. There is a free sauna for guests.

The abbey's restaurant **Il Cantico** (☎ 0744 780 005; mid-Mar–Oct; set veg/local/seafood/meat menu €34/38/40/40, mains around €14) has a well-deserved reputation as one of the better restaurants in all of Umbria. It's tucked under the abbey in a centuries-old vault and is surprisingly affordable, considering the quality and surroundings. Seasonal dishes include crayfish ravioli with Trasimeno bean soup, pumpkin flan with *pecorino* sauce and truffles and pigeon breast in sagrantino wine sauce, all made with fresh, local ingredients.

NORCIA
pop 4872

This eminently walkable town is the commercial and tourist hub of the surrounding Valnerina. It's certainly a pleasant enough town, but rather inexplicably, Norcia receives an enormous number of tourists. They are mainly day-trippers so avoid visiting on a Sunday (and Saturday, if you can help it) and you'll be able to explore the town at a more leisurely pace.

Orientation

The main gate for Norcia is the Porta Ascolana, also known as the Porta Massari, which is where buses arrive. Most of Norcia is pedestrian-only, but there are many pay car parks around the city walls, including one near Porta Ascolana.

Information

Casa del Parco (☎ 0743 81 70 90; cpnorcia@yahoo.it; Via Solferino 22; 9.30am-12.30pm & 3-6pm Mon-Fri, 9.30am-12.30pm & 3.30-6.30pm Sat & Sun) Offers tourist information and plenty of Monti Sibillini information, including guided trips, public transportation to the area, detailed walking maps and local products. During the summer, ask about low-priced English-language excursions throughout Monti Sibillini.
Norcia (www.norcia.net) Private tourist information.
Post office (next to Porta Romana)

Sights & Activities

The **Basilica di San Benedetto** (Piazza San Benedetto) is an impressive show of architectural know-how. Named after St Benedict,

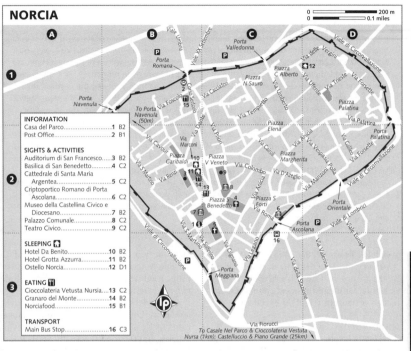

NORCIA

INFORMATION	
Casa del Parco......................**1** B2	
Post Office............................**2** B1	
SIGHTS & ACTIVITIES	
Auditorium di San Francesco.....**3** B2	
Basilica di San Benedetto...........**4** C2	
Cattedrale di Santa Maria	
Argentea.............................**5** C2	
Criptoportico Romano di Porta	
Ascolana.............................**6** C2	
Museo della Castellina Civico e	
Diocesano...........................**7** B2	
Palazzo Comunale.................**8** C2	
Teatro Civico.........................**9** C2	
SLEEPING	
Hotel Da Benito.....................**10** B2	
Hotel Grotta Azzurra...............**11** B2	
Ostello Norcia.......................**12** D1	
EATING	
Cioccolateria Vetusta Nursia....**13** C2	
Granaro del Monte.................**14** B2	
Norciafood..........................**15** B1	
TRANSPORT	
Main Bus Stop.......................**16** C3	

patron saint of Europe, who was born in Norcia, it was built in the shape of a Latin cross with a polygonal apse. The bell tower dates back to 1389 and its portico is Gothic. Frescoes inside the church date to the 16th century, including *Resurrezione di Lazzaro* (Resurrection of Lazarus) by Michelangelo Carducci (not *the* Michelangelo, but one from Norcia) and *San Benedetto e Totila* (St Benedict and Totila) by Filippo Napoletano, completed in 1621.

The **Museo della Castellina Civico e Diocesano** (La Castellina Diocesan Civic Museum; ☎ 0743 81 70 30; Piazza San Benedetto; adult/concession €4/2.50; �9 10am-1pm, 3-5pm winter, 4-6pm summer) contains a small collection of Roman artefacts and local artwork. It is open late some nights in August. The admission price also gains you entrance to the **Criptoportico Romano di Porta Ascolana** (Roman Crypt of Porta Ascolana), which is a remnant of a small Roman necropolis.

Next to the museum is the **Cattedrale di Santa Maria Argentea** built in 1560 but modified after several earthquakes in the 1700s. The weighty wooden doors are original. Also on Piazza San Benedetto is the **Palazzo Comunale**, parts of which date back to the 14th century. Its bell tower dates to 1713.

You can see a performance at either the **Teatro Civico** or the **Auditorium di San Francesco** (☎ 0743 816 44 88).

Festivals & Events

The last weekend in February and first weekend in March are dedicated to the **Mostra Mercata del Tartufo Nero** (Black Truffle Market) and display of black truffles, with lots of music and folkloric festivities.

Sleeping

BUDGET

Ostello Norcia (☎ 349 300 2091; www.montepatino.com in Italian; Via Ufente 1/b; dm incl breakfast €15) This new and modern hostel is in an old and beautiful building that is as clean as it is packed with information about hiking and wildlife in the area. Open year-round, it sleeps 52 in rooms of two to 10 people, all with private bathrooms. It can also arrange many local outdoor and sporting outings. Try calling ahead to book as it closes intermittently during the day. Bed sheets are included.

DETOUR: LA SCARZUOLA

Fans of architecture, theatre, philosophy, religion, history, horticulture or conspiracy theory should head out to the country to **La Scarzuola** (☎ 0763 83 74 63; http://grandigiardini.it/2005/eng/giardini /umbria/scarzuola.htm; Montegabbione; admission €10; ☉ year-round). Famous Milanese architect Tommaso Buzzi (1900–81) bought this property, the site of a 1218 Franciscan monastery, in 1956. Francis was said to have planted a bush here that developed into a spring, growing the *la scarza* (marsh plants) he and his followers used to build themselves shelter. Buzzi added onto the monastery – itself a treasure trove of relics – in a labyrinthine stone structure he called 'The Ideal City'. It symbolises the dance between the sacred and the profane, surrealism and simplicity, life without death. Ancient Greek architecture, monsters and a mysterious Egyptian third eye (his nephew, who runs La Scarzuola now, confirms Buzzi was a Mason) intertwine into the most curious of edifices. Starting in 2006, La Scarzuola will hold a series of evening concerts open to the public (check the website). To visit during the day, call ahead, as they require at least 10 visitors a day to open.

To arrive, head to the far central western part of Umbria, between Orvieto and Città della Pieve. On the road from Pornello to Montegiove, keep your eyes out for a tiny sign on the left for La Scarzuola. Head down a dirt road that's much longer than you'd expect and you'll see the expansive gates.

Hotel Da Benito (☎ 0743 81 66 70; guelsnc@virgilio .it; Via Marconi 5; s €27-40, d €30-75) Located perfectly in the centre of town, it's a friendly one-star hotel with eight modest rooms. The attached restaurant (right) is excellent.

MIDRANGE

Hotel Grotta Azzurra (☎ 0743 81 65 13; www.bianconi .com; Via Alfieri 12; s €37-88, d €44-125; 🖫) The Bianconi Ospitalità group also owns three McHotels outside the city centre (including a rare Umbrian chain hotel, a Best Western). This one has the most personality by far, and you can take advantage of all the activities the group offers: baby-sitting, evening events, gym classes and outdoor activities, like truffle hunts. The building dates back to the 16th century and has been an inn since 1850.

Casale Nel Parco (☎ /fax 0743 81 64 81; www.ca salenelparco.com; Loc. Fontevena 8; d incl breakfast €80, d incl breakfast & dinner €120, extra person €24; P 🖫) Only 1km from Norcia towards Castelluccio, this working organic *agriturismo* grows its own lentils, spelt and vegetables (which you can sample at dinner). Swim in the terracotta-tiled pool under the eye of snowcapped Monte Patino, ride the horses through the foothills of Monti Sibillini or ask your hosts to arrange any outdoor activity you can imagine. Fourteen rustic double rooms all come with private bathroom.

Eating

The town is full of norcinerias – butchers serving Norcia-produced dried meats. In fact, the word *norcineria* is now used to mean a butcher throughout all of Italy. Famous food items from the area also include *cinghiale*, lentils and *pecorino* cheese.

Granaro del Monte (☎ 0743 81 65 13; Via Alfieri 12; mains €7-24) One of the most famous restaurants in Umbria for visitors. It's filled with tourists, but the food is actually pretty good. With an enormous banquet-sized interior and pleasant outdoor dining area during summer, this is the place to try some of the trumpeted Norcineria specialities, including pork, sausage and *cinghiale*. Its signature dish is *Filetto Tartufato del Cavatore*, a veal dish sautéed in butter, black truffles and red wine – as rich as it is delicious.

Da Benito (☎ 0743 81 66 70; ristorante.benito@libero .it; Via Marconi 5; mains around €8; ☉ closed Mon) This simple but delicious restaurant within the hotel of the same name offers many dishes served with local meats and truffles.

Cioccolateria Vestusta Nursa (☎ 0743 81 73 70, shop 0743 82 80 70; Viale della Stazione 41/43) A kilometre outside Norcia on the road to Castelluccio you'll pass what looks like a boring warehouse. Step inside and you'll find the best prices on a huge selection of chocolate, wine, lentils and local (nonmeat) products. Best of all, there is always something available to taste. There's also a smaller and more expensive store in town at Via Mazzini 6.

Norciafood (☎ 0743 82 83 62; www.norciafood .com; Via dei Priori 38) This is one of the largest and most complete Norcineria and local produce shop. They ship to anywhere in the world and you can order many of their products on the website.

Getting There & Away

The closest train station is in Spoleto, so the best way to get to Norcia is by bus. The main bus stop is near Porta Ascolana. **SSIT** (www.spoletina.it; ☎ 0743 21 22 11) runs trips to Norcia from Spoleto (€4.40, one hour, five daily) and Perugia (€6.80, two hours, one daily at 2.10pm).

You can travel to Castelluccio only once a week, and Norcia is the town to do it from. The bus leaves Norcia at 6.25am and 1.30pm on Thursday only (€2.80, 40 minutes). It originates in Castelluccio, returning at 7.20am or 2.20pm, so if you just wanted to take a drive through the region, you could technically buy a return ticket and take it straight through.

MONTI SIBILLINI

Monti Sibillini is one of those places it would be great to discover by accident, but there's no way you're going to haul yourself up from Norcia (if you make it to Norcia at all) unless you hear how beautiful this area is.

This area is really, really, *really* beautiful. Really. Go. Even during summer, its jagged peaks keep a healthy dusting of snow. Mt Vettore – the highest peak in Monti Sibillini – stands at 2476m. In May and June, infinite expanses of wildflowers blanket the **Piano Grande**, the great plain surrounding Castelluccio. Wolves run free, icy streams flow and fairies dance. Well, so the story goes. During the Middle Ages, the Sibillini mountains were known throughout Europe as a place that held demons, necromancers and fairies. A woman named Sybil was said to live in a cave and tell fortunes. These days, the area is home to peregrine falcons, royal eagles and porcupines (brought over in the last few decades). Eighteen hundred botanical species have been counted just in this one area.

Before going off into the Monti Sibillini, you can pick up a host of maps at the **Casa del Parco** (p318) in Norcia, depending on how strenuous or leisurely you want to be. Any level of activity is possible here, spanning from day paths to week-long survival treks circling the mountain chain. The office has information on inexpensive guided trips in English, as well.

For information, try the official **Parco Nazionale dei Monti Sibillini** (www.sibillini.net).

Castelluccio

Visiting this little hamlet in the middle of the Piano Grande is like going back in time a few decades. There's only one hotel in town (and a bad *agriturismo*) and goats often meander the cobblestone streets. Stone buildings that were once houses and stores have fallen into artistically charming ruin.

Albergo Sibilla (☎ 0743 82 11 13; Via Piano Grande 2; s/d €36/60; P) has very basic rooms with rudimentary bathrooms. But they're clean and it's whisper quiet at night. The view is the reason you're staying here (that, and it's also the only hotel in town). There's a good restaurant downstairs, so consider the half-board option.

Pro Delta (☎ 0743 82 11 56, 339 5635456; www .prodelta.it; Via della Fate 3, Castelluccio) is one of the most well-respected hang-gliding institutions in Europe and has a solid reputation for safety. A basic five-day hang-gliding or paragliding course costs €400 and refresher courses start at €50. Those with a sense of adventure but neither time nor money can take a two-person paragliding and hang-gliding ride for €25 to €70. Check the requirements page of its website before arriving for a course.

Another school is **Fly Castelluccio** (☎ 0736 344 204; www.flycastelluccio.com; Via Copernica 12, Ascoli Piceno), in the neighbouring region of Le Marche. It offers weekend, five- or 10-day elementary courses in paragliding and hang-gliding, as well as paramotoring.

To hire bikes you could try the **Associazione Sportiva Piangrande** (☎ 0743 81 72 79; Castelluccio), which is open from Easter to October. They also arrange horseback riding. Before heading out, pick up the *Pedalling in the Park* brochure at any Casa del Parco office.

TOP FIVE WANDERABLE SMALL TOWNS IN UMBRIA

- Amelia (p331)
- Spello (p303)
- Bevagna (p307)
- Civita di Bagnoregio (p339)
- Castelluccio (above)

TODI

pop 17,000

As a traveller in Todi, you'll quickly adapt to its pace of life. Restaurants take longer, the entire town shuts down for a three-hour midday break and people walk a little slower. There are enough sights to keep a visitor occupied for a few days, but if you take it as leisurely as the locals, you might want to spend a week or two.

Todi has been thriving for millennia. Three thousand years ago, the Umbrii tribe developed the area, sharing it for a spell with the Etruscans. Rome conquered Todi around the 2nd century BC. Like rings in a tree, Todi's walls speak of its history; the interior city walls show Etruscan influences, a middle ring of walls known as *nicchioni* (little niches) is an enduring example of Roman know-how and the 'new' exterior walls date to the late Middle Ages. In Roman days, Todi was known as Tudernum and was home to temples of Jupiter and Minerva and Roman baths. The Dark Ages weren't terribly kind to Todi, but in 1213 the city cemented its reputation as an area powerhouse.

Information

EMERGENCY

Police station (☎ 075 895 62 43; Piazza Jacopone)

INTERNET ACCESS

Paolo M Fedrighini Centro Grafica Digitale
(☎ 075 894 2227; Piazza Umberto 1/17; per 15 min €1.55) Across from Tempio di San Fortunato.

INTERNET RESOURCES

Todi (www.todi.net)
Todi Comune (www.comune.todi.pg.it) The official governmental tourist site.

MEDICAL SERVICES

Hospital (☎ 075 8 85 81; Via Giacomo Matteotti)

POST

Post office (☎ 075 894 24 26; Piazza Garibaldi; ⏱ 8am-6.30pm Mon-Fri, Sat 8am-12.30pm)

TOURIST INFORMATION

Tourist office (☎ 075 894 33 95; www.todi.umbria2000.it; Piazza Garibaldi; ⏱ 9.30am-1pm & 3-6pm Mon-Sat, 10am-1pm Sun & holidays)

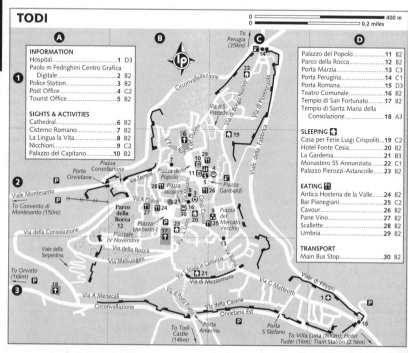

TODI

0 _____ 400 m
0 _____ 0.2 miles

INFORMATION
Hospital.....................................1 D3
Paolo m Fedrighini Centro Grafica
  Digitale..................................2 B2
Police Station...........................3 B2
Post Office................................4 C2
Tourist Office...........................5 B2

SIGHTS & ACTIVITIES
Cathedral..................................6 B2
Cisterno Romano.....................7 B2
La Lingua la Vita.....................8 B2
Nicchioni..................................9 C2
Palazzo del Capitano............10 B2

Palazzo del Popolo................11 B2
Parco della Rocca..................12 B2
Porta Marzia............................13 C3
Porta Perugina.......................14 C1
Porta Romana.........................15 D3
Teatro Comunale....................16 D3
Tempio di San Fortunato.......17 B2
Tempio di Santa Maria della
  Consolazione.......................18 A3

SLEEPING
Casa per Ferie Luigi Crispoliti...19 C2
Hotel Fonte Cesia...................20 B2
La Gardenia.............................21 B3
Monastero SS Annunziata......22 C1
Palazzo Pierozzi-Astancolle...23 B2

EATING
Antica Hosteria de la Valle......24 B2
Bar Pianegiani.........................25 C2
Cavour......................................26 B2
Pane Vino.................................27 B2
Scallette...................................28 B2
Umbria.....................................29 B2

TRANSPORT
Main Bus Stop..........................30 B2

To Perugia (35km)
Circonvallazione
Via di Borgo Nuovo
Via di Fiorenzuola
Via di S Prassede
Viale della Fabbrica
Via Paolo Rolli
V del Duomo
Piazza Consolazione
Porta Orvietana
Via Termoli
Piazza del Popolo
Piazza Jacopone
Piazza Garibaldi
Via A Ciuffelli
Parco della Rocca
Viale Montesanto
To Convento di Montesanto (150m)
Piazza Umberto I
Corso Cavour
Piazza del Mercato Vecchio
Via della Consolazione
Piazzale IV Novembre
Viale della Serpentina
Via della Rocca
Via Melsungen
To Orvieto (16km)
Via S Maria in Camucia
Via di Mezzomuro
Via A Menecali
Circonvallazione
Via di Porta Fratta
Via G Matteotti
Viale di Filippo
Via della Caselle
Orvietana Est
Porta Amerina
Porta S Stefano
To Todi Castle (14km)
To Villa Luisa (800m); Hotel Tuder (1km); Train Station (2.5km)

Sights & Activities

Todi's town centre, the Piazza del Popolo, is one of the most renowned squares in all of Italy. Its lugubrious medieval cathedral and buildings cradle the interior piazza, enclosed with four gates during the medieval years but now filled with bustling shops, cappuccino-sipping residents and travellers gazing in wonderment at living history.

Starting with the southeastern corner of the square, you'll find Todi's Gothic **Palazzo del Popolo** (Palace of the People), a 13th-century masterpiece built to honour Todi's standing as an autonomous free *comune*. The seemingly adjoining **Palazzo del Capitano** was built 30 years later, but architecturally tied in with a stone staircase and similar Gothic features. Nowadays, the two buildings are linked by the **Museo Pinacoteca di Todi** (City Museum and Art Gallery; ☎ 075 894 41 48; Piazza del Popolo; adult/concession €3.50/2-2.50; 10.30am-1pm & 2.30-6.30pm Tue-Sun Apr-Oct, to 5pm Tue-Sun Nov-Mar), an expansive museum housing exhibits on archaeology, numismatics (coins), weaving and ceramics, in addition to the impressive frescoed rooms of the pinacoteca. Artwork includes paintings by Giovanni di Pietro (Lo Spagna) and a copy of an Etruscan statue of the Roman god Mars (the original bronze is at the Vatican).

At the north end of the square is the **cathedral** (☎ 075 894 47 31; Piazza del Popolo; 8.30am-12.30pm & 2.30-6.30pm), a statuesque medieval building with a magnificent rose window and intricate doorway. The 8th-century crypt is worth a visit for the fine example of inlaid wooden stalls in the chancel.

Near the piazza is the **Cisterno Romano** (Roman Cistern; ☎ 075 894 41 48; adult/concession €2/1.50; 10.30am-1pm & 2.30-6.30pm Tue-Sun Apr-Oct, 10.30am-1pm & 2.30-5pm Tue-Sun Nov-Mar, Sat-Sun and holidays), a thorough example of Roman handiwork good enough to be used by residents for a water source until 1926.

Wander through Todi's medieval labyrinth and pop into some of the other churches, including the lofty **Tempio di San Fortunato** (Piazza Umberto 1; admission free; 10.30am-1pm & 3-7pm Apr-Oct, 10.30am-1pm & 2.30-5pm Nov-Mar, closed Mon morning), with frescoes by Masolino da Panicale and the tomb of San Jacopone, Todi's beloved patron saint. Inside, make it a point to climb the **Campanile di San Fortunato** (adult/concession €1.50/1; same as above, closed Mon), where you can gaze across the hills and castles surrounding Todi. Just across from the

> **COMBINED TICKET**
>
> If you'll be spending a day or two in Todi, it's a good idea to buy a **biglietto cumulativo** (adult/concession/child €6/5/4), which will allow you to gain entry into the Museo Pinacoteca, Cisterno Romano and the Tempio di San Fortunato. The ticket can be purchased at any of the museums or at the tourist office.

temple you'll find the **Teatro Comunale**, the municipal theatre inaugurated with a Verdi opera in 1876, that is still used today (check with the tourist office for a schedule).

The late-Renaissance **Tempio di Santa Maria della Consolazione**, considered one of the top architectural masterpieces of the 16th century, is just outside the city walls. Possibly designed by Donato Bramante in 1508 but not completed until 99 years later, the construction was a veritable modern feat in early Renaissance Italy and its Greek cross design was considered geometrically perfect. Visitors can admire its soaring cupola-topped dome from most of the Tiber valley.

The **Parco della Rocca** is at the highest point in Todi. It's got magnificent views of the surrounding countryside and contains the ruins of the old *rocca* (fort). From here you can see part of the old Roman wall, called the **Nicchioni**. Todi features a staggering amount of old city walls, some of them medieval, some Roman and some pre-Roman. The gates are a magnificent example of ancient architecture, especially the **Porta Romana** (Roman Gate), **Porta Perugina** (Perugia Gate) and **Porta Marzia** (Gate of Mars).

Just outside the main town walls you can see the **Convento di Montesanto**, now a working convent but built as a fortress in 1325 to guard against Orvieto.

Courses

Sign up for some courses at **La Lingua La Vita** (☎ 075 894 83 64; www.lalingualavita.com; Via Mazzini 18). While many students and younger folk head to Perugia to learn and party, the more mature student (meaning 25 plus) might enjoy studying Italian in Todi. You can sign up for group or individual lessons, but both options get to participate in a handful of activities including cooking classes, Italian films and field trips in and around Todi.

SOUTHERN UMBRIA

Costs start at €330 per week for accommodation and classes.

Festivals & Events

The **Todi Festival** (www.todiartefestival.it), held for 10 days each July/August, is a mixture of classical and jazz concerts, theatre, ballet and cinema.

Sleeping

BUDGET

Monastero SS Annunziata (☎ 075 894 2268; www.monasterosmr.com; Via San Biagio 2; s/d/tr incl breakfast €35/70/105) Get away to this tranquil retreat within the city walls. Set around a lovely garden, all rooms come with private bath, bed linens and some with furnishings from the 15th century. Try to catch a meal with your hosts, nuns from the Mary's Servant of Repair order.

Hotel Tuder (☎ 075 894 21 84; www.hoteltuder.it; Via Maesta dei Lombardi 13; s standard/comfort €45/60, d standard/comfort €75/97; P ❄) This three-star hotel is about a kilometre outside the city centre on the bus route from the train station. The 40 rooms are divided into 'standard' and 'comfort', and you'll get posher furniture, better showers, more space and higher prices in the comfort category. All rooms come with TVs and direct-dial phones.

Casa per Ferie Luigi Crispolti (☎ 075 894 53 37; www.crispoltiferie.it; Via Cesia 96; s/d incl breakfast €33/52) This former monastery-cum-orphanage is the least expensive place to stay in Todi. It's institutional and depressing, but if you don't mind feeling a little bit like Little Orphan Annie, the views are superb and it's centrally located.

MIDRANGE

Palazzo Pierozzi-Astancolle (☎ 320 273 1035; Piazza Umberto 1; www.palatodi.it; 2-8 guests daily €90-200, weekly €450-1000) Years of restoration went into creating this masterpiece of 16th-century Italian history and 21st-century Scandinavian minimalist design. The English-speaking Danish/Italian couple who oversee the apartments are charming and erudite hosts, armed with a wealth of knowledge of the area and Italy. Five apartments can be rented separately or together, but each is outfitted with a modern kitchen and various exquisite touches: balconies, fireplaces, antique tapestries, frescoes, plush living rooms and washing machines.

La Gardenia (☎ 347 611 52 20; www.lagardeniatodi.com; Via Santa Maria 45; weekly €450-500, monthly €800) A fruit basket greets you at your new home in Todi. This central apartment has everything to make you feel like Todi is home, including two double beds, one single bed, a washing machine, dining room, TV, stereo and iron. The view of Santa Maria dell Consolazione, the hills and the campanile will bring anyone to tears. Trade English and Italian lessons with your sweetheart of a host, Carlo.

Hotel Fonte Cesia (☎ 075 894 37 37; www.fontecesia.it; Via Lorenzo Leoni 3; s/d/ste incl breakfast €112/157/200; P ❄ 💻) The top hotel in Todi, the exquisitely decorated rooms have all the amenities: satellite TV, hairdryer, minibar etc. You can upgrade to a junior suite, some of which have private balconies and claw-foot bathtubs.

Villa Luisa (☎ 075 894 85 71; www.villaluisa.it; Via A Cortesi 147; s/d incl breakfast €80/120; P ❄ 🛗) This place is outside the city walls on the bus line coming in from the train station. It's set on parklike grounds with a pool, lift and restaurant.

TOP END

Todi Castle (☎ 0744 95 20 04; www.exclusive-umbria.com; Vocabolo Capecchio, Morre; weekly villa/castle for up to 10 people from €1500/4500; P 🛗) Here's your chance to live in an honest-to-goodness castle for a week, or an equally perfect (and much more affordable) private villa, set in the hills south of Todi. Stroll to the deer enclosure, swim in your private pool, watch as the vineyard soaks up the Umbrian sun ripening the grapes that will become the delicious house wine you'll be sipping all week. The best part about staying here is the incredible attention to detail the staff provides – help setting up visiting itineraries, freshly squeezed orange juice and cakes for breakfast, even a fabulous driver for hire.

Eating

Antica Hosteria de la Valle (☎ 075 894 48 48; Via Ciuffelli 17; mains around €11; ☯ closed Mon) Most of the time you'll be dining here with the locals or chatting with the family who owns the place. Pasta is homemade and delicious, but the traditional *farro* soup (€7) should not be missed.

Pane e Vino (☎ 075 894 54 48; Via Ciuffelli 33; ☯ closed Wed) Now you're definitely in Italy. Dine on dishes such as risotto with yellow pumpkin (€8) or just nibble on the antipasto plate (€11) while tasting from the extensive wine list that includes wines from all over Italy. Relax on the outdoor patio or at candlelit tables under the curved brick ceiling in this narrow, atmospheric *enoteca*.

Bar Pianegiani (☎ 075 894 2376; Corso Cavour 40; ☺ 6am-midnight) You'd never know it, but this nondescript village bar serves up some of the most incredible *gelato* in Umbria for practically nothing. Try the *spagnola* (black cherry) or the house speciality, *crema e pignoli* (cream with pine nuts).

Umbria (☎ 075 894 27 37; Via Santa Bonaventura 13; mains €9-23; ☺ closed Tue) What's more enjoyable, the food or the outdoor patio with a view back in time? Look in the display case to salivate over which goodies you'd like for your meal; perhaps some local meats or salami? Try the *palombaccio* (€13), a type of pigeon, or a risotto dish.

Scallette (☎ 075 894 44 22; Via delle Scalette 1; mains €5-11; ☺ closed Mon) Wander off the main road down this ancient stairway for a reasonably priced feast in a hobbitlike abode. This ancient farmhouse feels like it's practically in Middle Earth and, with its stone walls, roasted meat dishes and decadent desserts, is a precious spot for a minimedieval banquet.

Cavour (☎ 075 894 37 30; Corso Cavour 21; pizzas from €4.50; ☺ until 2am, closed Wed) A casual place populated with locals, this is where to come

---

BE THANKFUL FOR UMBRIAN OLIVE OIL

Most visitors to Umbria notice the bread right away. Many words have been used to describe it: namely 'bland', 'hard' and 'dry'. But Umbrians are intensely proud of their bread, partly due to the historical significance. In 1540, Pope Paul III levied a salt tax on Umbria. The hardy and self-reliant peasants refused to pay, and began baking bread without salt. They soon found out unsalted bread didn't spoil as easily, and spiffed up quickly when moistened with olive oil, topped with tomatoes, or added to soup or salad. Be sure to try the delicious bruschetta (toasted bread topped with olive oil, tomatoes, truffles, artichokes etc) or *panzanella* (bread salad), but try keep your appetite for your meal, not the bread bowl.

---

to get a light meal or pizza. Serves several different traditional soups (€4 to €5), a nice addition on a rainy day.

Getting There & Away

By road, Todi is easily reached on the SS3bis-E45, which runs between Perugia and Terni, or take the Orvieto turnoff from A1 Milano-Roma-Napoli.

APM (☎ 075 506 781) bus E12 leaves Perugia's Piazza Partigiani (€4.80, one hour) every hour or so, but only four reach Piazza Jacopone in the city centre. The rest stop at Piazza Consolazione, where it's possible to take city bus A or B or walk uphill 2km. Heading back to Perugia from Piazza Jacopone, buses depart at 6.35am, 12.42pm, 1.30pm, 3.38pm and 4.58pm (except Sunday). There is one daily service to Spoleto (€5.20, 1½ hours) at 6.50am. Pick up tickets in the fruit store on the piazza.

From Stazione Sant'Anna you can take the **Ferrovia Centrale Umbra** (☎ 075 575 401) from Perugia (€2.55, 50 minutes, 18 daily). Although the train station is 3km away, city bus C runs there (€0.80, 20 minutes) once an hour, or every other hour on Sundays.

MONTE CASTELLO DI VIBIO
pop 1700

The real draw in this tiny speck of a town about 20km from Todi is its even tinier speck of a theatre. Throw in sleeping (or dining) in a castle, gorgeous views and a working *agriturismo* and you're set for one or two days.

Monte Castello di Vibio feels like it's in the middle of nowhere, but it's just a few kilometres from the SS3Bis-E45 that links Perugia and Terni (just north of Todi). Tourist information can be found at the **Associazione Culturale** (Via Roma 1), which faces the theatre. The **post office** next door sells stamps with the image of the theatre.

In keeping with the proportions of the tiny town, **Teatro della Concordia**, (Teatro Piccolo; ☎ 075 878 07 37, 328 918 88 92; www.teatropiccolo.it; admission free; ☺ 10am-12.30pm & 3.30-6.30pm Oct-Apr, 10am-12.30pm & 4.30-7.30pm Jun-Sep) is billed as the smallest the-atre in the world. It seats 99 people, 32 on the main floor and 67 in the stalls. The theatre was built in 1808, when nine Monte Castello di Vibio families decided that their town needed a theatre. In 1850, residents added frescoes to the ceiling and stalls. Along

---

AUTHOR'S CHOICE

Agriturismo/Ristorante Fattoria di Vibio (☎ 075 874 96 07; www.fattoriadivibio.com; Località Buchella 9, Doglio; daily €80-105, weekly €455-735, 3-bdrm cottages per week €800-1900; mains around €11; P ✖ ❀) Four kilometres outside of Monte Castello di Vibio (towards Doglio) is an oasis of gastronomy, nature and tranquillity. It's worth every minute to head here from Todi or Orvieto, whether it be to stay a few days or just dine. The restaurant serves every local delicacy you could imagine – *cinghiale* with polenta, *carciofi alla romana* (artichokes), ravioli with porcini mushrooms – but it's the *strangozzi* pasta with truffles and cheese we still daydream about. They make their own olive oil, wine and (salted!) bread. The grounds offer a perfect after-lunch stroll, which you might need if you've tasted from their 17-page wine list. If you do stay the night, take advantage of the horseback riding, spa or dozens of nearby hiking trails. Only weekly rentals are available in August.

---

with red velvet seats, the theatre gained a sophisticated look to rival any larger, grander theatre. Gina Lollabrigida acted in her very first play here. In 1951 the theatre was almost shut down for lack of revenue, but the community voted to pay extra taxes to keep the theatre going. In 1993 the theatre teamed up with the theatre in Parma – one of the world's largest – to put on a series of events. Performances are staged for much of the year, especially on Saturday nights. The theatre is also open by appointment and an English audioguide is available.

A brilliant marketing campaign (and honestly, a really fun way to spend a day and a half) is to take advantage of the **Weekend in Umbria** (☎ 075 89 42 161; weekend@teatropiccolo .it) package (for one/two people €90/150). Available only on Saturday night, you arrive in Monte Castello di Vibio and are provided with accommodation at Hotel il Castello or one of the local *agriturismi*, as well as dinner, a show at the theatre and breakfast on Sunday morning. You can even arrange to be picked up.

Hotel Il Castello (☎ 075 878 06 60; www.hotel ilcastello.it; Piazza Marconi 5, Monte Castello di Vibio; s/ d €80/120; P ✖ ❀) A fascinating place to spend the night or, especially, to eat in the restaurant with suits of armour as your dining companions. The hotel was undergoing a renovation at the time of our visit; hope for the best, as previously rooms felt historical, but not necessarily in a good way. Ask for a discount during low occupancy.

Take the SS3bis-E45 from Todi to Perugia. Exit at the Monte Vibio sign and continue for about 4km (at the roundabout that doesn't tell you where to turn, veer left). It's on the S397 between Todi and Marsciano.

TERNI

pop 104,938

There are only two reasons to come to Terni – passing through on your way to the Valnerina, Norcia and Monti Sibillini or because you're an art historian. Terni is a major industrial city, virtually obliterated in WWII bombing raids and subsequently rebuilt. Known as 'the steel city' or 'the Manchester of Italy', its modern factories used to attract tourists in the early 1900s.

Terni's **tourist office** (☎ 0744 42 30 47; info@iat .terni.it; Viale Cesare Battisti 7; ☉ 9am-1pm & 3-6pm Mon, Tue, Thu, Fri) is south of the main train station and just west of Piazza C Tacito, near Largo Don Minzoni.

Art-lovers should stop by the **pinacoteca** (☎ 0744 459421; Via del Teatro Romano 13; adult/concession €4/2.50; ☉ 10am-1pm & 3-7pm) to have a look at one of the more important remaining works by Piero Matteo d'Amelia, *Pala dei Francescani*. He was the most important artist of his time but has been surpassed in history as his most important work, a certain Vatican chapel's ceiling, was painted over by some newcomer named Michelangelo.

One of Terni's charms is its devotion to that famous Umbrian pastime, the festival. Its most famous hometown hero is St Valentine, who was the bishop of Terni until Placidius Furius, on orders of Emperor Aurelius, got really angry and had St Valentine executed in 269. Well after Valentine's martyrdom, a legend was created. It was said that he would often give gifts of flowers from his own garden to his young visitors. Two of these visitors fell in love and married, forever linking St Valentine with love. Now, a huge feast engulfs the city on 14

February, but the entire month is dedicated to love and romance.

From Terni, you can catch an ATC Terni bus to Perugia (€6.40, 1¼ hours, three daily) and Narni (€1.60, 30 minutes, two daily). If you arrive in Terni by train and need to get to the bus station on Piazza Europa, or vice versa, catch local bus Nos 1 or 2.

CARSULAE

The most complete example of a Roman city in Umbria, **Carsulae** (☎ 0744 33 41 33; adult/concession €4/3; ☼ 10am-1pm & 4-7pm Tue-Fri, 10am-7pm Sat, Sun & public holidays), isn't quite the size of Pompeii or Rome, but it does offer some spectacular Roman history in a beautiful setting. During the reign of Augustus in the 3rd century BC, Romans took to the task of building the strategically important Via Flaminia. Carsulae was one of the many outposts systematically built along this Roman version of a highway. It was on the part of the road that joined Narnia to Vicus Martis Tudertium (Narni to the Todi region), so when reconstruction started on a more easterly route, Carsulae fell into decline. Then, barbarians from the north began using this part of the road to head towards Rome, and Carsulae had no chance.

To arrive here, take the road to Perugia from Terni. Look for the sign indicating SS75/San Gemini and you'll then see signs for Carsulae. The closest place to spend the night around Carsulae is in San Gemini.

NARNI

pop 20,054

While Umbria is called the 'Green Heart of Italy', the town of Narni could be called the true heart of Italy. It's the closest town to the geographic centre of the Italian peninsula, a symbolic position not lost on its inhabitants. Umbria is one of the more rural provinces in Italy, and Narni exudes the friendly, laid-back charm that's so pervasive throughout the region. You're not just imagining it: people here *are* friendlier.

As one Narni local puts it, 'We have the bread, but we don't have the teeth'. He's referring to the amazing array of tourist sites – a 13th-century hill-top *rocca* guarding mightily over the town; Narni Sotterranea, a subterranean world of caves that used to house Inquisition prisoners; churches and palaces galore – but practically no tourist structure. The *rocca* is difficult to get to and Narni Sotterranea is only open on public holidays, Sundays and a few Saturdays (the entrance is through a preschool playground). However, the tourist board just published its first Narni map, available in English, which will help ensure you don't miss its bread for lack of teeth.

Narni became a Roman stronghold in the 2nd century BC as the Via Flaminia ran from Rome to Rimini through Narni. It developed into a *comune* as early as the 11th century but was partially destroyed in the 14th century by northern mercenaries on their way home from sacking Rome. After rebuilding, Narni regained its status as a centre for art and goldsmithing, and held great artistic prominence throughout the Renaissance.

Orientation

Narni has two historic centres: the quieter Piazza dei Priori, which houses the tourist office and Palazzo del Podestà; and Piazza Cavour, home to the cathedral. Just outside the main town gate is Piazza Garibaldi, along the back of the cathedral, where you'll find restaurants, cafes and the bus stop. Everything is a short walk from these two, except for the *rocca*, which is either a drive or a pretty decent hike up the hill.

Information

EMERGENCY

Police station (☎ 0744 71 52 34; Via Portecchia)

INTERNET RESOURCES

Narnia (www.narnia.it)
Narnia Comune (www.comune.narni.tr.it) The government website for Narni.

CREEPY UMBRIA

Visit one of these places for a hair-raising experience:

▪ See medieval corpses frozen in time at the **Museo delle Mummie** (p317) in Ferentillo

▪ Get a history lesson on the Battle of Trasimeno and how to beat the Romans in **Tuoro** (p291)

▪ Visit **Narni Sotterranea** (p328) to see an Inquisition prisoner's desperate graffiti

---

SOUTHERN UMBRIA

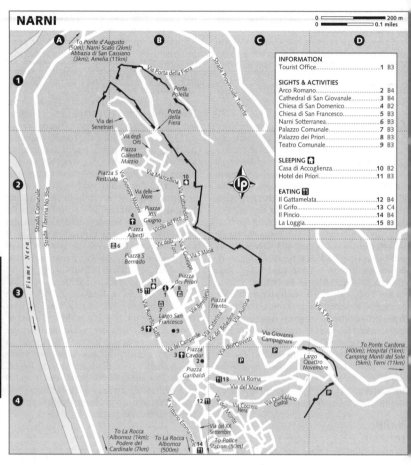

NARNI

0 ————— 200 m
0 ————— 0.1 miles

INFORMATION	
Tourist Office................................1	B3

SIGHTS & ACTIVITIES	
Arco Romano.................................2	B4
Cathedral di San Giovanale.........3	B4
Chiesa di San Domenico..............4	B2
Chiesa di San Francesco..............5	B3
Narni Sotterranea........................6	B3
Palazzo Comunale........................7	B3
Palazzo dei Priori.........................8	B3
Teatro Comunale.........................9	B3

SLEEPING	
Casa di Accoglienza...................10	B2
Hotel dei Priori..........................11	B3

EATING	
Il Gattamelata............................12	B4
Il Grifo.......................................13	C4
Il Pincio.....................................14	B4
La Loggia...................................15	B3

MEDICAL SERVICES
Hospital (☎ 0744 7401; Via Cappuccini Nuova)

TOURIST INFORMATION
Tourist office (☎ 0744 71 53 62 or 0744 74 72 47; www.comune.narni.tr.it; Piazza dei Priori 3; ⏱ 9.30am-12.30pm daily, 4.30-6.30pm Mon-Tue, 3.30-6.30pm Wed-Sun)

Sights
Plan your visit to Narni around the concise opening hours of the tortuously fascinating **Narni Sotterranea** (Narni Subterranean; ☎ 0744 72 22 92; www.narnisotterranea.it; Via S Bernardo 12; admission €5; ⏱ tours 10.15am, 12.15pm, 3.15pm, 4.15pm Sun & public holidays, 3pm & 6pm Sat Apr-Oct). The 1½ hour tour (in Italian, English or both) guides you

through millennia of history, starting with a look into Roman plumbing and an underground Romanesque frescoed church and moving on to an Inquisition prisoner's cell from 1759 and the torture devices with which he might have been familiar. Skulls and bones abound throughout the tour. The subterranean was rediscovered in 1979 on the advice of an older town resident whose grandfather had heard the stories passed down for centuries. The current archaeological director rents a tranquil apartment outside of town (Podere del Cardinale, p330) and guests or visitors might be able to lend a hand during the week for the ongoing archaeological excavations. In addition to the above hours the subterranean is also open weekdays during the Corso all'Anello and Ferragosto, or be appointment during the week.

Above the subterranean is the **Chiesa di San Domenico** where the Dominican inquisitors preached when they weren't inquisiting. There was a pathway recently discovered that led the monks from the church into the subterranean. Search for the hidden symbols – a Templar 'rosy' cross (a cross hidden in a four-sided rose) and the sun and the moon, the Lombard symbols for the beginning and the end.

The fortress **La Rocca Albornoz** (admission €3; 11am-7pm summer, 10am-5pm winter, weekends & holidays; P) was built by Cardinal Albornoz, who was the heavy charged with switching Narni from a free *comune* to a papal-controlled state in the 13th century. The pope needed an imposing bastion to guard against the pro-Emperor Ghibellines and to scare the people into submission. Some original frescoes still exist, but its use as a prison for hundreds of years took its toll on the building. The climb up the tower stairs is treacherous but worth it for the 360-degree perfect Umbrian view at the top. La Rocca now opens its doors to choirs and orchestras and has a collection of photos from its medieval festival. Also housed is a fascinating motorcycle collection, including a 1906 foldable motorcycle, a rare surviving joint venture from Aermacchi (a popular Italian manufacturer) and Harley Davidson. Imagine the bomber helmet you might have worn sitting in the 1938 BMW sidecar. Contact the tourist office for information.

The Romans built the **Ponte d'Augusto**, a bridge on the ancient route of the Via Flaminia, in 27 BC. The bridge now has only one remaining arch, but it's not everyday you see a giant Roman arch.

Around what was the Roman forum is now the municipal and social centre of Narni. The **Palazzo dei Priori** (10am-1pm & 3-7pm) construction is attributed to Gattapone in 1275. Look up at the balcony called the *loggia colpire*, from where a town crier used to yell the equivalent of the evening news. Across the street from the Palazzo dei Priori is the **Palazzo Comunale** (0744 74 72 69; Piazza dei Priori 1; admission free; 10am-1pm Mon, 10am-1pm & 4-7pm Tue-Sun summer, to 6pm Tue-Sun winter), a 13th-century building formed by the union of three towers. If no-one is inside, you can take a peek in the council chamber to see the *Pala*

di Ghirlandaio, the artist's representation of the coronation of the Virgin Mary. The 12th-century **Cathedral di San Giovenale** (Piazza Cavour; 7.30am-12.30pm & 3.30-7pm) is dedicated to Narni's patron saint, San Giovenale, who became the first bishop of Narni in AD 386.

The **Teatro Comunale** (0744 72 63 62; Via Garibaldi; admission free; 4-7pm Sat, 9am-1pm & 4-7pm Sun) is a glorious 19th-century theatre that can accommodate up to 500 patrons. You can visit it for free on the weekends, and it's also a lovely place to see a performance. Make sure you make an appointment first.

The simple **Chiesa di San Francesco** (Via Aurelio Saffi) was built several years after the death of St Francis on the same site of a place where the Assisian himself had briefly lived.

The geographic centre of Italy is just outside Narni at the **Ponte Cardona** (0744 72 22 92), a Roman bridge that is the only remnant of an old Roman aqueduct dating to the 1st century AD. It's off the Via Flaminia heading south towards Terni. Call for information or to book a guided tour.

Abbazia di San Cassiano is an imposing abbey dating back to the 11th century, built in the plan of a Greek cross. It's thought to have been the first Benedictine abbey constructed in the area.

Festivals & Events
Corso all'Anello (The Race for the Ring) The town's major festival of the year is held from the end of April to the beginning of May. The town goes all out for this festival. As a rare foreign tourist, you will be welcomed with open arms. There are all sorts of feasts, competitions and performances by the Anerio Choir, an ancient choir formed by Palestrina, who was one of the founders of baroque music. The race itself is held on the second Sunday of May.
International Folklore Festival Held from mid-July to mid-August and sees folklorist groups from all over the world perform nightly on a stage in the Piazza dei Priori.

Sleeping
Narni has very few hotels within the historic centre.

BUDGET
Casa di Accoglienza (Suore di Santa Anna; 0744 71 52 17; Via Gattemelata 74; s/d €19/38) This quiet and tranquil religious house is near the town centre along the ancient walls. It's got an internal garden used for reflection and meditation, as well as a view of the Nera river. It's in an austere 14th-century building.

Camping Monti del Sole (☎ 0744 79 63 36; montisole@libero.it; Str di Borgaria 22, SS Flaminia, Km 80.800; per car/tent/person €1.50/5.70/6.70; P ⊠) This camp site, 5km south of Narni, has a pool, restaurant and tennis courts. It's surrounded by forested grounds and is open from the beginning of April until the end of September.

Podere del Cardinale (☎ 0744 717 031; www .poderedelcardinale.com; Strada di Massa Bassa 7, Taizzano; per person €20-30) Archaeology buffs will most definitely enjoy staying at this absolutely charming country house. The owner is also the director of the Narni Sotterranea and during the week he often does digs there, and gladly invites guests along. The house itself is down a dirt road surrounded by olive trees. There's a gigantic wood-burning adobe oven that takes up half the kitchen. The furniture is what country chic strives to be: ancient gnarled farmhouse tables, huge wooden beds and a homey fireplace that makes this more of a retreat than a hotel. With a kitchenette, solar-powered shower and sofa bed the rooms can accommodate up to four comfortably. Roberto can also give you a tour of a nearby Romanesque church with Templar inscriptions and point you to horse riding facilities.

MIDRANGE

Hotel dei Priori (☎ 0744 72 68 43; www.loggiadeipriori .it; Vicolo del Comune 4; s/d €50/70; ⊠) In the centre of town is this three-star hotel, located in a 15th-century building with modern amenities – great showers, hairdryers, TV, minibar. It's got 17 beautiful rooms with incredible views, and some with balconies. The rooms become less charmingly historic the higher the floor, except for the penthouse *camere di torre* (tower room). Inside its walls is the charming restaurant, La Loggia.

Eating

Il Pincio (☎ 0744 72 22 41; Via XX Settembre 117; mains around €9; ⚇ closed Wed) Located under a beautiful old nobleman's palace is this restaurant that you might simply walk by if you didn't know part of it was literally inside a grotto. Ask chef Leonardo Passone to suggest a bottle of wine, and you'll soon be circling down a staircase into his famed wine cellar. Try the pasta with zucchini flowers.

Il Gattemelata (☎ 0744 71 72 45; Via Pozzo della Comunità 4; mains €8-14; ⚇ closed Mon) Named after the *capitani di ventura* Il Gattemelata, this simply decorated restaurant serves wonderful meals that are a little more inventive than the typical Umbrian cuisine. You can try dishes such as ravioli with smoked

---

LE STRADE DEL VINO

The Etruscans produced wine in the district, the Romans continued the tradition and today several regions around Umbria embrace their viticulture heritage.

However, although Umbria is a major wine-growing region, it is just starting to adopt the concept of wine tasting. Most visitors have simply tasted their wines one bottle or glass at a time with lunch and dinner, or in town at an *enoteca* (wine bar) or a shop that offers *degustazione* (tasting). But Umbria is starting to offer the driving wine routes many seasoned wine lovers would recognize.

If you do want to venture out to the countryside, pick up a brochure of one of these guided itineraries at any nearby tourist office. Umbria is divided into four wine routes known as the *strada dei vini* (wine trails, see p68). Each route is based not only on wine, but the history, culture, art, tradition and archaeology of a region. The routes are quite lengthy and seem to cover at least 80% of Umbrian secondary roads, but you can do just a section of the route. Check the website www.umbriadoc.com (in Italian) for more information on the routes and links to the wineries themselves.

Strada dei Vini del Cantico The most sprawling route, it crisscrosses a triangle between Perugia, Todi and Spello, stopping in Torgiano, Assisi and Marsciano.

Strada dei Vini Etrusco Romana Connects Orvieto with Amelia and many points in between.

Strada del Sagrantino The area surrounding Bevagna and Montefalco, the fastest growing wine area in the region.

Strada del Vino Colli del Trasimeno Starts at Corciano near Perugia and circles through the *colli* (hills) around the lake.

cheese in herb-infused butter (€8). However, the dish you can't leave without trying is the chocolate mousse pyramid dessert, flambéed with essence of vermouth. You can order from two tasting menus that feature foods served during medieval times.

La Loggia (☎ 0744 72 68 43; Vicolo del Comune 4) Owned by the Hotel dei Priori, this restaurant serves excellent dishes at even better prices. Bright yellow walls and small tables set in front of an open fireplace make for an intimate dinner. The menu blends typical Umbrian dishes with intricate flavours, such as lamb with artichokes (€11) or pork with juniper berries (€8).

Il Grifo (☎ 0744 72 66 25; Via Roma 3) Specialising in Umbrian and international cuisine, this large restaurant's view is as enticing as the food.

Getting There & Away

ATC Terni (☎ 0744 71 52 07) buses leave from Piazza Garibaldi, just outside the main gate. From Narni, you can travel by bus to Amelia (€1.60, 30 minutes, nine daily from Piazza Garibaldi, plus another 10 from Narni Scalo), Terni (€1.60, 30 minutes, almost hourly with a gap between 10.30am and 1pm) and Orvieto (€4.80, one hour and 20 minutes, five daily). To get to Perugia, switch in Terni (€6.40, 1½ hours).

To get to Narni from the A1 autostrada, take the Magliano Sabina exit if you're coming from the south. Take the Orte exit if you're coming from the north.

AMELIA

pop 11,090

Few other words describe this town as aptly as 'sweet'. Perhaps 'quaint', 'delightful' or 'adorable' come close. It's a tiny little village, unassuming and unspoiled, with one of the oldest histories in Umbria. The legend goes that Amelia was founded by a mythological king named Ameroe in the 12th century BC. Latin texts mention the existence of Amelia as a settlement as early as the 11th century BC (four centuries before Rome was founded). A good chunk of the original walls (believed to have been constructed sometime around the 6th century BC) can still be seen by the theatre, but much of the wall is of newer construction. You know, the 4th century BC.

For even more sweetness, take your sweetie down 'Girl-Kissing Alley' or try the town's delicacy, *fichi girotti*, an Amerino snack of fig and chocolate. Locals vie with Narnians for the friendliest people in Italy and, knowing Umbria, they just might invent a festival testing that theory one day.

Orientation

The town is still a walled city, with several *porte* (doors) leading in and out. The main entrance is the Porta Romana. Just outside of it is the tourist office, parking facilities, the bus station and several cafés (some selling *fichi girotti*). Signs posted in front of monuments are all listed in Italian and English, so it's easy to get around.

Information

For information on the town, try www
.amelia.it.

Pro Loco Città di Amelia (☎ 0744 98 25 59; web.tis cali.it/proloco.amelia; Piazza Augusto Vera 8; ✆ 9.30am-12pm & 4-7pm Mon-Fri, 9.30am-12pm Sat)
Tourist office (☎ 0744 98 14 53; info@iat.amelia. tr.it; Porta Romana; ✆ 3.30-6.30pm Mon, 9am-12.30pm Tue-Sat 15 Sep-30 May, 9.30am-12.30pm & 3.30-6.30pm rest of year) Bypass this horrendously unhelpful office for the Pro Loco.

Sights

Amelia is almost entirely surrounded by pre-Roman polygonal walls, possibly dating back to the 6th century BC. The huge stones have held together without mortar for over 2500 years. Piazza Matteotti was the site of an ancient Roman forum.

Don't miss the fascinating **Museo Archeologico di Amelia** (Archaeological Museum & Art Museum; ☎ 0744 97 81 20; www.sistemamuseo.it in Italian; Piazza Augusto Vera 10; adult/concession €5/4; ✆ 10.30am-1pm & 3.30-6pm Fri-Sun Oct-Mar, 10.30-1pm & 4-7pm Tue-Sat Apr-Jun & Sep, 10.30am-1pm & 4.30-7.30pm Tue-Sun Jul-Aug), with its famous bronze statue of Germanico, Roman captain and adopted son of Tiberius. Over two metres high, this almost fully restored statue is covered in armour featuring Achilles' ambush of Troilus in the Trojan War. You'll also find a painting by one of Amelia's most famous residents, Piermatteo d'Amelia. Piermatteo was instrumental in securing Christopher Columbus the three ships he used to discover America and was also the painter of the original Sistine Chapel ceiling.

An ancient **Roman cistern** (☎ 0744 97 84 36; ✆ 4.30-7.30pm Sat, 10.30am-12.30pm & 4.30-7.30pm Sun

Apr-Sep, 3-6pm Sat, 10.30am-12.30pm & 3-6pm Sun Oct-Mar) goes underneath Piazza Matteotti from what is now a private house to the youth hostel.

If you're with your darling be sure to walk down from Piazza Matteotti past the Palazzo Municipale to **Vicolo Baciafemmine** (Girl-Kissing Alley), so named because its narrowness has been known to cause passers -by to get close enough to let their passions run amok.

In 1783 Amelia's Theatrical Society (comprised of the middle class and bourgeoisie) decided that their hamlet needed some culture. They banded together and built the **Teatro Sociale** (☎ 0744 97 83 15; Via del Teatro), turning the theatre into the most important gathering spot in town. The moving wings still work on the original wood wheels. Domenico Bruschi frescoed the ceiling and booths in 1886. Most of the concerts begin at 8pm.

From the theatre, go to Via della Valle to get the best look at the **Mura Megalitiche**, stone walls built by the Etruscans in the 6th century BC. The rougher the texture, the older the stone. The builders didn't have mortar, but the walls were constructed well enough so that we can still see them.

The **Chiesa di San Francesco** (☎ 0744 97 81 20; ☼ 10am-noon & 3-6.30pm) was originally built in the 13th century, but most of the architecture now is from the 15th and 20th century. The façade is from 1406, and is decorated in the Romanesque and Gothic styles.

Since 872, there has been a religious institution on the site of the current **cathedral** (☼ 10am-noon & 3-6.30pm). The cathedral has been rebuilt after several disasters, and is certainly not the most impressive in Umbria, but there are several paintings and sculptures of interest inside. Next to the cathedral is the **Torre Civica**, which was built in 1050. Like many towers that were built in the medieval period, it was constructed on a dodecagonal (12-sided) plan based on the symbolic importance of the number 12 (12 apostles, 12 signs of the zodiac).

Courses

If you're looking for somewhere easy-going to learn Italian, try **Eurolinks** (☎ 0744 98 18 60; www.eurolinkschool.com; Viale Rimembranze 48), which runs live-in classes at all levels from €660 per week for a double room in a farmhouse to €1232 for two weeks full-board staying with a local family. It also arranges wellness retreats, cooking courses and tours of local wineries and *frantoio* (olive mills).

Festivals & Events

Amelia knows how to throw a party during its medieval *manifestazione* (event), the **Palio dei Columbi**. Every August, teams comprised of neighbourhood residents vie against each other in competitions recorded in the municipal records from the 14th century. Knights and crossbowmen are paired up to attempt to shoot an arrow through a target, which then sets free a dove. Practically every resident of the town is in full costume. The wooden doors you see on the Porta Romana are closed only on this day each year.

Sleeping

It's rather amazing, but there is not one hotel or B&B in the entire town of Amelia. Thankfully, there's a fabulous hostel with family rooms as good as any hotel.

Ostello per la Gioventù Giustiniani (☎ 0744 97 86 73, 348 764 56 64; www.ostellogiustiniani.it; Piazza Mazzini 9; dm/f per person incl breakfast €15.50/17.50; ☼ 8-10am & 4pm-midnight Mar-Oct) Whether bunking in a dorm room or with a friend in a two- or four-person family room, you'll appreciate the relaxing nature of this most comfortable of hostels. Atmospheric double oak doors add to the privacy feel. Lockout is virtually all day, so make sure you call ahead for a bed. An HI card is required, but can be issued upon arrival.

Eating

Be sure to try the local sweet *fichi girotti* at any shop in town. It's kind of like eating the hardened insides of a fig biscuit mixed in with chocolate and nuts.

Osteria dei Cansacchi (☎ 0744 97 85 57; Piazza Cansacchi 4; mains around €9) Set in a medieval atmosphere, this restaurant combines two excellent local delicacies by serving *bistecche di cinghiale e porcini* (wild boar with porcini mushrooms). Pizza is a good and inexpensive bet here.

La Gabelletta (☎ 0744 98 21 59; Str Tuderte Amerina 20) Its signature dish is *pappardelle al sugo di lepre* (pasta with wild hare sauce).

Getting There & Away

Amelia is serviced by ATC Terni. Buses leave from in front of the main gate. From Amelia, nine buses travel daily to the centre of Narni, plus another 10 to Narni Scalo and the train station (€1.60, 30 minutes). Buses also travel to Orvieto (€4, one hour and 10 minutes, seven daily; check with the driver as to whether the bus stops at the train station or Piazza Cahen) and Terni (€2.40, one hour, 16 daily). To get to Perugia, switch in Terni.

Getting Around
Bypass the paid parking near the centre and head towards the tourist office. Veer right into the little street along the city walls. At the end of this road, head left under the bridge to find a free car park. The entire town is within walking distance.

AROUND AMELIA
The area surrounding Amelia is known as the Amerino and has an untold amount of little treasures, natural and cultural. Holm-oak groves, ilex trees, and an ample amount of rivers and interesting geological terrain makes this area worthy of a country drive. But Sundays and public holidays – when the museums below are open and the rest of Umbria is closed – is the best time to visit.

In nearby Alviano you'll find the **Lago di Alviano** and **Oasi di Alviano**, which is more marshland than lake, formed when Lago di Corbara was dammed, and now a bird habitat. To go on a quest to learn about the *capitani di ventura* (mercenary captain or captain of fortune; see boxed text, p290), journey to the **Museo Storico Multimediale Bartolomeo d'Alviano e i Capitani di Ventura** (☎ 0744 905028, infoline ☎ 199 194 114; ☼ 10.30am-12.30pm year-round & 4.30-7.30pm Jul-Aug, 4-7pm Apr-Jun & Sep, 3-6pm Oct-Mar or by appt), which shares a castle with the **Museo della Civiltà Contadina** (Museum of Agricultural Heritage). Bartolomeo d'Alviano was a *capitani di ventura*. The Alviano family held a lot of clout over the centuries and was instrumental in building the Orvieto cathedral. Bartolomeo was so famous as a *capitano di ventura* that his likeness was minted on a Venetian coin.

ORVIETO
pop 21,600
The entire town is placed precariously on a cliff made of the area's tufaceous stone, a craggy porous limestone that seems imminently ready to crumble under the weight

of Orvieto's magnificent Gothic cathedral (or, at least under all the tourists who are now drawn to see it). Just off a main autostrada, Orvieto can get a bit crowded with summer bus tours, but they're all here for good reason.

Orientation
Trains pull in at Orvieto Scalo and from here you can catch bus No 1 up to the old town or board the cable car (funicular) to take you up the steep hill to Piazza Cahen.

Those with cars should head to a free car park behind the train station (at the roundabout in front of the station head in the direction of 'Arezzo' and turn left into the large parking lot). There's plenty of parking space in Piazza Cahen and in several designated areas outside the old city walls. The Orvieto Unica Card will buy you five hours of free parking at the former Campo della Fiera and a ride on the *ascensore* (lift) into the city centre.

Information
BOOKSHOPS
Libreria dei Sette (☎ 0763 34 44 36; Corso Cavour 85; ☼ 9am-1pm & 4-8pm) Stock up on a collection of maps, English-language books or Lonely Planets in Italian.

EMERGENCY
Police station (☎ 0763 39 21 11; Piazza Cahen)

INTERNET ACCESS
Caffè Montanucci (p338; per 30 min €3.10; ☼ closed Wed) Pick up a global supply of chocolate or a *panini* while you're here.

MEDICAL SERVICES
After-hours doctor (☎ 0763 301 884) Call here for the hospital at night and on the weekend.
Hospital (☎ 0763 30 71) In the Ciconia area, east of the railway station.

POST
Post office (☎ 0763 340 914; Via Largo M. Ravelli; ☼ 8.10am-6pm Mon-Sat)

TOURIST INFORMATION
ATC (☼ 8am-1.15pm & 4-6pm, closed Sat) Beside the railway station; sells Orvieto Unica Cards and has tourist information.
Tourist office (☎ 0763 34 17 72; info@iat.orvieto.tr.it; Piazza del Duomo 24; ☼ 8.15am-1.50pm & 4-7pm Mon-Fri, 10am-1pm & 3-6pm Sat, Sun & holidays)

www.lonelyplanet.co

SOUTHERN UMBRIA

ORVIETO

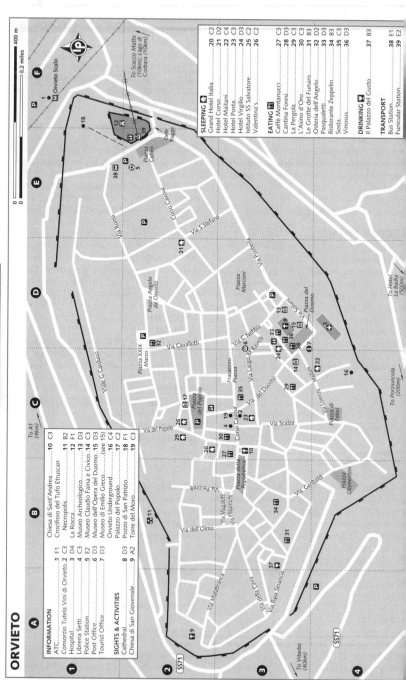

INFORMATION
ATC..1 F1	
Consorzio Tutela Vini di Orvieto.2 C3	
Hospital......................................3 D4	
Libreria Setti..............................4 C3	
Police Station............................5 E2	
Post Office.................................6 D3	
Tourist Office.............................7 D3	

SIGHTS & ACTIVITIES
Cathedral..................................8 D3	
Chiesa di San Giovenale..........9 A2	
Chiesa di Sant'Andrea............10 C3	
Crocifisso del Tufo Etruscan	
Necropolis............................11 B2	
La Rocca..................................12 F1	
Museo Archeologico................13 D3	
Museo Claudio Faina e Civico.14 C3	
Museo dell'Opera del Duomo..15 D3	
Museo di Emilio Greco......(see 15)	
Orvieto Underground...............16 C4	
Palazzo del Popolo..................17 C2	
Pozzo di San Patrizio...............18 F1	
Torre del Moro.........................19 C3	

SLEEPING 🛏
Grand Hotel Italia....................20 C2	
Hotel Corso.............................21 D2	
Hotel Maitani...........................22 C4	
Hotel Posta..............................23 C3	
Hotel Virgilio...........................24 D3	
Istituto SS Salvatore................25 C2	
Valentina's...............................26 C2	

EATING 🍴
Caffè Montanucci.....................27 C3	
Cantina Foresi.........................28 D3	
La Pergola...............................29 C3	
L'Asino d'Oro...........................30 C3	
Le Grotte del Funaro...............31 B3	
Osteria dell'Angelo..................32 D2	
Pasqualetti...............................33 D3	
Ristorante Zeppelin..................34 B3	
Sosta.......................................35 C3	
Vinosus...................................36 D3	

DRINKING 🍷
Il Palazzo del Gusto.................37 B3	

TRANSPORT
Bus Station..............................38 E1	
Funicular Station......................39 E2	

ights

ATHEDRAL

ittle can prepare you for the visual feast nat is the **cathedral** (☎ 0763 34 11 67; Piazza el Duomo; admission free; ◷ 7.30am-12.45pm & 2.30-.15pm Apr-Sep, 7.30am-12.45pm & 2.30-6.15pm Mar & ct, to 6.15pm Mar & Oct, to 5.15pm Nov-Feb). Origiating in 1290, this remarkable edifice vas originally planned in the Romanesque tyle but, as work proceeded and architects hanged, Gothic features were incorporated nto the structure. The black-and-white narble banding of the main body of the hurch, reminiscent of other great churches ou may already have seen in Tuscan cities uch as Siena and Pisa, is overshadowed by he rich rainbow colours of the façade. A armonious blend of mosaic and sculpture, lain stone and dazzling colour, it has been ikened to a giant outdoor altar screen.

Pope Urban IV ordered that the cathedral e built following the so-called Miracle of Bolsena in 1263. A Bohemian priest who vas passing through the town of Bolsena near Orvieto) had his doubts about tranubstantiation dispelled when blood began o drip from the Host onto the altar linen vhile he celebrated Mass. The linen was preented to Pope Urban IV, in Orvieto at the ime, who declared the event a miracle and et the wheels in motion for the construcion of the cathedral. He also declared the new feast day of Corpus Domini. The reliquary holding the blood-stained altar cloth now leads the Corpus Domini procession, held in June.

The building took 30 years to plan and three centuries to complete. It was probably started by Perugia's Fra Bevignate and coninued over the years by Lorenzo Maitani responsible for Florence's cathedral), Andrea Pisano, his son Nino Pisano, Andrea Orcagna and Michele Sanmicheli.

The façade appears almost unrelated to the main body of the church and has greatly benefited from meticulous restoration, completed in 1995. The three huge doorways are separated by fluted columns and the gables are decorated with mosaics that, although mostly reproductions, seem to come to life in the light of the setting sun and in the evening under spotlights. The areas between the doorways feature 14th-century bas-reliefs of scriptural scenes by Maitani and his pupils, while the rose window is by Andrea Orcagna.

The great bronze doors, the work of Emilio Greco, were added in the 1960s.

Reopened in late 1996 after years of painstaking restoration, Luca Signorelli's fresco cycle *The Last Judgement* shimmers with life. Look for it to the right of the altar in the **Cappella di San Brizio** (admission €3; ◷ 10am-12.45pm & 2.30-7.15pm Apr-Sep, to 6.15pm Mar & Oct, to 5.15pm Mon-Sat, to 5.45pm public holidays Nov-Feb). Signorelli began work on the series in 1499, and Michelangelo is said to have taken inspiration from it when he began the Sistine Chapel fresco of the same subject 40 years later. Indeed, to some, Michelangelo's masterpiece runs a close second to Signorelli's work. Not to be ignored in the chapel are ceiling frescoes by Fra Angelico. The chapel is closed during Mass.

The **Cappella del Corporale** (◷ 7.30am-12.45pm & 2.30-7.15pm summer, shorter hr winter) houses the blood-stained altar linen, preserved in a silver reliquary decorated by artists of the Sienese school. The walls feature frescoes depicting the miracle, painted by Ugolino di Prete Ilario. Mass is celebrated here daily at 9am (in Italian). Tickets for the Cappella di San Brizio are available from the tourist office; both *capella* are closed during mass.

PIAZZA DEL DUOMO

An absolutely fantastic museum for ancient history is the **Museo Claudio Faina e Civico** (☎ 0763 34 12 16; www.museofaina.it; Palazzo Faina, Piazza del Duomo 29; adult/child €4.50/3; ◷ 9.30am-6pm Mar-Oct, 10am-5pm Tue-Sun Nov-Feb), opposite the cathedral. Much of the display here comes from the Etruscan Necropolis found on the

SOUTHERN UMBRIA

COMBINED TICKET

If you plan to spend more than a day in Orvieto consider buying the **Orvieto Unica Card** (adult/concession €12.50/10.50, valid one year). It gives its owner admission to the four biggest attractions (the Cappella di San Brizio, Museo Claudio Faina e Civico, Orvieto Underground and Torre del Moro), five hours' free car parking at the train station or a return trip on the cable car and city buses, and offers discounts at many shops and restaurants in town. The card can be purchased at the parking lot Campo della Fiera, from each attraction listed, the tourist office or the cable car parking lot.

outskirts of town. There are examples of Gorgons, an incredibly thorough collection of numismatics (coins, many with the likeness of famous Roman emperors) and bronze figures from the 2nd and 3rd centuries BC. Kids will enjoy following the questions (in Italian and English) for developing little historians to ponder along the way.

Next to the cathedral is the **Museo dell'Opera del Duomo** (☎ 0763 343 592; Palazzo Soliano, Piazza del Duomo; admission €5; ☽ 10am-12pm Tue & Thu, 11am-1pm & 3-6pm Sat, 10am-1pm & 3-5pm Sun), which houses a clutter of religious relics from the cathedral, as well as Etruscan antiquities and works by artists such as Simone Martini and the three Pisanos: Andrea, Nino and Giovanni. The museum has been closed for restoration for ages; contact the tourist office to see if it has reopened.

Museo di Emilio Greco (☎ 0763 34 46 05; Palazzo Soliano, Piazza del Duomo; adult/concession €2.50/1.50; ☽ 10.30am-1pm & 2.30-6pm Apr-Sep, 10.30am-1pm & 2-5.30pm Oct-Mar, closed Mon) displays a collection of modern pieces donated by the creator of the cathedral's bronze doors. You can get a combined ticket (adult/child €5.50/4) for admission to the Pozzo di San Patrizio.

Around the corner, you can see Etruscan antiquities in the **Museo Archeologico** (☎ 0763 34 10 39; Palazzo Papale, Piazza del Duomo; adult/child €3/ 1.50; ☽ 8.30am-7.30pm). It doesn't have information in English, so visit the Museo Claudio Faina e Civico first to get your bearings.

The coolest place in Orvieto – literally – is the **Orvieto Underground** (☎ 0763 340 688, 339 733 27 64; Parco delle Grotte; adult/concession €5.50/3.30; ☽ tours 11am, 12.15pm, 4pm and 5.15pm Mar-Jan, Sat & Sun only Feb). The caves were initially used as wells by the Etruscans, who needed water but with the Romans about couldn't risk leaving the hill. During the Middle Ages, locals experiencing a high volume of sieges used the caves for protected sustenance, this time they trapped pigeons in dovecotes for food (pigeon is still found on Umbrian menus to this day – look for *palomba*). During WWII, the caves were turned into bomb shelters, but luckily they never had to be used, as the tufaceous volcanic rock that makes up the hill crumbles easily. Tours leave from in front of the tourist office at 11am, 12.15pm, 4pm and 5.15pm. During the summer, take the 12.15pm tour: you'll enjoy the year-round temperature of around 15°C while most sights and shops are closed.

OTHER SIGHTS & ACTIVITIES

Near the end of the main drag is the **Torre del Moro** (Moor's Tower; ☎ 0763 34 45 67; Corso Cavour 87; adult/concession €2.80/2; ☽ 10am-8pm May-Aug, 10am-7pm Mar, Apr, Sep & Oct, 10.30am-1pm & 2.30-7pm Nov-Feb). Climb all 250 steps (or take an elevator part-way) for a sweeping, pigeon's-eye view of the entire city.

To see a bit of striated history, the 12th-century **Chiesa di Sant'Andrea** (Piazza della Repubblica; ☽ 8.30am-12.30pm & 3.30-7.30pm) and its curious decagonal bell tower is a good choice. As with many Italian churches, it was built over a Roman structure, which itself incorporated an earlier Etruscan building. You can see the ancient foundations in the crypt. The piazza, once Orvieto's Roman forum, is at the heart of what remains of the medieval city.

North of Corso Cavour, the 12th-century Romanesque-Gothic **Palazzo del Popolo** presides over the piazza of the same name. At the northwestern end of town is the 11th-century **Chiesa di San Giovenale** (Piazza Giovenale; ☽ 8am-12.30pm & 3.30-6pm), its interior brightened by 13th- and 14th-century frescoes.

Standing watch at the town's easternmost tip is the 14th-century **La Rocca**, part of which is now a public garden. To the north of the fortress, the **Pozzo di San Patrizio** (St Patrick's Well; ☎ 0763 34 37 68; Viale Sangallo; adult/concession €4.50/3.50; ☽ 10am-6.45pm Apr-Sep, to 5.45pm Oct-Mar) is a well, testament to the hardy disposition of the townsfolk. More than 60m deep, it is lined by two staircases for water-bearing mules and a Latin inscription reading: 'What nature denied for defence, in this case water, was added by the work of man'. It was sunk in 1527 on the orders of Pope Clement VII. If you're planning on visiting the Museo di Emilio Greco, buy a combined ticket.

Besides the Hypogea di Volumni outside of Perugia, the **Crocifisso del Tufo Etruscan Necropolis** (☎ 0763 34 36 11; Loc. Le Conce, SS71, Km 1.6; adult/concession €3/1.50; ☽ 8am-7pm) is one of only two Etruscan necropolises that travellers can visit in Umbria. It dates back to the mid-6th century BC. Several series of burial chambers feature the etched names of their deceased residents. The manner in which the graves are laid out shows the preciseness of good ancient urban planning, albeit one whose residents couldn't quite appreciate it. Many of the furnishings from the Necropolis can be found at the Louvre, British Museum and various other museums, though some of the collection hasn't left: the Museo Claudio Faina e Civico still holds onto a good chunk.

Festivals & Events

Orvieto's most famous festival is the **Palombella**, held every year on Pentecost Sunday. Unusually, it is world-famous for its highlight event rather than the parades and crafts fairs. For traditionalists, the sacred rite has been celebrating the Holy Spirit and good luck since 1404. For animal rights activists, the main event celebrates nothing more than scaring the living crap out of a bewildered dove.

For six centuries, the ritual has gone like this: take one bewildered dove, cage it, surround the cage with a wheel of exploding fireworks, and hurtle the cage 300m down a wire towards the cathedral steps. If the dove lives (which it usually does), the couple most recently married in the cathedral become its caretakers (and, presumedly, the ones who pay for post-traumatic dove-stress disorder counselling). It's not likely you'll see a fake dove in the cage, but if so, you'll know who has won.

Umbria Jazz Winter is held from the end of December to early January, with a great feast and party on New Year's Eve. Ask at the tourist office for a programme. See p273 for details of the summer jazz festival.

Sleeping

Orvieto does not lack for hotels, and visitors will benefit from the highly competitive pricing. It's always a good idea to book ahead in summer or at the weekend, or if you're planning to come over New Year when the Umbria Jazz Winter festival is in full swing.

BUDGET

Porziuncola (☎ 0763 341 387; Loc. Cappuccini 8; dm €10-12; P) With only eight beds each in two separate single-sex rooms, you'd do best to call ahead. Take bus no 5 from Piazza Cahen to the Cappuccini neighbourhood just a few kilometres away.

Scacco Matto (☎ 0744 95 01 63; fax 0744 95 03 73; Lago di Corbara; per person/tent €4.15/4.65) The closest camp sites are about 10km east of Orvieto, on Lago di Corbara, near Baschi. Scacco Matto is tiny (just 12 pitches) and fairly basic, but stays open year-round.

Istituto SS Salvatore (☎ /fax 0763 342 910; www.argoweb.it/istituto_sansalvatore; Via del Popolo 1; s/d €35/55) Practise your Italian with these jovial nuns. There's a 10.30pm curfew, but the place is comfortable and clean and there's a lovely garden. Singles don't have bathrooms.

Hotel Posta (☎ 0763 34 19 09; www.orvietohotels.it; Via L Signorelli 18; s/d €31/43, s/d with bathroom €37/56, all incl breakfast) Rooms in this stolid, rather ramshackle but impressive 16th-century building are endearing, as if your quirky great-aunt with the big hoop earrings had decorated them. Great fluffy blankets.

Valentina's (☎ /fax 0763 34 16 07, 347 6527779; valentina.z@tiscalinet.it; Via Vivaria 7; s/d/tr incl breakfast €50/65/85, apt €130) As if being set back on a quiet street wasn't enough, the rooms are also soundproof, casually elegant and spacious. Valentina lives downstairs with two friendly dogs. All rooms have private bathrooms, TVs, and hairdryers, and a laundry service is available.

MIDRANGE

Hotel Maitani (☎ 0763 34 20 11; www.hotelmaitani.com; Via Lorenzo Maitani 5; s/d €75/124; P ♿) Every detail is covered, from a travel-sized toothbrush and toothpaste in each room to chocolates (Perugino, of course) on your pillow. Several rooms have views of the cathedral or the countryside. Rooms are pin-drop quiet, as they come with not one but two double-pane windows.

Hotel Corso (☎ /fax 0763 34 20 20; www.hotelcorso.net; Corso Cavour 343; s/d €60/82; ♿ 💻) Set a bit further away from the cathedral than most other hotels, this is nevertheless an excellent choice. Rooms are enveloped with wooden beamed ceilings, terracotta bricks or antique cherry furniture, allowing one to describe them as snug rather than tiny. The breakfast buffet is an extra €6.50 but it's worth it to sit on the outdoor terrace. A 10% discount applies to stays of more than two nights.

Grand Hotel Italia (☎ 076 334 32 75; www.grandhotelitalia.it; Via di Piazza del Popolo 13; s/d €80/130, superior €165, all incl breakfast; P) The rooms reflect the elegance of the 19th-century building, many with superb views and a few with balconies. Take note that school groups often stay here to take advantage of its conference rooms, so it can get filled with boisterous teenagers every so often. Some of the superior rooms have balconies with panoramic views. Parking will set you back €8.

Hotel Virgilio (☎ 0763 34 18 82; www.hotelvirgilio .it; Piazza del Duomo 5; s/d with bathroom €62/85) This three-star hotel has an unrivalled position on Piazza del Duomo. It has clean, bright basic rooms, most with views that could command admission they're so spectacular. It's not hard to understand why it's so popular, but with rooms this small, the staff could stand to be a little less gruff.

TOP END

Hotel La Badia (☎ 0763 30 19 59; www.labadiahotel.it; Loc. La Badia 8; d/ste €221/270; P ⛷ 🏊) Occupied 1200 years ago by Benedictine monks, this hotel – claimed to be the oldest in Italy – was once known as the Abbey of St Severo and Martirio. It's been a holiday retreat since the 15th century, with guests such as Pope Paul II, Borghese and Barberini. For the past century it's been under the ownership of a noble family who turned it into the hotel it is today. Twenty-one rooms and seven suites consist of modern comforts along with attractive antiques and furnishings, a swimming pool and tennis court. The hotel is closed early January to early March.

Eating
BUDGET

L'Asino d'Oro (☎ 0763 34 44 06; Vicolo del Popolo 9; mains around €9; ☾ closed Mon) Despite its modest appearance, L'Asino d'Oro has gained fame as one of the best trattorias in Italy. Meals are served outside on wooden tables under an arbour along a quiet street, and the menu changes daily.

Le Grotte del Funaro (☎ 0763 34 32 76; Via Ripa Serancia 41; mains around €10; ☾ closed Mon) Eating here, you'll think you have died and gone to…well, a funerary cave. This restaurant was created out of a cavern and drips with atmosphere. There's an amazing view through the narrow windows, as well as antique agricultural objects and a piano bar.

La Pergola (☎ 0763 34 30 65; Via dei Magoni 9b; mains around €9; ☾ closed Wed) The food here is typically Umbrian – good and filling – but the real draw here is dining in the flower-filled garden in the back. Try the *cinghiale*.

Sosta (☎ 0763 34 30 25; Corso Cavour 100a; mains around €5) This extremely simple self-service restaurant actually serves up some very good pizza and pasta. It's cafeteria-style so you order as much or as little as you like,

including meat and vegetable dishes. Students get a discount.

Pasqualetti (☎ 0763 34 10 34; Piazza del Duomo 14) This *gelateria* serves mouthwatering *gelato*, plus there are plenty of tables on the piazza for you to gaze at the magnificence of the cathedral while you gobble.

MIDRANGE

Ristorante Zeppelin (☎ 0763 34 14 47; Via Garibaldi 28; ☾ closed dinner Sun) This natty place has a cool 1920s atmosphere, jazz on the stereo and a long wooden bar where Ingrid Bergman would have felt right at home. It serves creative Umbrian food, including well-priced tasting menus for vegetarians (€25), children (€20), truffle-lovers (€40) and traditionalists (€25). Ask about the day-long cooking courses.

Vinosus (☎ 0763 341 907; Piazza Duomo 15; tapas €6-10; ☾ closed Mon) In photo-op range of the cathedral's northwest wall is this wine bar and eatery. The smattering of cheese plates makes this an elegant spot for a wine and cheese break. It is open until the wee hours for wine tasting.

Osteria dell'Angelo (☎ 0763 341 805; Piazza XXIX Marzo 8a; mains €22; ☾ closed Mon) Judged by local food writers to be one of the best restaurants in Umbria, this is certainly an elegant place. Your meal is being cooked by the winner of the 2000 'Chef to Watch' competition. The banana soufflé with a rum and cream sauce is recommended and the wine list is extensive.

TOP END

La Badia Ristorante (☎ 0763 30 19 59; Loc. La Badia 8; mains €13-25; ☾ closed Wed) The restaurant at La Badia is as refined as its hotel (left). The chef's speciality is suckling pig and *tagliolini* pasta with truffles. If you enjoy the Orvieto Classico here, tell the owner, Count Fiumi, as it's from his vineyards. Even if you don't stay or eat here, you can still see it; when you're in the Orvieto Underground, look for the 8th-century abbey in the fields below.

CAFÉS

Caffè Montanucci (☎ 0763 34 12 61; Corso Cavour 21; hot dishes from €3.60; ☾ closed Wed) An affable one-stop shop for espresso, *gelato*, *panini*, Internet access (per 30 minutes €3.10) and the best part: the wall o' chocolate. Hundreds of bars from all over the world congregate around a few tables, causing plenty of passing mouths to water.

Cantina Foresi (☎ /fax 0763 34 16 11; Piazza del Duomo 2) A family-run café serving up *panini* and sausages, washed down with wines from the ancient cellar.

Drinking

Il Palazzo del Gusto (☎ 0763 39 35 29; www.orvieto congusto.it; Via Ripa Serancia I 16; tastings €5-11; ⏰ 11am-1pm & 3-5pm winter, 11am-1pm & 5-7pm summer) This Etruscan subterranean wine cellar is infused with equal parts atmosphere and thousand-year-old yeast. Several tunnels have been updated for wine tastings and parties. Peek behind the glass doors for a look at ancient Etruscan tunnels. Check with the tourist office as to when they're open for tastings.

Shopping

Despite being a tourist town, Orvieto still has plenty of shops selling high-quality ceramics, lace and delicious sample packs of local wines, sausage, olive oil, cheeses and *funghi* (mushroom) products. Via Garibaldi is a pedestrian shopping street with as many clothiers as ceramicists.

Getting There & Away

Buses depart from the station on Piazza Cahen and make a stop at the train station as well. COTRAL buses connect the city with Viterbo in Lazio (€2.80, 1½ hours, seven daily) and Bagnoregio (€1.65, one hour, seven daily), where you can take another bus to the foot bridge to Civita di Bagnoregio. **ATC buses** (☎ 0763 34 22 65) run to Todi (€4.40, one hour) departing at 2.05pm and returning at 5.50am. **SIRA** (☎ 0763 417 30 053) runs a daily service to Rome at 8.10am, and at 7.10am on Sunday (€5.15, 1½ hours).

Trains travel to Rome (€6.82, 1¼ hours, hourly), Florence (€10.10-17.15, 1½ to 2½ hours, hourly) and Perugia (€6.10, 1¼ hours, at least every other hour).

The city is on the A1, and the SS71 heads north to Lago di Trasimeno.

Getting Around

A century-old cable car connects Piazza Cahen with the train station, with carriages leaving every 10 to 15 minutes from 7.15am to 8.30pm daily (€0.80, or €0.90 including the bus from Piazza Cahen to Piazza del Duomo). Bus No 1 also runs up to the old town from the train station (€0.80). Once in Orvieto, the easiest way to see the city is on foot, although ATC bus A connects Piazza Cahen with Piazza del Duomo and bus B runs to Piazza della Repubblica.

For a taxi, dial ☎ 0763 301 903 or swing by Piazza Matteotti.

CIVITA DI BAGNOREGIO

Civita di Bagnoregio is a tiny, ancient island of a village resting atop cliffs that rise from the valley floor. Accessible only by a 300m-long footbridge, as you approach you'd swear that it couldn't possibly still be inhabited. Once you walk through the gate of Santa Maria and notice the flowers decorating the homes, you'll realise that the town is still occupied. Well, technically. Only about 20 residents live here year-round, which expands to a whopping 300 in the summer.

Civita dates back to Etruscan times and is notable as the birthplace of St Bonaventure, as well as three other Christian saints. DH Lawrence mentioned Civita in his short story 'Etruscan Places'.

Once a thriving and important commercial and agricultural centre, Civita has been steadily disintegrating for centuries. Built on unstable clay and volcanic sediments, whole neighbourhoods have been lost to landslides, so what we see today is only the central and most ancient part of the city.

Orientation

The only way to get into the town is to walk across the footbridge from a car park in Bagnoregio. Only two cars are allowed into Civita: a Fiat Panda for the elderly or physically disabled, and a minitractor that brings goods in or rubbish out. Watch as either precariously manoeuvres the vertical steps as they splutter their way towards Civita.

Sights & Activities

Walking out of the east end of the city (opposite the main gate) you'll find a path that leads down some ancient steps to the right and along the base of the town. Ancient Etruscan tombs cut into the cliffs can be seen along the way. The path terminates at an **Etruscan tunnel** that runs north–south under the width of the town, and was used at various times as an access tunnel to the Etruscan necropolis, a water conduit and a footpath for farmers to reach their fields. If you look up from either side of the tunnel, you'll see first-hand the precarious nature of Civita's existence. Note: go back the way you came, as there is no other route back into town.

In town, the **Bruschetteria Antica** (bypass the one near the Piazza Duomo Vecchio and head almost to the end of the town) features a minimuseum that displays an ancient **frantoio** (olive-oil press) dating from the 1500s, used by the family of the *bruschetteria's* current owner (who also owns Agriturismo Le Corone). The **Chiesa di San Donato** on the east side of Piazza Duomo Vecchio in the town centre houses the remains of St Victoria.

Festivals & Events

Civit'arte In August, the local arts festival features all sorts of modern and traditional live arts performances.

La Tonna If you'd like to see grown men race jockeys through an ancient village, show up on the first Monday in June or the second Monday in September.

Sleeping

Romantica Pucci (☎ 0761 79 21 21; www.hotelromantica pucci.it; Piazza Cavour 1, Bagnoregio; d/tr incl breakfast €70/95) The breakfast alone is worth a stay here. The amicable host Pucci makes homemade blood-orange and kiwi jam. Special touches like cookies before bed, bottled water in the rooms and four-poster beds make this a truly Romantica spot.

Civita Bed & Breakfast (☎ 0761 76 00 16; www .civitadibagnoregio.it; Main square, Civita di Bagnoregio; s/d/tr with bathroom €45/68/73, s/d without bathroom €40/62) Eleven very basic rooms, some with shared bathrooms and rather hard mattresses. Remember that you're staying here for the charm. It's just off the main square to the left and there's an attached restaurant, Trattoria Antico Forno.

Agriturismo Le Corone (☎ 320 422 7244; www .agrilecorone.com; Loc. Palombaro, Strada per Vaiano, Km 4; per person €35) This *agriturismo* is as remote as it gets while still only an hour from Orvieto. Comfortable and authentic, the stone farmhouse holds up to a family of five. Owner Fabrizio Rocchi can trace his family's roots back to the 1500s, and he and his American-born wife now run an adjoining organic farm that grows wine and olive oil, and raises cattle. Stroll through the grounds to see Etruscan ruins, and be sure to take advantage of a guided tour of the area on horseback (or on foot). Civita is a short but steep climb up a well-marked path.

Eating

Trattoria Antico Forno (☎ 0761 76 00 16; Main square, Civita di Bagnoregio) This restaurant is attached to Civita Bed & Breakfast. In fact, it's the only restaurant in town. The menu is good country food: tagliatelle with a 'medieval' sauce of tomatoes, red peppers and sausages; pesto gnocchi; *piciarello* pasta with

---

SLOW FOOD, SLOW CITY

In 1986 McDonald's was about to open a restaurant at the famed Spanish Steps in Rome. Carlo Petrini, a wine writer, was so appalled that he started a movement that has grown to include around 80,000 members on five continents. Called 'Slow Food' (see p62), about half of the members are based in Italy, but conviviums are opening around the world at a rapid pace as people are adopting the Italian and, more so than any other province, Umbrian way of cooking and eating.

From the Slow Food Movement grew the Slow City Movement, whose current president is the mayor of Orvieto. Its members are concerned that globalisation is wiping out differences in traditions and culture and replacing it with a watered-down homogeneity.

To become a Slow City (or Città Lenta as they're known in Italy, where most of the Slow Cities are located), towns have to pass a rigid set of standards, including having a visible and distinct culture. The towns must follow principles such as relying heavily on autochthonous (from within) resources instead of mass-produced food and culture, cutting down on air and noise pollution, and relying more and more on sustainable development, like organic farming and public transport. Umbria boasts six Slow Cities: Trevi (p309), Todi (p322), San Gemini, Orvieto (p333), Città di Castello (p300) and Castiglione del Lago (p290).

As you travel through these towns, you will never hear a car alarm, you can be assured you'll find plenty of public space and there will never, ever be a McDonald's.

truffles or asparagus and mushrooms; and a good array of bruschetta.

Hostaria del Ponte (☎ 0761 79 35 65; Contrada Mercatello, Bagnoregio; mains around €13) A favourite of locals, this restaurant is at the foot of the bridge on the Bagnoregio side of Civita. A covered outdoor patio allows you to eat here even in winter, with a spectacular view of Civita. Specialities are truffles and *cinghiale*.

Shopping

Le Cordelier (☎ 0761 79 29 81; Via della Fraticella, Civita di Bagnoregio) This little shop sells books on Civita and beautiful local products. The owner studies the history of Civita's own St Bonaventure, and has been compiling a history that she hopes to turn into a book soon. For now, she's got a written history along the shop's walls. It's in Italian, but she's more than willing to explain anything about Bonaventure – or Civita – in English or French.

Getting There & Away

Buses leave from Piazza Cahen in Orvieto about every hour or so (€1.60, 50 minutes), with a gap between 9.10am and 12.40pm. The bus stops at Porta Albana in Bagnoregio and a smaller shuttle bus runs between there and the parking lot for Civita (or you can walk). By car, take the S71 south from Orvieto and get off in the direction of Bagnoregio. The cost to park in the car park in front of the footbridge is €1 per hour. Buy a parking ticket at any of the three businesses surrounding the car park.

DIRECTORY

Directory

CONTENTS

> ### PRACTICALITIES
>
> - Use the metric system for weights and measures.
>
> - Buy or watch videos on the PAL system.
>
> - Plugs have two or three round pins so bring an international adapter; the electric current is 220V, 50Hz.
>
> - If your Italian's up to it, try the following national newspapers: *Corriere della Sera*, the country's leading daily, or Rome's centre-left *La Repubblica*, which is published nationally. Florence-based *La Nazione* is the main regional broadsheet, and there is also Turin's *La Stampa*, which is widely available.
>
> - Tune in to state-Italian RAI-1 (1332AM or 89.7FM), RAI-2 (846AM or 91.7FM) and RAI-3 (93.7FM) for classical and light music with news broadcasts; Radio 105 out of Milan plays contemporary and rock music throughout Italy.
>
> - Turn on the TV to watch Italy's commercial stations Canale 5, Italia 1, Rete 4 and La 7, as well as the state-run RAI-1, RAI-2 and RAI-3.

ACCOMMODATION

Prices for accommodation quoted in this book are intended as a guide only. Accommodation rates fluctuate wildly; during summer weekends or festivals you can often pay double the price asked in the low season. Prices usually rise 5% or 10% semiannually, but they can remain fixed for years or even go down. Always check the room before plunking down your money.

High season is July and August, when most Italians take their holidays. Be prepared to book in advance during the summer and holidays such as Easter or Christmas or the two weeks surrounding Ferragosto (15 August), as it's nearly impossible to show up at the beach on a Saturday in August and find a room. If you're arriving quite late, it's advisable to call ahead.

January through to early March and November to mid-December are the quietest months. During this off-peak season, you should be able to bargain lower rates with hoteliers, especially if you show up towards the end of the day and the hotel is empty.

In this book we've generally used the term 'budget' to describe accommodation where a double costs less than €70 a night, 'midrange' for those places where a double costs between €70 and €150, and 'top end' where a double costs more than €150 a night. Overall, prices in some towns, like Florence, can be higher, while prices in other towns with plentiful accommodation, such as Assisi, might run a little lower. The author's favourite is listed at the top of each section.

Agriturismo

Agriturismo is a holiday on a working farm, and is particularly popular in Tuscany and Umbria. Italians love them, but foreigners are discovering the benefits. *Agriturismi* are, by law, supposed to grow at least one of their own products. Many make olive oil or wine, but some of the older, well-established farms produce wheat, jams, honey and even meats. Tourist offices can supply listings; online check out www.agriturismo.net or www .agriturist.com. For Umbria, try www.bellaumbria.net. Those interested in volunteering on an organic Italian farm should check out www.wwoof.it for a worldwide directory (requires membership) that includes many farms in the region. Touring Club Italiano (TCI) publishes *Agriturismo: The Guide to Farm Holidays in Italy* for €16.95, available on its website www.touringclub.it.

Camping

Camping is extremely popular in central Italy, but can be quite expensive once you add up the costs. You'll pay a separate charge for each person, child, car, tent, caravan, motorcycle, even dogs. Most camp sites are often away from the town centre, so public-transport users will need to factor in extra time for long walks or extra costs for bicycle rentals, buses or camp-site pickups. Camping rough is generally not permitted.

TCI publishes a biannual book, *Italian Camping: The Guide to Camping and Caravaning* (€9.95), which lists camp sites in Italy. Online, try www.campeggitalia.com or www.camping.it for regional and provincial listings.

Convents & Monasteries

Many of the more than 50 convents and monasteries scattered about the region offer some form of accommodation to outsiders. The rooms aren't luxurious, but they are generally quiet and clean. You almost always need to call or email ahead, and there is usually a two-night minimum and a curfew of around 10.30pm or 11pm. A handy book, available in good travel bookshops, is *Guida ai Monasteri d'Italia*, by Gian Maria Grasselli and Pietro Tarallo (around €10). Also, every tourist office in Tuscany and Umbria has a listing *Campeggi e Altra Ospitalita* that includes camp sites, *affittacamere* (rooms for rent), B&Bs and religious accommodation.

Hostels

Most youth hostels are run by the AIG (Associazione Italiana Alberghi per la Gioventù), which is affiliated to Hostelling International (HI). You need to be a member, but most places will let you buy an €18 membership card; it is good for one year at HI hostels around the world. Accommodation is usually in segregated dormitories and beds cost around €15 per night. Some hostels offer family rooms at a higher price. In the summer months you should book in advance, especially in Florence and Perugia. It is usually necessary to pay before 9am on the day of your departure, otherwise you could be charged for an additional night. There are also a few private hostels in Italy.

Visit www.ostellionline.com for a complete list of all AIG hostels in Italy, their services and how to book.

Hotels

Prices quoted in this book are intended as a guide only. Hotels are strictly regulated in Italy and are classified on a scale of one to five stars. They are known by many names, including *albergo, locande, affittacamere* or *pensione*. A *pensione* is no longer officially recognised, but if you do come across a place by this name it is most likely a small family-run one- or two-star hotel.

The quality of accommodation can vary a great deal. One-star hotels tend to be basic and usually do not have an en suite. Standards at two-star places are often only slightly better, but rooms will generally have a private bathroom. Once you arrive at three stars you can assume that the standards will be reasonable, although quality still varies dramatically.

PARKING AT YOUR ACCOMMODATION

Parking in rural and suburban accommodation is rarely a problem. In cities, most three-star-plus hotels offer parking either onsite or give guests a validation for nearby parking. You're usually on your own in hostels and smaller establishments. Some four- and five-star hotels have been known to charge €20 a day, and there's even a few hotels in Florence's city centre that charge €50 (!!) a day, at which rate you might as well sleep in your car.

Four- and five-star hotels are sometimes part of a group of hotels, and offer facilities such as room service, laundry and dry-cleaning.

Prices are highest in Florence and on Elba (in July and August). Some hotels, especially along the beach, may impose a multinight stay during high season.

A single room is called a *camera singola,* a double room with twin beds is a *camera doppia,* and a double room with a double bed is called a *camera matrimoniale.*

The tourist board can provide extensive accommodation listings.

Rental Accommodation

Finding rental accommodation in the cities can be difficult and time-consuming, but not impossible. Rental agencies will assist, for a fee, but it's best to keep your guard up (see boxed text, opposite). A one-room apartment with kitchenette in Florence or Perugia will cost anything from €400 to €800 a month, while renting or sharing a room starts at about €200. Renting in other towns can be considerably cheaper.

You can also look for rental ads in advert rags such as Florence's *La Pulce* and *Panorama* or Perugia's *Cerco e Trovo.*

Rifugi

If you are planning to hike in the Apennines, you should first obtain some information on the network of *rifugi* (mountain huts). The most common are the ones run by **Club Alpino Italiano** (CAI; www.cai.it in Italian). The accommodation is generally in bunk rooms sleeping anything from two to a dozen or more people. Half board (dinner, bed and breakfast) is often available.

In addition to CAI *rifugi,* there are some private ones and the occasional *bivacchio,* a basic, unstaffed hut. *Rifugi* remain open from mid-June to mid-September, but some at lower altitudes may remain open longer.

If you are counting on staying in a *rifugio,* always call ahead, or have someone do so for

---

VILLAS AMONG THE VINES

If you want to get away from it all and relax in style, then renting a villa just may be the ticket for you. In recent years it has become a popular accommodation option and villas are as common as vines in both Tuscany and Umbria.

Prices can range from €400 a week for two to four people to well over €10,000 for a 12-person castle with your own private chef. Most fall somewhere in the €800 to €2000 range and sleep four to eight people. If you average out the per-person, per-week price and factor in cooking several meals in the house, villa stays can actually be quite economical. Plus, many villa owners live on site and speak English, so you're essentially hiring a built-in concierge.

Ask a lot of questions about the villa's amenities, location and what is and is not included in the price. Remember: photos can be deceiving. You could get stuck at an enticingly beautiful stone farmhouse in an industrial suburb where you have to pay extra for toilet paper in the outhouse. Many villa renters contact the property themselves to save the expense of an agency. You can search online on Google or check reviews at a website such as www.slowtrav.com for recommendations and links.

Cottages to Castles (☎ 01622 77 52 17; www.cottagestocastles.com) Has an enticing collection of properties to choose from. This UK company has agents in New Zealand, Australia, South Africa, the US, Israel and across Europe. It is run by an Italian father and son, and caters to groups of two to 30 people. It can also arrange car hire and airport pickups.

Cuendet (☎ 800 370 477; www.cuendet.com) A large-scale operation since 1974 with offices in many European countries, this Italian-based company manages hundreds of villa rentals in Umbria and Tuscany, as well as Spain, France and Portugal.

Italian Villas (☎ 800-700-9549; www.italianvillas.com) This company, based in the US, manages several hundred villas and *agriturismi* all over Italy, including Tuscany and Umbria, catering to all price ranges. It has an extremely useful search engine that allows users to search for categories including most unusual, most historic, great for teenagers, for those who don't want to rent a car etc.

Traditional Tuscany (☎ 01553 810003; www.traditionaltuscany.co.uk) This is a specialist company with a wide range of rural villas and converted farmhouses in Tuscany, Umbria, Lazio and Le Marche. It has a good deal of low-priced accommodation and offers specials and last-minute offers on its website.

you, to check that it is open and has room for you. Where possible, let staff know approximately when you expect to arrive.

Student Accommodation

Those planning to study in Italy can usually organise accommodation through the school or university they will be attending. Options include a room with an Italian family, or a share arrangement with other students in an independent apartment. If you're willing to chance it, you can look through newspapers and on university notice boards after you've arrived. Many hostels and B&Bs give a weekly discount.

ACTIVITIES

Most people think of a visit to Tuscany and Umbria in terms of the familiar museum and church circuit, but both provinces have a plethora of outdoor activities on offer. Hiking, hang-gliding, rafting, fishing, kayaking, bicycling, rock climbing, truffle hunting and skiing are all popular. See the Outdoors chapter and the individual destination chapters for ideas.

BUSINESS HOURS

Shops are generally open 9am to 1pm or 3.30pm, and reopen in the afternoon from 4pm to 7.30pm or 8pm, Monday to Friday, but in main towns and cities it's increasingly popular for shops to remain open all day.

Bank hours are generally from 8.30am to 1.30pm and 3pm to 5pm on weekdays, but times can vary. Post offices open 8.30am to 1.30pm Monday to Friday and for several hours in the afternoon. In large towns, they might open on Saturday morning. Pharmacies open 9am to 12.30pm and 3.30pm to 7pm Monday to Friday, and are open on Saturday and Sunday mornings. It is the law that one pharmacy in every town has to stay open on the weekend, and all other pharmacies list that location on their front door.

Restaurants usually serve from 12pm to 2.30pm or 3pm and 7.30pm to 10pm or 11pm. Bars usually open at 8am until the early hours. The law requires restaurants to close one day a week, but some ignore this rule and others close two days a week. Nightclubs open their doors at about 10pm but don't usually start filling up until midnight.

CHILDREN

Your children will get a great reception in Tuscany and Umbria, and most places will happily accommodate them. Discounts are available for children (usually under 12 years of age) on public transport and for admission to museums, galleries etc. Hotels will almost always offer a child discount or not charge for children at all.

Travelling with children can be extremely rewarding with the right planning. For more information see Lonely Planet's *Travel with Children*.

Practicalities

If possible, families should book accommodation in advance to avoid any inconvenience. You might want to try a villa or some other self-catering accommodation so you can have your own kitchen facilities. If not, ask the tourist office for suggestions on hotels and guesthouses that cater specifically to children. A few of the larger hotels have kids-club options. Most places will have cots and highchairs available, if you request them in advance, although some hotels will charge an additional fee. Car seats can also be hired with rental cars, but if you plan to do a lot of travelling you might be better off taking your own: if you are flying, remember to check your luggage allowance.

Farmacie (pharmacies) sell baby formula in powder or liquid form as well as sterilising solutions. Disposable nappies are widely available at supermarkets and pharmacies. Fresh milk is sold in cartons in bars (which have a 'Latteria' sign) and in supermarkets. If it is essential that you have milk you should carry an emergency carton of UHT milk, which does not need to be refrigerated, since these bars usually close at 8pm.

Stock up on sunscreen as the sun can be particularly harsh on young skin, and try to schedule your day to fit in with the cooler periods (early morning and late afternoon).

Watch out for the amount of sugary sweets that are heaped upon kids by well-meaning locals.

CLIMATE CHARTS

Tuscany and Umbria both enjoy a typically Mediterranean climate, with a mean annual temperature of around 15°C. Summertime can be oppressive and hot, with temperatures reaching 35°C. For more information on when to go see p12.

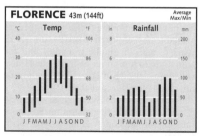

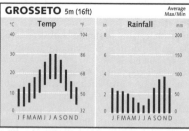

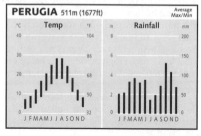

COURSES

Both Tuscany and Umbria are popular destinations for people who want to learn Italian. Universities and private schools throughout the region provide all levels and types of language courses, although the three main magnets are Florence, Perugia and Siena. Many also offer accommodation with families, making it an intimate way to experience the country.

Individual schools and universities are listed under Information in the relevant towns throughout this book. The handy website www.it-schools.com lists a slew of schools and courses. Accommodation can almost always be arranged through the school.

Many schools also offer courses in painting, ceramics, art history, sculpture, architecture and cooking at a wide range of prices. For cooking courses, see p70.

It is also possible to undertake serious academic study at a university, although obviously only if you have a solid command of the language. Perugia's Università per Stranieri (University for Foreigners; p273) offers accredited language courses for students and Italian teachers abroad.

CUSTOMS

Duty-free sales within the EU no longer exist. Under the rules of the single market, goods bought in and exported within the EU incur no additional taxes, provided duty has been paid somewhere within the EU and the goods are for personal consumption.

Travellers who are coming from outside the EU are permitted to import, duty-free: 400 cigarettes, one bottle of hard liquor, two bottles of wine, two still cameras and 10 rolls of film per camera.

DANGERS & ANNOYANCES
Theft

Pickpockets and bag-snatchers operate in the more touristy parts of the bigger cities, at train stations and in some of the coastal resort towns. Invest in a money belt to keep your important items safe, and pay attention to what's going on around you. In Florence and around train stations and tourist areas, watch out for groups of dishevelled-looking women and children, especially two or three together, holding some sort of distracting diversion such as a pile of papers or even a baby. Children as young as six or seven might be employed in the sleight-of-hand thefts, one of which is to have several children make a commotion in front of you or ask for money while an adult sneaks behind and cuts your bag straight off your back or shoulder. Never underestimate their skill – they are as fast as lightning and very adept. As soon as you notice a suspicious ruckus, hold on tight to all your possessions.

Parked cars, particularly those with foreign number plates or rental-company stickers, are also prime targets for thieves. Never leave valuables in your car, and make sure you are adequately insured. See p366 for more details. In case of theft or loss, always report the incident to the police within 24 hours and ask for a statement, otherwise your travel insurance company may not pay out.

Traffic

Italian driving varies dramatically between city and country driving, but expect to stay on your toes at all times. The city is fast, chaotic and not overly friendly to pedestrians. Crossing the street can be a life-threatening event, as Italians would rather swerve around a pedestrian than (god forbid) stop and wait. Scooter drivers often act more like bicyclists and it's not uncommon to see them driving on a sidewalk or going the wrong way down a one-way street. Always look both ways before crossing a street.

Driving in the countryside can be substantially more relaxing, but is not without its share of anxiety-provoking moments. Even secondary roads that look rather substantial on a map can be windy little two-lane roads. See p366 for a quick tutorial on overtaking.

DISABLED TRAVELLERS

Tuscany and Umbria are not the easiest places for travellers with physical disabilities. Cobblestone streets, common in many towns in the region, can be a nuisance for those who use wheelchairs, and many buildings (including hotels and monuments) don't have lifts.

Regency San Marino (www.accessibleitaly.com) runs tours and day trips as well as assists in arranging independent travel for customers with physical or visual disabilities. It can coordinate an entire holiday, including airport pickup and hotel reservations, and provide listings of accessible monuments.

Italy is very slowly working on outfitting public buildings with wheelchair-accessible ramps and elevators. Several cities are far ahead of the bunch. A paraplegic Assisian has created a website as a resource for travellers using wheelchairs to gauge the accessibility of hotels, restaurants and monuments in the city. Find it at www.assisiaccessibile.it (in Italian). Città di Castello is refreshingly free of hills, and many hotels have access for people with disabilities.

The Italian State Tourist Office in your country may be able to provide advice on Italian associations for the disabled and what help is available in the country. It may also carry a small brochure *Services for Disabled People*, published by the Italian railways, which details facilities at stations and on trains. There's an airline directory that provides information on the facilities offered by various airlines on the disability-friendly website www.everybody.co.uk.

DISCOUNT CARDS
Senior Cards

Seniors over 60 or 65 (the age limit depends on what you are seeking a discount for) can get many discounts simply by presenting your passport or ID card as proof of age.

Student & Youth Cards

These cards can get you worthwhile discounts on travel, and reduced prices at some museums, sights and entertainment spots. The International Student Identity Card (ISIC), for full-time students, and the International Teacher Identity Card (ITIC), for full-time teachers and professors, are issued by more than 5000 organisations around the world – the organisations are mainly student travel related, and often sell student air, train and bus tickets. In Australia, the USA or the UK, try **STA Travel** (www .statravel.com).

Anyone under 26 can get a Euro26 card. This gives similar discounts to the ISIC and is issued by most of the same organisations. See www.euro26.org for details.

CTS (Centro Turistico Studentesco e Giovanile) youth and student travel organisation branches in Italy can issue ISIC, ITIC and Euro26 cards.

Note that many places in Italy give discounts according to age rather than student status. An ISIC card may not always be accepted without proof of age (eg passport).

EMBASSIES & CONSULATES

It's important to realise what your own embassy can and can't do to help you if you get into trouble. Generally speaking, your embassy won't be much help in emergencies if the trouble you're in is remotely your own fault. Remember that you are bound by the laws of the country you are in. Your embassy will not be sympathetic if you end up in jail after committing a crime locally, even if such actions are legal in your own country.

In genuine emergencies you might get some assistance, but only if other channels have been exhausted. For example, if you need to get home urgently, a free ticket home is exceedingly unlikely – the embassy would expect you to have insurance. If you have all your money and documents stolen, it might help you get a new passport, but a loan for onward travel is out of the question.

Italian Embassies & Consulates

The following is a selection of Italian diplomatic missions abroad. As a rule, you will need to approach a consulate rather than an embassy (where both are present) on visa matters. Several countries have consulates in more than one city; check with the main consulate's website to see if there is one closer to you.

Australia (☎ 02-6273 3333; www.ambitalia.org.au; 12 Grey St, Deakin, Canberra, ACT 2600)
Canada (☎ 416-977 1566; www.toronto.italconsulate .org; 136 Beverley St, Toronto, Ontario M5T 1Y5)
Ireland (☎ 01-660 1744; www.italianembassy.ie; 63-65 Northumberland Rd, Dublin 4)
The Netherlands (☎ 070-302 1030; www.italy.nl; Alexanderstraat 12, 2514 The Hague)

New Zealand (☎ 04-4735 339; www.italy-embassy .org.nz; 34-38 Grant Rd, Thorndon, Wellington)
UK (☎ 020-7235 9371; www.embitaly.org.uk; 38 Eaton Pl, London SW1X 8AN)
USA (☎ 212-439-8600; www.italconsulnyc.org; 690 Park Ave, New York, NY 10021-5044)

Embassies & Consulates in Italy

Most countries have an embassy (and often a consulate) in Rome, though there are a few consulates in Florence. Passport enquiries should be addressed to the offices below.

Australia (☎ 06 85 27 21; Via Antonio Bosio 5, Rome)
Canada (☎ 06 44 59 81; Via G B de Rossi 27, Rome)
Germany (Map pp80-1; ☎ 055 29 47 22; Lungarno Amergio Vespucci 30, 50123 Florence)
Ireland (☎ 06 67 82 541; Largo Nazareno 3, Rome)
The Netherlands (☎ 06 322 11 41; Via Michele Mercati 8, Rome)
New Zealand (☎ 06 441 71 71; Via Zara 28, Rome)
UK Florence (Map pp82-3; ☎ 055 28 41 33; Lungarno Corsini 2); Rome (☎ 06 4220 0001; Via XX Settembre 80a)
USA Florence (Map pp80-1; ☎ 055 266 951; Lungarno Amerigo Vespucci 38, 50123); Rome (☎ 06 4 67 41; Via Vittorio Veneto 119a)

FESTIVALS & EVENTS

The calendar is full to bursting with events, ranging from colourful traditional celebrations with a religious and/or historical flavour, through to festivals of the performing arts, including opera, music and theatre. Occasionally celebrations are countrywide but more often than not the events relate specifically to a city or town. Details of destination-specific festivals and events can be found in the regional chapters; details of food-related festivals can be found on p66.

FEBRUARY & MARCH

Carnevale During the period before Ash Wednesday, in February or March, many towns stage carnivals and enjoy their last opportunity to indulge before Lent. Viareggio in Tuscany is particularly festive this day (see p166).
Settimana Santa Holy Week is marked by solemn processions and passion plays in various cities in March or April. In Florence the Scoppio del Carro is staged in the Piazza del Duomo at noon on Easter Saturday. This event features the explosion of a cart full of fireworks, a tradition dating back to the Crusades – it is seen as a good omen for the city if the explosion works.

APRIL & MAY

Corsa all'Anello (p329) Named for the Race of the Ring, which is held on the second Sunday in May in Narni, the two weeks leading up to the equestrian joust is filled with singing baroque choirs dressed in traditional garb and feasts.

Corsa dei Ceri (p297) The three neighbourhoods in Gubbio jostle against one another carrying gigantic 'candles' through the city streets on 15 May.

Palio della Balestra (p297) The men of Gubbio and its Tuscan neighbour Sansepolcro battle it out with antique crossbows while wearing medieval costume on the last Sunday in May.

JUNE

Festa di San Giovanni (p114) On 24 June medieval football matches end with a fireworks display over Piazzale Michelangelo in Florence.

Gioco del Ponte (p152) On the last Sunday in June two groups in medieval costume contend for the Ponte di Mezzo in Pisa.

L'Infiorata del Corpus Domini (p305) The best place to celebrate Corpus Domini, all of Spello's citizens decorate the streets with colourful flower petal designs on 21 June.

Palio delle Quattro Antiche Repubbliche Marinare (p152) This race between the four old-time maritime republics – Genoa, Amalfi, Pisa and Venice – is also a procession of boats and events. It is held in June in rotating cities, including Pisa in 2006.

JULY

Il Palio (p212; Siena; 2 July) Perhaps one of the most famous festivals in all of Italy, this is a rather dangerous horseback ride, held on 2 July, through a piazza in Siena. It is preceded by a parade of traditionally costumed supporters.

Spoleto Festival (p314) An international performing arts event held in Spoleto from early to mid-July, featuring music, theatre, dance, art and courtroom re-creations.

Summer Festival (p159) The best of international contemporary music shows up for this very reasonably priced Luccan music festival held in July. Acts have included Youssou N'Dour, Jamiroquai and Van Morrison.

Umbria Jazz (p273) The very best of the best flock to this international festival featuring traditional jazz, soul, experimental and New Orleans brass bands. It is held in Perugia in mid-July.

AUGUST

Ferragosto You can practically hear the crickets chirping on 15 August as virtually every Italian man, woman and child heads out of the cities to the coast or country, closing many of their shops and restaurants behind them (thus, a good time to stay away from either spot).

Palio dei Columbi (p332) The culminating event of this festival, dating from 1346, pairs a 'knight' on horseback with a crossbowman aiming at a target to free a dove, but for two weeks Amelia proffers medieval demonstrations

and taverns. It is held from the end of July to beginning of August.

SEPTEMBER

Giostro del Saracino (p257) This event is held in Arezzo at the end of August and the beginning of September. The first Sunday in September sees a medieval jousting competition.

Palio della Balestra (p260) Sansepolcro holds a rematch to Gubbio's May competition, Palio della Balestra, on the first Sunday in September.

OCTOBER

Harvest Known as Vendemmia in Chianti, late September and October is the prime season to sample the new wines, olive oils and cheeses at *agriturismi*, *sagre* (festivals) and restaurants all over Tuscany and Umbria.

DECEMBER & JANUARY

Natale During the weeks preceding Christmas there are many processions and religious events.

Umbria Jazz Winter (p337) Many of the world's great names in jazz take the stage in Orvieto with a spectacular New Year's Eve event. The festival begins at the end of December and goes through to the beginning of January.

FOOD

In this book we've used the term 'budget' to describe places where you can grab a meal for less than €15; 'midrange' places cost between €15 and €40, while the full works at a 'top-end' restaurant will cost over €40 per head.

For information on what to eat in Tuscany and Umbria, see p62.

GAY & LESBIAN TRAVELLERS

Homosexuality is legal in Italy and well tolerated outside of the south and in large cities, including Florence, Pisa and Perugia.

The fabulous English-language www.gay friendlyitaly.com (connected to the Italian-language site www.gay.it) helps with information on tour groups and gay-friendly hotels, and even has a homophobia rating system of Italian cities.

On the Tuscan coast, Versilia and Torre del Lago have a lively and popular gay scene. The gay community created **Friendly Versilia** (www .friendlyversilia.it) to direct the more than 100,000 gays and lesbians who visit during the 'season' from late April to September. The area is quite built up, but visitors can choose from tanning on the beach, horse riding in a nature preserve, or late-night discos.

Gay-friendly bars and clubs can be tracked down through local gay organisations or on the web at www.gayfriendlyitaly.com

ArciGay (☎ 051 649 30 55; fax 051 528 22 26; www .arcigay.it some English), the Italian gay association, is the main organisation campaigning for the rights of gays and lesbians in Italy. Its headquarters are located in Bologna. In Florence, check with **Azione Gay e Lesbica Finisterrae** (☎ /fax 055 67 12 98; www.azionegayelesbica .it in Italian) for many useful links.

See p125 for more information on Florence's gay and lesbian scene.

HOLIDAYS

It's a good idea to try to avoid Italy in mid-August, when most Italians take their holidays. The beaches are overly crowded and many restaurants and shops are closed, especially during the week of Ferragosto (15 August). The Easter break (Settimana Santa) is another busy holiday period and when many schools take pupils on cultural excursions. Museums and places of interest may be more crowded than usual. Allow for long queues and be sure to make hotel reservations in advance, especially on weekends.

Italian national public holidays include the following:

New Year's Day (Anno Nuovo) 1 January – the celebrating takes place on New Year's Eve (Capodanno)

Epiphany (Befana) 6 January

Easter Sunday (Pasqua) March/April

Easter Monday (Pasquetta) March/April

Liberation Day (Festa della Liberazione) 25 April – marks the Allied victory in Italy, the end of the German presence and Mussolini

Labour Day (Festa del Lavoro) 1 May

Foundation of the Italian Republic (Festa della Repubblica) 2 June

Assumption of the Virgin (Ferragosto) 15 August

All Saints' Day (Ognissanti) 1 November

Day of the Immaculate Conception (Concezione Immaculata) 8 December

Christmas Day (Natale) 25 December

St Stephen's Day/Boxing Day (Festa di Santo Stefano) 26 December

Individual towns also have public holidays to celebrate the feasts of their patron saints. Details can be found in the relevant chapters.

INSURANCE

Never leave home without travel insurance – it's just not worth the risk. Most policies will cover theft, loss and medical problems. Some policies offer lower and higher medical-expense options; the higher ones are chiefly for countries such as the USA, which have extremely high medical costs. There's a wide variety of policies available, so check the small print.

Some policies specifically exclude 'dangerous activities', which can include scuba diving, motorcycling and even trekking. Check your policy to be sure. A locally acquired motorcycle licence isn't valid under some policies.

You may prefer a policy that pays doctors or hospitals directly, rather than you having to pay on the spot and claim the money back later. If you do have to claim later, make sure you keep all of the documentation. Some policies ask you to call back (reverse charges) to a centre in your home country, where an immediate assessment of your problem is made.

Check that the policy covers ambulances or an emergency flight home. See p369 for more information.

If you are planning to travel by car in Italy, then insurance is not only recommended but legally required. See p366 for details.

INTERNET ACCESS

Travelling with a portable computer is a great way to stay in touch with life back home, but unless you know what you're doing it's fraught with potential problems. If you plan to carry your notebook or palmtop computer, remember that the power supply voltage in Italy may be different from that at home, so you could risk damage to your equipment. The best investment is a universal AC adaptor for your appliance, which will enable you to plug it in anywhere without frying the innards. You'll also need a plug adaptor for each country you visit – often it's easiest to buy these before you leave home.

Your PC-card modem may or may not work in Italy – you won't know for sure until you try it out. The safest option is to buy a reputable 'global' modem before you leave home, or buy a local PC-card modem when you're in Italy. If you're coming from the US, you'll have what's known as an RJ-11, for which, in order to adapt to Italian telephone sockets, you'll most likely need to buy a converter. A few hotels in Italy will already have this equipment, but these will be either very high-end outfits or business hotels. For some more information on travelling overseas with a notebook or laptop computer, see www.teleadapt.com, which also sells European-compatible adaptors.

A quickly developing service in Italy is the wireless access point. All you need is a wi-fi card in your laptop or palm and a bookstore, café or hotel that advertises wireless access. Considering the expense and bureaucratic hassle of obtaining a land line in Italy, expect this service to be a big hit soon.

Major Internet service providers such as **AOL** (www.aol.com) and **CompuServe** (www.compuserve.com) have dial-in nodes available in Italy – it's best to make sure you download a list of the dial-in numbers before you leave home. You can also sign up for a short-term account with an Italian Internet provider such as www.tiscali.it.

If you do intend to rely on Internet cafés, you'll need to carry three pieces of information with you to enable you to access your Internet mail account: your incoming (POP or IMAP) mail server name, your account name and your password. Your ISP or network supervisor will be able to give you these. Armed with this information, you should be able to access your email account from any Net-connected machine in the world, provided it runs some kind of email software (remember that Netscape and Internet Explorer both have mail modules). It pays to become familiar with the process for doing this before you leave home.

You'll find plenty of Internet cafés in larger towns. In smaller towns and villages, usually at least one copy store, pizzeria or bar will have an Internet terminal. Expect to pay anywhere between €1.50 and €6 per hour.

LEGAL MATTERS

For many Italians, finding ways to get around the law is a way of life. Some Italians are likely to react with surprise, if not annoyance, if you point out that they might be breaking a law. Few people pay attention to speed limits and many motorcyclists and drivers don't stop at red lights – and certainly not at pedestrian crossings. No-one bats an eyelid about littering or dogs pooping in the middle of the footpath, even though many municipal governments have introduced laws against these things. But these are minor transgressions when measured up against the country's organised crime, the extraordinary levels of tax evasion and corruption in government and business.

The average tourist will probably have a brush with the law only if they are unfortunate enough to be robbed by a bag-snatcher or pickpocket.

Drink Driving

The legal limit for blood-alcohol level is 0.05%. Random breath tests are carried out by the authorities, and penalties can range from an on-the-spot fine to the confiscation of your licence.

Drugs

Italy's drug laws are lenient on users and heavy on pushers. If you're caught with drugs that the police determine are for your own personal use, you'll be let off with a warning (and, of course, the drugs will be confiscated). If, instead, it is determined that you intend to sell the drugs, you could find yourself in prison. It's up to the police to determine whether or not you're a pusher, since the law is not specific about quantities. The sensible option is to avoid illicit drugs altogether.

Police

The *polizia* (police) are a civil force and take their orders from the Ministry of the Interior, while the *carabinieri* fall under the Ministry of Defence. There is a considerable overlap of their roles, despite a 1981 reform intended to merge the two forces.

The *carabinieri* wear a dark-blue uniform with a red stripe and drive dark-blue cars that also have a red stripe. Their police station is called a *caserma* (barracks).

The police wear powder-blue trousers with a fuchsia stripe and a navy-blue jacket, and drive light-blue cars with a white stripe and '*polizia*' written on the side. Tourists who want to report thefts, and people wanting to get a residence permit, will have to deal with them. Their headquarters are called the *questura*. This is where you get your *permesso di soggiorno* (permit to stay; see p356).

Other varieties of police in Italy include the *vigili urbani*, basically traffic police, who you will have to deal with if you get a parking ticket, or your car is towed away; and the *guardia di finanza*, who are responsible for fighting tax evasion and drug smuggling.

In an emergency, just go to the nearest people in uniform. Even if they're not the right uniforms, they'll know who to contact.

Italy has some antiterrorism laws that could make life difficult if you happen to be detained by the police. You can be held for 48 hours without a magistrate being informed and you can be interrogated without the presence of a lawyer. It is hard to obtain bail and you can be held legally for up to three years without being brought to trial.

MAPS

If you are driving around Tuscany and Umbria, the AA's *Road Atlas – Italy* is available in the UK for £13.99, and the AAA's *Deluxe Road Map Italy* is available in the US for US$8.95. Most car rental places will provide you with a national map if you ask. The AA also publishes maps for Tuscany and Umbria (£3.99 each). In Italy, Euro Cart publishes regional maps of Umbria at 1:170,000 and Tuscany at 1:300,000, both for €7.

Michelin produces a regional map specifically covering Tuscany, Umbria, Le Marche, Lazio, Abruzzo and San Marino (1:400,000), also for €7.

One of the best maps of Umbria is the Touring Club Italiano's *Carta Regionale* 1:200,000, a greenish topological foldout map available for free at most tourist offices and many hotels. It marks many features that make it extremely helpful: tertiary/dirt roads and sites of interest, including sanctuaries, Etruscan tombs, grottos, ruins and monasteries. On the reverse side are maps of major tourist towns such as Perugia, Castiglione del Lago and Todi. Most maps of Umbria are combined with either Le Marche or Tuscany, except Mappe Iter's Umbria 1:200,000 *Carta Turistica e Automobilistica* (€6). (A note about the terrain: 94% of Umbria is hilly. Industrial complexes have taken advantage of the remaining flat 6%, so if you want attractive landscapes, don't go towards anything white on your map, ie the flat areas directly around Perugia or Terni. Bevagna and Montefalco are exceptions.)

The city maps in this book, combined with tourist-office maps, are generally adequate to get you around. Many bookshops, with good selections of maps and guidebooks, are listed in each section.

The quality of city maps available commercially varies considerably, depending on the city. Most tourist offices stock free maps of their city, and commercial maps of larger cities are available from newsstands and bookstores. For suggestions on maps for the other main cities covered in this book, refer to each destination.

Tuscany and Umbria are great destinations for those who love the outdoors. Edizione Multigraphic publishes a couple of series designed for walkers and mountain-bike riders, scaled at 1:50,000 and 1:250,000. Where possible you should go for the latter. Ask for the *Carta dei Sentieri e Rifugi* or *Carta Turistica e dei Sentieri*. Another publisher is Kompass, which produces 1:50,000 scale maps of Tuscany and the surrounding areas. Occasionally you will also come across useful maps put out by the Club Alpino Italiano (CAI). For cycling enthusiasts, Verlag Esterbauer produces a *Cycling Tuscany: Cycle Guide and Map*, a spiral-bound 1:100,000 guide detailing the best cycling spots in the region.

Those planning a driving holiday should consult the AA's *Best Drives: Tuscany & Umbria*, which contains hand-picked car tours, essential motoring tips and specially designed maps.

MONEY

The unit of currency in Italy, 11 other EU countries and about a dozen overseas territories is the euro (€). The euro, which is the spelling in Italy whether it is singular or plural, is divided into 100 cents (known as *centesimi*). Coin denominations are one, two, five, 10, 20 and 50 cents, €1 and €2. The notes come in denominations of €5, €10, €20, €50, €100, €200 and €500. All euro notes and coins are identical on the side showing their value. The opposite side is the issuing country's design, but all denominations are accepted throughout the euro zone. For more information check out the website www.europa.eu.int/euro.

See the inside cover for a handy table to help you calculate the exchange rate. For information on costs see p13.

Money can be exchanged in banks, post offices and exchange offices. The best bet is to get money out of an ATM *(bancomat)*, but be aware that the bank charges a fee, so it's more advantageous to get out a large sum at once. Banks generally offer the best rates but shop around as they fluctuate considerably.

ATMs

You'll find ATMs in virtually every town or half-way populated village in Tuscany and Umbria. It's not uncommon for Italian ATMs to reject foreign cards for no reason whatsoever. If this happens, try a few branches or another day, and always make sure you're not down to your last *centesimi*. PIN codes need to be four digits.

Cash

Many smaller establishments (even some hotels) will only accept cash, so you'll need to carry a small amount of currency on you for day-to-day transactions. Other than that, keep cash to a minimum and store it in an under-the-clothes money belt if possible. Try and keep it separate from your other valuables in case your credit cards or travellers cheques are stolen.

Credit & Debit Cards

The simplest way to organise your holiday funds is to carry plastic (whether a credit, debit or ATM card). You don't have large amounts of cash or cheques to lose, you can get money after hours and on weekends, and the exchange rate is usually better than that offered for travellers cheques or cash exchanges. By arranging for payments to be made into your account while you are travelling, you can also avoid paying interest.

Most major credit/debit cards are accepted in Italy – for example, Visa, MasterCard, Eurocard, Cirrus and Eurocheque cards.

As well as making purchases and paying accommodation costs, credit cards can also be used in ATMs displaying the appropriate sign, or (if you have no PIN number) to obtain cash advances over the counter in many banks – Visa and MasterCard are among the most widely recognised for such transactions. Check charges with your bank before departure. Also, make sure your PIN code is exactly four digits and check the procedure on what to do if you experience problems or your card is stolen. Most card suppliers will offer you an emergency number you can call free of charge for help and advice.

Travellers Cheques

Although the simplicity of the ATM has now made them nearly obsolete, travellers cheques can be cashed at most banks and exchange offices. American Express (Amex), Thomas Cook and Visa are widely accepted brands.

It may be preferable to buy travellers cheques in euros rather than another currency, as they are less likely to incur commission on exchange. Amex and Thomas Cook don't charge commission, but other exchange places do have charges. Get most of the cheques in largish denominations to save on per-cheque exchange charges.

It's vital to keep your initial receipt, and a record of the cheque numbers you have used, separate from the cheques themselves. If your travellers cheques get stolen, you'll need these documents to get them replaced. You must take your passport with you when cashing travellers cheques.

PHOTOGRAPHY

Italy's airports are all fully equipped with modern inspection systems that do not damage most film or other photographic material that is carried in hand luggage. Getting a roll of film developed (24 exposure) costs anywhere between €8 and €13. Photographic services are often cheaper in the main towns and cities such as Florence and Perugia.

Photography is not allowed in many churches, museums and galleries. Look out for signs with a crossed-out camera symbol as you go in.

For tips on how to make the most of your camera, try Lonely Planet's *Travel Photography* Series.

POST

Italy's postal service is notoriously slow, unreliable and expensive. If you're sending a package, you might want to send your things home using DHL or FedEx. Shops such as Mail Boxes Etc can be found in most major towns.

Francobolli (stamps) are available at post offices and authorised tobacconists (look for the official *tabacchi* sign: a big 'T', often white on black). Main post offices in the bigger cities are generally open from around 8am to at least 5pm; many open on Saturday morning too. Tobacconists keep regular shop hours.

Postcards and letters up to 20g sent by airmail cost €1 to Australia and New Zealand, €0.80 to the USA, Asia and Africa and €0.62 within Europe. You can also send express letters *(posta prioritaria)* and registered letters *(raccomandata)* at additional cost. Charges vary depending on the type of post and weight of the letter. Normal airmail letters can take up to two weeks to reach the UK or the USA, while a letter to Australia will take between two and three weeks. The service within Italy is not much better: local letters take at least three days and up to a week to arrive in another city.

Poste restante is known as *fermo posta*. It's dying out because the widespread availability of Internet cafés makes email a much easier and quicker way to communicate, but it can be a good way to pick up care packages sent from home. Letters marked thus will be held at the counter of the same name in the main post office in the relevant town. Poste restante mail to Florence, for example, should be addressed as follows:

John SMITH
Fermo Posta
Posta Centrale
50100 Florence
Italy

You will need to pick up your letters in person and present your passport as ID.

SHOPPING

There are tour groups who come to Tuscany just for the shopping. Florence is famous for leather goods, jewellery, clothes and shoes. There are two brand-name factory outlets near the border between Tuscany and Umbria (see p127), lest you need a pair of €700 red alligator Prada shoes for 85% off. Umbria is the ceramics capital of Italy, and its centre, Deruta, is renowned for its centuries-old majolica technique.

Wine is obviously a popular take-home purchase, but consider several factors before laying down any euro. First, check with your country or state as to customs rules on alcohol. In the US, for example, many states do not allow international alcohol shipments to anyone except a licensed wine dealer. It costs around €156 to airmail a case (12 bottles) to North America or Australia. It's only slightly less to ship, but the extreme temperatures could destroy the quality. This is also true of an airplane's cargo hold, but ask your airline; they should know the estimated air temperature during your flight. Many oenophiles prefer to carry on three or four bottles. If you do use

checked luggage, bring special styrofoam bottle holders, but no bubble wrap.

But above all, check your local wine store. After all this hassle, you want to make sure you're not lugging home 70kg of wine that Aunt Bea just bought on sale down the street.

SOLO TRAVELLERS

Those travelling alone should experience few problems in Tuscany and Umbria. Although there are not large numbers of solo travellers as in other places with an established backpacking culture, you should not feel out of place and you will certainly not be made to feel uncomfortable. However, single room accommodation is usually around the same price as a double room. If you are travelling on a tight budget you may want to consider hostel accommodation – it will work out cheaper and it's also a great way to meet fellow travellers.

In general, normal common-sense rules apply. Avoid unlit streets and parks at night, and ensure your valuables are safely stored.

TELEPHONE

Privatised Telecom Italia is the largest phone company in the country and its orange public pay phones are liberally scattered all over the place. The most common accept only *carte/schede telefoniche* (telephone cards), although you will still find some that accept cards and coins. Some card phones now also accept special Telecom credit cards and even commercial credit cards. Phones can be found in the streets, train stations and some big stores, as well as in unstaffed Telecom centres. Most phones have clear instructions in English.

Telephone numbers change often in Italy so check the local directory for up-to-date information. For directory enquiries within Italy, dial ☎ 12.

Mobile Phones

Italy uses GSM 900/1800, which is compatible with the rest of Europe and Australia, but not with the North American GSM 1900 or the totally different system in Japan. Many mobile phones in America are now GSM compatible. Check with your manufacturer. When you arrive in Italy, you can sign up at any mobile-phone store for a pay-as-you-go plan. You just pop in an Italian SIM card, buy *ricarica* minutes (prepaid minutes) and gab all you want, for about €0.20 within Italy and €0.60 to North America.

Phone Codes
The international access code is ☎ 00 and the country code is ☎ 39.

Area codes all begin with zero and consist of up to four digits. The area code is followed by a telephone number of anything from four to eight digits.

Area codes are an integral part of all telephone numbers in Italy, even if you are calling within a single zone. For example, any number you ring in Florence will start with ☎ 055, even if it's next door. When making domestic and international calls you must always dial the full number including the initial zero.

Numeri verdi (free phone numbers) usually begin with ☎ 800 (some start with ☎ 199 and ☎ 848). Mobile phone numbers begin with a three-digit prefix such as ☎ 330, ☎ 339, ☎ 347 etc.

Phonecards
You can buy phonecards at post offices, tobacconists, newspaper stands and from vending machines in Telecom offices. They come with a value of €5 and €10. Remember to snap off the perforated corner before using them.

TIME
Italy operates on a 24-hour clock. It is one hour ahead of GMT/UTC. Daylight-saving time starts on the last Sunday in March, when clocks are put forward one hour. Clocks are put back an hour on the last Sunday in October.

TOURIST INFORMATION
Regional Tourist Offices
Tuscany's regional **tourist office** (☎ 055 43 82 111; www.turismo.toscana.it; Via di Novoli 26) can be found in Florence. Umbria's regional **tourist office** (☎ 075 575 951; www.umbria2000.it; Via Mazzini 21) is in Perugia. Neither office is open to the public, but a consortium of Azienda di Promozione Turistica (APT) offices, in all the provincial capitals, provide general information on the provinces. Helpful brochures include lists of outdoor activities, hotels and *agriturismi* guides, plus free maps.

Local Tourist Offices
The next rung down is the local city or town tourist offices. These can operate under various names but most commonly are known as Pro Loco. They may deal with a town only, or in some cases the surrounding countryside. English and French are widely spoken in Tuscany, but you might not find anyone who speaks English in many Umbrian tourist offices, even in the tourist hotspots of Perugia or Assisi.

The bigger tourist offices will often respond to written and telephone requests – for example, information about hotels or apartments for rent.

The addresses and telephone numbers of offices are listed under the relevant towns and cities throughout this book.

TOURS
Options for organised travel to Tuscany and Umbria abound, and come in many different forms, from intimate treks for adventuring bicyclists to cattle-call bus tours that have you following a microphone-wearing leader holding a giant umbrella. These kind of tours can provide seamless travel, new friends and often education, but can sometimes stifle independence, spontaneity and exploration. Participants from any country can join the tours listed below.

A company with an impressive commitment to sustainable tourism is **ATG Oxford** (☎ 01865 315 678 UK; www.atg-oxford.co.uk), which leads small walking, cycling and cultural tours, as well as arranges trips for independent walkers. Choose between comfortable strolls, grand hotels and wine-tasting or rugged hikes through mountains.

The Canadian outfitter **GAP Adventures** (☎ 800-465-5600 North America; www.gapadventures .com) takes 'Great Adventure People' on active tours made up of no more than 12 people. Trips throughout Tuscany and Umbria include family trips, bicycling and rafting, and a gourmand's dream.

There are several companies offering well-priced organised walking tours in Tuscany – try the UK's **Explore Worldwide** (☎ 01252-760000; www.exploreworldwide.com) or **Headwater** (☎ 01606-720033; www.headwater.com). The latter also offers cycling tours around both Tuscany and Umbria.

An outstanding cycling (and walking) tour company is **Backroads** (☎ 800-462-2848 US;

www.backroads.com; 7am-5pm Mon-Fri, 9am-3pm Sat PST), which runs dozens of trips to Tuscany from June to October, and an Umbrian itinerary in September and October. It's based in the US, but anyone can join. In the UK, **Cyclists' Touring Club** (☎ 0870 873 00 60; www.ctc.org.uk) can help you plan your own bike tour or organise guided tours for you. Membership costs as little as £12.

Adults aged 55 and over and their companions (of any age) can join **Elderhostel** (☎ 877-426-8056; www.elderhostel.org) for an educational and adventurous look into Tuscan and Umbrian art, nature and culture.

Tuscany and Umbria are made for motorcycle touring – the winding, scenic roads are ideal to explore. Advantages include the fact that motorcyclists rarely have to book ahead for ferries, and that you will be able to enter restricted traffic areas in Italian cities without any problems. Parking is also less of a headache for those on two wheels. **Beach's Motorcycle Adventures** (☎ 1-716-773-4960 US; www.beachs-mca.com) can arrange two-week tours within Italy in early May and early October. Riders need to have a motorcycle licence; an international one is best.

VISAS & PERMITS

The following information on visas was correct at the time of writing, but restrictions and regulations can change. Use the following as a guide only, and contact your embassy for the latest details. You may want to visit the websites of **Lonely Planet** (www.lonelyplanet.com), for useful links and up-to-date information, or the **Italian Ministry of Foreign Affairs** (www.esteri.it), for updated visa information, including links to every Italian consulate in the world and a database of the reasons and the nationalities that will need a visa.

Be sure that you understand the difference between a visa and a *permesso di soggiorno* (permit to stay; see below). You need a visa to enter the country and, once in Italy, a *permesso di soggiorno* to stay. To apply for a visa, visit an Italian consulate in your home country. To apply for a *permesso di soggiorno*, apply at a *questura* (police station) within eight days of your arrival.

Permits
PERMITS TO STAY
All *stranieri* (foreigners) staying in Italy for more than eight days, even tourists, are

technically supposed to obtain a *permesso di soggiorno* (PDS), roughly translated as 'permit to stay'. Tourists staying at hotels generally do not need to obtain one, as hoteliers are required to fill out paperwork on each guest (which is why they ask for your passport upon checking in).

The application process for one of these permits can take up to eight days if you don't follow the procedure exactly. For the most recent instructions, check the part-English-language sections of www.stranieriinitalia.it or call its outrageously expensive info line on ☎ 166 105 612.

To apply for any type of *permesso di soggiorno*, you'll need at least:
- Four passport-size photos
- Application form
- Legally stamped passport (and visa, if necessary) extending at least three months past your stay in Italy
- Proof of sufficient finances for your length of stay
- Marche da bollo (official tax stamp)

Depending on what type of *permesso di soggiorno* you're applying for, you might need to bring with you anything from eight extra photos to a vial of the blood of a six-toed cat born on a Tuesday. Check the website www.esteri.it/visti/index_eng.asp for information on both the *permesso di soggiorno* and visa requirements.

EU citizens supposedly do not need any permits to live, work or start a business in Italy. They are, however, advised to register with a *questura*, if they take up residence – in accordance with an anti-Mafia law that aims at keeping a watch on everyone's whereabouts in the country.

Once you've acquired a *permesso di soggiorno*, your next step, if you plan on living in Italy indefinitely, is to acquire a *carta d'identità*, or residence card. While you're at it, you'll need a *codice fiscale* (tax-file number) if you wish to be paid for working in Italy. You'll have to go through the *questura* for both of these.

WORK PERMITS
Non-EU citizens wishing to work in Italy will need to obtain a *permesso di lavoro* (work permit). If you intend to work for an Italian company and will be paid in euros, the company must organise the *permesso*

nd forward it to the Italian consulate in our country – only then will you be issued an appropriate visa.

If non-EU citizens intend to work for a non-Italian company or will be paid in foreign currency, or wish to go freelance, they must organise the visa and *permesso* in their country of residence through an Italian consulate. This process can take many months, so look into it early.

The *permesso per attesa occupazione* (job-seeking permit) has been abolished, even for EU citizens. Because of this, many foreigners arriving in Italy without jobs look for off-the-book work such as teaching English, bar work and seasonal jobs.

Visas

Italy is one of 15 countries that have signed the Schengen Convention, an agreement where thirteen of the original EU member countries (except the UK and Ireland), plus Iceland and Norway, have agreed to abolish checks at internal borders. The other EU countries are Austria, Belgium, Denmark, Finland, France, Germany, Greece, Luxembourg, the Netherlands, Portugal, Spain and Sweden. Legal residents of one Schengen country do not require a visa for another Schengen country. In addition, nationals of a number of other countries, including the UK, the US, Canada, Australia, Ireland, Japan, New Zealand, Mexico and Switzerland, do not need visas for tourist visits of up to 90 days in any Schengen country. There are several dozen countries whose citizens require tourist visas, including Bosnia and Hercegovina, Peru, India and South Africa. Check with your nearest Italian consulate.

At the moment, there are 21 different types of visas, depending on whether you're in Italy as a tourist, religious pilgrim, competitive athlete, fashion model etc. Visitors with visas should also insist on having their passport stamped on entry as, without a stamp, they could encounter problems when trying to obtain a *permesso di soggiorno*.

STUDY VISAS

Non-EU citizens who want to study at a university or language school in Italy must have a study visa. These visas can be obtained from your nearest Italian embassy or consulate. You will normally need confirmation of your enrolment and payment of fees, as well as proof of adequate funds to be able to support yourself. The visa will then cover only the period of the enrolment. This type of visa is renewable within Italy, but, again, only with confirmation of ongoing enrolment and proof that you are able to support yourself – bank statements are preferred.

TOURIST VISAS

The standard tourist visa issued by Italian consulates is the Schengen visa, valid for up to 90 days. A Schengen visa issued by one Schengen country is generally valid for travel in all other Schengen countries. However, individual Schengen countries may impose additional restrictions on certain nationalities. It is therefore worth checking the visa regulations with the consulate of each Schengen country you plan to visit.

It's mandatory that you apply for a visa in your country of residence. You can apply for no more than two Schengen visas in any 12-month period, and they are not renewable inside Italy.

WOMEN TRAVELLERS

Tuscany and Umbria are not dangerous regions for women, but women travelling alone will sometimes find themselves with unwanted attention from local and foreign men. This attention is usually nothing more than whistles or overly long stares, but women travelling alone will want to keep an eye open for more sinister attention, especially in nightclubs or discos.

As in many parts of Europe, lone women may at times find it difficult to be left alone. It is not uncommon for Italian men of all ages to try to strike up conversations with foreign women who just want to drink a coffee or are trying to read a book in the park. Usually the best response is to just ignore them, but if that doesn't work, politely tell them that you are waiting for your

---

COPIES

All important documents (passport data page and visa page, credit cards, travel insurance policy, air/bus/train tickets, driving licence etc) should be photocopied before you leave home. Leave one copy with someone at home and keep another with you, separate from the originals.

DIRECTORY

marito (husband) or *fidanzato* (boyfriend) and, if necessary, walk away. Florence can be a pain in this way, especially in the bars. It can also be an issue in some of the coastal resorts and on Elba.

Avoid becoming aggressive as this almost always results in an unpleasant confrontation. If all else fails, approach the nearest member of the police.

Avoid walking alone on deserted and dark streets, and look for centrally located hotels within easy walking distance of places where you can eat at night. Lonely Planet does not recommend hitchhiking, and women travelling alone should be particularly wary of doing so.

The book *A Journey of One's Own: Uncommon Advice for the Independent Woman Traveler* by Thalia Zepatos is in its 3rd edition and filled with practical advice for female adventurers.

WORK

It is illegal for non-EU citizens to work in Italy without a work permit (p356), but trying to obtain one can be time-consuming. EU citizens are allowed to work in Italy, but they still need to obtain a *permesso di soggiorno* from the main *questura* in the town where they have found work.

Baby-sitting and au pair work is possible if you organise it before you come to Italy. A useful guide is *The Au Pair and Nanny's Guide to Working Abroad,* by Susan Griffith and Sharon Legg.

The easiest source of work for foreigners i teaching English, but even with full qualifica tions a native English speaker might find i difficult to secure a permanent position. Mos of the larger, more reputable schools will hir only people with a *permesso di lavoro,* bu the attitude of the schools can become mor flexible if the demand for teachers is high and they come across someone with goo qualifications. The more professional school will require at least a TEFL (Teaching Englis as a Foreign Language) certificate. It is advis able to apply for work early in the year, ir order to be considered for positions available in September (language-school years corres pond roughly to the Italian school year: late September to the end of June).

Some people pick up private students by placing advertisements in shop windows and on university notice boards. Rates o pay vary according to experience.

Some travellers are able to pick up kitchen and bar work in the more tourist restaurants, particularly in Florence.

Further reading resources include *Work Your Way around the World* and *Teaching English Abroad,* both by Susan Griffith, and *Live & Work in Italy* by Victoria Pybus and Huw Francis, or *Living, Studying & Working in Italy* by Travis Neighbor and Monica Larner.

Transport

CONTENTS

GETTING THERE & AWAY

ENTERING THE COUNTRY

Entering Italy is relatively simple. Airport customs has tightened up a bit since 9/11, If you are entering Italy from neighbouring EU countries you don't require a passport check.

Passport

Citizens of EU member states can travel to Italy with their national identity cards. All non-EU nationals must have a valid passport. If applying for a visa, check that the expiry date of your passport is at least some months off. See p356 for more information about obtaining a visa.

Entry stamps may not be stamped in your passport, but if you plan to remain in the country for an extended period or wish to work, you should insist on having one. Without a stamp you could encounter problems when trying to obtain a *permesso di soggiorno* – in effect, permission to remain in the country (see p356).

If your passport is stolen or lost while you are in Italy, notify the police straight away and obtain a statement, and then contact your embassy or consulate as soon as possible.

THINGS CHANGE

The information in this chapter is particularly vulnerable to change: prices for international travel are volatile, routes are introduced and cancelled, schedules change, special deals come and go, and rules and visa requirements are amended. You should check directly with the airline or a travel agent to make sure you understand how a fare (or ticket) works and be aware of the security requirements for international travel.

You should try and get quotes from as many airlines and travel agents as possible. The details given in this chapter should be regarded as pointers and are not a substitute for your own careful, up-to-date research.

AIR

High season for air travel to Italy is June to September. Shoulder season will often run mid-September to the end of October and again in April. Low season is generally November to March, but fares around Christmas and Easter often increase or are sold out well in advance.

Airports & Airlines

Tuscany's main hub is Pisa's **Galileo Galilei** (code PSA; ☎ 050 50 07 07; www.pisa-airport.com) airport, where the bulk of European commercial and charter flights for this area land. Umbria has a small airport, **Sant'Egidio** (code PEG; ☎ 075 59 21 41; www.airport.umbria.it), on the outskirts of Perugia, serving mainly European Alitalia flights. Intercontinental flights use Rome's **Leonardo da Vinci** (Fiumicino; code FCO; ☎ 06 659 55 571; www.adr .it) airport. The small **Amerigo Vespucci** (code FLR; ☎ 055 37 34 98; www.aeroporto.firenze.it) airport, just outside of Florence, is a jumping-off point to nearby European countries.

Note that, in response to the threat of terrorism, getting through airport security takes longer than it did before 9/11. Ask your airline about hand-luggage restrictions and how long you need to allow for check-in.

Airlines flying into the region include: **Air Berlin** (code AB; ☎ 848 39 00 54; www.airberlin .com; hub Nuremberg)

TRANSPORT

Air France (code AF; ☎ 848 88 44 66; www.airfrance
.com; hub Paris)

Air One (code AP; ☎ 199 20 70 80; www.flyairone.it;
hub Rome)

Alitalia (code AZ; ☎ 06 2222; www.alitalia.it; hub
Rome)

British Airways (code BA; ☎ 199 712 266; www
.britishairways.com; hub Heathrow)

Delta (code DL; ☎ 06 4201 0332; www.delta.com; hub
Atlanta)

EasyJet (code U2; ☎ 848 88 77 66; www.easyjet.com;
hub Luton)

Lufthansa (code LH; ☎ 199 400 044; www.lufthansa
.com; hub Frankfurt)

Meridiana (code IG; ☎ 199 111 333; www.meridiana
.it; hub Olbia)

Ryanair (code FR; ☎ 899 67 89 10; www.ryanair.com;
hub London Stansted)

Thomsonfly (code 06; ☎ 02 36 00 3582; www
.thomsonfly.com; hub Coventry)

Virgin Express (code TV; ☎ 848 390 109; www
.virgin-express.com; hub Brussels)

Tickets

World aviation has never been so competitive, and the Internet is fast becoming the
easiest way to find reasonably priced seats.

Full-time students and those under 26
have access to discounted fares. You have
to show a document proving your date of
birth or a valid International Student Identity Card (ISIC) when buying your ticket.
Other cheap deals are the discounted tickets released to travel agents and specialist
discount agencies. Most major cities carry
a Sunday travel section with ads for these
agencies, often known as brokers in Europe
and consolidators in the US. Also check the
websites directly for low-cost carriers, such
as Ryanair and Easyjet.

Many of the major travel websites, such
as **Travelocity** (www.travelocity.com), **Expedia** (www
.expedia.com), **Kayak** (www.kayak.com) or **Booking
Buddy** (www.bookingbuddy.com), can offer competitive fares.

Australia

Cheap flights from Australia to Europe
generally go via Southeast Asian capitals.
Qantas, along with Alitalia, offer the only
direct flights from Melbourne and Sydney
to Rome, but also try the Star Alliance
carriers (Thai Air, Singapore Airlines or
Austrian Air) or Malaysian Air, as they are
often cheaper.

Quite a few travel offices specialise in
discount air tickets. Some travel agencies,
particularly smaller ones, advertise cheap
air fares in the travel sections of weekend
newspapers, such as the *Age* in Melbourne
and the *Sydney Morning Herald*.

STA Travel (☎ 1300 733 035; www.statravel.com.au)
has offices in all major cities and on many
university campuses. **Flight Centre** (☎ 131 600;
24hr; www.flightcentre.com.au) has dozens of offices throughout Australia.

Canada

Alitalia has direct flights between Toronto
and Rome. Air Transat flies nonstop from
Montreal to Rome in the summer months.
Scan the budget travel agencies' advertise-
ments in the *Toronto Globe & Mail, Toronto
Star* and *Vancouver Province*.

Air Canada flies daily from Toronto to
Rome, direct and via Montreal. British Airways, Air France, KLM and Lufthansa all fly
to Italy via their respective home countries.
Canada's main student travel organisation
is **Travel Cuts** (☎ 800 667 2887; www.travelcuts.com),
which has offices in all major cities.

Continental Europe

All national European carriers offer services
to Italy. The largest of these, Air France,
Lufthansa and KLM, have representative
offices in major European cities. Italy's national carrier, Alitalia, has a huge range of
offers on all European destinations. Several
airlines, including Alitalia, Qantas and Air
France, offer cut-rate fares between cities
on the European legs of long-haul flights.

In France, the student travel agencies **OTU
Voyages** (☎ 0820 817 817; www.otu.fr in French) and
Travel Club Voyages (☎ 0892 888 888) are a safe
bet for cut-price travel. In Germany, Munich
is a haven of budget travel outlets such as
STA Travel (www.statravel.de in German), which is one
of the best and has offices throughout the
country. **Kilroy Travel Group** (www.kilroygroups.se in
Swedish) offers discounted travel to people aged
16 to 33, and has representative offices in
Denmark, Sweden, Norway, Finland and the
Netherlands. In Athens, **ISYTS** (☎ 010 322 12 67;
www.travelling.gr/isyts/) is the official International
Student Youth Travel Service. **Virgin Express**
(www.virgin-express.com) has a whole host of flights
out of Brussels, including five daily flights
to Rome. Details of its offices in Belgium,
Denmark, France, Germany and Greece can

be found on the website. If you are searching online, try www.budgettravel.com.

Getting cheap flights between Spain and Italy is difficult; frequently the least expensive flights are routed through another European city (such as Munich). In Madrid, one of the most reliable budget travel agencies is **Viajes Zeppelin** (☎ 902 38 42 53; www.viajeszeppelin .com in Spanish) which also offers onward flights to South American destinations. The Italian airline, **Meridiana** (www.meridiana.it), has direct flights to Florence from Barcelona and Madrid. In the Netherlands, there are plenty of discount travel agents along Amsterdam's Rokin, but shop around to compare prices. One recommended travel agent **Holland International** (☎ 070 361 4561), has branches in most cities. Online, try www.airfair.nl (in Dutch).

New Zealand

Singapore Air flies from Auckland through Singapore to Rome's Fiumicino on Sunday, Tuesday and Friday from May to October. On New Zealand Air, you'll have to make at least two stops. The *New Zealand Herald* has a travel section in which travel agencies advertise fares. **Flight Centre** (☎ 0800 24 35 44; www.flightcentre.co.nz) has a large central office in Auckland and many other branches throughout the country. **STA Travel** (☎ 0800 24 35 44; www.statravel.co.nz) has offices in Auckland, as well as in Hamilton, Palmerston North, Wellington, Christchurch and Dunedin.

UK & Ireland

Discount air travel is big business in London. Advertisements for many travel agencies appear in the travel pages of the weekend newspapers, such as the *Independent* and the *Guardian* on Saturday, and the *Sunday Times*, as well as in publications such as *Time Out* and the *Big Issue*.

STA Travel (☎ 0870 160 0599; www.statravel.co.uk) and **Trailfinders** (☎ 020 7292 18 88; www.trailfinders .com), both of which have offices throughout the UK, sell discounted and student tickets. Other good sources of discounted fares are www.discount-tickets.com, www.ebookers .com and www.flynow.com.

Most British travel agents are registered with ABTA (Association of British Travel Agents). If you have paid for your flight with an ABTA-registered agent who then goes bust, ABTA will guarantee a refund or an alternative.

USA

Discount travel agencies in the USA are known as consolidators, and often advertise in Sunday newspaper travel sections, especially in the *New York Times*, the *Los Angeles Times*, the *Chicago Tribune* and the *San Francisco Chronicle*. Be careful when you purchase from a company you find on the Internet or in the back of a newspaper.

STA Travel (☎ 800 781 4040; www.statravel.com) has offices in Boston, Chicago, Los Angeles, New York, Philadelphia and San Francisco. Fares vary wildly depending on season, availability and a little luck. **Discover Italy** (☎ 866 878 74 77; www.discoveritaly.com) offers flight-, hotel- and villa-booking services.

Discount and rock-bottom options from the USA include charter, stand-by and courier flights. Stand-by fares are often sold at 60% of the normal price for one-way tickets. **Courier Travel** (☎ 303 570 7586; www .couriertravel.org) is a comprehensive searchable database for courier and stand-by flights.

LAND

There are plenty of options to consider for reaching Tuscany and Umbria by train, bus or private vehicle. If time does not equal money, bus travel is the cheapest option, but it takes significantly longer and is less comfortable than travelling by train.

Border Crossings

The main points of entry to Italy are the Mont Blanc Tunnel from France at Chamonix, which connects with the A5 for Turin and Milan; the Grand St Bernard tunnel from Switzerland, which also connects with the A5; and the Brenner Pass from Austria, which connects with the A22 to Bologna. All three are open year-round. Mountain passes are often closed in winter and sometimes even in autumn and spring, making the tunnels a more reliable option. Make sure you have snow chains if driving in winter.

Regular trains on two lines connect Italy with the main cities in Austria, Germany, France or Eastern Europe. Those crossing the frontier at the Brenner Pass go to Innsbruck, Stuttgart and Munich. Those crossing at Tarvisio in the east proceed to Vienna, Salzburg and Prague. Trains from Milan head for Switzerland and into France and the Netherlands. The main international train line to Slovenia crosses near Trieste.

TRANSPORT

In 2007, the world's largest land tunnel will open in Switzerland, providing a rail link under the Alps. The tunnel will be 34km long and carry passenger trains at 150km/h, cutting the time to cross from Germany to Milan from 3½ hours to two hours.

Bus

Eurolines (www.eurolines.com) is a consortium of European coach companies that operates across Europe, with offices in all major European cities. Italy-bound buses head to Milan, Rome or Florence, and all come equipped with onboard toilet facilities (necessary for journeys like London–Rome, which takes 30 hours). Discounts are available for seniors and travellers under 26 years.

Another option is the backpacker-friendly **Busabout** (☎ 020 7950 1661; www.busabout.com), which covers at least 60 European cities and towns with a hop-on, hop-off pass. It also books three- and four-day short break itineraries. In Italy, it covers Rome, Florence, Siena, Pisa, Ancona, Venice and La Spezia (for the Cinque Terre).

Car & Motorcycle

Coming from the UK, you can take your car across to France by ferry or via the Channel Tunnel on **Eurotunnel** (☎ 08705 35 35 35; www.eurotunnel.com). Eurotunnel runs four crossings (35 minutes) an hour between Folkestone and Calais during the high season. You pay for the vehicle only; fares vary according to the time of day, season and advance purchase, but start at £49 each way.

When driving in Europe, always carry proof of ownership of a private vehicle. Third-party motor insurance is also a minimum requirement in Italy and throughout Europe. Ask your insurer for a European Accident Statement (EAS) form, which can simplify matters in the event of an accident. A European breakdown assistance policy is a good investment. In Italy, assistance can be obtained through the **Automobile Club Italiano** (ACI; ☎ 06 4 99 81, 24hr information ☎ 166 664 477; www.aci.it in Italian).

Every vehicle travelling across an international border should display a nationality plate of its country of registration.

Train

Florence is an important hub so it's easy to get to Tuscany and Umbria from numerous European destinations. The *Thomas Cook European Timetable* has a complete listing of train schedules. It is updated monthly and available from Thomas Cook offices worldwide for about €20. It is always advisable, and sometimes compulsory, to book seats on international trains to and from Italy. Some of the main international services include transport for private cars – an option worth examining to save wear and tear on your vehicle before it arrives in Italy.

Consider taking long journeys overnight, as a €20 or so sleeper fee costs substantially less than Italian hotels.

The **Eurostar** (☎ 0870 518 61 86; www.eurostar.com) passenger-train service travels between London and Paris, and London and Brussels. The Eurotunnel vehicle service travels between Folkestone and Calais. Alternatively, you can get a train ticket that includes crossing the Channel by ferry, SeaCat or hovercraft.

Trenitalia (www.trenitalia.com) operates the entire Italian rail system. For information on trains visit the website or call ☎ 89 20 21 (Italian-speaking) from anywhere in Italy.

Main train timetables generally display *arrivi* (arrivals) on a white background and *partenze* (departures) on a yellow one. Imminent arrivals and departures also appear on electronic boards.

There are many types of trains and many ticketing possibilities. Apart from the division between 1st and 2nd class, you usually have to pay a supplement for travelling on a fast train. When enquiring about a route, check to see what type of train you are travelling on. Types to look out for include *regionali, inter-regionali, intercity* and *ETR*.

You can buy rail tickets for major destinations from most travel agents. If you buy them at the station, there are automatic machines that accept cash and credit cards.

Eurail (www.eurail.com), **InterRail** (www.inter-rail.co.uk), **Eurodomino** (www.eurodomino.it/eng) and the **Trenitalia Pass** (www.trenitalia.com), all of which can be bought in Italy and abroad, are valid on the national rail. They allow you unlimited rail travel for varying periods of time. The passes are only useful if you plan to travel extensively around Italy by train. Passes have their own validating rules, which are generally written inside the pass cover.

Special offers for families and group travel are also available. Check what reductions are available when booking your tickets.

SEA

Ferries connect Italy with countries all over the Mediterranean, but if you want to reach Tuscany directly by sea, the only options are the ferry crossings to Livorno from Sardinia and Corsica. See p179 for more details.

GETTING AROUND

Most of the towns and cities have a reasonable bus service, but you'll probably find that amenities and places of interest are usually within walking distance. Bus tickets should be bought from newsagents, tobacconists or kiosks before boarding, and validated in the machine once on board.

Buses and trains connect Pisa's Galileo Galilei airport with Pisa and Florence, while buses link Amerigo Vespucci airport, just outside of Florence, with central Florence. Buses from Piazza Italia coincide with flights at Perugia's Sant'Egidio airport.

Taxis are widely available. Travellers are advised to use only the official taxis, which are easily identifiable.

BICYCLE

Cycling is a national pastime in Italy. You would be wise to equip yourself with a helmet and lights. You cannot take bikes onto the autostrada. If you plan to bring your bike by air to Italy, you will either have to dismantle it or pay a fee of around €50. Contact your airline for details.

Bikes can be taken on any train carrying the bicycle logo. The cheapest way to do this is to buy a separate bicycle ticket, available even at the self-service kiosks, usually costing around €3.50. You can use this ticket for 24 hours, making a day trip quite economical. Bikes dismantled and stored in a bag can be taken for free, even on night trains, and all ferries allow free bicycle passage.

Check out p355 or p45 for more information on bicycle tours.

Hire

There are bikes available for hire in most Italian towns and many hire places can offer both city and mountain bikes. They are generally well priced with rental costs for a city bike start at €8/25 per day/week.

Purchase

If you shop around, bargain prices for bicycles range from about €100 for a standard bike without gears to €210 for a mountain bike with 16 gears. Check university bulletin boards for used bicycles.

BOAT

Regular *traghetti* (ferries) connect Piombino with Elba. In summer, trips depart from Portoferraio on Elba for the island of Capraia, and from Porto Azzurro to the tiny island of Pianosa. From Livorno, ferries run to Capraia via the prison island of Gorgona. You can reach the islands of Giglio and Giannutri from Porto Santo Stefano. See the relevant chapters for more details. Travellers can also check www.traghetti.com for information on ferry companies, schedules, fares and availability.

To search for every ferry service that goes in or out of Italy, check **Traghettionline** (www.traghettionline.com in Italian).

BUS

Although the Italian train service is the most convenient and cheapest way to get between major towns and tourist destinations, the bus is often the best way to get to small towns and villages. A few routes, such as between Florence and Siena, are better served by bus.

Dozens of different companies offer hundreds of constantly changing itineraries. Most companies lessen or even stop services on weekends, especially on Sundays, and holidays. It is usually possible to get bus timetables from local tourist offices, or they can call the companies for you.

In larger cities, ticket companies often have offices at the bus terminal. In some villages and even good-sized towns, tickets are sold in bars or on the bus.

Lazzi has buses from Florence to parts of Tuscany, mostly in the northwest, including Pisa, Lucca and Pistoia. The CAP and Copit companies also serve towns in the northwest. In Umbria, look out for the companies ATC and SSIT, which serve southern Umbria, and APM, which covers Perugia, Assisi and the north.

Tickets can be bought at most *tabacchi* (tobacconists) and newsstands, or from ticket booths or dispensing machines at bus stations and in underground stations. Tickets cost around €0.80 to €1. Most large cities offer good-value 24-hour or daily tourist tickets.

CAR & MOTORCYCLE
Automobile Associations

The ever-handy **Automobile Club d'Italia** (ACI; ☎ 06 42 12, 24hr 800 116 800; www.aci.it in Italian; Via Colombo 261, Rome) is a driver's best resource in Italy. They have a dedicated 24-hour phone line for foreigners in need of emergency assistance, weather conditions or even tourist information. In an emergency, you can dial ☎ 803 116 from any Italian phone, or ☎ 800 116 800 from a foreign mobile phone. Foreigners do not have to join to use its services, but will need to pay a fee at the time of services. To tow a broken-down vehicle to the nearest mechanic shop might cost about €150.

A European breakdown assistance policy is advisable. In the UK, try the **AA** (☎ 0870 550 06 00) Five Star Service or the **RAC** (☎ 0800 55 00 55) Eurocover Motoring Assistance. Holders of these policies will usually be provided with an emergency assistance number to use while travelling. In the US, try **AAA** (www.aaa .com) or contact the automobile association in your own country for more information.

Bringing Your Own Vehicle

Cars entering Italy from abroad need a valid national licence plate and an accompanying registration card. If you're bringing in a car imported from a country that does not use the Latin alphabet you will need to have the registration card translated at the nearest Italian consulate before entering the country.

If you ship your car, be aware you must have less than one-quarter tank of petrol. Unfortunately, you can't use your vehicle as a double for luggage storage; it is supposed to be empty besides any necessary car-related items. All vehicles must be equipped with any necessary adjustments for the Italian market; for example, left-side drive cars will need to have the headlamps adjusted.

Proof of ownership of a private vehicle should always be carried when driving through Europe. You should also display a sticker detailing the country of origin of your vehicle.

ROAD DISTANCES (KM)

	Arezzo	Assisi	Carrara	Cortona	Florence	Livorno	Lucca	Orbetello	Orvieto	Perugia	Pisa	Pistoia	Prato	Siena	Spoleto	Viareggio
Assisi	96															
Carrara	198	317														
Cortona	28	72	237													
Florence	80	172	122	109												
Livorno	195	266	72	224	115											
Lucca	155	243	52	184	74	45										
Orbetello	175	222	247	215	180	175	216									
Orvieto	104	87	282	94	156	264	230	118								
Perugia	78	38	256	30	153	268	227	204	86							
Pisa	175	263	57	203	95	20	21	190	246	245						
Pistoia	115	208	92	143	35	85	45	215	204	190	65					
Prato	99	189	109	128	19	95	55	199	188	170	84	20				
Siena	65	124	153	99	70	130	140	116	134	109	110	105	81			
Spoleto	133	49	355	108	249	336	307	197	80	78	323	284	248	187		
Viareggio	180	266	30	206	97	41	25	195	250	247	21	69	89	123	325	
Volterra	111	175	135	151	75	69	74	168	186	161	65	108	88	52	239	86

WHERE TO PARK

Parking spaces outlined in blue are designated for paid parking. White or yellow outlines almost always indicate reserved parking or residential permits needed. You buy your ticket at a machine that's usually a few metres from wherever you've parked and display it in the front window.

Driving Licence

All EU member states' driving licences are fully recognised throughout Europe. Drivers with a non-EU licence are supposed to obtain an IDP (International Driving Permit), which is only valid when accompanying a valid driver's licence from the country of residence. An IDP costs around €10 and is valid for 12 months. You need to purchase one from the automobile association of the country from which you received your driver's licence. People who have held residency in Italy for one year or more must apply for an Italian driving licence.

Fuel & Spare Parts

Italy is covered by a good network of petrol and repair stations. You'll have three choices at the tank – petrol *(benzina)*, unleaded petrol *(benzina senza piombo)* and diesel *(gasolio)*. Petrol is around €1.30 per litre and diesel a little less, at around €1.15.

For spare parts, check with a repair shop or call the 24-hour ACI motorist assistance number ☎ 06 4212. You'll almost always get connected to an operator who speaks English.

Hire

There are countless car rental agencies in Italy, both multinational and local. There's no one rule for finding the best-priced rates. Sometimes reserving online from a national company is cheaper, other times it's best to walk into a local agency. Your best bet is to check the multinationals online, then call ahead to a local agency listed in the book and decide between the two.

Most tourist offices and hotels can provide information about car or motorcycle rental. To rent a car in Italy you must be at least 25 years and you need a credit card.

Check with your credit card company to see if they offer a collision damage waiver,

which covers you for additional damage if you use that card to pay for the car. Many car rental agencies request that you bring the car back with a full tank, and will charge astronomically if it's not. Make sure you understand what is included in the price (unlimited kilometres, tax, insurance, collision damage waiver and so on) and what your liabilities are.

CAR

The most competitive multinational and Italian car rental agencies are listed.

Avis (☎ 199 100 133; www.avis.com)
Budget (☎ 800 472 33 25; www.budget-italy.com)
Europcar (☎ 800 014 410; www.europcar.com)
Hertz (☎ 091 213 112; www.hertz.com)
Italy by Car (☎ 800 846 083; www.italybycar.it)
Partners with Thrifty.
Maggiore (☎ 848 867 067; www.maggiore.it in Italian)

An interesting way to get around Italy (and Europe) is to rent or buy a camper van. If you are travelling for more than a few weeks, it's much more cost effective to purchase and then sell back the camper van, as rental fees start at about €60 per day. Check www.ideamerge.com or **Caravan Mec** (☎ 055 31 19 28; www.caravanmec.it in Italian).

MOTORCYCLE

You'll have no trouble hiring a small Vespa or moped. There are numerous rental agencies in cities where you'll also be able to hire larger motorcycles for touring. The average cost for a 50cc scooter is around €20/150 per day/week.

Most agencies will not rent motorcycles to people aged under 18. Note that many places require a sizeable deposit, and you could be responsible for reimbursing part of the cost of the bike if it is stolen.

You don't need a licence to ride a moped under 50cc, but you should be aged 14 or over and you can't carry passengers. The autostrada is no place for a moped or scooter, and those in the know recommend at least a 650cc engine to venture forth. On all two-wheeled transport, helmets are always required. The speed limit for a moped is 40km/h. To ride a motorcycle or scooter up to 125cc, you must be aged 16 or over and have a licence (a car licence will do). Helmets are compulsory. For motorcycles over 125cc you will need a motorcycle licence.

TRANSPORT

You will be able to enter restricted traffic areas in Italian cities on a motorcycle without any problems.

Check out p355 for information on motorcycle tours.

Insurance

Third-party motor insurance is a minimum requirement in Italy. The Green Card is an internationally recognised proof of insurance obtainable from your insurer, and is mandatory. Ask your insurer for a European Accident Statement form, which can simplify matters in the event of an accident. Never sign statements you don't understand – insist on a translation.

Purchase

Rock-bottom prices for a reasonable car that won't break down instantly will run about €2000 to €3000. The cost of a second-hand Vespa ranges from €200 to €700.

To find vehicles for sale, look in the classified sections of newspapers or go to an online auction site such as www.ebay.it.

Road Rules

In Italy, as in the rest of continental Europe, drive on the right side of the road and overtake on the left. On three-lane roads, the middle lane is reserved for overtaking. At crossroads, give way to traffic from the right.

All passengers must wear seatbelts wherever fitted. Children under 12 must travel in the back seat, and those under four must use child seats. It is compulsory for motorcyclists and their passengers to wear helmets.

A warning triangle (to be used in the event of a breakdown) is compulsory throughout Europe. Recommended accessories are first-aid kit, spare-bulb kit and fire extinguisher. If your car breaks down at night take note if you get out of the vehicle. You could be fined up to €138 unless you wear an approved yellow or orange safety vest (available at bicycle shops and outdoor stores).

Random breath tests now take place in Italy. If you're involved in an accident while under the influence of alcohol, the penalties can be severe. The blood-alcohol limit is 0.05%.

Drivers usually travel at high speeds in the left-hand fast lane on the autostrada so use that lane only to pass other cars. You have to pay a toll to use the autostrada, which can be paid by credit card (including Visa, MasterCard, American Express and Diners Club). For information on road tolls and passes, check online at www.autostrade.it, or call the **Società Autostrade** (☎ 0 436 31). In built-up areas the speed limit is usually 50km/h, rising to 90km/h on secondary roads, 110km/h (caravans 80km/h) on main roads, and up to 130km/h (caravans 100km/h) on the autostrada. Keep your running lights, or your headlights, on at all times when on the autostrada.

Off the beaten path you'll be doing most of your travelling on the larger system of *strade statali*. On maps they'll be represented by 'S' or 'SS', and can vary from four-lane highways (no tolls) to two-lane roads. These can be extremely slow, especially in mountainous regions. The third category is the

---

PASSING

You might call it passing or overtaking, but Italians call it a national pastime. On first glance, it seems as if the overtaker is going to be reunited soon with an undertaker, but there are actually a few rules in place.

The major hard-and-fast rule is: stay in the right lane unless you're passing or going Italian-driver-on-three-espressos fast!

Italians joke that they don't use their rear-view mirrors when driving. This means that you don't have to, either. When a driver is on your tail at 160km/h, it's not your responsibility to pull over or slow down. If they want to pass, they will have to wait until it is safe (or not humorously dangerous) to do so. If they pass when another car is passing on the opposite side of the road, you can manoeuvre gently to the right with a turn signal indicator to allow the cars not to careen into each other, but that's your only choice.

When you pass, make sure you have your left-turn signal on. Wait until the solid yellow middle line turns into dots or dashes. Don't even think about passing on a curve. Oh, yes, and make sure there isn't a car coming from the opposite direction.

ROAD SIGNS

You can save yourself some grief in Tuscany and Umbria by learning what some of the many road signs mean:

- *entrata* – entrance (eg onto an autostrada)
- *incrocio* – intersection/crossroads
- *lavori in corso* – roadworks ahead
- *parcheggio* – car park
- *passaggio a livello* – level crossing
- *rallentare* – slow down
- *senso unico* – one-way street
- *senso vietato* – no entry
- *sosta autorizzata* – parking permitted (during times displayed)
- *sosta vietata* – no stopping/parking
- *svolta* – bend
- *tutte le direzioni* – all directions (useful when looking for the town exit)
- *uscita* – exit (eg from an autostrada)

strade provinciali, which you'll find in rural areas and connecting small villages, and finally, *strade locali,* which might not even be paved. You'll often find the most beautiful scenery off the provincial and local roads.

Motoring organisations in various countries have publications that detail road rules for foreign countries. If you get an IDP, it should also include a road rules booklet.

HITCHING

Hitching is, for the most part, completely unheard of in Tuscany and Umbria. Locals never, ever hitch, and you might find yourself stranded for days. We don't recommend it out of safety considerations in any country, but here it's nigh on impossible.

TAXI

You can usually find taxi ranks at train and bus stations, or you can telephone for radio taxis. It's best to go to a designated taxi stand, as it's illegal for taxis to stop in the street if hailed.

TRAIN

The trains throughout Tuscany and Umbria are widespread and you can get to most tourist areas by train, with a few noted exceptions (the Chianti region in Tuscany and Monti Sibillini in Umbria). Be aware that trains on the minor routes, known as *regionali,* can be limited and slow.

Trenitalia (☎ 800 89 20 21 Italian-speaking; www .trenitalia.com) is the partially privatised state train system, which runs most of the services in Italy. Other private Italian train lines are noted throughout this book.

For **train information** (☎ 800 51 21 41; www.um briatrasporti.it) for Umbria, plus bus and ferry timetables, try this extremely helpful free information line. You will rarely be connected to someone who speaks English, but usually, if your number is in Italian and you can tell them the city, they'll patiently tell you the prices and depature times.

Almost every Italian train station has either a guarded left-luggage office or self-service lockers. The guarded offices are usually open 24 hours or 6am to midnight. The charge is around €3 per 12 hours for each piece of luggage.

Classes & Costs

There are 1st and 2nd classes on most Italian trains; a 1st-class ticket costs just under double the price of a 2nd-class ticket.

To travel on Intercity and Eurostar trains you are required to pay a supplement (€3 to €16) determined by the distance you are travelling. On the Eurostar, the cost of the ticket includes the supplement and booking fee. If you are simply travelling to a town a stop or two away, make sure you check

---

VALIDATE, VALIDATE, VALIDATE!

Almost every train (and several bus) journey requires passengers to validate their tickets *before* boarding. You simply punch them in the yellow *convalida* machines installed at the entrance to all train platforms. On local buses and trains run by some private railway companies, you validate your ticket on the bus or train itself. Getting caught with a ticket that hasn't been validated risks a hefty fine of up to €50, paid on the spot to an inspector who will be kind enough to escort you to an ATM if you don't have the cash on you. Don't even think about trying the *'Ma sono una turista!'* line; it hasn't worked in at least 15 years.

TRANSPORT

TRAIN ROUTES

Principal Train Lines
Local Train Lines

whether your 40-minute journey requires a supplement. You might arrive 10 minutes earlier, but pay €5 more for the privilege. Check up-to-date prices of routes on www .trenitalia.com.

Reservations

Reservations on trains are not essential, but without one you may not be able to find a seat. Bookings can be made when you buy your ticket, and usually cost an extra €2.50. Reservations are obligatory for many of the Eurostar trains.

You can make train bookings at most travel agencies, or you can simply buy your ticket on arrival at the station (allow plenty of time for this). There are special booking offices for Eurostar trains at the relevant train stations.

Train Passes

If you're just travelling within Tuscany and Umbria, train travel is inexpensive, and a train pass wouldn't make financial sense.

If you do require one, Trenitalia offers discount passes for foreigners travelling within Italy. These include the Carta Verde (€25, valid for one year), which offers a 20% discount for people aged from 12 to 26 years. Similarly, the Carta d'Argento (€25, valid for one year) offers the same discount to people aged 60 years and over. Children aged between four and 12 years are entitled to a 50% discount; those aged under four travel free.

Health

CONTENTS

BEFORE YOU GO

While Tuscany and Umbria have excellent health care, prevention is the key to staying healthy while abroad. A little planning before departure, particularly for pre-existing illnesses, will save trouble later. Bring medications in their original, clearly labelled, containers. A signed and dated letter from your physician describing your medical conditions and medications, including generic names, is also a good idea. If carrying syringes or needles, be sure to have a physician's letter documenting their medical necessity. If you are embarking on a long trip, make sure your teeth are OK (dental treatment is particularly expensive in Italy) and take your optical prescription with you.

INSURANCE

If you're an EU citizen, arm yourself with the new European Health Insurance Card, a handy piece of plastic, valid for two years, that entitles you to emergency treatment throughout the Union. Order on line or through your local Health Office. This card supersedes the E111 form that previously entitled you to treatment within the EU.

Citizens from other countries should find out if there is a reciprocal arrangement for free medical care between their country and Italy. If you need health insurance, get a policy that covers you for the worst possible scenario, such as an accident requiring an emergency flight home. Find out in advance if your insurance plan will make payments directly to providers or reimburse you later for overseas health expenditures.

RECOMMENDED VACCINATIONS

No jabs are required to travel to Italy. The World Health Organization (WHO), however, recommends that all travellers should be covered for diphtheria, tetanus, measles, mumps, rubella and polio, as well as hepatitis B.

ONLINE RESOURCES

The WHO's publication *International Travel and Health* is revised annually and is available online at www.who.int/ith/. Other useful websites include www.mdtravelhealth .com (daily health recommendations for every country), www.fitfortravel.scot.nhs .uk (general travel advice), www.agecon cern.org.uk (advice on travel for the elderly) and www.mariestopes.org.uk (information on women's health and contraception).

IN TRANSIT

DEEP VEIN THROMBOSIS (DVT)

Blood clots may form in the legs during plane flights, chiefly because of prolonged immobility; the longer the flight, the greater the risk. The chief symptom of DVT is swelling or pain of the foot, ankle, or calf, usually but not always on just one side. When a blood clot travels to the lungs, it may cause chest pain and breathing difficulties. Travellers with any of these symptoms should immediately seek medical attention. To prevent the development of DVT on long flights you should walk about the cabin, contract the leg muscles while sitting, drink plenty of fluids and avoid alcohol and tobacco.

JET LAG

To avoid jet lag try drinking plenty of nonalcoholic fluids and eating light meals. Upon arrival, get exposure to natural sunlight and readjust your schedule (for meals, sleep, etc) as soon as possible.

IN TUSCANY & UMBRIA

AVAILABILITY & COST OF HEALTH CARE

If you need an ambulance anywhere in Italy call ☎ 118. For emergency treatment, go straight to the *pronto soccorso* (casualty) section of a public hospital, where you can also get emergency dental treatment.

Excellent healthcare is readily available throughout Italy but standards can vary. Pharmacists can give valuable advice and sell over-the-counter medication for minor illnesses. They can also advise when more specialised help is required and point you in the right direction. In major cities you are likely to find English-speaking doctors or a translator service available.

TRAVELLERS' DIARRHOEA

If you develop diarrhoea, be sure to drink plenty of fluids, preferably in the form of an oral rehydration solution such as Dioralyte. If diarrhoea is bloody, persists for more than 72 hours or is accompanied by fever, shaking, chills or severe abdominal pain, you should seek medical attention.

ENVIRONMENTAL HAZARDS
Heatstroke

Heatstroke occurs following excessive fluid loss with inadequate replacement of fluids and salt. Symptoms include headache, dizziness and tiredness. Dehydration is already happening by the time you feel thirsty – aim to drink sufficient water to produce pale, diluted urine. To treat heatstroke drink water and/or fruit juice, and cool the body with cold water and fans.

Hypothermia

Hypothermia occurs when the body loses heat faster than it can produce it. As ever, proper preparation will reduce the risks of getting it. Even on a hot day in the mountains, the weather can change rapidly, so carry waterproof garments, wear warm layers and a hat, and inform others of your route. Hypothermia starts with shivering, loss of judgment and clumsiness. Unless re-warming occurs, the sufferer deteriorates into apathy, confu-

sion and coma. Prevent further heat loss by seeking shelter, warm dry clothing, hot sweet drinks and shared body warmth.

Bites, Stings & Insect-Borne Diseases

Tuscan beaches are occasionally inundated with jellyfish. Their stings are painful but not dangerous. Dousing in vinegar will deactivate any stingers that have not fired. Calamine lotion, antihistamines and analgesics may reduce the reaction and relieve pain.

Italy's only dangerous snake, the viper, is found throughout Tuscany and Umbria. To minimise the possibilities of being bitten always wear boots, socks and long trousers when walking through undergrowth where snakes may be present. Don't put your hands into holes and crevices, and be careful when collecting firewood. Viper bites do not cause instantaneous death and an antivenin is widely available in pharmacies. Keep the victim calm and still, wrap the bitten limb tightly, as you would for a sprained ankle, and attach a splint to immobilise it. Seek medical help, if possible with the dead snake for identification. Don't attempt to catch the snake if there is a possibility of being bitten again. Tourniquets and sucking out the poison are now comprehensively discredited.

Always check all over your body if you have been walking through a potentially tick-infested area as ticks can cause skin infections and other more serious diseases such as Lyme disease and tick-borne encephalitis. If a tick is found attached, press down around the tick's head with tweezers, grab the head and gently pull upwards. Avoid pulling the rear of the body as this may squeeze the tick's gut contents through the attached mouth parts into the skin, increasing the risk of infection and disease. Lyme disease begins with the spreading of a rash at the site of the bite, accompanied by fever, headache, extreme fatigue, aching joints and muscles and severe neck stiffness. If untreated, symptoms usually disappear but disorders of the nervous system, heart and joints can develop later. Treatment works best early in the illness – medical help should be sought. Symptoms of tick-borne encephalitis include blotches around the bite, which is sometimes pale in the middle, and headaches, stiffness and other flu-like symptoms (as well as extreme iredness) appearing a week or two after the bite. Again, medical help must be sought.

Leishmaniasis is a group of parasitic diseases transmitted by sandflies and found in coastal parts of Tuscany. Cutaneous leishmaniasis affects the skin and causes ulceration and disfigurement; visceral leishmaniasis affects the internal organs. Avoiding sandfly bites by covering up and using repellent is the best precaution.

TRAVELLING WITH CHILDREN

Make sure children are up to date with routine vaccinations and discuss possible travel vaccines well before departure as some vaccines are not suitable for children under a year old. Lonely Planet's *Travel with Children* includes travel health advice for younger children.

WOMEN'S HEALTH

Emotional stress, exhaustion and travelling through different time zones can all contribute to an upset in the menstrual pattern.

If using oral contraceptives, remember some antibiotics, diarrhoea and vomiting can stop the pill from working. Time zones, gastrointestinal upsets and antibiotics do not affect injectable contraception.

Travelling during pregnancy is usually possible but always consult your doctor before planning your trip. The most risky times for travel are during the first 12 weeks of pregnancy and after 30 weeks.

SEXUAL HEALTH

Condoms are readily available but emergency contraception is not so take the necessary precautions.

HEALTH

Language

Italian is a Romance language related to French, Spanish, Portuguese and Romanian. The Romance languages belong to the Indo-European group of languages, which includes English. Indeed, as English and Italian share common roots in Latin, you will recognise many Italian words.

Modern literary Italian began to develop in the 13th and 14th centuries, predominantly through the works of Dante, Petrarch and Boccaccio – all Tuscans to a man – who wrote chiefly in the Florentine dialect. The language drew on its Latin heritage and many dialects to develop into the standard Italian of today. Although many dialects are spoken in everyday conversation, standard Italian is the national language of schools, media and literature, and is understood throughout the country.

While standard Italian was essentially born out of the Florentine dialect, anyone who has learned Italian sufficiently well will find many Florentines surprisingly hard to understand, at least at first. Whether or not they have their own localised non-standard vocabulary you could argue about at length, but no-one can deny the peculiarity of the local accent. Here, and in other parts of Tuscany, you are bound to hear the hard 'c' pronounced as a heavily aspirated 'h'. *Voglio*

una cannuccia per la Coca Cola (I want a straw for my Coca Cola) in Florence sounds more like *voglio una hannuccia per la Hoha Hola*! Over the regional border in Umbria, you'll be spared the anomalies of Tuscan pronunciation, and understanding the local accent should be a lot easier.

If you've managed to gain more than the most fundamental grasp of the language, you'll be aware that many older Italians still expect to be addressed by the third person polite, that is, *lei* instead of *tu*. Also, it is not considered polite to use the greeting *ciao* when addressing strangers, unless they use it first; it's better to say *buon giorno* (or *buona sera*, as the case may be) and *arrivederci* (or the more polite form, *arrivederla*). We've used the polite address for most of the phrases in this guide. Use of the informal address is indicated by (inf). Like other Latin-based languages, Italian has both masculine and feminine forms (in the singular they often end in 'o' and 'a' respectively). Where both forms are given in this guide, they are separated by a slash, with the masculine form first.

Lonely Planet's *Italian Phrasebook*, packed with practical phrases and simple explanations, fits neatly into your pocket.

PRONUNCIATION
Vowels
Vowels are generally more clipped than in English:

a	as in 'art', eg *caro* (dear); sometimes short, eg *amico/a* (friend)
e	short, as in 'let', eg *mettere* (to put); long, as in 'there', eg *mela* (apple)
i	short, as in 'it', eg *inizio* (start); long, as in 'marine', eg *vino* (wine)
o	short, as in 'dot', eg *donna* (woman); long, as in 'port', eg *ora* (hour)
u	as the 'oo' in 'book', eg *puro* (pure)

Consonants
The pronunciation of many Italian consonants is similar to that of their English counterparts. Pronunciation of some consonants depends on certain rules:

c	as the 'k' in 'kit' before **a**, **o** and **u**; as the 'ch' in 'choose' before **e** and **i**
ch	as the 'k' in 'kit'
g	as the 'g' in 'get' before **a**, **o**, **u** and **h**; as the 'j' in 'jet' before **e** and **i**
gli	as the 'lli' in 'million'
gn	as the 'ny' in 'canyon'
h	always silent
r	a rolled 'rr' sound
sc	as the 'sh' in 'sheep' before **e** and **i**; as 'sk' before **a**, **o**, **u** and **h**
z	as the 'ts' in 'lights'; at the beginning of a word, it's most commonly as the 'ds' in 'suds'

Note that when **ci**, **gi** and **sci** are followed by **a**, **o** or **u**, the 'i' is not pronounced unless the accent falls on the 'i'. Thus the name 'Giovanni' is pronounced joh-*vahn*-nee.

A double consonant is pronounced as a longer, more forceful sound than a single consonant.

Word Stress

Stress is indicated in our pronunciation guide by italics. Word stress generally falls on the second-last syllable, as in spa-*ghet*-ti, but when a word has an accent, the stress falls on that syllable, as in cit-*tà* (city).

ACCOMMODATION

I'm looking for a ...	Cerco ...	*cher*·ko ...
guesthouse	una pensione	oo·na pen·*syo*·ne
hotel	un albergo	oon al·*ber*·go
youth hostel	un ostello per la gioventù	oon os·*te*·lo per la jo·ven·*too*

Where is a cheap hotel?
Dov'è un albergo a buon prezzo?   do·*ve* oon al·*ber*·go a bwon *pre*·tso

What is the address?
Qual'è l'indirizzo?   kwa·*le* leen·dee·*ree*·tso

Could you write the address, please?
Può scrivere l'indirizzo, per favore?   pwo *skree*·ve·re leen·dee·*ree*·tso per fa·*vo*·re

Do you have any rooms available?
Avete camere libere?   a·*ve*·te *ka*·me·re *lee*·be·re

I'd like (a) ...	Vorrei ...	vo·*ray* ...
bed	un letto	oon *le*·to
single room	una camera singola	oo·na *ka*·me·ra *seen*·go·la

double room	una camera matrimoniale	oo·na *ka*·me·ra ma·tree·mo·*nya*·le
room with two beds	una camera doppia	oo·na *ka*·me·ra *do*·pya
room with a bathroom	una camera con bagno	oo·na *ka*·me·ra kon *ba*·nyo
to share a dorm	un letto in dormitorio	oon *le*·to een dor·mee·*to*·ryo

---

MAKING A RESERVATION

(for inclusion in letters, faxes and emails)

To ...	A ...
From ...	Da ...
Date	Data
I'd like to book ...	Vorrei prenotare ... (see the list on this page for bed/room options)
in the name of ...	nel nome di ...
for the night/s of ...	per la/le notte/i di ...
credit card ...	carta di credito ...
number	numero
expiry date	data di scadenza
Please confirm availability and price.	Vi prego di confirmare disponibilità e prezzo.

How much is it ...?	Quanto costa ...?	*kwan*·to *ko*·sta ...
per night	per la notte	per la *no*·te
per person	per persona	per per·*so*·na

May I see it?
Posso vederla?   *po*·so ve·*der*·la

Where is the bathroom?
Dov'è il bagno?   do·*ve* eel *ba*·nyo

I'm/We're leaving today.
Parto/Partiamo oggi.   *par*·to/par·*tya*·mo *o*·jee

CONVERSATION & ESSENTIALS

Hello.	Buongiorno.	bwon·*jor*·no
	Ciao. (inf)	chow
Goodbye.	Arrivederci.	a·ree·ve·*der*·chee
	Ciao. (inf)	chow
Good evening.	Buonasera. (from early afternoon onwards)	bwo·na·*se*·a
Good night.	Buonanotte.	bwo·na·*no*·te
Yes.	Sì.	see
No.	No.	no
Please.	Per favore/ Per piacere.	per fa·*vo*·re per pya·*chay*·re

LANGUAGE

Thank you.	*Grazie.*	*gra*·tsye
That's fine/	*Prego.*	*pre*·go
You're welcome.		
Excuse me.	*Mi scusi.*	mee *skoo*·zee
Sorry (forgive	*Mi scusi/*	mee *skoo*·zee/
me).	*Mi perdoni.*	mee per·*do*·nee

What's your name?

| *Come si chiama?* | *ko*·me see *kya*·ma |
| *Come ti chiami?* (inf) | *ko*·me tee *kya*·mee |

My name is ...

| *Mi chiamo ...* | mee *kya*·mo ... |

Where are you from?

| *Da dove viene?* | da *do*·ve *vye*·ne |
| *Di dove sei?* (inf) | dee *do*·ve *se*·ee |

I'm from ...

| *Vengo da ...* | *ven*·go da ... |

I (don't) like ...

| *(Non) Mi piace ...* | (non) mee *pya*·che ... |

Just a minute.

| *Un momento.* | oon mo·*men*·to |

DIRECTIONS

Where is ...?

| *Dov'è ...?* | do·*ve* ... |

Go straight ahead.

| *Si va sempre diritto.* | see va *sem*·pre dee·*ree*·to |
| *Vai sempre diritto.* (inf) | va·ee *sem*·pre dee·*ree*·to |

Turn left.

| *Giri a sinistra.* | *jee*·ree a see·*nee*·stra |

Turn right.

| *Giri a destra.* | *jee*·ree a *de*·stra |

at the next corner

| *al prossimo angolo* | al *pro*·see·mo *an*·go·lo |

at the traffic lights

| *al semaforo* | al se·*ma*·fo·ro |

behind	*dietro*	*dye*·tro
in front of	*davanti*	da·*van*·tee
far (from)	*lontano (da)*	lon·*ta*·no (da)

EMERGENCIES

Help!

| *Aiuto!* | a·*yoo*·to |

There's been an accident!

| *C'è stato un* | che *sta*·to oon |
| *incidente!* | een·chee·*den*·te |

I'm lost.

| *Mi sono perso/a.* | mee *so*·no *per*·so/a |

Go away!

| *Lasciami in pace!* | *la*·sha·mi een *pa*·che |
| *Vai via!* (inf) | va·ee *vee*·a |

Call ...!	*Chiami ...!*	kee·*ya*·mee ...
	Chiama ...! (inf)	kee·*ya*·ma ...
a doctor	*un dottore/*	oon do·*to*·re/
	un medico	oon *me*·dee·ko
the police	*la polizia*	la po·lee·*tsee*·ya

| near (to) | *vicino (di)* | vee·*chee*·no (dee) |
| opposite | *di fronte a* | dee *fron*·te a |

beach	*la spiaggia*	la *spya*·ja
bridge	*il ponte*	eel *pon*·te
castle	*il castello*	eel kas·*te*·lo
cathedral	*il duomo*	eel *dwo*·mo
island	*l'isola*	*lee*·so·la
(main) square	*la piazza*	la *pya*·tsa
	(principale)	(preen·chee·*pa*·le)
market	*il mercato*	eel mer·*ka*·to
old city	*il centro*	eel *chen*·tro
	storico	*sto*·ree·ko
palace	*il palazzo*	eel pa·*la*·tso
ruins	*le rovine*	le ro·*vee*·ne
sea	*il mare*	eel *ma*·re
tower	*la torre*	la *to*·re

HEALTH

| I'm ill. | *Mi sento male.* | mee *sen*·to *ma*·le |
| It hurts here. | *Mi fa male qui.* | mee fa *ma*·le *kwee* |

I'm ...	*Sono ...*	*so*·no ...
asthmatic	*asmatico/a*	az·*ma*·tee·ko/a
diabetic	*diabetico/a*	dee·a·*be*·tee·ko/a
epileptic	*epilettico/a*	e·pee·*le*·tee·ko/a

I'm allergic ...	*Sono*	*so*·no
	allergico/a ...	a·*ler*·jee·ko/a ...
to antibiotics	*agli antibiotici*	a·lyee *an*·tee·bee·o·tee·chee
to aspirin	*all'aspirina*	a·*la*·spe·ree·na
to penicillin	*alla penicillina*	a·la pe·nee·see·*lee*·na
to nuts	*ai noci*	a·ee *no*·chee

antiseptic	*antisettico*	an·tee·*se*·tee·ko
aspirin	*aspirina*	as·pee·*ree*·na
condoms	*preservativi*	pre·zer·va·*tee*·vee
contraceptive	*contraccetivo*	kon·tra·che·*tee*·vo
diarrhoea	*diarrea*	dee·a·*re*·a
medicine	*medicina*	me·dee·*chee*·na
sunblock cream	*crema solare*	kre·ma so·*la*·re
tampons	*tamponi*	tam·*po*·nee

LANGUAGE DIFFICULTIES

Do you speak English?
Parla inglese?   *par*·la een·*gle*·ze

Does anyone here speak English?
C'è qualcuno che   che kwal·*koo*·no ke
parla inglese?   *par*·la een·*gle*·ze

How do you say ... in Italian?
Come si dice ...   *ko*·me see *dee*·che ...
in italiano?   een ee·ta·*lya*·no

What does ... mean?
Che vuol dire ...?   ke vwol *dee*·re ...

I understand.
Capisco.   ka·*pee*·sko

I don't understand.
Non capisco.   non ka·*pee*·sko

Please write it down.
Può scriverlo, per   pwo skree·ver·lo per
favore?   fa·*vo*·re

Can you show me (on the map)?
Può mostrarmelo   pwo mos·*trar*·me·lo
(sulla pianta)?   (soo·la *pyan*·ta)

NUMBERS

0	*zero*	dze·ro
1	*uno*	*oo*·no
2	*due*	*doo*·e
3	*tre*	tre
4	*quattro*	*kwa*·tro
5	*cinque*	*cheen*·kwe
6	*sei*	say
7	*sette*	*se*·te
8	*otto*	*o*·to
9	*nove*	*no*·ve
10	*dieci*	*dye*·chee
11	*undici*	oon·*dee*·chee
12	*dodici*	do·*dee*·chee
13	*tredici*	tre·*dee*·chee
14	*quattordici*	kwa·*tor*·dee·chee
15	*quindici*	*kween*·dee·chee
16	*sedici*	*se*·dee·chee
17	*diciassette*	dee·cha·*se*·te
18	*diciotto*	dee·*cho*·to
19	*diciannove*	dee·cha·*no*·ve
20	*venti*	*ven*·tee
21	*ventuno*	ven·*too*·no
22	*ventidue*	ven·tee·*doo*·e

30	*trenta*	*tren*·ta
40	*quaranta*	kwa·*ran*·ta
50	*cinquanta*	cheen·*kwan*·ta
60	*sessanta*	se·*san*·ta
70	*settanta*	se·*tan*·ta
80	*ottanta*	o·*tan*·ta
90	*novanta*	no·*van*·ta
100	*cento*	*chen*·to
1000	*mille*	*mee*·le

PAPERWORK

name	*nome*	*no*·me
nationality	*nazionalità*	na·tsyo·na·lee·*ta*
date of birth	*data di*	*da*·ta dee
	nascita	na·*shee*·ta
place of birth	*luogo di*	*lwo*·go dee
	nascita	na·*shee*·ta
sex (gender)	*sesso*	*se*·so
passport	*passaporto*	pa·sa·*por*·to
visa	*visto*	*vee*·sto

QUESTION WORDS

Who?	*Chi?*	kee
What?	*Che?*	ke
When?	*Quando?*	*kwan*·do
Where?	*Dove?*	*do*·ve
How?	*Come?*	*ko*·me

SHOPPING & SERVICES

I'd like to buy ...
Vorrei comprare ...   vo·*ray* kom·*pra*·re ...

How much is it?
Quanto costa?   *kwan*·to *ko*·sta

I don't like it.
Non mi piace.   non mee *pya*·che

May I look at it?
Posso dare   *po*·so *da*·re
un'occhiata?   oo·no·*kya*·ta

I'm just looking.
Sto solo guardando.   sto *so*·lo gwar·*dan*·do

It's cheap.
Non è caro/cara.   non e *ka*·ro/*ka*·ra

It's too expensive.
È troppo caro/a.   e *tro*·po *ka*·ro/*ka*·ra

I'll take it.
Lo/La compro.   lo/la *kom*·pro

Do you accept credit cards?
Accettate carte   a·che·*ta*·te *kar*·te
di credito?   dee *kre*·dee·to

I want to	*Voglio*	*vo*·lyo
change ...	*cambiare ...*	kam·*bya*·re ...
money	*del denaro*	del de·*na*·ro
travellers	*assegni dee*	a·*se*·nyee dee
cheques	*viaggio*	vee·*a*·jo

more	più	pyoo
less	meno	me·no
smaller	più piccolo/a	pyoo pee·ko·lo/la
bigger	più grande	pyoo gran·de

I'm looking for ...	Cerco ...	cher·ko ...
a bank	un banco	oon ban·ko
the church	la chiesa	la kye·za
the city centre	il centro	eel chen·tro
the ... embassy	l'ambasciata di ...	lam·ba·sha·ta dee ...
my hotel	il mio albergo	eel mee·o al·ber·go
the market	il mercato	eel mer·ka·to
the museum	il museo	eel moo·ze·o
the post office	la posta	la po·sta
a public toilet	un gabinetto	oon ga·bee·ne·to
the telephone centre	il centro telefonico	eel chen·tro te·le·fo·nee·ko
the tourist office	l'ufficio di turismo	loo·fee·cho dee too·reez·mo

TIME & DATES

| What time is it? | Che ore sono? | ke o·re so·no |
| It's (8 o'clock). | Sono (le otto). | so·no (le o·to) |

in the morning	di mattina	dee ma·tee·na
in the afternoon	di pomeriggio	dee po·me·ree·jo
in the evening	di sera	dee se·ra
When?	Quando?	kwan·do
today	oggi	o·jee
tomorrow	domani	do·ma·nee
yesterday	ieri	ye·ree

Monday	lunedì	loo·ne·dee
Tuesday	martedì	mar·te·dee
Wednesday	mercoledì	mer·ko·le·dee
Thursday	giovedì	jo·ve·dee
Friday	venerdì	ve·ner·dee
Saturday	sabato	sa·ba·to
Sunday	domenica	do·me·nee·ka

January	gennaio	je·na·yo
February	febbraio	fe·bra·yo
March	marzo	mar·tso
April	aprile	a·pree·le
May	maggio	ma·jo
June	giugno	joo·nyo
July	luglio	loo·lyo
August	agosto	a·gos·to
September	settembre	se·tem·bre
October	ottobre	o·to·bre
November	novembre	no·vem·bre
December	dicembre	dee·chem·bre

TRANSPORT
Public Transport

What time does the ... leave/arrive?	A che ora parte/arriva ...?	a ke o·ra par·te/a·ree·va ...
boat	la nave	la na·ve
(city) bus	l'autobus	low·to·boos
(intercity) bus	il pullman	eel pool·man
plane	l'aereo	la·e·re·o
train	il treno	eel tre·no

I'd like a ... ticket.	Vorrei un biglietto ...	vo·ray oon bee·lye·to ...
one-way	di solo andata	dee so·lo an·da·ta
return	di andata e ritorno	dee an·da·ta e ree·toor·no
1st class	di prima classe	dee pree·ma kla·se
2nd class	di seconda classe	dee se·kon·da kla·se

I want to go to ...
Voglio andare a ...   vo·lyo an·da·re a ...
The train has been cancelled/delayed.
Il treno è soppresso/   eel tre·no e so·pre·so/
in ritardo.   een ree·tar·do

the first	il primo	eel pree·mo
the last	l'ultimo	lool·tee·mo
platform (two)	binario (due)	bee·na·ryo (doo·e)
ticket office	biglietteria	bee·lye·te·ree·a
timetable	orario	o·ra·ryo
train station	stazione	sta·tsyo·ne

Private Transport

I'd like to hire a/an ...	Vorrei noleggiare ...	vo·ray no·le·ja·re ...
car	una macchina	oo·na ma·kee·na
4WD	un fuoristrada	oon fwo·ree·stra·da
motorbike	una moto	oo·na mo·to
bicycle	una bici(cletta)	oo·na bee·chee·(kle·ta)

Is this the road to ...?
Questa strada porta   kwe·sta stra·da por·ta
a ...?   a ...
Where's a service station?
Dov'è una stazione   do·ve oo·na sta·tsyo·ne
di servizio?   dee ser·vee·tsyo
Please fill it up.
Il pieno, per favore.   eel pye·no per fa·vo·re
I'd like (30) litres.
Vorrei (trenta) litri.   vo·ray (tren·ta) lee·tree

ROAD SIGNS

Dare la Precedenza	Give Way
Deviazione	Detour
Divieto di Accesso	No Entry
Divieto di Sorpasso	No Overtaking
Divieto di Sosta	No Parking
Entrata	Entrance
Passo Carrabile	Keep Clear
Pedaggio	Toll
Pericolo	Danger
Rallentare	Slow Down
Senso Unico	One Way
Uscita	Exit

diesel	*gasolio/diesel*	ga·zo·lyo/dee·zel
leaded petrol	*benzina con*	ben·dzee·na kon
	piombo	pyom·bo
unleaded petrol	*benzina senza*	ben·dzee·na
	piombo	sen·dza pyom·bo

(How long) Can I park here?
(Per quanto tempo) (per kwan·to tem·po)
Posso parcheggiare qui? po·so par·ke·ja·re kwee

Where do I pay?
Dove si paga? do·ve see pa·ga

I need a mechanic.
Ho bisogno di un o bee·zo·nyo dee oon
meccanico. me·ka·nee·ko

The car/motorbike has broken down (at ...).
La macchina/moto la ma·kee·na/mo·to
si è guastata (a ...). see e gwas·ta·ta (a ...)

The car/motorbike won't start.
La macchina/moto la ma·kee·na/mo·to
non parte. non par·te

I have a flat tyre.
Ho una gomma bucata. o oo·na go·ma boo·ka·ta

I've run out of petrol.
Ho esaurito la benzina. o e·zo·ree·to la ben·dzee·na

I've had an accident.
Ho avuto un incidente. o a·voo·to oon een·chee·den·te

TRAVEL WITH CHILDREN

Is there a/an ...?	*C'è ...?*	che ...
I need a/an ...	*Ho bisogno di ...*	o bee·zo·nyo dee ...
baby change	*un bagno con*	oon ba·nyo kon
room	*fasciatoio*	fa·sha·to·yo
car baby seat	*un seggiolino*	oon se·jo·lee·no
	per bambini	per bam·bee·nee
child-minding	*un servizio*	oon ser·vee·tsyo
service	*di babysitter*	dee be·bee·see·ter
children's menu	*un menù per*	oon me·noo per
	bambini	bam·bee·nee
(disposable)	*pannolini*	pa·no·lee·nee·
nappies/diapers	*(usa e getta)*	(oo·sa e je·ta)
formula (milk)	*latte in polvere*	la·te in pol·ve·re
(English-	*un/una*	oon/oo·na
speaking)	*babysitter (che*	be·bee·see·ter
babysitter	*parli inglese)*	(ke par·lee
		een·gle·ze)
highchair	*un seggiolone*	oon se·jo·lo·ne
potty	*un vasino*	oon va·zee·no
stroller	*un passeggino*	oon pa·se·jee·no

Do you mind if I breastfeed here?
Le dispiace se allatto le dees·pya·che se a·la·to
il/la bimbo/a qui? eel/la beem·bo/a kwee

Are children allowed?
I bambini sono ee bam·bee·nee so·no
ammessi? a·me·see

Also available from Lonely Planet:
Italian Phrasebook

Glossary

abbazia – abbey
aeroporto – airport
affittacamere – rooms for rent (relatively inexpensive and not part of the classification system)
agriturismo – tourist accommodation on farms
albergo – hotel
alimentare – grocery shop
alloggio – lodging (relatively inexpensive and not part of the classification system)
alto – high
ambulanza – ambulance
anfiteatro – amphitheatre
appartamento – apartment, flat
arco – arch
autobus – local bus
autostazione – bus station/terminal
autostop – hitching
autostrada – motorway, highway

baldacchino – canopy supported by columns over the altar in a church
basilica – Christian church with a rectangular hall, aisles and an apse at the end
battistero – baptistry
benzina – petrol
biblioteca – library
bicicletta – bicycle
biglietteria – ticket office
biglietto – ticket
biglietto cumulativo – combined ticket that allows entrance to a number of associated sights
binario – platform
borgo – ancient town or village

cabinovia – two-seater cable car
calcio – football
camera doppia – room with twin beds
camera matrimoniale – double room with a double bed
camera singola – single room
campanile – bell tower
campeggio – camping
campo – field
cappella – chapel
carabinieri – military police
carnevale – carnival period between Epiphany and Lent
carta d'identità – identity card
carta telefonica – phonecard (also *scheda telefonica*)
cartolina (postale) – postcard
casa – house, home
castello – castle

cattedrale – cathedral
cava – quarry
cena – evening meal
centesimi – cents
centro – city centre
centro storico – (literally, 'historical centre') old town
chiaroscuro – (literally, 'light-dark') artistic distribution of light and dark areas in a painting
chiesa – church
chiostro – cloister; a covered walkway around a quadrangle, which is usually enclosed by columns
circo – oval or circular arena
codice fiscale – tax number
colle – hill
colonna – column
comune – equivalent to a municipality; town or city council; historically, a commune (self-governing town or city)
contado – district around a major town (the area surrounding Florence was known as the *contado di Firenze*)
contrada – town district
convalida – ticket-stamping machine
coperto – cover charge
corso – main street, avenue
cortile – courtyard
cupola – dome

deposito bagagli – left luggage
distributore di benzina – petrol pump (see also *stazione di servizio*)
duomo – cathedral

enoteca – wine bar

farmacia – pharmacies
ferrovia – train station
festa – festival
fiore – flower
fiume – river
fontana – fountain
foro – forum
francobollo – postage stamp
fresco – painting method in which watercolour paint is applied to wet plaster
funicolare – funicular railway
funivia – cable car

gabinetto – toilet, WC
golfo – gulf
grisaille – technique of monochrome painting in shades of grey

grotta – cave
guardia di finanza – fiscal police

HI – Hostelling International

intarsio – inlaid wood, marble or metal
isola – island

lago – lake
largo – (small) square
lavanderia – laundrette
lavasecco – dry-cleaning
lettera – letter
libreria – bookshop
lido – beach
locanda – inn, small hotel (relatively inexpensive and not part of the classification system)
loggia – covered area on the side of a building; porch
lungomare – seafront road, promenade

macchia – scrub, bush
mare – sea
mercato – market
monte – mountain, mount
motorino – moped
municipio – town hall
museo – museum

navata centrale – nave; central part of a church
navata laterale – aisle of a church
nave – ship
necropoli – (ancient) cemetery, burial site

oggetti smarriti – lost property
ostello per la gioventù – youth hostel
osteria – simple, trattoria-style restaurant, often with a bar

palazzo – palace; a large building of any type, including an apartment block
parco – park
passaggio ponte – deck class
passeggiata – traditional evening stroll
pensione – small hotel
permesso di lavoro – work permit
permesso di soggiorno – residence permit
piazza – square
piazzale – (large) open square
pietà – (literally, 'pity' or 'compassion') sculpture, drawing or painting of the dead Christ supported by Madonna
pinacoteca – art gallery
piscina – pool
poltrona – (literally, 'armchair') airline-type chair on a ferry
polyptych – altarpiece consisting of more than three panels (see also *triptych*)

ponte – bridge
porta – door, city gate
portico – walkway, often on the outside of buildings
porto – port
presepio – nativity scene
profumeria – perfumery
pronto soccorso – first aid
pullman – long-distance bus

questura – police station

rifugio – mountain hut, alpine refuge
rocca – fort

sagra – festival (usually with a culinary theme)
sala – room in a museum or a gallery
santuario – sanctuary
scalinata – flight of stairs
scavi – excavations
scheda telefonica – phonecard
servizio – service fee
spiaggia – beach
spiaggia libera – public beach
stazione – station
stazione di servizio – service/petrol station (see also *distributore di benzina*)
stazione marittima – ferry terminal
strada – street, road
superstrada – expressway; highway with divided lanes (but no tolls)

tabaccheria/tabaccaio – tobacconist's shop/tobacconist
teatro – theatre
telefonino – mobile phone
tempio – temple
terme – thermal bath
tesoro – treasury
torre – tower
torrente – stream
traghetto – ferry
trattoria – simple restaurant
triptych – painting or carving over three panels, hinged so that the outer panels fold over the middle one, often used as an altarpiece (see also *polyptych*)

ufficio postale – post office
ufficio stranieri – (police) foreigners' bureau
uffizi – offices

via – street, road
via aerea – air mail
via ferrata – climbing trail with permanent steel cables to aid walkers, usually in a hilly area
vicoli – alley, alleyway
vigili urbani – traffic police, local police

Behind the Scenes

THIS BOOK

The 1st edition of *Tuscany* was researched and written by Damien Simonis, and the 2nd edition was updated by Neal Bedford with help from Damien Simonis and Imogen Franks. The 3rd edition, which was the first to include Umbria, was updated by Alex Leviton, Josephine Quintero, Rachel Suddart and Richard Watkins. This edition of *Tuscany & Umbria* was updated by Miles Roddis and Alex Leviton.

THANKS from the Authors

Miles Roddis Huge thanks, as ever, to Ingrid, who drove me the length and breadth of my patch, then proofed with a sharp eagle's eye. And to Paola Lazzarini who, once again, chased up fleeting facts so efficiently. And to fellow Florence-savvy author Damien Simonis, in whose sure footsteps I've so often trodden. In Florence, Marco was generous with budget hospitality and Maurizio Piegaja of Victoria Hotel, Pisa, gave me some useful leads.

Tourist office staff were, as ever and almost without exception, helpfulness itself. Especial thanks to Sabrina Mafara and Maria Laura Billeri, a hugely efficient pair in Florence, Antonella Arnesano (Fiesole), Chiara Marcucci (Livorno), Mariarosario Aliboni (Viareggio), Lucia (Pisa), Roberta (Volterra), Claudia (San Gimignano), Emanuela Lorenzetti (Siena), Barbara (Montalcino), Elisa (Montepulciano), Andrea (Pienza), Anna (Porto Santo Stefano), Marÿke van der Weide (Pitigliano), Silvia (Cortona) and Giampaolo (Arezzo).

Lastly and risking taunts of toadiness, a hug for Michala, the most efficient, understanding and cooperative commisioning editor an author could dream of. And a hey across the Atlantic to Alex, my sparky, committed companion in literary crime.

Alex Leviton This book would not be what it is without many Umbrian friends who went above and beyond to help me create something that would capture the spirit of Umbria: Carlo Rocchi Bilancini, Mario Santoro, Zach Nowak, Vibeke Cardelli, Lucca Urbani and his cashmere-outfitted dog Téa, Leo Pretelli, Rolando and family, Fabiano and Katya Spagnoli, Roberto Nini and Lady Giuliana. Also, thanks to my travelling companions/drivers, Greg DeWitt and Suzanne Bartholf (congratulations, you two!), and Thibault Worth. Back in non-on-the-road life, thanks to my magnanimous coauthor Miles Roddis, editors extraordinaire Michala Green and Kim Noble, freelance writer, co-conspirator and cheerleader Rah Bickley, endlessly patient Italian teacher Angelita Nitti and *tutta la classe*, and Italian tourism expert Emanuela Boni.

CREDITS

Commissioning Editor Michala Green
Coordinating Editor Kim Noble
Coordinating Cartographer David Connolly
Coordinating Layout Designer Wibowo Rusli
Managing Cartographer Mark Griffiths
Managing Editor Martin Heng
Assisting Editors Carly Hall, Roy Garner, Emma Gilmour, Joanne Newell
Cover Designer Annika Roojun
Project Manager Ray Thomson
Language Content Coordinator Quentin Frayne

THE LONELY PLANET STORY

The story begins with a classic travel adventure: Tony and Maureen Wheeler's 1972 journey across Europe and Asia to Australia. There was no useful information about the overland trail then, so Tony and Maureen published the first Lonely Planet guidebook to meet a growing need.

From a kitchen table, Lonely Planet has grown to become the largest independent travel publisher in the world, with offices in Melbourne (Australia), Oakland (USA) and London (UK). Today Lonely Planet guidebooks cover the globe. There is an ever-growing list of books and information in a variety of media. Some things haven't changed. The main aim is still to make it possible for adventurous travellers to get out there – to explore and better understand the world.

At Lonely Planet we believe travellers can make a positive contribution to the countries they visit – if they respect their host communities and spend their money wisely. Every year 5% of company profit is donated to charities around the world.

Thanks to David Burnett, Sally Darmody, Emma Koch, Rebecca Lalor, Celia Wood

THANKS from Lonely Planet
Many thanks to the travellers who used the last edition and contacted us with helpful hints, useful advice and interesting anecdotes:

Andrew Arditti, April Arnatt Chris Bachovchin, Mark Bauer, Svea Breckberg, Michael Buckley, Alessio Bulli Norman Cain, Paolo Gherardo Calisse, Gert Callaerts, Loyola Colebeck, Simon Cope, Kate Crane, Pietro Crivelli Suzanne Dalton, Andrea D'Avella, George Dehnel, Jim Derksen Lorenzo Frusteri Evan Gorman, Miriam Greenbaum, Erik Gronvall Mary Hackett, Reynold Harrs, Frederik Helbo, J Hunter Neil Jackson Ron Kaplan, Val Kaplan, Jodi Kensley Karen Lee Shaun McCann, John Meredith, Nina Miesmäki, Darlene Moak Barbara Parrini Vibeke Ranum, Heidi Reutter, Stuart Richards, F Ringenoldus, Marina Rizzetto Sandro Santagata, Lone Scherfig, Robin & Peter Scott, Egidio Sponza, Edith Springveld Noga Tarnopolsky John Widdup

ACKNOWLEDGMENTS
Many thanks to the following for the use of their content:
Globe on back cover © Mountain High Maps 1993 Digital Wisdom, Inc.

SEND US YOUR FEEDBACK
We love to hear from travellers – your comments keep us on our toes and help make our books better. Our well-travelled team reads every word on what you loved or loathed about this book. Although we cannot reply individually to postal submissions, we always guarantee that your feedback goes straight to the appropriate authors, in time for the next edition. Each person who sends us information is thanked in the next edition – and the most useful submissions are rewarded with a free book.

To send us your updates – and find out about Lonely Planet events, newsletters and travel news – visit our award-winning website: **www.lonelyplanet.com/feedback**.

Note: We may edit, reproduce and incorporate your comments in Lonely Planet products such as guidebooks, websites and digital products, so let us know if you don't want your comments reproduced or your name acknowledged. For a copy of our privacy policy visit www.lonelyplanet.com/privacy.

Index

INDEX

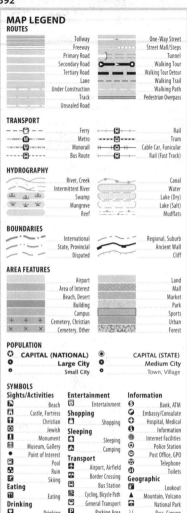

MAP LEGEND

ROUTES

Tollway		One-Way Street
Freeway		Street Mall/Steps
Primary Road		Tunnel
Secondary Road		Walking Tour
Tertiary Road		Walking Tour Detour
Lane		Walking Trail
Under Construction		Walking Path
Track		Pedestrian Overpass
Unsealed Road		

TRANSPORT

Ferry	Rail
Metro	Tram
Monorail	Cable Car, Funicular
Bus Route	Rail (Fast Track)

HYDROGRAPHY

River, Creek	Canal
Intermittent River	Water
Swamp	Lake (Dry)
Mangrove	Lake (Salt)
Reef	Mudflats

BOUNDARIES

International	Regional, Suburb
State, Provincial	Ancient Wall
Disputed	Cliff

AREA FEATURES

Airport	Land
Area of Interest	Mall
Beach, Desert	Market
Building	Park
Campus	Sports
Cemetery, Christian	Urban
Cemetery, Other	Forest

POPULATION

○ CAPITAL (NATIONAL)	◉ CAPITAL (STATE)
● Large City	◉ Medium City
● Small City	● Town, Village

SYMBOLS

Sights/Activities
- Beach
- Castle, Fortress
- Christian
- Jewish
- Monument
- Museum, Gallery
- Point of Interest
- Pool
- Ruin
- Skiing

Eating
- Eating

Drinking
- Drinking
- Café

Entertainment
- Entertainment

Shopping
- Shopping

Sleeping
- Sleeping
- Camping

Transport
- Airport, Airfield
- Border Crossing
- Bus Station
- Cycling, Bicycle Path
- General Transport
- Parking Area
- Petrol Station

Information
- Bank, ATM
- Embassy/Consulate
- Hospital, Medical
- Information
- Internet Facilities
- Police Station
- Post Office, GPO
- Telephone
- Toilets

Geographic
- Lookout
- Mountain, Volcano
- National Park
- Pass, Canyon
- River Flow

LONELY PLANET OFFICES

Australia
Head Office
Locked Bag 1, Footscray, Victoria 3011
☎ 03 8379 8000, fax 03 8379 8111
talk2us@lonelyplanet.com.au

USA
150 Linden St, Oakland, CA 94607
☎ 510 893 8555, toll free 800 275 8555
fax 510 893 8572, info@lonelyplanet.com

UK
72–82 Rosebery Ave,
Clerkenwell, London EC1R 4RW
☎ 020 7841 9000, fax 020 7841 9001
go@lonelyplanet.co.uk

Published by Lonely Planet Publications Pty Ltd
ABN 36 005 607 983

4th Edition - January 2006

First Published - July 2000

© Lonely Planet 2006

© photographers as indicated 2006

Cover photographs: Tuscany, Orcia Valley, Spring Landscape, Fabi
Muzzi/Picture Colour Library (front); Il Palio Contrada members i
Siena, Becca Posterino/Lonely Planet Images (back).

Printed through Colorcraft Ltd, Hong Kong.
Printed in China